③ PMS.
IJM 420
BLO

An introd
psychoth

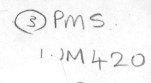

An introduction to the psychotherapies

FOURTH EDITION

Edited by

Sidney Bloch

Professor of Psychiatry,
Department of Psychiatry and Centre for Health and Society,
University of Melbourne, Australia

OXFORD
UNIVERSITY PRESS

Great Clarendon Street, Oxford OX2 6DP

Oxford University Press is a department of the University of Oxford.
It furthers the University's objective of excellence in research, scholarship,
and education by publishing worldwide in

Oxford New York

Auckland Cape Town Dar es Salaam Hong Kong Karachi
Kuala Lumpur Madrid Melbourne Mexico City Nairobi
New Delhi Shanghai Taipei Toronto

With offices in

Argentina Austria Brazil Chile Czech Republic France Greece
Guatemala Hungary Italy Japan Poland Portugal Singapore
South Korea Switzerland Thailand Turkey Ukraine Vietnam

Oxford is a registered trade mark of Oxford University Press
in the UK and in certain other countries

Published in the United States
by Oxford University Press Inc., New York

British Library Cataloguing in Publication Data

Data available

Library of Congress Cataloging in Publication Data

Data available

Typeset by Newgen Imaging Systems (P) Ltd., Chennai, India
Printed in Great Britain
on acid-free paper by
Ashford Colour Press Ltd

ISBN 0–19–852092–1   978–0–19–852092–4

10 9 8 7 6 5 4 3 2

Preface to the fourth edition

The decade that has passed since the third edition has witnessed exciting and pleasing developments in the psychotherapies, both conceptual and empirical. The field continues to mature in such a way that newcomers can potentially receive systematic training, which encompasses coherent theory and a growing body of knowledge derived from systematic research. I hope the book with its 12 updated and 5 new chapters reflects these positive trends.

The new chapter on research, by Frank Margison and Anthony Bateman, certainly attests to the benefits for the field stemming from empirical research while the new chapters on attempts at theoretical integration, namely cognitive—analytic (by Ian Kerr and its progenitor Tony Ryle), and conversational (by its foremost representative, Russell Meares), similarly reflect how 'schools' of therapy can evolve coherently and flexibly to meet the needs of various clinical groups. A patient group that has been ignored by therapists until very recently are older adults; the new chapter by Jane Garner is therefore most welcome.

The first edition of *An introduction to the psychotherapies*, was published almost three decades ago. During that time the subject has undergone an exciting history. It therefore dawned on me that the novice might have a need for an historical context within which to train. The new chapter by Bloch and Harari provides a succinct framework.

I extend a warm welcome to all therapist-writers mentioned above as well as to Brett Kennedy (who has joined forces with Lynne Drummond to update the chapter on behavioural psychotherapy), Ricky Emanuel (who has taken on the child and adolescent psychotherapy chapter following Sula Wolff's retirement), Edwin Harari (co-author on the history chapter and a new one on family therapy in the adult psychiatric setting) and Allen Dyer (who has co-authored the chapter on ethical issues in psychotherapy practice).

Jerome Frank's chapter has attained classic status and will, I hope, constitute an invaluable legacy of a great contributor to the psychotherapies. Jerry, a wise, gentle, and decent colleague, who I had the privilege of meeting during one of his visits to Oxford, died at the ripe old age of 95 in March 2005. I would like to dedicate this edition to his memory.

I very much hope that the fourth edition will continue to meet the needs of the newcomer to the psychotherapies by fulfilling its original four objectives: to make the process of the psychotherapies more understandable; to highlight features that are common to the many approaches used in mental health practice; to bridge research and practice; and to guide trainees in their further reading.

Melbourne   S.B.

February 2006

Preface to the third edition

An Introduction to the Psychotherapies has carved a niche for itself in the training in the psychotherapies of mental health professionals since 1979. It has been a great pleasure to edit this new edition, which I hope will prove as useful as its predecessors to students who need a 'gentle' guide to what is commonly experienced as a bewildering subject.

Both content and the team of contributors have undergone some changes since the second edition. First, cognitive psychotherapy and behavioural psychotherapy have been uncoupled, with each now having a chapter to itself, written by Nicholas Allen and Lynne Drummond, respectively. A new chapter, authored by Byram Karasu, has been included to cover the important topic of the ethical dimension of psychotherapy practice. Previous chapters have been updated by the authors, in some cases with the collaboration of new co-authors, namely Mark Aveline on group psychotherapy, Jeremy Holmes on individual long-term psychotherapy, and Cynthia Graham on crisis intervention.

The original objectives set out in the preface to the first edition remain as pertinent as ever. I hope this new edition succeeds in fulfilling those aims.

Melbourne   S. B.
November 1995

Preface to the second edition

For the second edition, coverage of the psychotherapies has been broadened by the inclusion of new chapters on brief, focal psychotherapy and child psychotherapy. In addition, the existing chapters have been updated by their authors to take into account recent developments in each particular field.

I hope the book will continue to prove helpful to students seeking an introduction to what remains a most complex subject.

Oxford   S. B.
April 1985

Preface to the first edition

The most striking memory I have of my first few months in psychotheraphy training was how bewildering it all seemed. No one could define it, controversy raged over the qestion of its effectiveness, different schools engaged in constant warfare with one another, and the training programme itself lacked goals and a coherent structure. I realized later when I continued my training in the United States and Britain that this sense of bewilderment was not indigenous to my native Antipodes. The 'acute confuisional state' was universal! In recent years I have noted, as a teacher of psychotherapy, that contemporary trainees still undergo a similar type of experience to the one I had.

This situation is not at all surprising. Psychotherapy after all is a nebulous term with widely differing connotations; the controversy over its value is still with us; dozens of psychotherapy schools, each with its own theories on psychopathology (often contradictory) and particular set of techniques, compete for the trainee's attention; and there is no apparent link between research and clinical practice—psychotherapists are influenced only occasionally by the results of research.[1] Overwhelmingly, theory determines practice and works vigorously to protect itself from forces that might lead to change.

I hope that this book, mainly an introduction for students in the mental health professions, will help to remove at least some of hurdles that commonly obstruct them in approaching the complex and demanding subject of psychotherapy. The general objectives of the book are: (a) To make the concept of psychotherapy more understandable. To this end I have used the term *psychotherapies* in the sense that there are several forms of psychotherapeutic treatment which can be distinguished from one another according to their goals, techniques, and target of intervention. We can therefore differentiate, for example, between crisis intervention, supportive psychotherapy for chronically disabled psychiatric patients, family therapy, sex therapy, long-term intensive individual psychotherapy, and so forth. The clinician's task is to match the needs of the patient, couple, or family with the appropriate psychotherapy rather than the converse of fitting the patient to

---

[1] Malan, D.H. (1973). The outcome problem in psychotherapy research. A historical review. *Archives of General Psychiatry*, 29, 719–29.

the treatment. By using this approach psychotherapy as a generic term may fade into oblivion. (b) To minimize the differences between schools of psychotherapy and to emphasize the features they have in common. Alongside this aim, the book attempts to eschew the dogmatism and doctrinaire attitudes that have tended to permeate the field. Jerome Frank, who has made such a valuable contribution in bringing the issue of 'shared factors' to our attention, considers it in his introductory chapter and the other contributors have been guided by it. A central focus in this book is on what Yalom refers to as 'core' factors (in contrast to 'front' factors).[2] The significance of theory is not denied; trainees must ultimately familiarize themselves with various models for each of the psychotherapies but they should not be swamped by them before they have grasped basic common principles. Each contributor therefore comments on theoretical aspects and provides a guide to further reading. (c) To draw a relationship between research and clinical practice. Although psychotherapy research is still in its infancy, the therapist needs to keep abreast of it in order to maximize his effectiveness. For example, the value of preparing the patient for psychotherapy has been replicated in several studies and the procedure should logically be incorporated into clinical work. When appropriate, reference is made to the contribution of such investigations on clinical practice. By taking cognizance of research findings, I hope that the heat will also be removed from the lingering debate over whether psychotherapy works or not. This debate is futile because we have no way as yet of even attempting to answer the basic questions. In any event, a more suitable question is whether each of the psychotherapies is of value, for whom and in what circumstance. Limitations of space do not allow more than a superficial examination of pertinent research but references are recommended for the interested reader at the end of each chapter. (d) To guide the trainee in his reading. A common problem in psychotherapy education is the bombardment of the novice with references. Inevitably, he wonders how to get into the material, and once having entered, often how to extricate himself. Since the literature is voluminous, reading must of necessity be done rationally. The contributors hope that the recommended reading lists following each chapter will help the trainee to reconnoitre without injury.

I hope that the book comes some way in meeting these objectives.

The presentation of eight different psychotherapies does not mean that the reader should be able to master them all. Presumably, he will select therapies which are intrinsic to his particular work and those which he finds

----

[2] Yalom, I. D. (1975). *The theory and practice of group psychotherapy*. Basic Books, New York.

interesting. However, he should also be in a better position to refer appropriately patients who require one of the treatments in which he has not trained.

The masculine pronoun is used, where appropriate, to represent both sexes so as to avoid clumsiness and unnecessary repetition.

Oxford   S. B.
April 1978

Dedicated to the memory of Jerome Frank (1910-2005), a pioneer of research in the psychotherapies, who respected the complementarity between the sciences and the humanities masterfully.

Acknowledgements

First edition
I have been helped by many colleagues in editing this book. To the contributors, with whom collaboration proved smooth and pleasant, my thanks. I am grateful to several colleagues who reviewed sections of the manuscript and offered valuable suggestions—Derek Bergel, Pepe Catalan, Michael Gelder, Dave Kennard, Michael Orr, William Parry-Jones, Bob Potter, and Nick Rose. Professor Gelder was helpful in many ways and I thank him for his support.

I would like to pay special tribute to the late Dr Phyllis Shaw. She not only provided the encouragement I needed to initiate the project but also agreed to contribute the chapter on supportive psychotherapy. Many ideas contained in this chapter come from her preparatory notes.

I am grateful to several secretaries in the Oxford University Department of Psychiatry who helped to prepare the manuscript. Finally, I thank my wife, Felicity, for her constant support and editorial suggestions.

Second edition
Again it is a pleasure to thank the contributors for their helpful collaboration. Gillian Forrest, Ian Goodyer, Keith Hawton, and David Mushin reviewed sections of the manuscript—to them my gratitude. My secretary Ann Robinson was most obliging in helping to prepare the final typescript.

Third edition
My gratitude to the contributors is boundless; their colleagueship has been a source of much pleasure. I thank Nicholas Allen, George Halasz, and Edwin Harari who provided valuable advice on parts of the manuscript. Julie Larke has proved time and time again through the editing process how blessed one is when assisted by a bright and congenial secretary; I am most grateful to her. I would like to thank Sandra Russell and Gillian Hiscock and their respective staff in the Mental Health Library of Victoria and St Vincent's Hospital Library for their unstinting assistance in tracking down references. The Victorian branch of the Australian and New Zealand Association of Psychotherapy has generously permitted the use of its logo for the cover—a wonderful representation of the therapeutic process. Finally, I thank Felicity, Leah, David, and Aaron for putting up with a husband and father who has not always been accessible in recent months, especially as nasty deadlines loomed!

Fourth edition

Many of the contributors to the new edition were part of the original team. Amazingly, we have collaborated to common purpose for well over a quarter of a century. I thank them profusely for their commitment and conscientiousness. I am most grateful to the rest of the 'team' for their wonderful support and dedication.

Catherine Roberts and Renee Best provided secretarial and administrative help—thank you for your spirited and efficient help. I could not have asked for a better pair to assist me in the myriad tasks involved in producing a multi-authored volume. The staff of the Victorian Mental Health Library and the St Vincent's Hospital Library have, as always, been extraordinarily obliging in tracking down elusive references. My wife, Felicity, and children, Leah, David, and Aaron, have always provided a congenial and stimulating ambience in which I could pursue my editorial functions; my gratitude to them is boundless.

Contents

4 Specific clinical groups

List of Contributors

Nicholas B. Allen
Associate Professor of Psychology,
ORYGEN Research Centre and
Department of Psychology,
The University of Melbourne,
Melbourne, Australia

Mark Aveline
Honorary Professor of
Counselling and Psychotherapy,
Institute of Lifelong Learning,
Leicester; Emeritus Consultant,
Nottighamshire Healthcare
NHS Trust, UK

John Bancroft
Senior Research Fellow,
The Kinsey Institute for
Research in Sex, Gender and
Reproduction, Indiana University,
Bloomington, Indiana, USA

Anthony Bateman
Consultant Psychiatrist and
Psychotherapist, Halliwick Unit,
Barnet, Enfield, and Haringey
Mental Health Trust;
Visiting Professor, University College
London, London, UK

Sidney Bloch
Professor of Psychiatry,
Department of Psychiatry and
Centre for Health and Society,
University of Melbourne, Australia

Michael Crowe
Formerly Consultant Psychiatrist,
South London and Maudsley
NHS Trust, and Senior Lecturer,

Institute of Psychiatry
(King's College London),
London, UK

Lynne M. Drummond
Consultant Psychiatrist and
Senior Lecturer, Department
of Mental Health, St George's
Hospital Medical School,
London, UK

Allen R. Dyer
Department of Psychiatry,
East Tennessee State University,
Johnson City, TN, USA

Ricky Emanuel
Consultant Child and Adolescent
Psychotherapist; Head of Child
Psychotherapy Services,
Department of Child and
Adolescent Psychiatry, Royal
Free Hospital, London;
Clinical Lead Child and Adolescent
Mental Health Services, Camden
Primary Care Trust,
London, UK

Jerome D. Frank
Formerly Emeritus Professor
of Psychiatry, Johns Hopkins
University, Baltimore, Maryland,
USA

Jane Garner
Consultant Psychiatrist in Psychiatry
of the Elderly,
Department of Old Age Psychiatry,
Barnet, Enfield and Haringey Mental
Health Trust, Enfield, UK

Cynthia Graham
Research Tutor, Oxford Doctoral
Course in Clinical Psychology,
Isis Education Centre, Warneford
Hospital, Oxford, UK

Edwin Harari
Consultant Psychiatrist,
The University of Melbourne,
St Vincent's Hospital, Melbourne,
Australia

Michael Hobbs
Medical Director, Oxfordshire
Mental Healthcare Trust,
Warneford Hospital, Oxford, UK

Jeremy Holmes
Department of Psychiatry,
North Devon District Hospital,
Barnstaple, UK; Visiting Professor,
University of Exeter and
University College London, UK

Brett Kennedy
Specialist Registrar, Springfield
University Hospital, London, UK

Ian B. Kerr
Psychotherapist and Consultant
Psychiatrist, Sheffield Care Trust,
Sheffield, UK

Frank Margison
Manchester Mental Health and
Social Care NHS Trust,
Manchester, UK

Russell Meares
Emeritus Professor of Psychiatry,
University of Sydney;
Joint Centre of Mental Health
Excellence, Westmead Hospital,
Westmead, Australia

Susan Mizen
Consultant Psychiatrist and
Psychotherapist, Wonford House
Hospital, Exeter, UK

Anthony Ryle
Formerly Consultant
Psychotherapist,
St Thomas' Hospital,
London, UK

Part 1

Key contexts

Chapter 1

An historical context

Sidney Bloch and Edwin Harari

Our purpose in including this chapter is to offer the newcomer to the psychotherapies a historical context. We hope this will enable the future practitioner to appreciate that psychological treatments in the setting of psychiatry, and mental health more generally, have proceeded through a series of identifiable stages, some leading to advances of the subject, others to *cul de sacs*.

Since all contributors to this volume have included a focused historical background to the psychotherapy they deal with in their chapter, we have opted to provide a more general account which is necessarily brief and relatively schematic.

Psychotherapy—the systematic application of psychological principles to accomplish symptomatic or more substantial personality change—has its origins in two healing traditions—the magico-religious and the medico-scientific (Bromberg 1954). The idea that human experience is influenced by supernatural forces and that certain people have the power to intercede with these forces dates back to antiquity. Shamans and sorcerers have resorted to amulets, magical potions, and incantations for centuries. They have also conducted exorcism and induced altered states of consciousness.

With the Age of Reason, interest was aroused in the newly discovered phenomena of electricity and magnetism. Anton Mesmer (1734–1815), a brash physician, drew on the latter when propounding his theory of animal magnetism. Since the body contained 'magnetic fluid', and this could become disturbed, by applying magnets to various parts, a patient could be relieved of pain and other ailments. While Mesmer's work was ultimately denounced by a Royal Commission and he was forgotten, the observation that his methods appeared to help patients continued to attract attention. James Braid

Based on a chapter by the authors in Smelser, N. and Battes, P. (eds) (2001). *International Encyclopedia of the Social and Behavioural Sciences*, 18, 1248–91. Elsevier, Amsterdam.

(1795–1860), a Manchester doctor, noted that he could induce a similar trance-like state by getting people to fix their gaze on a luminous object. Labelling the phenomenon hypnotism, he proceeded to demonstrate its effectiveness in treating a range of conditions.

The doyen of French neurology, Jean Martin Charcot (1835–1893), considered hypnosis a neurophysiological process, and set about its study in states like somnambulism and hysteria. His pupil, Pierre Janet (1859–1947), suggested that the latter was brought about by weakening of higher brain function, resulting in a constriction of consciousness. In this 'dissociated' state thoughts could not be integrated, and symptoms were beyond the reach of consciousness.

In an alternative explanation, Ambroise Liebeault (1823–1904), and Hippolyte Bernheim (1840–1919), posited a narrowing of attention in hypnosis which rendered the patient vulnerable to the therapist's influence by suggestion. Far from invalidating hypnosis, the power of suggestion could be investigated scientifically and accepted as a *bona fide* therapy.

Freud (1856–1939) had briefly studied with Charcot in 1885–1886 and became enthusiastic about new possible treatments for hysteria. Freud's mentor, a respected Viennese physician, Josef Breuer (1842–1925), had described the treatment of a young women who suffered from an array of marked hysterical symptoms. Instead of suggesting disappearance of the symptoms, Breuer had encouraged Anna O (the pseudonym given to her), to talk freely about her life. She did so and over time began to share memories about her father's illness. Breuer noted that his patient became less distressed after each session and her symptoms improved. Anna herself referred to this approach as her 'talking cure' or 'chimney sweeping'; Breuer termed it 'catharsis'. Whereas Charcot had described physically traumatic events as possibly causal in his hysterical patients, Breuer and Freud's interest focused on psychological trauma, such as humiliation and loss. Freud also became less keen on applying hypnosis.

Breuer and Freud's (1955) volume, *Studies on hysteria*, published in 1895, which included the case of Anna O, and four others treated by Freud himself, also contained ideas on defence mechanisms and an account of various techniques including suggestion, hypnosis, and catharsis. Most importantly, however, was the new concept of 'free-association': the patient instructed to disclose whatever came into their mind, without any censoring, while the analyst adopted an attitude of 'evenly suspended attention' in listening to, and interpreting, the material.

On the basis of his subsequent self-analysis and further clinical experience, Freud elaborated his theory of infantile sexuality. Sexual fantasies in young children centred around the triangular relationships of love and rivalry with their parents (the Oedipal complex). Promoting free association of this theme, as well as of dreams, slips of the tongue, and other unconsciously based thoughts, feelings, and fantasies, Freud emphasized the centrality of the complex in the neuroses. While catharsis and insight (making the unconscious conscious) seemed pivotal to therapy, Freud soon realized that other factors also operated, particularly the role of transference, that is, how feelings, thoughts, and fantasies stemming from childhood experiences and revived in current relationships are 'transferred' onto the analyst. Interpretations were directed at this three-fold nature of the analytic experience. The therapist's response to transference (counter-transference) led to analysts having their own personal therapy, the aim being to minimize it, and thus to be thoroughly objective in attending to the patient's disclosures (Ellenberger 1970).

In summary then, psychoanalytic psychotherapy elaborated the following processes: the patient's unbridled disclosure of whatever enters his mind—free association; the transference of infantile and childlike feelings and attitudes to the therapist which were previously directed to key figures in the patient's earlier life; interpretation of the transference as well as of defences the patient applies to protect himself and the resistance he manifests to self-exploration; and finally, the repeated working through of the discoveries made in treatment. The ultimate aim is insight with translation into corresponding change in behaviour and personality.

Variations on a theme

Freud revised his theories at numerous points in his long professional life. In addition, many of his colleagues extended the boundaries of psychoanalytic thinking. But differences of opinion soon surfaced, some radical. The nature of psychoanalysis then, especially Freud's intolerance of dissent, led notable figures to leave the fold and to evolve their own models on which corresponding schools of therapy were established. Jung and Adler were two foremost European dissidents; Karen Horney, Erich Fromm, and H. S. Sullivan were pioneering neo-Freudians in the United States; and W. D. Winnicott and Melanie Klein were prominent in Britain (Mitchell and Black 1995).

Carl Gustav Jung (1875–1961) was perhaps the most critical dissenter since he was clearly being groomed to take over the leadership of the psychoanalytic movement. But he was also celebrated because of his own contribution. Specifically with regard to psychotherapy, he advanced the notion of 'individuation'—the aim was to discover all parts of oneself and one's creative potential. Jung was less concerned than Freud with the biological roots of behaviour, especially infantile sexual development, but rather emphasized social and cultural factors. The role of transference was replaced by a more adult type of collaboration.

Furthermore, the unconscious for Jung is not merely the repository of the individual's history but also a wider social history, a phenomenon Jung labelled the collective unconscious. He arrived at this notion through a study of myths, legends, and symbols in different cultures, and in different epochs. That these are shared by a variety of cultures is not fortuitous but reflects cosmic mythical themes or archetypes, a salient feature of man's collective history.

Alfred Adler (1870–1937), a Viennese physician, was like Jung a prominent dissenter. Adler joined Freud's circle in 1902 but broke away to form his own school of 'individual psychology' in 1911. An important tenet concerns individual development. We begin life in a state of inferiority, weak and defenceless, for which we compensate by striving for power and by evolving a lifestyle to make our lives purposeful. The pattern that emerges varies and may include such goals as acquisition of money, procreation, high ambition, or creativity. The drive for power and choice of lifestyle may, however, go awry in which case a neurosis results. A path is followed which leads to ineffective efforts to cope with the feeling of inferiority and assumption of a facade or false self.

Adler regarded therapy as a re-educative process in which the therapist, who serves as model and source of encouragement, engages in a warm relationship with the patient and enables him to understand the lifestyle he has assumed. Unconscious determinants of behaviour are less crucial than conscious ones and the term 'unconscious' is used only descriptively to refer to aspects of the person that are not understood by him.

Freud's insistence on innate drives and infantile sexuality not only led to the schisms with Jung and Adler but also spurred a new generation of analytically oriented analysts to concentrate on interpersonal aspects of psychological experience. In the United States, Sullivan pioneered the school of 'interpersonal psychiatry', in which the therapist adopted the role of participant observer in treatment, the transference providing one opportunity to explore communication and its breakdown in the patient's interpersonal world.

We can consider the chief features in the approach of the neo-Freudians by looking briefly at Karen Horney (1885–1952). She became disenchanted with Freud's rigid focus on instinctual biological factors, arguing that cultural factors were more salient, as reflected in the differences in psychological development and behaviour among different sociocultural groups. Indeed, behaviour regarded as normal in one culture could be viewed as neurotic in another.

In line with her emphasis on culture, Horney advanced the role of parental love in the life of a young child. Children typically suffer anxiety, a consequence of feeling helpless in a threatening world. The child reared in a loving atmosphere succeeds in overcoming basic anxiety. By contrast, the deprived child comes to view the world as cruel and hazardous. An inevitable result is low self-esteem.

The task of therapy is to examine the patient's defective patterns in relating to others. In part, this is achieved through study of what transpires between patient and therapist. But there is no emphasis on transference as occurs in Freudian analysis. Therapy aims to enable the patient to move *with* others, by engaging in relationships which are reciprocal and mutual. Another goal is greater self-realization, with freedom from determined modes of thought and action.

While the neo-Freudians were establishing a new pathway for psychoanalysis, a group were equally innovative in the United Kingdom and France. In the United Kingdom, Melanie Klein (1882–1960), a physician hailing from Berlin, concluded from her study of children's play that the Oedipal complex, as described by Freud, was a late expression of primitive unconscious anxieties which children experienced in the first 18 months of life. Given that these states could be reactivated in adult life, Klein labelled them 'positions' rather than stages of psychological development. She also supported the move away from Freud's formulation of instincts and psychosexual energy towards one of object relations, namely the representations of the perception and experience of significant others. Similarly, transference was to be understood not only as a repetition of past or current relationships, but also as evidence of relational patterns in the patient's current *internal* world.

In tandem with Klein, other analysts in Britain proposed ways in which significant early relationships, particularly between infant or young child and its mother, exerted a formative influence on the developing psyche. John Bowlby (1907–1990), in particular, observed that children who had suffered prolonged separation from their mother underwent a grief experience which predisposed them to a range of psychopathology in later life. Donald Winnicott (1896–1971), a paediatrician and analyst, proposed that a mother's attunement to her child, enabling him to feel psychologically 'held' and understood, was an essential ingredient for a stable sense of self. The American psychoanalyst, Heinz Kohut (1913–1981), advanced a similar concept in the 1970s, but highlighted the place of empathy whereby the mother functions as a 'self object' for the child.

Wilfred Bion (1897–1979), a student of Klein, suggested that the analyst functions as a 'container' into whom the patient projects their 'unprocessed' feelings and experiences; the analyst returns them later in a form accessible to him to work on. This experience is deemed to be crucial to the development of a person's ability to examine his own state of mind and that of others.

Michael Balint (1896–1970), an analyst at the Tavistock Clinic, worked along similar lines as Winnicott, focusing on the opportunity for the patient to 'regress' in the safety of the therapeutic relationship to a state of mind in which differentiating between patient and therapist may blur. The features of the encounter—its regularity, predictability, and the therapist's empathic attitude—creates circumstances for such regression which can then be used to examine and alter defence mechanisms.

These models have implications for practice in that the therapist expresses moment-to-moment empathic understanding of the patient's inner experiences and, as this is repeated time and again, the process promotes the evolution of a coherent identity.

Jacques Lacan (1901–1981), the maverick French analyst, claimed a 'return to Freud', his early work in particular, but through the prisms of semiotics and linguistics. These disciplines, he contended, do not see language as a value-free means to express ideas and convey meaning but as a system of signs that communicate symbolically tacit rules and power arrangements. Language imposes on the child awareness of a separateness from its mother who represents a fantasized internal object (the imaginary mother), in whose eyes the child mirrors itself in an attempt to achieve a state of psychological unity. Lacan's controversial proposals regarding variable duration of treatment and trainees themselves determining their competence to qualify as psychoanalysts, led to his expulsion from the International Psychoanalytic Association, albeit with a dedicated following.

Humanistic experientially oriented schools of therapy became popular in the 1960s and 1970s, mainly in the United States. Their chief features were challenging patients with the way they avoid emotionally significant matters in the 'here and now', increasing awareness of non-verbal aspects of communication, facilitating emotional arousal, and providing a forum in which patients were encouraged to experiment with new behaviours.

The most influential humanistic school has been the client-centred therapy of Carl Rogers (1902–1987), although it has been absorbed into psychotherapy generally, and not always with appropriate acknowledgement. Its premise is that if the therapist creates an atmosphere that is non-judgemental, empathic, and warm, people can realize their potential for self-expression and self-fulfilment.

Feminist-based psychotherapies began to evolve in the 1980s, reflecting a range of opinion from that which condemn Freud as a misogynist who deliberately recanted his discovery of the actuality of childhood sexual abuse to those who appreciate his linkage of life experience, innate drives, and corresponding defence mechanisms in influencing vulnerability to psychopathology (Elliot 1991; Appignanesi and Forrester 1992). The latter point of view, echoing a broader debate within psychoanalysis of the respective roles of internal and external reality, has led some feminist therapists to stress social reality, others psychical reality.

A radical conceptual departure

Cognitive therapy (or cognitive behavioural therapy as it is widely referred to on the grounds that many behavioural therapy techniques have been incorporated into the cognitive model) has achieved an increasingly prominent position among the psychotherapies since the 1960s, thanks to the industry and persistence of its progenitor, Aaron Beck. After training in psychoanalytically oriented psychiatry, he turned to psychoanalysis *per se*, excited about the prospect of exploring new psychological worlds, and applying this knowledge to his patients.

During the course of researching the psychodynamics of depression empirically in the 1960s, Beck reached the fateful conclusion that Freud's theoretical postulates were not confirmed. Instead, he advanced his own cognitions-based theory at whose core is the notion that depressed people feel gloomy as a result of the way they regard themselves. Thus, their feelings and behaviour are governed by their negative beliefs about themselves, the world, and the future. Having established a cardinal role for such negative thinking, Beck (1976) advanced a new therapeutic procedure whose goal is to challenge and correct erroneous beliefs, without the need to delve into childhood material or penetrate the unconscious layers of the mind (see Bloch's 2004 interview of Aaron Beck for considerably more detail about the evolution of cognitive theory and its applications).

Since this pioneering work, cognitive therapy has been widely embraced by the mental health professions, particularly clinical psychology, and tested empirically in a range of psychological problems across the lifespan: mood disorders, anxiety syndromes, substance abuse, personality disorders, somatoform disorders, and marital discord. Its potential role in the psychoses has also been under active study since the late 1990s (see Chapter 7 for further details).

The development of other modes of psychotherapy

Our focus, hitherto, has been on psychotherapy of the individual patient. The second half of the twentieth century saw the evolution of treatments conducted with more than one person: groups of strangers (see Chapter 11) and families (see Chapter 18).

Although therapy of stranger groups was experimented early on in the century, it was not until the Second World War that major developments ensued. The exigencies of war were the spur in that the group format proved highly economical to deal with huge numbers of soldier-patients. The Northfield Military Hospital in the United Kingdom was a centre of remarkable innovation, led by psychoanalytically oriented therapists like Wilfred Bion and S.H. Foulkes (1898–1976). Bion's (1961) influence pervaded subsequent work at the Tavistock Clinic while Foulkes (1965) was the founding father of the Institute of Group Analysis (both in London).

In the United States, the move to the study of group process was spearheaded by social psychologists, particularly Kurt Lewin (1890–1947). A national centre was established to train people in human relations and group dynamics. Participants from diverse backgrounds studied group functioning in order to act more effectively in their own work settings. Parallelling the human potential movement in the 1960s, the group movement transferred its focus from group to personal dynamics, and before long the encounter group movement had evolved with its thrust of promoting greater self-awareness and personal growth. Encounter groups became widespread during the 1960s and 1970s but after an initial fervour, declined both in terms of membership and appeal.

Formal group therapy under professional leadership then assumed a more prominent role. The most popular model was fathered by Irvin Yalom. He drew upon an interpersonalist approach, one originally moulded by Harry Stack Sullivan who proposed that personality is chiefly the product of a person's interaction with other significant people. Yalom pioneered the study of therapeutic factors specific to the group rather than following the pattern of transposing psychoanalytic or other theories from the individual setting. His *Theory and practice of group psychotherapy* (Yalom and Leszcz 2005) became exceedingly influential, attested to by the appearance of five editions.

Constrained perhaps by medicine's focus on the individual patient, psychiatry was slow to develop an interest in the family (Gurman and Knistern 1991). Scattered through Freud's writings are interesting comments about family relationships and their possible roles in both individual development and psychopathology. His description of processes like introjection, projection, and identification explained how individual experiences could be transmitted across the generations in a family. Influenced by the work in the United Kingdom of Anna Freud, Melanie Klein, and Donald Winnicott, the child guidance movement developed a model of one therapist working with a disturbed child and another with the parents, most often the mother on her own. The two clinicians collaborated in order to recognize how the mother's anxieties distorted her perception and handling of her child, which were added to the child's own anxieties.

Things took a different turn in the United States. There, Nathan Ackerman (1958) introduced the idea of working with the family of a disturbed child using psychoanalytic methods in the 1950s. An interest in working with the family, including two or more generations, arose concurrently. Thus, Murray Bowen (1971) found that the capacity of psychotic children to differentiate themselves emotionally from their families was impaired by the consequences of unresolved losses, trauma, and other upheavals in the lives of parental and grandparental generations.

Boszormenyi-Nagy (1984) also addressed this transgenerational theme by describing how family relationships were organized around a ledger of entitlements and obligations which conferred upon each participant a sense of justice about their position. This, in turn, reflected the experience in childhood of neglect or sacrifices for which redress was sought in adult life.

Bowen also introduced the principles of Systems Theory into his work but it was Salvador Minuchin, working with delinquent youth in New York, who highlighted the relevance of systems thinking to their interventions. The youngsters often came from emotionally deprived families, headed by a demoralized single parent (most often the mother) who alternated between excessive discipline and helpless delegation of family responsibilities to a child. Minuchin's Structural Family Therapy deploys a series of action-oriented techniques and powerful verbal metaphors which enable the therapist to join the family, and to re-establish an appropriate hierarchy and generational boundaries between the family subsystems (marital, parent/child, siblings).

Another major development took place in Palo Alto, California, where a group of clinicians gathered around the anthropologist Gregory Bateson (1972) in the 1950s. They noted that implicit in communication were *meta-communications*, which defined the relationship between the participants. Any contradiction or incongruence carried great persuasive, moral, or coercive force and formed part of what they labelled a 'double-bind'; they proposed this as a basis for schizophrenic thinking.

All these system-oriented views assume that the family is a system observed by the therapist. However, therapists are not value-neutral. They may take an active role in orchestrating change in accordance with a model of family functioning. Yet, these models ignore therapists' biases as well as the relevance of their relationships with families. This probably reflected the determination of some American family therapists to distance themselves from psychoanalytic theory, and also led them to neglect the family's history, how it changed throughout the lifecycle, and the significance of past traumatic and other notable life events.

In response to these criticisms, there was a move away from the problem-focused approach which had characterized most behavioural and communication views of psychopathology. The Milan school (Selvini-Palazzoli et al. 1980), whose founders were psychoanalysts, developed a new method of interviewing families in conjunction with observers behind a one-way screen formulating and then presenting to the family and therapist hypotheses about 'their' system.

Family therapists also began to consider that families might be constrained from experimenting with new solutions because of the way they had interpreted their past experiences or internalized explanatory narratives of their family, the expert's or society at large. This led to a shift from considering the family as a social to a linguistic system. The narrative a family conveys about their lives is a construction which organizes past experience in particular ways; other narratives are excluded. When a family with an ill member talks to a professional, conversations are inevitably about problems (a problem-saturated description). The participants ignore times when problems were absent or minimal, or when they successfully confined problems to manageable proportions. A different story might be told if they were to examine the context that might have led, or could still lead, to better outcomes.

A number of narrative approaches have applied these concepts. Philosophically, they align themselves with postmodernism, which challenges the notion of a basic truth known only by an expert.

Many criticisms of systems approaches have been levelled including the disregard of the subjective and intersubjective experiences of family members, neglect of their history, and denial of unconscious motives which affect relationships.

This critique has led to growing interest in integrating systems-oriented and psychoanalytic ideas, particularly those derived from object-relations theory. One variant is John Byng-Hall's (1995) synthesis of attachment theory, systems-thinking, and a narrative approach.

A further criticism of systems-oriented approaches is that they minimize the impact of external reality, such as physical handicap or biological factors in the aetiology of mental illness and socio-political phenomena like unemployment, racism, and poverty. One result is the 'psycho-educational' approach, which has evolved in the context of the burden schizophrenia and other psychotic disorders place on the family and the potential for its members to influence its course. This has led to a series of interventions including educating the family about the nature, causes, course, and treatment of the particular condition; providing them with opportunities to discuss their difficulties in caring for the patient, and to devise appropriate strategies; and helping them to resolve any conflict, which may be aggravated by the demands of caring for a chronically ill person.

The scientific era (see Chapter 3 on research for a fuller account)

Systematic research in the psychotherapies was a low priority for many decades; instead, practitioners' interests focused on theory and technique. Investigation of the subject only took off in earnest in the early 1950s. A notable impetus was the critique by H. J. Eysenck (1952) in which he argued that treatment of neurotic patients was no more effective than no treatment at all. Two-thirds of both groups showed improvement with time. In later reviews, Eysenck was even more damning: the effects of psychoanalysis in particular were minuscule. The attack led to much rancour and an extended battle between the psychoanalytic and behavioural camps (Eysenck featured prominently in the latter). Fortunately, a positive repercussion was the sense of challenge experienced by the analytic group. They had been riding high for several years, particularly in the United States, and barely questioned whether their concepts and practice required scientific appraisal. Thus, although Eysenck's interpretation of the research literature was flawed and biased, he had stirred a hornet's nest.

Since the 1950s, research has burgeoned and yielded much knowledge about whether psychotherapy works (outcome research), and how it works (process research). These developments were not without incident. Many therapists challenged the relevance of conventional research methodology to psychotherapy. A key argument was that the encounter between therapist and patient is unique, involving two people in a complex collaborative venture, and cannot be subject to the same form of scrutiny as occurs in the natural sciences. Moreover, the latter approach is necessarily mechanistic and reductionistic.

There is merit to the argument but actual research practice reveals that methodology can accommodate, at least in part, respect for the highly personal nature of psychological treatment. Sophisticated statistical procedures can also contribute to maintaining an appreciation that many characteristics in both patient and therapist are relevant, and they cannot be viewed as homogeneous groups. An illustration is the multidimensional measurement of outcome. Instead of restricting this to one or two variables only, several can be examined concurrently which together encompass the patients internal and interpersonal world, for example, quality of life, self-awareness, authenticity, self-esteem, target problems, and social adjustment.

Another criticism of outcome research is examining effectiveness without adequate treatment being given. Duration of research-bound therapy in fact is often much briefer than in customary practice, because of funding constraints. A similar objection relates to the follow-up period usually set. A robust test of effectiveness entails examining outcome one or more years following the end of therapy in order to judge clinical progress independent of the therapist.

The effectiveness of the psychotherapies

Several reviews have been conducted since the 1970s. A sophisticated method—meta-analysis—which relies on a rigorous statistical approach, points to psychotherapy overall generating benefits for patients who have been suitably selected. Encouragingly, better designed studies show positive results more commonly than inadequate ones. In one trail-blazing meta-analysis, levels of effectiveness were computed from 375 studies in which some 25,000 experimental and 25,000 control patients were tested (Smith et al., 1980). The average patient receiving psychological treatment of one kind or another was better off than 75% of those who were untreated—a clear demonstration of the beneficial effects of treatment in general. Several other meta-analyses have followed; see Chapter 3.

With tens of 'schools' available, many of them claiming a distinctive approach, the obvious question arises as to whether some are superior in producing benefit. This question of comparative effectiveness is complicated in that not only may 'schools' be compared but also specific procedures, such as setting a time limit or not or conducting therapy individually or within a group. Notwithstanding these difficulties, considering research on comparative effectiveness is worthwhile. Several reviews show a consistent pattern— that 'everyone has won and must have prizes'. This was of course the judgement of a race handed down by the dodo bird in *Alice in Wonderland*. In the psychotherapy stakes, it appears that everyone has won too, a finding probably attributable to factors common to all therapeutic approaches. These factors, originally set out by Jerome Frank (see Chapter 4 pp. 67–70), include a confiding relationship with a helping person, a rationale which provides an account of the patient's problems and of the methods for remedying them, instillation of hope for change, opportunity for 'success experiences' during treatment, facilitating emotion in the patient, and providing new knowledge, thereby promoting self-awareness. These 'non-specific' factors comprise a significant theme in psychotherapy; they probably serve as a platform for benefits from all treatments (Frank and Frank 1991).

Any consideration of effectiveness brings up the issue of harm. In other words, treatment may be for better or for worse. After a long gestation, the concept of a 'negative effect' attracted widespread attention from the 1970s (Hadley and Strupp 1976). A growing sense of confidence perhaps permitted therapists to be more open to a potential harmful impact.

To distinguish between a patient becoming worse because of their intrinsic condition or following an adverse life event, a negative effect has been defined as deterioration directly attributable to treatment itself. Such a causal link is difficult to prove but genuine negative effects certainly do occur. The definitional difficulty, however, leads to estimates of prevalence ranging from rare to common. The type of therapy appears to influence the rate. Evidence points to worsening in about 5–10% of cases in psychotherapy generally. The reasons for deterioration are not well established although a common view is that patient factors probably contribute, particularly selecting people for treatments for which they are unsuited. In this situation, refining assessment, thus enhancing clinicians' ability to predict response to specific treatments, is deemed as helpful to reduce the casualty rate.

Another obvious facet is the therapist and/or technique. Here, inadequate training has emerged as salient, with poor judgement leading to inappropriate interventions. It has also been recognized that a proportion of therapists perform poorly because of their personality traits, no matter what their level of training or experience. In other words, the role of therapist does not suit all those who wish to practise. In a noteworthy study (Lieberman et al. 1973) of different forms of encounter group, a substantial percentage of 'casualties' were produced by four leaders, who typically pummelled members to disclose personal information and express intense emotion.

During the half century of systematic research, attention has also been devoted to the processes that take place in the therapeutic encounter. Process and outcome research are inevitably linked. If we can identify factors that promote or hinder effectiveness, we may be able to modify these and then note the result. Advent of recording techniques, such as audio and video, has facilitated studies of process and a wide range of observations of both verbal and non-verbal behaviour, in both therapist and patient and their interaction, have been made. One illustration is the premise that a necessary condition for effective group therapy is group cohesiveness. It follows that anything enhancing cohesiveness could be advantageous. Compatibility between members has been proposed as pertinent and indeed been shown to relate to cohesiveness. Group therapy therefore could conceivably be more effective if, in selecting members, compatibility were taken into account. For example, a patient incompatible with all his peers would presumably not be placed in that group.

Research on process has been shown to be as salient as that on outcome since only with the study of what occurs in treatment can therapists appreciate its inherent nature and the factors for optimal improvement of participants. Diligent process research has provided solid foundations for establishing hypotheses about outcome.

We have dealt in general terms with the theme of psychotherapy research. The second half of the twentieth century and the beginning of the twenty-first century has been a fertile period and seen much achieved; to do it justice is beyond our remit. The interested reader is recommended to consult the four editions of the *Handbook of psychotherapy and behaviour change* (Bergin and Garfield 1994) which has served the field well in distilling work done and providing a critique of its quality.

References

Ackerman, N. W. (1958). *The psychodynamics of family life*. Basic Books, New York.

Appignanesi, L. and Forrester, J. (1992). *Freud's women*. Virago, London.

Bateson, G. (1972). *Steps to an ecology of mind*. Ballantine, New York.

Beck, A. (1976). *Cognitive therapy and the emotional disorders*. International Universities Press, New York.

Bergin, A. and Garfield, S. (eds) (1994). *Handbook of psychotherapy and behaviour change*. 4th edn. Wiley, New York.

Bion, W. (1961). *Experiences in groups*. Tavistock, London.

Bowen, M. (1971). *Family therapy in clinical practice*. Jason Aronson, New York.

Boszormenyi-Nagy, I., and Spark, G. (1984). *Invisible loyalities: Reciprocity in intergenerational family therapy*. Brunner/Mazel, New York.

Bromberg, W. (1954). *The mind of man: A history of psychotherapy and psychoanalysis*. Harper, New York.

Breuer, J. and Freud, S. (1955). *Studies on hysteria*. Standard edition, Volume 2. Hogarth Press, London.

Byng-Hall, J. (1995). *Rewriting family scripts. Improvisation and systems change*. Guilford, London.

Ellenberger, H. (1970). *The discovery of the unconscious*. Basic Books, New York.

Elliot, P. (1991). *From mastery to analysis, theories of gender in psychoanalytic feminism*. Cornell University Press, Ithaca, NY.

Eysenck, H. (1952). The effects of psychotherapy. *Journal of Consulting Psychology*, **16**, 319–324.

Foulkes, S. and Anthony, E. (1965). *Group psychotherapy: The psychoanalytic approach*. Penguin, Harmondsworth.

Frank, J. and Frank, J. (1991). *Persuasion and healing: A comparative study of psychotherapy*. 3rd edn. Johns Hopkins University Press, Baltimore.

Gurman, A. and Knistern, D. (eds). (1991). *Handbook of family therapy, Volume II.* Brunner/Mazel, New York.

Hadley, S. and Strupp, H. (1976). Contemporary views of negative effects in psychotherapy. *Archives of General Psychiatry*, **33**, 1291–1302.

Lieberman, M. Yalom, I., and Miles, M. (1973). *Encounter groups: First facts.* Basic Books, New York.

Mitchell, S. and Black, M. (1995). *Freud and beyond: A history of modern psychoanalytic thought.* Basic Books, New York.

Selvini-Palazzoli, M., Boscolo, L., Cecchin, G., and Prata, G. (1980). Hypothesising-circularity-neutrality: Three guidelines for the conductor of the session. *Family Process*, **19**, 3–12.

Smith, M., Glass, G., and Miller, T. (1980). *The benefits of psychotherapy.* Johns Hopkins University Press, Baltimore.

Yalom, I. and Leszcz, M. (2005). *The theory and practice of group psychotherapy.* 5th edn. Basic Books, New York.

Recommended reading

Ellenberger, H. (1970). *The discovery of the unconscious.* Basic Books, New York. (A magisterial, unrivalled history of the dynamic psychotherapies.)

Frank, J. and Frank, J. (1991). *Persuaion and healing.* 3rd edn. Johns Hopkins University Press, Baltimore. (Provides a panoramic view of the psychotherapies including their history by a pioneering scholar of the field and his daughter.)

Beck, A. (1976). *Cognitive therapy and the emotional disorders.* International Universities Press, New York. (Early account of cognitive theory and its therapeutic application.)

Bloch, S. (2004). A pioneer in psychotherapy research: Aaron Beck. *Australian and New Zealand Journal of Psychiatry*, **38**, 855–867. (An interview in which Beck describes the evolution of cognitive therapy—its theory and practice.)

Gay, P. (1988). *Freud: A life for our time.* Dent, London. (A splendid account of the life and ideas of Freud, including an illuminating chapter on his association with Jung.)

Freud, S. (1922). *An autobiographical study.* Standard edition, Vol. **20**, 1–74, Hogarth Press, London. (Invited to write a 'self-portrait' at the age of 68, Freud provided a lively account of the development of his key concepts; this is an essential read.)

Shamdasani, S. (2005). 'Psychotherapy': The invention of a word. *History of the Human Sciences*, **18**, 1–22. (An interesting examination of the origin of the term 'psychotherapy' in the English, French and German-speaking medical worlds of the nineteenth century.)

Chapter 2

Ethical aspects of psychotherapy practice

Allen R. Dyer and Sidney Bloch

Ethics is fraught with ambiguity both theoretically and in its application. Who should judge what is right and wrong? What principles, methods, and sources should be used? Ethics and morality may be used synonymously. Alternatively, a distinction is made, morality referring to the correctness of personal behaviour and ethics connoting more objective standards of behaviour, particularly as they might apply to professional practice. The ethics of psychotherapy fall into the latter category, although the practice itself—given that it entails self-reflectiveness—contributes to an understanding of moral action that transcends philosophy.

Psychotherapy, like a telescope, can be viewed from either end since it is both the object of ethical consideration and the instrument that helps us to scrutinize morality. Unlike the cold physics of an optical instrument, psychotherapy is a profoundly human activity. The subject of study is in a process of change, the observer an integral part of that process. Psychotherapy is, in this sense, more like quantum physics with its uncertainty principle—participant observation and change in the person being observed are inextricably linked.

Most psychotherapies, if they work successfully, move people to a deeper understanding of their motives and needs, strip them of self-deceiving defences (or, at least help them to understand such defences), and bring them to a point where they can respond empathetically to others (family, friends, the broader community). The key objective is self-understanding, which enables the person to live adaptively and fulfillingly.

The matter, however, is not quite so straightforward since various 'schools' of psychotherapy have elaborated their own views on what constitute the desiderata for successful treatment. Freud (1937, p. 250) for example, remarks in *Analysis terminable and interminable* that although it is 'not easy to foresee a natural end', the aim of psychoanalysis is: '... not to rub off every peculiarity of human character for the sake of a schematic "normality", nor yet to demand that the person who has been "thoroughly analysed" shall feel no passions and develop no internal conflicts. The business of the analysis is to secure the best possible psychological conditions for the functions of the ego; with that it has discharged its tasks'.

Whatever outcome is regarded as clinically desirable, all forms of psychotherapy are, in addition, moral in that patients are offered the opportunity to live their lives in a way that is integrated with their past (and future aspirations) and in the context of relationships, past and present, in a particular social community. The goals of the treatment are inherently idealistic although qualified by the need to live within a constraining reality.

Psychotherapy as a health profession

The concept of a health profession first evolved in Greece in the 4BC. The resultant Hippocratic Oath derives from a time when the distinction first emerged between shamanistic healers, with the power to heal or harm, and a new kind of practitioner devoted entirely to healing (Mead 1976). The Oath stipulates who may practice by extending training to a 'family' of clinicians which agrees to a common set of standards (Edelstein 1943).

The Oath's purposes are a mix of what is good for the patient and what upholds the professional group's reputation. The tone of reverence and invocation of the gods elevate the latter. For instance, the principle of confidentiality, 'Keeping to myself things which should not be noised abroad', makes it possible for a patient to trust in the doctor in a unique way. Beneficence, promoting the good of the patient, is stressed throughout. Specific prohibitions, against abortion and euthanasia, distinguish the modern practitioner from the shaman of old. And 'not cutting on the stone' is understood to denote not practicing beyond one's competence.

Psychotherapy, like contemporary medicine, draws on the Oath by requiring that its practitioners promote their patient's best interests by fulfilling a series of principles. On the other hand, psychotherapy is seen by some observers as an 'impossible profession' since it steers a precarious course between the ideal and the necessary, and the therapist herself is engaged in a process of self-discovery that resembles the patient's experience. Thus, no ethical codes or formulas answer the dilemmas of practice in a concrete way; instead, only broad principles may give guidance.

There is in fact no profession of psychotherapy as such. Rather, it is a set of skills shared by various groups: psychoanalysts, psychiatrists, psychologists, social workers, nurses, pastoral counsellors, family counsellors, marriage guidance counsellors, and others. In many instances, these groups have devised codes of ethics which guide in particular situations and set standards to define membership. Violating the latter may result in reprimand, censure, even expulsion. Psychotherapy does not necessarily require a license to practice, though professions that apply its skills may be subject to registration and regulation by a statutory authority. It is often claimed that ethical standards set by the practitioners themselves exceed those deemed adequate by an authority. Codes are explicit but at the cost of being simplistic. Professional ideals are, by contrast, tacit and lofty.

Values in psychotherapy

A goal of psychotherapy for both therapists and patients is to learn and appreciate what is valued, and esteemed by the latter. Even in a treatment limited to behavioural change, underlying values in the person, presenting with say, a social phobia may well determine what change is regarded as desirable. Given that the problems for which the patient seeks help are inextricably bound up with the basic question of how he should live his life, the therapist inevitably faces the risk of imposing his own values, consciously or unwittingly (Strupp 1974).

Some therapists have therefore espoused the notion of a value-free treatment. Carl Rogers (1979), for example, in labelling his model 'client-centred', argued for the therapist restricting his role to 'facilitator' in the pursuit of goals set by the patient. Although he asserted that 'one of the cardinal principles in client-centred therapy is that the individual must be helped to work out his *own* value system . . .' he also conceded the therapist's potential influence when he added '. . . with a minimal imposition of the value system of the therapist'.

A similar view, proposed by Engelhardt (1973), involves a shift in focus—psychotherapy is not about ethics but about what he calls *meta-ethics* in that it paves the way for ethical decision-making by the patient but not his adopting a *particular* set of values in treatment. The therapist takes care to avoid offering specific recommendations about how the patient should live his life. Instead, the patient is helped to reach a point where he can make his own choices *freely*, that is, unhindered by influences of which he was previously unaware. The problem with this position is that in advocating autonomy as a foremost objective of treatment and particularly one which allows choice about how to live one's life, the therapist is, in effect, conducting no more than another form of value-laden therapy. By stressing autonomy, the therapist makes a fundamental ethical statement.

Freud (1924, p. 118) was also intent on promoting treatment as value-free. He argued that 'The [therapist] should be opaque to his patients and, like a mirror, should show them nothing but what is shown to him'. He insisted, moreover, that the task was limited to the 'freeing of someone from his neurotic symptoms, inhibitions, and abnormalities of character' (Freud 1937, p. 216).

On the other hand, he pointed out the therapist's educative role. As he put it '[the analyst] must possess some kind of superiority, so that in certain analytic situations he can act as a model for his patient and in others as a teacher' (Freud 1937, p. 248).

It is difficult to conceive of this hybrid role of mirror, model, and teacher being value-free, even if goal is to rid the patient of neurotic features in order that he may no longer be governed by unconscious and irrational forces.

A reappraisal by influential therapists suggests that they inevitably incorporate values into their work. Thus, Strupp (1974, p. 200) asserts 'There can be no doubt that the therapist's moral and ethical values are always 'in the picture'. . . he cannot really espouse a 'value-free' position. . . . the therapist, whether he acknowledges it or not, does influence the patient's moral and ethical values'.

Sidney Crown (1977) reminds us that the therapist's influence concerning values occurs at verbal *and* non-verbal levels. While he may be aware of his utterances and attempt to control these, 'his non-verbal communication through gesture, facial expression, nods of approval or disapproval, can be almost unconscious', with the result that the patient is at risk of becoming exposed to a process of conditioning.

Erik Erikson (1976, p. 411) echoes the views of Strupp and Crown in proposing that psychotherapy is an explicit ethical intervention: 'What the healing professionals advocate . . . is always part of the value struggle of the times and, whether "avowed" or not, will be—therefore had better be—ethical intervention'.

If treatment amounts to ethical intervention, the obvious corollary follows: how shall the therapist go about this task? He could pursue the Rogerian position and make every effort to minimize moral agency. But the chance of success is slim—his 'unavowed' values will, in all likelihood, manifest through non-verbal cues.

A second option for the therapist is to accept that among his roles *is* that of 'ethical interventionist', but that this is his 'problem', not the patient's. She is thus not 'burdened' by a dilemma that does not belong to her in the first place. The therapist has the responsibility to be aware of his potential function as moral agent (Serota 1976). As part of this process, he is sensitive to his own values and monitors his unconsciously motivated impulse to influence the patient.

Illustrative is the case of a student who had won a prestigious fellowship to write a book but who had failed to write a word after nine months. It soon emerged that her motivation to do the project was derived from an unconscious wish to please her father, from whom she had always craved, but never received, affection. Presenting him with academic accomplishments was her only means to fulfil this need. The therapist, himself an academically ambitious person, had to grapple with his own confusion, wanting the patient to succeed with the book—in accordance with a strongly held value that academic achievement was a worthy pursuit—and yet, knowing through considered clinical judgement that her 'ambitiousness' was ill-conceived and had caused her much misery in the past. Thus, a sort of 'value-testing' is needed to ensure that intrusion of values into the therapeutic relationship is handled appropriately.

A more radical option is for the therapist to make the declaration of his personally held values a value in itself. The argument runs as follows: psychotherapy is a means of social influence; the therapist is more powerfully placed to influence his patients than the other way round; the therapist acknowledges this state of affairs; and he is 'transparent' regarding the values he espouses.

The American psychoanalyst, Robert Jay Lifton (1976), is an eloquent representative of this position. In his work with veterans of the Vietnam War, he elaborated a view in which the professional avoids the 'trap of pseudo-neutrality . . .' Instead, he combines advocacy and detachment, the process entailing 'moral advocacies' and, at the same time, 'maintaining sufficient detachment to apply the technical and scientific principles of one's discipline'. In the case of the veterans, Lifton articulated his anti-war position according to a principle he dubbed 'affinity'. This involved the coming together of veterans who had undergone the experience of fighting a purportedly unjust war and wished to make sense of it. Lifton participated in this affinity by dint of his avowed political and ethical sympathies.

Other examples of affinity have evolved in psychotherapy, all typified by the therapist assuming moral advocacy. Some homosexual therapists have aligned themselves with the 'gay movement' in providing therapy for homosexual patients (Bancroft 1981); a prominent doyen of American psychotherapy research, Alan Bergin (1980), evolved a school of 'theistic realism' for patients with religious convictions in which the therapist avows values derived from a Judeo-Christian tradition; these include forgiveness, reconciliation, spiritual belief, supremacy of God, marital fidelity, and primacy of love; and a few therapists, who worked in the context of *apartheid* South Africa, proclaimed their rejection of racism by committing themselves to supporting traumatized Blacks, especially those who had been victims of detention and torture (Steere and Dowdall 1990).

In these four illustrations, particular constituencies are served: war veterans, homosexuals, those with a religious commitment, Black victims of *apartheid*. However, a therapist's avowal of a value system can apply more generally.

Hence, he may adopt an approach with *all* his patients in which he is transparent about his ethical position in diverse clinical circumstances. As Aponte (1985) contends, the therapist does this on the premise that: 'Values are integral to all social systemic operations and therefore to the heart of the therapeutic process. Values are an essential component in defining and assessing a problem, determining goals, and selecting therapeutic strategies'. The corollary is unambiguous: 'Therapists do not have a choice about whether they need to deal with their values in therapy, only how well'. Aponte's contribution is helpful in offering a coherent account of how they may optimize their ethical task.

Marital therapy with a devout Christian couple serves as a useful example. Both partners subscribed to the chapter in Ephesians (5: 22–33) in which husbands are enjoined to love their wives 'as their own bodies', and wives are instructed to 'submit to their husbands in everything'. Aware of his motives, the non-Christian therapist not only helped the couple to clarify how each partner interpreted these verses in order to suit their own needs but also contributed his own view of marriage when pressed by both husband and wife. He felt it would be disingenuous to participate in a discussion about a crucial ethical matter without sharing his own position. He did not seek to impose his personal values but to ensure that the couple knew about them, thereby forewarning them of the potential influence of these values in the proceedings.

Ethical principles and informed consent

Standard accounts of ethics divide its theories into two major groups: rule or principle based. The most prominent example of the first is that of Kant with his categorical imperative: 'Act only according to that rule (or maxim) which you would want to be a universal principle'. Bearing this in mind offers guidance (especially for the rationally inclined) when trying to make an ethical decision. Utilitarian theories—the greatest good for the greatest number—are based on the ideas of Jeremy Bentham and John Stuart Mill, and weigh good according to a principle-governed calculation. Both approaches require analysis, and presume an attempt to determine what is right and good in a particular situation.

Ethical codes of the professions practicing psychotherapy are generally lists of rules that are articulated as principles. The resultant guidelines tend to be a consensus of professional leaders or 'elders'; the analogy with a religious community is noteworthy.

Four principles in particular—beneficence, respect for autonomy, non-maleficence, and justice—are prominent in contemporary psychotherapy.

Beauchamp and Childress (2001) have developed these over many years to assist all health professionals. The shift from medical-to bio-ethics is relevant in the recognition that decisions once made by practitioners paternalistically have broad social repercussions. Patients and their families have a legitimate say, indeed a right according to some ethicists, to participate actively in health decision-making. Consideration of the four principles reveals sociocultural tensions in which psychotherapy is carried out; the practice itself informs philosophical consideration of the principles.

Beneficence, doing good for others, a prominent feature of the Hippocratic tradition, has been a cornerstone of clinical practice, in the nineteenth and twentieth centuries. However, its role in ethical judgements has been challenged since the advent of the civil rights movement in 1960s. That 'Doctor knows best' is no longer regarded as sacrosanct, at least in Western societies.

Respect for autonomy emerged with the appreciation of a person's right to self-determination. The current emphasis on autonomy also follows in the wake of the civil rights movement in which choices are framed in terms of individual rights. It also parallels innovations in medical research and technology, such as chemotherapy and organ transplantation, where a patient may not want to face major risks of the treatments doctors propose. The place of autonomy was also reinforced by a greater awareness of the impact of unwanted research (as was conducted by Nazi physicians—an extreme but historically critical example). Informed consent has thus become the standard for health decision-making, not just as a perfunctory ritual, but also as a key consideration of the benefits and risks of the proposed treatment.

The similarities and differences between surgery and psychotherapy are worth noting in the context of informed consent. Whereas a plan for surgery can in virtually all cases be made explicit, the unpredictability of the psychotherapeutic process makes it less subject to specificity. (Freud likened it to a chess game!) Even the ambiguity of the distinction between 'patient' and 'client' hinges on assumptions about what is understood by autonomy. Patients treated by doctors for instance tend to be recipients of beneficence whereas clients 'shop in the marketplace', more or less autonomously, with their wits about them. As members of the medical profession, psychiatrists may be more inclined to see those they serve as patients whereas psycho-therapists belonging to other disciplines like psychology and social work tend to regard them as clients, even consumers. The distinction is sufficiently pertinent that we will return to it after reviewing the principles of non-maleficence and justice.

Non-maleficence was introduced as a neologism to capture the Hippocratic principle often cited by physicians, *Primum non nocere*—First, do no harm. Harm is not always easy to define, but certainly, the kind of psychological distress often experienced in recalling traumatic memories in psychotherapy would be a relevant example.

Justice is an abstract principle that has not received as much attention as it deserves. Justice is best understood as fairness, that is, treating similar situations in the same way. Justice as fairness also includes consideration of allocation of limited resources. For instance, is it preferable for a psychotherapist to treat a small number of patients intensively (as occurs in psychoanalysis) or to devote her expertise to a much larger clientele (e.g. supportive therapy for the long-term mentally ill)?

The pendulum has swung from beneficence to autonomy and perhaps back again. On the one hand, autonomy may be viewed philosophically as a basis for decision-making in the professional–patient relationship; it may also be construed as a goal of the therapeutic work. At a time of psychological distress and dysfunction, a person may be in such need of support or guidance or protection that dependence on a paternalistic therapist supersedes his capacity to act autonomously. Beneficence and autonomy in the context of psychotherapy are not mutually exclusive but part of a developmental mosaic. One may move from dependence towards autonomy but, at times of illness or stress, revert to a more dependent position in the interest of recovery.

Men may be more likely to favour autonomy and women more apt to look to the therapeutic relationship for support (Jordan et al. 1991). While stereotyping should be viewed cautiously, there is an inherent tension which bears scrutiny. Is autonomy meant to be self-sufficiency and total avoidance of dependence on another? Is autonomy, in this sense, a defensive posture? Alternatively, should gratifications encountered in the relationship with the therapist—the care and the nurturance—serve as a compensation for disappointments experienced elsewhere. Differences in theoretical orientation notwithstanding, men and women therapists need to be sensitive to these sorts of issues, and respond in ways that help the patient to pursue goals agreed on as part of the process of informed consent.

Informed consent, a hallmark of bioethics since the Second World War, reflects a shift from paternalism to autonomy. Extreme abuse of autonomy by Nazi physician-scientists in the extermination camps pointed to a radical new principle in medical practice and research, the right to self-determination. This was articulated dramatically in the Nuremburg statement, promulgated in the framework of the Nazi war crimes trials immediately after the War. Informed consent has become increasingly cogent as advances in medical science lead to complex treatments, entailing marked risks to which patients might not want to subject themselves. Consent requires provision of detailed information, the patient fully understanding it, appreciating the implications of various treatment options, and having the capacity to decide freely. Informed consent must have all four components for its ethically sound application.

An admirable model provided by Carl Goldberg (1977) calls for the concept of a 'therapeutic partnership', with its cornerstone of a 'mutually agreed upon and explicitly articulated working plan'. This becomes subject to reviews throughout therapy. Among its elements are: identifying goals and the methods to reach them; monitoring the effectiveness of treatment; and permitting either partner to voice dissatisfaction at any stage. Moreover, the respective roles, tasks, and responsibilities of both therapist and patient are outlined, discussed, and examined as necessary.

The partnership does not imply an equal share of power, rather an agreement about how the power will be allocated at various times. Thus, complete patient autonomy in which he enjoys the capacity to reflect, decide, and act freely on the basis of reflections may not always be a feature of the encounter, no matter how desirable this may seem. A patient in the throes of a severe crisis, for instance, may lack the wherewithal to consider what constitutes his best interests and, in collaboration with the therapist as partner, agree to a redistribution of responsibility; the therapist is then assigned a more paternalistic role. As the crisis wanes, so will this aspect of the partnership require renegotiation, paving the way for a restoration of the patient's autonomous state. A key feature of such shifts is their *joint* determination by the partners.

Dyer and Bloch (1987), in reviewing models which could be applied to informed consent in a therapeutic relationship, have proposed that the fiduciary approach is most apt by virtue of its emphasis on trust and time. Arguing against exclusive reliance on either respect for autonomy or paternalism they suggest that a relationship built on trust is more relevant. Thus, the therapist operates to manifest his trustworthiness and this in turn encourages the patient to invest his trust in him. The process occurs over time and is not a function of a one-off negotiation at the outset of treatment.

Moreover, the fiduciary quality enhances in the therapist a sense of responsibility in that he seeks to identify the patient's needs and to respond to them at all times. Although autonomy is viewed as a legitimate goal of the encounter, it is not the exclusive basis for the therapist's ethical concern for his patient; he may be required to act paternalistically on occasion, paternalism comparable to the concern manifest by responsible parents for a vulnerable or needy child.

The acceptance of a therapeutic partnership based on the fiduciary model obviates the ethical pitfalls that inevitably permeate the psychotherapeutic enterprise. The partnership is a necessary but *not* sufficient condition for sound practice.

In Goldberg's partnership model, either protagonist can raise the issue of the effectiveness of treatment. This also includes lack of progress or deterioration. The goal of helping someone overcome his problems seems unambiguous but treatment is a complex process that can go awry. Not every person benefits. Like the natural developmental process which therapy seeks to imitate and promote, numerous pitfalls are possible. Failures of interpretation and empathy, for instance, can lead to adverse sequelae.

Winnicott's (1990) concept of 'good enough' mothering is pertinent in this regard. Perfection is neither possible nor desirable in human interactions, including the one that typically evolves in treatment. Therapists should strive to be good enough rather than flawless in their role and functioning. Indeed, the latter may well undermine the patient's ability to participate. The therapist may be seduced unwittingly by the patient's praise in the transference and shy away from the necessary task of helping him grapple with ambivalent feelings. All intimate relationships, including that with a therapist, are marked by such ambivalence. Good enough therapy requires that therapists tolerate this insightfully. Voltaire's dictum: *Le mieux est l'ennemi du bien* (The perfect is the enemy of the good) is most apposite.

Dealing with traumatic memories is a prominent contemporary example of how the therapist needs to be content with good enough practice. Treating patients affected by traumatic memories is challenging to say the least. Some therapists espouse the notion that no healing can occur until the perpetrator has been confronted, even brought to justice. Others are of the equally sincere view that the patient *must* forgive the perpetrator. These divergent approaches share the feature of suggestion. The course of therapy may be predetermined by the therapist's premises rather than by the patient's needs.

A tenet of many 'schools' is that childhood experiences have influenced the course of psychological development and that adult personality is shaped by what preceded it. Freud used the concept of 'overdetermination' to indicate the many paths to symptoms. For example, incest would almost certainly be traumatic and lead to symptoms later. But the presence of symptoms does not necessarily mean they are linked to a particular traumatic episode.

We have come to assume that childhood experiences will be recalled in therapy. However, these may be long forgotten or repressed. In practice, what is remembered are associated feelings. We tend to forget a disappointment of childhood and replace a child-like outlook with the thoughts of adulthood. We forget, for example, how confused we felt at the birth of a sibling. We extinguish the suffering that accompanied a loss. These forgotten aspects may, however, be recovered in treatment.

Good enough therapy creates a forum in which it is safe to remember and share memories, thoughts, feelings, and fantasies. The patient then acquires the opportunity both to understand how she came to be the person she is and how she may choose to change.

With regard to memories of childhood sexual abuse, a balance between *belief* and *suggestion* may prevail. The therapist's *belief* that early traumatic experience can be reconstructed creates fertile ground for both implicit and explicit *suggestion* which, in conjunction with a vulnerable patient, may lead to the production of false memories. The therapist must be not only willing to believe but also remain sceptical in an empathic way, which does not invalidate the patient's experience. The therapist has the challenging task of helping the patient sort out whether the clinical material she shares are actual memories or fantasies. The process takes time and skill; it is not infallible and there are no short cuts. The therapist needs to know the patient exceedingly well and she must, ideally, get to know herself well too.

Confidentiality

Confidentiality is a vital feature of psychotherapy. Tracing its central principle back to Hippocrates, we can appreciate its profundity. How could a patient trust a therapist if he 'noised abroad that which is too shameful to be spoken?' We might imagine a time before Hippocrates when knowledge one had of another was public. Healers in pagan cultures were in effect mediators with the spiritual world. They were not—as Margaret Mead (1976) points out—constrained to heal only, but also extended their powers to causing harm to enemies and to people who had transgressed. In the small communities of ancient Greece, what one person knew about another was accessible to all for example, who was ill and unable to perform their usual work, who had violated a social norm. Everyone participated in decisions about how to bring the person back in line.

The respect for privacy we take for granted and as required by contemporary psychotherapy is a radical departure from what prevailed in ancient times. The right to have one's own thoughts became a novelty. Relating with the healer became more personal, and no longer mediated by the community.

Privilege, a related concept, refers to the right of a person to determine what information will be divulged in a judicial or administrative context and prevails when legal statute specifies its function. The clearest illustration of its role in psychotherapy is articulated in Jaffee v. Redmond (1996), where the US Supreme Court ruled that communication between therapist and patient is privileged and '. . . rooted in the imperative need for confidence and trust'. Mary Redmond, a policewoman, shot and killed a man while on duty. She soon started to receive therapy from a social worker. The deceased's relatives then sued Ms Redmond and asked to access the therapist's notes. This was refused on the grounds of its privileged status.

As can be seen in this example, confidentiality pertaining to the clinical sphere has special relevance in psychotherapy. The nature of the patient's disclosures to the therapist is frequently personal in the extreme. An account of sexual abuse or a shameful act or a guilt-laden experience are but a few instances which testify to the salience of the therapist–patient relationship as a forum for sharing intensely private information. As Sissela Bok (1982) puts it: 'People benefit from confidentiality because it allows them to seek help they might otherwise fear to ask for'.

That confidentiality cannot be absolute raises genuine ethical dilemmas for health professionals. Siegler's (1982) radical description of it as a 'decrepit concept' reflects his pessimism that the principle can be sustained. He points out, for instance, that tens of people have legitimate access to the hospital medical record but the corollary that the principle of confidentiality '. . . no longer exists' does not follow. On the contrary, it means that clinicians have to work that much harder to safeguard patients' private information. Joseph and Onek (1999) have pointed this out comprehensively when covering such aspects as the interface between confidentiality and the law; clinical records (this is especially problematic in an era of information technology when much clinical data are computerized, transferred between information systems including databases, and accessible to the patient); the requirements of, and pressures from, third parties (e.g. insurers, employers, statutory authorities); the Tarasoff situation (see below); sexual abuse; group, family and couple therapy; teaching; and medical writing.

We have opted to focus on a topic which challenges the therapist, namely the potential breach of confidentiality when a patient threatens to harm others.

A landmark case is the *Tarasoff v. Regents of the University of California* (1976). A student, Prosenjit Poddar, murdered Tatiana Tarasoff, whom he was eager to befriend, after divulging his intention to do so to his therapist two months earlier. Concerned by the prospect of harm befalling Ms Tarasoff, the therapist consulted his seniors and the police. The latter questioned Mr Poddar, concluded that he did not pose a threat to Ms Tarasoff but extracted a promise that he would not contact her.

The 1976 judgement can be summarized as follows: In the event of a patient intending to harm an identified person, 'protective privilege ends when the public peril begins'. In other words, the therapist is duty-bound to protect an intended victim if that person can be identified. The 1974 decision referred only to a 'duty to warn'.

The judgement has endured for over three decades and been taken up in various ways by several other jurisdictions in the United States. However, we should note arguments mounted against the judgement, including a dissenting opinion in the original decision. Virtually all criticism revolves around the threat Tarasoff poses to the integrity of the therapeutic relationship. As Stone (1984) proclaimed at the time of the 1976 judgement, using an utilitarian argument (also the basis of the dissenting opinion in the Californian Supreme Court decision), imposing a duty to protect would undermine a patient's expectation of confidentiality and so jeopardize treatment. Gurevitz (1977) has argued that a Tarasoff duty leads to a situation in which the therapist is more concerned to protect society than treat patients.

Ironically, a professor of law, has argued for a shift in how clinicians should deal with the patient threatening harm and the intended victim. The law, David Wexler (1979) avers, has played itself out but paved the way for a 'post-Tarasoff scenario' whose principal feature is abandonment of an intrapsychic model of interpersonal violence in favour of an interactionist framework. Wexler's sights are on *both* patient and intended victim. The latter, is typically a family member or other known person who is aware of the patient's participation in treatment and of his hostility. The therapist, accordingly, strives to obtain the patient's consent to establish contact with the potential victim. The advantage of a meeting between therapist and the person at risk is acquisition of valuable knowledge about the patient's motives as well as the intended victim's possible contribution to the problematic interaction. This additional body of information is, in Wexler's thesis, likely to enhance treatment. The proposition to exploit the patient's trust in therapist and treatment is designed to prevent a breach of confidentiality, with all the ethical and legal repercussions that ensue.

Boundaries and violations

We can trace contemporary considerations of professional boundaries and their transgressions to the Hippocratic Oath in which practitioners are warned to remain free of all injustice and to refrain from sexual relations with either men or women, whether free or enslaved. An absolute rule in ancient Greece, it is as unambiguous as a moral precept can possibly be.

Boundaries today are defined as the limits of appropriate therapist behaviour in a professional setting (Gabbard 1999). Gutheil and Gabbard (1993) have distinguished between boundary crossings and boundary violations. A crossing deviates from conventional therapeutic norms but does not exploit the patient. Crossings, such as having a social chat with a patient encountered in a supermarket or extending the duration of a session to accommodate a patient's wish to be special or scheduling sessions in the evening after fellow therapists have departed, are not in and of themselves harmful but do run the risk of disrupting the therapeutic process.

Boundary violations go beyond crossings inasmuch as patients are definitely exploited and therapy placed in jeopardy. They take varied forms, for example, financial associations, such as receiving advice from a stockbroker patient, extraprofessional social encounters, such as dining with a patient, religious links, such as inviting a patient to join one's church. On the other hand, inflexible rules can disrupt treatment. A behaviour therapist, for instance, may take a patient to a shopping centre as part of a desensitization program in treating agoraphobia or to a cemetery to carry out grief work.

Sexual relations with a patient definitely constitute a boundary violation. Gabbard (1999) has made a notable contribution to an understanding of sexual boundary violations, especially in differentiating four psychodynamically based categories. The psychopath and severe narcissistic personality are grouped together to constitute a predator category. They are typically sadistic, exploitative, unempathetic, guiltless, and remorseless. Given the power differential in the therapist–patient relationship, they can readily manipulate the patient to their advantage.

A second category covers therapists who have a need to be loved as a means of bolstering their self-worth. They characteristically have one sexual relationship only. In what Gabbard terms the lovesick sub-type they desperately seek to obtain the patient's love although they dupe themselves with the belief that they are actually offering love.

The masochistic category covers therapists who have a deep-seated need to be controlled, and enact this with a demanding 'difficult' patient. Thus, they subject themselves to the patient's escalating requests, perhaps starting with making themselves accessible at all times through physical embrace to a sexual relationship. The psychotically disturbed make up the last, and smallest category. A good example is the manic therapist who is completely convinced that loving his patients can bring about their improvement.

Given these variegated reasons for violating sexual boundaries, a detailed analysis is indicated in order that appropriate treatment and rehabilitation can be instituted.

It is obvious that prevention is the best policy. All therapists, from the inception of their training, should be fully cognizant of the factors contributing to a sexual boundary violation and alert to their own vulnerability. Supervision is clearly the forum to share any concerns and to prevent a crossing becoming a violation. The supervisor bears the responsibility to offer a troubled therapist a safe and private space. The seasoned therapist, by no means less immune than the novice, needs to be equally vigilant and recruit the assistance of a trusted colleague should he find himself deviating from ethically sound norms.

Since transference patterns endure, it is generally agreed that a sexual relationship with an ex-patient exploits unconscious feelings that were part of the previous therapy (Dyer 1988). This has not always been the case. In the past, it was regarded by many therapists that an intimate relationship with an ex-patient was acceptable. Controversy then raged over this question from the 1990s, with various attempts at a compromise. For instance, Appelbaum and Jorgensen (1991) proposed a 1-year prohibition of a sexual relationship following the end of treatment. This is a pragmatic but arbitrary limit. It could also lend itself to abuse inasmuch as a therapist might be tempted to end treatment prematurely to circumvent the "rule".

Major psychiatric bodies like the American Psychiatric Association and the Royal Australian and New Zealand College of Psychiatrists have stood by the principle, 'Once a patient, always a patient' as the safest guideline for their members.

Conclusion

In an illuminating essay, Susan Sontag (2001) highlights obligations of conscience that stem from looking at photographs of war and bearing witness to the suffering of others. If war is understood as traumatic in the way therapists apply the concept, then her thesis applies equally to psychotherapy.

Never does Sontag (2003) hint that studying the suffering of others is voyeuristic. Instead, she avers that those who are 'surprised that depravity exists continue to feel disillusioned... when confronted with evidence of what humans are capable of inflicting in the way of gruesome cruelties upon other humans, has not reached moral or psychological adulthood.... No one after a certain age has the right to this kind of innocence...'

Psychotherapy performs a similar function in that its practitioners bear witness to the suffering of others. Such witnessing is an ethical act, which has intrinsic value. Thus, therapists should never allow their patients to suffer alone or to feel that their pain is too severe to bear by the professional carer.

References

Aponte, H. (1985). The negotiation of values in therapy. *Family Process*, **24**, 323–38.

Appelbaum, P. and Jorgenson, L. (1991). Psychotherapist-patient sexual contact after termination of therapy: An analysis and a proposal. *American Journal of Psychiatry*, **148**, 1466–73.

Bancroft, J. (1981). Ethical aspects of sexuality and sex therapy. In *Psychiatric ethics* (ed. S. Bloch and P. Chodoff), pp. 160–84. Oxford University Press, Oxford.

Beauchamp, T. and Childress, J. (2001). *Principles of biomedical ethics*. 5th edn. Oxford University Press, New York.

Bergin, A. (1980). Psychotherapy and religious values. *Journal of Consulting and Clinical Psychology*, **48**, 95–105.

Bok, S. (1982). *Secrets*. Oxford University Press, Oxford.

Crown, S. (1977). Psychotherapy. In *Dictionary of medical ethics* (ed. A. S. Duncan, G. R. Dunstan, and R. B. Wellbourn). pp. 264–8. Darton, Longman and Todd, London.

Dyer, A. and Bloch, S. (1987). Informed consent and the psychiatric patient. *Journal of Medical Ethics*, **13**, 12–16.

Dyer, A. (1988). *Ethics and psychiatry: Toward professional definition*. American Psychiatric Publishing Press, Washington, DC.

Edelstein, L. (1943). The Hippocratic oath. *Bulletin of the History of Medicine* (Suppl. no. 5, 1:1–64).

Engelhardt, H. T. (1973). Psychotherapy as meta-ethics. *Psychiatry*, **36**, 440–5.

Erikson, E. (1976). Psychoanalysis and ethics-avowed and unavowed. *International Review of Psychoanalysis*, **3**, 409–15.

Freud, S. (1924). *Recommendations to physicians practising psychoanalysis*. Standard edition, **12**, 111–20. Hogarth Press, London.

Freud, S. (1937). *Analysis terminable and interminable*. Standard edition, **23**, 211–53. Hogarth Press, London.

Gabbard, G. (1999). Boundary violations. In *Psychiatric ethics* (ed. S. Bloch, P. Chodoff and S. Green) pp. 141–160. Oxford University Press, Oxford.

Goldberg, C. (1977). *Therapeutic partnership: ethical concerns in psychotherapy*. Springer, New York.

Gurewitz, H. (1977). Tarasoff: protective privilege versus public peril. *American Journal of Psychiatry*, **134**, 289–92.

Gutheil, T. and Gabbard, G. (1993). The concept of boundaries in clinical practice: theoretical and management decisions. *American Journal of Psychiatry*, **150**, 188–196.

Jaffee v. Redmond, 116S. Ct. 1923, 1996.

Jordan, J., Kaplan, A., Miller, J., Stiver, I. and Surrey, I. (1991). *Women's growth in connection—Writings from the Stone Center*. Sone Centre, Wellesly, MA.

Joseph, D. and Onek, J. (1999). Confidentiality in psychiatry. In *Psychiatric Ethics* (ed. S. Bloch, P. Chodoff and S. Green), pp. 105–140, Oxford University Press, Oxford.

Lifton, R. J. (1976). Advocacy and corruption in the healing professions. *International Review of Psychoanalysis*, **3**, 385–98.

Mead, M. (1976). Quoted in Levine, M. (1976). *Psychiatry and ethics*. Holt, Rinehart and Winston, New York.

Rogers, C. (1979). *Client-centred therapy*. Constable, London.

Siegler, M. (1982). Confidentiality in medicine. *New England Journal of Medicine*, **307**, 1518–21.

Serota, H. (1976). Ethics, moral values and psychological interventions. *International Review of Psychoanalysis*, **3**, 373–5.

Sontag, S. (2003). *Regarding the pain of others*. Picador, New York.

Sontag, S. (2001). *On photography*. Picador, New York.

Steere, J. and Dowdall, T. (1990). On being ethical in unethical places: the dilemma of South African clinical psychologists. *Hastings Center Report*, **20**, 11–15.

Stone, A. (1984). The Tarasoff case and some of its progeny: Suing psychotherapists to safeguard society. In *Laws, psychiatry and society*. American Psychiatric Press, Washington DC.

Strupp, H. (1974). Some observations on the fallacy of value-free psychotherapy and the empty organism. *Journal of Abnormal Psychology*, **83**, 199–201.

Tarasoff v. *Regents of the University of California*. 131 Cal Rptr 14, 17 Cal 3rd 425, 551P, 2d 334, 1976.

Wexler, D. (1979). Patients, therapist, and third parties: The victimological virtues of Tarasoff. *International Journal of Law and Psychiatry*, 2, 1–28.

Winnicott, D. W. (1990). *Collected papers: From paediatrics through psychoanalysis*. Karnac, New York.

Recommended reading

Bloch, S., Chodoff, P. and Green, S. (1999). *Psychiatric ethics*. 3rd edn. Oxford University Press, Oxford. (Contains several useful chapters for the psychotherapist including on confidentiality, boundary violations, and allocation of resources, as well as a chapter by Jeremy Holmes specifically on ethical aspects of the psychotherapies.)

Bloch, S. (ed.) (1996). Special section: Ethics and psychotherapy. *American Journal of Psychotherapy*, **50**, 257–335. (Six papers make up this guest-edited section covering such subjects as the ethics of family and child psychotherapy, repressed memories, values and sexual boundary violations.)

Dyer, A. (1988). *Ethics and psychiatry: Toward professional definition*. American Psychiatric Publishing Press, Washington, DC. (Clear account of foundational topics such as what is a profession, the therapeutic alliance, informed consent, the place of virtue and moral agency.)

Gabbard, G. (ed.) (2002). Ethics in psychiatry. *Psychiatric Clinics of North America*, **25**, 509–524, 547–559, 575–584, 585–592, 593–603, 605–621. (Six papers in this guest-edited volume are devoted to ethical aspects of psychotherapy including confidentiality, boundary violations, the place of religion and gay and lesbian patients.)

Holmes, J. and Lindley, R. (1989). *The values of psychotherapy*. Oxford University Press, Oxford. (Covers a wide range of pertinent topics e.g. the role of values, codifying ethical behaviour, conflict of interest, allocation of psychotherapy resources and sexual exploitation.)

Lakin, M. (1988). *Ethical issues in the psychotherapies*. Oxford University Press, New York. (Covers a wide range of topics with specific chapters on ethical aspects of individual, group, couple and family therapy.)

Chapter 3

Research in psychotherapy

Frank Margison and Anthony Bateman

Our aim in this chapter is to outline fundamental principles of research in psychotherapy and to challenge the assumption that research is a specialized area and only the concern of the researchers themselves. Core knowledge of psychotherapy research is required by therapists for a number of reasons. First, an understanding of how to apply research thinking to daily practice is fundamental to being a good clinician. We cover this in the section on applying research methods to practice. Second, good practice depends on a working knowledge of what has already been discovered, with an ability to sort the wheat from the chaff by knowing what constitutes good psychotherapy research and what is meaningful to clinical practice. This forms the major part of the chapter. Third, an ability to appraise new research critically in the context of previous findings enables practitioners to adapt their practice according to contemporary findings. Finally, knowledge of the research literature enables experienced practitioners to train others more effectively. The history of psychotherapy research since the 1960s suggests that it has had a major influence on clinical psychotherapy and led to changes in practice and re-organization of training.

It is not possible to cover comprehensively all the research on the different models of psychotherapy. We therefore attempt (1) to highlight the main trends, (2) to provide key studies as examples, (3) to discuss the main research methods used because there are specific problems in investigating psychotherapy, and (4) to provide the main 'headline' findings.

Psychotherapy research myths

Psychotherapy is inherently 'unresearchable' and there is little evidence for its efficacy

Psychotherapy 'is the best documented medical intervention in history' according to Howard and his colleagues (Howard et al. 1995). Roth and Fonagy (2005) reviewed the outcome research of different models in various psychiatric disorders and found good evidence for the effectiveness of some therapies in some disorders. Also, the effect sizes (effect size is a standardized way of comparing change between therapies) were comparable to many other non-psychotherapeutic treatments, from all branches of medicine.

Sessions of psychotherapy can be counted like doses of a drug

This is not true but it is equally erroneous to assume that drug dosages themselves necessarily equate in a simple manner. Furthermore, many drugs have therapeutic 'windows' or effects that occur earlier and later in treatment. No researcher would simply count sessions alone because there are systematic differences in therapies of various lengths. In general, the impact of each successive session lessens and so the graph of change against number of sessions shows a 'law of diminishing returns'. For example, 16 sessions does not give twice the benefit of 8. Also, the course of improvement for any individual may be quite erratic. But, there are still systematic patterns. Continuing with the drug analogy, the ED50, the effective dose to produce recovery in 50% of patients, suggests that there are repeatable patterns found in all psychotherapies. Initial 'remoralization' has a low ED50 (4–6 sessions) whereas typical symptoms, say of depression or anxiety, have ED50s of about 10–12 sessions, and long-standing problems in interpersonal relation ED50s of 40+ sessions. Indeed, some patterns of relating (conflicted) respond quicker than others (passivity and detachment). Sometimes remarkably low doses can be effective, for example, a study of 2+1 therapy (two sessions plus a follow-up) was effective for people with mild depression (Barkham and Hobson1990).

Different sessions of a therapy vary so much that you are not comparing like with like

Early sessions differ in content from middle and last sessions and different therapists deliver the 'same' therapy but within the context of their own personal style. These variations can be minimized by training practitioners to follow manuals and by checking their 'adherence' through audio or video recording. But some would argue that this makes the therapy even more alien to practitioners and therefore unrepresentative of customary practice. It is true though that the 'drug analogy' breaks down when looking at individual sessional change. Patients report certain sessions as 'special' in that there is a moment of insight or breakthrough that persists and can often generalize. Sometimes these 'moments' are not what the therapist expected; the 'great interpretation' may be mystifying, but a moment of mutual understanding may profoundly affect the participants.

Psychotherapy is an art rather than a science—it is intuitive and relies on clinical experience rather than research knowledge

We would argue that good psychotherapy needs to combine art in the sense of intuition and the judicious use of subjectivity with robust science. In the preceding paragraph, we noted that experience may have profound effects and this cannot be predicted accurately. This is reminiscent of Thomas Edison's comment that 'Genius is one per cent inspiration and 99 per cent perspiration'. For these reasons of unpredictable responses and imperfectly understood causation, research knowledge is notoriously difficult to embed into regular practice. Many practitioners have never tried, arguing that their cases are different (more ill, more complex, etc.), or that they want the freedom to shift focus and goals as the need arises.

However, research across therapies shows that there are advantages in treatment being structured, with a formulated set of goals, clear processes, and a clear rationale that can be conveyed to the patient.

Psychodynamic therapy has no evidence base

All research goes through different stages. This has been conceptualized as an 'hourglass' model (Salkovskis 1995). Initially, clinicians work with individual patients conducting 'messy' research, refining theoretical views, and trying out different strategies. They operate within a wide frame and give little consideration to cause and effect. Gradually this becomes more refined as clinicians begin to recognize, for example, that certain strategies succeed with some patients and not others. Patients are selected more carefully, protocols defining interventions are developed, and gradually a model of therapy is defined. Carefully conducted trials are implemented and used to inform additional strategies; there may even be a need to return to the beginning to refine the treatment further. The model is not sequential but dynamic with each aspect informing others.

In essence, the psychotherapies are at different stages in this 'hourglass' process. Until recently psychodynamic psychotherapy relied on single case studies that have been rich in clinical detail but of limited value in determining effectiveness. Dynamic therapy remained reliant on anecdotal data in which practitioners found clinical evidence consistent with their predictions. Psychodynamic therapists have been severely criticized for this on the basis that knowledge gleaned from such case studies is unreplicable, non-falsifiable, less valid, and less generalizable than that obtained from groups of people in comparative trials. There is merit in this criticism. However, we should not throw the baby out with the bath water. Psychodynamic therapy may have been constrained, in part, by historical forces. The model and method of treatment evolved within a different environment from the current evidence-based one, and reducing reliance on out-dated investigative methods is taking time. More recent therapies such as Interpersonal Therapy (IPT) and Cognitive Behavioural Therapy (CBT) have incorporated research concepts into treatment itself and have not faced the problem of shifting from a century-old culture in which practitioners argued that 'scientific' research is not an appropriate paradigm with which to investigate psychoanalytic treatments, or that it was so intrusive as to compromise therapy.

An evidence-based approach

An evidence base implies that we can determine the value of an intervention as judged by its consequences for the person receiving it. The world is not so simple. For example, even effective treatments are only so for a proportion of patients (typically 60–70%). Therapy is only any good for that patient if he or she gets better, whatever the evidence base claims.

Evidence of effectiveness has other limitations. First, it tells us nothing about *how* a patient improves. Only process and process–outcome research can answer this question in any detail. Process research identifies critical ingredients and underlying mechanisms of change. Process-outcome research also yields data that is meaningful to therapists and may influence practice.

Second, there is difficulty in identifying *meaningful measures of outcome* that properly reflect improvement in terms the patient understands. Psychotherapy is an elaborate intervention and rarely used to target symptoms alone although this may be the case in behavioural treatment. The tendency can be to over-simplify problems. For example, depression is reduced to a score on the Beck Depression Inventory or the Hamilton Rating Scale. Change on the scale is then equated with a good outcome. These measures become shorthand for the problem itself when in reality they can only ever be a summary of specified features.

Measures cannot represent the complexity and heterogeneity of illness or indicate change in an individual's life. To circumvent this problem researchers have used batteries of measures, looking at different domains, such as interpersonal functioning and social adjustment as well as symptoms. This approach adds to the richness of measuring outcome, but can lead to problems when different measures favour different treatments. Interestingly, this is rarely a problem since most measures correlate with each other to a surprising extent, possibly signifying that the person responds to an overall feeling of 'wellness' when scoring purportedly specific questions.

Third, relying on symptomatic improvement may be a poor measure of the benefit of treatment. Symptom distress may be unchanged, suggestive of a poor outcome, but the patient may show improvement in subtle areas of personal functioning. Such outcomes can be extremely difficult to measure and large samples may be needed to find significant differences between treatments. The reverse is also true. In research into outcome for personality disorder, there is often evidence that symptomatic improvement occurs which implies good outcome. But functional impairment, for example, social adjustment and interpersonal relating, remain quite unchanged.

Finally, who is the arbiter of outcome? The patient may hold a different view to the therapist, and both may differ from an 'outside observer'. Some patients do their best to please the researcher, others may want to spoil the study and deliberately mark questionnaires negatively. Researchers often find differences between self-report and observer-rated outcomes although there is no consistent pattern.

Patient satisfaction as a measure of outcome has become increasingly relevant. Long-term therapy does well in this regard. The Consumer Reports study (Seligman 1995), based on self-report, concluded that long-term worked better than short-term therapy, and that satisfaction with treatment was high. This is a comforting finding for those who favour long-term therapies, but satisfaction alone is not an acceptable outcome measure even though it may be superficially appealing. Which other treatment would judge its worth on the fact that the patient wants it to last longer. It is difficult to imagine this applying to any other branch of medicine. We can only assume that the patient is reflecting on the way the relationship with the therapist has an intrinsic value. There is nothing shameful about this, but it makes it difficult to compare long-term therapy with other interventions.

Methodology

A principal problem in evaluating evidence is the gap between 'efficacy' and 'effectiveness'. Efficacy refers to results that are achieved in carefully designed trials so that causal inferences can be made. As many factors as possible are controlled so that the major variable is the intervention itself. In this way, any change is likely to be a consequence of treatment rather than result from other factors, such as passage of time. But too great an emphasis on this internal validity compromises external validity, with treatment found to be efficacious in carefully specified conditions not generalizing to everyday practice. In general, interventions found to be efficacious in trials are less effective when studied in clinical populations. This has led to calls for 'effectiveness' research, that is, how therapy performs in hard-pressed services with few fully trained staff. A further advantage of research in clinical services is that we learn that implementation of treatment is feasible in routine practice. In effect, it bridges the gap between research interventions and everyday work. This 'gap' should not be underestimated. Family therapy for schizophrenia was shown to reduce rates of relapse and hospitalization as long ago as the early 1980s. It has taken over two decades to introduce family interventions as part of early intervention approaches. This is strikingly different from the introduction of new drugs, where there is much less of a 'lag time'.

Single-case studies

The belief that clinical description of a single group of cases is relevant beyond the specific locus of discovery is fatally flawed (Fonagy and Moran 1993) and no longer an acceptable method in psychotherapy research unless it is a first step towards more refined designs.

Quantitative single-case studies do not suffer from these problems. Appropriate baseline measures may be taken and interventions given or withdrawn systematically, and the effects monitored. When replicated across randomly sampled cases they have excellent generalizability, particularly the effectiveness of an intervention on specific symptoms. The patient acts as his own control. This has been used in CBT and psychoanalytic therapy. An example of the process in CBT is summarized by Salkovskis (1995) who developed a theoretically driven approach to treat panic disorder. In psychoanalytic research, Fonagy et al. (1987) followed the progress of the psychoanalysis of a 13-year-old diabetic girl, using blood sugar readings as a marker of her internal psychological world and relating these to the analyst's session records. Using 'lag correlation', they showed a temporal relationship between the interpretation of Oedipal conflicts and better diabetic control, and argued that such results counter Grunbaum's (1986) claim that psychoanalysis is based on 'suggestion', since the analyst was ignorant of, and made no reference to, the state of the patient's diabetic control.

Cohort studies

Cohort studies reflect a naturalistic approach to studying a group of patients undergoing treatment and have been used most commonly to investigate longer-term therapies. Patients may have to satisfy strict criteria to enter a trial but there is no randomized control group. As a result, change may be an effect of other factors, such as passage of time. However, if a cohort is large enough, it is possible to draw conclusions about the value of a treatment, particularly if it is possible to compare outcomes with those of a similar group who have not received the intervention. This method has been used particularly to study effectiveness of services treating patients in therapeutic communities (Rosser et al. 1987; Najavits and Gunderson 1995; Blatt 1996; Dolan et al. 1997; Blatt 1998). Patients treated for 1 year in inpatient settings show symptomatic improvement over time (Dolan and Evans 1992) but this is difficult to evaluate since most of the research is uncontrolled. However, Dolan and colleagues (1997) used a non-admitted comparison sample to assess the effectiveness of a therapeutic community. Of 137 patients studied, 70 were admitted and 67 not admitted for clinical or financial reasons. One year after treatment there was significantly greater reduction in core features of personality disorder in the treated than non-admitted group.

A mixed approach has also been taken using cohorts allocated to different treatments non-randomly but on another basis, such as domicile. The effectiveness of three psychodynamically oriented models for a mixed group of personality disorders—(1) long-term residential treatment using a therapeutic community; (2) briefer inpatient treatment followed by community-based dynamic therapy (step-down programme); and (3) general community psychiatric treatment—was studied in this way. The brief inpatient treatment followed by outpatient dynamic therapy was more effective than the other two approaches on most measures including self-harm and readmission rates to general psychiatric wards as well as being more cost-effective (Chiesa et al. 2002). Follow-up at 36 months confirmed these results (Chiesa and Fonagy 2003).

Stevenson and Meares (1992) used a cohort design to great effect in establishing the efficacy of a psychodynamic therapy in an outpatient setting for borderline personality disorder. The researchers later reported the 5-year follow-up of these patients, a remarkable achievement given the difficulties of long-term follow-up (Stevenson et al. 2005). Patients treated with 1-year dynamically based psychotherapy twice a week showed considerable improvement at the end of treatment and maintained their gains over 5 years. The improvement was not predicted by the hypothetical natural history suggesting that relatively brief, low-intensity therapy can influence the course of severe personality problems.

In another field study, the Stockholm Outcome of Psychotherapy and Psychoanalysis Project (Blomberg et al. 2001; Sandell et al. 2002), 405 patients in psychoanalysis (4–5 sessions a week) or psychoanalytic psychotherapy (1–2 a week) were compared. The groups were matched on several variables and followed for up to 3 years following termination. Outcome was similar at the end of treatment, but at a 3-year follow-up of 156 patients, psychoanalytic psychotherapy patients had not changed further whereas the psychoanalytic group continued to improve to the point where they were indistinguishable from a normal population sample. This suggests that long-term reconstructive personality change may be associated with the more frequent therapies. Despite the useful information that may be derived from both single case and cohort studies and their ease of implementation, greater emphasis has been given to the randomized controlled trial, which has become the gold standard.

Randomized controlled trial (RCT)

The application of RCTs to psychotherapy is deceptively simple. A homogeneous group of patients with a specific problem is allocated randomly to different treatments. Skilled therapists deliver interventions in a pure and measurable form and in a specific dose, for example, 16 sessions, and outcome is reliably measured.

Despite the popularity of RCTs there are problems with them. First, randomization of patients does not represent customary entry into therapy. Strict randomization may lead to patients being allocated to treatments they would not usually accept or be offered. Second, there is increasing evidence that expectation of therapy is pertinent for outcome (Horowitz et al. 1993). Third, sample size is often small and attrition substantial leading to a situation in which those patients remaining in a trial are far from random. Patients respond differently to the same treatment leading to variation in outcome in the same group. Fourth, the 'named' treatment is often delivered by different therapists; even if a manual is followed, patients may get treatment that differs in salient respects. Therapists show considerable flexibility in interpreting manuals even after training (Gibbons et al. 2003). Fidelity of application is commonly measured by recording sessions and randomly transcribing them to ensure therapists keep to the model of therapy. Few studies, however, record all sessions. In any case, manualization has been found wanting. Henry et al. (1993) demonstrated that adherence to protocols obtained by additional training resulted in a *decrease* in quality of therapist functioning. This may either reduce effectiveness of therapy or, at least, not improve it (Bein et al. 2000). Fifth, therapists themselves are rarely matched to patients even though patient–therapist fit may influence outcome (Rubino et al. 2000, Lambert 2004). Sixth, non-specific factors powerfully influence outcome and blind evaluations are hard to achieve. Finally, and possibly most pertinently, investigator allegiance affects outcome (Gaffan 1995). Professionals closely identified with a therapy are more likely to show a better outcome for that therapy than an alternate control. Luborsky and colleagues (1999) found researcher allegiance accounted for 70% of the variance in outcome.

Many of these difficulties are not specific to psychotherapy research and it is to the credit of psychotherapy investigators that they take them seriously. Research into effectiveness of medication is beset with similar problems. First, outcomes of treatment with medication are better in trials conducted by pharmaceutical companies than those conducted by independent investigators (Freemantle et al. 2000). Second, trials are rarely performed using an active placebo which means 'blindness' of participants and researchers is unlikely, as most medication has unwanted effects obvious to patient and researcher.

In randomization, the ideal control group may be no treatment at all but this is rarely ethically or practically possible and does not control for the effect of attention. A placebo treatment is impossible since it is inconceivable that any activity between two people would have no positive or negative therapeutic effect. Researchers have therefore tended to compare an active treatment with treatment as usual in the case of longer-term therapies or with another active therapy in the case of short-term therapies.

RCTs tend to focus on short-term treatments. In long-term treatment patients drop out, (although this is more likely early in treatment), receive additional treatment, or begin to resent the repetitive intrusion of data collection. This disadvantages research in longer-term therapy which has been under-represented other than through the 'open trial' or cohort study. There are notable exceptions. Some RCTs have been done of longer-term treatment of personality disorders with reasonable follow-up (Linehan et al. 1991, 1993; Bateman and Fonagy 1999, 2001).

Outcome studies

Eysenck (1952) in his often-quoted review of evidence then available asserted that two-thirds of neurotic patients improve irrespective of whether they are treated with psychotherapy or not. But his view has been sharply criticized. Re-analysis of the data (McNeilly and Howard 1991) showed that the impact of a few months of psychotherapy was equal to the impact of 2 years of all other forms of help available to a patient, confirming the potency of psychotherapy. Even though the original review was flawed, it was hugely influential in shaking the psychotherapy community out of complacency and into an active engagement with research.

A notable outcome study that attempted to surmount many of the problems we have cited was conducted by the National Institute of Mental Health (NIMH) in the United States. The Treatment of Depression Collaborative Research Programme (TDCRP) (Elkin et al. 1989) had two major aims: to see if collaborative trials of psychotherapy on a large scale were feasible, and to compare the effectiveness of two brief psychotherapies with standard medical treatment using antidepressants. Two hundred and fifty depressed patients were randomly assigned to one of four treatment conditions—cognitive-behavioural therapy (CBT), interpersonal psychotherapy (IPT), imipramine plus clinical management (IMI-CM), and placebo plus clinical management (PLA-CM). Psychotherapists were trained and supervised regularly. Sessions were recorded to ensure therapist fidelity. Allegiance effects were controlled for by therapy being given in centres whose clinical facilities were well versed in providing the treatment but not involved in setting up the study, and outcome measures were extensive and meaningful.

Patients were assessed for depression and social function before treatment and at 4, 8, 12, and 16 weeks and followed up at 6, 12, and 18 months. Inevitably, the results are complicated but, in essence, there was little difference in outcome between the groups. Patients receiving medication were least symptomatic and those receiving placebo the most symptomatic at the end of treatment. Recovery rates showed some differences but these were not marked; patients receiving medication or IPT were most likely to recover. This was upsetting to those vociferously supporting CBT, who argued that it was given inadequately at one site although there is little data to support this (Hollon 1994). Reanalysis (Elkin et al. 1995) confirmed the equivalence of treatments for less-depressed patients. There was greater differentiation between treatments for more severely ill patients.

Similar results were found in three English studies, which looked at the outcome of depression treated with CBT or psychodynamic-interpersonal therapy (PI). The latter is a manualized therapy derived from psychodynamic principles with humanistic and interpersonal elements. The studies were the Sheffield Psychotherapy Project (SPP-1) (Shapiro and Firth-Cozens 1987), the Second Sheffield Psychotherapy Project (SPP-2) (Shapiro et al. 1994, 1995), and the Collaborative Psychotherapy Project (CPP) (Barkham 1996). All three were rigorously designed taking into account the problems of RCTs discussed above.

The first study used a crossover design in that each patient was treated by the same therapist with CBT and PI, each for eight sessions but the order randomly determined. There were only minor differences in outcome during each type of treatment while the order of therapy was of no consequence.

In the second study, comparing 8 or 16 sessions of either therapy, therapists had equal allegiance to the two therapies. More severely depressed patients showed better outcomes with 16 sessions compared to those receiving only 8 and PI therapy did less well than CBT over 8 sessions. Follow-up at 1 year confirmed these patterns.

The third study took place in routine practice, again with either 8 or 16 sessions of either PI or CBT. There were three main findings. Effects were less marked than in a research clinic but still substantial, patients did better with 16 sessions, and the immediate post-therapy gains were not maintained at follow-up.

Many other comparative studies have found little difference between treatments for a number of conditions. One of the best known was conducted by Sloane and colleagues (Sloane et al. 1975) who studied patients suffering from moderately severe neuroses and personality disorders. They were randomly allocated to one of three conditions for 4 months: behaviour therapy, analytically oriented therapy, or a waiting list. Severity of target symptoms declined in all three groups, but more so in the treated conditions than the waiting-list one. In both therapies outcome correlated with the quality of the relationship between patient and therapist. At the subsequent 8 month follow-up the analytical group continued to improve on social adjustment (indicating a need for follow-up of patients after the end of therapy).

In another well-crafted study Snyder and Willis (1989) compared behavioural marital therapy (BMT) with insight-oriented marital therapy (IOMT). Both were better than no treatment and equivalent at the end of the trial and at 6-month follow-up. Later, when couples were followed up at 4 years (Snyder et al. 1991), there was a marked difference in divorce rates between the two groups—38% of the BMT group but only 3% of the IOMT group. There was something particular about IOMT that had a continuing effect. Other explanations may apply but adherence to treatment was monitored and it was established that both treatments had been given appropriately. This study again underscores the need for long follow-up in psychotherapy research.

Another example of the need for follow-up came from a comparison of a CBT-based treatment for psychosis which was compared with 'befriending', on the basis that both were supportive but only one was thought to have the active therapeutic ingredient. Against expectations, outcomes were equivalent at the end of therapy, but at 1-year follow-up the CBT group had maintained their gains whereas the befriending group had slipped back to baseline levels (Sensky et al. 2000).

The consistent finding of equivalence of therapies is known as the 'dodo verdict' (Luborsky et al. 1975) after the story in *Alice's adventures in wonderland* in which— 'everybody has won and all must have prizes'. Certainly, the verdict remains plausible and difference in outcome between therapies needs more careful consideration than discovering similarity. It may be that we do not have the capability to detect difference or that therapies share many factors which are agents of change. They are often subsumed under the rubric of the therapeutic or working alliance (see below).

Meta-analytic studies

Meta-analytic studies collect data from separate outcome studies, allowing calculation of an effect size (ES). The ES refers to group differences in standard deviation units—basically the degree to which the average treated patient is better off than the controls. This technique has been used to investigate outcome and cost-effectiveness. ESs show that psychotherapy is better than placebo (ES=0.46) and substantially better than no psychotherapy (ES=0.82) (Wampold et al. 1997). The small differences reported among mainstream therapies suggest that they may be more or less equivalent. Some therapies show superior ESs to others under specific conditions. For example, CBT shows a greater ES in the treatment of anxiety than other therapies. Psychodynamic therapy may have a greater ES than CBT in personality disorder (Leichsenring and Leibing 2003).

Caution should be exercised when assessing meta-analyses. First, the quality of studies included varies considerably. Second, studies should be comparable and yet this is often not the case. Between studies, patients may have been diagnosed according to different criteria, therapies given for different lengths of time, and therapists not comparable in terms of experience and training. Third, in the case of meta-analyses comparing ESs of active control conditions, it is important to examine specifically the control condition in each study. Finally, ESs comparing different therapies need to be considered as quite different from ESs measured before and after therapy for the same patients, which typically have much larger ESs.

There is limited research on cost-effectiveness of psychotherapy but meta-analyses suggest that considerable savings can be made in health service utilization and other costs (Gabbard et al. 1997).

Therapeutic alliance

As mentioned earlier, the relationship between therapist and patient as a contributor to outcome is crucial. In one meta-analytic study (Horvath and Simmonds 1991) there was a 26% difference in level of success dependent on the alliance.

It may be thought that the alliance is likely to be most pertinent in dynamically oriented therapies since they explicitly use the relationship as a mediator of change. However, it seems equally relevant in other therapies. Castonguay and colleagues (1996) found significant associations between alliance and outcome in patients receiving CBT and CBT plus an antidepressant.

The impact of the alliance was demonstrated in the NIMH project we discussed earlier (Krupnick 1996); it was pertinent across all treatments including medication and placebo. In the Sheffield studies Stiles et al. (1998) a significant link between outcome and the relationship was detected.

We can summarize the above evidence thus:

* Specific treatments are better than 'treatment as usual'
* A substantial body of evidence shows that psychotherapy works, although some therapies have been studied more extensively than others
* When treatments are compared there are few advantages shown of one over another
* Effectiveness studies show smaller effects than efficacy studies
* Participation in a study seems to improve outcomes of 'treatment as usual' so there are likely to be benefits from the attention given in a research setting
* The therapeutic alliance is a key factor in change

Process research

It could be argued that excessive effort has been expended in chasing small differences in the comparative outcome research. This has led to more interest in process and process–outcome research—that is, how patients improve. Studying process represents an attempt to move research away from quantification of outcome towards meaning. But, conceptually the term 'process' needs some clarification.

Observational perspective

Like outcome, process can be examined from the perspectives of patient, therapist, and independent observer. This has led to recognition that different observational points do not necessarily correlate. For example, in personality disorder research, observer-rated improvements are often higher than self-rated change; this may result from obvious improvement in external behaviour but less change in the internal experience of the patient.

Treatment vs change process

Psychotherapy processes are often considered separately from intrinsic treatment components. The former refers to general psychological features in the therapy, the latter to the actual interventions delivered or the purported active ingredients of therapy. This confusion has been remedied to an extent by researchers looking at all events in therapy without taking an a priori view of sources of change. Actions, perceptions, feelings, intentions, thoughts, and verbalizations of both patient and therapist are all examined as well as their interrelationships. The alliance, for example, becomes a process contributed to by both patient and therapist rather than one solely from the patient's view. This approach suggests that while there may be equivalent outcomes between therapies there is a notable non-equivalence in process. Stiles (1979, 1986) found evidence of technical non-equivalence, as therapists of different persuasions gave interventions consistent with their model. Psychoanalytically oriented therapists restricted themselves, for instance, to interpretations, clarifications, acknowledgements, and reflections whereas gestalt therapists 'stayed in the 'now' and client-centred therapists used reflections and acknowledgement as their primary interventions.

Technical aspects of therapy

Therapeutic techniques have come under considerable scrutiny and research has begun to unravel the complex process of psychological treatment, looking at what makes people better. The most widely known attempt to put technical aspects on a reliable, replicable, and scientifically reputable basis is the Core Conflictual Relationship Theme (CCRT) method (Luborsky and Crits-Christoph 1990). This is laborious but yields psychodynamically meaningful data about the patient's inner world. Luborsky and others have used CCRTs to research salient psychoanalytic concepts. CCRT 'pervasiveness' diminishes in the course of successful therapy, so that by its termination patients are less dominated by core conflicts. Therapeutic change is associated particularly with the capacity to cope with negative responses and to elicit more positive ones from others, rather than an idealized 'resolution of underlying conflict'.

Another study used CCRTs to look at the relationship between the 'accuracy' of interpretations, as measured by their closeness to CCRTs, and change. The more skilful the therapist, the better the outcome, especially insofar as they were able to identify wishes, responses elicited, and reactions. While accuracy of interpretation was related to outcome, the type of interpretation was not—that is, non-transference interpretations were just as effective as transference ones (Fretter 1994).

Luborsky and Crits-Cristoph (1990) believe that the CCRT approach provides the first scientific confirmation and objective measure of the concept of transference. By comparing the features of CCRT with Freud's statements about transference they confirm that (1) people have only a few basic transference patterns, (2) these are manifest both in their relationships generally and with the therapist, (3) they seem to derive from early parental relationships, (4) they are as evident outside therapy as in it, and (5) they are susceptible to gradual change in the course of treatment.

Applying research to practice

Evidence-based practice and practice-based evidence

A new approach involves pooling results from many therapists, working routinely across several sites. These Practice Research Networks (PRNs) (Audin et al. 2001) rely on a willingness to use common instruments and to share data. Typically, an academic centre can help with analysis and inter-pretation of data to support several PRNs. One such outcome measure, used widely in the United Kingdom, is CORE-OM (Clinical Outcomes in Routine Evaluation-Outcome Measure) (Evans 2002), used by many psychotherapy centres.

Pooling of data allows the outcomes of different therapists who are treating similar patients to be compared. It may emerge that some therapists achieve better outcomes, less dropouts, or have poorer outcomes with specific types of patients. This information can then be used for training, to explore the possible reasons for differences, and to reorganize services.

Learning from evidence

There are standard methods of drawing inferences from a body of research but there are also difficulties applying them coherently (Margison 2001) when the evidence base is equivocal or the values supporting the therapy clash with methods used to evaluate evidence. This is striking when therapies claim to be about 'personal growth', without specific measurement reflecting such growth. Therapies focusing on symptom reduction that can be explicitly measured using established instruments are more easily understood and incorporated into services and training.

Whether outcome findings are meaningful in terms of drawing implications relevant to clinical practice is pivotal. A model that can be used on small samples or for whole departments relies on the concept of clinically significant and reliable change (CSRC). The method only requires two points of measurement for each patient (typically before and after therapy).

In Figure 3.1, each dot represents a patient. The same outcome scale is used on the horizontal scale (pre-therapy score) and the vertical scale (post-therapy score). It follows that the diagonal line represents patients who have not changed at all. Those above and to the left have worsened and those to the right and below have improved. The dotted 'tramlines' represent the imprecision of the measure and any dots falling within these lines cannot be interpreted.

Anyone to the upper left beyond the tramlines has *reliably deteriorated* and anyone below and to the right has *reliably improved*. Simply examining these figures is of value in assessing a service or a particular therapist.

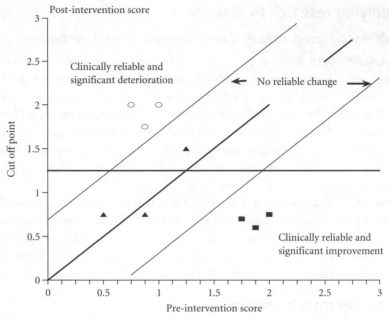

Fig. 3.1 Graphical plot of reliable and clinically significant change parameters. Reproduced by kind permission of Evidence-Based Mental Health, BMJ Publishing Group.

A second issue is whether the patient has shown *clinically significant improvement*. This is a different issue, which looks at whether the magnitude of change makes a clinical difference. Anyone falling below the horizontal line (which represents the cut-off between well and clinical samples) can be said to show clinically significant improvement.

It is possible to plot patients for an individual therapist or for a whole department, and the results are a good and readily accessible form of quality monitoring. The chart can also be used for quality improvement by using it to select patients who have deteriorated and focusing attention and supervision on them.

Conclusion

Considering the limited funds for psychotherapy research, its depth and breadth is impressive. Outcome for different conditions is well documented. Process research has contributed enormously and given us an understanding of how psychotherapy works. Even so, we know little about mediating factors. Social class, age, ethnicity, and gender are not relevant. There is greater need to study the interactions between patient features, therapist attitudes, and treatment methods. Researchers take all these aspects seriously. In its joint focus on outcome and process, psychotherapy remains the 'best documented medical interventions in history' (Howard etal.1995) and research on it continues to be rewarding.

References

Audin, K., Mellor-Clark, J., Barkham, M., Margison, F., McGrath, G. L., S., Cann, L., Duffy, J. and Parry, G. (2001). Practice research networks for effective psychological therapies. *Journal of Mental Health*, **10**, 241–251.

Barkham, M., Shapiro, D.A., Hardy, G.E., Rees, A. (1999). Psychotherapy in two-plus-one sessions: Outcomes of a randomized controlled trial of cognitive behavioural and psychodynamic interpersonal psychotherapies for subsyndromal depression, **67**, 201–211.

Barkham, M., Rees, A., and Shapiro, D. A. (1996). Outcome of time-limited psychotherapy in applied settings: replication the Second Sheffield Psychotherapy Project. *Journal of Consulting and Clinical Psychology*, **64**, 1079–1085.

Bateman, A. and Fonagy, P. (1999). The effectiveness of partial hospitalization in the treatment of borderline personality disorder—a randomised controlled trial. *American Journal of Psychiatry*, **156**, 1563–1569.

Bateman, A. and Fonagy, P. (2001). Treatment of borderline personality disorder with psychoanalytically oriented partial hospitalisation: An 18-month follow-up. *American Journal of Psychiatry*, **158**, 36–42.

Bein, E., Andersen, T., Strupp, H. H., Henry, W. P., Schacht, T. E., Binder, J. L. and Butler, S. F. (2000). The effects of training in time-limited dynamic psychotherapy: changes in therapeutic outcome. *Psychotherapy Research*, **10**, 119–132.

Blatt, S., Berman W, Cook B. P. and Ford R. Q. (1998). Effectiveness of long-term, intensive, in-patient treatment for seriously disturbed young adilts: A reply to Bein. *Psychotherapy Research*, **8**, 42–53.

Blatt, S. J., Stayner, D. A., Auerbach, J. S. and Behrends, R. S. (1996). Change in object and self-representations in long-term, intensive, inpatient treatment of seriously disturbed adolescents and young adults. *Psychiatry*, **59**, 82–107.

Blomberg, J., Lazar, A. and Sandell, R. (2001). Long-term outcome of long-term psychoanalytically oriented therapies: First findings of the Stockholm Outcome of Psychotherapy and Psychoanalysis study. *Psychotherapy Research*, **11**, 361–382.

Castonguay, L., Goldfried, M., Wiser, S., Raue, P. and Hayes, A. M. (1996). Predicting the effect of cognitive therapy for depression: A study of unique and common factors. *Journal of Consulting and Clinical Psychology*, **64**, 497–504.

Chiesa, M. and Fonagy, P. (2003). Psychosocial treatment for severe personality disorder: 36-month follow-up. *British Journal of Psychiatry*, **183**, 356–362.

Chiesa, M., Fonagy, P., Holmes, J., Drahorad, C. and Harrison-Hall, A. (2002). Health Service use costs by personality disorder following specialist and non-specialist treatment: A comparative study. *Journal of Personality Disorders*, **16**, 160–173.

Dolan, B. and Evans, C. (1992). Therapeutic community treatment for personality disordered adults: changes in neurotic symptomatology on follow-up. *International Journal of Social Psychiatry*, **38**, 243–250.

Dolan, B., Warren, F. and Norton, K. (1997). Change in borderline symptoms one year after therapeutic community treatment for severe personality disorder. *British Journal of Psychiatry*, **171**, 272–279.

Elkin, I., Gibbons, R. D., Shea, M. T., Sotsky, S. M., Watkins, J. T., Pilkonis, P. A. and Hedeker, D. (1995). Initial severity and differential treatment outcome in the National Institute of Mental Health Treatment of Depression Collaborative Research Program. *Journal of Consulting and Clinical Psychology*, **63**, 841–847.

Elkin, I., Shea, M. T., Watkins, J. T., Imber, S. D., Sotsky, S. M., Collins, J. F., Glass, D. R., Pilkonis, P. A., Lever, W. R., Docherty, J. P., Fiester, S. J. and Parloff, M. B. (1989). National Institute of Mental Health Treatment of Depressoin Collaborative Research Program: General effectiveness of treatments. *Archives of General Psychiatry*, **46**, 971–982.

Evans, C., Connell, J., Barkham, M., Margison, F., Mellor-Clark, J., McGrath, G. and Audin, K. (2002). Towards a standardised brief outcome measure: Psychometric properties and utility of the CORE-OM. *British Journal of Psychiatry*, **180**, 51–60.

Eysenck, H. J. (1952). The effects of psychotherapy: An evaluation. *Journal of Consulting Psychology*, **16**, 319–324.

Fonagy, P. and Moran, G. S. (1993). Selecting single case research designs for clinicians. In *Psychodynamict treatment research: A handbook for clinical practice* (eds. Miller, N. E., Luborsky, L., Barber, J. P. and Docherty, J. P.). Basic Books, New York, pp. 62–95.

Fonagy, P., Moran, G. S., Lindsay, M. K. M., Kurtz, A. B. and Brown, R. (1987). Psychological adjustment and diabetic control. *Archives of Disease in Childhood*, **62**, 10009–11013.

Freemantle, N., Anderson, I. M. and Young, P. (2000). Predictive value of pharmacological activity for the relative efficacy of antidepressant drugs. Meta-regression analysis. *British Journal of Psychiatry*, **177**, 292–302.

Fretter, P., Bucci, W. and Broitman, J. (1994). How the patient's plan relates to the concept of transference. *Psychotherapy Research*, **4**, 58–71.

Gabbard, G. O., Lazar, S. G., Hornberger, J. and Spiegel, D. (1997). The economic impact of psychotherapy: A review. *American Journal of Psychiatry*, **154**, 147–155.

Gaffan, E. A., Tsaousis, I. and Kemp-Wheeler, S. M. (1995). Researcher allegiance and meta-analysis: the case of cognitive therapy for depression. *Journal of Consulting and Clinical Psychology*, **63**, 966–980.

Gibbons, M. C., Crits-Christoph, P., Levinson, J. and Barber, J. (2003). Flexibility in manual-based psychotherapies: Predictors of therapist interventions in interpersonal and cognitive-behavioral therapy. *Psychotherapy Research*, **13**, 169–185.

Grunbaum, A. (1986). Precis of the foundations of psychoanalysis: A philosophical critique, with commentary. *Behavioural and Brain Sciences*, **9**, 217–284.

Henry, W. P., Strupp, H. H., Butler, S. F., Schacht, R. E. and Binder, J. L. (1993). The effects of training in time-limited psychotherapy: Changes in therapists' behaviour. *Journal of Consulting and Clinical Psychology*, **61**, 434–440.

Hollon, S. D. and Beck A. T. (1994). Cognitive and cognitive behavioural therapies. In *Handbook of psychotherapy and behaviour change* (eds. A. Bergin, and S. L. Garfield) Wiley, New York.

Horowitz, L. M., Rosenberg, S. E. and Bartholomew, K. (1993). Interpersonal problems, attachment styles and outcome in brief dynamic therapy. *Journal of Consulting and Clinical Psychology*, **61**, 549–560.

Horvath, A. O. and Simmonds, B. D. (1991). Relation between working alliance and outcome in psychotherapy: A meta-analysis. *Journal of Consulting and Clinical Psychology*, **38**, 139–149.

Howard, K. I., Orlinsky, D. E. and Lueger, R. J. (1995). The design of clinically relevant outcome research: Some considerations and an example. In *Research foundations for psychotherapy practice* (eds. M. Aveline, and D. A. Shapiro,) John Wiley, Chichester, pp. 3–47.

Krupnick, J. L., Sotsky, S. M., Simmons, S., Moyer, J. and Elkin, I. (1996). The role of the therapeutic alliance in psychotherapy and pharmacotherapy outcome: Findings in the NIMH Collaborative Research Programme. *Journal of Consulting and Clinical Psychology*, **64**, 532–539.

Lambert, M. J. (2004). *Handbook of Psychotherapy and Behaviour Change*, Wiley, New York.

Leichsenring, F. and Leibing, E. (2003). The effectiveness of psychodynamic therapy and cognitive behavior therapy in the treatment of personality disorders: a meta-analysis. *American Journal of Psychiatry*, **160**, 1223–32.

Linehan, M. M., Armstrong, H., Suarez, A., Allmon, D. and Heard, H. (1991). *Archives of General Psychiatry*, **48**, 1060–1064.

Linehan, M. M., Heard, H. L. and Armstrong, H. E. (1993). Cognitive-behavioural treatment of chronically parasuicidal borderline patients. *Archives of General Psychiatry*, **50**, 971–974.

Luborsky, L. and Crits-Christoph, P. (1990). *Understanding transference: The CCRT method*, Basic Books, New York.

Luborsky, L., Diguer, L., Seligman, D. A., Rosenthal, R., Krause, E. D., Johnson, S., Halperin, G., Bishop, M., Berman, J. S. and Schweizer, E. (1999). The researcher's own therapy allegiances: A 'wild card' in comparisons of treatment efficacy. *Clinical Psychology: Science and Practice*, **6**, 95–106.

Luborsky, L., Singer, B. and Luborsky, L. (1975). Comparative studies of psychotherapies: is it true that 'everybody has won and all must have prizes'? *Archives of General Psychiatry*, **37**, 471–81.

Margison, F. (2001). Practice based evidence in psychotherapy. In *Evidence in the psychological therapies: A critical guide for practitioners* (eds. C. Mace, S. Moorey and B. Roberts,) pp. 174–198 Brunner-Routledge, Hove.

McNeilly, C. L. and Howard, K. I. (1991). The effects of psychotherapy: A re-evaluation based on dosage. *Psychotherapy Research*, **1**, 74–78.

Najavits, L. M. and Gunderson, J. G. (1995). Improvements in borderline personality disorder in a 3 year prospective outcome study. *Comprehensive Psychiatry*, **36**, 296–302.

Rosser, R., Birch, S., Bond, H., Denford, J. and Schachter, J. (1987). Five year follow-up of patients treated with in-patient psychotherapy at the Cassel Hospital for Nervous Diseases. *Journal of the Royal Society of Medicine*, **80**, 549–555.

Roth, A. and Fonagy, P. (2005). *What works for whom? A critical review of psychotherapy research. 2nd Edition*, Guilford, New York.

Rubino, G., Barker, C., Roth, T. and Fearon, P. (2000). Therapist empathy and depth of interpretation in response to potential alliance ruptures: the role of therapist and patient attachment styles. *Psychotherapy Research*, **10**, 408–420.

Salkovskis, P. (1995). Demonstrating specific effects in cognitive and behavioural therapy. In *Research foundations in psychotherapy practice*. (eds. M. Aveline and D. A. Shapiro) Wiley, Chichester.

Sandell, R., Blomberg, J. and Lazar, A. (2002). Time matters: on temporal interactions in long-term follow-up of long-term psychotherapies. *Psychotherapy Research*, **12**, 39–58.

Seligman, M. E. P. (1995). The effectiveness of psychotherapy. *American Psychologist*, **50**, 965–974.

Sensky, T., Turkington, D., Kingdon, D., Scott, J. L., Scott, J., Siddle, R., O'Carroll, M. and Barnes, T. R. (2000). A randomized controlled trial of cognitive-behavioral therapy for persistent symptoms in schizophrenia resistant to medication. *Archives of General Psychiatry*, **57**, 165–72.

Shapiro, D. and Firth-Cozens, J. (1987). Prescriptive v. exploratory therapy: outcomes of the Sheffield psychotherapy project. *British Journal of Psychiatry*, **151**, 790–799.

Shapiro, D. A., Barkham, M., Rees, A., Hardy, G. E., Reynolds, S. and Startup, M. (1994). *Journal of Consulting and Clinical Psychology*, **62**, 522–534.

Shapiro, D. A., Rees, A., Barkham, M., Hardy, G., Reynolds, S. and Startup, M. (1995). Effects of treatment duration and severity of depression on the effectiveness of cognitive-behavioral and psychodynamic-interpersonal psychotherapy. *Journal of Consulting and Clinical Psychology*, **63**, 378–387.

Sloane, R. B., Staples, F. R., Cristol, A. H., Yorkston, N. J. and Whipple, K. (1975). Short-term analytically oriented psychotherapy versus behaviour therapy. *American Journal of Psychiatry*, **132**, 373–377.

Snyder, D. and Willis, R. (1989). Behavioural versus insight-oriented marital therapy: effects on individual and interspousal functioning. *Journal of Consulting and Clinical Psychology*, **57**, 39–46.

Snyder, D. K., Willis, R. M. and Grady-Fletcher, A. (1991). Long-term effectiveness of behavioral versus insight-oriented marital therapy: A 4-year follow-up study. *Journal of Consulting and Clinical Psychology*, **59**, 138–141.

Stevenson, J. and Meares, R. (1992). An outcome study of psychotherapy for patients with borderline personality disorder. *American Journal of Psychiatry*, **149**, 358–362.

Stevenson, J., Meares, R. and D'Angelo, R. (2005). Five-year outcome of outpatient psychotherapy with borderline patients. *Psychological Medicine*, **35**, 79–87.

Stiles, W. (1979). Verbal response modes and psychotherapeutic technique. *Psychiatry*, **42**, 49–62.

Stiles, W. B. (1986). Development of a taxonomy of verbal response models. In *The psychotherapeutic process: A research handbook* (eds. Greenberg, L. and Pinsof, W. M.) Guilford Press, New York.

W. B. Stiles, Agnew-Davies, R., G. E. Hardy, Barkham, M., and D. A. Shapiro, (1998). Relations of the alliance with psychotherapy outcome: Findings in the second Sheffield Psychotherapy Project. *Journal of Consulting and Clinical Psychology*, **66**, 791–802.

Wampold, B. E., Mondin, G. W., Moody, M., Stich, F., Benson, K. and Ahn, H. (1997). A meta-analysis of outcome studies comparing bona fide psychotherapies: Empirically, 'All must have prizes'. *Psychological Bulletin*, **122**, 203–215.

Recommended reading

Bateman, A. and Fonagy, P. (1999). The effectiveness of partial hospitalization in the treatment of borderline personality disorder—a randomised controlled trial. *American Journal of Psychiatry*, **156**, 1563–1569. (Shows that psychotherapy in a partial hospitalisation setting is effective.)

Henry, W. P., Strupp, H. H., Butler, S. F., et al. (1993). The effects of training in time-limited psychotherapy: Changes in therapists' behaviour. *Journal of Consulting and Clinical Psychology*, **61**, 434–440. (A key study showing that the therapist's internal world affects later outcome.)

Lambert, M. J. (2004). *Handbook of psychotherapy and behaviour change*. New York, Wiley. (A key book summarising a vast amount of research in psychotherapy.)

Luborsky, L. and Crits-Christoph, P. (1990). *Understanding transference: The CCRT method*. New York, Basic Books. (A readable summary of the CCRT method.)

Luborsky, L., Singer, B. and Luborsky, L. (1975). Comparative studies of psychotherapies: is it true that 'everybody has won and all must have prizes'? *Archives of General Psychiatry*, **37**, 471–481. (A frequently-quoted paper drawing attention to the 'dodo effect'.)

Piper, W. E., Azim, H. F. A., Joyce, A. S., et al. (1991). Transference interpretations, therapeutic alliance, and outcome in short-term individual psychotherapy. *Archives of General Psychiatry*, **48**, 946–953. (A model of good research measuring key psychodynamic variables and studying them in a well conducted trial.)

Roth, A. and Fonagy, P. (2005). *What works for whom? A critical review of psychotherapy research*. 2nd edn, New York, Guilford. (A good summary of outcome research.)

Chapter 4

What is psychotherapy?

Jerome D. Frank

In this introductory, now classic chapter, the late, much esteemed
Jerome Frank (1910–2005) attempts to answer the complex
question 'what is psychotherapy?' by approaching the subject in
historical and cultural contexts. After describing psychotherapy's
practitioners, the kinds of treatment they offer, and the patients
who receive it, he pays particular attention to the common
therapeutic functions of the rationales and procedures of all
psychotherapies. The chapter ends with general principles and
guidelines for the trainee setting out to practise psychotherapy.

As social beings, humans are totally dependent on each other for maintenance
of their biological and psychological well-being. When this is threatened in
any way, they typically turn to each other for help, whether this be protection
against a physical danger, such as an enemy group, protection of a food supply
endangered by drought, or for assuagement of distress created by the vicissitudes of life.

This book is concerned with the attempt of one person to relieve another's
psychological distress and disability by psychological means. These are
typically words, but include other communicative or symbolic behaviours,
ranging from laying a ressuring hand on someone's shoulder to elaborate
exercises aimed at combating noxious emotions and promoting inner
tranquillity.

Informal psychological help in the form of solace, guidance, advice, and
the like is frequently sought and received from family members and other
intimates. Other sources may sometimes be casual acquaintances and
even strangers, especially if they occupy roles like that of the bartender, for
example, that create the expectation that they will be good listeners.

Psychotherapy, the form of help-giving with which we are here concerned,
differs from such informal help in two significant ways. First, the practitioners

are specially trained to conduct this activity and they are sanctioned by their society or by a subgroup to which they and the patients belong. Second, their activity is systematically guided by an articulated theory that explains the sources of the patients' distress and disability, and prescribes methods for alleviating them. Psychotherapy differs from medical and surgical procedures in its major reliance on symbolic communications as contrasted with bodily interventions. This implies that it is concerned with the content of the symptoms and their meaning for the patient's life, for example, what the hallucinated voices are saying, or what the patient is depressed about, or what he fears when anxious. Drugs, when used, are regarded as facilitative adjuncts, and their choice is determinted by the form and severity of the patient's symptomatology, such as auditory hallucinations and depressed mood.

An important consequence of the primacy of communication as the medium of healing is that the success of all forms of psychotherapy depends more on the personal influence of the therapist than do medical and surgical procedures. Even when the success of psychotherapeutic procedures is believed to depend solely on their objective properties, as some behaviour therapists maintain, the personal influence of the therapist determines whether the patient carries out the prescribed treatment in the first place, as well as having healing effects in itself. While important in all medical treat-ment, the personal impact of the therapist is crucial to psychotherapy (Greben 1983; Frank and Frank 1991).

A historical-cultural perspective

Although there are a bewildering number of schools of psychotherapy, each proclaiming its own special virtues, viewed from a historical-cultural stand-point, all can be subsumed under two categories: the religio-magical and the empirical-scientific (Zilboorg and Henry 1941; Frank 1977). The former is as old as human culture and continues to predominate in most non-industrialized societies. Although viewed askance by many persons in industrialized societies, healing cults continue to have large followings in them as well.

Religio-magical therapies are grounded in what has been termed the perennial philosophy (Huxley 1941). This underlies all major religions and avers that humans are manifestations of the 'Divine Ground' which links us into a kind of seamless web. Each individual, as it were, contains the universe. The conventional or sensory reality in which we live is only one of reality. Health is harmonious integration of forces within the person coupled with a corresponding harmony in his relations with other persons and the spirit world. Illness is a sign that he has transgressed the rules of nature or society, thereby disrupting his internal harmony and creating vulnerability to harmful influences from other persons and spirits.

Such a conceptualization takes for granted that mental states can powerfully affect bodily functions and that the state of bodily health, conversely, can affect mental functions. The therapist's goal is to restore the patient's harmony within himself, with his group, and with the spirit world through special rituals requiring the participation of the patient and, usually, those important to him, the purpose of which is to intercede with the spirit world on the patient's behalf. The religio-magical healer is as well trained in special techniques as his scientific colleague but attributes his heading powers to supernatural sources which are linked to a religious system that he and the patient share. Healing involves a special state of consciousness of both healer and patient, in which both temporarily enter another reality characterized by such phenomena as clairvoyance, communion with the spirit world, and out-of-the-body experience.

Empirical-scientific psychotherapy was foreshadowed by Hippocrates. It has been practised continuously in the West since the mid-eighteenth century, beginning with the charismatic physician, Anton Mesmer, who viewed his treatment as the scientific application of animal magnetism. Although his theories and he himself were discredited, empirical-scientific psychotherapy continued as hypnosis and then experienced a sharp rise in popularity and influence thanks to the genius of Freud. More recently empirical-scientific psychotherapy has been expanded by therapies based on the theories of Pavlov and Skinner, and therapies that seek to help the patient correct pathogenic cognitions (Beck 1976).

The empirical-scientific approach is conducted with the patient in an unaltered state of consciousness but may involve hypnotic states, fantasies, dreams, and the state of reverie which may accompany free association in psychoanalysis. The therapies which appear most scientific, however, notably cognitive therapy and behaviour therapy, depend on full utilization of the patient's waking intellect. Healers in the scientific tradition, instead of basing their powers on supernatural sources, invoke science as the sanction for their methods.

Despite striking differences in their underlying world views, religio-magical and empirical-scientific therapies have much in common. They share the aim of restoring the patient's harmony with himself and with his group. Both approaches, furthermore, depend on a belief system shared by the patient and the therapist that the treatment has been empirically validated. This is as true for the religio-magical systems of pre-scientific cultures as for the supposedly scientifically based systems in our own. The therapeutic procedures express the belief system in tangible form, thereby reinforcing it. In both, a trained healer derives his power from the belief system—whether it be as scientifically grounded Western practitioner or a supernaturally inspired shaman—and in both he serves as an intermediary between the patient and his group. Finally, empirical-scientific healers, no less than shamans, expend considerable effort to mobilize the patient's faith in their procedures.

Practitioners of psychotherapy

Starting with Mesmer and until the middle of the twentieth century, empirical-scientific psychotherapy was conducted by physicians, initially neurologists, later psychiatrists. In recent decades they have been joined by psychiatric social workers and later by clinical psychologists and psychiatric nurses. These mental health professionals often work under medical supervision but some have achieved virtually complete autonomy. To these must be added clergy-men, for whom psychotherapy is a natural extension of pastoral counselling.

In addition, especially in the United States, the excess of demand for help over the supply of trained practitioners has led to a proliferation of self-appointed healers and cult leaders, with or without training, who work not only in conventional settings but in ones specially designated as 'growth centres' as well as in hotel rooms, meeting halls, and private homes. Most utilize group approaches, some of which are similar to those of healing religious cults such as 'scientology'. Although many do not set themselves up as therapists, the great majority of their clientele have had previous psychotherapy or are currently in treatment.

Also important are groups composed of fellow sufferers. These 'peer self-help psychotherapy groups' function autonomously and maintain various degrees of rapport with the medical profession. Some welcome all comers, but most, such as Alcoholics Anonymous, are offered only for those suffering from a specific common problem.

Kinds of psychotherapy

The goal of all forms of psychotherapy is to enable a person to satisfy his legitimate needs for affection, recognition, and sense of mastery through helping him to correct the maladaptive attitudes, emotions, and behaviour that impede the attainment of such satisfactions. In so doing, psychotherapy seeks to improve his social interactions and reduce his distress, while at the same time helping him to accept the suffering that is an inevitable aspect of life and, when possible, to utilize it in the service of personal growth.

Although all psychotherapies take into account all aspects of personal life, different schools vary considerably in emphasis. They can be roughly ordered in accord with their primary target, their temporal orientation, and whether they seek primarily to modify thoughts and attitudes, emotional states, or behaviour.

To oversimplify vastly, insight-therapies focus on the individual patient and see distress as arising primarily from unresolved internal conflicts. Some, such as psychoanalysis, focus on the past. They see the internal conflicts as caused by traumatic experiences of early life and seek to unearth their sources and thereby resolve them. Behaviour therapies also are primarily concerned with counteracting the effects of previous damaging experiences.

Other behaviour therapists who emphasize modelling or operant conditioning view the primary difficulties as located at the interface between the patient and his immediate social environment and are oriented to the present; that is, they try to help the patient identify and modify the proximate causes and consequences of behaviour that create distress. Existentially oriented therapists are apt to emphasize helping the patient to open up the future, that is, to discover new potentialities for personal satisfaction and growth.

Therapists who regard the primary focus of treatment as the patient in his family (see Chapters 16 and 18) or in an artificially composed group (see Chapter 11) pay particular attention to the patient's reactions to other family or group members as casting light on the sources of their symptoms and seek to mobilize therapeutic group or family forces. Family and group therapists differ in the extent to which they search in the patient's past for sources of current problems, and in whether they focus on the individual patient or on the pathogenic or healing potentials of the family or group as a system.

For psychoanalytically derived therapies, the kind of treatment the patient receives depends primarily on the therapeutic school of the therapist to whom he is referred. That is, these therapists tend to apply their particular method to all their patients, and justify this on the grounds that their goal is to enhance the patient's general integration or to foster personality growth. Relief of specific symptoms is assumed to follow automatically. Cognitive and behaviour therapists reverse this. They believe that the patient's success in correcting faulty cognitions or overcoming specific symptoms will promote more general improvement by enhancing social competence and self-confidence. Hence, they attempt to tailor their methods to combat the patient's specific complaints. As is reported in Chapter 8, behaviour therapists have succeeded to some extent with complaints that are fairly circumscribed. Unfortunately, patient whose chief complaints are of this kind represent a very small proportion of those seeking help. Most feel a pervasive distress or sense of incompetence or alienation, and evidence is still lacking that they respond better to one approach than another, a point to be considered more fully below.

Receivers of psychotherapy

Since psychotherapy is a cultural institution, those who are considered suitable candidates for it vary among different societies. In the West, psychotherapy is believed to be appropriate for all persons in whom psychological factors are perceived as causing or contributing significantly to distress and disability. Although this criterion is more generously applied in the United States than elsewhere, by and large, individuals are selected from the following categories in Western societies:

1 *The psychotically disturbed*, such as schizophrenic patients, whose symptoms in all likelihood stem predominantly from an organic source. The aim of psychotherapy for these patients is to help them to recognize and try to deal more effectively with life stresses to which they are particularly vulnerable (see Chapter 10).

2 *The neurotically and personality disordered*, who suffer from persistent faulty strategies for dealing with the vicissitudes of life, based presumably on important early experience that were either damaging or lacking, thereby distorting the processes of maturation and learning. These patients and those in the next category constitute the vast majority of individuals in psychotherapy.

3 *The psychologically shaken*, who are temporarily overwhelmed by current life stresses such as bereavement (see Chapter 9). Relatively brief help usually suffices to restore their emotional equilibrium. Since such individuals can manifest the entire gamut of clinical symptoms and respond gratifyingly to any form of help, they fan the competitiveness between different schools of psychotherapy.

4 *The unruly*, whose behaviour upsets other people but is attributed to illness rather then wickedness. This category includes 'acting-out' children and adolescents, spouses whose heedless or self-indulgent behaviour distresses their partners, as well as antisocial personalities and substance abusers. Some could be classified under the preceding categories. The distinguishing feature is, perhaps, the degree of motivation for help; the unruly are brought to it by others, which makes them, by and large, poor candidates.

Two additional categories of persons receiving psychotherapy exist in affluent or intellectual circles: the discontented, struggling with boredom or existential problems; and professionals who undergo training in psychotherapy as a prerequisite to offering it to others.

How effective is psychotherapy?

This is an easy question to ask but a surprisingly hard one to answer. Evaluation of therapies bristles with methodological problems of which two important ones are how to measure improvement and how to disentangle the effects of psychotherapy from those of other concurrent life experiences.

Criteria of improvement, to the extent that they depend on the conceptualizations of therapeutic schools, are not readily comparable. Thus, psychoanalysts define improvement in part as being able to experience consciously previously unconscious feelings and thoughts, while behaviour therapists look for overcoming of symptoms elicited by particular situations. They are interested in whether the agoraphobic patient can leave the house or the socially inhibited one can enjoy a party, not in the relationship of unconscious to conscious experiences.

Moreover, improvement is not unitary, and so can change in different directions on different criteria. If a husband's chronic abdominal pain disappears after he takes to mistreating his wife instead of submitting to her, is he better or worse? Another problem of evaluation arises from the fact that psychotherapeutic sessions constitute only a small proportion of a person's waking life and he may well be seeking informal help at the same time. Hence, improvement during therapy may primarily reflect this outside help or beneficial changes in his life situation. To complicate matters further, these changes may be the result of shifts in the patient's attitudes and behaviour resulting from psychotherapy.

These and other problems present more difficulties for the evaluation of long-term psychotherapy with loosely defined, open-ended goals, such as increased personality integration than of short-term therapies focused on the relief of particular target complaints.

Nevertheless, findings from many studies have consistently found that all the types of psychotherapy that have been studied produce greater beneficial change than 'spontaneous improvement'; that is, improvement occurring over the same time interval in the absence of psychotherapy (Smith et al. 1980, p. 183): 'Psychotherapy is beneficial, consistently so and in many different ways. Its benefits are on a par with other expensive and ambitious interventions, such as schooling and medicine'. Findings are less clear with regard to the relative effectiveness of various types of therapy for different conditions.

It must be emphasized that failure to demonstrate significant differences between various therapies by no means excludes the possibility that such differences exist; failure may be due to the lack of criteria for classifying patients with respect to their relative response to various therapeutic approaches. As a result, if a cohort of patients, selected by any criterion, are divided into two groups, one receiving therapy A and one receiving therapy B, each may contain some patients who respond to neither and some who do well with both, and those respond differentially may get lost in the statistical shuffle.

Improvement in methods of diagnosis and evaluation of change may yet reveal some differences in effectiveness of different therapies that present methods fail to detect. In the meanwhile, a reasonable conclusion is that, whatever their specific symptoms, most patients share a source of distress that responds to the common features of all forms of psychotherapy (Frank and Frank 1991).

See Chapter 3 for elaboration of the above account.

The demoralization hypothesis

A common source of distress may be termed 'demoralization'—a state of mind that ensues when a person feels subjectively incompetent, that is, unable to cope with a problem that he and those about him except him to be able to handle (Frank 1974; DeFigueiredo and Frank 1982). Demoralization can vary widely in duration and severity, but the full-blown form includes the following manifestations, not all of which need be present in any one person. The individual suffers a loss of confidence in himself and in his ability to master not only external circumstances but his own feelings and thoughts. The resulting sense of failure typically engenders feelings of guilt and shame. The demoralized person frequently feels alienated or isolated, as well as resentful because others whom he excepts to help him seem unable or unwilling to do so. Their behaviour in turn may reflect their own irritation with him, thus creating a vicious circle. With the weakening of his ties often goes a loss of faith in the group's values and beliefs, which have formerly helped to give him a sense of security and significance. The psychological world of the demoralized person is constricted in space and time. He becomes self-absorbed, loses sight of his long-term goals, and is preoccupied with avoiding further failure. His dominant moods are usually anxiety, ranging from mild apprehension to panic, and depression, ranging in severity from being mildly dispirited to feeling utterly hopeless.

Most episodes of demoralization are self-limiting. These responses to crisis can enhance a person's mental health by stimulating him to seek better solutions to his problems, strengthening his emotional ties with others, and demonstrating to himself that he can overcome obstacles. Prolonged states of demoralization, however, are self-perpetuating and self-aggravating, since they lead to increasing discouragement which impedes recovery. Those who seek psychotherapeutic help are usually in the middle range of demoralization. Mild forms are relieved by advice or reassurance from family or friends, or changes in life situation, such as a change of job, as a result of which the person regains his sense of mastery and links with his group. At the other extreme, if demoralization is sufficiently severe, the person believes he is beyond help and simply withdraws into a shell. Such individuals do not seek help and some, such as derelicts, seem unable to use it.

In order to come to psychotherapy, the patient must experience certain symptoms, which are viewed as especially amenable to this form of treatment. Many of these, such as anxiety, depression, and feelings of guilt, seem to be direct expressions of demoralization. Others, such as obsessions, dissociate phenomena, and hallucinations have a variety of causes, many of which are still not understood. Sometimes, they seem to be symbolic ways through which the patient expresses or attempts to resolve the problems which demoralize him.

Whatever their ultimate aetiology, symptoms interact in two ways with the degree of demoralization. First, the more demoralized the person is, the more severe these symptoms tend to be; thus patients troubled with obsessions find them becoming worse when they are depressed. Second, by crippling the person to some degree, symptoms reduce his coping capacity, thereby aggravating his demoralization. The demoralization hypothesis asserts that the shared features of psychotherapies, which account for much of their effectiveness, combat demoralization, as a result of which symptoms diminish or disappear.

Features of all psychotherapies that combat demoralization are:

1 An intense, emotionally charged, confiding *relationship* with a helping person, often with the participation of a group. In this relationship the patient allows himself to become dependent on the therapist for help because of his confidence in the latter's competence and goodwill. The patient's dependence is reinforced by his knowledge of the therapist's training, the setting of treatment (see below), and by the congruence of his approach with the patient's expectations. While these factors determine the therapist's power increasingly becomes his personal qualities, especially his ability to convince the patient that he can understand and help him; that is, his ability to establish what has been termed 'a therapeutic alliance'.

2 A *healing setting* which reinforces the relationship by heightening the therapist's prestige through the presence of symbols of healing: a clinic in a prestigious hospital, or an office complete with bookshelves, impressive desk, couch, and easy chair. The setting often contains evidence of the therapist's training, such as diplomas and pictures of his teachers.

Furthermore, the setting is a place of safety; that is, the patient is secure in the knowledge that his self-revelation will have no consequences beyond the walls of the office. As a result, he can dare to let into awareness of, and come to terms with, thoughts and feelings that had been avoided or repressed.

3 A *rationale* or conceptual scheme that explains the cause of the patient's symptoms and prescribes a ritual or procedure for resolving them. The rationale must be convincing to the patient and the therapist; hence it is validated by being linked to the dominant world view of their culture and cannot be shaken by therapeutic failures. In the Middle Ages, the belief system underlying what we today call psychotherapy was demonology. In many primitive societies it is witchcraft. In the Western world today it is science.

4 Linked to the rationale is a *procedure* that requires active participation of both patient and therapist and which is believed by both to be the means for restoring the patient's health. Proponents of all schools of psychotherapy agree that they offer essentially the same kind of therapeutic relationship, but each claims special virtues for their particular rationales and procedures.

Shared therapeutic functions of the rationales and procedures of psychotherapy

Despite marked differences in content, all rationales and procedures in psychotherapy, reinforced by the setting, share six therapeutic functions:

1 *They strengthen the therapeutic relationship.* Since the therapist represents society, his mere acceptance of the patient as worthy of help reduces the latter's sense of isolation and re-establishes his sense of contact with his group. This is further reinforced by the fact that therapist and patient adhere to the same belief system, a powerful unifying force in all groups. Explanations of the patient's symptoms or problems in terms of a theory of therapy, moreover, implicitly convey to him that he is not unique, since the rationale obviously must have developed out of experiences with many patients. The treatment procedure also serves as a vehicle for maintaining the therapist–patient relationship over stretches when little seems to be happening, by giving both participants work to do.

2 The rationales and procedures of all therapies inspire and maintain the patient's *hope for help*, which not only keeps him coming but is a powerful healing force in itself. Hope is sustained by being translated into concrete expectations. Thus, experienced therapists spend considerable time early in treatment teaching the patient their particular therapeutic 'game' and shaping his expectations to coincide with what he will actually experience.

3 The rationales and procedures provide the patient with opportunities for both *cognitive and experiential learning* by offering him new information about his problems and possible ways of dealing with them, or new ways of

conceptualizing what he already knows. All schools of psychotherapy agree that intellectual insight is not sufficient to produce change. The patient must also have a new experience, whether this be related to reliving the past, discovering symptom-reinforcing contingencies in the environment, or becoming aware of distortions in interpersonal communications. Experiential learning occurs through, for example, emotionally charged self-discovery, transference reactions, and the feelings aroused by attempts to change the contingencies governing behaviour. It is facilitated by the therapist and, in therapy groups, by the group members, both of whom the patient uses as models and as sources of knowledge.

4 Experiential learning implies *emotional arousal*; this supplies the motive power for changes in attitudes and behaviour (Frank et al. 1978). The revelations emerging in psychotherapy may be pleasant surprises, but more often they are unsettling shocks, as the patient discovers features of himself he had previously not let himself face. Some therapists deliberately cultivate emotional arousal, since they see it as central to treatment.

5 Perhaps the chief therapeutic effect of the rationales and procedures is enhancement of the patient's sense of mastery, self-control, competence, or effectiveness. Ability to control one's environment starts with the ability to accept and master one's own impulses and feelings, an achievement which in itself overcomes anxiety and strengthens self-confidence. Nothing is more frightening than feeling oneself to be at the mercy of inchoate and mysterious forces. A powerful source of a sense of mastery is being able to name and conceptualize one's experiences, an activity facilitated by each of the therapeutic rationales. That naming a phenomenon is a means for gaining dominance over it is a frequent theme in folklore and religion as in the fairy tale of Rumpelstiltskin, and the book of Genesis in which the first task God assigns Adam is to name the animals, thereby asserting his dominion over them.

The sense of mastery is reinforced by *success experiences*, which all therapeutic procedures provide in one form or another. These successes maintain the patient's hopes, increase his sense of mastery over his feelings and behaviour, and reduce his fear of failure. The role of success experiences is most obvious in behaviour therapy, which is structured to provide continual evidence of progress and aims to have every session end with a sense of attainment. For example, exposure, by showing the patient that he can survive the full impact of feelings he feared would destroy him, powerfully enhances his sense of self-mastery. Psychoanalytically and existentially oriented therapies, being less clearly structured, yield more subtle but equally potent successes. Patients who respond well to these approaches master problems through verbalization and conceptualization, so that the achievement of a new insight or ability to formulate clearly previously muddled thoughts can powerfully raise their self-confidence.

6 Finally, all therapies tacitly or openly encourage the patient to digest or '*work through*' and practise what he has learned in his daily living, thereby fostering generalization of the therapeutic gains beyond the psychotherapy situation itself. Some therapies assign homework and require the patient to report back how well he has carried out his assignment. For others, this remains an implicit, but nevertheless strong, expectation.

Differences in the length of therapy used by different schools depend in part on the expectations implicit in their rationales. Behaviour therapies are expected to be brief, those that are psychoanalytically oriented long. Within each school, differences in duration may depend primarily on how long it takes to establish a genuine therapeutic alliance (i.e. win the patient's trust), and how much practice he needs to unlearn old attitudes and habits and develop new, healthier ones.

In short, evidence available to date strongly suggests that in treating most conditions for which persons come or are brought into psychotherapy, the shared functions of different rationales and procedures, not their differing content, contribute most of their therapeutic power. These functions, which are interwoven, all help to re-establish the patient's morale by combating his sense of isolation, reawakening his hopes, supplying him with new information as a basis for both cognitive and experiential learning, stirring him emotionally, providing experiences of mastery and success, and encouraging him to apply what he has learned.

Implications for psychotherapy practice

The probability that the rationales and procedures of all psychotherapies differ little in their effectiveness for most patients by no means implies that familiarity with a particular psychotherapeutic rationale and procedure in unnecssary. Most psychotherapists need a conceptual framework to guide their activities, maintain self-confidence, and provide adherents of similar orientation to whom they can turn for support.

The demoralization hypothesis does imply, however, that a therapist will probably do best with the method most congenial to his personality. Some therapists are effective hypnotists, others are not; some welcome emotional outbursts, others avoid them; some work best with groups, others with an individual patient; some enjoy exploring the psyche, others prefer to try to change behaviour. As far as possible, therefore, the trainee therapist would do well to look into a variety of approaches with the aim of mastering one or more that best accord with his won personal predilection and, if he can handle several, selecting the one most appropriate for a given patient. Criteria that could help guide his choice, as well as the procedures themselves, are described in the remainder of this volume.

This chapter concludes with some general principles and guidelines on which almost all school of psychotherapy agree, and which therefore can be put to immediate use while the student is learning to master a particular approach. The suggestion concern primarily the first encounter with the patient but apply in varying degrees throughout treatment.

Most patients enter therapy with more or less covert conflicts and doubts that distort or impede free communication with the therapist. Your success in overcoming these obstacles in the initial interview may determine whether the patient returns for a second visit as well as the course of therapy thereafter. Hence, from the very beginning, cultivate sensitivity to patients' attitudes that may be blocking the interview. They can be grouped into three classes: (1) those arising from the patients' internal state; (2) those reflecting his attitude towards the interview situation; and (3) those springing from his feelings towards you.

With respect to patients' internal states, most are more or less demoralized; their self-esteem damaged. They may also experience a conflict between wanting to change and unwillingness to surrender their habitual ways of dealing with life, especially since change usually entails the distress felt in confronting their own repressed feelings and the anxiety of venturing into new, uncharted territory. Like Hamlet, many prefer to bear the ills they have than fly to others they know not of.

As to the interview situation, patients have a wide range of sophistication concerning psychotherapy. Some are fully informed; others are bewildered, even frightened, and do not know what to expect. They may suspect that referral to a psychotherapist means that others regard them as crazy, and they may fear what you may discover about their less admirable qualities. The route by which they have arrived at your office influences their initial attitude. A self-referred patient usually feels differently than one who has been referred by his physician in such a way that he experiences it as a brush-off, or one who faces criminal charges or has been referred by his probation officer.

Finally, many patients have doubts about your competence and trustworthiness, especially if you are young and inexperienced. It is prudent to assume that the patient is covertly forming an impression of you at the same time that you are evaluating him. Hence your initial aim is to help the patient to overcome these blocks to open communication. Central to this is your ability to convince the patient that you desire to help him and are competent to do so. To this end, try to act in such a way as to show that you are trustworthy, concerned about his welfare, and seeking to understand him. Try to elicit hidden doubts and misgivings and respond appropriately. The sense that one's message is being received and understood by someone who cares is a powerful reliever of anxiety.

This implies suggestions as to some general attitudes and specific procedures that facilitate patient–therapist communication, thereby supplying the necessary basis for the success of all forms of psychotherapy:

1 *Be yourself.* Within the boundaries of the professional role. A stiff, artificial therapist discourages communication. Accordingly, you should not fear being spontaneous within wide limits, expressing pleasure, concern, sorrow, or even anger, admitting when you are sleepy or uncertain as to what is going on, and the like. If humour is within you repertoire, it can be a great help in enabling the patient to achieve some detachment from his troubles, as long as he feels that you are laughing with him and not at him (Bloch and McNab 1987).

By being open with the patient you make it easier for him to be open with you and also to use you as a model. While relying on spontaneity increases the likelihood of making errors, if the patient is convinced that you genuinely care about his welfare, he will forgive and forget almost any blunder you may commit.

2 *Maintain an attitude of respectful, serious attention.* For many patients, especially socially disadvantaged ones, the psychotherapist may be the first person with status who is willing to hear them out. You should keep in mind that, especially in early interviews, the patient is covertly testing you to see how understanding and trustworthy you are. The best way to pass the test is to maintain an attitude of respectful attention no matter how shocking, trivial, or ridiculous the patient's productions are. This does not mean that the patient should be allowed to ramble. It is possible, tactfully, to guide the patient while preserving a respectful attitude.

3 Throughout the interview *emphasize the positive.* It is necessary, of course, to explore what is going wrong in the patient's life. After all, it is because of this that he has come for help. Exclusive pursuit of this goal, however, can increase the patient's demoralization by turning the interview into what has been aptly described as a degradation ceremonial. Remember that patients would not have survived to be in your office today unless they had some assets and coping skills. So be sure to listen for these and remind the patient of them, especially after particularly damaging self-disclosures. This must be done with care. Nothing is more harmful to the progress of an interview than unwarranted or empty reassurance, because the patient hears it as evidence that you do not

take his troubles seriously or have not understood their gravity. It is always reassuring, however, after listening to a patient's worst misgivings without implying that you share them, to utilize every appropriate opportunity to remind him of what is going well, or of latent abilities that he is not fully utilizing.

In prolonged therapy, a patient's goals often seem to become more ambitious as he improves. Because the goals keep receding in this way, he may fell he is making no progress. If you sense this, a reminder of the patient's state when he first entered therapy and the gain he has made since can be powerfully reassuring.

4 *Make sure the patient understands the interview situation.* Depending on the patient's sophistication, take sufficient time to find out his understanding of the nature and purpose of the interview and, to the degree necessary, explain them to him. Let him know how much, if any, of what he reveals will be reported back to the referring agent. Usually the patient can be reassured that information he reveals will be given to other only with his explicit permission. In the rare cases where complete confidentiality in this sense cannot be guaranteed, as in some court referrals, the patient should be so informed at the start.

5 *Pay attention to physical arrangements.* The chairs should not be separated by a desk, and be so placed that you and the patient can comfortably maintain or avoid eye contact. It may be facilitative sometimes, for example, for you to avert your gaze when the patient embarks on an acutely embarrassing topic. The lighting should be arranged so that illumination is equal for both parties, or more on you that the patient, to avoid the impression that the patient is being interrogated.

6 *Be alert to the patient's non-verbal behaviour.* These include tone of voice, hesitancies of speech, facial expression, as well as gestures and bodily postures. Is the patient's manner ingratiating, challenging, tense? Does he maintain eye contact? Are his responses forthright or defensive and evasive? Such clues as to covert attitudes may help you to evaluate what the patient is saying.

Evidence of autonomic activity like sweating or flushing may signal that the topic under discussion is emotionally significant. If a patient indicates that he has non-visible autonomic responses such as heart-pounding, abdominal pain, or headache during the interview, he should be asked to report when they occur.

Since commenting on non-verbal communication may increase the patient's uneasiness, you should reserve comment until you are sure that his trust in you is sufficiently strong to enable him to hear and use the information. Then you may offer immediate feedback of your own reactions, so as to clarify for the patient responses of others that have disturbed him in the past. This is most apt to happen when the patient is unaware of aspects of his communicative behaviour is to call the patient's attention to discrepancies between his verbal and non-verbal communications (e.g. that he states he is angry in a sweet tone of voice while smiling). Video-tape playback, by sharply confronting a patient with the way he presents himself to other, can enhance this aspect of therapy.

7 *Focus on the present.* The patient comes to therapy for help in resolving current problems, however long-standing they may be. He wants to talk about the here and now, and encouraging this helps to establish rapport. It is also the most direct route towards understanding the patient's characteristic ways of coping. Another reason for focusing primarily on the present is that, although maladaptive patterns of perceiving, feelings, and behaving rooted in the past, they are sustained by present forces and, therefore, it is these that must be changed.

8 *Take a history.* Emphasis on the present must not preclude taking a history, especially in the first interview, and returning to aspects of it periodically when relevant. Irrespective of its contents, and therapists of different persuasions emphasize different aspects, taking a full history is the best way to get acquainted with someone. Moreover, it is essential to a full understanding of the patient's current reactions, for we perceive events and react to them not as they exist objectively but in terms of what they mean to us. The same objective event, such as the death of a close relative, may be experienced as a tragedy or a relief. Since the meaning of present events is largely determined by past experiences, considerable review of the latter may be needed to understand the patient's predicament today.

Sometimes a review of the past serves to enhance rapport: a patient may be able to reveal embarrassing or anxiety-provoking features of his history before he can discuss his current difficulties, and may need to test the therapist's reactions to remote material before he can bring up present feelings. As the patient progresses in therapy, moreover, changes in his interpretations of past events may be important clues as to his progress.

9 *Repeat what you have heard.* Repeating back what the patient has said, either precisely or with modifications to emphasize a point, is evidence that you are listening attentively and are not angered, frightened, or otherwise disturbed by what you have heard. This implicitly encourages the patient to continue.

10 *Interpret, but sparingly.* Calling attention to points a patient has overlooked, bringing together statements he had not realized were linked, or

offering explanations for his feeling and actions, if skilfully done, shows that you not only heard him but can make sense of what you have heard in ways he had not considered, thereby demonstrating your competence. Premature or implausible interpretations, however, may have the opposite affect, so it is well to be sure of one's ground before offering them.

11. *Ending the interview.* At the close of the first interview offer the patient an opportunity to make comments and ask questions. He may need encouragement to bring up matters of concern that were not adequately dealt with, seek additional information, ask for further clarification of some of your comments, and the like. Review the mundane aspects of therapy with the patient including the fee (if appropriate), frequency of interviews, and tentative duration. If possible, try to establish with the patient preliminary goals of therapy, recognizing that they might require subsequent revision. At the close of every interview, it is well to sum up the major topics and call attention to significant points. Sometimes it is also possible to offer a formulation in terms of a theme that links the topics together. Finally, when appropriate, suggest homework. This may be to think more about a certain issue, to record dreams, to keep a diary noting when certain symptoms occur, or to try to put into action what has been learned. At the next interview ask the patient to report on the assignment. This helps to preserve the continuity of psychotherapy during the intervals between sessions.

Summary

This chapter has attempted to answer the question: what is psychotherapy? by considering it in an historical-cultural perspective and by discussing its practitioners, the kinds of therapies they offer, and to whom. Particular emphasis has been placed on the shared therapies functions of the rationales and procedures of all psychotherapy. Finally, some general principles and guidelines common to all the psychotherapies covered in this book are briefly dealt with.

References

Beck, A. (1976). *Cognitive therapy and the emotional disorders.* International Universities Press, New York.

Bloch, S. and McNab, D. (1987). Humour in psychotherapy, *British Journal of Psychotherapy*, **3**, 216–25.

Defigueiredo, J. M. and Frank, J. D. (1982). Subjective incompetence, the clinical hallmark of demoralization. *Comprehensive Psychiatry*, **23**, 353–63.

Frank, J. D. (1974). The restoration of morale. *American Journal of Psychiatry*, **131**, 271–4.

Frank, J. D. (1977). The two faces of psychotherapy. *Journal of Nervous and Mental Disease*, **164**, 3–7.

Frank, J. D. and Frank, J. (1991). *Persuasion and healing: A comparative study of psychotherapy*, 3rd edn. Johns Hopkins University Press, Baltimore.

Frank, J. D., Hoehn-Saric, R., Imber, S. D., Liberman, B. L., and Stone, A. R. (1978). *Effective ingredients of successful psychotherapy*. Brunner/Mazel, New York.

Greben, S. E. (1983). *Love's labor: Twenty-five years in the practice of psychotherapy*. Schocken, New York.

Huxley, A. (1941). *Introduction to Bhagavad-Gita* (trans. by Swami Prabhavananda and C. Isherwood). New American Library, New York.

Smith. M. L., Glass, G. V., and Miller, T. I. (1980). *The benefits of psychotherapy*. Johns Hopkins University Press, Baltimore.

Zilboorg, C. and Henry, G. W. (1941). *History of medical psychology*. Norton, New York.

Part 2

Principal approaches

Chapter 5

Individual long-term psychotherapy

Susan Mizen and Jeremy Holmes

Long-term therapy is usually correctly equated with psychoanalysis, which, unlike almost all other forms of therapy, values the importance of treatment over a matter of years. Supportive psychotherapy (see Chapter 10) also implies long-term treatment. In this chapter, we shall be concerned mainly with psychoanalysis (usually 3–5 sessions a week, lasting 2–5 years) and its derivative, psychoanalytic psychotherapy (commonly 1–2 sessions per week, lasting 18 months–3 years). Other forms of therapy, such as Cognitive Behaviour Therapy and Dialectical Behaviour Therapy, when applied to people suffering from complex problems may last longer than was originally envisaged. We hope that the principles we explore will also illuminate themes that arise when these shorter therapies become prolonged.

A historical context (see Chapter 1)

Individual long-term therapy in its most established form has its roots in psychoanalysis. Freud's theories formed the underpinning of a treatment for psychological disorders, as well as a model of mental functioning and psychological development.

Freud was initially a neurologist who, following a visit to Charcot in Paris, explored the role of hypnosis with patients suffering from hysterical conversion. This led him to the view that 'conversion symptoms' were the result of trauma, of which the patient was unaware. Through abreaction, Freud sought to bring the trauma into consciousness and so deal with the symptoms. Freud, however, was dissatisfied with this technique, and subsequently developed the psychoanalytic method, in which the patient lay upon a couch and revealed whatever came into his mind ('free association'). He was increasingly aware of the 'transference' relationship between himself and the patient, feelings that resembled those described towards significant figures from the patient's past. The transference, now held to reveal the fundamental constellation of the patient's inner world, determines assumptions and preconceptions, which he or she brings into relationships.

Freud's first model of the mind, the topographical, differentiated mental functioning into unconscious, preconscious, and conscious aspects. He later developed the structural model comprising Id, Ego, and Superego. He saw psychopathology arising from the discrepancy between instinctual impulses, located in the Id, mostly aggressive and sexual, and societal and parental expectations as represented by the Superego, resulting in psychic conflict and compromise formation through the ego's application of defence mechanisms.

Freud's daughter, Anna Freud, later systematized the subject of defences. Her ideas were further elaborated in the United States by Heinz Hartmann into Ego Psychology, which emphasizes the ego's role in adapting to the environment and the use of defences to protect it from the effects of stress and adverse environments and from disruptive inner feelings (Erikson 1965).

British psychoanalytic thought, dominated by Object Relations Theory (ORT) from the 1030s, stems from the work of Klein, Fairbairn, Balint, Bion, and Winnicott (Greenberg and Mitchell 1983; Kohon 1986). All of these were reacting in various ways against Freud's initial emphasis on 'Drive Theory', and adopting his later concept of internal psychic representations of significant figures and relationships.

Melanie Klein's psychoanalytic therapy with children from the 1930s led her to the view that the sexual and aggressive drives mapped out by Freud were inseparable from those to whom they were directed—that is, figures (objects) in the child's early life. Both Balint and Fairbairn also emphasised the relationship-seeking nature of drives. Based on her play technique with children and regressed states in adult psychoanalysis, Klein (Segal 1964; Mitchell 1985; Hinshelwood 1989) detected internal representations of parents, siblings, the self, and parts of the body (part objects) such as breast, mouth, and penis in various relations to one another in unconscious fantasy in the infant and young child's mind. These latter representations were thought to predominate during the first 6 months of life.

Because at this stage 'good' (loving responsive, nurture-providing) representations of the mother were split off from 'bad' (withholding, unavailable, persecuting) images, and because Klein wanted to identify infantile precursors of adult psychopathology, the child was described as occupying the 'paranoid-schizoid position' (PSP) during this phase of development. The PSP is viewed as a way of the infant organising experience in order to defend itself from anxiety about annihilation. Klein postulates this anxiety as arising from within through the action of the death instinct. The baby defends against this by splitting itself and its objects into a loving self and a hating self, and loved and hated objects, good and bad. The world is experienced in terms of feelings and fantasies.

Thus, aggressive feelings, experienced as badness, are 'projected' into the mother's breast, which is then experienced as persecuting. In this way the baby's good self in relation to a part object good mother is 'uncontaminated' by destructive impulses. Analysts see this mechanism as predominating in Borderline Personality Disorder (Kernberg 1977).

In normal development, from 6 months, 'good' and 'bad', love and hate, come to be recognized as two sides of the relationship with the same 'whole object'. The child then enters the 'depressive position' (DP), so called because Klein imagined guilt in the child when he discovers that the mother whom he has hated is one and the same as his good object—and, again, because she was searching for infantile origins of adult psychological illness. The depressive position is characterized by anxiety about loss which the child may seek to overcome by making reparation—through creativity and play.

For Bion (1967b) this movement from PSP to DP is mediated by the mother's 'reverie' and 'containment', her capacity to tolerate and 'detoxify' the infant's rage so that, at the appropriate moment, it can be reunited with love, and so be transformed into healthy self-assertiveness. The therapist similarly provides 'containment' in order to help the patient progress from splitting to integration. Bion also shifted the emphasis of Kleinian thinking beyond the intrapsychic to an interpersonal slant.

Donald Winnicott (1971; Phillips 1988) differed from Klein in that he adopted a more benign view of the mother—infant interaction. Mother's 'good enough' care facilitates the infant's maturation. Winnicott is best known for his concept of transitional space, an intermediate and overlapping zone between the unconscious of infant and mother (and, by extension, therapist and patient), within which emotional development, including the reparative creativity mentioned above, occurs. He saw the use of 'transitional objects' (i.e. teddy-bears and comfort blankets) as manifestations of this process. Another major notion was the authentic or 'true self', which could be facilitated by a sensitive, attuned but not overprotective maternal response. When the caregiver is controlling or neglectful or unattuned, a compliant 'false self' would develop.

American psychoanalysis came under the influence in the 1980s of Heinz Kohut (1977) when he developed a model of self-psychology derived from Freud's distinction between self-preservative or narcissistic drives and those which led to relationships with others. In contrast to Freud, Kohut saw narcissistic needs not as primitive precursors of relationship needs but as coexisting with them from birth, continuing through life, and as normal.

He viewed idealization of the therapist, a common feature of therapy, as a positive manifestation of narcissistic needs, similar to idealization of parents by their children. This was gradually replaced with a more realistic appraisal. Psychopathology arose from environmental failure or deficit, mainly lack of developmentally appropriate maternal empathy (rather than, as in the Kleinian model also espoused by the Klein-influenced American psycho-analyst, Otto Kernberg 1984), the result of intra-psychic conflict such as excessive aggression. Psychotherapists influenced by Kohut therefore highlight empathy as a central therapeutic tool.

The history of psychoanalysis is replete with controversy and schism, the ideas of several outstanding figures who disagreed with Freud continuing to influence psychoanalytic psychotherapy. Jung, for instance, thought that Freud neglected man's spiritual aspirations and overemphasized sexuality as central to neurosis (Stevens 1991). Jungian analytic theory postulates the presence of the 'collective unconscious', a source of fantasy life lying deeper than the individual unconscious, emerging in different but related forms across cultures. Archetypes are proposed as pre-existing, possibly genetically determined, unconscious structures, around which significant experience is organized. Jung used the term 'individuation' to describe the inclination of the self towards development, maturation, and fulfilment of its potential. The process of active imagination is proposed as the therapeutic technique which facilitates this process of extricating oneself from collective and archetypal psychological origins (Samuels 1985).

In the United States, Harry Stack Sullivan (1953) emphasized the role of the social environment in psychopathology. The relationship with the analyst was the key process around which both theory and therapy should center. In contrast to classical psychoanalytic and object relations theory, inter-personal psychoanalysis (Mitchel 1985; Stolorow and Atwood 1987) focuses on the joint contribution of analyst and patient's unconscious to the therapeutic relationship. Interpersonal psychoanalysis draws on infant observation studies (e.g. Stern 1985) and attachment theory (see below) for its observational and theoretical base.

Non-psychoanalytic contributions to long-term psychotherapy

Several non-psychoanalytic influences have, often unobtrusively, affected the evolution of psychoanalytic psychotherapy. Jerome Frank and J. B. Frank (see Chapter 4) (1991) believed that therapies have more in common than their quarrelsome proponents would like us to believe. In comparing outcome of various forms, Luborsky et al. (1975) invoked the 'dodo-bird verdict': 'All have won and everyone shall have prizes'. Frank's discussion of healing suggested that 'common factors' are found in all effective methods of psychological treatments. He summarized these as: (1) instilling hope; (2) providing a relationship with the therapist; (3) offering an explanatory theory or rationale of the illness or problem; and (4) suggesting practical steps to be taken to overcome the difficulty. Each of these applies to psychoanalysis: the last comprising the commitment to attend regular sessions, to 'associate' freely (i.e. communicate everything that arises in the mind, however irrelevant, trivial or embarrassing it may seem), and an emphasis on dreams.

Carl Rogers (1951) introduced 'client-centred therapy' in the 1950s. The research findings based on his ideas suggest that effective therapists possess (and can be trained to develop) empathy, genuineness, and 'non-possessive warmth' (Truax and Carkhuff 1967). These attributes are no less relevant to psychoanalysis as they are to other therapies.

Finally, the work of Aaron Beck (Beck et al. 1979) has had a huge impact since the 1970s. Cognitive therapy, originally developed as an alternative to psychoanalysis, has much in common with it, especially when it moves into longer-term, 'schema-focused' treatments for patients with personality disorders (Beck 1993). Schemata, reflecting fundamental dispositions of the self in relation to others, can be seen as analogous to object relationships as described by psychoanalysts. Similarly, interpretations of splitting used by psychoanalytic psychotherapists have much in common with cognitive challenges to the patient. For example, when questioning dichotomized or catastrophizing assumptions (that underlie the transference), it might be suggested to a patient who had been physically abused by his father and whose attitude towards the therapist is one of sulky compliance: 'It looks as though you assume I can only be either a depressed mother or a violent father'.

How verifiable is the theory underlying long-term dynamic psychotherapy? The contribution of research on infant development

Daniel Stern's (1985) research in developmental psychology established objectively how infants experience themselves, others, and their relationships. His observations led him to postulate four stages of development of the self in infancy. First is the sense of 'emergent self', occurring between birth and 2 months, in which the infant actively engages in organising its experience of the world and locating itself within it.

This is followed between 2 and 7 months by the development of the 'core self', in which the baby has a sense of himself as a coherent whole, and of others as separate, complete persons. During this phase, the infant also develops a sense of self-with-other, but this is achieved from a position of having clearly established self and object as discrete entities.

In the next phase between 7 and 9 months, the infant develops a sense of 'subjective self'. The baby discovers that he and other people have minds and that he can share his feelings with others, facilitating intersubjectivity.

During the second year of life, the 'verbal sense of self' evolves which both extends the domain of intersubjective experience and distinguishes between life as it is experienced and as it is verbally represented.

These types of studies view the infant's emotional world from a different viewpoint than the clinician engaged with the adult's representations of early infantile experience and fantasy life, through the filter of subsequent life.

Stern's conclusions differ from those of classical analysis. The infant's intense interest in the outside world from the outset is in contrast to Freud's view of barriers to engagement because of primary narcissism. Observational studies do not support a single motivational drive but several hierarchically organized drives. 'Internal working models' of relationships with parents are developed which can be grouped by the baby into those with negative and positive hedonic tone. Stern argues that these come to be designated good and bad by the verbal child rather than being associated with good and bad emotional states resulting from libidinal and destructive drives from the outset (as Klein would posit). This research has opened up a new dialogue between analytic theory and observational research to the advantage of both.

The contribution of neurobiology

As mentioned, Freud trained as a neurologist and hoped to find a physical basis for the psychological constructs he was describing. As psychoanalysis became increasingly psychological in orientation, that hope faded. However, the notion that much mental life operates unconsciously has gained wide acceptance in contemporary cognitive neuroscience. A basic distinction is made between unconscious or implicit memory, and conscious or explicit memory (Siegel 1999). Implicit memory operates from birth if not before; infants demonstrate recall for experiences derived from behavioural, perceptual, and emotional learning. This involves the amygdala and other limbic circuits in the case of emotional memory, and basal ganglia and motor cortex for behavioural memory, neither of which require conscious processing during either encoding or retrieval. These 'memories' have implications for a sense of self, being the means by which mental models of the world are built up. None can be consciously recalled, since this requires the hippocampus which only matures sufficiently at around the age of 18–24 months.

Consider a key concept in psychoanalysis—repression. Thoughts and feelings remain unconscious not because of neurological immaturity, but through active prevention of them reaching consciousness. Based on studies of brain injured patients, Solms (2000) argues that the 'superego' (i.e. that part of the mind concerned with conscience, doing what is 'right and proper'), which is closely bound up with the ventromedial region of the prefrontal lobe, acts as a repressive 'stimulus barrier' between instinctual drives (especially sexual and aggressive) arising in the limbic system.

A simplistic account of the differences between psychoanalytic and cognitive therapy is that the former is concerned with affect, the latter with cognition. Experimental psychologists have, however, become interested in the role of emotion in determining behaviour. Another intriguing field of enquiry has explored the neurobiology of interpersonal experience and its influence on the developing mind. Activation of neural pathways directly influences neuronal connections especially during the first 3–4 years of life. Schore (1994) suggests that brain development is 'experience-dependent'. Thus, emotional experiences in early life and the quality of relationship with parents becomes a 'hard-wired' aspect of a person's neurological make-up. Interpersonal relationships determine how genes express themselves in the brain. For example, privation results in neurological 'pruning'; conversely, rich emotional and cognitive experiences lead to increased activity of neurones, and the development of new synaptic connections. Trauma or stress in early life is possibly linked to impaired neuronal development and susceptibility to psychiatric disorder in later life (Schore 1997).

Attachment theory-research findings relevant to psychotherapy

John Bowlby, a psychoanalyst at the Tavistock Clinic in London for many years, was keen to establish a scientific basis for psychoanalytic concepts, particularly, the link between early childhood adversity ('maternal deprivation') and long-term personality difficulties and psychopathology. His colleague, Mary Ainsworth, devised ways to classify the quality of attachment between parent and child. She studied their responses to what was called the 'Strange Situation'. In this 20-min laboratory test, a child is exposed to brief separations from the parent. The reaction to these separations led to a classification of children as securely attached (healthy protest followed by soothing on reunion and return to exploratory play), anxious-avoidantly attached (with a damped down 'hypoactivated' response), anxious-ambivalent or resistant ('hyper-activated', that is aroused and hard to soothe) in their attachment style, or disorganized/disoriented (no recognizable strategy for maintaining contact with the caregiver).

These tend to be stable, and can be extrapolated to adult relationships as follows: (1) secure/autonomous people who value attachment relationships; (2) insecure/dismissing who deny, devalue, idealize or denigrate current and past attachments; (3) insecure/preoccupied who are overwhelmed or confused by current and past attachment relationships and cling to intimates, including therapists; and (4) disorganized or 'unresolved' who have often suffered neglect or trauma and whose attachment patterns are chaotic.

Compared to other psychoanalytic 'schools' rigorous empirical research underlies attachment theory. For instance, expectant parents' models of attachment predict subsequent patterns of attachment between mother and infant (Fonagy 2001). A key concept is *mentalization*, the capacity to understand that one's own behaviour and that of others is motivated by internal states such as thoughts and feelings (Fonagy 1998). Mentalization also implies an understanding that one's perceptions of others are representations rather than the way reality actually is. The caregiver's capacity to observe the infant's intentional state and internal world influences the evolution of secure attachment which in turn influences the child's capacity to mentalize. Thus the sequence is: secure attachment in childhood—parental mentalization of the child—the child's capacity to mentalize himself and others—effective and satisfying interpersonal strategies. The opposite process results in psychopathology.

How does long-term psychotherapy work?

Long-term psychodynamic therapy effects psychological change in many ways. Theoretical models of what is effective in bringing about change are very much in the making. The models represent important differences, affecting the emphasis given to patient's feelings about ends of sessions, breaks and all aspects of the analyst's separateness.

The therapeutic relationship itself. The therapeutic relationship has long been thought to be central to change in dynamic therapy. Views vary as to how the relationship brings about change. Followers of Kohut argue that the relationship is a 'corrective emotional experience', that the experience of a good enough relationship makes up for deficiencies in formative relationships. Others argue that change occurs not through the therapist's availability (positive transference), but through disappointment with the therapist (negative transference). A 'Kleinian' view is that change occurs through the analyst's ability to contain the patient's destructiveness without being overwhelmed by it.

Disconfirming assumptions. When the therapist is perceived to behave in ways which resonate with internal object relationships, those internalizations are amenable to change if the therapist does not behave in the expected way. Expectations are disconfirmed, and the patient brings a new set of assumptions into play in order to continue to operate in a coherent way. If uncertainty can be tolerated and held within the therapeutic situation, psychological growth can occur. One can conceptualize this as occurring through the activation of neural networks, one network being modified and weakened while a new neural network comes to hold sway (Westen and Gabbard 2002a, b).

Fostering the capacity for mentalization. One important aspect of the therapeutic relationship is the capacity to tolerate and reflect upon feelings. This starts with the therapist, and is internalized by the patient. Once this process is firmly established the patient will continue to use therapy or analysis long after sessions have ended. Fonagy and Target (1996) describe this in terms of the therapist's capacity for mentalization.

Outcome studies have verified these assumptions. Blatt and Auerbachs (2001) studied 40 treatment-resistant young adults and adolescents using the Differentiation–Relatedness Scale. They were tested at the start and finish of psychoanalytic inpatient treatment of 1-year duration. Internal self- and object representations underwent significant changes from being dominated by splitting and polarization at the outset towards more integrated descriptions of self and others after treatment.

Insight. Fostering insight was classically thought to be the mode of operation of psychoanalysis. Unconscious themes in free association would be brought to consciousness. The development of insight into unconscious processes as a means to obtaining more conscious control of behaviour rather than being driven by unconscious defensive motives is still understood to be one of the primary means by which therapy works.

Non-analytic techniques. Techniques used in other models of therapy also come into play in psychoanalytic therapy while not easily sitting with analytic theory. These include suggestion, most evident when the analyst is confronting the patient about self-destructive behaviour, and the behavioural technique of exposure, the patient being exposed to feared emotional situations in sessions and finding them less terrifying than imagined. Negative cognitions are challenged in a way, which has some parallels with cognitive therapy through, for example, identifying expectations of criticism in the transference as manifestations of punitive superego activity.

Neurobiological speculations. From a neurobiological perspective, Schore (1996) marshals convincing evidence that neurological development in the early years of life is experience-dependent (see p. 85). Experience of early relationships becomes 'hard wired' into the developing brain during critical periods of development. The important question from the psychotherapist's point of view is whether such neurologically established patterns of relating are amenable to change later in life or, as is the case with cortical blindness, once the critical period has passed in which the part of the brain is 'wired up', the emotional damage becomes irreparable. It would appear that animal models of critical periods and imprinting are not directly translatable to humans who retain a capacity to learn and use dependent neuronal plasticity throughout life and there is a body of evidence indicating that experience-dependent maturation continues into adult life, and may be the neurological substrate of long-term psychological change (Cozolino 2002).

The therapeutic process

Psychoanalysis and psychoanalytic psychotherapy

We have referred hitherto to psychoanalysis and psychoanalytic psychotherapy interchangeably. Although they have much in common there are also substantive differences between them. Psychoanalysis is expensive; there are few third-party payers—insurance companies, private health insurance agencies, or health departments—who are willing to pay for it. In publicly funded settings, psychoanalytic psychotherapy is therefore the norm. The patient is seen once or twice a week for a limited period, often not exceeding 3 years. The patient tends to sit up rather than lie on a couch. Regression is less likely to occur. A more supportive component influences some therapist interventions. Research evidence to answer the question of the differential indications for psychoanalytic psychotherapy and full psychoanalysis is scanty. The former is more suitable for those who are too disturbed to undergo a full analysis (which might precipitate a 'breakdown') or sufficiently well functioning not to warrant it. A study which tried to address this issue (Sandell et al. 2000) suggests that the outcome of psychoanalysis may be superior and more durable than that of psychoanalytic psychotherapy, but methodological difficulties characterised the research.

Assessment

People seek out psychoanalytic therapy for many reasons, and in diverse ways. Some come through word of mouth, whereas others are referred by GPs, psychiatrists or psychologists. Many have been in therapy which may have had short-term effects but have not changed enduring dysfunctional patterns. The quasi-medical term, 'referral', implies a passivity in the patient that is inimical to the psychoanalytic contract. Ultimately, the patient has to 'own' the need for help and commitment to treatment.

The term 'assessment' derives from the Latin word *assidere*, 'to sit beside', but also has connotations of the reckoning of assets (Holmes 1991). Assessment for long-term therapy can be considered to contain both elements: an empathic attempt to understand the patient's inner world and an analysis of strengths and weaknesses. Another view is to construe the preliminary meetings as a consultation, an opportunity for the patient to have an experience of what therapy is like, particularly, the intimacy involved, to enable them to arrive at their own decision, about whether it is what they are looking for.

A number of constructs predict good outcome (Sifneos 1969; Malan 1973): motivation for change, a capacity to express emotion, a positive working alliance (Bergin and Lambert 1986) and 'psychological-mindedness'. The latter captures such features as the ability to see oneself from the outside (i.e. to mentalize), tolerate psychic pain and a capacity for fluidity of thought.

However, most patients with long-standing difficulties or personality disorders have problems in all these areas. What is being assessed is whether the difficulties show signs of being amenable to change or present an insurmountable obstacle. Research and clinical experience indicate that a *robust working alliance*—that is, a collaborative atmosphere as viewed by the assessor and a positive view of therapy and the therapist in the patient—early in treatment is the best predictor of good outcome.

Therapists implicitly or explicitly adopt the following framework to think through the implications of 'taking on' a patient for psychoanalytic psychotherapy.

Diagnostic considerations

Psychoanalysis was originally devised by Freud and Breuer as a treatment for neurosis, especially conversion hysteria. Freud soon came to see the Oedipus complex as the 'kernel of the neuroses' and conceptualized anxiety disorders, including obsessional neurosis, sexual dysfunction, and psychosomatic problems in Oedipal terms. The Oedipal situation was seen as a 'three-person problem' (Balint et al. 1972): the male child competing with father for exclusive possession of mother and fearing reprisal in the form of castration anxiety (the situation supposedly reversed in girls). The resultant conflict between impulse and societal/parental prohibition was thought to be dealt with by defence mechanisms, especially repression, the breakdown of which leads to neurotic symptoms.

Effective non-psychoanalytic psychotherapies are available today for specific neurotic disorders. These include cognitive behaviour therapy and medication for obsessional neurosis, cognitive behaviour therapy and antidepressants for uncomplicated depressive illness, couple therapy and behaviour therapy for sexual dysfunction and anxiety management for anxiety states. These therapies predominate in the public sector where resources are limited and the need to maximize symptomatic benefit in a limited number of sessions is paramount.

At the same time, object relations theory and self-psychology, as mentioned above, have opened up understanding of 'pre-Oedipal' or 'two-person' psychology. This refers to the first year or two of life in which the infant's world is concerned with himself and that of his principal caregiver, usually mother, and where anxieties defended against are not of partial loss (as is the case in castration anxiety) but of total loss, that is, the infant's very survival is at risk. Difficulties in this period are linked with more global problems in personality development than those seen in Oedipal conflicts alone. The focus of psychoanalytic psychotherapy has therefore shifted increasingly towards the personality disorders.

Candidates for long-term individual therapy usually have enduring personality difficulties and symptoms which are pervasive rather than circumscribed. Patients with recurrent depressive disorders or prolonged grief reactions, long-standing and intractable anxiety, repeated relationship difficulties, and especially borderline and narcissistic personality disorders, form much of the work of psychoanalytic psychotherapists. Many patients will have experienced severe childhood trauma, including neglect and/or sexual and physical abuse.

An optimum level of disturbance for psychoanalytic psychotherapy is likely (Horowitz et al. 1984; Wallerstein 1986). The very disturbed need considerable support, often from a psychiatric service, while the less complicated can be managed with cognitive and other techniques. Those in between—'ill enough to merit it, well enough to benefit from it' (Bateman and Holmes 1995)—are potential patients. Where the line is drawn depends on how much support is available between sessions from the psychiatric service or other agencies and how well links can be made between this and the work in therapy itself.

Inclusion and exclusion criteria

The principle of 'to whom it hath it shall be given . . .' applies, however unfairly, to psychoanalytic psychotherapy. Research shows that patients with certain attributes are more likely to benefit from all types of therapy than those who lack them. Young, attractive, verbal, intelligent, and successful (YAVIS) people tend to do well (Luborsky et al. 1971). Malan (1976, 1979) found that a history of at least one meaningful relationship or evidence of positive achievement in work, sport, artistic talent, or even a good sense of humour, was associated with good outcome in brief dynamic therapy (see Chapter 6).

Malan also proposed his 'law of increased disturbance', suggesting that a person's previous history of disturbed behaviour—addiction, promiscuity, violence, or self-harm—is likely to manifest in therapy. This implies that those with a history of substance abuse, recurrent self-harm, psychosis, entrenched somatiation and obsessional neurosis should only be taken on for long-term therapy with careful thought, considering, particularly, what support is available should such eventualities arise. Treatment *is* possible but requires collaboration between therapist and other professionals, such as the GP, psychiatrist, or community psychiatric nurse, with the option of brief admission at times of crisis.

What does the assessor look for?

The assessment interview is a microcosm of future psychoanalytic therapy. Patients are no doubt anxious about revealing intimate details to a stranger. The way they deal with this highly charged situation reveals much about their strengths and weaknesses in the capacity to relate. The capacities to relate and to mentalize are most pertinent in determining whether psychoanalytic therapy is likely to be of use. The therapist can test this by observation and trial interpretations. For example, patients may respond to the therapist's apparently accurate attempts to understand them paradoxically—the closer the therapist approaches to the truth the more the patient withdraws, an interpretation is not feasible, which enables the patient to feel the therapist has understood their need to withdraw—creating a moment of understanding and contact—this difficulty may recur throughout therapy and prevent change.

A good outcome is likely if what Malan (1979) calls 'leapfrogging' occurs—a dialogue in which the patient describes an aspect of their feelings, the therapist responds with a comment or interpretation, the patient opens up in response to that, and so on. For example (simplified):

> *Patient*: (with a depressive illness precipitated by divorce): 'Whenever I begin to get close to someone I seem to back off and try to escape . . .'
>
> *Therapist*: 'Do you think that could have something to do with your mother's death when you were young, and a feeling that it just isn't safe to trust anyone, including me . . .' [transference interpretation]
>
> *Patient* (silence, cries): 'I remember at the funeral how my granny tried to put her arms around me and I just pushed her away. My dad really had a go at me about that, it was embarrassing in front of everyone, I just hated him for it . . .'

A moment in which understanding has been reached is often followed by an expression of feeling in the patient and deepening contact with the therapist.

The psychodynamic formulation

As part of the process of thinking about the patient's suitability and offering a trial interpretation, the therapist will *formulate* the totality of the presentation in an attempt to identify a core theme which underlies the patient's presenting problems (Hinshelwood 1991). Patient and therapist act like interpreters of a literary text or musical score, trying to grasp the underlying structure (Holmes 1992). The formulation brings together the presenting problem, past difficulties or trauma and the transference into what Malan (1979), following Menninger and Holzman (1958), has called the 'triangle of insight' (see Chapter 6).

Luborsky and colleagues (Luborsky and Crits-Cristoph 1988) have systematized the process of formulation in order to sharpen therapeutic thinking and for the purposes of research. For the Luborsky group the formulation consists in identifying an underlying need, desire or *wish* (the use of the latter word is based on Freud's conceptualization of dreams as disguised wish-fulfilments) in the patient, the *responses of others* to that wish, and the *response of the self* to those responses (i.e. in the above case, wishing to be close, anxiety about loss and avoidance of closeness, respectively). Similarly, Ryle (1990) emphasizes the self-fulfilling nature of neurotic difficulty, in which a person's core state— an inner loneliness in the example—is reinforced and maintained by his reactions and behaviour: the more the patient rejects and pushes away, the more the feeling of isolation is maintained.

During the assessment, having the formulation in mind enables the therapist to think about:

—The likely reactions of the patient to the therapist.

—The impact of breaks and the ending.

—The implications of the patient's defences being altered in therapy.

—The likelihood that defences will not be touched by therapy, given the intensity of underlying anxiety.

—The support needed to enable the person to face such anxiety in therapy.

—How to discuss with the patient the likely implications of embarking on therapy to enable them to decide whether to proceed.

Assessment effects

The reaction after this initial assessment is usually a good indicator of possible reactions to therapy overall. Patients may self-harm, report profound dreams, sustain accidents, have seminal conversations with partners or relatives and the like. A follow up meeting can therefore be pivotal to reach a conclusion about the likely value of therapy. Failure to show up for a scheduled meeting, needless to say, indicates poor prognosis or early drop out. In some instances, it is not possible to establish potential benefits of therapy after one or two meetings and a 'trial of therapy' of around six sessions may be offered.

Goals of therapy

Setting goals is a controversial subject. The assessor establishes what the patient hopes will change through therapy as part of the decision-making about whether to proceed. But free association demands that the patient discloses whatever comes into his mind as a means of gaining access to unconscious material masked by day-to-day mental activity. Setting goals can be a disadvantage in getting to grips with often-elusive psychodynamics. In addition, if the therapist joins the patient in mapping out objectives, she has given up a degree of neutrality. There *are* goals in the broadest sense since both protagonists are working on what they know to be the patient's difficulties with a view to resolving them. The way patients address or avoid this task is constantly subject to interpretation. There is a marked contrast here with brief therapy, even if psychoanalytic in orientation. As time-limited therapists like Malan (1976) and Sifneos (1969) suggest, a clear focus on specified goals is mandatory (see Chapter 6). On the other hand, Thoma and Kachele (1987) regard psychoanalysis as a focal form of therapy in that a dynamic focus exists at any developmental stage around which the work is organized, although this may shift gradually over time.

The early sessions

Arrangements made at the outset of therapy constitute the therapeutic contract. This includes the times, length and frequency of sessions. The message is conveyed that treatment involves a reliable relationship with the therapist. Missed sessions undermine the possibility of useful therapeutic work. Therapist and patient undertake to let one another know, with notice where possible, of any planned or unexpected breaks. Throughout therapy, any alteration is not made impulsively, but thoroughly discussed. This allows an understanding of the full implications of change in terms of the patient's personality, problems, life-situation, relation with the therapist (transference); this can contribute usefully to insight.

The patient is bound to feel anxious at first. Often preconceptions or fantasies about what the therapist will be like or what will happen are revealing about the patient's difficulties. 'Staying with' the anxiety means ascertaining the patient's concerns without immediately reassuring them. For example, a patient may wait for the therapist to ask her questions, because she is uncomfortable about needing something from another person. The patient may project a neediness into the therapist by perceiving the therapist's questions as a reflection of his need for answers, thus defending herself against facing a needy aspect of herself. If the therapist promptly relieves the patient's anxiety by actually asking many questions, the defence is *enacted* but is unavailable for *understanding*. *Au contraire*, if the therapist's comments on the patient's tendency to do this, her anxiety commonly diminishes because a habitual pattern has been spotted and understood. Interpreting thus may be more reassuring than reassurance!

Many patients are intolerant of anxiety or take time to learn the value of staying with their distressing affect. The first session should not be an agony. More disturbed patients, such as those with borderline psychopathology, are apt to find it difficult to tolerate the anxiety of this approach. Patients unable to articulate feelings can respond to suggestions about how to start. A simple strategy like pursuing an obvious part of the history is useful. The patient will need assistance less and less later. Whenever possible, the patient's own words and imagery, rather than technical or abstract terminology should be used. This enables the therapist to stay as close as possible to the material the patient raises.

Working through

Freud introduced the concept of 'working through' partly to differentiate purely intellectual insight from emotional acceptance of an interpretation, and partly to describe the way in which ideas and feelings generated in therapy need to generalize into everyday life and the totality of personality. The value of working through is a key justification for long-term treatment.

After an initial honeymoon phase, progress may become more difficult as resistance or unconscious blocks to progress emerge. Symptoms may be 'overdetermined', serving multiple functions. They will therefore not resolve if only one function alone is addressed; they need to be tackled at many levels.

In order to overcome these difficulties, the therapist uses core therapeutic techniques of active listening and observing transference and countertransference. He also uses, at different times, (guided by tact and countertransference based on his personal therapy and training), all five types of intervention: clarification, linking, reflecting, interpretation, and confrontation. These are covered in the next section.

Free association and active listening

Long-term psychotherapy continues to use Freud's already mentioned 'fundamental rule'—that the patient tries to say everything that comes into his mind without censure. This is an ideal and not truly possible. Some patients have a facility to work in this way; others learn to do so; yet others continue to encounter great difficulty. This in itself can be informative. 'Autobiographical competence' (Holmes 1992)—the capacity to describe facts and feelings about oneself in a fluent and coherent way—is linked to secure attachment in childhood, whereas insecure patterns are associated with alexithymia (a difficulty in finding words to express feeling) or an emotional enmeshment in past trauma (Holmes 1993). Note, however, that fluent free association can be used defensively—to placate the therapist. In any event, the principle remains: once therapy is under way, it is the patient who initiates the sessions and sets the agenda. The therapist accepts whatever the patient brings—even if ostensibly mundane, practical, or irrelevant—as primary data.

The counterpart to free association is active listening. When silent, the therapist aims for a state of active receptiveness, 'beyond memory and desire' (Bion 1978, quoting Eliot), based on what Freud called 'evenly suspended attention', empathically attuned to the emotional import of the patient's material, and his own counter-transferential reactions. Winnicott (1971), Kohut (Stolorow et al. 1987), and others (see Stern 1985; Holmes 1994) have linked this aspect with the sensitivity shown by effective parents to their children's needs, provision of a 'holding environment', and a secure and self-absorbed child happily playing 'alone' in the presence of a watchful but non-intrusive parent.

Transference and counter-transference

The hallmark of psychoanalytic psychotherapy is the understanding and use of transference and counter-transference, which can be defined as unconscious aspects of the relationship as they affect patient and therapist. Freud originally conceived them as impediments but both are now seen as central since they bring the patient's interpersonal difficulties directly into the consulting room where they can be worked on.

Two vital distinctions need to be made here. Sandler and Sandler (1984) differentiate 'past transference', which corresponds with the classical Freudian view of a repetition in therapy of feelings, attitudes, and assumptions derived from early parental relationships with 'present transference', which is more akin to the notion of the 'pre-conscious'—referring to the immediate impact of the therapist on the patient and 'what is going on' between them.

Understanding and interpreting current transference should precede that of past transference which otherwise may seem stereotyped and unconvincing. Transference is not an esoteric concept only available to the cognoscenti but an everyday phenomenon. For example, on meeting a patient—a young man with paranoid feelings—in the waiting area the therapist noted that he looked startled. When asked about this later in the session the patient reported that he had expected the therapist to be short, fat, bald, bearded, and with a middle-European accent, and had assumed therefore that he was facing an impostor! This misperception in the 'present transference', and the general suspicious-ness, could be linked later to a disrupted childhood in which his mother had frequently been hospitalized with depression and, at times of her illness, seemed alien and changed in a frightening way to him.

Freud's notion of counter-transference as comprising the therapist's blind spots, responsible for his misperceptions of the patient, based on his own childhood experience, remains valid. For instance, the 'compulsive caring syndrome', seen in some health workers, may be an attempt to assuage guilt about childhood aggression towards siblings or be a continuation of a child-hood role reversal in which the therapist-to-be was expected emotionally, even physically, to look after her parent. The unconscious element would be due to the therapist's inability to recognize what she needs directly, gratifying it vicariously through his patients.

Heimann (1950), Winnicott (1971), and others have emphasized the positive aspects of counter-transference. Emotions and fantasies aroused in the therapist are a vital guide to the inner world of the patient (see Casement 1985). This links with the Kleinian concept of *projective identification*, a primitive non-verbal communication in which difficult feelings belonging to a person are induced in another, in the first instance between mother and baby, later in adult relationships including that with the therapist. Thus, benignly, a mother vicariously feels her baby's fear and rage, and is able to assuage them through feeding and soothing. When this process continues into adult life, however, as it does with most people when extremely stressed, and regularly in those suffering from Borderline Personality Disorder, caregivers and therapists may be overwhelmed by strong feelings—anger, disgust, erotic interest, intense desire to rescue or retreat—which *feel* like their own, but ultimately emanate from the patient.

The therapist's task is to observe his counter-transference, sifting that which relates to his own life from what has been projected, containing rather than acting on it, and translating these feelings into interpretations, which can be useful to the patient. The process need not be complicated: the patient who makes one angry is probably furious himself; a patient in tears may arouse in the therapist a variety of feelings, such as overwhelming sadness, irritation, anguish, or indifference, each of which can be tied to the patient's particular situation and problems. This task is facilitated by the therapist having under-gone his own therapy or analysis through which they have learned to observe and think about the manifestations of their own unconscious, as well as learning about their own unconscious dispositions to become aware of them before they are enacted.

Transference and counter-transference reflect a growing recognition that the classical view of the therapeutic relationship as a one-way street with therapist as neutral observer of the 'seething cauldron' of the patient's emotions is no longer appropriate. More relevant to a postmodernist world is a model in which patient and therapist each contribute to a 'bipersonal field' (Langs 1976), albeit asymmetrical in that each is assigned a different role, but to which each contributes both consciously and unconsciously.

Clarification

Since patients often talk in vague generalities, it is frequently illuminating to seek more information. The devil is in the detail. Language can be used to hide feelings as well as reveal them. A patient might say, 'I'm not feeling very good today'. This needs to be clarified: in what way 'not good', what sort of a feeling is 'not good'? Does it have a specific bodily sensation—in the stomach or head, for example? What might have precipitated the feeling? Might it be worth going through the events in detail that led up to it? (the therapist might have said something in the previous session that the patient experienced as rejecting).

At another, and less therapeutic, level clarification may help cross cultural or technical barriers. If the therapist is not acquainted, for example, with marital or family customs in a particular culture he simply asks. Similarly, if patients have technical expertise with which the therapist is unfamiliar, for example, instrumental technique in a musician which is relevant to his problem. Another use of clarification, described by Kernberg (1977), is to detect more serious disturbance than the therapist suspected: unclear speech, for instance, may reflect unclear thought which in turn may reflect severe anxiety or schizophrenic thought disorder. As a generalization, when asked to clarify, a neurotic patient does so, whereas a psychotic patient's thinking may be thrown further into disarray.

Linking

A therapist may explicate links he has noted but the patient has missed—for example, between the depression of a man who feels himself to be always an outsider and his growing up as an adoptive child in a family which later had a much longed for child of their own. Indeed, the aim of therapy is an attempt to link, and therefore make more coherent, a life that feels fragmented and inchoate. An emotionally powerful form of linking is the use of metaphor (Holmes 1992). Much therapeutic conversation is metaphorical ('I always feel

I'm on the fringe of things'—a young man with sexual difficulties, especially with penetration). Metaphor and transference are etymologically identical: both mean a 'carrying across'. Being able to make links closely relates to the capacity to symbolize. This in turn is associated with the capacity to establish mental representations of experience. Bion (1967a) asserts that the capacity to make links is often disrupted in more severe psychological disorder, because of difficulties in the mother–infant relationship.

Malan (1979) describes the 'triangle of person' (or triangle of transference) in psychotherapy which links the relationship with the therapist, the patient's current relationship patterns with significant others, and parental relationships in childhood (see also Chapter 6, pp. 123–126). At each 'point' of the triangle—therapist, other, parent—there is a second triangle—'triangle of conflict'—comprising anxiety, defence, and hidden fear. The work of therapy can be understood as making conscious the links between different aspects of these triangles. Through his studies of brief psychoanalytic therapy, Malan (1973) identified interpretations which made links with the transference as most clearly related to a good outcome. For example, the adoptee patient, who suffered from bipolar disorder, started off a session unable to get words out, as though they were stuck in his throat; this was followed by an unstoppable flow. The therapist linked his feelings of being an outsider to his feelings when depressed. As he came to sense he was understood in the session, his wishful fantasy of being totally known, with no barriers at all between him and the therapist was seen in his unrestrained flow of talk and associated sense of elation. This was linked with his childhood fantasies about the relationship he had lost with his biological mother in which he made a division between an inner mother who really wanted only to keep him and the authorities who had removed him from her and rendered him forever an outsider.

Reflecting

In reflecting, derived from Rogerian client-centred therapy, a problem or situation presented by the patient is 'sifted' through by the therapist, drawing on his experience, and reflected back in a way that helps to make it clearer. Even simple reflection can be immensely helpful. For example, in a patient faced with a career decision, the therapist comments: 'I think this conflict is between what you want to do and what you feel you should do'. The chief feature here is that nothing, or at least very little, is added to what comes from the patient.

Interpretation

Interpretation, a fundamental psychoanalytic technique, is an attempt to make unconscious motives, attitudes, and feelings conscious and thus promote insight. Interpreting applies to any facet of unconscious activity the therapist thinks may be relevant. Interpretations can be subdivided into transference (i.e. unconscious thoughts and feelings involving the therapist are brought to light and linked with past experience), and non-transference (the focus is on an extra-therapeutic aspect of the patient's life and its connections with the past).

Dream interpretation remains a central feature of psychoanalytic therapy (Freud 1900; Flanders 1993). Dreams reflect both present preoccupations, as well as those in the past, and represent an unwilled or 'innocent' account of the patient's current state of mind (Rycroft 1979). When a patient describes a dream (manifest content), the therapist enquires about what the elements of the dream bring to mind, inviting a train of associations. Therapist and patient then collaborate to establish the underlying significance of the dream (latent content). It often has a bearing on patient's perception of the relationship between himself and the therapist.

Malan's ideas, described earlier, can be traced to Strachey's (1934) seminal paper on the 'mutative interpretation', bringing together the patient's current difficulty, his relationship with the therapist, and the past into a single theme. This has led to the view that transference interpretations are powerful in effecting change. This was not Freud's original view, since he believed non-transference interpretations were equally cogent. Indeed, a study (Piper et al. 1991) suggests that a high frequency of transference interpretations can even be associated with deterioration. This may occur when the therapist is desperately salvaging an ineffective therapeutic alliance.

Offenkrantz and Tobin (1974) have spelt out four conditions under which transference should be interpreted: the patient shows undue emotion with no obvious cause, particularly if this occurs repeatedly; the flow of associations becomes blocked; the therapist considers it likely that a transference interpretation will increase understanding; and the link between attitudes to pivotal figures in the past and attitudes to the therapist are close to the patient's awareness.

Conscience (superego) manifestations like excessive guilt, common in depressive disorders, need interpretation in an effort to discover their source and to modify their harmful effects; like in cognitive therapy, analytically oriented therapists aim to free patients from 'oughts' and 'shoulds' which unconsciously (and sometimes masochistically) dominate their lives.

Steiner (1993) has usefully distinguished between 'patient-centred' and 'therapist-centred' interpretations. In early stages of therapy, the therapist may have to contain and 'metabolize' (Bion 1978) projections without translating them into interpretations. Therapist-centred interpretations are usually reserved for later and deeper phases of therapy.

An interpretation is an hypothesis to account for a certain attitude, emotion, or behaviour. If accurate change towards increased insight, modified attitude or more adaptive behaviour should ensue. If inaccurate there will be no effect. This is how the hypothesis is tested. A 'correct' interpretation may be rejected because it is given too early but is accepted later (Balint et al. 1972). This is not unlike the expanding understanding that comes from repeated reading of a complex novel or listening to a piece of music. The therapist should not be easily put off by a negative response or, conversely, be too gratified by an overly eager acceptance; these reactions may be defences and call for further interpretation (Blackwell 1976).

Confrontation and acting-out

Periodically, patients need to be confronted with the consequences of their actions, although interpretation is preferable and should accompany it. Confrontation is a challenge. For example, merely exploring the meaning of recurrent lateness may not be enough; the patient may need to be faced with the fact that treatment is rendered useless and may have to cease.

Acting-out, a problem that may need interpretation and, later, confrontation, reflects an unconscious enactment of a problem, often a defence against acknowledging it. The action is often self-destructive. For this reason impulsiveness can be difficult to handle in therapy. A patient with substance misuse, for example, may binge to alleviate the first sign of anxiety. Impulsiveness can take other forms, such as suicidal behaviour, self-mutilation, reckless driving, and an action which threatens a relationship. Confronting patient's with the self-destructive implications of their behaviour is almost always necessary.

Ending therapy

There are both positive and negative reasons for finishing treatment. A positive reason arises when patient and therapist agree that therapy has achieved as much as it is likely to, albeit not necessarily achieving all changes considered desirable, and an agreed date to terminate is set. The date is set well in advance. A minimum of 10 weeks is needed if the patient has been seen for a year or more, and it is often set to coincide with a readily identifiable date, such as Christmas, Easter, or Summer. Endings are significant and a time for much therapeutic work. This is because psychoanalytic theory affords a central place to separation and loss. A 'negative therapeutic reaction' may occur, with an apparent return of symptoms and loss of progress. This is often a regression in the face of impending loss of the therapist, and resolves after the therapy has ended or when it is examined and understood.

Therapists are increasingly called on to quantify the 'health gain' of their treatments and may use standard questionnaires such as the Beck Depression Inventory, Social Adjustment Scale, or the Adult Attachment Interview (Main 1991) to measure progress (Bergin and Garfield 2004). Patients usually evaluate their progress subjectively. The therapist's task is to help the patient reach realistic conclusions about ways in which therapy has made a difference and about aspects which have not shifted. This process is also a way of the patient articulating appreciation, and perhaps disappointment, for unfulfilled wishes.

Negative reasons for ending may be situational (e.g. a job move) or as summed up in the term 'therapeutic failure'. In the latter, the therapist tries to ascertain where the problem lies: severity of symptoms, personality structure, therapist's actions, the patient–therapist relationship, an incorrectly chosen modality of treatment, and so forth. Even if the patient is implacably determined to quit, one or more 'termination sessions' should be arranged. Since the therapist may be able to help the patient decide on the next course of action, for example, no further therapy, a different therapy, or similar treatment with another therapist; although these 'post-mortems' are painful for both protagonists, they can be constructively useful.

Patients may reveal themselves as unsuitable for long-term insight-oriented therapy in a way that was not detectable at assessment—perhaps because they are impulsive, distrustful, histrionic, or hold religious or political convictions impervious to intervention. Management includes altering the basic approach from interpretive to supportive. This includes decreasing frequency of sessions; applying more explicit support and less interpreting of unconscious motives; focusing less on reconstruction of the past; and emphasizing current reality (e.g. job and relationships).

Further treatment

Patients may contact therapists for help after treatment has ended. Further treatment with the same therapist is an option but the possibility that there are unresolved issues about the ending of the current therapy needs to be borne in mind. Returning to therapy with the same therapist can be a means of therapist and patient avoiding the painful reality of a final goodbye, with the opportunity lost to deal with separation and loss.

Does long-term dynamic psychotherapy work? (see Chapter 3)

Psychoanalysts and psychodynamic therapists have historically been far too complacent about the paucity of evidence substantiating the efficacy of their treatments. In some respects, the scarcity of efficacy data based on randomized controlled trials is understandable in light of the unique methodological problems associated with studying long-term psychoanalytic treatment (Gabbard 2005). A long-term follow-up study would be prohibitively expensive, as the project would have to persist for 10 years or more to accumulate a large enough sample for statistically valid analyses to be possible. A suitably matched control group would also be difficult to recruit. Self-selection of treatment is considered important to analysts and analytically oriented therapists because of the motivation necessary to engage in psychodynamic exploration. Patients who are not given the treatments they prefer might well drop out of a randomized, controlled study. Indeed, a substantial number of dropouts would create major problems for a long-term study. Finally, over a period of a decade, uncontrolled variables, such as life events, serious illness, medication changes, and the co-morbidity with Axis I disorders might well affect the meaningfulness of the results.

The psychodynamic approach generally has been given credibility by a substantial body of research on brief psychodynamic therapy. A meta-analysis performed on 26 studies between 1974 and 1994 (Anderson and Lambert 1995) found that short-term psychodynamic therapy was equally effective as other therapies at post-treatment and indeed showed slight superiority in follow-up assessment. In addition, three separate studies have demonstrated that accurate interpretation of core conflicts predicts better treatment outcomes within sessions and across sessions (Silberschatz et al. 1986; Crits-Christoph 1988; Joyce and Piper 1993). A review of studies with patients suffering from personality disorders (Leichsenring and Liebing 2003) found that both psychodynamic and cognitive behaviour therapies are effective treatments for these conditions.

When we examine long-term psychoanalytic treatments effectiveness, that is, psychoanalysis and intensive psychoanalytic therapy, there is suggestive evidence for child psychoanalysis (Heinicke and Ramsey-Klee 1986; Target and Fonagy 1994a,b) but for adults there are currently only two relevant outcome studies.

In one of them, 38 patients with borderline personality disorder were randomly assigned to a psychoanalytically oriented partial hospital treatment or to standard psychiatric care as a control group (Bateman and Fonagy 1999). The primary treatments in the partial hospital cell consisted of once-weekly individual psychoanalytic psychotherapy and three-times-weekly group psychoanalytic psychotherapy. The control subjects received no psychotherapy. At the end of treatment at 18 months, the patients who received the psychoanalytically oriented treatment showed significantly more improvements in

depressive symptoms, social and interpersonal functioning, need for hospitalization, and suicidal and self-mutilating behaviour. These differences were
maintained during an 18-month post-treatment follow-up period with assessments every 6 months (Bateman and Fonagy 2001). Moreover, the treatment
group continued to improve during the 18-month follow-up period, and a
cost–benefit analysis showed that the money they consumed in psychotherapy
they saved in health and social service utilization.

The Stockholm Outcome of Psychoanalysis Psychotherapy Project (Sandell
et al. 2000) was not a randomized controlled trial, but was able to follow-up a
large number of patients treated with psychoanalysis and psychoanalytic psychotherapy. This study can best be categorized as a large pre-post design.
Random assignment was attempted but was unsuccessful. Some patients
refused to be assigned, and others who agreed to be assigned did not get the
treatment they preferred, so they sought it privately. The patient sample
included 756 people who were subsidized for up to 3 years in psychoanalysis
or psychotherapy, or were on the respective waiting lists for those treatments.
Complete data for three panel waves were obtained from a group of 331
patients in various phases of long-term psychodynamic psychotherapy and
from a group of 74 in various phases of psychoanalysis. The psychoanalytic
treatments were defined as occurring four to five times a week, while psychotherapy consisted of one to two sessions per week. Improvement during
the 3 years after treatment was related to treatment frequency and duration,
with patients in psychoanalysis doing better than those in psychoanalytic
psychotherapy. This finding may be confounded, however, by the possibility
that the psychoanalysts doing once or twice weekly psychotherapy were not
conducting their preferred modality. Patients in psychoanalysis continued to
improve after termination, a finding not generally noted in outcome studies of
other psychotherapies.

Several similar prospective studies using a pre-post design have suggested
substantial improvements in patients given psychoanalytic therapies for personality disorders (Stevenson and Meares 1992; Høglend 1993; Monsen et al.
1995a,b). Additional data (Stevenson et al. 2005) from one of these studies
suggest that gains from 1-year of dynamic therapy were maintained at 5-year
follow-up. Uncontrolled studies, however, particularly those with relatively
small sample sizes and clinical populations whose condition is known to fluc-
tuate wildly, do not give a clear understanding about what type of treatment is
likely to be effective and for whom.

Clearly there is much work still to be done both in evaluating overall
outcomes of psychoanalytic treatments, and, perhaps more importantly, in
linking process with outcome. For example, a study by Diamond et al. (2003),

using the Adult Attachment Interview, showed how the quality of therapy was a bi-directional phenomenon involving the therapist's capacity to mentalize as well as the patient's, and to adjust his interventions to the level of the patient. Such nuanced strategies point to the next generation of studies focusing on the subtleties of therapist–patient interaction.

Training

Therapists bring their own personalities into their work in the fullest sense, and will, with increasing experience, develop their particular style. Some are able to challenge without being destructive; some reveal something about themselves without jeopardizing therapy. Humour is probably a vital, if little discussed, part of an effective repertoire (Bloch and McNab 1987). An experienced therapist uses his personal attributes to good effect.

Just as the therapist provides a safe space with firm but flexible boundaries within which the patient explores and matures, so he needs to function in a secure framework of ethics, supervision, and training (Holmes and Lindley 1997; Bloch and Chodoff 1999). Ethical issues are mainly concerned with the boundaries of therapy, for example, contract, fees if relevant, confidentiality, absolute prohibition of sexual contact, and discouragement of social interaction. The last does occasionally occur—for example, between trainees and their therapists in training organizations, or in small towns—and needs to be handled sensitively (see Chapter 2 for an account of the ethical dimension).

In principle, therapists should work under supervision (Pedder 1986) since they have to deal with counter-transference reactions, such as love, hatred, anger, frustration, stuckness, fear, and detachment. Supervision puts such feelings into perspective so that they can be put to good use as a direct communication of feelings from the patient, as well as providing an opportunity to observe and consider how these feelings have arisen and their meaning.

Supervision helps the therapist when he becomes over-involved, under-involved, or bored. It has the capacity to keep therapy on track. Simply talking about a session can, without changing the approach, help resolve a problem. Supervision is the most critical safeguard against breaching of ethical principles. It is ideally offered individually or in a group by an experienced therapist. A mutual supervision model with a peer or group of peers is appropriate in the absence of a 'senior' therapist.

Even for those who have the knack of helping others, formal training develops these talents and deals with any defences which might stand in the way of effective therapeutic work through the therapist in-training undergoing personal therapy.

Formal psychoanalytic training highlights personal analysis. This commonly takes place with a training analyst, a senior member of an analytic society. Such analyses last a number of years; and are complemented by theoretical seminars, infant observation, and supervised clinical experience. Training in psychoanalytic psychotherapy is less intensive.

University-based courses tend to place more weight on theory rather than clinical work. Training also occurs as part of professional qualifications in psychology, nursing, social work, and psychiatry. Psychotherapy training for example, is now a requirement for psychiatric qualification in the United Kingdom and Australasia (Grant et al. 1993).

Conclusion

Long-term individual therapy continues to be central to the psychotherapy community, both as a touchstone for the most intensive therapy available with the best chance for producing fundamental change. Its value and efficacy is likely to be both challenged and robustly defended well into the twenty-first century.

References

Anderson, E. M. and Lambert, M. J. (1995). Short-term dynamically oriented psychotherapy: a review of meta-analysis. *Clinical Psychological Review*, **15**, 503–14.

Balint, M., Ornstein, P. and Balint, E. (1972). *Focal psychotherapy*. Tavistock, London.

Bateman, A. and Fonagy, P. (1999). The effectiveness of partial hospitalization in the treatment of borderline personality disorder: A randomized controlled trial. *American Journal of Psychiatry*, **156**, 1563–69.

Bateman, A. and Fonagy, P. (2001). Treatment of borderline personality disorder with psychoanalytically oriented partial hospitalization: an 18-month follow-up. *American Journal of Psychiatry*, **158**, 36–42.

Bateman, A. and Holmes, J. (1995). *Introduction to psychoanalysis: Contemporary theory and practice*. Routledge, London.

Beck, A. (1993). Cognitive therapy: Past, present and future. *Journal of Consulting and Clinical Psychology*, **2**, 194–8.

Beck, A., Rush, A., Shaw, B. and Emery, G. (1979). *Cognitive therapy of depression* (3rd edn.). International Universities Press, New York.

Bergin, A. and Lambert, M. (1986). The evaluation of therapeutic outcomes. In *Handbook of psychotherapy and behavior change*. (ed. S. Garfield and A. Bergin) (2nd edn.) Wiley, Chichester.

Bion, W. (1967a). *Second thoughts. Attacks on linking*. Heinemann, London

Bion, W. (1967b). *Second thoughts*. Heinemann, London.

Blackwell, B. (1976). Treatment adherence. *British Journal of Psychiatry*, **129**, 513–31.

Bloch, S. Chodoff, P, and Green, S. (1999). *Psychiatric ethics*. (3rd edn). Oxford University Press, Oxford.

Bloch, S. and McNab, D. (1987). Humour in psychotherapy. *British Jorunal of Psychotherapy*, **3**, 216–25.

Cozolino, L. (2002). *The neuroscience of psychotherapy*. Norton, New York.

Crits-Christoph, P., Cooper, A. and Luborsky, L. (1988). The accuracy of therapists' interpretations and the outcome of dynamic psychotherapy. *Journal of Consulting and Clinical Psychology*, **56**, 490–95.

Diamond, D., Stovall-McCloough, C., Clarkin, J. and Levy, K. (2003). Patient-therapist attachment in the treatment of borderline personality disorder. *Bulletin of the Menninger Clinic*, **67**, 227–59.

Erikson, E. H. (1965). *Childhood and society*. Penguin, Harmondsworth.

Flanders, S. (ed.) (1993). *The dream discourse today*. Routledge, London.

Fonagy, P. (1998). An attachment theory approach to treatment of the difficult patient. *Bulletin of the Menninger Clinic*, **62**, 147–169.

Fonagy, P. (2001). *Attachment theory and psychoanalysis*. Other Press, New York.

Fonagy, P. and Target, M. (1996). Playing with reality, I: Theory of mind and the normal development of psychic reality. *International Journal of Psycho-Analysis*, **77**, 217–33.

Frank, J. D. and Frank, J. B. (1991). *Persuasion and healing: A comparative study of psychotherapy*, (3rd edn.) Johns Hopkins University Press, Baltimore.

Freud, S. (1900). The interpretation of dreams. In *Standard edition*, (Vols **5–6**, pp. 1–625). Hogarth, London.

Gabbard, G. (2005). Psychoanalytic psychotherapies. In *Oxford textbook of psychotherapy*. (eds. G. Gabbard, J. Beck, and J. Holmes). Oxford University Press, Oxford.

Grant, S., Holmes, J. and Watson, J. (1993). Guidelines for training in psychotherapy as part of general professional training. *Psychiatric Bulletin*, **17**, 168–71.

Greenberg, J. and Mitchell, S. (1983). *Object relations in psychoanalytic theory*. Guilford, New York.

Heimann, P. (1950). On countertransference. *International Journal of Psychoanalysis*. **31**, 81–4.

Heinicke, C. M. and Ramsey-Klee, D. M. (1986). Outcome of child psychotherapy as a function of frequency of session. *Journal of the American Academy of Child Psychiatry*, **25**, 247–53.

Hinshelwood, R. (1989). *A dictionary of Kleinian thought*. Free Association, London.

Hinshelwood, R. (1991). Psychodynamic formulation in assessment for psychotherapy. *British Journal of Psychotherapy*, **8**, 166–74.

Høglend, P. (1993). Personality disorders and long-term outcome after brief dynamic psychotherapy. Journal of Personality Disorders, **7**, 168–81.

Holmes, J. (ed.) (1991). *A textbook of psychotherapy in psychiatric practice*. Churchill Livingstone, Edinburgh.

Holmes, J. (1992). *Between art and science: Essays in psychotherapy and psychiatry*. Routledge, London.

Holmes, J. (1993). *John Bowlby and attachment theory*. Routledge, London.

Holmes, J. (1994). Clinical implications of attachment theory. *British Journal of Psychotherapy*, **11**, 62–76.

Horowitz, M., et al. (1984). Brief psychotherapy of bereavement reactions: The relationship of process to outcome. *Archives of General Psychiatry*, **41**, 438–48.

Joyce, A. S. and Piper, W. E. (1993). The immediate impact of transference in short-term individual psychotherapy. *American Journal of Psychotherapy*, **47**, 508–26.

Kernberg, O. F. (1977). The structural diagnosis of borderline personality organization. In *Borderline personality disorders*, (ed. P. Hartocollis). International Universities Press, New York.

Kernberg, O. (1984). *Severe personality disorders: Psychotherapeutic strategies*. Yale University Press, New Haven, CT.

Kohon, G. (1986). *The British school of psychoanalysis: The independent tradition*. Free Association, London.

Kohut, H. (1977). *The restoration of the self*. International Universities Press, New York.

Langs, R. (1976). *The bipersonal field*. Jason Aronson, New York.

Leichsenring, F. and Leibing, E. (2003). The effectiveness of psychodynamic therapy and cognitive behavior therapy in the treatment of personality disorders: A meta-analysis. *American Journal of Psychiatry*, **160**, 1223–32.

Luborsky, L., Chandler, M., Auerbach, A. H., Cohen, J. and Bachrach, H. M. (1971). Factors influencing outcome of psychotherapy: A review of quantitative research. *Psychological Bulletin*, **75**, 145–85.

Luborsky, L., Singer, B. and Luborsky, L. (1975). Comparative studies of Psychotherapies: Is it true that 'everyone has won and all must have prizes'? *Archives in General Psychiatry*, **35**, 471–81.

Luborsky, L. and Crits-Cristoph, P. (1988). Measures of psychoanalytic concepts- the last decade of research from the 'Penn studies'. *International Journal of Psychoanalysis*, **69**, 75–86.

Main, M. (1991). Metacognitive knowledge, metacognitive monitoring, and singular (coherent) vs. multiple (incoherent) models of attachment. In *Attachment across the life cycle* (ed. C. Parkes, J. Stevenson-Hinde, and P. Marris). Routledge, London.

Malan, D. (1973). The outcome problem in psychotherapy research. A historical review. *Archives of General Psychiatry*, **29**, 719–29.

Malan, D. (1976). *The frontier of brief psychotherapy: an example of the convergence of research and clinical practice*. Plenum, New York.

Malan, D. (1979). *Individual psychotherapy and the science of psychodynamics*. Butterworths, London.

Menninger, K. and Holzman, P. (1958). *Theory of psychoanalytic technique*. Basic Books, New York.

Mitchell, J. (ed.) (1985). *The selected Melanie Klein*. Penguin, London.

Monsen, J. T., Odland, T., Faugli, A., Daae, E. and Eilertsen, D. E. (1995a). Personality disorders and psychosocial changes after intensive psychotherapy: A prospective follow-up study of an outpatient psychotherapy project, 5 years after end of treatment. *Scandinavian Journal of Psychology*, **36**, 256–68.

Monsen, J. T., Odland, T., Faugli, A., Daae, E. and Eilertsen, D. E. (1995b). Personality disorders: Changes and stability after intensive psychotherapy focusing on affect consciousness. *Psychotherapy Research*, **5**, 33–48.

Offenkrantz, W. and Tobin, A. (1974). Psychoanalytic psychotherapy. *Archives of General Psychiatry*, **30**, 593–606.

Pedder, J. (1986). Reflections on the theory and practice of supervision. *Psychoanalytic Psychotherapy*, **2**, 1–12.

Phillips, S. A. (1988). *Winnicott*. Fontana, London.

Piper, W., Hassan, F., Joyce A. and McCallum, M. (1991). Transference interpretations, therapeutic alliance, and outcome in short-term individual psychotherapy. *Archives of General Psychiatry*, **48**, 946–53.

Rogers, C. (1951). *Client-centred therapy*. Constable, London.

Rycroft, C. (1979). *The innocence of dreams*. Oxford University Press, Oxford.

Ryle, A. (1990). *Cognitive Analytic Therapy: Active participation in change*. Wiley, Chichester.

Samuels, A. (1985). *Jung and the Post-Jungians*. Routledge and Kegan Paul, London.

Sandell, R., Blomberg, J., Lazar, A., Carlsson, J., Broberg, J. and Schubert, J. (2000). Varieties of long-term outcome among patients in psychoanalysis and long-term psychotherapy: a review of findings in the Stockholm Outcome of Psychoanalysis and Psychotherapy Project (STOPP). *International Journal of Psycho-Analysis*, **81**, 921–42.

Sandler, J. and Sandler, A. (1984). The past unconscious, the present unconscious, and interpretation of the transference. *Psychoanalytic Enquiry*, **31**, 54–61.

Schore, A. N. (1994). *Affect regulation and the origin of the self: The neurobiology of emotional development*. Erlbaum, Hillsdale, NJ.

Schore, A. N. (1996). The experience dependent maturation of a regulatory system in the orbital prefrontal cortex and the origin of developmental psychopathology. *Development and Psychopathology*, **8**, 59–87.

Schore, A. N. (1997). Early organization of the nonlinear right brain and development of a predisposition to psychiatric disorders. *Development and Psychopathology*, **9**, 595–631.

Segal, H. (1964). *Introduction to the work of Melanie Klein*. Heinemann, London.

Siegel, J. (1999). *The developing mind; Toward a neurobiology of interpersonal experience*. Guilford, New York.

Sifneos, P. (1969). Short-term anxiety-provoking psychotherapy. *Seminars in Psychiatry*, **1**, 389–98.

Silberschatz, G., Fretter, P. B. and Curtis, J. T. (1986). How do interpretations influence the process of psychotherapy? *Journal of Consulting and Clinical Psychology*, **54**, 646–52.

Solms, M. (2000). *Clinical studies in neuro-psychoanalysis*. Karnac, London.

Stern, D. (1985). *The interpersonal world of the infant*. Basic Books, New York.

Steiner, J. (1993). *Psychic retreats*. Routledge, London.

Stevens, A. (1991). *On Jung*. Penguin, London.

Stevenson, J. and Meares, R. (1992). An outcome study of psychotherapy for patients with borderline personality disorder. *American Journal of Psychiatry*, **149**, 358–62.

Stevenson, J., Meares, R. and D'Angelo, R. (2005). Five-year outcome of outpatient psychotherapy with borderline patients. *Psychological Medicine*, **35**, 79–87.

Stolorow, R., Brandchaft, B. and Atwood, G. (1987). *Psychoanalytic treatment: An intersubjective approach*. Analytic Press, Hillsdale, NJ.

Strachey, J. (1934). The nature of the therapeutic action of psycho-analysis. *International Journal of Psycho-Analysis*, **15**, 127–59.

Sullivan, H. (1953). *The interpersonal theory of psychiatry.* Norton, New York.

Target, M. and Fonagy, P. (1994a). The efficacy of psychoanalysis for children: prediction of outcome in a developmental context. *Journal of the American Academy of Child and Adolescent Psychiatry*, **33**, 1134–44.

Target, M. and Fonagy, P. (1994b). The efficacy of psychoanalysis for children with emotional disorders. *Journal of the American Academy of Child and Adolescent Psychiatry*, **33**, 361–71.

Thoma, H. and Kachele, H. (1987). *Psychoanalytic practice.* Springer, London.

Truax, C. and Carkhuff, R. (1967). *Towards effective counseling and psychotherapy: Training and practice.* Aldine, Chicago.

Wallerstein, R. (1986). *Forty two lives in treatment: A study of psychoanalysis and psychotherapy.* Guilford, New York.

Westen, D. and Gabbard, G. O. (2002a). Developments in cognitive neuroscience II: implications for theories of transference. *Journal of the American Psychoanalytic Association*, **50**, 99–134.

Westen, D. and Gabbard, G. O. (2002b) Developments in cognitive neuroscience I: conflict, compromise, and connectionism. *Journal of the American Psychoanalytic Association*, **50**, 53–98.

Winnicott, D. (1971). *Playing and reality.* Penguin, Harmondsworth.

Recommended reading

Bateman, A. and Holmes, J. (1995). *Introduction to psychoanalysis: A contemporary synthesis.* Routledge, London. (An attempt to bring together the major psychoanalytic schools—Object relations, contemporary Freudian, Kleinian, self psychology—in a readable practical guide, illustrated with case examples.)

Casement, P. (1985). *On learning from the patient.* Tavistock, London. (A sensitive, jargon-free account of what goes on in the therapist's mind while with the patient, and, through self-supervision, how to make good therapeutic use of this.)

Fonagy, P. and Target, M. (2003). *Psychoanalytic theories.* Whurr, London. (In-depth exposition by two world-leaders in attachment and psychoanalytic research.)

Freud, S. (1916–1917). *Standard edition, Introductory lectures on psychoanalysis*, Vol. **15/16**. Hogarth, London. (Perhaps the most accessible of all Freud's texts.)

Gabbard, G., Beck, J. and Holmes, J. (2005). *Oxford textbook of psychotherapy.* Oxford University Press, Oxford. (Comprehensive, integrative text including essays on aspects of psychoanalysis, and the main psychotherapeutic methods for treating the range of psychiatric diagnoses.)

Holmes, J. (2001). *The search for the secure base: Attachment theory and psychotherapy.* Brunner/Routledge, London. (How attachment theory can inform the practice of psychoanalytic psychotherapy.)

Malan, D. (1995). *Individual psychotherapy and the science of psychodynamics.* 2nd edn. Arnold, London. (Clear, logical account of the complexities of psychodynamic formulation and interpretation. Many fascinating case examples.)

Rycroft, C. (1972). *A critical dictionary of psychoanalysis.* Penguin, Harmondsworth. (Lucid exposition of psychoanalytic concepts by a master of psychological prose. Invaluable vade-mecum.)

Symington, N. (1986). *The analytic experience*. Free Association, London. (Personal account, written with great *élan*, of the history and theory of psychoanalysis, with chapters on major figures like Klein and Fairbairn. Many illuminating case examples.)

Winnicott, Donald. (1968). *Playing and reality*. Penguin, London. (Classic text expounding the concept of 'transitional object' and the importance of play in child development and psychotherapy.)

Chapter 6

Short-term dynamic psychotherapy

Michael Hobbs

Short-term dynamic psychotherapy (STDP) has been the subject of renewed clinical and research interest since the third edition of this textbook, both in its own right and in conjunction with other models of short-term psychological therapy. This heightened interest reflects the increasing demand for psychological ('talking') treatments from patients resistant to the ready prescription of psychotropic medications, the contemporary expectation for rapidly effective treatments, and the economic imperatives of health care provision.

Characterized by its relative brevity, short-term dynamic psychotherapy emphasizes a focus on identified core problems, an active therapist style, and therapeutic exploitation of a time limit. Contemporary practice has emphasized flexibility, and modification of aims and techniques for specific patient groups.

Contrary to earlier misconceptions, short-term dynamic psychotherapies are *not* truncated versions of analytical psychotherapy, but planned treatments with an inherent rationale. Fundamental is the recognition that a focused, circumscribed intervention can stimulate a powerful developmental process which, under the influence of ongoing life experience, continues over time to generate substantial and enduring change.

STDP is not only effective in its own right but also, although it may seem paradoxical, casts light on key therapeutic processes including those fundamental to long-term analytical psychotherapies. Small (1971) referred to the wisdom of therapists who had 'penetrated the time barrier' in psychotherapy.

Definition

This chapter describes a number of discrete but functionally interrelated short-term approaches which, by virtue of their common psychodynamic basis, are collectively called short-term dynamic psychotherapies. These encompass treatments entitled historically by their authors 'focal psychotherapy' (Balint et al. 1972), 'brief psychotherapy' (Malan 1963, 1976), 'short-term anxiety-provoking psychotherapy' (Sifneos 1972, 1987), 'time-limited psychotherapy' (Mann 1973), 'time-limited dynamic psychotherapy' (Strupp and Binder 1984), 'intensive short-term dynamic psychotherapy' (Davanloo 1980), and 'short-term psychotherapy' (Wolberg 1980). An influential recent model is Vaillant's (1996) 'short-term anxiety-regulating psychotherapy'.

STDPs are related to a number of other short-term psychological treatments, such as the eclectic psychotherapies of Garfield (1989), cognitive analytic therapy (Ryle 1990), interpersonal psychotherapy (Klerman et al. 1984), and psychodynamic interpersonal therapy (Guthrie 1999). STDP also relates in application and technique to aspects of crisis intervention (Sifneos 1972; Hobbs 1984), an integrative short-term therapy drawing on psychodynamic, behavioural, cognitive, systemic, and pragmatic principles (see Chapter 9).

Although differing in practice, all variations of STDP are conducted within a conceptual framework which gives prominence to internal psychological processes, especially those of which the person is unconscious. In addition, they emphasize the relationship between patient and therapist as both the medium for therapy and, through analysis of transference phenomena, its most important tool.

Despite their brevity, STDPs offer the patient an opportunity for reflective exploration and a search for meaning in experience. Self-awareness, understanding, and self-efficacy are promoted rather than the resolution of symptoms; although, of course, symptomatology often recedes with resolution of internal and interpersonal problems and the growth of insight. At its best, STDP promotes empowerment and self-determination. In these ways, STDPs share the expected outcomes of psychoanalytic psychotherapies.

Historical development

STDP has its origins in psychoanalysis. Although some of its defining characteristics, particularly the brevity and focus, represent notable divergences from psychoanalysis, its theoretical basis and core methods are unequivocally psychoanalytic.

Nowadays, psychoanalytic psychotherapy is typically prolonged and intensive. As is stressed in most accounts of STDP, this was not always the case. Freud's early treatments were aimed at the relief of neurotic symptoms, particularly those of conversion hysteria, and were surprisingly short. Derived from his earlier experimentation with hypnosis, his method was active and directive. Bruno Walter, the orchestral conductor, was treated by Freud in six sessions for a paralysis of his conducting arm. The composer Gustav Mahler's impotence was treated (although we cannot be sure about the outcome) by Freud in a single 4-hour session.

As theory and practice evolved, treatment became progressively longer. Malan (1963) identified reasons for this, including the growing complexity of psychoanalytic theories of personality development and symptom formation, therapeutic perfectionism of practitioners, and expectation that exhaustive 'working through' would be accomplished during therapy, all of which conveyed a sense of timelessness to the patient. Eventually Freud (1937–1964) himself, in *Analysis terminable and interminable*, questioned the inexorable lengthening of psychoanalytic treatment.

Some of Freud's contemporaries, opposing the tendency towards longer treatment, challenged, particularly, the apparent passivity of the therapist. Ferenczi (1950), for example, actively confronted unconscious resistance by using techniques like touch and embrace to remedy purported deficiencies in the patient's formative experience. His methods, however, eventually provoked Freud's displeasure (Marmor 1979), promoting hostile reaction in the psychoanalytic community to short, active therapies.

Rank (1936), best known for his identification of 'birth trauma' and separation anxiety, highlighted a time limit in order to promote the patient's 'will' or motivation for the required work. In this, he pre-figured a central aspect of Mann's (1973) time-limited psychotherapy.

Alexander and French (1946) challenged the tendency of psychoanalysts to embark on treatment without taking a detailed history, arguing that the focus and effectiveness depended on an accurate psychogenetic formulation of the patient's problems. They also questioned the apparent emphasis on intellectual exploration, advocating instead promotion of emotional experiencing and arguing that the recovery and expression of repressed feelings, in an empathic atmosphere linked to increased self-awareness, offered the patient a 'corrective emotional experience'.

Despite clinical evidence for the effectiveness of planned short treatments and the fact that most psychotherapies were actually brief by design or default, most practitioners resisted development of shorter psychotherapies (Garfield 1989). Then, during the 1960s, several clinicians began independently to devise short-term models which incorporated contemporary developments in psychoanalysis, particularly interpretation of defences and transference. Balint (Balint et al. 1972) and Malan (1963) at the Tavistock Clinic, Sifneos (1972) and Mann (1973) independently in Boston, and Davanloo (1980) in Montreal, developed short-term psychotherapies which differed substantially but shared a common psychodynamic identity. These models represent the basis for the contemporary practice of STDP. Details of their respective concepts and techniques are outlined below.

Several notable clinical developments in STDP have taken place since the 1980s. First, selection and technique have been modified to permit extension of STDP to more diverse populations (e.g. Vaillant 1996; Binder 2004). Second, integrative models, combining features of STDP and other approaches, have evolved. One example, widely practised in Britain, is cognitive-analytic therapy (Ryle 1990; see Chapter 12). Another example is psychodynamic interpersonal therapy, which develops on the 'conversational model' of Hobson (1985; see chapter 13). Time-limited dynamic group therapies have also been devised, applicable both to broad diagnostic groups (MacKenzie 1990) and to specific problems, such as pathological grief (Piper et al. 1992).

Over the same period, increasingly sophisticated research has examined the process and outcome of short-term psychotherapies.

Aims and objectives

Despite the brevity of STDP, its aims are radical. Small (1971) suggested that the primary goal was to ameliorate or remove specific presenting symptoms; but, under favourable conditions, the dynamic intervention leads secondarily to progressive personality change. The current emphasis is on resolution of internal conflicts which have arrested, retarded, or distorted personality development and relationships.

STDP entails exploration of the historical origins of a patient's difficulties; but, more relevantly for change, attention is directed to underlying dynamic processes as evidenced by ways of feeling, thinking, communicating, and relating in therapy. Examination of habitual patterns of relating (particularly, in the therapeutic relationship) serves to elucidate 'internal object relationships' or 'internal working models' (Bowlby 1979) which, derived from formative developmental experiences, have left their mark on adult interpersonal relationships. These internal templates or 'blueprints' for relating give rise to characteristic 'reciprocal role relationships' (Sandler 1976) in which both the individual and those with whom he interacts are drawn unconsciously to repeat interpersonal patterns which may be highly destructive. This analytic work is the basis of the encounter in which problems are examined *in vivo* within the therapeutic relationship. It is also the basis for a 'corrective emotional experience', for the patient is enabled to examine uncomfortable personal aspects in a relatively safe, non-judgemental, and accepting atmosphere.

The high level of therapist activity, the focus, and the short duration of STDP are used to combat development of transference-based problems of regression and acting-out. Short-term therapies entail a challenge to the universal illusion of timelessness, which is regarded by Mann (1973) as a core feature of neurosis. From the existential perspective then, STDP requires that the patient (and therapist) confronts and comes to terms with the finiteness of time. This is uncomfortable, even disturbing, but offers a crucial step towards redefining personal reality in a way which promotes responsibility and autonomy, and so ultimately reduces alienation from self and others.

In contrast to the wide-ranging exploratory remit of classical analytic therapy, STDP emphasizes specific, personalized aims for treatment. These are defined operationally in relation to the focus chosen for therapy; then progress and outcome are measured against them as well as more generally. This approach lends itself to individualized measures of progress and outcome.

In summary, the objective in STDP is to engage the patient in active examination of his difficulties, including how these impact on the therapeutic relationship, and thereby to liberate adaptive capacities and developmental potential. This objective is addressed through deployment of highly specific techniques.

Assessment, selection, and preparation

The related processes of assessment and selection are vital for the competent practice and effective outcome of STDP. As with any powerful treatment, STDP should be prescribed with care only to those who have the potential to benefit.

Indications

In terms of diagnostic categories, indications are

- 'neurosis' manifest by anxiety, depression, or generalized dysphoria, especially when internal or interpersonal conflicts and problems predominate;
- unresolved developmental crises (e.g. separation conflict, morbid grief); and
- uncomplicated post-traumatic disorders.

Sifneos (1987) advocated that patients who benefited most were those manifesting Oedipal-type difficulties, particularly those who 'lingered too long' in patterns of relating typical of a child's relationships with each parent. Other amenable interpersonal dynamics include those associated with rivalry, separation, and loss. Mann (1973) and Malan (1976) recommended STDP for a wider range of neurotic disorders. Davanloo (1980) treated patients with entrenched obsessive-compulsive disorder and moderately severe personality disorder, asserting that they were responsive to his confronting style providing that core dynamics could be identified and addressed.

Other practitioners argued for broad applicability. Ashurst (1991) suggested that a spectrum of neuroses and personality disorders are treatable by STDP if the patient has the capacity for adaptation; but she cautioned the therapist to be realistic about the aims of therapy and (while maintaining optimism) to avoid over-ambition. Levenson (1995) and Vaillant (1996) have developed models of STDP which are anxiety-regulating in order to treat patients with longstanding dysfunctional patterns of relationship characteristic of personality disorder. This breadth of selection criteria is consistent with other contemporary short-term models including cognitive analytic therapy and psychodynamic interpersonal therapy.

Assessment

Cautions have been demonstrated by clinical experience, particularly in relation to the earlier models of STDP which emphasized anxiety-provoking challenges to psychological defences. More recent models of treatment have been developed for those patients who are unable to tolerate high levels of anxiety without decompensation.

Assessment begins at the point of referral. Anxiety-provoking models of STDP may be contraindicated when a patient has a history of any disorder which might be reactivated by excessive emotional arousal: psychotic illness; severe depression; gross destructive or self-destructive behaviour; marked somatizing disorder; severe personality disorder, especially when characterized by negativism or poor impulse control; gross substance misuse; and excessive dependency in relationships. Some may benefit, however, from anxiety-regulating STDP (see below).

The initial interview incorporates a comprehensive psychiatric history and examination to identify psychologically fragile people who might be harmed by anxiety-provoking approaches. For example, a patient preoccupied with self-destructive thoughts could be precipitated into suicidal action.

Patients might not have been selected previously for STDP if evidence was found of: failure to make positive emotional contact with the therapist; rigid or primitive defences; a propensity for regression manifest by seeking reassurance or advice; low tolerance of frustration or anxiety; lack of motivation for the work of therapy; absence of a feasible focus; a negative response to a 'trial' intervention designed to test defences; and lack of capacity to use a focused approach. Now such attributes would be indications for an anxiety-regulating STDP or a similar model of therapy, such as psychodynamic interpersonal therapy.

Prognostic criteria

Certain criteria have positive prognostic significance (Sifneos 1987): capacity to identify a 'circumscribed chief complaint' and to prioritize difficulties; a history of at least one 'meaningful' relationship; flexible interaction with the assessor; capacity to express feelings, both directly and in words; psychological-mindedness, including reflectiveness, an ability to make mental links, and the capacity to construe experience in terms of internal psychological processes rather than attributing difficulties to bodily dysfunction or external events; motivation for change, as evidenced by open and honest participation in the assessment, introspective curiosity, realistic expectations of therapy, and a wish for significant internal change rather than symptom relief alone.

Malan (1976) also emphasized capacity for insight or self-scrutiny, as tested by trial interpretations.

Clinical experience points to other useful attributes in selecting patients: humour (Bloch and McNab 1987), an inclination to play with ideas (Winnicott 1971), concern for others, sense of responsibility and capacity to feel appropriate guilt. These qualities, in conjunction with evidence of achievement in study, work, and relationships can be regarded as evidence of *ego strength*, a prognostic attribute which correlates positively with change in STDP.

Social support helps to sustain commitment to an anxiety-provoking therapy. Further, evidence for the prognostic significance of a history of mutual relationships, and capacity to interact flexibly with the therapist, derives from research which points to a correlation between pre-therapy patterns of relating and the rapid establishment of an effective therapeutic alliance (Piper et al. 1991). The strength of this alliance at sessions 3–4 has been shown to correlate positively with outcome (Morgan et al. 1982; Gaston 1990).

Preparation for therapy

Assessment may extend beyond one interview, and ideally leads directly into therapy. Selection may conclude, and therapy may begin, with agreement on the focus and negotiation of a contract. The latter includes a clear statement that therapy will be short term, even if its exact duration is not determined at the outset, and sets administrative boundaries. Experience and empirical research show that patients engage in therapy more successfully if properly prepared.

The initial consultation can be therapeutic in itself since assessment and trial interpretation generate greater awareness and self-understanding. Some practitioners, notably Davanloo and Mann, propose a preliminary screening and then proceed to an encounter with the patient designed to be both diagnostic and therapeutic. In this sense, assessment embodies a trial of therapy.

Dynamic focus

The focus, central to STDP, is *not* the principal presenting complaint but a psychodynamic hypothesis which links the patient's current experience (including presenting problem) with formative past experiences, both recent and remote. The focus is derived during the psychodynamic assessment, both from historical information elicited and the interaction. By definition, the focus is circumscribed. Patients requiring an extended, complex dynamic formulation are less likely to benefit from STDP. The focus must also be feasible for short-term work. For example, a patient's self-defeating guilt may be formulated succinctly in terms of a repressed wish for revenge towards his sadistic father; but it may not be possible for this to be explored safely in a brief therapy without risk of the vengefulness surfacing explosively into action.

Dynamic focus: clinical illustration

A feasible focus for STDP was identified in a young man who presented with a generalized anxiety state. Mr A's academic achievements at school and university were substantial, and he was expected to accomplish rapid promotion in his chosen profession. Instead, he became progressively more anxious and was passed over for prestigious assignments. Furthermore, after a brief sexual relationship in his teens with an older married woman, his fear of sexual impotence had caused him to avoid intimate relationships. He returned each weekend to his parents' home, where his doting mother laundered his clothes and prepared his meals for the week. The warm tones with which he spoke of his mother contrasted with his anxious, negative account of his father who was described as formidably high-powered, critical, and intimidating.

At interview, Mr A was conspicuously anxious and related deferentially to the male therapist. Eventually the latter began to feel irritated by the deference and associated passivity, but construed this as an unconsciously projected facet of the patient's own anger. He used the information derived from Mr A's account of his father and the transference/counter-transference development to construct a trial interpretation, suggesting that the patient's deference to his father masked a deep, unacknowledged resentment. The young man appeared momentarily furious; but, after reflection, he agreed that he felt very angry towards his father for belittling him repeatedly.

This simple dynamic intervention proved therapeutic by enabling Mr A to confront his repressed anger. It also provided the therapist with the material with which to formulate the dynamic focus for the STDP he then recommended. The patient's anxious deference, which prevented him from asserting himself confidently in front of his (male) employers, was a product of his fear of standing up to his intimidating father; or, more accurately, stemmed from his fear of the potential destructiveness of his anger. This unconscious process was linked inextricably to Mr A's continued, exclusive intimacy with his mother. With unconscious but disabling guilt, he identified his mother in each potential girlfriend. His impotence with men and women in adulthood was the result of an enduring dynamic process (characterized in psychoanalytic terms as an Oedipal conflict) which offered a coherent focus for STDP.

The dynamic foci most readily amenable to STDP are associated with such internal conflicts.

For STDP to be most effective, the focus is adhered to throughout treatment. Although other issues may emerge these are not pursued unless they can be examined in terms of the focus. The focus can be refined to increase accuracy and specificity, and may be modified if shown to be inaccurate; but divergence on to other dynamic themes diminishes the power of therapy. Maintenance of high motivation and high 'focality' are associated with maximal effect (Malan 1976).

The process and techniques of STDP

STDP is demanding emotionally for both patient and therapist. The required level of activity and sustained tolerance of powerful emotions tests commitment and adaptive strength to the full.

Earlier models of STDP are intentionally anxiety provoking for the patient. Well-established defences are challenged putting him in touch with intense feelings and memories which have been hidden hitherto. Powerful negative feelings, perhaps anger and fear, are rekindled and may be focused on the therapist. The patient's trust in the therapist, and his security in the relationship, are tested.

As the core conflict is exposed and examined, the patient alternates between experiencing and reflecting on that experience. He may be gripped by discomfort in his relationship with the therapist which gives expression to unresolved childhood experience, and then be required by the therapist's observation or interpretation to examine the origins and impact of the recapitulated experience. The oscillation between experience and reflection is taxing, particularly when pressed by the time limit of therapy. Furthermore, the patient cannot slip back into past defensive patterns between sessions. He is likely to remain unsettled, but is expected to maintain the introspective process in his personal and interpersonal experience outside between sessions.

For the therapist, repeatedly challenging the patient's defences, and exploring uncovered material within a time limit, requires sustained vigilance, activity, and commitment. At the same time, he must maintain empathic contact and an analytic stance. If not, the danger is that confronting therapeutic activity will feel persecutory to the patient and repeat, rather than resolve, past conflicts.

Newer anxiety-regulating models of STDP (Levenson 1995; Vaillant 1996) involve more gentle exploration and clarification, rather than direct challenge, of defences. This still requires high levels of empathy, activity, and commitment. STDP contrasts markedly with the relatively leisurely exploration typical of longer-term analytic psychotherapy. Just as some patients are not able to tolerate or benefit from STDP, certain therapists are not suited temperamentally or technically to practise it.

Although STDP is characterized by specific principles and techniques, which will be outlined below, the way therapist and patient work together depends on the latter's needs. The process with a patient suffering internal conflict, as in the example of Mr A above, will differ substantially from that of a moody adolescent, or of someone traumatized psychologically by bereavement. For the spectrum of STDPs, however, there is a common structure and technical repertoire which is set out below.

Contract for therapy

The therapeutic contract may be established during the initial assessment but, if another clinician has undertaken the assessment, the therapist needs to renew the contract at the start of treatment. Although neither legalistic nor necessarily written, it emphasizes key features including focus and time limit.

Focus

The dynamic focus derived from assessment is reviewed and, if necessary, revised. Most practitioners see it as necessary to state their understanding of the dynamic factors underlying the presenting problems, and to obtain the patient's agreement to both its validity and the adopted focus. The focus may be revised in the light of emerging material, but adherence to it is essential.

Time limit

The other central component is the limited duration of therapy, and arrangements for it. Sessions are usually held weekly at a regular time, but flexibility is possible. Practitioners vary in their management of the time limit. Mann (1973) adopts a universal policy of 12-hours, usually involving 1-hour sessions at weekly intervals but, where considered necessary, beginning twice weekly or concluding with shorter (perhaps 30-minute) sessions at increased intervals. In this way of working, the time limit is explicit and the date of the last session identified from the outset. Mann uses the limit as a subsidiary focus to combat the patient's illusion of timelessness and to promote a sense of reality and responsibility.

Other therapists do not establish duration so firmly but specify that this will be short and within certain limits, for example, a maximum of 20 weekly sessions.

Setting

Face to face

Whereas in long-term analytic psychotherapy the patient may be encouraged to lie down on a couch in order to facilitate free association and 'therapeutic regression', the patient in STDP sits up, facing the therapist. This promotes the tension, transference development, and direct interaction required for anxiety-provoking STDP.

Privacy

As in any psychotherapy, the consulting room must afford the quiet, neutral environment, and privacy essential for the patient to feel secure enough to express innermost thoughts and feelings. Although they can often tolerate routine audio and video recordings if valid reasons for this are presented, few can work successfully if exposed to unexpected intrusions.

Therapeutic alliance

The process of therapy may be challenging and unsettling to the patient. The early creation and ongoing maintenance of an alliance between patient and therapist is a prerequisite for effective work and a successful outcome.

The strength of the alliance will be tested, on occasions to its limits, if the therapist confronts defences and when the transference embodies anger, fear, or other negative feelings. The therapist interprets such negative trans-ference actively, but sparingly, in order to preserve the alliance. It is from a secure base (Mackie 1981) that the patient may explore his anxiety and inner conflicts, as they become evident in uncovered memories, feelings, and transferences.

Therapist style

Within appropriate technical limits and professional boundaries, the therapist adopts an active, interactive, and flexible style. Touch is rarely appropriate, except at times with elderly patients. Within treatment, there is no time for lengthy monologues by patient or therapist, or for prolonged reflective silences. The emphasis is on *active* reflection and *interactive* dialogue, reinforcing the value of the patient's ability to express feelings and thoughts openly.

The therapist should communicate in everyday language, free from jargon. A competent practitioner does not need the illusion of superiority which comes with mystifying the patient. On the other hand, there is no place for collusive familiarity which avoids honest and therapeutic self-reflection.

The face-to-face setting and interactive style enables the therapist to use his own positive attributes to maximum effect in relating and communicating. Nothing is gained by adopting an inscrutable 'blank screen' facade, a caricature of the psychoanalyst. The patient will develop transferences regardless of the therapist's relative openness. However, he will need to monitor the significance of his emotional and other reactions to the patient rather than giving direct expression to them. His counter-transferences will be used as sources of information with which to generate or confirm hypotheses and to guide interventions.

Therapist technique

The therapist's activity should have purpose and direction. Interventions are designed to facilitate patient disclosure, exploration of salient feelings, thoughts, and perceptions within the framework of the focus. To this end, interventions tend to be comments, statements, or (sparingly) questions which aim to facilitate, clarify, challenge, or interpret the patient's verbal and non-verbal expressions. The purpose of challenges and interpretation will be examined further below.

Adherence to focus

As mentioned earlier, the elucidation and agreement of a focus is central, and adherence to it correlates positively with good outcome (Malan 1976; Keller 1984). This need not be rigid or restrict the content of the dialogue. Since the focus is a dynamic formulation, it is possible to link a broad range of material to it. The patient is encouraged to associate freely and to express thoughts openly, the therapist maintaining focality through 'selective attention' to relevant material and 'selective neglect' of extraneous matters (Balint et al. 1972).

Challenge to defences

STDP involves active exploration, and when clinically appropriate, challenge of the patient's defences. This is quite different from confronting the patient as a person, although it may feel like this initially. The therapist utilizes the alliance to foster a collaborative analysis of the nature and unconscious functions of the defences.

Assessment should establish whether the patient is able to withstand the therapist's challenge to their defences as a basis for therapeutic work. Evidence that they cannot tolerate the levels of anxiety generated, without potential decompensation, necessitates a more supportive anxiety-regulating approach.

When anxiety-provoking STDP is undertaken, the degree of confrontation should be titrated to the patient's capacity to use such challenge. Among practitioners of STDP, emphasis on challenge differs. Both Sifneos (1992) and Davanloo (2001) espouse particularly confrontative models, which were endorsed by Malan (1980).

Sifneos's technique consists of repeated confrontations but without any systematic attempt to explain or interpret unconscious factors. A successful challenge releases feelings and memories which leads to further exploration. The method works if the patient can tolerate the anxiety generated and if the core conflict is not overly complex.

Davanloo's method goes further, starting with the identification and 'relentless' challenge of defences, but proceeding to an active exploration and explanation of their dynamic purpose. Although persistent in this pursuit, and thereby appearing persecutory, even sadistic, to sceptical observers, Davanloo works empathically. He seeks to break through defences to repressed feelings, permitting uncovering and active analysis of the core conflict. He attaches importance to addressing the development of negative feelings towards the therapist, encouraging the release of anger, and the patient's discovery that such expression can be healing rather than destructive (Molnos 1986). Davanloo aims to achieve this breakthrough and demonstrate the healing potential of therapy in the first or second session. Like Malan, his reconstructive work draws on his understanding of the dynamic relationship between defences, anxiety, and the unconscious feelings and motives central to the core conflict.

Although the challenge of defences has its place, a wider range of patients can benefit from methods which moderate or regulate, rather than provoke and heighten anxiety during exploration of unconscious processes (Levenson 1995; Vaillant 1996). These still permit constructive therapeutic work.

Reconstructive analysis

In psychodynamic terms, the task is to enable the patient to understand and resolve his internal conflict and its relationship to people in his life, both past and present. This is achieved through analysis of the patient's current patterns of relating, especially as they manifest through transference, and through linking these patterns to formative past experiences in relationships.

The two triangles

Malan (1979) introduced a graphic representation of the unconscious processes which underpin and maintain conflict. The triangles of conflict and of person offer a guide for navigating the patient's unconscious.

The triangle of conflict (Fig. 6.1) represents the dynamic conflict associated with a hidden feeling (F) or impulse (e.g. Mr A's anger towards his controlling and belittling father), the potential expression of which generates such anxiety (A) of the fantasized consequences (e.g. Mr A's destruction of his father, or his father's retaliatory destruction of him) that defences (D) operate to render the forbidden feeling unconscious (e.g. Mr A represses all awareness of his anger, and manifests instead a compliant deference to older male figures).

The triangle of person (Fig. 6.2) represents the interaction between the patient's perception of, and feelings or attitudes towards, significant figures in his past (P) and current (C) life, including the therapist as a transference (T) figure. For Malan, the aim of most dynamic psychotherapy is 'to reach, beneath the defence and the anxiety, to the hidden feeling, and then to trace this feeling back from the present to its origins in the past', usually to the relationships with one or both parents. This certainly applies to STDP, although it should be remembered that the formative experience (P) may have occurred in the more recent past, and the hidden feeling (F) may be intense sadness, grief, or fear rather than anger.

Utilization of the two triangles can be illustrated by the following development of the case of Mr A.

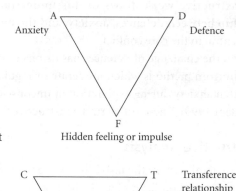

Fig. 6.1 Triangle of conflict

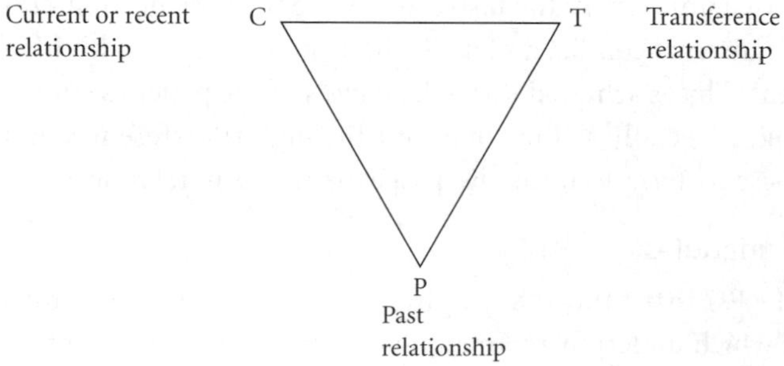

Fig. 6.2 Triangle of person

In STDP with the male therapist who originally assessed him, Mr A remained deferential and passively compliant, again masking unconsciously the anger which had been exposed during assessment by the trial interpretation.

Although appearing to work in therapy, Mr A showed little emotion and talked about his problems in an intellectualized manner. The therapist, in the second session, challenged defences: 'You're talking now about your father in a very detached way, as if you have no feelings for him'. The patient, visibly irritated and anxious, started to disagree but then fell silent.

Later in the same session, the therapist again challenged the defence, but this time the patient concurred passively and without evident feeling: 'I suppose you're right'. This time the therapist pursued his challenge: 'Now hold on, you're avoiding my point by just agreeing with me'. The patient became most anxious, again apparently irritated, but said nothing.

Drawing on his understanding of the triangle of conflict, the therapist made an interpretation of the manifest conflict: 'I think you're cutting off [D, defence] from your irritation with me because you're afraid [A, anxiety] that you'll hurt me with your anger [F, hidden feeling]—or that I will retaliate and hurt you'.

The patient responded, atypically, with an angry outburst: 'Oh, you think you're so bloody clever. You psychotherapists are all the same'. Without rising to the bait of the transference, the therapist asked what the patient meant. Initially the latter remained angry, but then became deflated and apologetic.

Pursuing the defence, now manifest by apology, the therapist pointed out that the patient was hiding his anger again and asked whether this pattern was usual in his relationships. The patient mulled this over sullenly, then burst out angrily: 'I'd tell my boss to get lost except that he would fire me'.

At this point the therapist made a full transference interpretation, drawing on the triangle of person: 'Your problem in expressing your anger towards me [T] is the same one you experience with your male superiors at work [C]. This is just how you've always been with your father [P], isn't it, because you're terrified that, if you showed your anger, he'd 'fire' you—whatever that would mean'.

The patient became tearful but calmer. He thought for a bit before responding: 'Yes, that's right. I was always afraid that, if I showed I was hurt or angry, he would blow up and reject me altogether'. The patient's need for his father's love prevented him from giving any expression to the pain and anger caused by his father's insensitive criticism.

This model was extended usefully by Molnos (1984) who demonstrated both graphically and technically that the two triangles could be combined (Fig. 6.3). Her framework reminds us that it is possible, and often necessary, to analyse the core conflict (D–A–F) successively in relation to people representative of two or more corners of the triangle of person.

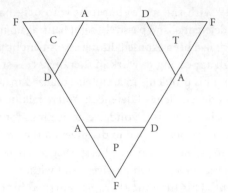

Fig. 6.3 Combined triangles

In the example of Mr A, the therapist worked with the (triangle of) conflict in each of the three corners of the triangle of person, first, with the transference (T), then with the current relationship (C) with his employer, and finally linking the common pattern of conflict to the formative past (P), but continuing, relationship with his father. In analytic therapy, long or short, the TCP interpretation is considered to be most powerful and mutative.

Work with emotions

The example demonstrates the need to galvanize feelings. The impact of exploratory and interpretive work is much diminished if the patient operates exclusively in an intellectual mode. The power of the experience is heightened when the patient is emotionally charged, getting in touch with and expressing hitherto repressed feelings.

Sometimes the emotional experience is therapeutic in itself. To be able to release feelings without receiving the anticipated and feared reaction from the therapist, as in Mr A's case, offers a 'corrective emotional experience' which can pave the way for change.

Adherence to the time limit

Treatment which draws on the above principles and techniques can bring about a breakthrough to a core conflict and the beginning of powerful reconstructive changes in early sessions. Davanloo would expect, with suitable patients, to achieve this point within the first session or two. Thereafter, therapy consists of a systematic reworking of the dynamic focus from successive perspectives, and in progressively greater depth. This process is akin to the working through of long-term psychoanalytic psychotherapy.

However, tempting it may be for patient and therapist to extend treatment, the cogency of STDP requires adherence to the set time limit. Each session is used to maximum effect. For Mann, the middle phase revolves around the confrontation of the finite reality of time. The patient's unconscious fixation in past patterns of perceiving and relating, and his longing for the illusory timelessness of dependent childhood relationships, are challenged by emphasis of the time limit. His disappointment and disillusionment is addressed, paving the way for the end phase.

Ending

For many patients, the time limit and emphatic ending activate issues to do with unresolved experiences of loss. If not included in the primary focus, these become a subsidiary focus.

Whether or not a specific number of sessions was identified at the outset, the therapist's initial statement of the finite duration of therapy and his progressive emphasis of the limited time available ensures that the ending is well anticipated. Practitioners who decide the ending date once the focal work has been largely completed nevertheless ensure that adequate time remains for dealing with ending.

The focus of the end phase is on the patient's anticipation of loss, and all that this stirs up. Of course, a focus on loss is central to the therapy for patients suffering unresolved grief, as will be addressed below. For them, the end phase may be particularly powerful, even painful. Other patients too may recover buried feelings associated with frustration, separation, and perceived rejection in previous relationships, including those in early life. Many are ambivalent about ending, relishing the prospect of independence on one hand but fearing loss of security and increased responsibility on the other. This ambivalence, which may reflect a similar pattern in other relationships, can be elucidated in the end phase. The therapist works with the framework of the triangles of conflict and person to illuminate how earlier experiences have influenced expectations and reactions in later relationships.

The aim of the end phase then is to enable the patient to learn from his emotional experience of separation and loss, and thereby to promote autonomy and individuation. The opportunity to examine emotional reactions, in the relative security afforded even by the ending relationship, ensures that the patient does not experience the loss alone. Of itself, this may constitute a corrective experience.

Sifneos (1992) encourages the patient to initiate the ending but takes responsibility for doing so if the patient avoids the issue. He also introduces an educative dimension, encouraging the patient to anticipate what could happen after therapy is concluded, thereby pre-empting avoidable crises. A problem-solving approach is promoted for any expected difficulties. The patient is encouraged to experiment with his newfound awareness outside of therapy, so promoting increasing confidence, adaptive coping, and independence. New ways of coping and relating are rehearsed.

Although active work is continued until the very end, the dynamic process initiated by therapy can continue under its own momentum. This will be so, particularly for young people and others whose natural development has been freed from neurotic or other obstacles. The patient becomes the agent of further change, having internalized the therapist's function. In this way, the end result may extend far beyond the point achieved at the final session.

Modifications of technique for specific groups

STDP has been advocated particularly for adult patients presenting with neurotic problems which have a clear psychodynamic basis, and the prognostic framework outlined above reflects this. Practitioners have also used the model successfully with patients presenting with more complex problems, including those complicated by a degree of personality disturbance, for whom modifications of technique are required. For some an anxiety-regulating STDP is effective. For the most dysfunctional, successive short, structured, anxiety-reducing therapies during times of crisis may be beneficial in restoring limited adaptive capacities. For others, change and maturational development, if any is viable, can be achieved only through more prolonged treatment, particularly in group-based programmes.

Adolescents (see Chapter 14)

Many adolescents who present with emotional or behavioural disorders are struggling with dynamic conflicts which, with appropriate technical modifications, respond well to STDP. Indeed, in view of the adolescent's age, temperament, and developmental potential, STDP may be the treatment of choice (Shefler 2000). Yet, if conventional selection criteria were applied rigidly, few adolescents would be offered it.

The developmental tasks of adolescence, the phase of transition from childhood dependence to adult independence, revolve around the impact of bodily changes and issues of separation and individuation. The adolescent who, for internal or external reasons, experiences difficulty in negotiating these tasks may be volatile emotionally, oppositional in attitude, particularly with parents and other authority figures, and preoccupied with body image and identity (Wilson 1991).

Consequently, the adolescent, especially if referred unwillingly, may react negatively to the therapist at first. He may be passive, uncommunicative, and hostile, keeping thoughts and feelings to himself. He is unlikely to relate flexibly and may display little capacity to express his difficulties or to co-operate in identifying a focus. He appears to have little psychological-mindedness and poor motivation for therapy.

Nevertheless, the therapist who appreciates the phase-dependent dynamics underlying the adolescent's truculence will not be deceived. Despite initial resistance, the adolescent may respond more readily to STDP than other treatment because it is short, active, oriented to present issues outside and within therapy, and directed primarily towards emotions rather than cognitions. The therapist is experienced as authentic exactly because he addresses the adolescent's stormy transferences without fear or rejection.

At first, the patient may be unco-operative and dismissive. The therapist works flexibly to minimize the intensity of resistances; and, in particular, to avoid being provoked into an authoritarian stance. With tact, consistency, and a willingness to confront the patient's mistrust and hostility, the therapist is able gradually to overcome initial resistance and engage him in the alliance (Uribe 1988). The adolescent develops a degree of trust which allows him to disclose his troubles with disarming openness. Fired by his youthful energy, therapy may progress rapidly.

Some notable modifications of structure and technique are necessary. Initially, the frequency of sessions may need to be greater than weekly to engage the patient, particularly for the adolescent with limited adaptive capacity; but should be reduced progressively to promote autonomy. Reflective silences are avoided since they are experienced as persecutory: a conversational style is maintained. The therapist works actively with aggressive and sexual transferences, where necessary setting limits gently but firmly on behaviours which threaten progress. In the same way, the therapist monitors his own counter-transference, for adolescents can provoke powerful aggressive or sexual feelings.

Uribe (1988) suggests that it may be necessary, with the patient's consent, for the therapist to meet with the parents to explore the contribution of family processes in the adolescent's problems. Where indicated parents may be referred for couple therapy, or the whole family may be engaged in parallel family therapy.

Elderly patients (see Chapter 15)

Many elderly people can benefit from psychodynamic psychotherapy (Ardern 2002), including STDP. Advancing age does not diminish psychological-mindedness, the ability to mobilize feelings or motivation for change. Although the elderly may have time for a long-term approach, goals must be realistic and increasing awareness of the finite duration of life lends itself to STDP.

The demands and developmental tasks of advancing age are concerned primarily with loss. In particular, the elderly person is having to come to terms with diminishing physical and mental powers, changing sexuality, the upsurge of old unresolved emotions, the relinquishing of aspects of their earlier lives, and the accelerating succession of external losses—of spouse, other relatives, and friends. Perhaps the most painful loss is loss of independence. Ultimately, the prospect of loss of life itself looms large (Porter 1991).

Establishing an alliance may be difficult if the patient is wary or envious of the therapist's relative youth, or if the therapist is threatened by the patient's ostensible helplessness, dependence, or fear of death. The patient may perceive the therapist, transferentially, as a child or grandchild at one time but as a parent or authority figure at another. Such transferences may be unfamiliar to the younger therapist, as may the powerful counter-transferences evoked.

Therapy with an elderly patient may be less confronting than with a younger and more robust patient, but it is still possible to challenge defences and to release repressed feelings. Interpretations addressing links between present and past may be central, encouraging recollection and reminiscence, and promoting re-establishment of the continuity of life. In addition, particularly in the end phase, the patient is encouraged realistically to anticipate the future—with all it meanings, including further loss and mortality. Because of the powerful meaning of ending in late life, the ending of therapy is handled carefully (Ardern 2002). However, many elderly people do welcome the opportunity to talk honestly about their hopes and fears.

In this way, the patient is offered an opportunity to bring together past, present, and future. The ending may even constitute a new beginning.

Pathological grief

STDP has a notable place in treating abnormal grief, particularly when it is prolonged, exaggerated or masked by somatic or behavioural symptoms (Worden 1991). It is effective for unresolved grief following loss of a spouse (Marmar et al. 1988) or infant (Leon 1987).

Grief therapy is not to be confused with grief counselling, the goal of which is to facilitate grieving in a recently bereaved person. Its goal is to identify and resolve obstacles to mourning. Worden identifies factors which complicate mourning:

+ the nature of the relationship with the deceased, particularly ambivalence and unacknowledged hostility, intense dependency, or a history of sexual or physical abuse;
+ the circumstances of the loss, such as sudden and unexpected death, the absence of a body, multiple losses, or violent and mutilating death;

- a history of previous unresolved loss, including loss of a parent in early life;
- personality factors such as vulnerability or its converse, the 'strong' type who does not grieve but cares for others; and
- social factors that discourage active grieving such as the absence of a supportive family, social network, or cultural rituals which sanction mourning.

Time-limited therapy is indicated for all but the most complicated grief reactions, because the time limit and emphasis on ending serve to highlight the focus on loss without fostering an unhealthy dependency on the therapist. A psychodynamic approach is appropriate when significant degrees of repression, ambivalence, or other unconscious factors are encountered in pathological grief. Gentle challenging of defences, recovery of repressed memories and feelings, and interpretive linking of present with past experience are salient techniques. The therapist may become a transference representation of the deceased, a target perhaps for the ambivalence which characterized the lost relationship. Its analysis can facilitate recognition of feelings and dynamic processes impeding mourning, such as anger or guilt. This unblocks grieving and permits acceptance of the finality of the loss. Sensitive handling of the ending is essential, for the conclusion of treatment acts as a symbolic opportunity to say goodbye and move on to a new phase.

Post-traumatic disorders

As with pathological grief, which itself may be the result of traumatic loss, post-traumatic disorders may be amenable to STDP. Traumatic events are those which, by virtue of being sudden, unexpected, violent or violating, penetrate the person's defences to injure the very core of the self. Such events usually involve death, the threat of death, or grave threat to a person's physical and psychological integrity. Psychological reactions to trauma are immediate or delayed; but, like grief, are construed as abnormal only if prolonged, disabling, or masked by somatic or behavioural symptoms. Although early proactive interventions (psychological debriefing) which confront denial, ostensibly to promote emotional and cognitive processing of the traumatic experience, do not reduce subsequent post-traumatic disorder, later exploration of the traumatic experience can be beneficial.

Post-traumatic symptoms are categorized as (1) re-experiencing (e.g. intrusive recollections, flashbacks, nightmares); (2) avoidance (e.g. emotional numbing or denial, avoidance of the scene of the incident or any reminder of it, social withdrawal); and (3) arousal (e.g. persistent tension, irritability, hypervigilance). Only if features of all three clusters persist is a formal diagnosis of post-traumatic stress disorder (PTSD) made, but other permutations can be as disabling. Apart from a symptomatic presentation, severe trauma can affect personality development, giving rise to disturbed interpersonal functioning.

Terr (1991) differentiates two types of trauma. Short, intense, and unanticipated experiences (Type 1), for example, involvement in a road accident, gives rise to reactions characterized by vivid, detailed, and intrusive recollections, associated with intense arousal and avoidant behaviour, the pattern typical of uncomplicated PTSD. Prolonged, repeated, and anticipated traumatic experiences (Type 2), such as repeated sexual abuse in childhood, torture or exposure to prolonged danger, or depravity in warfare, result in reactions typified by psychic numbing, denial, dissociation, extremes of passivity, rage and guilt, and disruption of personality functioning. This pattern typifies post-traumatic personality deterioration.

STDP can be an effective treatment for Type I reactions, even years after the traumatic experience (Marmar 1991). Complicated PTSD and post-traumatic personality disturbance require prolonged treatment.

STDP addresses the dynamic experience of the trauma as the focus and gives subsidiary prominence to issues of loss, particularly of the ubiquitous illusions of invincibility and immortality. An exposure strategy is central, the patient is encouraged in the secure therapeutic context to recollect and narrate the traumatic experience with its associated emotions, repeatedly if necessary. He thereby becomes desensitized and integrates the experience into a revised view of his life and identity.

Again, it may be necessary to challenge maladaptive defences against the fear, anger, sadness, and guilt generated by the trauma, and to explore unconscious links to previous unresolved traumatic experiences or losses if these obstruct emotional and cognitive processing of the more recent trauma. However, there is a danger of re-traumatizing the patient if the therapist cuts through defences prematurely or forcibly; or allows uncovering to proceed unchecked, without active processing of recovered memories and feelings. Particular risks are evident when the therapist makes incisive challenges to the defences of a patient who suffered penetrative sexual abuse or rape, and especially if the therapist is of the same sex as the perpetrator. For these reasons, the pace and style are managed sensitively.

The end phase represents a chance to render the trauma past, and to incorporate the experience into the continuity of life. In this way, the victim becomes a survivor: wiser, more compassionate, and more appreciative of life.

Problems encountered in STDP

These can be categorized as the product of faulty assessment or technique.

Faults in assessment

Attention has been drawn to the problems which can result from inadequate assessment. Particular risks may arise if anxiety-provoking STDP is used to treat borderline patients (who may become psychotic or act-out self-destructively) or patients with a propensity to become suicidal. Those with strong regressive potential may decompensate at the conclusion of short-term therapy (Malan and Osimo 1992).

Difficulties can emerge in STDP, even when assessment was apparently thorough, if aspects of the patient or his history remain concealed. This occurs particularly if the patient is aware that he is being assessed for short-term therapy, for he may present only the 'short-term' part of himself (Coren 2001). During the course of STDP, a history of severe childhood abuse or other Type 2 trauma may emerge which cannot be ignored, but which is not a feasible focus. Discretion is then the better part of valour. The therapist acknowledges that another form of treatment is required and either prolongs the present therapy, or ends it cautiously while arranging to transfer the patient to a suitable alternative therapist.

Faults in technique

The therapist's failure to adhere to the defined focus and/or time limit are obvious sources of failure. Therapists trained in long-term psychotherapies and accustomed to a different pace and an expansive framework are particularly at risk.

Other technical faults are associated with over-zealousness in confrontation of defences and premature uncovering of unconscious material. It is essential to provide a supportive therapeutic relationship and opportunity to address actively material which is uncovered, especially memories and feelings associated with traumatic experience.

Specific problems are presented by the generation of powerful transferences. If the patient develops a pervasive negative transference, which may be the result of the therapist's faulty technique, the alliance may be paralysed and the patient may drop out. As hazardous is the emergence of an idealizing or even eroticized transference, both likely to be the product of an undiagnosed personality disorder.

The therapist's counter-transference may be problematic because the brevity and high activity level of STDP both diminish his ability to monitor his reactions and create an atmosphere in which a predisposed therapist becomes persecutory. The repeated challenge to defences, in particular, requires that the therapist maintains empathic contact and control of his own aggressive impulses to prevent an unwarranted attack on the patient. Continuing supervision is therefore essential for sound practice, even for experienced therapists.

Research

A number of earlier reviews summarized the evolution of STDP and research evidence for its effectiveness (Koss and Butcher 1986; MacKenzie 1988; Hobbs 1989). The power of short-term psychotherapies was confirmed by a study of the dose–effect relationship: half the patients sampled showed improvement by the eighth session and three quarters by session 26 (Howard et al. 1986). Although this suggests that a 'law of diminishing returns' applies, Coren (2001) reminds us that a proportion of patients will only benefit through more prolonged therapy.

Research has added to our understanding of the change process in STDP. Llewelyn et al. (1988), through study of the patient's perception of significant events in therapy, found that those which enhanced awareness (particularly, getting in touch with previously hidden feelings), a sense of relief and hope, the relationship with the therapist as a person, and the opportunity to identify and rehearse new ways of problem solving were particularly valued in short dynamic therapy. The experience found to hinder progress most was for the therapist to focus on unwanted feelings and thoughts in an 'unhelpful' way. This suggests that it may be counterproductive to expose uncomfortable thoughts and feelings without addressing and resolving them, a danger identified particularly in work with people who have been abused sexually or otherwise traumatized.

A collaborative alliance is fundamental and interpretations are framed in a way which promotes it at the same time as extending insight and conscious control over patterns of thought, feeling, and behaviour (Westen 1986; Piper et al. 1991). This process of 'making the unconscious conscious' is tolerable and productive only if managed sensitively in patients carefully selected and prepared for it (Ogrodniczuk et al. 1999).

Comparative studies e.g. Shapiro and Firth 1987) and meta-analyses (e.g. Svartberg and Stiles 1991; Crits-Christoph 1992) showed STDPs to be similar in effectiveness to other psychotherapies and medication for a range of neurotic presentations, though inferior to cognitive behaviour therapy for major depression. Later studies have suggested that STDP is an effective treatment for depression (Hilsenroth et al. 2003), and that STDP may enhance the benefit of antidepressant medication (Burnand et al. 2002).

Of particular interest are two randomized studies (Hellerstein et al. 1998; Svartberg et al. 2004) and a meta-analysis ((Leichsenring and Leibing 2003) which demonstrate the value of short/medium-term (40 sessions) psychodynamic therapies for personality disorders (especially cluster C: avoidant, dependent, and obsessive-compulsive disorders).

Two process studies illustrate the value of research into technical aspects of STDP. Joyce et al. (2003) confirmed that the therapeutic alliance is a powerful mediator between pre-therapy expectancy of improvement and outcome, accounting for one-third of the impact. A note of caution derives from the work of Ogrodniczuk et al. (1999) which detected an inverse relationship between the *frequency* of transference interpretations and both patient-rated alliance and outcome.

Training

Malan and Osimo (1992) confidently assert that supervised practice of STDP is an excellent training experience. Working with patients, selected for their capacity to interact dynamically with the therapist and for the clarity of their psychopathology, trainees learn principles of active dynamic therapy, appreciate the psychodynamic structure of psychopathology, and experience the satisfaction of early, tangible results. Many therapists contend, however, that it is not possible to learn the skills of STDP before becoming competent in long-term analytic psychotherapy, particularly because it takes time to appreciate and work effectively with resistance and transference.

The therapists in Malan and Osimo's (1992) study were senior trainees obtaining specialized training experience in dynamic psychotherapy. Nevertheless, more junior trainees can develop skills and confidence in STDP, if they work with carefully selected patients and are supervised closely (Ashurst 1991). In parallel with training in other brief psychological treatments, such as cognitive therapy, exposure to basic training in STDP is highly relevant for the development of effective therapeutic skills. Trainees should learn to recognize both the indications for and limitations of STDP.

Conclusion

STDP is an effective and cost-effective treatment for a wide spectrum of clinical problems, ranging from entrenched neuroses to developmental disorders to unresolved grief. Technical ingredients, particularly the degree of challenge, are modified according to the patient's personal characteristics and psychopathology. Attention to preliminary assessment, dynamic focus, analysis of defences, and adherence to time limit are defining features.

STDP is no panacea. Not all patients will benefit. Some are too vulnerable or disturbed for a short anxiety-provoking therapy. They may require a short-term approach which regulates rather than provokes anxiety and other affects, or a longer therapy.

Clinical and research evidence suggests that STDP, in common with other psychological treatments, unlocks adaptive psychological processes. The effects may generalize and extend over time, but additional programmes of treatment may be required. The patient with more complex problems may benefit from further episodes of focal psychotherapy, perhaps complemented by family, couple, or group therapy. We are yet to identify with certainty the patient characteristics and therapist techniques which optimize STDP.

STDP is an exciting and rewarding model of treatment since progress may be rapid, and the outcome tangible. Further application and study of STDP is likely to enhance future development of the psychotherapies.

References

Alexander, F. and French, T. (1946). *Psychoanalytic therapy: principles and application.* Ronald Press, New York.

Ardern, M. (2002). Psychodynamic therapy. In *Psychological therapies with older people: Developing treatments for effective practice.* (ed. J.Hepple, J.Pearce, and P.Wilkinson), pp. 21–44. Brunner-Routledge, Hove.

Ashurst. P. M. (1991). Brief psychotherapy. In *Textbook of psychotherapy in psychiatric practice*, (ed. J. Holmes), pp. 187–212. Churchill Livingstone, Edinburgh.

Balint, M., Ornstein, P. H. and Balint, E. (1972). *Focal psychotherapy: An example of applied psychoanalysis.* Tavistock, London.

Binder J. L. (2004). *Key competencies in brief dynamic psychotherapy: Clinical practice beyond the manual.* Guilford Press, New York.

Bloch, S. and McNab, D. (1987). Attitudes of British psychotherapists towards the role of humour in psychotherapy. *British Journal of Psychotherapy*, **3**, 216–225.

Bowlby, J. (1979). *The making and breaking of affectional bonds.* Tavistock, London.

Burnand, Y., Andreoli, A., Kolatte, E., Venturini, A. and Rosset, N. (2002). Psychodynamic psychotherapy and clomipramine in the treatment of major depression. *Psychiatric Services*, **53**, 585–590.

Coren, A. (2001). *Short-term psychotherapy: A psychodynamic approach.* Palgrave, Basingstoke.

Crits-Christoph, P. (1992). The efficacy of brief dynamic psychotherapy: A meta-analysis. *American Journal of Psychiatry*, **149**, 151–8.

Davanloo, H. (ed.) (1980). *Short-term dynamic psychotherapy.* Aronson, Northvale, NJ.

Davanloo, H. (2001). *Intensive short-term dynamic psychotherapy: Selected papers of Habib Davanloo.* Wiley, New York.

Ferenczi, S. (1950). *Further contributions to the theory and technique of psychoanalysis*. Hogarth, London. (Originally published 1926.)

Freud, S. (1964). In Standard edition, *Analysis terminable and interminable*, Vol. **23**. Hogarth, London. (Originally published 1937.)

Garfield, S. L. (1989). *The practice of brief psychotherapy*. Pergamon, New York.

Gaston, L. (1990). The concept of the alliance and its role in psychotherapy: theoretical and empirical considerations. *Psychotherapy: Theory, Research and Practice*, 27, 143–153.

Guthrie, E. (1999). Psychodynamic interpersonal therapy. *Advances in Psychiatric Treatment*, 5, 135–145.

Hellerstein, D. J., Rosenthal, R. N., Pinsker, H., Samstag, L. W., Muran, J. C. and Winston, A. (1998). A randomized prospective study comparing supportive and dynamic therapies. Outcome and alliance. *Psychotherapy Practice and Research*, 7, 261–271.

Hilsenroth, M. J., Ackerman, S. J., Blagys, M. D., Baity, M. R., and Mooney, M. A. (2003). Short-term psychodynamic psychotherapy for depression: An examination of statistical, clinically significant, and technique-specific change. *Journal of Nervous and Mental diseases*, 191, 349–357.

Hobbs, M. (1984). Crisis intervention in theory and practice: A selective review. *British Journal of Medical Psychology*, **57**, 23–34.

Hobbs, M. (1989). Short-term dynamic psychotherapy. *Current Opinion in Psychiatry*, **2**, 389–92.

Hobson, R. F. (1985). *Forms of feeling: The heart of psychotherapy*. Tavistock, London.

Howard, K. I., Kopta, S. M., Krause, M. S. and Orlinsky, D. E. (1986). The dose-effect relationship in psychotherapy. *American Psychologist*, **41**, 159–64.

Joyce, A. S., Ogrodniczuk, J. S., Piper, W. E. and McCallum, M. (2003) The alliance as mediator of expectancy effects in short-term individual therapy. *Journal of Consulting and Clinical* Psychology, 71, 672–679.

Keller, A. (1984). Planned brief psychotherapy in clinical practice. *British Journal of Medical Psychology*, **57**, 347–61.

Klerman, G. L., Weissman, M. M., Rounsaville, B. J., and Chevron, E. S. (1984). *Interpersonal psychotherapy for depression*. Basic Books, New York.

Koss, M. P. and Butcher, J. N. (1986). Research on brief psychotherapy. In *Handbook of psychotherapy and behaviour change*, (2nd edn), (ed. S. L. Garfield and A. E. Bergin). Wiley, New York.

Leichsenring, F. and Leibing, E. (2003) The effectiveness of psychodynamic therapy and cognitive behavior therapy in the treatment of personality disorders: a meta-analysis. *American Journal of Psychiatry*, 160, 1223–1232.

Leon, I. G. (1987). Short-term psychotherapy for perinatal loss. *Psychotherapy*, **24**, 186–95.

Levenson, H. (1995). *Time-limited dynamic psychotherapy: A guide to clinical practice*. Basic Books, New York.

Llewelyn, S. P., Elliott, R., Shapiro, D. A., Hardy, G. and Firth-Cozens, J. (1988). Client perceptions of significant events in prescriptive and exploratory periods of individual therapy. *British Journal of Clinical Psychology*, 27, 105–14.

MacKenzie, K. R. (1988). Recent developments in brief psychotherapy. *Hospital and Community Psychiatry*, **39**, 742–52.

MacKenzie, K. R. (1990). *Introduction to time-limited group psychotherapy*. American Psychiatric Press, Washington, DC.

Mackie, A. (1981). Attachment theory: Its relevance to the therapeutic alliance. *British Journal of Medical Psychology*, **54**, 203–12.

Malan, D. H. (1963). *A study of brief psychotherapy*. Tavistock, London.

Malan, D. H. (1976). *The frontier of brief psychotherapy*. Plenum, New York.

Malan, D. H. (1979). *Individual psychotherapy and the science of psychodynamics*. Butterworths, London.

Malan, D. H. (1980). The most important development in psychotherapy since the discovery of the unconscious. In *Short-term dynamic psychotherapy* (ed. H. Davanloo), pp. 13–23. Aronson, Northvale, NJ.

Malan, D. H. and Osimo, F. (1992). *Psychodynamics, training, and outcome in brief psychotherapy*. Butterworths-Heinemann, Oxford.

Mann, J. (1973). *Time-limited psychotherapy*. Harvard University Press, Boston.

Marmar, C. R., Horowitz, M. J., Weiss, D. S., Wilner, N. R., and Kaltreider, N. B. (1988). A controlled trial of brief psychotherapy and mutual-help group treatment of conjugal bereavement. *American Journal of Psychiatry*, **145**, 203–9.

Marmar, C. R. (1991). Brief dynamic psychotherapy of post-traumatic stress disorder. *Psychiatric Annals*, **21**, 405–14.

Marmor, J. M. (1979). Short-term dynamic psychotherapy. *American Journal of Psychiatry*, **136**, 149–55.

Molnos, A. (1984). The two triangles are four: a diagram to teach the process of dynamic brief psychotherapy. *British Journal of Psychotherapy*, **1**, 112–25.

Molnos, A. (1986). Anger that destroys and anger that heals: handling hostility in group analysis and in dynamic brief psychotherapy. *Group Analysis*, **19**, 207–21.

Morgan, R., Luborsky, L., Crits-Christoph, P., Curtis, H. and Solomon, J. (1982). Predicting the outcomes of psychotherapy by the Penn Helping Alliance Rating Method. *Archives of General Psychiatry*, **39**, 397–402.

Ogrodniczuk, J. S., Piper, W. E., Joyce, A. S. and McCallum, M. (1999) Transference interpretations in short-term dynamic psychotherapy. *Journal of Nervous and Mental Diseases*, 187, 571–578.

Piper, W. E., Azim, H. F. A., Joyce, A. S. and McCallum, M. (1991). Transference interpretations, therapeutic alliance, and outcome in short-term individual psychotherapy. *Archives of General Psychiatry*, **48**, 946–53.

Piper, W. E., McCallum, M., and Azim, H. F. A. (1992). *Adaptation to loss through short-term group psychotherapy*. Guilford, New York.

Porter, R. (1991). Psychotherapy with the elderly. In *Textbook of psychotherapy in psychiatric practice*, (ed. J. Holmes), pp. 469–87. Churchill Livingstone, Edinburgh.

Rank, O. (1936). *Will therapy: an analysis of the therapeutic process in terms of relationship*. Knopf, New York.

Ryle, A. (1990). *Cognitive-analytic therapy: Active participation in change*. Wiley, Chichester.

Sandler, J. (1976). Counter-transference and role-responsiveness. *International Review of Psychoanalysis*, 3, 43–47.

Shapiro, D. A. and Firth, J. (1987). Prescriptive v. exploratory psychotherapy: outcomes of the Sheffield psychotherapy project. *British Journal of Psychiatry*, **151**, 790–9.

Shefler, G. (2000). Time-limited psychotherapy with adolescents. *Journal of Psychotherapy Practice and Research*, 9, 88–99.

Sifneos, P. E. (1972). *Short-term psychotherapy and emotional crisis.* Harvard University Press, Boston.

Sifneos, P. E. (1987). *Short-term dynamic psychotherapy: Evaluation and technique*, (2nd edn). Plenum, New York.

Sifneos, P. E. (1992). *Short-term anxiety-provoking psychotherapy: A treatment manual.* Basic Books, New York.

Small, L. (1971). *The briefer psychotherapies.* Brunner/Mazel, New York.

Strupp, H. H. and Binder, J. L. (1984). *Psychotherapy in a new key.* Basic Books, New York.

Svartberg, M. and Stiles, T. C. (1991). Comparative effects of short-term psychodynamic psychotherapy: a meta-analysis. *Journal of Consulting and Clinical Psychology*, 59, 704–714.

Svartberg, M., Stiles, T. C., Seltzer, M. H. (2004). Randomized, controlled trial of the effectiveness of short-term dynamic psychotherapy and cognitive therapy for cluster C personality disorders. *American Journal of Psychiatry*, 161, 810–817.

Terr, L. C. (1991). Childhood traumas: an outline and overview. *American Journal of Psychiatry*, **148**, 10–20.

Uribe, V. M. (1988). Short-term psychotherapy for adolescents: management of initial resistances. *Journal of the American Academy of Psychoanalysis*, **16**, 107–16.

Vaillant, L. M. (1996). *Changing character: short-term anxiety-regulating psychotherapy for restructuring defences, affects and attachment.* Basic Books, New York.

Westen, D. (1986). What changes in short-term psychodynamic psychotherapy? *Psychotherapy*, **23**, 501–12.

Wilson, P. (1991). Psychotherapy with adolescents. In *Textbook of psychotherapy in psychiatric practice*, (ed. J. Holmes), pp. 443–67. Churchill Livingstone, Edinburgh.

Winnicott, D. (1971). *Playing and reality.* Tavistock, London.

Wolberg, L. R. (1980). *Handbook of short-term psychotherapy.* Grune & Stratton, New York.

Worden, J. W. (1991). *Grief counselling and grief therapy* (2nd edn). Routledge, London.

Recommended reading

Binder, J. L. (2004). *Key competencies in brief dynamic psychotherapy: Clinical practice beyond the manual.* Guilford, New York. (Updates time-limited model he developed with Hans Strupp and sets out key ingredients and skills.)

Coren, A. (2001). *Short-term psychotherapy: A psychodynamic approach.* Palgrave, Basingstoke. (An excellent contemporary account of short-term psychodynamic psychotherapies.)

Davanloo, H. (2001). *Intensive short-term dynamic psychotherapy: Selected papers of Habib Davanloo.* Wiley, New York. (Includes verbatim transcripts which give a clear picture of his challenging method of STDP.)

Levenson, H. (1995). *Time-limited dynamic psychotherapy: A guide to clinical practice.* Basic Books, New York. (Transcripts of trainee supervision sessions illustrate treatment of people with longstanding dysfunction.)

Malan, D. H. (1995). *Individual psychotherapy and the science of psychodynamics. 2nd edn.* Arnold, London. (In this readable book, which is peppered with clinical illustrations, there is a valuable account of the application of the 'two triangles' in therapy.)

Mann, J. (1973). *Time-limited psychotherapy.* Harvard University Press, Boston. (Mann's influential text includes a lucid rationale for his emphasis of a time limit and an annotated transcript of a 12-session treatment.)

Sifneos, P. E. (1992). *Short-term anxiety-provoking psychotherapy: A treatment manual.* Basic Books, New York. (A clear presentation of Sifneos's short-term anxiety-provoking psychotherapy, including illustrated accounts of his selection process and method.)

Vaillant, L. M. (1996). *Changing character: Short-term anxiety-regulating psychotherapy for restructuring defences, affects and attachment.* Basic Books, New York. (Key account of a model developed for treatment of personality disorder.)

Chapter 7

Cognitive psychotherapy

Nicholas B. Allen

This chapter begins by recognizing the difficulty of providing an exhaustive definition of cognitive therapy while its applications and concepts are diversifying rapidly. The cognitive model of psychopathology and therapy is presented in the context of its historical development, where it can be seen as a distillation of certain themes from experimental psychology, behaviour therapy, and psychodynamic therapy. The seminal work of Aaron Beck and his colleagues is emphasized, and the therapy is presented as a directive and time-limited approach, which focuses on helping patients to gain new skills in managing distressing emotions and other psychological symptoms. Other important features of cognitive therapy include its provision of detailed treatment guidelines, and its commitment to rigorous outcome assessment. The limitations of this approach are also discussed, as are some of the more recent theoretical and technical developments designed to overcome these.

Definition

Defining any approach to psychotherapy is difficult because the various schools often use different language to describe similar phenomena and techniques. A particular school may also encapsulate a wide variety of emphases, with resultant overlap between approaches. This is particularly the case with cognitive therapy. Although a prototypic version of cognitive therapy can be described, approaches identifying themselves as 'cognitive' include those highlighting a highly prescriptive approach with a focus on behavioural change (e.g. Meichenbaum 1977), exploratory approaches that stress cognitive and affective change (e.g. Guidano and Liotti 1983), to more recent developments that emphasize awareness and acceptance of thoughts and feelings more than change (e.g. Hayes et al. 2004a). The reasons for this breadth are most likely due to the stage of development of cognitive therapy (i.e. it is still in a phase of evolution), and to diverse interpretations of its central construct—cognition.

Dobson and Block (1988) suggest that cognitive behaviour therapies[1] share three propositions: (1) cognitive activity affects behaviour; (2) cognitive activity may be monitored and altered; and (3) desired behavioural change is achievable through cognitive change. Although this is a sound starting definition, its capacity to describe cognitive therapy relies on a clear definition of the term 'cognition'. By and large this definition has been an everyday version of the concept, rather than the more technical definition used by cognitive scientists (Teasdale 1993). For instance, Beck describes cognitions as 'any ideation with verbal or pictorial content' (Beck et al. 1979a) or as 'stream-of-consciousness or automatic thoughts that tend to be in an individual's awareness' (Beck et al. 1983). This definition, which emphasizes conscious experience, differs from that of a cognitive scientist who regards cognition as any phenomena pertinent to human information processing, including memory and attention, as well as mechanisms that occur very early in the processes of human perception and are non-conscious (Neisser 1967). Other debates regarding the relationship between cognition and emotion have also highlighted how the definition of 'cognition' can influence the way in which cognitive phenomena are construed (Zajonc 1980; Lazarus 1982). Thus, depending on the phenomena subsumed under 'cognition', Dobson and Block's (1988) principles could be used to cover almost all psychotherapies involving mental phenomena, including, for instance, psychodynamic and experiential approaches. However, their principles operate best as a definition of current cognitive behavioural practice when 'cognition' relates to consciously experienced verbal and pictorial phenomena.

An alternative way to define cognitive therapy is to consider its *modus operandi*. Hawton et al. (1989) offer such a process-oriented definition proposing that cognitive behaviour therapy is typified by its:

- expression of concepts in operational terms,
- empirical validation of treatment,

[1] The terms 'cognitive therapy' and 'cognitive behaviour therapy' often cause confusion. In general the two terms mean the same thing, except that the term 'cognitive behaviour therapy' makes explicit reference to the fact that techniques derived from behaviour therapy (see chapter 8) are usually included in the treatment protocol. This should be seen as reflecting a form of technical rather than theoretical eclecticism (i.e. that although behavioural techniques are recognized as effective, the mechanisms by which they achieve change are understood in terms of cognitive constructs and models). For our purposes the terms will be used interchangeably.

- specification of treatment in operational terms,
- evaluation of treatment with reliable and objective measures,
- emphasis on the 'here and now',
- objective to help patients to bring about desired changes in their lives,
- focus on new learning and changes outside the clinical setting,
- explicit description of therapeutic procedures to the patient,
- collaboration of the patient and therapist to deal with identified problems,
- use of time limits and explicitly agreed goals.

This definition has the advantage over more substantive ones in avoiding the debate about the nature of cognition. Most mainstream approaches, however, include both content- and process-oriented definitions.

Theoretical background: A historical context

Three traditions—experimental psychology, behaviour therapy, and psycho-dynamic therapy—have influenced the development of cognitive therapy.

The notion of cognition in experimental psychology goes back to the nineteenth century, when two pioneering psychologists, Wilhelm Wundt and William James, defined their subject as the science of mental life. This early research chiefly concerned itself with matters of cognition, such as the processes whereby information was perceived, stored, and used. The method-ology involved subjects trained in introspection, who examined their own cognitive processes during experimental tasks. This phase of research was overtaken by the behaviourist framework during the 1920s, largely due to difficulties in demonstrating the validity of self-report data generated by introspective methods, and resultant concerns that this would compromise psychology's standing as a legitimate science (MacLeod 1993). Behaviourism offered an alternative in which phenomena had to be observable and objectively quantifiable. This limited the data of experimental psychology to overt behaviour. Although behaviourism employed cognitive constructs to explain observed behaviour (e.g. classical and operant conditioning involve storage and retrieval of information in order to exert an enduring influence on behaviour), these were kept to a minimum, and consideration of subjective phenomena eschewed.

Behaviourist research flourished as investigators conducted controlled experiments designed to examine the role of various processes, especially learning, in determining behaviour. By the 1950s and 1960s, however, psychol-ogists became dissatisfied with the capacity of the model to explain complex behaviour. This was particularly relevant in areas like natural language acquisition, where children learn linguistic skills of such idiosyncrasy and complexity that they are well beyond the capacity of adults to reinforce discriminately (Chomsky 1959; Vygotksy 1962). Other challenges to the paradigm included Bandura's (1977) work on vicarious learning, and Mischel's on delay of gratification (Mischel et al. 1972). Even ostensibly simple behaviour, such as a reaction time task, was shown to contradict predictions from behavioural accounts (e.g. Crossman 1953). Attempts to deal with these aspects without threatening the behaviourist framework included using the notion of 'covert' behaviour to explain the role of thoughts (Homme 1965). George Kelly's (1955) work on personal constructs and Jean Piaget's (1954) studies of child development also strongly influenced interest in cognitive concepts.

An alternative framework, based on information processing, thus emerged in psychology, linguistics, computer science, neuroscience, and philosophy. This 'cognitive science' (Gardner 1985) utilized information processing and the computer as the metaphor to explain intelligent behaviour; cognitive psychology began to be accepted as an alternative to behaviourism. Information processing concepts like parallel and serial processing, limited capacity and multiple channel systems, temporary storage buffers, and selective filters were used to extend the models developed by psychologists (MacLeod 1993). Experimental psychologists were then able to predict more precisely the behavioural performance of research participants during various tasks. This new model has developed to the point where the cognitive approach represents the pre-eminent paradigm in contemporary psychology.

As behaviourism in psychological *science* was questioned, its limitations in clinical *practice* were also noted. Prominent behaviourally-oriented therapists not only felt they were required to ignore important mental phenomena, but some of the disorders they treated entailed symptoms that were inherently cognitive (Dobson and Block 1988). One obvious example is obsessive-compulsive disorder. Although compulsive behaviour lent itself to behavioural analysis, the obsession often went unexplained. Thus, although the emphasis in traditional behaviour therapies on overt behaviour provided a marked increase in efficacy of treatment, especially those for disorders chiefly defined by their behavioural correlates (e.g. phobic anxiety), the need to extend the application of these therapies created an impetus for a model that could guide treatment of non-behavioural symptoms.

The most influential pioneering work to emerge from behaviourism was that of Donald Meichenbaum (1977). His research on training schizophrenic patients to use 'healthy talk' stimulated his curiosity regarding the relationship between self-instruction (including thoughts) and behaviour modification. He proposed that these 'covert behaviours' were subject to the same laws of conditioning as overt behaviours, and also reasoned that self-instructions were crucial to the voluntary control of behaviour. Meichenbaum developed Self-Instructional Training (SIT) programs designed for difficulties related to self-control (e.g. impulsivity in children). Later SIT was extended to other disorders like schizophrenia and anxiety. Skills taught were: (1) problem definition, (2) problem approach, (3) attention-focusing, (4) coping statements, (5) error-correcting options, and (6) self-reinforcement. Although dealing directly with cognitive phenomena, this pioneering endeavour had a strong behavioural flavour with its emphasis on modelling, graded tasks, and self-reinforcement.

Introducing cognitive phenomena into behaviour therapy was initially treated with suspicion, but the work of Meichenbaum and others, who presented this change as a logical evolution of behavioural technique and philosophy, did much to allay these concerns. The other crucial development in the acceptance of cognitive approaches was the rigorous assessment of outcome to which the cognitive behavioural treatments have been subjected, some of which show a superiority of cognitive behavioural techniques over purely behavioural ones (e.g. Dobson 1989). More explicitly cognitive approaches such as those of Beck (1967) and Ellis (1962), were accepted more hesitantly.

Questions were also raised by cognitive therapists regarding the psychodynamic model of personality and its associated treatment. In particular, emphases on long-term therapy, the unconscious, detailed scrutiny of personal history, and insight into the transference as the main vehicle for change, were questioned (Ellis 1962; Beck 1967). In addition, outcome reviews of traditional psychotherapy suggested there was little evidence for their efficacy (Eysenck 1969; Rachman and Wilson 1980).

Roots of cognitive therapy are also detectable in neo-Freudian models: Sullivanian (Arieti 1980), Adlerian (Schulman 1985), Logotherapy (Frankl 1985), and Horneyan (Rendon 1985). Indeed, Albert Ellis and Aaron Beck, two central figures in cognitive therapy, were originally trained in psychoanalysis. Ellis became frustrated with standard psychoanalysis upon observing that 'patient after patient would say to me: "Yes, I see exactly what bothers me now and why I am bothered by it; but I nevertheless still am bothered. Now what can I do about that?' " (Ellis 1962). He began to experiment with more active, directive, and short-term treatments. The resultant Rational-Emotive Therapy (RET) regards emotional disturbance in terms of an A–B–C model, where A refers to an activating event, C to the consequence for the person (usually an emotional response), and B refers to the beliefs or cognitive processes that mediate the relationship between A and C. Neurosis comes about through irrational beliefs, which are essentially related to unrealistic or absolute expectations (Ellis 1970). The similarity between these irrational 'musts' (i.e. 'I must be approved of by others') and Karen Horney's notion of 'the tyranny of the shoulds' clearly indicates part of Ellis's intellectual heritage. By replacing irrational beliefs with more realistic ones, reductions in distressing emotion follow. Although RET employs a range of behavioural and emotive techniques, the pre-eminent activity is the logical examination of the patient's beliefs through questioning, challenge, and debate.

Beck noted consistent themes in the conscious ideation of his patients, especially those with depression. His 'cognitive triad of depression' comprises negative views of the self, the world, and the future (Beck 1967). These phenomena, he asserted, were neglected in psychoanalytic treatment in favour of emotional and motivational material (Bloch 2004). Depressed patients also showed distorted thinking patterns, focusing on negative aspects of experience or explanations for events that result in self-criticism and perceived rejection. Schemata, a term derived from cognitive psychology, are cognitive structures that guide this information processing. In those vulnerable to emotional disorders, schemata from early life experiences are unrealistic and distorted, and these facilitate dysphoric responses to stressful situations. Once a dysphoric response is established, negative schemata continue to exert an effect on information processing, which in turn serves to maintain and exacerbate the dysphoric emotional state.

Beck's theory, conceptually similar to that of Ellis, entails techniques similar to those used in RET. Differences between them relate to RET's emphasis on more logical-philosophical discussion wedded to the ethos of 'rational hedonism' (the belief that taking a rational view of life will lead to the greatest long-term happiness and pleasure), compared to Beck's cognitive therapy which is more deductive, gathering evidence for and against particular conclusions.

Cognitive therapy has diversified both in application and range of models, including emphasis on problem solving (e.g. D'Zurilla and Goldfried 1971), coping (Meichenbaum 1977), self-control (Rehm 1977), and mindfulness and acceptance (Hayes et al. 2004a). The latter approaches are notable for their inclusion of concepts from Eastern meditation traditions, which emphasize observing the mind with a non-judgemental attitude rather than changing cognitive activity. A trend has also emerged for cognitive models to move from 'rationalist' (i.e. promoting more accurate perception in the belief that inaccurate perception lies at the heart of neurosis) to constructivist models that stress a person's active role in the construction of *any* perceived reality (Mahoney 1991). Thus, the constructivist approach emphasizes the utility (i.e. is it helpful) rather than the validity (i.e. is it true) of a way of thinking, and a less directive and more exploratory approach to psychotherapy has emerged as a result. Although some of these developments have been criticized for ignoring the programmatic approach inherited from behaviour therapy, and for losing touch with scientific psychology (Ross 1991; MacLeod 1993), it has been counter-argued that the changes have permitted therapy to be directed to more difficult and complex conditions (Neimeyer 1993).

Among these many approaches, that described by Beck and his colleagues (i.e. Beck et al. 1979a, 1985, 1990; Wright et al. 1993) is most useful in encapsulating the defining features of cognitive therapy, and has been carefully assessed in a series of outcome studies (Dobson and Craig 1998). This chapter will therefore focus principally on Beck's work.

Objectives

The aims of cognitive therapy are two-fold: to reduce distress by teaching skills to recognize, evaluate, and change relevant cognitive processes; and, in later phases, to engender an understanding of themes in maladaptive cognitions, and their autobiographical roots, in order to modify enduring sets of attitudes and beliefs that are the basis of the patient's vulnerability. The approach to a problem involves the following steps: eliciting automatic thoughts; testing their accuracy and viability; developing realistic alternatives; and identifying and challenging underlying maladaptive schemata.

Three types of cognitive phenomena determine psychopathology: *automatic thoughts, cognitive distortions*, and *schemata*. Automatic thoughts, the 'surface level' of cognition, are the often-transitory verbal or pictorial experiences associated with particular mood states. They are automatic in as much as they emerge spontaneously, and are difficult to resist. Despite their ubiquitous nature, many people are only partially aware of them, and need to develop the skill of 'thought catching' before therapy proceeds. These thoughts have a specific relationship to the kind of mood they engender. For instance, depression relates to thoughts about loss, defeat, rejection, and hopelessness, whereas anxiety is associated with thoughts of threat and danger, and panic to a catastrophic interpretation of bodily symptoms (Clark and Beck 1989).

Cognitive distortions refer to misinterpretations of reality that reinforce negative conclusions regarding the self, world, or future (i.e. the cognitive triad of depression). Beck (1967) describes specific kinds of distortions: overgeneralizing (a single instance is taken as an example of a wide range of situations), dichotomous thinking (only extreme points of view are considered), selective abstraction (attending solely to negative aspects of a situation), 'personalising' (assuming that one is the cause of an event or of another's actions), 'should' statements (absolute imperatives are applied to one's own or another's behaviour), 'catastrophizing' and minimizing (emphasizing negative and downplaying positive outcomes).

Information about oneself and one's environment is perceived, stored, and recalled through schemata, which are assumed to evolve during recurrent experiences. These help a person to recognize consistencies in experience so that new information is linked to current knowledge efficiently. Since a bias towards schema-congruent information occurs, psychopathological states result from schemata that facilitate interpretation of situations in terms of threats to the self, such as loss, failure, rejection, and danger. These are inaccessible without considerable introspection; although it is possible to describe them in verbal terms (such as 'If I am a good person, bad things will not happen to me'), it is not expected that they exert their influence through conscious processes. In other words, the nature of schemata is usually deduced on the basis of an observed pattern of recurrent cognitive distortions and automatic thoughts. Once a schema is activated it dominates perceptions of current and future situations.

In summary, cognitive therapy aims to elicit, evaluate, and modify negative automatic thoughts, cognitive distortions, and maladaptive schemata using a range of cognitive, emotive, and behavioural techniques see below.

Selection

The first step in selection is in terms of diagnosis. Most therapists agree that cognitive therapy is indicated for non-psychotic forms of depression, anxiety disorders, eating disorders, substance abuse, and most personality disorders. Therapy may also be useful as an adjunct to other treatments in psychotic depression, bipolar disorder, schizophrenia, schizo-affective disorder, and mild dementia. It is not suitable for severe dementia, delirium, and moderate to severe mental retardation. These assertions are not based solely on out-come research but also on the premise that where intellectual functioning is compromised by organicity, applying cognitively-based techniques may be limited.

Many conditions treated by cognitive therapy may also be dealt with by alternative approaches, including medication. Attempts to demonstrate that either cognitive behaviour therapy or medication are more effective for the treatment of depression have failed to find consistent effects in favour of one or the other treatment approach (Hollon et al. 2002). More promising is the idea that symptom profiles are associated with greater responsiveness to medication or psychotherapy, especially the idea that severe forms of depression respond better to medication (Elkin et al. 1989), but even in such profiles the results are mixed (e.g. DeRubeis et al. 1999). The most compelling differences between the two treatment modes relate to the time course of response. Thase and colleagues (1997) found that adding medication to cognitive treatment accelerated recovery time. However, beneficial effects of medication seem to be limited in that they do not persist after it is withdrawn; cognitive behaviour therapy, on the other hand, reduces relapse of depression, even in long-term studies that assess participants years after initial treatment (e.g. Hollon et al. 1992b; Segal et al. 1999).

Aside from depression, cognitive therapies are well established as efficacious treatments for anxiety and stress disorders (especially generalized anxiety and panic disorder, see Beck 1993; Landon and Barlow 2004; Lang 2004) and bulimia (Ricca et al. 2000; for an overview of empirically validated psychological therapies across a range of disorders see Chambless et al. 1998). 'Either–or' type decisions between medication and cognitive therapy are often unnecessary. Moreover, given that research suggests medication may be more efficacious for severe depression and/or facilitates faster recovery, and that cognitive therapy may offer superior relapse prevention, combining the two probably yields the best outcome. Consistent with this, several studies show that the combination is superior to either approach by itself in depression (e.g. Keller et al. 2000; TADS 2004).

In determining suitability for cognitive therapy on the basis of clinical features, most attention has been paid to depression. As noted above, antidepressants are more effective than cognitive therapy in severe depression in one large study (Elkin et al. 1989), but replication has not been achieved (Thase et al. 1991c; Hollon et al. 1992a; McLean and Taylor 1992; DeRubeis et al. 1999). Indeed Thase et al. (1991a) reported an uncontrolled trial in which cognitive therapy was effective for a group of unmedicated, 'endogenously' depressed in-patients. Furthermore, cognitive therapy is equally effective across groups with and without 'endogenous' symptoms as indicated by abnormal sleep electroencephalograph patterns (Simons and Thase 1992), abnormal dexamethasone suppression (considered a biological marker for melancholic depression) (McKnight et al. 1992), or Research Diagnostic Criteria endogenous diagnosis (Thase et al. 1991a). Thus, cognitive therapy's efficacy appears to extend beyond mild and moderate depression.

A third approach to selection is to consider psychological features that may enhance responsiveness to cognitive therapy. Problem-solving ability, intact cognitive function, and high motivation for symptom improvement are examples. In Safran and Segal's (1990) assessment interview, which aims to determine suitability for short-term cognitive therapy, the patient should display:

- the capacity to access and identify automatic thoughts,
- awareness and differentiation of emotions,

- acceptance of responsibility for change,
- understanding and acceptance of the cognitive rationale,
- the capacity to form a therapeutic alliance, as reflected in both therapist–patient interaction and past relationships,
- shorter rather than longer duration of problems,
- a low propensity to use avoidant information processing to reduce anxiety, and
- the ability to maintain a problem focus.

Safran et al. (1993) have found that a semi-structured interview to assess these criteria can predict outcome. Another criterion correlating with outcome is the willingness and capacity to complete prescribed homework tasks (Fennell and Teasdale 1987; Persons et al. 1988).

As already mentioned, cognitive therapy is unsuitable for people whose capacity to engage in its logical and empirical procedures is limited. Organic brain syndromes and acute psychotic states are examples, although it should be noted that cognitive therapies are regarded as pertinent to manage certain psychotic symptoms (e.g. Morrison et al. 2004). Another way to tackle suitability emerges from research that shows non-responders having severe symptoms (especially hopelessness), interpersonal problems (e.g. marital discord), and more difficulties establishing an effective working relationship within therapy (Robins and Hayes 1993). On the other hand, new techniques are being devised with these patients in mind (Safran and Segal 1990; Linehan 1993; Young 1999).

Cognitive therapists typically apply self-report inventories to assess symptoms and cognitive processes. Beck's inventories to assess depression (Beck et al. 1979a), hopelessness, (Beck et al. 1974), suicidal ideation (Beck et al. 1979b), and anxiety (Beck et al.1988) are used in the initial assessment and during the course of treatment. Other relevant questionaries include the Automatic Thoughts Questionnaire (Hollon and Kendall 1980), which measures the frequency of thoughts typical of depression, and the Dysfunctional Attitudes Scale (Weissman and Beck 1978), which focuses on dysfunctional beliefs.

As in many forms of psychotherapy, assessment and treatment are iterative processes. Indeed, given cognitive therapy's empirical nature, the patient is encouraged to participate actively in assessment and to collaborate in modifying procedures in the light of new circumstances. Assessment usually involves self-monitoring and is part of homework. The aim is to establish a coherent cognitive behavioural analysis of the patient's problems. In this respect the initial interview shares many features with behavioural interviewing (see chapter 8), by describing the problem in terms of its behavioural, cognitive, affective, and physiological components, as well as situational and maintaining factors (Kirk 1989). The emphasis on specific detail (e.g. What? Where? When? How often? With whom? How distressing? How disruptive?) typifies assessment, as does the focus on avoidant behaviour, coping style, and personal resources. The focus on conscious thoughts and images, and their role as symptomatic, precipitating, and maintaining factors in dysphoric mood and problem behaviour is especially pertinent during the initial assessment phase, but also typically continues throughout the therapeutic process.

Process

Cognitive therapy entails a set of techniques and a specific therapeutic relationship known as 'collaborative empiricism' (Beck et al. 1979). The therapist creates an atmosphere where resistance and competition between therapist and patient are reduced by a task-oriented alliance. The therapist blends empathy with an active and problem-oriented focus. The main tool used is 'Socratic questioning' (Beck et al. 1979a) in that it attempts to imitate a philosophical dialogue. Socrates often used questions rather than assertions to expose the illogical or inconsistent quality of a position. Patients are expected to develop a questioning and curious attitude towards their condition, which extends to expressing hypotheses about links between thoughts and feelings or other problematic behaviours, and testing these out. The therapist's stance is prescriptive in so far as she makes certain assumptions about the phenomena upon which to focus, and plays an active role in structuring sessions and setting homework. The role is not entirely directive since she looks to the patient to provide crucial information and to participate in gaining understanding.

Just as the therapist is expected to be active, so is the patient. He completes homework from the very first session in order to generalize skills acquired in therapy to situations in everyday life. Completion of the exercises is associated with better outcome, an effect not merely due to motivation or use of active coping strategies (Burns and Nolen-Hoeksema 1991).

A typical session begins with a review of homework, followed by the drawing up of an agenda. Only a limited number of issues can be covered during a single session. Many patients find it difficult to focus on a distinct issue without straying into other ostensibly relevant areas, but which may not facilitate resolution of the matter at hand. This is not surprising given that patients commonly experience their situation as a complex tangle of intertwined problems; this contributes to a perception of being 'stuck' and unable to change self-defeating behaviours. A cardinal technique is to inculcate the idea of dealing with one problem at a time, or even to divide the problem into sub-tasks. Accordingly, the therapist re-directs a patient back to the task at hand, while empathically confirming that any related aspects raised will be attended to at another time.

The therapist seeks to identify salient cognitive and behavioural dimensions of the problem. Specifically, she tries to evaluate the adaptiveness of the patient's idiosyncratic cognitive appraisal of events, and related emotional reactions. Once these are delineated, therapist and patient try to identify one or two automatic thoughts inherent in the emotional response. With these cognitions mapped out, strategies are deployed to evaluate their accuracy and adaptiveness, and to devise more realistic and useful alternatives. At the end of the session the therapist reviews material covered, seeks the patient's feedback, and sets homework.

Techniques relate to aims: to elicit and test automatic thoughts, provide rational alternatives, and identify and modify underlying dysfunctional schemata. Early on, when symptom reduction is the goal stressed, work focuses on automatic thoughts. It is helpful to work efficiently in order to achieve prompt symptomatic relief, especially in a state like depression where motivation is a key factor and the risk of suicide may loom. Therapy is thus more prescriptive, behaviourally-focused, and structured in early sessions.

Behavioural techniques (called thus because they emphasize overt behaviour, not because they fail to target cognitive mechanisms) include scheduling activities, graded task assignment, behavioural and cognitive rehearsal, and diversion techniques (Beck et al. 1979a). Exposure may also be used extensively, especially to overcome anxiety, and is described in chapter 8 (see page 167–196). Scheduling activities begins with recording what is done on an hourly basis. Activities are rated for both mastery (i.e. level of achievement for the patient to do an activity) and pleasure on 10-point scales. This is usually the first task, especially in the case of depression, since it helps both therapist and patient to observe links between activity and mood. It also helps to break down perceptions of being in a consistently dysphoric mood, whatever the circumstances. With these links established, activity scheduling is used to lift mood (or at least to alleviate the worst periods), as well as to enhance the sense of achievement.

Graded task assignments help patients to achieve difficult goals (e.g. challenging a superior at work) by breaking down the activity into achievable sub-tasks. These assignments are a good 'tonic' for those who try to achieve everything at once or, alternatively, for those who procrastinate. They also help those unwilling to accept limitations imposed by their clinical status (i.e. being severely depressed). Where poor concentration, low self-efficacy, or social skill deficits interfere with task completion, behavioural and cognitive rehearsal is conducted during the session or as homework to enhance the capacity to overcome these obstacles. Rehearsal is particularly effective to improve skills to manage anger and conflict. Diversion techniques such as physical activity, social contact and soothing imagery, such as imagining relaxing scenes or other pleasurable situations, are used to achieve temporary relief from dysphoric emotions.

Techniques are applied early to identify and test automatic thoughts. Their nature is first explained, including their role in maintaining unwanted emotional states and problem behaviours. One way to identify these thoughts is to ask patients what goes through their mind when they experience an unpleasant emotional state or face a difficult situation. Although some recall and report these phenomena readily, recollection may be biased by the *post hoc* nature of the task. Various strategies are deployed to examine the relationship between automatic thoughts and problematic behaviour and emotions as realistically as possible. For instance, a change in mood during the session is an ideal opportunity to inquire about accompanying thoughts, for example, a depressed patient who becomes upset while reflecting on a past rejection, or an anxious patient apprehensive about the consultation itself. Imaginal recall also helps to conjure up the full emotional context of a situation. The therapist works with the patient to paint as vivid a picture as possible, while the latter reports associated thoughts and feelings. Role-playing also provides vital cues to recall cognitive-emotional links.

The 'downward arrow' technique (Burns 1980) is used to explore the relationship between conscious cognitions and dysfunctional assumptions. The therapist repeatedly asks 'So what if that is true, what does that mean?' (with appropriate variation in phrasing) to the thoughts a patient associates with a dysphoric state. This is pertinent when automatic thoughts appear to be much less potent than the emotional response engendered by them. Insight into the link between a relatively innocuous automatic thought and a strong basic fear, such as of loneliness, failure, subordination, or being overwhelmed by one's own emotions, often ensues. The technique also enables hypothesis development about the schemata that underlie vulnerability.

Another strategy to assess negative automatic thoughts is self-monitoring, such as the daily record of dysfunctional thoughts (Beck et al. 1979a). Patients are required to record unpleasant emotions, the situation or thought that triggered them, and associated automatic thoughts. They do this during, or as close to, actual experiences as they are able in the hope that the quality of information gained will be optimal. The next step is to test the accuracy and adaptiveness of negative thoughts. Much time is devoted to this, and to developing rational alternatives. Socratic questioning models for the patient questions to be asked of any thought related to problematic emotions and behaviour. These questions are: (1) What is the evidence to support the thought? (2) Are there any alternative interpretations? (3) Am I totally to blame for this negative event, and can I do anything about it? and (4) What if my interpretation is true? How will I manage then? (Thase and Beck 1993). These questions aim to establish to what degree particular thoughts are biased or exaggerated, and if they do reflect a real difficulty or skill deficit, how the patient can best cope with a 'worst case scenario'.

The final step in dealing with negative automatic thoughts is to develop rational alternatives. The therapist leads a problem-solving exercise to test current thoughts and alternatives by posing the above questions. The daily record of dysfunctional thoughts is used extensively at this point, first during, and then between, sessions, at times of distress. The record asks the patient to consider realistic alternatives to specific negative automatic thoughts, and to re-rate their emotional state and level of belief in the original thoughts. The therapist guides this process initially in the anticipation that the patient will eventually apply the procedure in the 'heat of the moment'. When facing an emotionally demanding situation she first records her thoughts *in vivo*, and then collaboratively works on developing alternatives during a session. A phase follows in which the patient is encouraged to become more independent at this task until she is able to apply it during the most difficult episodes between sessions.

Evolution of realistic cognitions may prompt further negative automatic thoughts which, ironically, make it seem that realistic thoughts cause further distress. For instance, a patient responding to the thought 'Because a person only spoke to me briefly, he must be angry with me' with a realistic response 'If he were really angry with me he probably would have expressed it more obviously' may be reminded of previous occasions when people expressed anger towards him, and of his perceived inability to cope with this experience. These second-order automatic thoughts are dealt with directly to ensure they do not hinder therapy. With progress the patient is encouraged to 'internalize' these new skills by relying less on 'external' techniques, such as the daily record of dysfunctional thoughts, and more on internal self-monitoring using introspection.

During therapy, consistent themes in the negative automatic thoughts that a patient experiences in a number of circumstances usually emerge. These indicate underlying dysfunctional assumptions. All the aforementioned procedures are relevant to detect them. Autobiographical techniques are applied to examine the evolution of these assumptions (Beck et al. 1979). This process may begin in the first few sessions or at a later point after a measure of symptomatic control has been achieved. Techniques to bring about change in basic attitudes resemble those used with automatic thoughts in that they involve logical, philosophical, and empirical examination. However, the process is slower, entailing more exploration and reflection than modifying thoughts.

Conducting 'behavioural experiments' in which a patient acts in accordance with an alternative to a customary dysfunctional assumption provides crucial experiential evidence that she need not be bound by these maladaptive beliefs. For instance, in a patient living by the rule 'If I disagree with someone, even in the smallest way, she will reject me', an experiment in which she voices polite disagreement with others in order to find that this is not necessarily followed by rejection, may provide compelling evidence for an alternative viewpoint.

Termination

Cognitive therapy was conceived of as short term and time limited. Explicit goals and timetables for achieving them are therefore set. Termination is usually not as complex as for more open-ended treatments, but is still addressed by emphasizing that indefinite treatment is unnecessary. Indeed, the therapist's objective is to impart knowledge and techniques in order that the patient may apply gains to problems in the future and to those not fully addressed during the current treatment. Dependence on the therapist is discouraged and patients are expected to become more self-reliant as therapy proceeds.

Poorly handled termination is problematic and interferes with the capacity to maintain the process of change. As the ending approaches, patients may express concern about relapse or the capacity to apply cognitive techniques without support (e.g. 'I'll forget what I've learned' or 'I won't be able to discipline myself when therapy ends'). These concerns are approached similarly to other negative thoughts in therapy. It is helpful to emphasize a patient's consistent use of treatment by recalling achievements. Role-plays in which the therapist presents worst-case scenarios, with accompanying negative thoughts and interpretations, and the patient plays the therapist's role by guiding the problem-solving process and proposing more realistic alternatives help in the termination phase. A commonly utilized option is to offer a 'booster session' to review progress, usually a month or so after the final meeting.

Problems encountered during therapy

Problems encountered are either therapist- or patient-based, although a blend of the two is most common. The chief caveat is to not to lose sight of the uniqueness of the patient while working energetically on her problems and applying techniques to deal with them. The risk is that the patient's resources and assets may be overlooked, and not harnessed to good purpose.

In the face of what can be intense hopelessness in the patient's interpretation of a situation, the therapist maintains optimism and a positive solution-oriented focus. This can be demanding when hopeless scenarios are presented that are ostensibly convincing. At these times the therapist re-emphasizes core problem-solving principles and/or deploys new tactics. Many patients may appear to reject the therapist's encouragement but report later that this was pivotal in stemming the tide of hopelessness and pessimism. To this end, the therapist learns to deal with her own negative thoughts, particularly regarding tardy progress or ingratitude. Thoughts like 'If all my patients do not get better I must be an incompetent therapist' or 'After all my efforts this patient should be more thankful' exemplify dysfunctional interpretations. Recognition of these thoughts helps to reduce frustration, and facilitates optimism and an empathic, action-oriented attitude. Patients may harbour counter-therapeutic beliefs, ranging from 'Maybe I want to be depressed' to 'I am too disorganized to do homework tasks' (Beck et al. 1979). Since these beliefs can impede progress if left unchecked, they require attention, using the same techniques described earlier.

Short-term forms of cognitive therapy may not suit all patients, for instance, those with personality disorder (Young 1999). Assumptions that need to be examined include the following: (1) patients can access feelings, thoughts, and images with minimal training, (2) identifiable problems exist upon which to focus, (3) patients are motivated to complete homework and learn self-control strategies, (4) they engage collaboratively after a few sessions, (5) any difficulties in the therapeutic relationship are not critical, and (6) all cognitions can be altered through empirical analysis, logical discourse, and graded practice. Young (1999) proposes specific modifications to treat personality disorder as part of his 'Schema Focused Cognitive Therapy'. This resembles aspects of psychodynamic therapy and entails more challenging of the patient regarding cognitive and behavioural avoidance of emotion and makes more explicit use of the therapeutic relationship through examination of transference. Treatment is typically longer in order to overcome resistance and examine developmentally early origins of beliefs. Even these initiatives may not help certain patients who may be better served by another approach altogether. The cognitive therapist needs to recognize her limits and refer patients when necessary.

Developments in cognitive therapy

Understanding how it works

Given that cognitive therapy has been repeatedly demonstrated to be beneficial in many clinical situations, research has increasingly focused on whether change is mediated by the specific cognitive processes targeted by the therapy. This is not a trivial matter. If cognitive change is not required for improvement, the emphasis should shift to aspects that do promote change. A paradigm to evaluate these issues compares depressed people treated successfully with cognitive therapy to those treated successfully with an approach that does not target cognitive change, for example, antidepressants. For example, DeRubeis et al. (1990) found that cognitive change mediated improvement in the cognitive therapy group, but not those on medication. Segal and colleagues (1999) have found that people who had been effectively helped with cognitive therapy show less negative thinking during a mood challenge (i.e. a mild depressed mood induced by sad music and autobiographical recall) than patients successfully treated with medication. Furthermore, the level of negative thinking in response to the mood challenge is related to the likelihood of relapse, suggesting that change may reflect specific effects of cognitive therapy and also operate to prevent relapse.

In a neuroimaging study of depressed patients before and after cognitive-behavioural treatment, Goldapple and colleagues (2004) found that although this therapeutic approach and antidepressants both affected certain limbic and cortical regions in the brain, the psychotherapy alone had an effect on the frontal cortex, anterior cingulate, and hippocampus. This suggests that cognitive behaviour may have unique biological and psychological mechanisms of action.

Knowledge about mechanisms of change in cognitive therapy has also come from intensive study of the therapeutic processes. For example, Tang and De Rubeis (1999a) observed that many patients experience, between sessions, reductions in symptoms at highly specific point in treatment. Cognitive change is more likely to occur in sessions preceding 'sudden gains' (i.e. rapid between-session symptomatic improvement), supporting the notion that cognitive change is the crucial mediator of improvement. Despite these results notable caveats remain. For instance, Ilardi and Craighead (1994) observed that most of the improvement occurs in the first 4 weeks, and questioned whether cognitive techniques could have been adequately applied in such a brief period. Despite a challenge to this interpretation (Tang and De Rubeis 1999b), the dilemma remains unresolved. Perhaps the most parsimonious explanation for the varied findings is that while cognitive change is a key factor in outcome, non-specific mechanisms also have a positive effect.

A third wave? Incorporating new concepts into cognitive therapy

Attempts to apply cognitive therapy to a broader range of problems, together with questions raised by studies of change mechanisms, have resulted in major alterations to both theory and practice. Apart from Young's (1999) approach to personality disorder mentioned earlier, attention has been devoted to interpersonal processes (Safran and Segal 1990), the role of emotion (Greenberg and Safran 1987) and 'core' versus 'peripheral' schemata (Guidano and Liotti 1983). Core schemata include a person's sense of reality, identity, value, and control and may be more basic, and therefore more resistant to change, than schemata peripheral to these issues. For example, a person's sense of self-worth (value) is likely to be more 'core' than their beliefs about a specific circumstance, such as their relationship with their boss. However, if change is achieved in these core schemata, the change is expected to be more profound. Clearly such concepts are vital if cognitive therapy is to be used for the personality disorders.

A notable development is Linehan's (1993) Dialectical Behaviour Therapy for borderline patients. This combines training in 'mindfulness' (a Buddhist term to describe non-judgemental awareness of one's own moment-to-moment experience), interpersonal effectiveness, emotional regulation, and tolerance of distress, with exposure to disturbing memories, and training in self-validation (i.e. the ability to experience one's own thoughts, feelings, and actions as understandable within the context of one's life). Applied both individually and in group settings, it is effective for parasuicidal women who satisfy criteria for borderline personality disorder (Linehan et al. 1991).

Another set of problems that have led to innovation are those associated with prevention. For example, depression is often worse over the course of repeated episodes in terms of severity, frequency needing lesser precipitants, and lack of response to previously effective treatments (Post et al. 1996; Kendler et al. 2000). A major limitation of typical cognitive therapy in this group is that phenomena addressed by standard techniques remit with other symptoms when depression remits (Eaves and Rush 1984; Simons et al. 1984; Persons and Rao 1985). An intervention designed to prevent relapse in recovered patients is Mindfulness-Based Cognitive Therapy (MBCT; Segal et al. 2002). The core skill taught is—at times of potential relapse—to disengage mentally from states typified by self-perpetuating patterns of ruminative, negative automatic thoughts. MBCT trains the patient to observe her own mind non-judgementally and to become aware of constantly repeated thoughts, themes, and images and her reactions to these mental events. Teasdale et al. (2000) and Ma and Teasdale (2004) have evaluated the effect of an 8-week MBCT program on recurrently, but recovered, depressed people and found significantly reduced relapse rates for patients who had three or more previous episodes.

Dialectical Behaviour Therapy, MBCT, and related approaches are examples of a 'third wave' of cognitive-based treatments (Hayes, 2002) the first being behaviour therapy, the second cognitive-behaviour therapy. These new approaches share the goal of promoting awareness of inner experience through techniques that promote self-observation. There is also a deliberate focus on techniques promoting acceptance rather than change. Thus, the capacity to 'think about one's thinking' is emphasized (Wells 1994). This is often observed during therapy and is exemplified by shifts from 'I am a loser' to 'Today I am feeling quite sad and I notice I am saying to myself "I am a loser"'. In other words, even negative thoughts can be neutralized when they are experienced as temporary and erroneous rather than as unquestioned truths. Most importantly, these new approaches rely on empirical evaluation of outcomes (as has always been central to the cognitive therapy tradition, Hayes et al. 2004b).

Training

Despite the highly structured nature of cognitive therapy, its practitioners need to cultivate non-specific skills, such as genuineness and the capacity for empathy and understanding (Mahoney 1991). A synergistic effect of core clinical skills and specific cognitive interventions is likely (Persons and Burns 1985). The therapist must also understand the cognitive model of psychopathology, its specific applications to different disorders and the full range of techniques.

Cognitive therapy has been clearly operationalized as a series of guidelines. Beck's manuals shine as coherent and comprehensive (Beck et al. 1979a, 1985, 1990, 1993; Wright et al. 1993). Other useful guides are those of Hawton et al. (1989) and Barlow (2001).

The most effective route to competence is combining reading, observation of experienced therapists, and, above all, supervised clinical practice. The latter includes training experiences in delivering therapy in both individual and group settings. Although personal therapy is not usually required, many programs incorporate exercises applying cognitive behavioural techniques to trainees' own difficulties. Specialized centres exist in many countries to provide these programs; indeed, training in cognitive therapy is a common component of educational programs in clinical psychology, psychiatry, and social work.

Conclusion

Cognitive therapy, a brief empirically based treatment, emphasizes collaborative problem solving by focusing on how cognitive processes maintain emotional distress and self-defeating behaviours. It embodies clear guidelines and has been studied extensively. It maintains a dialogue with basic sciences—social and cognitive psychology, artificial intelligence, and neuroscience. Cognitive therapy seeks to extend its area of operation, altering techniques where appropriate to suit new clinical groups. The model has played a leading role in the psychotherapy integration movement. According to Beck (1991), cognitive therapy is integrative since cognitive change underlies all effective treatment. As the approach has evolved, it has assimilated concepts and methods from several sources in an effort to assist people with a broad range of problems. Whether this expansion turns out to be a form of *hubris or* a genuine leap forward is best left to history to judge. The capacity of cognitive therapy to maintain its emphasis on integration with process and outcome research, and basic sciences relevant to human behaviour, will, in large measure, determine its fate.

References

Arieti, S. (1980). Cognition in psychoanalysis. *Journal of the American Academy of Psychoanalysis*, **8**, 3–23.

Bandura, A. (1977). Self efficacy: Toward a unifying theory of behaviour change. *Psychological Review*, **84**, 191–215.

Barlow, D. H. (2001). *Clinical handbook of psychological disorders* (3rd ed). Guilford, New York.

Beck, A. T. (1967). *Depression: Clinical, experimental and theoretical aspects*. Harper and Row, New York.

Beck, A. T. (1991). Cognitive therapy as *the* integrative psychotherapy. *Journal of Psychotherapy Integration*, **3**, 191–198.

Beck, A. T., Weissman, A., Lester, D., and Trexler (1974). The measurement of pessimism: The Hopelessness Scale. *Journal of Consulting and Clinical Psychology*, **42**, 861–865.

Beck, A. T., Rush, A. J., Shaw, B. F. and Emery, G. (1979a). *Cognitive therapy of depression*. Wiley, New York.

Beck, A. T., Kovacs, M., and Weissman, A. (1979b). Assessment of suicidal intention: The Scale for Suicidal Ideation. *Journal of Consulting and Clinical Psychology*, **47**, 343–352.

Beck, A. T., Epstein, N. and Harrison, R. (1983). Cognitions, attitudes and personality dimensions in depression. *British Journal of Cognitive Psychotherapy*, **1**, 1–16.

Beck, A. T., Emery, G., and Greenberg, R. L. (1985). *Anxiety disorders and phobias: A cognitive perspective*. Basic Books, New York.

Beck, A.T., Epstein, N., Brown, G., and Steer, R. A. (1988). An inventory for measuring clinical anxiety: Psychometric properties. *Journal of Consulting and Clinical Psychology*, **56**, 893–897.

Beck, A. T., Freeman, A. and Associates. (1990). *Cognitive therapy of personality disorders*. Guilford, New York.

Beck, A. T., Wright, F. D., Newman, C. F., and Liese, B. S. (1993). *Cognitive therapy of drug abuse*. Guilford, New York.

Bloch, S. (2004). A pioneer in psychotherapy research: Aaron Beck. *Australian and New Zealand Journal of Psychiatry*, **38**, 855–867.

Burns, D. D. (1980). *Feeling good: The new mood therapy*. Morrow, New York.

Burns, D. D. and Nolen-Hoeksema, S. (1991). Coping styles, homework compliance, and the effectiveness of cognitive behavioural therapy. *Journal of Consulting and Clinical Psychology*, **59**, 305–311.

Chambless, D. L., et al. (1998). Update on empirically validated therapies, II. *The Clinical Psychologist*, **51**, 3–16.

Chomsky, N. (1959). [Review of B. F. Skinner's *Verbal behaviour*]. *Language*, **35**, 26–58.

Clark, D. A. and Beck, A. T. (1989). Cognitive theory and therapy of anxiety and depression. In *Anxiety and depression: Distinctive and overlapping features* (eds P. C. Kendall and D. Watson). Academic Press, San Deigo.

Crossman, E. R. F. W. (1953). Entropy and choice time: The effect of frequency unbalance on choice responses. *Quarterly Journal of Experimental Psychology*, **5**, 41–51.

DeRubeis, R. J., Gelfand, L. A., Tang, T. Z., and Simons, A. D. (1999). Medications versus cognitive behaviour therapy for severely depressed outpatients: Mega-analysis of four randomized comparisons. *American Journal of Psychiatry*, **156**, 1007–1013.

DeRubeis, R., Hollon, S., Grove, W., Evans, M., Garvey, M., and Tuason, V. (1990). How does cogntive therapy work? Cognitive change and symptom change in cognitive therapy and pharmacotherapy for depression. *Journal of Consulting and Clinical Psychology*, **58**, 862–869.

Dobson, K. S. (1989). A meta-analysis of the efficacy of cognitive therapy for depression. *Journal of Consulting and Clinical Psychology*, **57**, 414–419.

Dobson, K. S. and Block, L. (1988). Historical and philosophical bases of the cognitive behaviour therapies. In *Handbook of cognitive-behavioural therapies* (ed K. S. Dobson) Hutchinson, London.

Dobson, K. S. and Craig K. D. (1998). *Empirically supported therapies: Best practice in professional psychology*. Sage, Thousand Oaks, CA.

D'Zurilla, T. J. and Goldfried, M. R. (1971). Problem solving and behaviour modification. *Journal of Abnormal Psychology*, **78**, 107–126.

Eaves, G. and Rush, A. (1984). Cognitive patterns in symptomatic and remitted unipolar major depression. *Journal of Abnormal Psychology*, **93**, 31–40.

Elkin, I., Shea, T., Watkins, J. T., Imber, S. D., Sotsky, S. M. Collins, J. F., et al.(1989). National Institute of Mental Health treatment of depression collaborative research program:1. General effectiveness of treatments. *Archives of General Psychiatry*, **46**, 971–982.

Ellis, A. (1962). *Reason and emotion in psychotherapy*. Citadel, Secaucus NJ.

Ellis, A. (1970). *The essence of rational psychotherapy: A comprehensive approach to treatment*. Institute for Rational Living, New York.

Eysenck, H. J. (1969). *The effects of psychotherapy*. Science House, New York.

Fennell, M. J. V. and Teasdale, J. D. (1987). Cognitive therapy for depression: Individual differences and the process of change. *Cognitive Therapy and Research*, **11**, 253–271.

Frankl, V. (1985). Cognition and logotherapy. In *Cognition and psychotherapy* (eds M.Mahoney and A. Freeman). Plenum, New York.

Gardner, H. (1985). *The mind's new science: A history of the cognitive revolution*. Basic Books, New York.

Goldapple, K., Segal, Z., and Garson, C. et al. (2004). Modulation of cortical-limbic pathways in major depression: treatment-specific effects of cognitive behavior therapy. *Archives of General Psychiatry*, **61**, 34–41.

Greenburg, L. S. and Safran, J. D. (1987). *Emotion in psychotherapy*. Guilford , New York.

Guidano, V. F. and Liotti, G. (1983). *Cognitive processes and emotional disorders*. Guilford, New York.

Hawton, K., Salkovskis, P. M., Kirk, J., and Clark, D. M. (1989). *Cognitive behaviour therapy for psychiatric problems: A practical guide*. Oxford University Press, Oxford.

Hayes, S. (2002). Acceptance, mindfulness and science. *Clinical Psychology: Science and Practice*, **9**, 101–106.

Hayes, S., Follette, V., and Linehan, M. (2004a). *Mindfulness and acceptance: Expanding the cognitive behavioural tradition*. Guilford, New York.

Hayes, S., Masuda, A., Bissett, R., Luoma, J., and Guerrero, L., (2004b). DBT, FAR and ACT: How empirically oriented are the new behavior therapy technologies? *Behavior Therapy*, **35**, 35–54.

Hollon, S. D. and Kendall, P. C. (1980). Cognitive self statements in depression: Development of an Automatic Thoughts Questionnaire. *Cognitive Therapy and Research*, **4**, 383–395.

Hollon, S. D., DeRubis, R. J., Evans, M. D., Wiemer, M. J., Garvey, M. J., Grove, W. M., et al. (1992a). Cognitive therapy and pharmacotherapy for depression: Singly and in combination. *Archives of General Psychiatry*, **49**, 774–781.

Hollon, S., DeRubeis, R., and Seligman, M. (1992b). Cognitive therapy and the prevention of depression. *Applied and Preventive Psychology*, **1**, 89–95.

Hollon, S. D., Thase, M. E., and Markowitz, J. C. (2002). Treatment and prevention of depression. *Psychological Science in the Public Interest*, **3**, 39–77.

Homme, L. E. (1965). Perspectives in psychology:XXIV. Control of coverants, the operants of the mind. *Psychological Reports*, **15**, 501–511.

Ilardi, S. S. and Craighead, W. E. (1994). The role of non-specific factors in cognitive behaviour therapy for depression. *Clinical Psychology: Science and Practice*, **1**, 138–156.

Keller, M. B., McCullough, J. P., and Klein, D. N. et al. (2000). A comparison of nefazodone, the cognitive behavioral-analysis system of psychotherapy, and their combination for the treatment of chronic depression. *New England Journal of Medicine*, **342**, 1462–1470.

Kelly, G. A. (1955). *The psychology of personal constructs*. Norton, New York.

Kendler, K., Thornton, L., and Gardner, C. (2000). Stressful life events and previous episodes in the etiology of major depression in women: an evaluation of the 'kindling' hypothesis. *American Journal of Psychiatry*, **157**, 1243–1251.

Kirk, J. (1989). Cognitive-behavioural assessment. In *Cognitive behaviour therapy for psychiatric problems: A practical guide* (eds K. Hawton, P. Salkovskis, J.Kirk, and D. Clark). Oxford University Press, Oxford.

Landon, T. M. and Barlow, D. H. (2004). Cognitive behavioural treatment for panic disorder: Current status. *Journal of Psychiatric Practice*, **10**, 211–26.

Lang, A. J. (2004). Treating generalised anxiety disorder with cognitive behaviour therapy. *Journal of Clinical Psychiatry*, **65**, supplement, **13**, 14–19.

Lazarus, R. S. (1982). Thoughts on the relations between emotion and cognition. *American Psychologist*, **37**, 1019–1024.

Linehan, M. M. (1993). *Cognitive-behavioural treatment of borderline personality disorder.* Guilford, New York.

Linehan, M. M., Armstrong, H. E., Suarez, A., Allman, D., and Heard, H. L. (1991). Cognitive-behavioural treatment of chronically parasuicidal borderline patients. *Archives of General Psychiatry*, **48**, 1060–1064.

Ma, S. H. and Teasdale, J. D. (2004). Mindfulness-Based Cognitive Therapy for Depression: Replication and exploration of differential relapse prevention effects. *Journal of Consulting and Clinical Psychology*, **72**, 31–40.

MacLeod, C. (1993). Cognition in clinical psychology: Measures, methods or models? *Behaviour Change*, **10**, 169–195.

Mahoney, M. J. (1991). *Human change processes.* Basic Books, New York.

McKnight, D. L., Nelson-Grey, R. O., and Bernhill, J. (1992). Dexamethasone suppression test and response to cognitive therapy and antidepressant medication. *Behaviour Therapy*, **23**, 99–111.

McLean, P. and Taylor, S. (1992). Severity of unipolar depression and choice of treatment. *Behaviour Research and Therapy*, **30**, 443–451.

Meichenbaum, D. H. (1977). *Cognitive behaviour modification.* Plenum, New York.

Mischel, W., Ebbesen, E. B., and Zeiss, A. (1972). Cognitive and attentional mechanisms in delay of gratification. *Journal of Personality and Social Psychology*, **21**, 204–218.

Morrison, A., Renton, J. Dunn, H., Williams, S. and Bentall, R. (2004). *Cognitive Behaviour Therapy for psychosis: A formulation based approach.* Routledge, London.

Neimeyer, R. A. (1993). An appraisal of constructivist psychotherapies. *Journal of Consulting and Clinical Psychology*, **61**, 221–234.

Neisser, U. (1967). *Cognitive psychology.* Appleton-Century-Crofts, New York.

Persons, J. B., and Burns, D. D. (1985). Mechanisms of action of cognitive therapy: The relative contributions of technical and interpersonal interventions. *Cognitive Therapy and Research*, **9**, 539–551.

Persons, J. B. and Rao, P. (1985). Longitudinal study of cognitions, life events, and depression in psychiatric inpatients. *Journal of Abnormal Psychology*, **94**, 51–63.

Persons, J. B., Burns, D. D., and Perloff, J. M. (1988). Predictors of drop out and outcome in cognitive therapy for depression in a private practice setting. *Cognitive Therapy and Research*, **12**, 557–575.

Piaget, J. (1954). *The construction of reality in the child.* Basic Books, New York.

Post, R. M., Weiss, S., Leverich, G. S., and George, M. S. (1996). Developmental psychobiology of cyclic affective illness: Implications for early therapeutic intervention. *Development and Psychopathology*, **8**, 273–305.

Rachman, S. J. and Wilson, G. T. (1980). *The effects of psychological therapy*, (2nd edn). Pergamon, Oxford.

Rehm, L. (1977). A self control model of depression. *Behaviour Therapy*, **8**, 787–804.

Rendon, M. (1985). Cognition and psychoanalysis: A Horneyan perspective. In *Cognition and Psychotherapy* (eds M.Mahoney and A. Freeman). Plenum, New York.

Ricca, V., Mannucci, E., Zucchi, T., Rotella, C. M., and Faravelli, C. (2000). Cognitive-behavioural therapy for bulimia nervosa and binge eating disorder. A review. *Psychotherapy and Psychosomatics*, **69**, 287–295.

Robins, C. J. and Hayes, A. M. (1993). An appraisal of cognitive therapy. *Journal of Consulting and Clinical Psychology*, **61**, 205–214.

Ross, A. (1991). Growth without progress. *Contemporary Psychology*, **36**, 743–744.

Safran, J. D. and Segal, Z. V. (1990). *Interpersonal process in cognitive therapy*. Basic Books, New York.

Safran, J. D., Segal, Z. V., Vallis, T. M., Shaw, B. F., and Samstag, L. W. (1993). Assessing patient suitability for short-term cognitive therapy with an interpersonal focus. *Cognitive Therapy and Research*, **17**, 23–38.

Schulman, B. H. (1985). Cognitive therapy and the individual psychology of Alfred Adler. In *Cognition and Psychotherapy* (eds M.Mahoney and A. Freeman). Plenum, New York.

Segal, Z. V., Gemar, M., and Williams, S. (1999). Differential cognitive response to a mood induction following successful cognitive therapy and pharmacotherapy for depression. *Journal of Abnormal Psychology*, **108**, 3–10.

Segal, Z., Williams, J. M. G., and Teasdale, J. (2002). *Mindfulness-Based Cognitive Therapy for depression. A new approach to preventing relapse*. Guilford, London.

Simons, A. D, Garfield, S. and Murphy, G. (1984). The process of change in cognitive therapy and pharmacotherapy for depression. *Archives of General Psychiatry*, **41**, 45–51.

Simons, A. D. and Thase, M. E. (1992). Biological markers, treatment outcome, and one year follow up in endogenous depression: Electroencephalographic sleep studies and response to cognitive therapy. *Journal of Consulting and Clinical Psychology*, **60**, 392–401.

Treatment of Adolescents with Depression Study (TADS) Team. (2004). Fluoxetine, cognitive behaviour therapy, and their combination for adolescents with depression. *Journal of the American Medical Association*, **292**, 807–820.

Tang, T. and DeRubeis, R. (1999a). Sudden gains and critical sessions in cognitive-behavioral therapy for depression. *Journal of Consulting and Clinical Psychology*, **67**, 894–904.

Tang, T. and DeRubeis, R. (1999b). Reconsidering rapid early response in cognitive behavioral therapy for depression. *Clinical Psychology: Science and Practice*, **6**, 283–288.

Teasdale, J. D. (1993). Emotion and two kinds of meaning: cognitive therapy and applied cognitive science. *Behaviour Research and Therapy*, **31**, 339–354.

Teasdale, J. D., Segal, Z. V., Williams, J. M. G., Ridgeway, V. A., Soulsby, J. M., and Lau, M. A. (2000). Prevention of relapse/recurrence in major depression by Mindfulness-Based Cognitive Therapy. *Journal of Consulting and Clinical Psychology*, **68**, 615–623.

Thase, M. E. and Beck, A. T. (1993). An overview of cognitive therapy. In *Cognitive therapy with inpatients: Developing a cognitive milieu*. (eds J. H. Wright, M. E. Thase, A. T. Beck, and J. W. Ludgate). Guilford, New York.

Thase, M. E., Bowler, K., and Harden, T. (1991a). Cognitive behaviour of endogenous depression: Part 2: Preliminary findings in 16 unmedicated inpatients. *Behaviour Therapy*, **22**, 469–478.

Thase, M. E., Simons, A. D., Cahalane, J., and McGreary, J. (1991b). Cognitive behaviour therapy of endogenous depression: Part 1: An outpatient clinical replication series. *Behaviour Therapy*, **22**, 457–468.

Thase, M. E., Simons, A. D., Cahalane, J., McGreary, J., and Harden, T. (1991c). Severity of depression and response to cognitive behaviour therapy. *American Journal of Psychiatry*, **148**, 784–789.

Thase, M. E., Greenhouse, J. B., and Frank, E. et al. (1997). Treatment of major depression with psychotherapy or psychotherapy-pharmacotherapy combinations. *Archives of General Psychiatry*, **54**, 1009–1015.

Vygotsky, L. S. (1962) *Thought and language*. MIT Press, Cambridge, MA.

Weissman, A. N. and Beck, A. T. (1978). *Development and validation of the Dysfunctional Attitude Scale: A preliminary investigation*. Paper presented at the annual meeting of the American Psychological Association, Toronto, Canada.

Wells, A. (1994). Attention and the control of worry. In *Worrying: Perspectives of theory, assessment, and treatment*. (eds G. Davey and F. Tallis) (pp. 91–114). Wiley, Oxford.

Wright, J. H., Thase, M. E., Beck, A. T., and Ludgate, J. W. (1993). *Cognitive therapy with inpatients: Developing a cognitive milieu*. Guilford Press, New York.

Young, J. E. (1999). *Cognitive therapy for personality disorders: A schema focused approach* (3rd edn). Professional Resource Exchange, Sarasota FL.

Zajonc, R. (1980). Feeling and thinking: Preferences need no inferences. *American Psychologist*, **35**, 151–175.

Recommended reading

Barlow, D. H. (2001). *Clinical handbook of psychological disorders* (3rd edn.). Guilford, New York. (The third edition of this manual, with chapters on major applications of cognitive-behavioural therapy, remains indispensable; its content is up to date, and the chapters written by experts in their field.)

Beck, A. T., Emery, G., and Greenberg, R. L. (1985). *Anxiety disorders and phobias: A cognitive perspective*. Basic Books, New York. (This manual represents innovations in technique, such as the imagery-based interventions, as well as a sophisticated cognitive theory.)

Beck, A. T., Rush, A. J., Shaw, B. F., and Emery, G. (1979). *Cognitive therapy of depression*. Wiley, New York. (This is a classic 'how to do it' manual; clear and comprehensive, it offers a detailed account of cognitive therapy process.)

Brewin, C. R. (1988). *Cognitive foundations of clinical psychology*. Erlbaum, Hove. (A clear introduction to the relationship between psychological research and cognitive models of psychopathology.)

Guidano, V. F. and Liotti, G. (1983). *Cognitive processes and emotional disorders*. Guilford, New York. (An early account of a constructivist approach to cognitive therapy; notable for its integration of attachment theory principles.)

Hawton, K., Salkovskis, P. M., Kirk, J., and Clark, D. M. (1989). *Cognitive Behaviour Therapy for psychiatric problems: A practical guide*. Oxford University Press, Oxford. (An excellent book with chapters on treatment of a range of psychiatric conditions, including marital problems, and chronic psychiatric handicaps, as well as the usual fare.)

Linehan, M. M. (1993). *Cognitive-behavioural treatment of borderline personality disorder*. Guilford, New York. (Linehan's innovative work, described here in detail, represents an exciting development of cognitive therapy.)

Morrison, A., Renton, J. Dunn, H., Williams, S., and Bentall, R. (2004). *Cognitive Behaviour Therapy for psychosis: A formulation based approach*. Routledge, London. (Includes a description of a sophisticated cognitive model of psychosis and of cognitive therapy for psychotic symptoms.)

Segal, Z., Williams, J. M. G., and Teasdale, J. (2002). *Mindfulness-Based Cognitive Therapy for depression. A new approach to preventing relapse*. Guilford, London. (The integration of mindfulness principles with cognitive therapy is clearly described: this is part treatment manual, part diary of the personal and scientific issues in developing an innovative approach.)

Wright, J. H., Thase, M. E., Beck, A. T., and Ludgate, J. W. (1993). *Cognitive therapy with inpatients: Developing a cognitive milieu*. Guilford, New York. (This manual aimed at integrating cognitive therapy into the inpatient setting is of great value to those working with more severe disorders.)

Young, J. E. (1999). *Cognitive therapy for personality disorders: A schema-focused approach* (3rd edn). Professional Resource Exchange, Sarasota FL. (This volume is one of the best accounts of the adjustments required to standard cognitive techniques when working with patients with long-standing personality difficulties.)

Chapter 8

Behavioural psychotherapy

Lynne M. Drummond and Brett Kennedy

Behavioural psychotherapy is surprisingly difficult to define. Whereas it has been referred to as a group of treatments based on the application of learning theory, this is only partly correct. Many behavioural treatments have been discovered and refined by trial and error, and by clinicians examining what is beneficial. In many cases, learning theory has been modified to incorporate clinical findings.

It has been suggested that behavioural psychotherapy is merely the application of common sense. This again is only partially so. Whereas exposure can be seen as a variant of common sense, that if a person has a car accident they should soon drive again, the relevance of duration and other factors involved in exposure are not commonly appreciated. Similarly, some treatments appear to be contrary to a common sense view.

A brief definition of behavioural psychotherapy is as follows: it is a collection of treatments whose central thesis is that psychological distress results from learned behaviour and that this behaviour can be unlearned (Stern and Drummond 1991). This definition covers most behavioural treatments. However, behavioural psychotherapists do not ignore possible genetic, structural, and biochemical factors in the development of psychiatric syndromes. A good behavioural clinician considers the whole patient and his or her environment in a behavioural formulation and then tries to identify potential targets for change.

The mainstay of much behavioural therapy is exposure. Other frequently used treatments are self-imposed response prevention; sexual skills exercises; modeling; stimulus control techniques; role-play and rehearsal; contingency management and reinforcement schedules, and covert sensitization. Educating the patient about their condition and the rationale for treatment is a first step in treatment. Most programmes require the patient to complete homework tasks.

An historical context

Research on behavioural psychotherapy has developed from several strands. For example, the work of Masters and Johnson (1966, 1970) generated effective treatments of sexual dysfunction. The techniques used are similar to other behavioural treatments but were devised in parallel to developments in treating other anxiety disorders. For simplicity, this section will concentrate on the historical development of behavioural treatment for phobic and obsessive-compulsive disorder.

An early example of what appears to be exposure treatment for phobic disorder is mentioned by Freud (1919). In 1909, he described the treatment of a boy with a fear of horses using the exposure technique of encouraging him to gradually approach the feared object. Similarly, the French psychologist, Pierre Janet (1903), described exposure treatment in a patient with obsessive-compulsive disorder.

The concept of behaviourism and viewing behaviour as the result of learned experience became popular at the beginning of the twentieth century. This movement adopted a philosophical framework that all experience could be explained by behavioural theory. This is, of course, simplistic; any theory is only a model and can never represent absolute truth. Some early views about children being born *tabula rasa* whose personality is totally determined by learned experience appear excessively naive today. However, interesting experiments were performed to demonstrate a model for the development of phobias.

In their famous case of Albert, Watson and Rayner (1920) revealed that an 11-month-old child with a positive interest in furry animals developed a fear of rats after a steel bar was struck making a loud noise whenever he put out his hand towards a white rat. This case was not replicated, however, and the theory of a direct relationship between genesis of phobias and classical conditioning was modified; other researchers commented on individual differences in the susceptibility to aversive stimuli (e.g. Pavlov 1927). Later, Eysenck (1957) suggested that people who condition easily are more likely to develop phobias. Other researchers emphasized that the intensity and level of reinforcement following any action also had an effect on the degree of conditioning which occurred (Spence et al. 1958).

In the initial development of behavioural treatment for phobias, Mowrer's (1950) notion of fear acquisition was accepted as a model, that is, classically conditioned fear lead to avoidance behaviour; a reduction of fear and avoidance behaviour was reinforced by lowered anxiety levels.

Several investigators challenged this model. First, it was found that many patients could not recall a traumatic experience relating to the onset of their phobia (Buglass et al. 1977; Goldstein and Chambless 1978). Second, several workers failed to replicate Watson and Rayner's (1920) findings (English 1929; Thorndike 1935). Third, it did not appear compatible with the gradual onset of phobias often seen clinically (Emmelkamp 1985). Finally, it did not explain stereotyped patterns of fear-provoking objects and situations. In a series of laboratory-based experiments with adult volunteers, Ohman and his colleagues (1984) demonstrated that human beings are more likely to be aversively conditioned to phylogenetically old fear-relevant stimuli (e.g. snakes, spiders) than to neutral ones (e.g. flowers, mushrooms).

The finding that situations evoking fear is non-random led Marks (1969) to propose the concept of prepotency. This is the tendency for a particular species to attend preferentially to certain stimuli of evolutionary importance (rather than evolutionary irrelevant stimuli) even when encountered for the first time. Seligman's (1971) concept of preparedness extends this evolutionary model. Preparedness refers to the idea that certain stimuli are more likely to be associated with one another, and with certain responses.

Behavioural psychotherapy was popularized in the United States by Joseph Wolpe. He used systematic desensitization (SD) for simple phobias. This is based on the principle of reciprocal inhibition which refers to the idea that if a state incompatible with anxiety can be produced, then that anxiety cannot occur. Since relaxation is incompatible with anxiety, this was applied in SD (Wolpe 1958).

SD in phobic disorder was examined widely. For example, Gelder et al. (1967) compared it with individual and group psychotherapy. SD was found to be consistently more effective than the other treatments. Although successful, SD is time consuming for both patient and therapist.

In vivo exposure, originally called flooding, was then introduced (Stampfl and Lewis 1967). The term has since been dropped as it was prone to be misunderstood. The erroneous belief that it involved exposing the patient to the highest order item in the fear hierarchy led to many dropouts. *In vivo* exposure was pioneered with phobic patients (e.g. Watson et al. 1971). They were treated with rapid exposure in real life with much success. Concerns that anxious patients would be made worse and other symptoms would emerge proved unfounded.

Treatment of agoraphobia by exposure was also tackled (e.g. Mathews et al. 1976) and found to be effective. Over a decade, exposure treatments were refined and therapeutic factors identified. For example, optimal duration of exposure was sorted out (Stern and Marks 1973). *In vivo* exposure was also found to be more effective than exposure in imagination (Emmelkamp and Wessels 1975).

Group behavioural treatment of agoraphobia was studied. Hand et al. (1974) compared 'structured' with 'unstructured' groups, and found progress was greater in the former. Only the structured group continued to improve after treatment and up to 3 month follow-up. Group exposure required less professional time. However, it is often difficult in practice to compose a group of similar phobic patients at the same time. Also, progress of the group as a whole is limited by the rate of progress of the slowest member.

Work in the development of self-exposure methods resulted in a great diminution of therapist time. Marks et al. (1983) showed that brief therapist-aided exposure was a useful adjunct to self-exposure homework instructions. Even self-exposure homework instruction alone is a potent treatment for agoraphobia. Current experience supports the use of this approach, although involvement of family members in the treatment wherever possible is thought to be beneficial.

Exposure was also investigated in obsessive-compulsive disorder. Marks et al. (1975) reported the results of 20 patients with long-standing obsessive rituals. This treatment was as effective in three-fourths of the patients. In obsessive-compulsive patients, exposure was generally combined with modelling and self-imposed response-prevention. The term modelling means that the therapist demonstrates the desired behaviour to the patient. Self-imposed response prevention is asking the patient not to ritualize. These techniques are described in detail in the treatment section of the chapter. The principles outlined by Janet were refined in a series of studies over the years (Levy and Meyer 1971; Rachman et al. 1971, 1973) until the present time when a truly effective therapy can now be offered to most patients with compulsive rituals.

Similar optimism was not justified, until the mid-1980s, for patients with obsessive ruminations as the main problem. The only technique available until then was thought stopping. This aimed to reduce ruminations by aversive techniques. The patient was asked to ruminate and the therapist would then shout loudly. This was repeated several times until the patient had difficulty in concentrating enough to ruminate. Gradually the therapist reduced the volume of the shouting until the patient could imagine the shouting without any therapist input. Although this technique helped a few patients it was not generally effective and is virtually obsolete.

The technique of audio-taped habituation was developed in the 1980s and appeared more effective. This has been demonstrated both by case reports (Salkovskis 1983; Headland and McDonald 1987) and by a controlled trial (Lovell et al. 1994). Audio-taped habituation is described fully below.

Cognitive therapy can be applied to anxiety and depressive disorders. Although this therapy is covered in Chapter 7, it is worthwhile noting that these techniques can often be usefully incorporated in or used as an adjunct to a behavioural programme. A demonstration of this is the use of Danger Ideation Reduction Therapy (DIRT) for patients with contamination fears

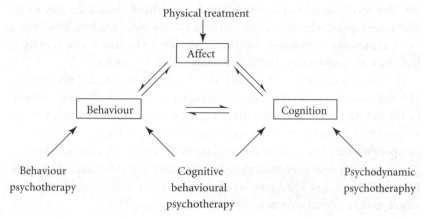

Fig. 8.1 The components of psychiatric syndromes and the site of action of the various types of therapy. NB These components interact with each other and thus a treatment acting on affect will also alter behaviour and cognition

(Jones and Menzies 1997). Although this treatment contains elements of Rational Emotive Therapy, much of the treatment involves behavioural methods.

Aims

Behavioural psychotherapy aims to alter symptoms by modifying behaviour. Psychological symptoms consist of three main components, affective, cognitive, and behavioural, and are often associated with coexistent physical symptoms.

For example, a woman fears spiders; intense anxiety is felt in their vicinity (affective); a fear that the spider may crawl onto her body makes her worry that she is 'going mad' due to anxiety (cognitive); this results in her running away from the feared situation and avoiding any stimuli which remind her of spiders (behavioural). Theoretically, treatment is aimed at any component. She could be offered anxiolytics to reduce anxiety (affective) or be treated psychoanalytically to explore the roots of her fear (cognitive), or be encouraged through behavioural therapy to approach the feared object (behavioural). In reality, the three components interact so that an alteration in one affects the others. However, the behavioural component is often the quickest way of tackling the problem. If the patient is offered anxiolytics, she may be able to approach the feared object and have fewer fearful thoughts but once the drug is withdrawn, she may well relapse. Psychoanalytically based therapy would take several months before she felt confident to approach a spider. Behavioural treatment would encourage her from the start to confront and remain in fear-provoking situations. Treatment usually takes 4–6 weeks.

The aim of behavioural treatment is thus to establish more adaptive patterns of behaviour and unlearn maladaptive behaviours which fuel the problem. In the previous example, the patient's escape behaviour was worsening the situation. The presence of a spider made her feel intensely anxious. She escaped from the situation by running from the room. This reduced anxiety. The escape was thus reinforced by reduced anxiety and this increased the likelihood she would escape again, leading to complete avoidance of situations where spiders might be encountered.

A comprehensive history and behavioural assessment is essential to ensure that all aspects are covered. For example, a 26-year-old man presented with an 8-year history of exposing himself to women in the park. Whereas this target problem could be dealt effectively with the aversion technique of covert sensitization, this would leave him with the tendency to relapse. A detailed history revealed that this was his only sexual outlet. He therefore needed sexual skills training to encourage him to take up non-deviant sexual fantasies and to seek appropriate sexual outlets.

Selection

Indications

A patient should have a condition known to be amenable to treatment. Behavioural psychotherapy has been shown to be effective, indeed the treatment of choice, for phobic disorders including agoraphobia; obsessive-compulsive disorder and sexual dysfunction. It has also been demonstrated to be helpful for habit disorders including many tics; obesity, bulimia nervosa and anorexia nervosa; sexual deviation; social skills problems including anger control; marital difficulties, and abnormal illness behaviour. It has been found to play a part in treating a range of physical problems including hypertension and post-myocardial infarction; the rehabilitation of chronic schizophrenia; managing depression; alcohol and drug abuse; and in childhood and adult behavioural disturbances. This list can be extended to include any condition where behavioural analysis reveals that the patient's behaviour contributes to the disorder.

With most behavioural techniques, it is vital that the patient is motivated to change and willing to engage in treatment. The only exception is in certain operant reinforcement regimes with patients with long-standing conditions, but here rigorous ethical standards must be applied.

Contraindications

In most cases where patients are unwilling or unable to embark on behavioural psychotherapy, the nature of the treatment should be carefully described. They should be told how to seek help in the future following reconsideration or changed circumstances.

In the case of substance abuse or dependence, patients should undergo detoxification prior to behavioural treatment given the risk of state-dependent learning, that is, skills learned in an intoxicated state are not usually present in the non-intoxicated state. In treating anxiety, alcohol and many drugs complicate the picture since withdrawal symptoms may be indistinguishable from those of anxiety.

Benzodiazepines are contraindicated in behavioural psychotherapy due to concerns about state-dependent learning and withdrawal effects. There is no objective evidence to demonstrate that state-dependent learning is a problem. However, psychological factors can be important and patients on drugs often attribute improvement to the drug than to their own efforts. For all these reasons, patients should be weaned off benzodiazepines prior to behavioural therapy or, in the case of the chronic benzodiazepine user with difficulty in withdrawing, reducing the drug to an evenly spaced dose of less than the equivalent of 15 mg diazepam a day.

Depression also has to be tackled cautiously. Severely depressed patients should be treated ahead of behavioural therapy since they do not habituate to anxiety induced by exposure programmes (Foa 1979). Moreover, they do not learn new skills effectively and construe events negatively. However, when patients have mild or moderate depression associated with their condition, treatment of the latter usually alleviates the mood problem.

Schizophrenia and related psychoses need to be approached carefully. A small proportion of patients with obsessive-compulsive symptoms who fail to respond to exposure treatment have over-valued ideas that their preoccupations are correct. Some schizophrenic patients present with bizarre obsessive-compulsive symptoms but do not do well with exposure (Foa 1979). However, reinforcement programmes (operant) are often used to rehabilitate patients with long-standing psychosis.

Behavioural analysis

When assessing a patient for behavioural treatment, a full psychiatric history and mental state examination are necessary. Any contraindications are noted.

A behavioural assessment is straightforward but there may be copious information to elicit, especially if the problem is long-standing, (see chapters on assessment in Stern and Drummond 1991). The patient is first asked to describe the main problem briefly; detailed information is then needed.

Therapists may benefit from a mnemonic to organize their questions so that nothing is omitted. Two ABCs and three Ps are helpful in this regard.

The first ABC covers antecedents, behaviours and beliefs, and consequences (O'Leary and Wilson 1975). The antecedents and consequences of a behaviour as well as the patient's beliefs about it can modify frequency of that behaviour. These factors are examined since treatment is geared to modify them.

The second ABC deals with affective, behavioural, and cognitive aspects which were discussed on page 171.

The three Ps represent predisposing, precipitating, and perpetuating factors of the problem, all of which are assessed.

Abbreviated assessment (BASIC ID)

It maybe necessary to do an abbreviated assessment due to lack of time, as described by Lazarus (1973); this provides minimum information to devise a behavioural programme. The scheme follows the mnemonic—BASIC ID:

BEHAVIOUR

AFFECT

SENSATIONS

IMAGERY

COGNITION

INTERPERSONAL RELATIONSHIPS

DRUGS

Most of these aspects have been discussed earlier. Physical sensations which accompany symptoms fuel patients' beliefs. Imagery refers to thoughts which are formed in pictures in the imagination. Since the patient's family and social circumstances may affect therapy, they need to be inquired about. Finally, a full drug history is done since side effects may impede progress.

It is important to ascertain why the patient has presented at this time, and his aims and expectations of treatment.

At the end of the evaluation, the therapist determines if behavioural treatment is indicated and presents the patient with a formulation and rationale for treatment. Baseline measures are taken and a plan devised if the patient accepts treatment.

Behavioural formulation

The behavioural formulation is a hypothesis about a disorder, behaviour, or symptom which attempts to identify predisposing, precipitating, and perpetuating factors. It is not cast in stone and may alter with treatment and as other factors come to light. The formulation should be shared with the patient since it is helpful to hear their problem summarized. This is particularly true when the problem seems insurmountable; a summary can demonstrate that it is manageable. Discussing the formulation also allows the therapist to ensure that she has understood the problem fully.

The behavioural formulation for the woman with a spider phobia might be presented thus: 'You have told me that you have been frightened of spiders for as long as you can remember. Your mother was similarly frightened. This is not unusual. A tendency to develop phobias is often passed from one generation to the next. Your mother's fear and avoidance of spiders would have taught you to regard them as creatures best avoided. Many children have specific animal fears from the age of about three. You developed this fear but your mother's reaction to spiders probably contributed to you not overcoming it as you grew to adolescence.

Once you had this fear, you would run away if you saw a spider or even a picture of one in a book or on television. This served to strengthen your fear. High anxiety is unpleasant and therefore a reduction in it is like a reward. In your case escaping from, or avoiding, the situation reduced your anxiety. These behaviours were then "rewarded" by diminished anxiety. If you reward any behaviour, you elevate the risk of it recurring. Therefore, every time you avoided contact with spiders, you increased your fear and strengthened your belief that it was the only way to spare yourself unpleasant sensations. You therefore became increasingly phobic of spiders'.

Use of change measures

Measurement is taken seriously, with each patient considered as a single-case experiment. There are several advantages:

1 In the initial stage the patient identifies targets and goals. This prevents the therapist from pursuing a course of action without the patient's motivation.

2 It allows patient and therapist to monitor progress. Poor progress is recognized early and treatment modified.

3 As treatment progresses, the patient may have a dim memory of the severity of the original problem and misjudge progress.

4 The therapist may also only vaguely recollect the presenting problem and underestimate or, more commonly, overestimate progress.

Questionnaires

Questionnaires are commonly used. It is best to become familiar with a few of proven reliability and validity. They should measure target symptoms and behaviours.

Objectivity and types of measurement

Self-report or therapist-report questionnaires combined with observation by the patient, relatives, and therapist usually suffice. The list below, which covers the main categories, is given in order of increasing objectivity.

1 *Self-report*. Asking a question like, 'How often do you experience panic in a day?' provides a guide to frequency of behaviours. Self-report can be more useful through standardized questionnaires and visual analogue scales. Once the patient has completed a questionnaire, an element of self-observation operates and subsequent ratings are often more valid.

2 *Relatives' report*. Family and friends who are in close contact are asked questions like, 'How often does he wash his hands?'

3 *Self-observation*. This requires patients to monitor and observe their own behaviour over a period of time; a diary is frequently applied for this purpose.

4 *Relatives' observation*. Family and friends are asked to monitor the target behaviour over time and to record this in a diary.

5 *Impartial professional interview and rating*. These measures and question-naires are often used in research and involve a professional who is blind to the patient's self ratings.

6 *Direct observation using role-play*.

7 *Direct observation in vivo*. With certain behaviours the therapist can observe progress in real life, for example, a patient with contamination fears may initially be unable to touch a door handle but achieves this during treatment. The reliability of this type of measure is increased by setting up a standard 'behavioural avoidance test' which is performed repeatedly during treatment. An example is a journey for an agoraphobic patient which follows a set route, starting with a walk, continuing with a visit to a small shop to buy a newspaper, then moving on to a bus trip, a supermarket, and eventually a train journey.

8 *Direct observation of the results of behaviour change*. An obvious example is in treating over-eating where weight can be measured directly. Unfortunately, objective criteria are rarely available.

Process

Exposure treatment

Exposure treatment is effective in most agoraphobic (Mathews et al. 1981) and obsessive-compulsive patients (Foa and Goldstein 1978; Rachman et al. 1979). It is also highly beneficial for specific and social phobia (Marks 1981).

Despite its efficacy, concern about exposure arises from erroneous views about its applicability, value, and the time required for it to work. Behavioural psychotherapy is actually efficient and easily applied in many settings (Marks 1981, 1987; Stern and Drummond 1991). Training can be achieved by reading texts on techniques (e.g. Hawton et al. 1989; Stern and Drummond 1991) and obtaining supervision from an experienced therapist.

The most effective exposure is prolonged rather than brief (Stern and Marks 1973), applied in real life rather than in fantasy (Emmelkamp and Wessels 1975) and practised regularly in the form of homework (McDonald et al. 1978).

Example of exposure treatment

Jill, a 40-year-old married secretary, came to the clinic accompanied by her husband and teenage daughter. She gave a 20-year history of a fear of travelling on her own and staying alone in the house. These problems had worsened over the previous 2 years following a move some distance from her family of origin. Her husband worked shifts in a factory, often all night. Jill would not let her daughter leave the home at such times but she worried she was being unreasonable and that this might interfere with her going to University.

A full history was obtained. Jill, the youngest in a family of three daughters, had always been anxious and shy. At age 12, she had once felt unwell and fainted during a school assembly. Following this she had been unwilling to return to school. After a week at home she had been persuaded to return if her elder sister accompanied her to the gate and met up with her at break times. Thereafter, she was always accompanied to and from school until she left at 16.

After leaving school she got a job as a typist and later became a secretary in a solicitors' office. Since the office was close to where her sister worked, Jill always had her accompany her to the office. She avoided travelling on buses or trains for fear she might faint.

Jill married Roy at the age of 21. They described their relationship as happy. They had had only one daughter since they felt a bigger family would restrict their lifestyle. Initially, they had lived in rented accommodation near to Jill's parents and her siblings. Two years previously they had bought a house 5 miles away which required her to use a bus or train. She had attempted to travel to work but had panicked at the bus stop and returned home. She had remained off work since then.

A provisional hypothesis for the origin and maintenance of Jill's symptoms was established from the history. The therapist explained:

> 'Although you have always been a shy and nervous person, it seems that your problems really began after you fainted at school. This was an unpleasant experience which you learned to associate with being away from your family. Following this, you avoided going anywhere alone and therefore strengthened the belief. You never allowed yourself to discover whether or not you could be alone without fainting. Although you managed to cope when you were near to your parents and brother and sister, the house move meant that it was no longer convenient for them to accompany you whenever you went out.
>
> Currently, whenever you are in danger of being alone, you take precautions to prevent this. When you went to catch the bus, you were tense because of an expectation that something dreadful might happen. Due to the tension, you noticed physical symptoms of anxiety, such as your heart pounding, and believed that this was evidence that something terrible was about to happen and that you might die'.

The next step was to tell Jill and Roy about the nature of anxiety and its treatment. First, the physical and emotional features of anxiety were clarified. Then it was explained how avoidance of feared situations led to further avoidance. Third, the way anxiety eventually diminishes during prolonged exposure to fear provoking situations, even though this might take up to 2 hours, was elaborated. Also, that if exposure exercises were practised regularly, the anxiety would gradually decline in intensity and duration. Finally, they were given the three golden rules for exposure treatment:- (1) Anxiety is unpleasant but does not harm a person— 'I will not die; go mad, or lose control'; (2) Anxiety does eventually diminish— 'It cannot continue indefinitely if I face up to the situation'; and (3) Practice makes perfect— 'The more I repeat the exposure exercise the easier it becomes'.

Targets were then identified. She chose four tasks she wished to carry out by the end of treatment which would demonstrate improvement: to travel to work alone on the bus during the rush hour; to travel to work alone on the train during the rush hour; to travel alone by bus and underground train into the centre of town and visit the main shopping areas; and to remain in her home alone overnight while Roy was on night shift.

Jill decided it would be easiest to tackle the problem of walking alone. Roy and her daughter, Louise, were willing to help by acting as 'co-therapists'. All agreed that every evening, when either Louise or Roy arrived home, they were to go out for a walk. Jill was to leave first and walk along a predetermined route; the 'co-therapist' was to wait for 5 minutes and then follow. They were to take care that the exposure time was long enough for Jill's anxiety to reduce (habituation) (usually 1–2 hours). Jill was to record details of the exposure process and to note anxiety levels at the beginning, middle, and end of the task, using a 0–8 scale where 0 means no anxiety and 8 extreme anxiety or panic. If Jill found anxiety levels diminishing during the week, she was to go out for a long walk alone.

At the second session the following week, Jill was delighted with her progress. She had managed not only to walk alone but had visited local shops and done some shopping while Louise remained at home. The therapist praised her for this excellent progress. The session was then used to tackle bus travel.

Initially, Jill wanted Roy to sit beside her but eventually agreed to sit at the front of the bus while he and the therapist sat at the rear. After a few minutes, Jill became very anxious and complained of symptoms of panic. She was gently reminded that this feeling, although unpleasant, would pass, whereas if she gave up, her anxiety might be worse next time. She returned to her seat and after a further 45 minutes looked more relaxed and cheerful. At the prearranged stop, Jill, Roy, and the therapist left the bus. Jill was praised by the therapist who said, 'You have done extremely well. Despite feeling panicky you managed to face up to your fear and learned that these frightening and nasty symptoms do eventually lessen'.

On the return journey, Jill sat alone upstairs while husband and therapist sat downstairs. Again, she coped excellently and readily agreed to continue this practice with Roy the following week. She was to use driver-only buses once her confidence increased and to tackle bus travel alone.

Over the next six sessions, Jill faced the problems of underground train travel, shopping, and being alone in the house. Much of this was done by Jill practicing at home. If it was necessary for the therapist to assist in the exposure this was always followed by Jill practicing the same exercise daily before the next appointment.

The target of remaining alone at home was difficult to achieve since Louise would always come in at some point even if she did stay out late. Jill was particularly keen to stay alone all night. It was arranged that Louise would spend a week away from home during the school holidays when Roy was due for a week of night shifts. On the first night, Jill's sister agreed to be at home and be telephoned if Jill felt overly anxious. Jill was delighted that she managed the task without resorting to the telephone.

By the 8th session all targets had been achieved. The principles of treatment which Jill had learned and applied successfully were reiterated. The therapist advised her to practice the new behaviours over the following months. Everyone had good and bad days, weeks, or months; the important thing would be for Jill to face up to difficult situations even during the 'bad' times when she felt more anxious. A period of illness which restricted her activities might well lead to a slight elevations in fear when she returned to health. Finally, she was congratulated and arrangements made for reviews at 1, 3, 6, and 12 months to ensure that gains were maintained.

A concern about exposure treatment is that it requires considerable professional input to accompany a patient into fear-provoking situations. Fortunately, self-exposure instruction can be all that is needed (Ghosh et al. 1988; Marks et al. 1988). The efficacy of self-exposure has led to the development of self-help manuals (e.g. Marks 1987). However, few patients can complete a program successfully without professional guidance: educating the patient and helping to devise targets, monitor progress and encourage and advise in the face of difficulty.

Self-imposed response prevention

Although exposure is the cornerstone of treatment for obsessive-compulsive disorder, it is not sufficient to overcome the problem: rituals lessen anxiety and prevent habituation. Although compulsions or rituals initially reduce anxiety, they only reduce it by a small amount and for a limited time. This limited efficacy of the rituals leads to their repetition. Overall, they prolong anxiety and do not allow it to diminish naturally.

It is necessary to ask the patient not to perform rituals. This can be achieved by educating the patient about their effect. Exposure tasks should be graded, with tasks which cause anxiety but at a level which is tolerable without rituals. Even with the best motivated patient, slips occur and rituals recur. The patient is told that this is expected occasionally but will not interfere with therapy as long as they repeat the exposure task immediately.

An identical approach is taken with seeking reassurance which also interferes with habituation by causing temporary relief from anxiety. It is necessary to educate relatives and friends who reassure so that they respond appropriately. It is difficult for them to withhold reassurance. Role-play is useful here— where reassurance is requested they should reply, 'Dr X has asked me not to answer questions like that'.

Audiotaped habituation treatment for obsessive ruminations

Audio-taped habituation involves finding out the complete sequence of thoughts in a rumination. It is then determined that some thoughts will cause anxiety and are obsessional in nature whereas others are anxiolytic and covert rituals. The patient is asked to record the anxiety-producing thoughts on audiotape without the anxiety-reducing words and phrases. A continuous loop tape as used in answering machines is used since this saves the patient having to record the same thoughts repeatedly. The patient is then asked to play the tape back to themselves several times a day. The tape is, in effect, an exposure exercise and must be listened to until anxiety consistently diminishes by at least half. As with all exposure programs it must be carried out regularly, until ruminations cease to be problematic.

New cognitive methods in treating obsessive-compulsive disorder

The high success rates achieved with patients who receive behavioural treatment for obsessive-compulsive disorder has been covered as has the minority who fail to respond. Another group find engaging in exposure therapy too daunting; the use of cognitive therapy to complement exposure therapy has been considered here.

Cognitive behaviour therapy (CBT) has been advocated as the first line treatment for obsessive compulsive disorder (OCD), but results are no better than exposure and response prevention (James and Blackburn 1995; Cottreaux et al. 2001; McLean et al. 2001). CBT is more time-consuming and requires more training than exposure treatment. Nevertheless, targeted cognitive techniques are useful to overcome specific problems in exposure therapy; for example, by reducing the strength of belief in an obsession (Salkovskis and Warwick 1985) or the heightened sense of responsibility. Salkovskis (1999) believes that the key problem in OCD is that patients feel responsibility for things that others would see as beyond their control. This results in an increase in anxiety and excessive checking behaviour.

Not all workers concur with the idea that an exaggerated sense of responsibility is core to OCD. A new treatment based on cognitive therapy for patients with contamination fears who refuse or fail in exposure therapy, Danger Ideation Reduction Therapy (Jones and Menzies 1998; Krochmalik et al. 2001), encourages patients to confront the feared contaminant and focuses on changing thoughts of danger rather then over-inflated ideas of responsibility, the backbone of cognitive approaches (Salkovskis 1999). The treatment consists of:

1 *Cognitive restructuring.* Based on the techniques of Rational Emotive Therapy (Ellis 1962), the patient is taught to re-evaluate unrealistic thoughts about contamination. Rational responses are recorded and the patient asked to learn the responses and repeat them daily.

2 *Filmed interviews.* These consist of interviews with people who work in situations commonly feared by obsessive-compulsive patients, for example,

tellers handling money or cleaners using detergents and cleaning other peoples' dirt.

3 *Corrective information.* Patients view a list of facts about their feared contaminant; for example, the number of health-care workers who have contracted HIV through their work. Patients are also informed about the deleterious effects of overzealous hand washing.

4 *Microbiological experiments.* Results of experiments are discussed with the patient. For example, subjects were asked to touch feared contaminants, such as money or toilet door handles, frequently with one hand while keeping the other 'clean'. Fingerprints from both were imprinted on blood agar plates. No pathogens were found on either hand.

5 *Probability of catastrophe.* Patients initially asked to estimate the probability of catastrophe occurring in different situations examine their component parts and judge the chance of the feared consequence of each part separately. The latter is compared with the original estimate. For example, a woman who feared touching rubbish bins lest she contract salmonella infection estimated the risk as 90%. When asked how often rubbish contained salmonella, she rated this as 50% and the risk of salmonella on the exterior of the bin as 50%. Bin to fingers was 80%; ingestion 80%. The risk of her immune defences not coping was 60%. This yields a figure of the likelihood of contracting salmonella from touching a rubbish bin as 9.6%, not the 90% she first believed.

6 *Attentional focusing.* A form of meditation, patients are taught to steer their mind away from intrusive thoughts and focus on benign, non-threatening stimuli.

Outcome with exposure treatment

Exposure treatment is effective in two-thirds of agoraphobia patients (Mathews et al. 1981) and highly effective (Marks 1981) in patients with specific and social phobia.

Self-exposure—encouraging patients to engage in therapy on their own or with friends and relatives—is clearly more cost-effective than when therapist-aided. At least for mild and moderate disorders instructions can be given by a professional (e.g. Mathews 1981) or with the use of a computer programme (Ghosh et al. 1988; Greist et al. 2002; Kenwright et al. 2004).

Social phobia has been extensively researched given that its response to medication differs compared to other forms of phobia and the effectiveness to exposure varies. A specific social phobia, for example, in a person who fears carrying out a specific activity such as eating or drinking in public, the response may be better to exposure on its own. More generalized social phobias may require social skills training in addition to exposure.

The generalized nature of fear in social phobia and agoraphobia suggests the need for cognitive therapy, not exposure, but there is little evidence for this. A study on agoraphobic patients failed to show any benefit of adding cognitive sessions to exposure (Burke et al. 1997). Targeted cognitive techniques may be useful to overcome specific problems; for example, cognitive therapy is used to alter faulty beliefs in social phobia (Marks 1995; Coupland 2001). Clark's (1988) model of panic incorporates an associated treatment of hyperventilation while cognitive therapy is pertinent for patients experiencing both agoraphobia and panic.

Treatment of OCD with graded exposure and self-imposed response prevention is effective in most cases. In the early days of exposure treatment for OCD the therapist would actively prevent the patient from performing rituals. This can be counterproductive and cause poor therapeutic relationships and so the stopping of rituals is done by education and encouragement. This is known as self-imposed response prevention. Therapist modelling does not alter the response to exposure but family participation is helpful (Emmelkamp 1982). Gains made are maintained without symptom substitution (Marks 1981).

Behavioural therapy of obsessional ruminations is less successful. (Emmelkamp and Kwee 1977). Audiotaped habituation may have a role (Lovell et al. 1994). See pp. 180–1.

Cognitive therapy is no better than behavioural therapy in treating OCD. Rational Emotive Therapy (Emmelkamp et al. 1988; Emmelkamp and Beens 1991) or cognitive therapy directed at an undue sense of responsibility do not have any advantage (James and Blackburn 1995; van Oppen et al. 1995; McLean et al. 2001).

One option is to target specific problems which have lead to failure of exposure treatment using cognitive therapy or medication (Drummond 1993).

Other uses of exposure

Exposure can be applied to any condition where avoidance is central, for example, in morbid grief in which the bereaved person avoids facing her loss (Mawson et al. 1981). Similarly, a patient with PTSD often avoids thinking about aspects of the trauma and related activities and places. This can confuse the therapist since flashbacks, nightmares, and reliving the trauma may suggest that avoidance is not a feature. However, further analysis may reveal the patient's efforts to blank out specifics of the trauma. Imaginal exposure, including dwelling on these 'hot spots', promotes habituation and can be combined with cognitive therapy (Keane et al. 1989; Foa et al. 1991).

Table 1 Techniques to overcome treatment failures

Possible explanation of previous failure	Action
Lack of motivation to change	Consider cognitive therapy or family therapy or psychodynamic therapy, Educate patient about the problem and discharge (can be re-referred if motivation changes)
Inappropriate previous treatment	Exposure and response prevention (E + r.p.)
Treatment in hospital/clinic has not generalized to home	Home-based treatment or treatment in hospital with weekend leave and domiciliary treatment
Cognitive rituals	Education plus *Either* Audiotape of anxiogenic obsessions (Salkovskis 1983; Headland and McDonald 1987) *Or* High-intensity exposure and response prevention
Major depressive illness	Antidepressant drug followed by exposure and response prevention; cognitive therapy for depression as necessary
Overvalued ideation that obsessions are realistic	High-intensity exposure and response prevention *Or* Cognitive restructuring (Salkovskis and Warwick, 1985) followed by exposure and response prevention
Failure to habituate without major depression or overalued ideation	Cognitive therapy based on ideas of faulty sense of responsibility (Salkovskis 1999) *Or* SSRI plus E + r.p. *Or* Neuroleptic plus E + r.p. *Or* SSRI plus neuroleptic plus E + r.p. *Or* Benzodiazepine plus E + r.p. *Or* Psychosurgery (when all of above failed)

Source: Adapted form Drummond (1993) British Journal of Psychiatry. 163, 223–229.

Many patients with hypochondriasis or abnormal illness behaviour have similar symptoms as those with OCD. They worry that they have a serious illness and manifest excessive checking and reassurance-seeking behaviours. Treatment comprises exposure, response prevention, and cognitive therapy (Warwick et al. 1996; Barsky and Ahern 2004).

Body Dysmorphic Disorder is also similar to OCD in that patients have a preoccupation about their appearance which leads to avoidance, checking, and reassurance-seeking. Repeated requests for plastic surgery also occur. Indeed, many of these patients have undergone procedures but remain dissatisfied. Exposure to the perceived unsightly feature is used together with response prevention, a ban on reassurance-seeking (including surgery consultations) and cognitive therapy (Veale 2004).

Reduction of undesirable behaviour

Exposure is useful to overcome anxiety in most forms of anxiety disorder. However, maladaptive behaviour may develop in response to stimuli unrelated to fear and in these cases alternative strategies are indicated. The therapist has the option of several strategies depending on the nature of the problem:

1 Eliminating the behaviour using aversive stimuli (only indicated if the behaviour is life-threatening or constitutes a major public nuisance), for example, covert sensitization.

2 Modifying the stimulus leading to the response, for example, orgasmic reconditioning.

3 Modifying the response to the stimulus, for example, stimulus control techniques.

4 Replacing the problem behaviour with alternative adaptive responses, for example, habit reversal.

5 Reducing the desirability of the problem behaviour, for example, mass practice and response cost. Response cost involves a penalty requiring time and effort on the part of the patient and aims to undo the harm of the target behaviour, for example, a patient throws a glass of water but is expected to mop the whole room in response.

These strategies are not mutually exclusive; a therapist who tries to eliminate a specific behaviour without helping the patient to develop alternative strategies will fail at the task.

Application of covert sensitization in the treatment of sexual deviance

Indications for aversion therapy are few and it is rarely applied due to ethical considerations. However, antisocial sexual behaviour which threatens others requires action. The form of aversion used, covert sensitization, involves asking the patient, almost always a man, to describe two or three aversive scenes and to rate their degree of aversiveness. An aversive scene may be related to the deviant behaviour (e.g. being attacked by fellow prisoners following conviction) or unrelated (e.g. falling into a vat of vomit). Scripts describing arousing and aversive scenes are prepared. The patient is instructed to relax and imagine an arousing scene, taking the therapist through their fantasy. Before he reaches the end of the scene the therapist asks him to shift to an aversive scene which is then also carefully described. This is repeated five or six times in a session. The patient reads through the scripts in a similar way at home. Alternatively, the scripts are taped and played back at home. It is necessary to check the anxiety level caused by the aversive scene frequently as habituation may occur, reducing its aversive value. Changing aversive scripts regularly is done to prevent habituation. As therapy proceeds the aversive scene is introduced progressively earlier in the arousing scene until anxiety results as soon as the patient thinks about his deviant fantasy.

Treatment requires motivation to improve general personal functioning (including sexual).

Application of orgasmic reconditioning in the treatment of sexual deviance

If a patient has a sexual preference which concerns him and his partner but is not inherently dangerous, less radical treatment is applied. In orgasmic reconditioning, originally described by Marquis (1970), the patient masturbates regularly to his troublesome fantasies but, at the point of orgasmic inevitability, switches to the desired, 'non-deviant' fantasy. As treatment evolves, the latter is introduced progressively earlier in the arousal process until masturbation is achieved without the deviant fantasy. Sexual and/or social skills training ensures that the arousal to non-deviant stimuli persists.

Realistic goals are set when dealing with distressing sexual urges. It is not possible, and many would argue not desirable, to change the orientation of an exclusively homosexual person. In this case counselling to help accept the sexual preference may be indicated. Similarly, if a person with homosexual paedophilia is referred for treatment, it is unrealistic to aim for adult heterosexual involvement. An adult homosexual orientation is more realistic.

Application of stimulus control techniques in treating obesity

Although obesity is a great threat to health in the Western world, prevailing public health methods have failed to exert any beneficial effects.

Medical and psychodynamic treatments are not particularly useful. Behavioural therapies have proved more successful (e.g. Stuart 1967). The programme consists of

1 Description of the behaviour to be controlled. Patients keep a daily diary of the amount of food ingested, and the time and circumstances of eating.

2 Modification and control of the discriminatory stimuli governing eating is introduced. Patients limit their eating to one room, use distinctive table settings and make eating a 'pure' experience unaccompanied by other activities like reading or watching television.

3 Development of techniques to control the act of eating, such as counting each mouthful, replacing utensils on the table after each bite and leaving food on the plate at the end of the meal.

4 Prompt reinforcement of behaviours which delay or control eating.

Weight loss usually follows but as with all other dietary regimes many patients regain it. For this reason, booster sessions, often lead by lay-therapists and available at the worksite, have been recommended (Stunkard 1977).

There are two aspects to obesity. Preventive programs may be applied to try to reduce the population rate. With obesity rampant in the Western world, it may be timely to re-examine basic behavioural techniques, combined with education about healthy eating and graded exercise.

In treating seriously overweight people, surgery alone has a durable effect. Its poor outcome is predicted by binging and mood disorder, with dysfunctional eating modulating negative emotions. Preoperative psychological assessment and behavioural intervention boosts the chance of a good outcome.

Treatment using habit reversal

Problem behaviours may take the form of habits learned in response to a range of stimuli. Azrin and Nunn (1973) pioneered the treatment of habit reversal for such behaviours as tics, nail biting, and neurodermatitis. Treatment has these components:

1 Awareness training since habits occur repeatedly without the patient realizing it. The first step is to encourage awareness by discussing the habit and its triggers and asking the patient to monitor and record frequency.

2 Competing response training entails identifying an activity incompatible with the habit and encouraging the patient to carry it out whenever the urge occurs. For example, a woman with a facial tic first furrowed her forehead and then grimaced with her whole face and bent her neck. Applying firm pressure to lift her eyebrows aborted the tic.

3 In habit control motivation, the patient is encouraged to consider the habit's negative effects and to focus on improvements in her life which would ensue from overcoming it.

4 In generalization training, the competing response is incorporated into daily life in an unobtrusive way. For example, the woman with facial tics

worked at a desk and found she could control them by resting her forehead onto her hand and pushing her eyebrows upwards. The manoeuvre was not noticeable to others since she appeared to be resting her head and thinking. She also wore a hair band to remind herself not to contract the muscles of her forehead.

Applying operant techniques to long-standing problems

With behavioural problems of long duration, such as in some institutionalized psychotic patients, operant conditioning can be used. This has been described as applying 'sticks and carrots' but careful analysis is needed since one person's 'carrot' may be another person's 'stick'. Premack (1959) addressed this by observing that high frequency preferred activity can be used to reinforce lower frequency, non-preferred activity. If children, for instance, spend most of their time playing with toy soldiers, this high frequency, preferred activity can be used to reinforce lower frequency, non-preferred activity of helping to wash-up. Positive reinforcement is the most appropriate strategy. Negative reinforcement is barely ever used and confined to hazardous or life-threatening situations. The types of reinforcers are listed below:

Reinforcers which increase specified activities

Positive reinforcers

(1) Social approval, for example, nurse's praise of a patient's improved self-care.

(2) Higher frequency preferred activities.

(3) Feedback reinforcement, for example, constructive comments in a social skills group.

(4) Food reinforcers.

(5) Tokens—awarded for certain activities which can be 'spent' on other reinforcers.

Negative reinforcers

This entails removal of an aversive event after a specific response is obtained (aversive relief); it has virtually no place in contemporary treatment. It may be used covertly in the management of deviant sexual behaviour.

Reinforcers which reduce specified activities

Punishment

This refers to applying an aversive stimulus in response to certain behaviours. It should have no role in therapy.

Response cost

(1) Penalty involving some time and effort in response to certain behaviours.

(2) A positive reinforcer is removed if certain non-desired activities are practiced. Time out—removing a person from a reinforcing environment—is one category, for example, a child who slaps another child is removed from the room for a few minutes.

Problems in the course of therapy

Many problems can be obviated if a complete history and behavioural assessment are carried out. Educating the patient about the nature of their condition and the treatment plan follows. An integral feature is to convey that treatment is rational and relevant. Some patients, particularly those who have had other forms of help which have not worked, may be more difficult to convince, and need an explanation in lay terms of research evidence, including on efficacy. Spending extra time with sceptical patients to ensure they are satisfied with the treatment plan is required. 'Bargaining' is a particularly useful strategy. For example the therapist states:

> 'I understand your reluctance for behavioural treatment as you have been treated with several drugs, without success. I am confident that you will benefit from this treatment. We know that 7 out of 10 people with agoraphobia improve. Before you worry that you may be one of those who do not, let me tell you we know about the complications which make treatment less effective; you have none of those. The only other factor which influences outcome is how much you want to get better and how determinedly you stick to treatment. I suggest we try it for 2 weeks. If you are improving at the end of this time, we should continue; if not, we can rethink'.

Negotiating the number of sessions after which progress will be reviewed is useful. Setting an agenda and detailing goals is another salient component. This leads to clarifying when therapy should end. The agenda, however, should be revised during therapy , if necessary.

Despite these measures, not all potential beneficiaries accept an offer of therapy. Some have become so accustomed to the problem that the prospect of treatment seems worse than the condition itself. For others family and friends seek change whereas the patient is content to remain as they are. About a quarter of patients who could benefit refuse the offer of treatment, but their behavioural assessment is still worthwhile. It may, for instance, reveal family factors influencing their decision and family therapy may be indicated. Other patients may have personality difficulties better suited to a psychoanalytically oriented approach. Another group may be best treated with drugs initially. In all cases, patients should know they have the right to refuse treatment and that their decision will not jeopardize receiving behavioural treatment in the future.

A minority of patients fail to improve with behavioural treatment. This usually emerges early on when outcome measures fail to reveal change. The therapist then ensures that the behavioural assessment and treatment plan are correct and realistic. For example, a woman with obsessive-compulsive disorder failed to respond to exposure treatment for her fears of contamination. These had begun in the wake of her mother's death. Further enquiry revealed that she had not grieved. Guided mourning was provided with good effect and exposure treatment resumed.

The therapist also ensures that treatment is carried out correctly. This may involve accompanying the patient while the relevant task is performed. Patients may misunderstand instructions. For example, an agoraphobic woman failed to improve with an exposure task of travel on buses. The therapist accompanied her and discovered that she constantly wore dark glasses and listened to taped music to distract herself from the task. Their removal lead to more anxiety initially but she then began to improve.

Other conditions may impede treatment. Foa (1979) examined the reasons for a failed treatment in patients with obsessive-compulsive disorder. One group had an overvalued idea that the obsessional fear was rational. Although they demonstrated habituation of anxiety during prolonged exposure, this was not maintained between sessions. The second group was depressed and failed to achieve any sustained reduction in anxiety.

Another reason for failure in obsessive-compulsive disorder is covert rituals. For example, a man with checking rituals failed to respond to treatment. Whenever he performed an exposure task he would think, 'God, please make sure no harm will come'. This impeded habituation of the anxiety. He had difficulty stopping this 'prayer' since it automatically came into his mind. Treatment continued with him wearing a tape player onto which he recorded, 'I have not checked and disaster will occur'. This phrase was repeated continuously during exposure by it being recorded on a loop tape.

Training

Training in behavioural psychotherapy is obtained through direct experience. Several handbooks (e.g. Stern and Drummond 1991) and texts about theory and research are available. The best way to learn is to consult a handbook and treat 'simpler cases' under supervision. Academic texts can be used to deepen understanding of techniques.

An intensive training usually results in a professional able to perform independently. This does not, however, necessarily result in better outcome with selected patient groups. In a series of studies (reviewed by Marks 1981), psychiatric nurses given a circumscribed course in behavioural psychotherapy demonstrated that they could treat patients with phobias, obsessive-compulsive rituals, sexual dysfunction, and sexual deviation and obtain equivalent outcomes to trained psychologists and psychiatrists. Lay therapists can also be trained in exposure techniques for certain problems through self-help organizations.

Concern has been expressed about people with limited training treating psychiatric patients. However, with a 6-month prevalence of between 5% and 13% for phobic disorders (Myers et al. 1984), it is obvious that no service could provide sufficient resources. Lay therapists can help those with uncomplicated phobic conditions although it is essential that screening is done to confirm that suitable patients are so treated. This requires GPs to be informed about diagnosis and treatment of phobic disorders. A professional service is also required to which patients can be referred should lay treatment fail.

Another approach to increase availability of behavioural treatment is computer-aided. Using limited therapist input and the patient following instructions, this is effective for phobic disorders and panic (Kenwright et al. 2004), obsessive-compulsive disorder (Greist et al. 2002), and depression with anxiety (Osgood-Hynes et al. 1998).

With the contribution of lay and nurse therapists and computer-assisted programs, it could be argued that psychiatrists may not need in-depth knowledge of behavioural therapy. Nothing could be further from the truth. Psychiatrists are often referred complex patients, with multiple problems, and are in a position to offer several forms of treatment flexibly. For example, a patient may present with severe depression, obsessive-compulsive disorder, and anorexia nervosa. Treatment would probably start with medication for the depression. Behavioural treatment of the other two conditions would then follow. Even if the psychiatrist believes the latter can be administered by colleagues she will still have to refer appropriately, and may also need to assist if treatment does not run smoothly.

Conclusion

Behavioural psychotherapy is effective and cost-effective for most anxiety, habit, appetitive disorders, and sexual problems. Other conditions are being shown, through controlled trials, to respond to treatment. Research has also shown more cost-effective ways to treat (Marks et al. 1998).

It is vital to understand and manage patients who fail to improve. There may be many reasons, as discussed earlier. Additional behavioural analysis and applying other treatments in conjunction with or prior to behavioural therapy are options (Drummond 1993).

References

Azrin, N. H. and Nunn, R. G. (1973). Habit reversal: A method of eliminating nervous habits and tics. *Behaviour Research and Therapy*, 11, 619–628.

Barsky, A. J. and Ahern, D. K. (2004). Cognitive behaviour therapy for hypochondriasis; a randomised controlled trial. *Journal of the American Medical Association*, 291, 1464–1470.

Buglass, D., Clarke, J., Henderson, N., Kreitman, N., and Presley, A. S. (1977). A study of agoraphobic housewives. *Psychological Medicine*, 7, 73–86.

Burke, M., Drummond, L. M., and Johnson, D. W. (1997). Treatment choice for agoraphobic women: Exposure or cognitive-behaviour therapy? *British Journal of Clinical Psychology*, 36, 409–420.

Cottraux, J., Note, I., Yao, S. N., Lafont, S., Note, B., Mollard, E., Bouvard, M., Sauteraud, A., Bourgeois, M., and Dartigues, J. F. (2001). A randomized controlled trial of cognitive therapy versus intensive behaviour therapy in obsessive-compulsive disorder. *Psychotherapy and Psychosomatics*, 70, 288–297.

Coupland, N. J. (2001). Social phobia: etiology, neurobiology and treatment. *Journal of Clinical Psychiatry*, 62 suppl.1, 25–35.

Drummond, L. M. (1993). The treatment of severe, chronic, resistant obsessive-compulsive disorder: An evaluation of an inpatient programme using behavioural psychotherapy in combination with other treatments. *British Journal of Psychiatry*, 163, 223–229.

Ellis, A. (1962). *Reason and emotion in psychotherapy*, Lyle-Stuart, New York.

Emmelkamp, P. M. G. (1982). *Phobic and obsessive-compulsive disorders theory, research and practice*. Plenum, New York.

Emmelkamp, P. M. G. (1985). Anxiety and Fear. In *International handbook of behavior modification and therapy* (eds A.S. Bellack, M. Hersen and A.E. Kazdin), Plenum, New York.

Emmelkamp, P. M. G. and Wessels, H. (1975). Flooding in imagination vs flooding *in vivo* in agoraphobics. *Behaviour Research and Therapy*, 13, 7–9.

Emmelkamp, P. M. G. and Kwee K. G. (1977). Obsessional ruminations: a comparison between thought-stopping and prolonged exposure in imagination. *Behaviour Research and Therapy*, 15, 441–4.

Emmelkamp, P. M. G. and Beens, H. (1991). Cognitive therapy with obsessive-compulsive disorder: a comparative evaluation. *Behaviour Research and Therapy*, 29, 293–300.

Emmelkamp, P. M. G., Visser, S., and Hoekstra, R. J.(1988). Cognitive therapy versus exposure in vivo in the treatment of obsessive-compulsives. *Cognitive Therapy and Research*, 12, 103–114.

English, H. B. (1929). Three cases of the 'conditioned fear response.' *Journal of Abnormal and Social Psychiatry*, 34, 221–225.

Foa, E. B. (1979). Failure in treating obsessive-compulsives. *Behaviour Research and Therapy*, 17, 169–176.

Foa, E. B. and Goldstein, A. (1978). Continuous exposure and complete response prevention in the treatment of obsessive-compulsive neurosis. *Behavior Therapy*, 9, 821–829.

Foa, E. B, Rothbaum, B. O., Riggs, D. S., and Murdoch, T. B. (1991). Treatment of posttraumatic stress disorder in rape victims: a comparison between cognitive-behavioural procedures and counselling. *Journal of Consulting and Clinical Psychology*, 59, 715–723.

Freud, S. (1919). Turnings in the ways of psychoanalytic therapy. In: *Standard edition*, Vol II. Hogarth Press, London.

Gelder, M. G., Marks, I. M., and Wolff, H. H. (1967). Desensitization and psychotherapy in the treatment of phobic states: a controlled enquiry. *British Journal of Psychiatry*, **113**, 53–73.

Ghosh, A., Marks, I. M., and Carr, A. C. (1988). Therapist contact and outcome of self-exposure treatment for phobias: a controlled study. *British Journal of Psychiatry*, **152**, 234–238.

Goldstein, A. J. and Chambless, D. (1978). A reanalysis of agoraphobia. *Behavior Therapy*, **9**, 47–59.

Greist, J. H., Marks, I. M., Baer, L., Kobak, K. A., Wenzel, K. W., Hirsch, M. J., Mantle, J. M., and Clary, C. M. (2002). Behaviour therapy for obsessive compulsive disorder guided by a computer or by a clinician compared with relaxation as a control, *Journal of Clinical Psychiatry*, **63**, 138–145.

Hand, I., Lamontagne, Y., and Marks, I. M. (1974) Group exposure (flooding) in vivo for agoraphobia. *British Journal of Psychiatry*, **124**, 588–602.

Hawton, K., Salkovskis, P. M., Kirk, J., and Clark, D. M. (1989). *Cognitive behaviour therapy for psychiatric problems: a practical guide*. Oxford University Press, Oxford.

Headland, K. and McDonald, R. (1987). Rapid audiotaped treatment of obsessional ruminations. *Behavioural Psychotherapy*, **15**, 188–192.

James, I. A. and Blackburn, I. M. (1995). Cognitive therapy with obsessive-compulsive disorder. *British Journal of Psychiatry*, **166**, 444–450.

Janet, P. (1903). *Les obsessions et la psychasthenie*. Bailliere, Paris.

Jones, M. K. and Menzies, R. G. (1997). Danger Ideation Reduction Therapy (DIRT): preliminary findings with three obsessive-compulsive washers. *Behaviour Research and Therapy*, **35**, 955–960.

Jones, M. K. and Menzies, R. G. (1998). Danger Ideation Reduction Therapy (DIRT) for obsessive-compulsive washers. A controlled trial, *Behaviour Research and Therapy*, **8**, 121–125.

Keane, T. M., Fairbank, J. A. Caddell, J. M., and Zimering, R. T. (1989). Implosive (flooding) therapy reduces symptoms of PTSD in Vietnam combat veterans. *Behaviour Therapy*, **20**, 245–260.

Kenwright, M., Gega, L., Mataix, D., and Marks, I. M. (2004). Computer-aided self-help for phobia/panic via home internet or standalone computer at a clinic: Pilot comparison. *British Journal of Psychiatry*, **184**, 448–449.

Krochmalik, A., Jones, M. K., and Menzies, R. G. (2001). Danger Ideation Reduction Therapy (DIRT) for treatment resistant compulsive washing. *Behaviour Research and Therapy*, **39**, 897–912.

Lazarus, A. A. (1973). Multimodal behaviour therapy: treating the 'Basic ID'. *Journal of Nervous and Mental Disorders*, **156**, 404–411.

Levy, R. and Meyer, V. (1971). Ritual prevention in obsessional patients. *Proceedings of the Royal Society of Medicine*, **64**, 115–120.

Lovell, K., Marks, I. M., Noshirvani, H., and Qullivan, G. (1994). Should treatment distinguish anxiogenic from anxiolytic O. C. ruminations? Results of a pilot controlled study and of clinical audit. *Psychotherapy and Psychosomatics*, **61**, 150–155.

Marks, I. M. (1969). *Fears and phobias*. Academic Press, New York.

Marks, I. M. (1981). *Cure and care of neurosis: Theory and practice of behavioural psychotherapy.* Wiley, New York.

Marks, I. M. (1987). *Fears, phobias and rituals.* Oxford University Press, Oxford.

Marks, I. M. (1995). Rapid audit of clinical outcome and cost by computer. *Australian and New Zealand Journal of Psychiatry,* **29**, 32–7.

Marks, I. M., Hodgson, R., and Rachman, S. (1975). Treatment of chronic OCD 2 years after *in vivo* exposure. *British Journal of Psychiatry,* **127**, 349–364.

Marks, I. M., Gray, S., Cohen, D., Hill, R., Mawson, D., Ramm, E., and Stern, R. (1983). Imipramine and brief therapist-aided exposure in agoraphobics having self-exposure homework. *Archives of General Psychiatry,* **40**, 153–162.

Marks, I. M., Lelliot, P., Basoglu, M., Noshirvani, H., Monteiro, W., Cohen, D., and Kasvikis, Y. (1988). Clomipramine, self-exposure and therapist-aided exposure for obsessive-compulsive rituals. *British Journal of Psychiatry,* **152**, 522–534.

Marquis, J. N. (1970). Orgasmic reconditioning: Changing sexual object choice through controlling masturbation fantasies. *Journal of Behavior Therapy and Experimental Psychiatry,* **1**, 263–270.

Masters, W. H. and Johnson, V. E. (1966). *Human sexual response.* Churchill, London.

Masters, W. H. and Johnson, V. E. (1970). *Human sexual inadequacy.* Churchill, London.

Mathews, A. M., Johnston, D. W., Lancashire, M. et al. (1976). Imaginal flooding v. real exposure in agoraphobics: Outcome. *British Journal of Psychiatry,* **129**, 362–371.

Mathews, A. M., Gelder, M. G. and Johnston, D. W., (1981). *Agoraphobia: Nature and treatment.* Guilford, New York.

Mawson, D., Marks, I. M., Ramm, E, and Stern, R. S. (1981). Guided mourning for morbid grief: a controlled study. *British Journal of Psychiatry,* **138**, 185–193.

McDonald, R., Sartory, G., Grey, S. J., Cobb, J., Stern, R., and Marks, I. M. (1978). Effects of self-exposure instructions on agoraphobic outpatients. *Behaviour Research and Therapy,* **17**, 83–85.

McLean, P. D., Whittal, M. L., Thordarson, D. S., Taylor, S., Sochting, K. W. J., Paterson, R., and Anderson, K. W. (2001). Cognitive versus behaviour therapy in group treatment to Obsessive-compulsive disorder. *Journal of Consulting and Clinical Psychology,* **69**, 205–214.

Mowrer, O. H. (1950). *Learning theory and personality dynamics.* Arnold, New York.

Myers, J. K., Weissman, M. M., Tischler, G. L. et al., (1984). Six month prevalence of psychiatric disorders in three communities. *Archives of General Psychiatry,* **41**, 959–967.

Ohman, A., Dimberg, U., and Ost, L. G. (1984). Animal and social phobias: Biological constraints on learned fear responses. In *Theoretical issues in behavior therapy.* S. Reiss and R.R. Bootzin (eds.) Academic Press, New York.

O'Leary, K. D. and Wilson, G. T. (1975). *Behavior therapy: Application and outcome.* Prentice Hall, New Jersey.

Osgood-Hynes, D. J., Greist, J. H., Marks, I. M., Baer, L., Heneman, S. W., Wenzel, K. W., Manzo, P. A., Parkin, J. R., Spierings, C. J., Dottl, S. L., and Vitse, H. M. (1998). Self-administered psychotherapy for depression using a telephone-accessed computer system plus booklets: An open US-UK study. *Journal of Clinical Psychiatry,* **58**, 358–365.

Pavlov, I. P. (1927). *Conditioned reflexes.* Academic Press, London.

Premack, D. (1959). Toward empirical behaviour laws: 1. Positive reinforcement. *Psychological Review,* **66**, 219–233.

Rachman, S., Hodgson, R., and Marks, I. M. (1971). Treatment of chronic obsessive-compulsive neurosis. *Behaviour Research and Therapy*, **9**, 237–247.

Rachman, S., Marks, I. M., and Hodgson, R. (1973). The treatment of obsessive-compulsive neurotics by modelling and flooding *in vivo*. *Behaviour Research and Therapy*, **9**, 237–247.

Salkovskis, P. M. (1983). Treatment of an obsessional patient using habituation to audiotaped ruminations. *British Journal of Clinical Psychology*, **22**, 311–313.

Salkovskis, P. M. and Warwick, H. M. C. (1985). Cognitive therapy of obsessive-compulsive disorder: treating treatment failures. *Behavioural Psychotherapy*, **13**, 243–255.

Salkovskis, P. M. (1999). Understanding and treating Obsessive-compulsive disorder. *Behaviour Research and Therapy*, **37**, suppl.1, 29–52.

Seligman, M. E. P. (1971). Phobias and preparedness. *Behavior Therapy*, **2**, 307–320.

Spence, K. G., Haggard, P. F., and Ross, L. G. (1958). UCS intensity and the associated (habit) strength of the eyelid CR. *Journal of Experimental Psychology*, **95**, 404–411.

Stampfl, T. J. and Levis, D. G. (1967). Essentials of implosive therapy: a learning theory based psychodynamic behavior therapy. *Journal of Abnormal Psychology*, **72**, 496–503.

Stern, R. S. and Drummond, L. M. (1991). *The practice of behavioural and cognitive psychotherapy*. Cambridge University Press, Cambridge.

Stern, R. S. and Marks, I. M. (1973). Brief and prolonged flooding: A comparison in agoraphobic patients. *Archives of General Psychiatry*, **28**, 270–276.

Stuart, R. B. (1967). Behavioral control of overeating. *Behaviour Research and Therapy*, **1**, 357–365.

Stunkard, A. J. (1977). Obesity and the social environment: Current status and future prospects. *Annals of the New York Academy of Sciences*, **300**, 298–320.

Thorndike, E. L. (1935). *The psychology of wants, interests and attitudes*. Appleton-Century, London.

Veale, D. (2004). Body dysmorphic disorder. *Postgraduate Medical Journal*, **80**, 67–71.

Van Oppen, P., de Haan, E., van Balkom, A. J., Spinhoven, P., and van Dyck, R. (1995). Cognitive therapy and exposure *in vivo* in the treatment of obsessive-compulsive disorder. *Behaviour Research and Therapy*, **33**, 379–390.

Warwick, H. M. C., Clark, D. M., Cobb, A. M., and Salkovskis, P. M. (1996). A controlled trial of cognitive-behavioural treatment of hypochondriasis. *British Journal of Psychiatry*, **69**, 189–195.

Watson, J. P. and Marks, I. M. (1971). Relevant and irrelevant fear in flooding—a crossover study of phobic patients. *Behavior Therapy*, **2**, 275–293.

Watson, J. B. and Rayner, R. (1920). Conditioned emotional reactions. *Journal of Experimental Psychology*, **3**, 1–14.

Wolpe, J. (1958). *Psychotherapy by reciprocal inhibition*. Stanford University Press, Stanford.

Recommended reading

Marks, I. M. (2001). *Living with far*. McGraw-Hill, New York. (A self-help book for anxious patients. Written for a lay audience but full of case histories demonstrating the treatments in practice.)

Marks, I. M. (1981). *Cure and care of neurosis: Theory and practice of behavioural psychotherapy*. Wiley, New York. (Although now somewhat out of date, this gives an excellent background to the theoretical and clinical background of behavioural psychotherapy.)

Marks, I. M. (1986). *Behavioural psychotherapy*. Wright, Bristol. (Contains questionnaires commonly used in behavioural psychotherapy.)

Marks, I. M. (1987). *Fears, phobias and rituals*. Oxford University Press, Oxford. (A full account of research in animal and human behaviour related to behavioural psychotherapy as well as a full clinical section concentrating on syndromes and their treatment and covering all major areas of research.)

Stern, R. S. and Drummond, L. M. (1991). *The practice of behavioural and cognitive psychotherapy*. Cambridge University Press, Cambridge. (A practical guide with minimum reference to research but which concentrates on teaching how the techniques are performed in practice. Case histories of patients are used to demonstrate the techniques.)

Chapter 9

Crisis intervention

Cynthia Graham and John Bancroft

Since the book's third edition in 1996, several notable developments have occurred in 'crisis intervention' (CI). Professional (and public) interest in CI has grown substantially, as evidenced by new books (Aguilera 1998; Roberts 2000; James and Gilliland 2005) and journals (e.g. Brief Treatment and Crisis Intervention, Crisis Intervention and Time-Limited Treatment). In North America, Europe, and Asia, many treatment programs have evolved. Crises are affecting an ever-increasing number of people. Lifetime prevalence for exposure to trauma is escalating (Kessler et al. 1995) to such a degree that mass disasters have been regarded as 'virtually epidemic' in nature (Everly et al. 2000, p. 77). CI has been applied to an expanding range of high-risk groups, such as victims of school violence (MacNeil and Stewart 2000), HIV-positive women (Lewis and Harrison 2000), and women affected by domestic violence (Roberts and Roberts 2000).

In parallel with these developments, the terminology in the context of CI has become quite confusing. Crisis management, critical incident stress debriefing, emotional first aid, crisis and disaster management are used, sometimes interchangeably and usually without clear definition. Moreover, while CI is still applied widely in social work, this is not the case in other disciplines, such as psychiatry. Instead, specific aspects of dealing with people in crisis, including assessment and particular therapeutic approaches such as problem solving and brief cognitive behavior therapy (Hawton 2004) are focused upon.

Roberts (2000) has highlighted the debates in the field of CI among 'competing professional groups'. Differences prevail in the models applied, the definition and scope of intervention, and the level of training required. Much controversy relates to rigid adherence to a particular approach.

Paradoxically, the debates and controversies have drawn attention to an aspect of health care where the overlap between the roles of psychiatrist, psychologist, emergency department doctor, general practitioner, social worker, probation officer, and lay counsellor is considerable. While each of these groups may contribute specific professional skills, most people in crisis benefit from non-specific skills. We will consider the latter below.

The term crisis intervention originated in relation to basically stable people, with a history of adequate coping resources, facing a major life crisis (Caplan 1961). Our focus will be on the use of CI with such individuals. While we cannot deal with all crisis situations, we will provide a framework that can be applied flexibly. The model described below was presented in the first edition of this book (Bancroft 1978). It evolved in the setting of a general hospital psychiatric service dealing predominantly with attempted suicide, using a multidisciplinary team. However, it has wider relevance. Before outlining the approach, we will first describe the principal tenets of crisis theory, the nature of a crisis, coping and its failure, the circumstances that overextend coping resources and the need for treatment.

Definition

Given the broad range of problems to which it has been applied, it is not surprising that disagreement prevails about what constitutes CI. Features common to all approaches are:

1 prompt assessment and provision of services for the person or family in crisis;

2 a time-limited, goal-directed intervention directed at 'here and now' problems; and

3 an active and flexible therapeutic style.

It is also generally agreed that CI encompasses a first phase immediately after the acute crisis has occurred (or within 48 h), and a second phase, typically lasting up to several weeks (Roberts 2000).

Theory

Erich Lindemann (1944) introduced the concept of time-limited CI, based on observations of 'acute grief' in survivors and relatives of victims of the Coconut Grove nightclub fire in Boston. Another influential pioneering theorist was Gerald Caplan (1961), who defined a crisis as occurring 'when a person faces an obstacle to important life-goals that is, for a time, insurmountable through the utilization of customary methods of problem solving. A period of disorganization ensues, a period of upset, during which many abortive attempts at solution are made'. The crisis is seen as a turning point. If the situation is well resolved, new skills will have been learned which could be applied in future crises. Conversely, with a poor outcome, a maladaptive pattern, possibly psychiatric disturbance, may ensue. Caplan emphasized that crisis is self-limited, lasting 4–6 weeks. Immediate but short-term help is therefore required, provided in medical or non-medical settings such as social work departments or 'Samaritan' organizations. For the doctor, the relationship between CI and conventional medical treatment needs to be clarified while for the non-medical therapist, knowing when to consult medical colleagues is a pertinent question.

Basic concepts—coping and failure to cope

We respond to a threatening or demanding situation with some type of coping process. Traditional accounts of coping emphasized traits or 'styles', that is, stable personality features. In contrast, certain theorists such as Lazarus (1993) depict coping as a process. Although acknowledging that patterns of coping may be stable, they stress that coping is principally situation-specific and cognitive appraisal is crucial. Thus, a coping response depends on a consideration of whether anything, and what, can be done to alter the situation. Two principal types of coping processes can be differentiated:

1 *Problem-focused*. When appraisal suggests that something can be done, a problem-focused response (and corresponding problem solving) is usually deployed.

2 *Emotion-focused*. When appraisal suggests that nothing can be done, coping processes that only change the *way* we interpret or attend to a situation ensue. Denial is a typical example: perception of reality is so distorted that the problem is no longer recognized. Denial may succeed if the situation resolves spontaneously but usually it only postpones and aggravates the problem. Regression, in which a person resorts to behaviour learned at an earlier stage of development may have helped in the past, at least temporarily, by transferring responsibility to others. Resort to alcohol or drugs may be used in this way. Inertia, a state of inaction based on a person's conclusion that there is nothing useful he or she can do is yet another emotion-focused strategy. While inertia can be appropriate, it usually reflects a state of hopelessness typical of depression.

Some researchers have discerned gender differences in coping, with women more likely to show emotion-focused and men more problem-focused styles (Vingerhoets and Van Heck 1990; Wadsworth et al. 2004). However, a series of experimental studies demonstrated that faced with similar stressors, men and women used similar coping patterns (Lazarus 1993). Interestingly, there is some evidence that women may respond better to CI than men (Viney et al. 1985; Cluse-Tolar 1997). Cluse-Tolar (1997) for instance evaluated the response to treatment for people presenting to a psychiatric emergency service and found only women showed psychological improvement.

Perception of a threatening situation usually generates an emotional response. For example, anger leading to aggressive behaviour is a direct, and possibly adaptive, way to cope with a threat (e.g. the enemy retreats). The emotional reaction is a motivating force. However, this may become a problem in its own right. Unless we handle anger, anxiety, grief, and the like appropriately, our ability to cope becomes impaired. This can be regarded as 'second order' coping, that is, dealing with the emotional reaction.

Coping responses may fail. Various factors contribute; for example, the threatening situation is overwhelming; it is unfamiliar; the person uses maladaptive coping methods; physical or mental ill-health impairs the person's resources; support from friends or family is unavailable.

When coping fails, Caplan's (1961) *the four phases of crisis* ensue: phase 1— emotional arousal and attempts to 'problem solve' increase; phase 2—due to the excessive arousal, impaired functioning occurs with resultant disorganization and distress. Thus, the person becomes, for instance, overly anxious or angry, is too aroused to sleep, becomes fatigued, and so on; phase 3—emergency resources, internal and external, are mobilized and new methods of coping tried; and phase 4—continuing failure culminates in a state of progressive deterioration, exhaustion and 'decompensation'. Help can be offered in two distinct ways during the above sequence: at an early stage when the person attempts to mobilize help and later in the decompensation phase when intervention by others is necessary to prevent further deterioration. Before developing these themes, let us briefly consider the types of situations that commonly require CI.

Selection

The diversity of circumstances to which CI is applied has been mentioned. Aguilera (1998) distinguishes two categories of stressors that precipitate crises: situational crises such as role and status change, rape, and physical illness, and life cycle stressors such as parenthood and retirement. We divide stressors into four groups:

1 Loss. This may involve loss of a loved person through death or separation, loss of self-esteem, loss of a bodily function (e.g. amputation, paralysis, colectomy), and loss of resources, such as financial or material. In the aftermath of a traumatic event like a sexual assault or disaster, a person may experience reduced trust, freedom, and sense of identity. A pattern characteristically seen in bereavement (Lindemann 1944; Parkes 1986) follows.

Initially the person is in a state of shock; then follows denial of reality which gives way to a feeling of grief. When the latter is 'worked through', the person gradually restructures her life and fills the 'gap'. Intervention is concerned with aiding the person to experience and express and hence 'work through' the affect of grief.

2 Change. Here the source of the problem is a new situation that has to be faced rather than loss of a previous one. Principal forms are in role, such as work, marital status, and parenthood; and in identity that accompanies a change in role (the transitional or maturational crises of Erikson (1969) fall into this category). A positive aspect usually occurs—the element of challenge in expecting a new and potentially rewarding development. Nevertheless, it can be intensely threatening. A particular form of role change which overlaps with the effect of loss is entry into a 'sick' role where the threat or reality of loss of health and function are central.

3 Interpersonal. Profound stress can stem from troubled interpersonal relationships, especially between spouses or other family members. This is the most common context for deliberate self-harm (Hawton et al. 1997; Williams and Pollack 2000). Interpersonal crises are also associated with the onset of depression, as demonstrated by Brown et al. (1987) in their classic studies. The therapist needs to promote constructive communication with the goal of resolving the relational 'tensions'.

4 Decisional conflict. The person faces a difficult or seemingly impossible choice between two or more alternatives. A typical example would be whether to remain in a long-standing relationship or leave and start a new one. Problem solving in such a case involves realistic appraisal of each set of the two alternatives.

Whatever the type of stressor involved, the therapist either offers help to someone mobilizing resources—in phase 1 or 2 of crisis—or assumes responsibility temporarily—in phase 3 or 4.

Initial assessment

A tenet of crisis theory is that there is a 'critical period' during which a person responds readily to intervention (Rapaport 1967). The initial contact is therefore pivotal, and aims to win trust and establish rapport. A related goal is identifying recent events, particularly those that have influenced the person to seek help. A detailed inquiry using open-ended questions, such as 'What led you to seek help?', usually reveals the principal problems, though their precise nature may not emerge until later. Clarifying the demands facing the person at this time, including practical obligations, is done. Attention is paid to mental state: suicidality, anxiety, agitation, or other distress; and whether any practical steps are immediately called for. The therapist assesses the person's support network, including the home situation. The ultimate aim is not only to ascertain more about the evolution of the problems, but also how the person has fared with similar challenges in the past and the quality of her available coping resources. The latter may have to wait until the decompensated state abates or another informant can be interviewed.

By the end of this assessment, the first decision has to be taken: does responsibility for the person's affairs need to be taken over temporarily? If yes, a form of intervention, 'intensive care', is launched; 'care' since the person has to be looked after and 'intensive' in that concentrated assistance will be required. If intensive care is not indicated, 'crisis counselling' is provided. The distinction between the two types of help may be clear cut, or responsibility may be transferred partially.

Aims and objectives

The primary goal of CI is to restore 'equilibrium' by reducing subjective discomfort, promoting effective coping strategies, and facilitating the return to the previous level of functioning. However, new coping skills and resources, designed to buffer in future stressful situations, is an added goal of effective crisis work (Aguilera 1998; Roberts 2000). We will now outline the stages and techniques of CI.

Process

Intensive care

The chief objective is to reverse the state of decompensation, enabling a prompt return to normal functioning. The sequence is:

1 Explicitly transferring responsibility. The patient is told that her customary responsibilities will be taken over by others for the time being. Whether this is justified on grounds of illness is determined after carefully considering potential implications.

2 Organizing the takeover of tasks. The therapist ensures that the patient's current obliations are taken over by others. For instance, children may need to be sent to relatives or an employer contacted. Houses need to be made secure, pets fed, and so on. The help of relevant family and friends is mobilized as far as possible though social services or community agencies such as 'Meals on Wheels' may need to be recruited.

3 Removing the patient from a stressful environment. This is not always necessary or possible and depends on how relevant the home

environment is in aggravating the current situation or in providing support. A move to stay with friends or relatives may suffice. Admission to hospital or to a 'crisis unit' is an option which permits close, and continuing, contact with the therapist.

4 Lowering arousal and distress. The patient is commonly distressed, excessively aroused, and exhausted. Arousal is best lowered psychologically by relating to the patient reassuringly. Teaching anxiety management techniques, such as deep breathing exercises or progressive relaxation, is helpful. Medication has a place, particularly if arousal is intense and unresponsive to psychological methods, or sleep severely impaired. However, this is presented to the patient as an interim measure.

5 Reinforcing appropriate communication. Decompensation may present as the aforementioned exhausted, distressed state or, less commonly, as a state of 'shock', perhaps of sudden onset, in which the patient becomes virtually immobile. In either case, the objective is to re-establish normal communication: to reinforce normal, relevant conversation and to discourage agitated, perseverative or non-communicative forms of behaviour.

6 Showing concern and warmth and encouraging hope. Underlying the two previous steps is a need for the therapist to demonstrate empathy and instill hope for a resolution of the crisis (Rapoport 1967). Rapoport suggests that a collaborative approach and defining goals and tasks clearly facilitates a sense of enthusiasm. Additional ways to help the patient during intensive care, particularly following a diminution in state of over-arousal or shock, are also used in crisis counselling and therefore described in the next section.

Crisis counselling

The key difference between crisis counselling and intensive care is in the nature of the patient–therapist relationship. Whereas intensive care involves explicit transfer of responsibility, crisis counselling requires the person in crisis to accept responsibility for further developments while striving to benefit from the guidance and support of the counsellor. The nature of the relationship is made explicit, particularly if preceded by a phase of intensive care. Objectives are agreed, frequency and duration of treatment sessions spelt out, and the role of the patient emphasized. As counselling proceeds and circumstances change, this 'agreement' is often modified as necessary, but always unambiguously. For example, an initial aim may be to define problems before deciding on what further steps might be taken. Having achieved this, a new 'contract' highlighting problem solving might be made.

The therapist then adopts any of the following as appropriate, the choice determined by the nature of the crisis and the patient's resources.

1 Facilitating expression of affect. As mentioned above, affect may become a problem in its own right and impede crisis resolution. To illustrate: where cultural, family, or personality factors inhibit the expression of grief and prevent its resolution (Lindemann 1944); or early acquired attitudes to anger (e.g. 'It is wrong to lose your temper') or fear of its consequences may inhibit its expression. Unexpressed, lingering anger, manifest by sulking, and other negativistic behaviour, can have a devastating effect on a relationship. Conversely, expression of anger, if appropriate, can improve the situation dramatically.

The therapist facilitates emotional expression by listening for cues, encouraging the patient to talk about feelings, and reassuring her that their release will not be judged. Exchange of feelings between patient and partner or relatives is also promoted. Affect may be a feature of a disturbed mental state (e.g. agitated depression, morbid jealousy), and its expression likely to magnify tensions but, generally, if feelings are perceived by the therapist as understandable reactions and have not been appropriately ventilated, then this is likely to be beneficial (Aguilera 1998).

2 Facilitating communication. Problems also arise in conveying thoughts clearly. This may be a reaction to the crisis, or reflect a difficulty in communication which renders the patient and family more vulnerable. The patient's customary methods of communication are observed in the context of the therapeutic relationship or in a family interview. Feedback helps to point out how certain patterns of communication affect others and how these can be improved.

3 Facilitating understanding. Much distress results from failure to understand how a crisis situation has come about and the reasons for feeling so upset. A vivid example is the tendency for women who have been raped to question, and feel guilty about, their responses during the assault ('Why did I not fight back?') (Koss and Harvey 1991). A therapist then discusses the nature of shock and the sequence of emotions commonly experienced following rape. Similarly, survivors of a disaster are told that feelings of guilt or self-blame are common. Helping patients to appreciate these sorts of issues is intrinsically therapeutic and serves to identify problems and their potential remedies.

4 Showing concern and empathy and bolstering self-esteem. We have stressed empathy in relation to intensive care but it is just as relevant to crisis counselling. Although difficult when the patient is enveloped by failure,

bolstering self-esteem is a central task. A focus on 'protective factors' and resilience (Seligman 1995; Walsh 1998), the latter defined as the ability not only to survive and cope with the stressful situation but also to 'bounce back' and continue to develop psychologically and emotionally, is cogent in this respect. Assessment of the patient's life together with observation of current behaviour can provide the therapist with material to identify strengths and assets. This perspective (Rapp 1998) highlights inherent coping abilities that are either not being used at all or are being underused.

5 Problem solving. Distressed people are not efficient problem solvers. Instead, they tend to use more impulsive or aggressive strategies (Williams and Pollack 2000); recall Caplan's (1961) point that 'many abortive attempts at solution are made' to deal with a crisis.

The therapist adopts a stepped approach to assist the patient to resolve the current crisis as well as promote skills to deal with future demands. Problem solving is collaborative, reflecting the adult–adult nature of the therapeutic relationship.

The following techniques are pertinent:

(a) Explain the underlying principles: that distress and maladaptive behaviour often result from impaired problem solving.

(b) Help the patient to define the problem realistically, for example, by giving the patient information and feedback from other relevant sources and in terms that suggest potential methods to deal with it. A diary to monitor mood and other states can be helpful in this process.

(c) Identifying and recording treatment goals. One strategy is to ask patients what they would like to change if they had a magic wand to wave.

(d) Much problem solving depends on creative thinking which yields novel ideas. Through 'brainstorming', the patient generates multiple solutions, however implausible. The therapist can lend her own creative thinking to this process.

(e) Assessing coping resources used in the past points to strengths and limitations of various options.

(f) Ensure the patient has realistically considered the consequences and implications of various alternatives (i.e. further reality testing).

(g) Encourage the patient to make a choice when this 'feels right'.

(h) Help the patient to break down the selected strategy into manageable steps and to anticipate likely consequences, including obstacles.

(i) 'Negotiate' a contract incorporating short- and long-term goals; this is written down, with a copy for both therapist and patient.

The above approach has much in common with problem solving to treat emotional problems in general practice (Mynors–Wallace et al. 1997). It is also similar to solution-focused therapy (DeShazer et al. 1986) in which the emphasis is on working collaboratively with the patient to seek solutions rather than to solve problems.

The above framework can also accommodate a range of psychotherapeutic skills. By agreeing on goals and analysing them in detail, any difficulties the patient has in pursuing them are examinable, including salient attitudes and resistance to change.

6 Advice. Occasionally, advice offered by the therapist or another relevant agency (e.g. medical, family planning, legal, or financial) plays a role in CI. Citizens Advice Bureaux and rape crisis centres are examples of community-based organizations. A patient may be advised to defer a course of action (e.g. divorce proceedings) given the possibility, even remote, of improvement in specific situations. The therapist is aware of the rationale underlying the advice and its appropriateness in the specific circumstances.

7 Psychotropic drugs. In intensive care (see p. 202) use of psychotropic drugs presents no problem for the patient–therapist relationship. By contrast, when medication is used during crisis counselling it is crucial to counteract any implication that the need for a 'prescription' equals 'illness' and hence transfer of responsibility to the therapist. She needs to stress that the drug is only an adjunct to other methods and an aid to the patient's own efforts. Indications for medication are:

(a) To lower emotional arousal when it is jeopardizing the ability to implement problem solving or arrive at decisions or after psychological methods have failed. The aim is to reduce arousal so that effective coping manoeuvers can be resumed.

(b) To elevate mood where depression is so severe that patients are unable to participate in any problem solving. An antidepressant may have a role in elevating mood so allowing the patient to collaborate actively in CI strategies. Longer-term use will depend on clinical factors, such as severity of depression and any history of previous episodes.

(c) To improve sleep—insomnia needs special attention given its deleterious effects on coping abilities and emotional well-being. Care is taken to avoid dependence on the hypnotic, which should only be taken on a short-term basis and then gradually withdrawn.

Practical aspects of crisis counselling

The provision of intensive care requires special resources. Family or friends can often provide these but there will be many clinical situations where the professional looks for other options, such as a crisis centre offering inpatient facilities. Traditional psychiatric facilities should be used sparingly as these are not designed to provide the type of support intrinsic to crisis counselling and may only serve to prolong the initial stage of dependency.

Crisis counselling can be conducted in the patient's home or in a clinic setting and may involve family or friends. Duration of therapy is commonly between 6 and 8 weeks, but spacing of sessions is governed by the needs of the particular individual. Group approaches have been applied (Everly et al. 2000), although individually based treatment is by far the most common practice.

The patient–therapist relationship

The relationship between therapist and the person in crisis is the key aspect of CI and yet often ignored. A crisis is not inherently a psychopathological state, although its sequel might be so. As discussed earlier, transfer of responsibility may be indicated but this does not necessarily imply that the patient's condition results from a morbid process. On occasion the label of illness does serve to protect self-esteem. In other circumstances, it may discourage a person from learning new coping skills to handle future stresses. Two decisions have to be taken therefore at an early stage. Is this person in, or about to descend into, a decompensated state which requires urgent intervention and transfer of responsibility? And is designating the person as ill appropriate? These decisions are based on astute clinical judgement, confounded by people presenting in a state of decompensation as a regressive method of coping; they have learnt to do this in the past and found that it worked, at least in the short-term. Knowledge of past history, particularly evidence of similar reactions on previous occasions, eases the task.

A final aspect of the therapeutic relationship revolves around what the therapist can offer in terms of contact between sessions, duration of therapy, and 'boundaries'. People in crisis are often profoundly distressed and are apt to feel vulnerable and helpless. The therapist may be tempted to provide more than is clinically appropriate, thereby fostering undue dependency, even regression.

A typical example of CI

The following case history illustrates the type of problem and objectives involved in both intensive care and crisis counselling.

Gerald, a 38-year-old accountant, and Elizabeth, a full-time homemaker, had been married for 12 years; they had two children aged 11 and 8. For the previous 3 months, an old family friend, Brian, whose marriage had broken up and who was in financial difficulty, had been staying with them. Twelve hours before being referred by his general practitioner to the local Crisis Unit, Gerald had discovered Brian and Elizabeth having sexual intercourse in their house. After an angry scene he had told them both to get out. They had both departed at midnight, driving off in Brian's car. A neighbour found Gerald, the next morning, in an agitated state. The two children were distressed and frightened, having witnessed the ejection of their mother.

When assessed by the crisis counsellor, Gerald was still acutely agitated, expressing intense anger with Elizabeth and Brian and alarm at the prospect of being left on his own with the children. He was making distinct suicidal threats if his wife was not prepared to care for them. The counsellor determined that Gerald's reaction—a combination of anger, humiliation, and the threat of a single parental role—rendered him unable to care for the children or safe to be left on his own. Immediate intensive care was therefore indicated and the following plan implemented: he was strongly advised to enter the unit for 2–3 days, and to hand over responsibility for the children to the unit staff; arrangements were made for the children to be looked after by a family friend; he was encouraged to ventilate his feelings of hurt and resentment; and he was given a mild hypnotic to help him sleep (he was utterly exhausted).

He had largely regained his composure within a day and a half, and although still intensely angry he was deemed capable of returning home to look after the children. The intensive care phase ended at this stage. It was then agreed that he would resume responsibility for himself and the children but if he felt at any time he was unable to maintain this, he was to contact the unit immediately. Crisis counselling was started and an appointment set for the next day. Three such sessions were held over the following week, during which a range of problems were dealt with. A key component of therapy was the use of problem-solving techniques, for example, clarifying and defining the problems, generating possible solutions, selecting a preferred solution, exploring various coping methods, and evaluating the effectiveness of any actions taken. Problem solving was used in particular to deal with the following two issues:

1 how to deal with the needs of the children in the short term—it was agreed that he would take time off work to be at home until the situation became clearer.

2 what to do about the marriage—after further ventilation of feelings occurred, it was agreed that the therapist should contact Elizabeth with the view to recommending a joint session.

After additional sessions during the subsequent 3 weeks, it emerged that couple therapy was unlikely to alter the situation and that Elizabeth had opted to remain with Brian. She revealed long-standing discontent with the marriage. Gerald then arranged for a part-time housekeeper so that he could return to work. He also launched divorce proceedings.

This case demonstrates the utility of brief intensive care, paving the way for crisis counselling (of six sessions over a month).

Ending CI

Because of the short-term and collaborative nature of CI, the likely duration of therapy is determined explicitly as is the expectation that the patient will assume an active role, during the sessions themselves as well as between them. At an early stage in crisis counselling, it is helpful to propose a predetermined number of sessions (i.e. a 'limited contract') although these can be extended if necessary. Criteria for ending treatment should be relatively clear at the onset of crisis counselling. In most cases, these involve goals that should be reached to enable the patient to return to his previous level (possibly a higher level) of functioning, rather than fully resolving all problems (Roberts 2000). The final session should be one in which therapist and patient focus on progress accomplished, as well as anticipate possible setbacks and how to handle them. Ideally, a follow-up appointment should be scheduled at the last session. Its precise timing will vary according to clinical circumstances but will usually occur 1–2 months later.

Problems encountered in the course of therapy

Patients who encounter difficulty in agreeing to a limited therapeutic contract or to the collaborative requirement may be seeking a more dependent relationship. In such a case it becomes a key task to discuss the likely repercussions of passivity and dependency and the constraints these impose on CI. Reluctance to modify these expectations may suggest the need for longer-term psychotherapy to deal with long-standing personality traits and defences.

Another common problem is that limited improvement may occur because the patient's family and friends continue to exert a negative, disruptive influence, effectively 'sabotaging' CI. This is more common when the therapist has had no contact with the patient's 'significant others'.

Training

CI offers much scope for the deployment of empathy and sensitivity, attributes some therapists are fortunate to have as part of their overall personality, but which all can enhance through monitoring their own performance. Clinical practice, ideally with a range of people in crisis, under supervision of an experienced therapist, is a pivotal component of training. Observation of a veteran at work using videotapes or a one-way screen is most valuable. Supervision is often done in the context of regular meetings of the crisis team where ongoing cases are presented, and there are opportunities to practice role-plays (e.g. of methods of interventions, problems encountered in crisis counseling, etc.). Knowledge of the clinical and research literature is another facet of training (see the recommended reading provided at the end of the chapter).

Novices need to recognize their limitations. Communicating a sense of competence in tandem with empathic concern is a major therapeutic achievement, particularly in the course of intensive care. Inexperienced therapists may feel insecure since they suspect there are forms of help with which they are unfamiliar. Although the complexity of crisis and CI cannot be fully done justice to in the space available, the essence has been more or less covered. For the most part CI relies on skilful use of common sense rather than highly specialized professional skills.

Research

Given the range of approaches under the rubric of CI, a firm conclusion about effectiveness is elusive. The difficulties in carrying out outcome research with heterogeneous types of crisis and considerable variability in levels of competence to cope are formidable. However, studies on specific approaches with particular clinical groups are very much needed. CI has only been examined systematically in a few of these (e.g. suicidal behaviour, psychiatric emergencies, and crime victimization) (see Corcoran and Roberts 2000). Even in the case of suicidality, where substantial research has been carried out, few studies involve randomized controlled trials (Neimeyer and Pfeiffer 1994). In a review evaluating the benefits of suicide prevention centres in a number of countries, Lester (1997) found a modest effect (effect size of 0.16). People aged 15–24 and 55–64, and women in general, showed the best response.

In a study of the treatment of depression, problem-solving treatment was found effective when administered by professionals with varied backgrounds and training (e.g. psychiatrists, general practitioners, and community nurses) (Mynors-Wallace et al. 1997). In another study, problem-solving therapy produced better results than control treatment in symptom improvement for deliberate self-harm patients (Townsend et al. 2001).

Studies on CI in psychiatric emergencies have mostly used symptom improvement and hospital admission rates as outcome measures. Overall, this work has found positive results but, as Corcoran and Roberts (2000) point out, these studies have had methodological shortcomings including lack of comparison or control groups, lack of standardized measures, and poor description of treatments used.

Recommendations have been made about research designs and assessment measures that are most appropriate to evaluate CI (Neimeyer and Pfeiffer 1994; Dziegielewski and Powers 2000). We may hope that these will stimulate good quality research, especially on the components that contribute to change.

Conclusion

In this chapter we have provided a framework encompassing a series of explicit interventions. Although many approaches to CI have evolved since the 1960s, they share much in common. There is clearly a need for more outcome research, but the widespread and increasing use of CI techniques is testimony to their usefulness.

References

Aguilera, D. C. (1998). *Crisis intervention: Theory and methodology*. (8th edn). Mosby, St. Louis, Mo.

Bancroft, J. (1978). Crisis intervention. In *Introduction to the psychotherapies*. (1st edn). (ed S. Bloch). Oxford University Press, Oxford.

Brown, G. W., Bifulco, A., and Harris, T. O. (1987). Life events, vulnerability and onset of depression. *British Journal of Psychiatry*, 150, 30–42.

Caplan, G. (1961). *An approach to community mental health*. Tavistock, London.

Cluse–Tolar, T. (1997). Gender differences in crisis theory recovery: rethinking crisis theory. *Crisis Intervention*, 3, 189–198.

Corcoran, J. and Roberts, A. R. (2000). Research on crisis intervention and recommendations for future research. In *Crisis intervention handbook. Assessment, treatment and research*. (2nd edn), (ed A. R. Roberts), pp. 453–486. Oxford University Press, New York.

DeShazer, S., Berg, I. K., Lipchik, E., Nunnally, E., Molnar, A., Gingerich, W., and Weiner–Davis, M. (1986). Brief therapy: Focused solution development. *Family Process*, 25, 207–221.

Dziegielewski, S. F. and Powers, G. T. (2000). Designs and procedures for evaluating crisis intervention. In *Crisis intervention handbook. Assessment, treatment, and research*. (2nd edn), (ed A. R. Roberts), pp. 487–511. Oxford University Press, New York.

Erikson, E. H. (1969). *Childhood and society*. Penguin, Harmondsworth.

Everly, G. S., Lating, J. M., and Mitchell, J. T. (2000). Innovations in group crisis intervention. In *Crisis intervention handbook. Assessment, treatment, and research*. (2nd edn), (ed A. R. Roberts), pp. 77–97. Oxford University Press, New York.

Hawton, K., Fagg, J., Simkin, S., Bale, E., and Bond, A. (1997). Trends in deliberate self-harm in Oxford, 1985–1995. Implications for clinical services and the prevention of suicide. *British Journal of Psychiatry*, **171**, 556–560.

James, R. K. and Gilliland, J.(2005). *Crisis intervention strategies*. (5th edn), Wadsworth, Belmont, CA.

Kessler, R. C., Sonnega, A., Bromet, E., Hughes, M., and Nelson, C. (1995). Posttraumatic stress disorder in the National Comorbidity Survey. *Archives of General Psychiatry*, **52**, 1048–1060.

Koss, M. P. and Harvey, M. R. (1991). The rape victim: Clinical and community interventions (2nd edn). Sage, Newbury Park, California.

Lazarus, R. S. (1993). From psychological stress to the emotions: A history of changing outlooks. *Annual Review of Psychology*, **44**, 1–21.

Lester, D. (1997). The effectiveness of suicide prevention centers: A review. *Suicide and Life-threatening Behavior*, **27**, 304–310.

Lewis, S. J. and Harrison D. F. (2000). Crisis intervention with HIV–positive women. In *Crisis intervention handbook. Assessment, treatment, and research.* (2nd edn), (ed A. R. Roberts), pp. 337–356. Oxford University Press, New York.

Lindemann, E. (1944). Symptomatology and management of acute grief, *American Journal of Psychiatry*, **101**, 101–48.

MacNeil, G. and Stewart, C. (2000). Crisis intervention with school violence problems and volatile situations. In *Crisis Intervention Handbook. Assessment, Treatment, and Research.* (2nd edn), (ed A. R. Roberts), pp. 229–249. Oxford University Press, New York.

Mynors-Wallis, L., Gath, D. H., Davies, I., Gray, A., and Barbour, F. (1997). A randomized controlled trial and cost analysis of problem-solving treatment given by community nurses for emotional disorders in primary care. *British Journal of Psychiatry*, **170**, 113–119.

Neimeyer, R. A. and Pfeiffer, A. M. (1994). Evaluation of suicide intervention effectiveness. *Death Studies*, **18**, 131–166.

Parkes, C. M. (1986). *Bereavement: Studies of grief in adult life.* (2nd edn). Penguin, Harmondsworth.

Rapoport, L. (1967). Crisis-oriented short-term casework. *Social Service Review*, **41**, 31–43.

Rapp, C. A. (1998). *The strengths model: Case management with people suffering from severe and persistent mental illness.* Oxford University Press, New York.

Roberts, A. R. (2000). *Crisis intervention handbook. Assessment, treatment, and research.* (2nd ed). Oxford University Press, New York.

Roberts, A. R. and Roberts, B. S. (2000). A comprehensive model for crisis intervention with battered women and their children. In: *Crisis intervention handbook. Assessment, treatment, and research.* (ed A. R. Roberts), pp. 177–208. Oxford University Press, New York.

Seligman, M. E. P. (1995). *The optimistic child.* Houghton Mifflin, Boston.

Townsend, E., Hawton, K., Altman, D. G., Arensman, E., Gunnell, D., Hazell, P., House, A., and van Heeringen, K. (2001). The efficacy of problem-solving treatments after deliberate self-harm: Meta-analysis of randomized controlled trials with respect to depression, hopelessness and improvement in problems. *Psychological Medicine*, **31**, 979–988.

Viney, L. L., Benjamin, Y. N., Clarke, A. M., and Bunn, T. A. (1985). Sex differences in the psychological reactions of medical and surgical patients to crisis intervention counselling: Sauce for the goose may not be sauce for the gander. *Social Science and Medicine*, **20**, 1199–1205.

Vingerhoets, A. J. M. and Van Heck, G. L. (1990). Gender, coping and psychosomatic symptoms. *Psychological Medicine*, **20**, 125–35.

Wadsworth, M. E., Gudmundsen, G. R., Raviv, T., Ahlkvist, J. A., McIntosh, D. D., Kline, G. H., Rea, J. and Burwell, R. A. (2004) Coping with terrorism: Age and gender differences in effortful and involuntary responses to September 11th. *Applied Developmental Science*, **8**, 143–157.

Walsh, F. (1998). *Strengthening family resilience*. Guilford, New York.

Williams, J. M. G. and Pollack, L. R. (2000). The psychology of suicidal behaviour. In *The International Handbook of Suicide and Attempted Suicide*. (ed. K. Hawton and K. van Heeringen), pp. 79–93. Wiley, Chichester.

Recommended reading

Aguilera, D. C. (1998). *Crisis intervention: Theory and methodology*. (8th edn). Mosby, St. Louis, Mo. (a concise and useful text; chapters 8 and 9 on situational and life cycle stressors are most informative.)

Caplan, G. (1974). *Support systems and community mental health*. Grune and Stratton, New York. (Chapter 1 contains a helpful account of the concept of support in relation to crisis.)

Cluse-Tolar, T. (1997). Gender differences in crisis theory recovery: rethinking crisis theory. *Crisis Intervention*, **3**, 189–198. (interesting study on gender differences in response to CI.)

Corcoran, J. and Roberts, A. R. (2000). Research on crisis intervention and recommendations for future research. In *Crisis intervention handbook. Assessment, treatment, and research*. (2nd edn), (ed A. R. Roberts), pp. 453–486. Oxford University Press, New York. (useful and practical recommendations for future research on outcome of CI.)

James, R. K. and Gilliland, J. (2005). *Crisis intervention strategies*. (5th edn), Wadsworth, Belmont, CA. (useful handbook covering all aspects of CI.)

Mynors-Wallis, L. (2002). Does problem-solving treatment work through resolving problems? *Psychological Medicine*, **32**, 1315–1319. (empirical study that provides a good overview of problem-solving treatment used in general practice.)

Rapp, C. A. (1998). *The strengths model: Case management with people suffering from severe and persistent mental illness*. Oxford University Press, New York. (interesting book that outlines the 'Strengths perspective', which is highly relevant to CI.)

Roberts, A. R. (2000). *Crisis Intervention Handbook. Assessment, Treatment, and Research*. (2nd edn). Oxford University Press, New York. (a comprehensive handbook covering all aspects of CI; the Introduction and chapters 1, 2, and 20 are particularly useful.)

Chapter 10

Supportive psychotherapy

Sidney Bloch

Supportive psychotherapy has several meanings. In this chapter I will refer to a form of psychological treatment used for patients with enduring and disabling psychiatric conditions for whom basic change is an unrealistic goal. Applying the term in this way, supportive therapy is probably one of the most commonly practised psychotherapies. In addition to its use in psychiatry, the therapy is also applied by, among others, general practitioners and social workers.

Supportive therapy as a mode of psychological treatment can be traced back to the 1930s when Paul Schilder (1938) referred to supportive techniques such as advice, catharsis, reassurance, and modelling. A few years later, Alexander and French (1946) referred to patients with a 'warped ego' where 'there is little hope of effecting permanent change' in whom long-term, sometimes interminable, guidance, strengthening of defences, reassurance and 'protection' were required.

The growing interest in the role supportive therapy can play in mental health practice is reflected in the publication of a range of relevant books, articles, and chapters (e.g. Rockland 1989a; Berlincioni and Barbieri 2004; Novalis et al. 1993). Reviews by Rockland (1993), Van Marle and Holmes (2002), and Winston et al. (1986) are noteworthy and well worth reading. I make further reference to this material in the sections that follow. We now turn to a definition of supportive therapy and consider its aims, indications, therapeutic components, and problems that may arise in the course of treatment.

Definition and theoretical considerations

An agreed upon definition of supportive therapy has proved elusive, principally because not all contributors to the subject regard it as a treatment for the chronically ill and there is continuing conflation between supportive therapy as a *bona fide* psychological treatment in its own right and the place of support as a potential ingredient of all psychotherapies (Holmes 1988; Novalis et al. 1993; Pinsker 1994). We should note that our focus here is on a form of treatment in which therapist support is paramount. Other therapies may well entail a degree of support but this is only one of several therapeutic components deployed, not the principal one.

The derivation of the work 'support' helps us to understand the therapy under consideration: Supportare: Sup = Sub + portare—to carry (*Oxford English Dictionary*, Oxford University Press, Oxford 1978). In essence, the therapist helps to sustain and bolster the patient. An implication follows: that some patients are so affected by their psychiatric state or limitations of personality that they depend on professional assistance in order to 'live to fight another day'.

Supportive therapy can thus be defined as a psychological treatment provided to a patient over an extended period, often years, with the aim of sustaining him psychologically, given his inability to function adequately on his own. An alternative definition by Gilbert and Ugelstad (1994) stresses: '. . . supporting and strengthening the potential for better and more mature ego functioning in both adaptational and developmental tasks'. Piper and his colleagues (2002) put it this way: '. . . supportive therapy is a treatment principally focused on strengthening mental structures that are actively or chronically deficient, in contrast to the focus on facilitating insight in interpretive therapy'. Their list of its features alongside those of interpretive psychotherapy in a table (see p. 52) is a most useful elaboration of their definition.

Obviously, an inability to cope on one's own may be transitory or long term. In the former situation, a person typically is overwhelmed by a stressful life event such as bereavement, divorce, or loss of job, which leads to a degree of emotional upheaval not countered by his internal resources and usual supports. The person is in crisis and crisis intervention indicated; this is dealt with in Chapter 9.

Enduring incapacity to manage independently is found in people who are disabled by a chronic psychotic or neurotic condition or by marked personality dysfunction; they may require supportive therapy indefinitely.

A distinction between supportive and exploratory (or interpretive, insight-oriented, dynamic, expressive) psychotherapy is a subject of much debate among psychoanalysts (Berlincioni and Barbieri 2004). Kernberg (1984), for example, refers to a spectrum with supportive and expressive at the two ends, with movement possible depending on the degree of patient impairment and clinical progress. Pine (1986) also advances the notion from a psychoanalytic perspective of how interpretations are given in specific ways for the psychologically vulnerable, namely the therapist applies only supportive strategies, thus making interventions possible.

Pinsker's (1994) contribution on theoretical aspects illuminates further the complexity of arriving at a uniform definition. He concludes that since supportive therapy is 'not based upon a theory of mind or personality or psychopathology, it should not be thought of as a unique modality of treatment but rather as a body of techniques or tactics that function with various theoretical orientation.' Barber et al. (2001) also concentrate on technique in their conceptual account by asserting that supportive strategies pervade the psychotherapies but are used to achieve specific purposes (see Alford and Beck (1997) below). Drawing on empirical evidence, a mere four studies, the authors conclude that: (1) supportive techniques and the therapeutic alliance are different entities and (2) we need to differentiate between the supportive value of an aspect of treatment and an explicitly supportive manoeuvre in the therapist's set of methods. This chapter is written with the same observation in mind but with a crucial proviso: a range of theoretical principles derived from several schools and systems—psychoanalytic, behavioural, cognitive, self-psychology, attachment, and object-relations among them—are relevant to supportive therapy, and usefully incorporated according to clinical need.

Thus, Dewald (1994) when describing pertinent principles, applies psychoanalytic terms but avoids equating supportive therapy with a modified form of psychoanalysis. Buckley (1994) roams onto other theoretical terrain to understand both the techniques and value of supportive therapy. For example, he cites Kohut's emphasis on empathy as a means to foster a positive transference while still appreciating that an 'idealized object is unavailable or imperfect'. Buckley also embraces Winnicott's 'holding environment' as another concept which pertains to creating a suitable framework; the patient feels sufficiently secure to feel real and to relate authentically to others.

Alford and Beck (1997) have contributed usefully to the topic of support in psychotherapy, with a particular focus on its role in cognitive therapy (CT). They regard CT as a supportive therapy in the sense that the therapist is a 'helper', a 'benefactor', who encourages the patient within the domain of cognitive theory. Responsible dependency is carefully distinguished from regression—the therapist directs treatment but ensures that the patient is an active collaborator. In addition to the director role, the cognitive therapist also assumes supportive functions. What is supported, in effect, are the patient's efforts to work at the task of correcting maladaptive schemas.

As Berlinicioni and Barbieri (2004) note, the precise theoretical foundation of supportive therapy remain elusive, and subject to debate. The relationship between supportive and exploratory approaches in the area of psychoanalytic therapy is especially problematic. How theory will finally be sorted out is a key question, for example, is supportive therapy best regarded as an eclectic-driven treatment or should it fall under the psychodynamic rubric or should other specific theories, such as attachment theory (Holmes 1996) and ego psychology, be harnessed to constitute an integrated framework?

Background

Provision of support to vulnerable, needy people has a long tradition. Religious orders particularly have played, and continue to play, the part of 'therapist'. Relatives and friends may obviously serve as sources of long-term support to those in need. With the advent of 'professional' psychotherapy in the 1890s, psychiatrists and other mental health practitioners systematically applied psychological strategies in their work, but tended to concentrate on neurotic and, later, personality disordered patients. Chronically mentally ill patients, particularly those with psychosis, were relegated by contrast to the back wards of mental hospitals and only given custodial care.

The advent of antipsychotic medication in the 1950s and associated community-based treatment from the 1970s enabled an increasing proportion of patients with long-term psychiatric conditions to be cared for outside the hospital. A corollary was the central role of supportive therapy for them. The salient question remains how mental health professionals can best care effectively for people with long-term disability who live outside of institutions, often isolated and with minimal natural support.

Aims

The aims of supportive therapy are shaped in part by features of the patient—diagnosis, severity, social circumstances, personal resources, and the like—but common objectives are:

1 to promote his best possible psychological and social adaptation by restoring and/or reinforcing the ability to cope with life's vicissitudes and challenges;

2 to strengthen adaptive defence mechanisms and discourage those that are maladaptive;

3 to bolster self-esteem by identifying and highlighting assets and achievements;

4 to make the patient cognizant of the reality of the situation, for example, of his intrinsic limitations and those of treatment and of what is and is not achievable;

5 to forestall relapse, thus striving to avoid deterioration and re-institutionalization;

6 to enable the patient to use only that level of professional support which will result in his best possible adaptation, so avoiding undue dependency;

7 to transfer sources of support (not necessarily all of it) from professionals to relatives or friends, provided the latter are available and equipped psychologically and materially, to assume the role of caregiver.

Indications

Supportive psychotherapy is indicated in psychiatric patients who are severely impaired emotionally, cognitively, behaviourally, and interpersonally and in whom there is, realistically, negligible prospect of basic improvement. Werman (1984) sums it up this way: '... supportive psychotherapy assumes that the patient's psychological equipment is fundamentally inadequate'. Their condition means they cannot live adaptively without external sources of help. They are vulnerable to life's stresses, even minor pressures. They may encounter difficulty in requesting help, whether professional or from others, or in making use of help that is offered. Life events tend to disrupt their equilibrium, leading to symptom formation or increased dependency. Relatives and friends who might be sources of support are often absent, or unable or unwilling to respond satisfactorily to the patient's needs. The severity of their condition and associated fragility preclude applying forms of psychotherapy that entail acquisition of insight and aim for 'structural' change.

Dewald (1994) captures the gist of these criteria. Supportive therapy is usually indicated for people who have difficult, unstable, or limited interpersonal relationships; for those who are not introspective or curious about themselves and their psychological functioning; for patients whose reality resources preclude the necessary frequency or expense of intensive psychotherapy; or for those whose interest is predominantly in symptomatic change and whose capacity for self-initiating behaviour is limited.

In terms of conventional diagnosis suitable candidates come from the following categories:

1 Chronic schizophrenia and related psychoses including delusional and schizo-affective disorders (Kates and Rockland 1994);

2 Recurrent or chronic affective disorders including unipolar, bipolar, cyclothymia and dysthymia, and unresolved grief (Müller and Barash-Kishon 1998);

3 Long-standing neurotic and somatoform disorders including phobic and anxiety states, adjustment disorders, somatization, and hypochondriasis (Kellner 1985; Karasu 1986);

4 Marked disorders of personality such as dependent, paranoid, schizotypal, schizoid, borderline, narcissistic, and histrionic (Kernberg 1984; Rockland 1992; Paris 1993; Stone 2000; Aviram et al. 2004).

Obviously not all patients with these diagnosis are impaired; indeed, many may make good progress with exploratory psychotherapies and/or medication. We are concerned here with an enduringly impaired group, whose needs are considered in terms of how they might be best helped to accomplish and maintain their best possible adjustment.

Determining whether patients are suitable for supportive therapy does not usually pose a problem. Conversely, the treatment has no place in those in whom there is clear evidence of personal resources and strengths, sufficient to meet life's demands.

The therapeutic relationship

As is obvious in Sally's case below, the typical patient for whom supportive therapy is indicated has much difficulty in maintaining relationships, both intimate and general. An intense relationship entailing closeness and trust poses a distinct threat. This is borne in mind when considering the type of link between patient and therapist in supportive therapy. This is well illustrated in a classical study by Balint et al. (1970). Patients who requested repeat prescriptions (mainly for psychotropics) from their GPs made frequent contact with them but always obliquely. They were isolated, showed long-standing maladaptive traits, and 'tolerated badly any proximity or intimacy with their partners'. They maintained a safe distance from their doctors, chiefly by 'offering them bodily complaints' and receiving in return repeat prescriptions; the drug represented the 'something' they needed. The patients seemed incapable of making use of a warm alliance, the basis of psychotherapy.

The relationship therefore between patient and therapist in supportive therapy is of a particular kind: the therapist assumes a helping role, attends sensitively to the patient's needs through various strategies (to be discussed below), but promotes only a modest level of closeness (Crown 1988).

Another reason for this type of relationship is pragmatic. Patients receiving supportive therapy are enduringly impaired and require help for extended periods, usually lifelong. The same therapist will often be unavailable for such a long-term commitment since he may well move to another position. Fostering an overly intense relationship paves the way for a greater sense of loss and the risk of deterioration when the therapist departs. An obvious alternative is for the patient to develop an institutional alliance, that is, a relationship with the clinic rather than with a single therapist. The clinic is *always* there, a dependable and secure framework.

Transference is always present as part of therapist–patient interaction. In contrast to psychoanalytic treatment in which transference patterns are identified and interpreted, the supportive therapist 'manages' transference phenomena (Misch 2000). Positive forms are used to enhance the working alliance; negative forms are corrected promptly but sensitively.

Another feature typifying the therapist–patient relationship is the therapist's directive role. He assumes a relatively elevated measure of responsibility—not seen in other forms of psychotherapy—on the premise that the patient finds it too demanding to live autonomously. To an extent the bond resembles that between parent and child, the therapist creating a link through which she offers the security and care the patient needs (Winnicott 1965; Meyer 1993; Misch 2000). Misch is emphatic about the type of role needed: 'What would a good parent do in this situation with this person?' The therapist also uses the relationship as a vehicle to implement a number of therapeutic strategies which we now describe.

Components of supportive therapy

Although we discuss each of the following components separately, they are not discrete in practice. Teasing them out, however, clarifies their specific application. They are not considered in any order since they are applicable at any time and in varying combination (see Pinsker 1997 and Misch 2000 for clear and comprehensive accounts).

1 *Reassurance.* The therapist reassures patients in two main ways: by removing doubts and misconceptions, and by pointing to their assets. Patients commonly harbour thoughts about themselves which are ill-founded and distressing. For example, a married man who believed he was losing his sanity was relieved at being reassured that he was definitely not destined for such a fate and that his feelings of jealousy were an exaggeration of a normal emotion and quite understandable in the light of his deprived upbringing. Reassurance is used to good effect to relieve such fears in the patient as that he is crazy or becoming so, will be detained in a hospital, has a serious physical illness, and his symptoms are unique.

The long-term psychiatric patient has invariably lost self-confidence. On reviewing his life he can discern nothing but failure and missed opportunities. Although this may partially be true, he omits from the self-appraisal any positive qualities or other assets. The therapist can bolster his esteem by point-ing these out. A caveat applies. To be effective, reassurance must be realistic. To promote hope and morale unreasonably through reassurance that is ground-less may be effective in the short term but is bound to backfire later. The ther-apist therefore aims to create a climate of positive expectation but shorn of disingenuousness.

2 *Explanation.* This strategy is used very differently in supportive therapy compared to psychotherapy in which the chief goal is to promote insight (see Chapter 5). In the former, explanation (or to use the customary term, inter-pretation) of such phenomena as transference, resistance, defences (Van Marle and Holmes 2002), and unconscious determinants of behaviour, is inappro-priate and best avoided. Instead, explanation relates to day-to-day practical questions and to the external reality with which the patient grapples. The goal is not to promote psychodynamic self-understanding but to enhance the abil-ity to cope by clarifying the nature of the problems and challenges the patient faces and how he can best manage them. The generic term, psycho-education, is often applied to cover the associated learning that the patient needs to do.

This 'reality testing' is crucial for the impaired patient since he has to become aware of the nature of his condition and of any unrealistic fantasies he may nurture. He must also appreciate the limits of the therapist and of his techniques (i.e. 'I cannot expect a magic cure'). Following appropriate explanation, he is better equipped to accept that he must live in spite of his long-standing difficulties in the best way possible. He should acknowledge: 'I have to live with this for a long time to come, perhaps lifelong; what can I do in collaboration with the therapist to face the future?'

The therapist may clarify an array of issues among which are the nature of the symptoms (e.g. 'These headaches are due to your scalp muscles tightening up when you feel tense and not to a brain tumour'); the reason for taking medication (e.g. 'These tablets will make you feel more relaxed and this in turn will help to prevent your breaking down again'); the reason for a relapse (e.g. 'It's not surprising you are feeling distressed given the pressure you have been under since you husband became ill'). Note that all these examples are couched in straightforward, everyday language. Explanations using technical terms or peppered with jargon exert little impact since they are often beyond the patient's comprehension.

3 *Guidance.* Supportive therapy entails guiding the patient in many ways, mainly through direct advice. As with explanation, the stress is on practical matters, including the most fundamental—budgeting, personal hygiene, nutrition, and sleep. Advice may be necessary in respect of work (e.g. how to

apply for a position, whether to change jobs, how to approach a boss to make a reasonable request); or about family (e.g. how best to relate to an aged parent, what to do about a rebellious son); or about leisure (e.g. how to join a social club, how to pursue a hobby).

The goal is not merely to assist the patient to deal with a particular issue but also to teach him requisite skills for coping with other similar problems. Ideally, he learns to assess common pressures and identify corresponding measures to deal with them. He thus becomes better placed to handle stress and to tackle decisions. Particularly pertinent is teaching the patient how and when to seek help appropriately. Many patients have been unable to do this throughout their lives, often calling for aid when the situation is dire or, conversely, frustrating their caregivers, professional or natural, by insatiable or pervasive demands. Moreover, they may have expressed their difficulties in terms of bodily symptoms or made impulsive suicide attempt or delayed consultation until they were either intensely distressed or functioning poorly. In summary, the therapist tries to enhance the patient's coping skills and to teach him how to ask for help when this is necessary.

Occasionally, when advice proves inadequate, *persuasion* is another option. The therapist shifts from a gently directive to a more controlling stance as he tries to convince the patient to think or act in a particular way. This may relate, for example, to a decision the patient has to make or to specific action the therapist senses he should pursue. The therapist must feel confident of his ground before resorting to this strategy and preferably use advice and explanation first. A risk always lurks that persuasion reflects the therapist's personal attitudes and beliefs rather than being objectively grounded.

4 *Suggestion*. In this strategy, similar to guidance, the patient is offered less 'freedom' to comply. The therapist aims to induce change by influencing him implicitly or explicitly. An example of implicit influence is the therapist manifesting approval of desirable behaviour: 'The way you stood up for yourself was terrific', with the obvious implication that the patient will benefit by replicating the specific behaviour. As with persuasion, guidance and explanation, in which the patient plays a more collaborative role, are preferable to suggestion, and should be attempted first.

5 *Encouragement*. To encourage a patient is such common sense that we are likely to take it for granted. Effective use of encouragement is made, however, when the therapist is keenly aware of what he is trying to achieve. Patients with long-standing difficulties need 'injections of courage' repeatedly but this is best done in relation to particular circumstances in their lives or therapy. Rather than encourage in nebulous terms, the therapist does so in specific

contexts. These vary from patient to patient but what remains consistent are its objectives: to combat feelings of inferiority, to promote self-esteem, and to urge the patient to adopt courses of action or behaviours of which he is hesitant or anxious.

The therapist encourages in myriad ways according to need and circumstance. For example, he can use the full force of an authoritative, benevolent role by commenting: 'From my long experience in dealing with this sort of problem, I am fully confident you will be able to master it'. She may also demonstrate her sense of optimism non-verbally through a display of eagerness. As with reassurance, the therapist exploits past or current progress by positive reinforcement, explicit or tacit. He may comment: 'Last year you proved how effectively you could discuss your work schedule with your boss—I'm certain you have it in you to do it this time too'.

Caution is required regarding encouragement. Its use may not only be futile but also counter-therapeutic if given inappropriately. To encourage a patient unrealistically, towards a goal, way out of his reach, may have a contrary result to that intended. He becomes dispirited as he battles to attain what the therapist hopes for but which he himself finds daunting. Limitations imposed by the patient's condition and impaired resources must be respected. In any event, he is encouraged to take small steps, thereby increasing the chance of negotiating them successfully. Each experience of mastery then promotes self-confidence and serves as a source of encouragement for subsequent initiatives (see Chapter 4).

6 *Effecting changes in the patient's environment.* Patients with a long-standing psychiatric condition or disorder of personality are markedly influenced by social forces, both human and institutional. The deleterious effects on the schizophrenic patient of a family atmosphere typified by high 'emotional expressiveness' is a good illustration (Leff and Vaughn 1985). In supportive therapy a cardinal consideration is the patient in his social context; the goals are to remove or alter detrimental elements and, conversely, to maximize potentially beneficial ones. The therapist regularly asks herself: 'How can I help to modify my patient's social environment to his best advantage?'

Stressful factors are carefully assessed so that they can be modified. The range is infinite, the following common: the patient's job has outstretched his psychological resources; the family atmosphere is tense; the housing situation is poor; he is socially isolated; and financial pressures are mounting. Environmental changes of a more positive kind (i.e. adding to the patient's world) are as relevant as removing a stressor. Encouraging the patient to participate in social activities like those found in community centres or helping him to try out or resume creative hobbies and pastimes, can be of considerable value. Social contact is enhanced in a protective setting, and the patient derives pleasure from intrinsically worthwhile pursuits.

Note the two dimensions of this strategy: (1) working directly with the patient by helping him, for example, to obtain a suitable job or to approach the appropriate authorities for sickness or other benefits, or putting him in touch with social clubs (social workers are most helpful with these aspects); and (2) working with people who are significant for the patient, particularly relatives. Here, straightforward counselling often helps both relatives and, indirectly, the patient. If we recall that an aim of supportive therapy is to transfer some of the sources of support from professionals to family or friends (assuming they exist) it follows that the better equipped they are for the task, the more apt they are to succeed. The job is no easy matter (Van Marle and Holmes 2002). Caring for a chronically ill patient calls for perseverance and discretion (Bloch et al. 1994). The therapist helping relatives or friends can use many of the strategies we discussed above, including guidance, encouragement, and reassurance.

Failure of supportive therapy may well be due, at least in part, to the therapist neglecting the family's needs. He may have overlooked the positive effects on a patient's welfare that can ensue when optimizing the family's role as ally. The family's successful recruitment, however, requires they be fully informed and counselled, and then instructed as to what to do, and how to do it. Family members also need help in their own right to care for their relative since the process can be burdensome and frustrating.

The need may arise to alter the patient's environment radically because his condition has deteriorated or he has become exposed to a particularly noxious situation. Options include admission to a psychiatric ward, attendance at a day hospital, or participation in a sheltered workshop or occupational therapy programme. Such a development need not be construed by either therapist or patient as a failure if both appreciate that the latter's resources will periodically be outstretched by circumstances.

7 Permission for catharsis. The relative security typifying the therapeutic relationship in supportive therapy permits the patient to share, with a sense of relief, pent-up feelings like fear, grief, sorrow, concern, frustration, and envy. The clinic is commonly the sole place where the patient can feel safe enough to do this. The therapist, by showing that he is an empathic, active listener who accepts the patient unconditionally, facilitates the disclosure of 'secrets', however painful or embarrassing. Although sharing emotionally charged material is not necessarily effective in and of itself, the process does lead to a sense of relief and serves as a vehicle for other therapeutic strategies.

Associated components of therapy

Other therapeutic methods can complement supportive therapy when appropriate. Drug treatment may well have a place (e.g. maintenance antipsychotics in chronic schizophrenia or lithium to prevent recurrent mood swings). The therapist clarifies the precise role of psychotropic medication in a particular patient and only uses it when solid clinical criteria are met.

Other methods include relaxation training, social skills training, and occupational therapy. Seeing the patient together with family members may be indicated but the approach is usually psychoeducational and supportive rather than interpretive and systems-oriented. The therapist uses the strategies we discussed above in order to help the family cope more effectively as a group (Bloch et al. 1994).

Supportive psychotherapy in practice

More often than not, trainees are assigned to patients for long-term support rather that for supportive therapy *per se*. Typically the therapist 'slides' into the work rather than mapping out clear objectives. Therapy can, as a result, be unfocused, even haphazard.

When initiating support therapy , it is helpful to pose a series of interlocking questions. How often will I see the patient? How long will each session be? How long will therapy continue for? Is it desirable that I collaborate with the GP? How often will I review effectiveness? Should anyone else be involved in treatment, for example, relatives? Should I draw on community resources, such as a support organization, (e.g. Schizophrenia Fellowship)? Is medication necessary? If yes, who should prescribe?

Accompanying the above inquiry is the attempt to establish in what areas help is necessary. The use of a problem-oriented approach not only guides therapists to set goals but also enables them to assess the value of their interventions. Much of this work is carried out collaboratively with the patient.

Anticipating hurdles is wise from the outset. In particular, what is the risk of undue dependence? Is it necessary to set any limits? What arrangement should I make regarding extra sessions requested between appointments, the patient's use of emergency services, and of my availability on the telephone?

Periodic review is an inherent feature of a continuing treatment like supportive therapy. As mentioned earlier the problem list is valuable for this purpose. In addition, certain questions need to be asked: Is my original plan working? Am I making the patient worse in any way? Is he becoming unduly dependent? Have any new problems arisen? Should I modify goals set previously? Am I still the most appropriate person to provide help? If not, who is best suited—the general practitioner, the family?

Clinical illustration

Sally was born into a professional family, the oldest of three siblings. Her father, an eminent lawyer, and her mother, a dedicated school teacher, tended to be emotionally unavailable as the children grew up. Moreover, father was persistently irascible and critical of all of them when they did not meet his expectations. Sally had little to do with her two brothers, 4 and 7 years her junior. Each child seemed to retreat into a world of their own. Growing up in this 'cold' family was a lonely, distressing experience for Sally. She did not find solace elsewhere. Although she acquitted herself well at school, she could not sustain friendships. The result was an isolated, ultra-sensitive teenager, exquisitely vulnerable to even the mildest pressure.

The same pattern prevailed at university. By dint of hard slogging, Sally graduated in her early twenties with an arts degree but her achievement brought little joy and nothing in the way of family congratulation. She could not land a suitable job, not for want of trying, and wandered from one temporary or part-time post to another. Still threatened by intimacy, she remained a lonely soul. Casual sexual relationships ensued, reflecting a desperate strategy to make contact. On becoming pregnant in one of these encounters, she was determined to bear the child despite the partner's disinterest and her parents' ambivalence. She was supported materially by the latter for the first 2 years of David's life but mounting conflict culminated in a breakdown of the arrangements. Sally was then truly on her own—a single mother, jobless, friendless, and on a pension—at the age of 32.

Sally's psychiatric 'career' had begun with her self-referral 5 years earlier. Buffeted by feelings of rejection and low self-regard, she highlighted her need for 'emotional support'. She could no longer cope with what she saw as the family's rejection of her and a harsh world. Although no frank psychotic phenomena were identified, Sally's paranoid-like stance was noted, as was her incapacity to trust the ward staff. An assessment pointed to notable personality difficulties, with schizoid and avoidant features to the fore. A recommendation for a trial of exploratory psychotherapy was made but with the caveat that her fragile sense of self and tendency to use primitive defences, such as projective identification, might well preclude application of psychodynamic techniques, especially interpreting unconscious conflict, defences, and transference.

It required only a matter of weeks to reveal that the caveat had been justified. Sally became progressively more distressed in the course of the early sessions, to the point of growing suspicious about the therapist's intentions. The latter fearing an impending psychotic break, consulted with a colleague. They agreed that Sally was not a suitable candidate for an insight-oriented approach.

Instead, her vulnerability pointed to supportive therapy. This was begun by the same therapist following a careful description to her of the rationale and aims of the substitute treatment. Sally appeared to be comfortable by the prospect of emotional support as a primary element.

This clinical judgement proved accurate. Sally continued to be seen in the clinic, and weathered the original therapist's replacement following her departure for another job. Frequency of sessions varied from weekly to monthly, dependent on Sally's clinical state and overall situation. For example, she was seen weekly during the last trimester of her pregnancy and in the puerperium, as well as for the duration of a conflict-laden episode with her parents. Apart from the centrality of the therapeutic alliance, an assortment of strategies were deployed, according to clinical necessity (see below). Attempts were made to promote more effective maternal coping by arranging for her to join a mother's club. Minimal family intervention was attempted; the aims were modest given the entrenched history of conflict. For instance, links between the grandparents and their sole grandchild were encouraged. Sally's efforts to exploit her own assets were reinforced. Thus, she participated in a social club's activities and did voluntary teaching in a literacy programme.

As the months, and then years, went by the likelihood of Sally requiring indefinite supportive therapy was confirmed. Mostly monthly attendances appeared adequate, admission to a psychiatric hospital unlikely (unless a major crisis supervened).

(For other vivid case illustrations, see Pinsker 1997; Holmes 1998; and Aviram et al. 2004).

Problems in the course of treatment

A notable risk in supportive therapy is fostering dependency; the patient then relinquishes any responsibility for himself and comes to rely entirely on the therapist. As Kolb (1973) cautions: 'In employing supportive therapy, the physician should bear in mind the dangers that he may thereby encourage dependence and a regressive passivity in the patient'. Dependency is inevitable in every therapist–patient relationship but even more so in supportive therapy where the patient is actually sanctioned to 'lean on' the therapist. The thorny question arises as to how much support is appropriate? The condition of the patient often dictates the answer but generally the goal is to promote self-sufficiency to a level that is realistically possible and to transfer some of the source of support to family and other intimates.

One could argue that dependence on the therapist in the enduringly impaired is of little consequence. The drawback, however, is that he is robbed of an opportunity to act autonomously and to benefit from a corresponding sense of mastery.

A therapist may assume a supportive role but later encounter difficulty in trying to reduce the level of support offered. He may resort to setting inappropriate limits or 'withdraw'. The relationship inevitably is strained and therapy thrown into disarray. The patient may cling all the harder as the therapist, angry and frustrated, endeavours to keep him at bay.

A therapist may instil dependency unwittingly out of a need to 'prove' that he exerts a pivotal role in helping patients. He may deflect the uncertainty of his helpfulness by relying on the concept of support. Since supportive therapy denotes an active role he can derive comfort in his benevolence.

Supportive therapy is regarded by many therapists as less satisfying than psychotherapy in which one participates in a journey of discovery with goals often accomplished. For the long-term patient an explicit 'cure' is unattainable and the therapy less engaging. Moreover, therapists are confronted with their relative ineffectiveness in the face of a range of conditions.

Supportive therapy practised in an appropriate setting can, despite what we have noted, satisfy and challenge. A patient achieving a goal, no matter how limited, can be rewarding for him and his therapist. A positive experience for the latter is more likely to occur if she remembers to '. . . content herself with settling for what is possible' (Lamb 1981).

Research

The effectiveness of supportive psychotherapy is difficult to assess (Conte and Plutchick 1986; Rockland 1993; Conte 1994). Criteria of outcome have to be tailored to patients who are enduringly impaired. Moreover, we are dealing with a diagnostically heterogenous group. We would also need to note other treatments being given (e.g. medication, non-professional support like social clubs, and so on). Forming a control group for a long-term therapy against which to test effectiveness is ethically problematic.

With regard to the problem of outcome assessment, suitable criteria might include: the pattern of clinic attendance (e.g. failure to keep appointments, dropping out of treatment, excessive use of the clinic); rate of psychiatric hospitalization; use of emergency facilities; the overall pattern of help-seeking; quality of relationships with family and others; work performance and ability to cope with everyday tasks.

Given the hurdles it is no surprise that outcome studies are uncommon. Brandwin et al. (1976) in assessing a 'continuing-care clinic' used hospitalization as a criterion and compared the rate for a period before and after patients began their clinic attendance. The proportion of those admitted and total number of inpatient days were substantially reduced when treated in the supportive clinic. Although an 'old' study its utility endures. The same can be said for the investigation by Masnik et al. (1980) who followed-up patients after they had received supportive therapy for an average 5 years. According to therapists' ratings, patients improved symptomatically and in their ability to cope, albeit modestly. Readmission rates also declined. Improvement only correlated with attendance, suggesting that the clinic served as a support system.

Research carried out since the last edition of this book, while still uncommon, has been methodologically more sophisticated, with greater attention paid to sample specificity, description of the treatment, and relevant outcome measurement.

For example, a British study (Tarrier et al. 1998) of patients with clinical schizophrenia, schizo-affective psychosis, or delusional disorder compared their responses to intensive cognitive behaviour therapy or 'supportive counselling' or routine care. In a randomized control trial, patients in the two treatment conditions were seen twice weekly over 10 weeks. The supportive therapy offered emotional support through promoting rapport and 'unconditional regard'.

The emphasis was on optimizing 'non-specific' effects (Frank and Frank 1991). Fidelity of treatments given was satisfactorily examined. Assessment of outcome, multidimensional in nature, was limited to a 3-month follow-up. The supportive approach was intermediate in clinical effect, between cognitive behaviour therapy and routine care. Specifically, the two treatments seemed to protect against relapse. Two major caveats are noteworthy—the follow-up period was obviously brief and medication was not controlled for. Nonetheless, it is striking how useful supportive counselling was for this group of chronically ill patients.

A small number of researchers have confirmed this modest role for supportive therapy in schizophrenia. The question of how benefits are mediated is still to be answered. David Penn and his colleagues (2004) have carefully considered this issue, especially the place of support in the context of cognitive behaviour therapy, and offered an account of possible mechanisms. Patients may learn, for instance, that social interaction is possible given the positive way they are treated by their therapists. Indeed, patients value the 'friendship' therapists extend to them rather than their expertise.

Another theoretical possibility revolves around patients' perceptions, interpretations, and processing of social information. Supportive therapy may yield positive effects by dealing with patients' concerns about their role in the 'social world' and promoting self-confidence.

Another relatively new target for the empirical investigator examining the potential role of supportive therapy is borderline personality disorder. A major project comparing a psychodynamically-based approach, Dialectical Behaviour Therapy, and supportive therapy is in progress under the direction of Otto Kernberg and John Larkin (Fox-Fliesser 2002). A treatment manual has been prepared for the latter in which the principal therapeutic factors include the therapist's modelling of reflective functioning and his creating safe conditions for the patient to develop a more 'cohesive sense of self and other'.

The odd outcome study including a supportive therapy condition has been done on Axis I—conditions such as social phobia (Cottraux et al. 2000), anxiety disorders (Barrowclough et al. 2001), and depression (Thase et al. 2000), but little substantial knowledge has emerged hitherto.

A methodologically reasonable randomized clinical trial comparing manualized short-term dynamic and supportive therapies in a heterogeneous sample of both Axis I and II disorders shows equivalent outcomes at a 6-month follow-up in terms of symptomatic change, target problems, and interpersonal functioning (Hellerstein et al. 1998). We must bear in mind, however, that the sample comprised relatively high-functioning patients, mostly employed college graduates, and thus are not representative of the patients we have been considering in this chapter.

Training

Instruction on theory is arguably less pertinent than in other psychotherapies since no conceptual model has stood out as relevant. On the other hand, psychodynamically-oriented theorists like Kernberg (1984) and Rockland (1989; 1993) have sought to clarify how psychoanalytic concepts are applied, albeit in modified form, in supportive therapy. Alongside this movement has been the participation of behaviourally-focused practitioners. Treatment is more empirically than theoretically-driven and comprises an array of related methods that clinical experience suggests are beneficial.

As pertinent as theoretical knowledge is familiarity with the nature of chronic psychiatric illness and severe personality disorders—course, complications, co-mobility, prognosis—for which supportive therapy is indicated. With such information the therapist is more aware of the needs and problems of those receiving supportive therapy.

Practical experience under supervision is undoubtedly the key component of training. By treating various types of patients over a year or more, the novice accomplishes several tasks. Attitudes to their care becomes more realistic and positive. Instead of regarding them nihilistically, the therapist appreciates that a highly specific approach is being used, whose goals are limited. To the novice, these may seem minuscule but later he can come to understand that, for the patient, their attainment may be most rewarding. Therapists learn through this feedback that they can help. Another myth, that supportive therapy is little more than 'brief, commonsensical chats... which consist of little more than sympathetic listening and more-or-less considered advice' (Smail 1978), is also dispelled. Trainees learn that they have to acquire specific skills.

Continuing learning ideally is related closely to clinical care. Therapists benefit by comparing their work with those of peers. A useful spin-off is mental health professionals from psychiatry, clinical psychology, social work, nursing, and occupational therapy participating in the same programme, with the advantage of interdisciplinary exchange and sharing of different perspectives in the care of the long-term patient.

Conclusion

Supportive therapy is a *bona fide* therapeutic approach, not merely the application of common sense. Indeed, as Kernberg (1984) stresses: 'Supportive therapy begins where the effectiveness of common sense ends.' As Piper et al. (2002) asserts: '... there is good reason to recognize supportive psychotherapy as a legitimate form of therapy with identifiable features'.

Supportive therapy with long-term patients aims to promote their best possible adjustment. To achieve this, the therapist develops a particular relationship, and applies a range of strategies, such as explanation, reassurance, and guidance. Undue dependency is a critical problem, its prevention requiring careful skill. The concept of an 'institutional alliance' helps to minimize the problem as well as to provide suitable care. Supportive therapy has a prominent role, especially in the era of deinstitutionalization, and should be part of the armamentarium of every mental health professional.

References

Alexander, F. and French, T. (1946). *Psychoanalytic therapy: Principles and applications.* University of Nebraska Press, Lincoln.

Alford, B. and Beck, A. (1997). Therapeutic interpersonal support in cognitive therapy. *Journal of Psychotherapy Integration,* 7, 105–117.

Aviram, R., Hellerstein, D., Gerson, J., and Stanley, B. (2004). Adapting supportive psychotherapy for individuals with borderline personality disorder who self-injure or attempt suicide. *Journal of Psychiatric Practice,* 10, 145–155.

Balint, M., Hunt, J., Joyce, D., Marinker, M., and Woodcock, J. (1970). *Treatment or diagnosis: A study of repeat prescriptions in general practice.* Tavistock, London.

Barber, J., Stratt, R., Halperin, G., and Connolly, M. (2001). Supportive techniques: Are they found in different therapies? *Journal of Psychotherapy Practice and Research*, **10**, 165–172.

Barrowclough, C., King, P., Colville, J., Russell, E., Burns, A., and Tarrier, N. (2001). A randomised trial of the effectiveness of cognitive-behavioural therapy and supportive counselling for anxiety symptoms in older adults. *Journal of Consulting and Clinical Psychology*, **69**, 756–762.

Berlincioni, V. and Barbieri, S. (2004). Support and psychotherapy. *American Journal of Psychotherapy*, **58**, 321–334.

Bloch, S., Hafner, J., Harari, E., and Sznukler, G. (1994). The family in clinical psychiatry. Oxford University Press, Oxford.

Brandwin, M. A., van Houten, W. H., and Neal, D. L. (1976). The continuing care clinic: outpatient treatment of the chronically ill. *Psychiatry*, **39**, 10317.

Buckley, P. (1994). Self psychology, object relations theory and supportive psychotherapy. *American Journal of Psychotherapy*, **48**, 519–29.

Conte, H. (1994). Review of research in supportive psychotherapy: An update. *American Journal of Psychotherapy*, **48**, 494–504.

Conte, H. and Plutchik, R. (1986). Controlled research in supportive psychotherapy. *Psychiatric Annals*, **16**, 530–3.

Cottraux, J., Note, I., Albuisson, E., Yao, S., Note, B., Mollard, E., Bonasse, F., Jalenques, I., Guerin, J., and Coudert, A. (2000). Cognitive behavior therapy versus supportive therapy in social phobia: A randomised controlled trial. *Psychotherapy and Psychosomatics*, **69**, 137–146.

Crown, S. (1988). Supportive psychotherapy: A contradiction in terms? *British Journal of Psychiatry*, **152**, 266–9.

Dewald, P. A. (1994). Principles of supportive psychotherapy. *American Journal of Psychotherapy*, **48**, 505–18.

Fox-Fliesser, J. (2002). Scientific meeting of the American Institute for Psychoanalysis. *American Journal of Psychoanalysis*, **62**, 201–202.

Frank, J. and Frank, J. (1991). *Persuasion and Healing*. 3rd ed. Johns Hopkins University Press, Baltimore.

Gilbert, S. and Ugelstad, E. (1994). Patients' own contributions to long-term supportive psychotherapy in schizophrenic disorders. *British Journal of Psychiatry*, **164** (Suppl. 23), 84–8.

Hellerstein, D., Rosenthal, R., Pinsker, H., Samstag, L., Muran, J., and Winston, A. (1998). A randomised prospective study comparing supportive and dynamic therapies: Outcome and alliance. *Journal of Psychotherapy Practice and Research*, **7**, 261–271.

Holmes, J. (1988). Supportive analytical psychotherapy. *British Journal of Psychotherapy*, **152**, 824–829.

Holmes, J. (1996). *Attachment, intimacy, autonomy. Using attachment theory in adult psychology*. Jason Aronson, Northvale, NJ.

Karasu, T. (1986). Supportive psychotherapy. Psychosomatic medicine and psychotherapy. *Psychiatric Annals*, **16**, 522–5.

Kates, J. and Rockland, L. H. (1994). Supportive psychotherapy of the schizophrenic patient. *American Journal of Psychotherapy*, 48, 543–61.

Kellner, R. (1985). Functional somatic symptoms and hypochondriasis. *Archives of General Psychiatry*, **42**, 821–33.

Kernberg, O. (1984). Supportive psychotherapy. In *Severe personality disorders*. Yale University Press, New Haven, CT.

Kolb, L. C. (1973). *Modern clinical psychiatry*. Saunders, Philadelphia. Lamb, H. R. (1981). Individual psychotherapy. In *The chronically mentally ill*, (ed. J. A. Talbot). Human Sciences Press, New York.

Lamb, H. R. (1981). Individual psychotherapy. In *The chronically mentally ill* (ed. J. Talbot). Human Sciences Press, New York.

Leff, J. and Vaughn, C. (1985). *Expressed emotion in families*. Guilford Press, New York.

Masnik, R., Olarte, S., and Rosen, A. (1980). 'Coffee groups': a nine-year follow-up study. *American Journal of Psychiatry*, **137**, 91–3.

Meyer, W. (1993). In defense of long-term treatment: On the vanishing holding environment. *Social Work*, **38**, 571–8.

Misch, D. (2000). Basic strategies of dynamic supportive therapy. *Journal of Psychotherapy Practice and Research*, **9**, 173–189.

Müller, U. and Barash-Kishon, R. (1998). Psychodynamic-supportive group therapy model for elderly holocaust survivors. *International Journal of Group Psychotherapy*, **48**, 461–475.

Novalis, P. N., Rojcewicz, S. J., and Peele, R. (1993). *Clinical manual of supportive psychotherapy*. American Psychiatric Press, Washington, DC.

Paris, J. (1993). The treatment of borderline personality disorder in light of the research on its longterm outcome. *Canadian Journal of Psychiatry*, 38 (Suppl. I), 28–34.

Penn, D., Mueser, K., Tarrier, N., Gloege, A., Cather, C., Serrano, D., and Otto, M. (2004). Supportive therapy for schizophrenia: Possible mechanisms and implications for adjunctive psychosocial treatments. *Schizophrenia Bulletin*, **30**, 101–112.

Pine, F. (1986). Supportive therapy: A psychoanalytic perspective. *Psychiatric Annals*, **16**, 526–9.

Pinsker, H. (1994). The role of theory in teaching supportive psychotherapy. *American Journal of Psychotherapy*, **48**, 530–42.

Pinsker, H. (1997). *A primer of supportive psychotherapy*. Analytic Press, Hillsdale, NJ.

Piper, W., Joyce, A., McCallum, M., Azim, H., and Ogrodniczak, J. (2002). *Interpretive and supportive psychotherapies*. American Psychological Association, Washington, DC.

Rockland, L. H. (1989). Psychoanalytically-oriented supportive therapy: Literature review on techniques. *Journal of the American Academy of Psychoanalysis*, **17**, 451–62.

Rockland, L. H. (1989a). *Supportive therapy: A psychodynamic approach*. Basic Books, New York.

Rockland, L. H. (1992). *Supportive psychotherapy for borderline patients: A psychodynamic approach*. Guilford Press, New York.

Rockland, L. H. (1993). A review of supportive psychotherapy, 1986–1992. *Hospital and Community Psychiatry*, **44**, 1053–60.

Schilder, P. (1938). *Psychotherapy*. Norton, New York.

Smail, D. J. (1978). *Psychotherapy: A Personal approach*. Dent, London.

Stone, M. (2000). Clinical guidelines for psychotherapy for patients with borderline personality disorder. *The Psychiatric Clinics of North America*, **23**, 193–210.

Tarrier, N., Yusupoff, L., Kinney, C., McCarthy, E., Gledhill, A., Haddock, G. and Morris, J. (1998). Randomised controlled trial and intensive cognitive behaviour therapy for patients with chronic schizophrenia. *British Medical Journal* **317**, 303–307.

Thase, M., Friedman, E., Berman, S., Fasiczka, A., Lis, J., Howland, R. and Simons, A. (2000). Is cognitive behaviour therapy just a 'nonspecific' intervention for depression? A retrospective comparison of consecutive cohorts treated with cognitive behaviour therapy or supportive counseling and pill placebo. *Journal of Affective Disorders*, **57**, 63–71.

Van Marle, S. and Holmes, J. (2002). Supportive psychotherapy as an integrative psychotherapy. In *Integration in psychotherapy: Models and methods* (ed. J. Holmes and A. Bateman). Oxford University Press, Oxford.

Werman, D. (1984). *The practice of supportive psychotherapy.* Brunner/Mazel, New York.

Winnicott, D. W. (1965). *The maturational process and the facilitating environment.* International Universities Press, New York.

Winston, A., Pinsker, H., and McCullough, L. (1986). A review of supportive psychotherapy. *Hospital and Community Psychiatry*, **37**, 1105–14.

Recommended reading

Kernberg, O. (1984). Supportive psychotherapy. In *Severe personality disorders.* Yale University Press, New Haven, CT. (A thought provoking chapter by one of the 'masters' of the therapy of the severely disordered personality.)

Novalis, P. N., Rojcewicz, S. J., and Peele, R. (1993). *Clinical manual of supportive psychotherapy.* American Psychiatric Press, Washington, DC. (As the title suggests, a 'how-to book', concentrating on principles and detailed clinical applications.)

Pinsker, H. (1997). *A primer of supportive psychotherapy.* Analytic Press, Hillsdale, NJ. (An eminently practical volume with many passages of therapeutic dialogue.)

Rockland, L. H. (1989). *Supportive therapy: A psychodynamic approach.* Basic Books, New York. (A clinical account of supportive therapy applied within a psychoanalytic framework.)

Rockland, L. H. (1992). *Supportive therapy for borderline patients.* Guilford Press, New York. (A psychodynamically oriented model of supportive therapy directed towards the special needs of the borderline patient.)

Chapter 11

Group psychotherapy

Mark Aveline

The goals of long-term individual therapy discussed in Chapter 5 can also be tackled in group therapy. In this chapter, an interpersonal model of small group therapy is described with special emphasis on therapeutic factors. Selection, group composition, preparation of members, group development, the mature group, and ethical issues are covered. The final section deals briefly with other applications of the group approach and with training.

Human beings live, work, and play in diverse groups, and find and express their identity through social interaction. Not surprisingly, many of the psychological problems they experience stem from disturbed relationships within the groups in which they have learned to be the people they are. With increasing recognition of the interpersonal factor in psychiatric theory and practice has come the development of psychotherapies that have as their target problems between people rather than within the individual. Chapters in this volume on family, marital and sex therapy reflect this focus. In addition to these naturally occurring groups, 'stranger' group therapy, both small and large, has been used in a variety of settings: psychiatric wards, the therapeutic community, the outpatient clinic, the private therapist's office, self-help, and many more. Groups may be used to deliver specific psychological treatments or address interpersonal relationship issues. Group therapy is commonly used although it is also one of the more difficult modes of therapy to practice well.

This chapter considers the long-term small group composed of patients who appreciate they have recurrent difficulties in relating and wish to change them. A typical group has eight members and two leaders and meets weekly for one and a half hours. The group might be *closed*, that is, all the members starting together and continuing until the preset end of the group, or *open* with members joining and leaving, as need dictates. In either form, 12–18 months, with an upper limit of 2 years, of membership is common. The model is based on the interpersonal theory of Harry Stack Sullivan (1953). For comprehensive accounts of this model, see Yalom (1995) and Whitaker (1985) and, for a summary, Ratigan and Aveline (1988). A long-term group provides the optimum training for the novice and much of what she learns there can be transferred to other settings. Brief mention is made of other uses of the group and further reading recommended.

Background

The systematic use of therapy groups is a twentieth-century development (Fuhriman and Burlingame 1994; Scheidlinger 1994), but their healing properties have long been recognized, particularly in a religious context; the shrine at Lourdes is an excellent example.

Joseph Pratt (1974), a Boston physician, is usually credited as the father of group therapy. At the turn of the twentieth century, he brought together patients with tuberculosis in order to educate them on medical aspects of their illness. He also promoted a group climate through which patients provided mutual support. Later a number of American psychiatrists incorporated Pratt's ideas, forming structured groups of patients who were viewed as 'students' and tutored on mental ill-health. This approach soon waned, to be replaced by the efforts of psychoanalysts treating patients in groups. Freud himself never practiced group therapy but recognized the significance of group phenomena, as reflected in his *Group psychology and the analysis of the ego* (Freud 1955). Jung was biased against the therapy group; since psychological illness was an individual experience, it required individual analysis. Adler, in contrast, embraced social factors in treatment and used the group format in child guidance centres and with alcoholic patients. Moreno, whose name is synonymous with psychodrama, emphasized group dynamics.

The Second World War was a watershed in the evolution of group therapy in that it proved an economical method to cope with the large patient numbers among the military. The Northfield Military Hospital was a centre of innovation and there Wilfred Bion (1961) and S. H. Foulkes (1946) tried out new approaches. Bion's work later influenced therapists at the Tavistock Clinic while Foulkes was the force behind the founding of the Institute of Group Analysis in London.

Another key contribution was that of a team of social psychologists led by Kurt Lewin in the United States (Lewin 1951). His field theory—that a person's dynamics are intimately associated with the nature of the social forces around him—was the basis for research into group process. In 1946, the State of Connecticut invited Lewin to help train community leaders in an effort to reduce interracial tensions. In this way the sensitivity-training group was born. Four years later, the National Training Laboratory (NTL) was formed as a training centre for human relations and group dynamics. Participants from a range of backgrounds could experience and study interpersonal functioning in a group workshop, and as a result act more effectively in their home settings.

A decade later, the NTL's emphasis changed from group to personal dynamics, paralleling the swell of interest in the human potential movement. The goals became greater self-awareness and personal growth. Before long, it spawned the encounter-group movement. This subsequently declined in membership and originality of concepts.

Groups are often used to deliver individual treatments, for example, anxiety or anger management. This structured approach is cost-effective but makes little use of such unique therapeutic factors in group therapy as group cohesion and interpersonal learning. In research trials, the strongest effect sizes are found when these special factors are exploited (Fuhriman and Burlingame 1994; Burlingame et al. 2004). These groups are referred to as *process groups*; they focus on the *here and now* of interaction within the group.

Yalom has been an inspiring advocate for interpersonally focused group therapy for nearly 40 years. Personal history as told is supplanted by history as shown in the 'social microcosm' of the group, setting the stage for 'interpersonal learning' (Yalom and Leszcz 2005). His use of the research method of the Q-sort highlighted the value that successful group participants place on self-disclosure, peer acceptance, and honest feedback. He urges all people to be courageous in facing existential realities (Yalom 1980) and illustrates points through vivid storytelling.

Assessment

Indications for group therapy depend largely on the kind of treatment offered. Obviously, a self-help group like Alcoholics Anonymous (AA) suits a specific range of people only. Indications are not as clear-cut for the long-term therapy group, the focus of this chapter, whose aim is personality change. Research to assist in selection is limited, and yet a group's success hinges on the patients chosen (Bond and Lieberman 1978; Piper 1994; Aveline 1997) and on the group's culture. Nonetheless, a range of problems can be dealt with in a group; desirable patient features are specifiable, and particular attitudes, perceptions, and behaviours pave the way for effective participation.

Problems commonly tackled include:

Interpersonal—pervasive difficulty in initiating and sustaining relationships is a pre-eminent indication. The patient may identify an inability to achieve intimacy, discomfort in social situations, and maladaptive interpersonal style (e.g. lacking trust, overly dependent, abrasive).

Emotional—unawareness of feelings in oneself and/or in others, inability to express feelings, poor emotional control, obsessive.

Self-concept—blurred identity, poor self-esteem, lack of purpose.

Symptomatic—anxiety, depression, poor work, or study performance, ineffective coping with stress. These need to be seen, or potentially seen, by the patient as secondary to problems in relationships.

More suited to group than individual therapy—some patients pose major difficulty when treated individually, for example, the person who settles into an intense, regressed relationship or the sadistic patient who may 'damage' the therapist. These sorts of patients may benefit from a group experience if they are not in the majority: individual therapy may be a useful or a necessary precursor.

Desirable patient characteristics

—He is motivated to change and prepared to work for it; his wish for therapy is his choice, not the result of pressure by others.

—He has sufficient trust to share his life, and enough capacity for mature relationships so that when interpersonal conflicts occur in the group, he can examine them constructively.

—He expects that the group will prove beneficial and, ideally, has a high opinion of group therapy.

—He is psychologically minded, and able to use verbal and conceptual skills in order to engage in self-exploration and reflect on group process. He is willing to consider conflicts in interpersonal terms. Psychological-mindedness is not synonymous with intelligence, professional occupation, or high socio-economic status. Indeed, patients from diverse backgrounds can participate in the same group to everyone's benefit. Systematic research from Edmonton/Vancouver demonstrates a differential effect for psychological mindedness (PM) and quality of object relations (QOR) in interpretive group therapy. Low PM was linked to increased dropout rate and high QOR with improved outcome. Patients with low QOR did better with supportive groups (Piper et al. 2001). German research indicates that attachment style may be a useful indicator; ambivalent attachment predicts better, and dismissive poorer, outcome (Strauss 2000).

See Burlingame et al. (2004) for a review of effectiveness of small group therapy in terms of diagnostic categories and Roth and Fonagy (2004) for a comprehensive review of psychological therapies in general.

Diagnoses presenting particular problems for interpersonal group therapy include:

Diagnostic categories in ICD 10 and DSM-IV are a relatively poor guide to assessment of suitability. Categorical diagnosis is best viewed in terms of particular difficulties a person brings to the group and wrestles with in order to benefit (for a discussion of the relative advantages of formulation, see Aveline (1999)). Should the difficulties prove severe, the likelihood of productive engagement diminishes. Some of these patients may be helped by more structured group approaches.

1 The *severely depressed*. Mild or moderate depression is a common feature of patients entering groups. Signifying a human reaction to problems, it often lifts or at least improves after the first few months of therapy. The severely depressed patient, in contrast, may be too withdrawn, pessimistic, and hopeless even to begin participation in the group. Efforts by therapists and fellow members to reach out fail and result in frustration and guilt. Unable to influence the patient, the group itself becomes dispirited. The patient may need antidepressants or other psychiatric intervention, either as a prelude or concurrently, in order to raise his level of functioning to the point where psychological issues can be explored.

2 The *acute schizophrenic patient*. A patient in the midst of an acute episode is an inappropriate candidate. Out of contact with reality and disturbed in thinking, he has little chance of engaging. In contrast, a patient who has emerged from such an episode and is now stable is a potential beneficiary.

3 *Severe personality disorders*

(a) The *paranoid personality*—Crucial questions are the degree of suspiciousness and the capacity to be flexible. Marked paranoid attitudes preclude the establishment of trusting relationships, an essential component for participation.

(b) The *severe schizoid personality*—group therapy challenges members to do interpersonally what they find most difficult. Patients with marked traits of detachment, coldness, and hypersensitivity manifest a style that is the antithesis of the group's striving to achieve open communication. The less severely schizoid person is a good candidate since the group establishes a cohesive, trusting environment in which he is encouraged to risk involvement.

(c) The *antisocial personality*—low frustration threshold, deficient capacity to empathize with others, and lack of a sense of responsibility make both for poor candidacy and a potentially disruptive influence.

The patient is likely to profit more from a homogeneous group in which limits are set and a solid structure provided for example, a therapeutic community. In that setting, being an 'expert' in antisocial behaviour enables him to recognize it in others and challenge it (Gabbard et al. 2000).

(d) The *borderline personality*—pervasive instability of self-image, relationships, and mood, uncertain identity, switching between idealization and devaluation, fear of abandonment, and impulsive action often leading to angry attacks or self harming make for a roller coaster ride for the group. The group needs to be robust and mature in its development to cope but such patients can do well. It is prudent not to have more than two borderline patients in a group.

(e) The *narcissistic personality*—insensitive to others, he alienates himself from the group. He claims attention exclusively and has great difficulty in learning how to interact.

4 *The patient with substance abuse.* He tends not to make a long-term commitment. Easily frustrated, and intolerant of the anxieties inherent in group work, he seeks relief from the drug on which he is dependent, often with disastrous effects for the group. He tends to benefit more from a structured group composed entirely of patients with the same problems.

5 *The somatizing patient.* Patients in group therapy commonly present with somatic complaints as part of their clinical picture but the intense somatizer who cannot be deflected from bodily concerns or translate them into psychological terms does not gain. Moreover, his relentless focus on the body frustrates other members.

Selection

Since a group's fate is bound so closely to the patients who constitute it, selection is done methodically. Therapists are often eager to launch their group and in their haste may generate avoidable difficulties for themselves. Long before any patient is seen, the leaders, preferably in conjunction with a supervisor, should have worked out a format and aims, and addressed personal preferences that may affect their collaboration. Selection is both for group therapy and for a particular group. Furthermore, the process of selection is closely linked to preparation for optimal participation.

Each referred patient should be assessed over two occasions. A useful procedure is to conduct an interview in which information is gathered, the capacity to construe problems in interpersonal terms tested, willingness to have them examined in the group explored, and risk factors considered. To help the patient make an informed choice, goals and process are elaborated; in written form, they constitute the basis of an informal agreement (see Appendix 1). As well as describing the process, such guidelines spell out the importance of confidentiality, regular attendance, and punctuality. A useful way to introduce the group is to show potential members a video, which opens with an account of how groups work, followed by a discussion among members of a well-established group about their experience, and ends with a member reviewing his progress after 'graduating'.

Before the second interview, a homework assignment is given entailing preparation of a list of problems the patient wishes to tackle and their anticipated resolutions. As well as orientating the patient to the focus of the group, how this task is done helps to assess motivation. The second session is used to review suitability for the group after which therapists and patient can jointly reach their decision. Joint decision-making is important, as patient and therapists must sense they can work well together. Once the patient is selected, the therapists prepare him for the endeavour as outlined later. Occasionally, a third session is required.

Having accepted a patient, the therapists then pose questions based on observed and inferred interpersonal style: 'How will this patient manifest interpersonal difficulties in the group?' 'What, if any, are the likely challenges of his participation?' 'Will he monopolize, withdraw, moralize, and the like?' 'How may these manifestations be addressed therapeutically?'

Composition

That a patient may be suitable for treatment but not necessarily for the group being formed raises the question of composition. Should a group be balanced in a specific way or admit all patients assessed as likely to benefit? Some principles help selection.

Homogeneous groups, comprising patients with similar problems (e.g. alcohol abuse or obesity), are relatively easy to form as they entail common goals. Heterogeneous groups require care. Patients presenting with a variety of problems, need a multifaceted 'social world' (or 'social microcosm' in Yalom's apt phrase (Yalom and Leszcz 2005)) to learn about themselves and others and to try out new adaptive behaviours. This implies diversity in composition. For instance, a group consisting only of dependent or schizoid members permits minimal scope for learning alternative ways of relating. Similarly, a unisex group is limited in helping a patient with heterosexual difficulties.

A typical group has eight members (a minimum of five is necessary for learning to occur while more than eight prevents members obtaining sufficient time for themselves). It is characterized by an equal balance of men and women, an age range of about 20–60, mixed social, economic, and occupational backgrounds, and a wide assortment of clinical problems and personality types. The therapist avoids including a patient who obviously stands out, for example, one woman only or a patient markedly older than the rest; such members tend to drop out.

Whitaker (1985) advocates formation of a group in which patients have a variety of problems and coping styles but are similar in severity and tolerance of anxiety. This principle is an excellent basis for selection. In practice, most groups contain patients with a range of problem severity. Too great a span is to be avoided lest the more disabled impede the development of the more fortunate members, thereby generating frustration and a sense of failure.

Groups may be *open or closed*. The closed group begins and ends with the same membership. For pragmatic reasons this arrangement is uncommon in long-term therapy since some patients 'graduate' early whereas others drop out prematurely. The closed system is appropriate for relatively short term and training groups. The open group permits members to terminate at different points and their substitution by new patients. The disadvantages are obvious: cohesiveness is threatened with each departure and arrival and a new patient must integrate into an established group. These difficulties, however, are transient since the robust working group can afford to lose and absorb members. Advantages of the open model include flexibility in duration of membership, the potential for a successful graduate to inspire all, and the way in which newcomers invigorate the group and provide new opportunities for interpersonal learning.

Preparation

Both clinical and research evidence confirm the value of preparing patients for their experience (Kaul and Bednar 1994); novices have similar concerns: Is group therapy not inferior to individual treatment? Will I be forced to make a confession? Can I be assured that confidentiality will be respected? Will I be affected adversely by other members? How can others with problems help me? How can I manage to voice my problems? The concept and the initial experience of group therapy are often baffling and unsettling; indeed, most dropouts take place in the first 3 months. The guidelines in the Appendix ask new members to commit themselves for 6 months, a period necessary to experience how the group can confer benefits.

Establishing the expectation that the patient's problems will be addressed, albeit at a pace that he and the group can handle, is a vital aspect of preparation. It is helpful to identify explicitly problematic aspects of interaction that will inevitably manifest in the group, and need to be 'owned' and worked on by the patient. The expression of these problems often leads to premature termination. As an example, Jonas had never experienced an intimate relationship. He expected others to attack him even while holding out a hand of friendship. His remedy was to attack and to annihilate others pre-emptively. Once they got too close, few were given a second chance. Having agreed on the nature of this pattern, preparatory work was directed towards how this problem would be tackled. Jonas agreed to disclose the pattern, invite the group to intervene when it happened, and try to let people get closer than was his wont. The benefit would be in learning to do precisely what he found so daunting.

On a lesser level, Alice was overly cautious; she was apt to make carefully considered comments but, by the time she spoke, the conversation had moved on. Her caution had resulted in an isolated life. Alice was able to see that she ran the risk of becoming an outsider in the group. The task was agreed upon; she would try to act more spontaneously.

This procedure of anticipating problematic interactions and making them a focus can be formalized. Prior to joining the group, the patient documents his problems and their impact on his relationships, and prepares a 'wish list' of changes that, realistically, he intends to grapple with. Every 4 months, all members review work done by each other, taking as their baseline what has been documented. A new wish list of hoped for achievements is formulated. Though laborious, the procedure helps to maintain focus and makes it more likely that members will continue to examine their interpersonal difficulties.

Therapeutic factors

The novice is apt to become bewildered by the diversity of theoretical schools, each claiming merit for its own approach (see Recommended reading). Fortunately, the methodical study of therapeutic factors helps to deal with this. Certain components of group therapy are of value. For a full account of the relevant research see Bloch and Crouch 1985; Crouch et al. 1994. Note that therapeutic factors depend on the group's goals and that different factors are relevant at particular times.

Corsini and Rosenberg (1955) were the first to review the group therapy literature on these factors, delineating nine categories. Later workers refined these. What follows is a brief account of these factors. The list is to an extent arbitrary and factors are not discrete.

Group cohesiveness (acceptance)

This factor is a *sine qua non* for an effective group and a foundation for all other factors. A group is cohesive when members have a sense of belonging and support one another. Members feel secure, enjoy close contact with their peers and the therapists, take risks without disastrous repercussions, and do not feel judged. Lest this sounds like a glorious haven, we should note that cohesiveness also entails negative feedback and conflict but all expressed as a feature of caring. As William Blake once said: 'Opposition is true friendship'. Research confirms the pre-eminent role of cohesiveness (Bloch and Crouch 1985; Crouch et al. 1994; Burlingame et al. 2002) Cohesive groups have better attendance, punctuality, member activity, and stability.

Learning from interpersonal action

A patient's behaviour within group typically resembles the way he acts generally. For example, clinging, explosive, or self-centred members enter the group with these patterns, which have proved troublesome in their lives, and before long they became obvious to the membership. This makes it possible to address in treatment what is problematic beyond it.

Commonly the pattern is first addressed by feedback from others about its impact and disclosure of trigger feelings, and past, formative interactions by the initiator. Reasons for the genesis and maintenance of the 'publicly' identified interpersonal problem , are explored, and the stage set for trials of new ways of relating (Ratigan and Aveline 1988). In practice, the sequence moves fitfully. There are various views in the group. Insight is resisted. Patterns gradually become clearer and problems owned. Insight deepens as the question of 'why' is tackled. While it is not clear if linking present behaviour to past influences is necessary, it helps place behaviour in context. What is important is interpersonal learning through novel action in the *here and now* (see the mature working group).

As an example, Bill had a record of failed relationships and had never achieved intimacy with men or women. In the first few meetings, he monopolized the group and sulked when deprived of centre stage.

Schematically, learning from interpersonal action follows the above. First, Bill perceives that a problem exists; he relates poorly. Members tell Bill that his insensitivity angers them and point out that fear of Bill monopolizing the session prompts avoidance of engaging with him, a strategy that counter-productively stimulates further attempts by Bill to dominate. He accepts the feedback though resistance may render him defensive and willing to see himself as he is seen. He evaluates the interactions with his fellows and learns that his domineering style is responsible. The interpersonal learning is not just for Bill. Fellows reflect on their engagement in the issue: altruistic concern, combatants, placators, or mini-Bills.

Bill now has to commit himself to becoming less egocentric. It is one thing to be aware of an undesirable trait, quite another to eradicate it. Yet, there is no change without interpersonal action. The group encourages and reinforces

Bill's efforts. It applauds the risks he takes. On discovering that he survives and is rewarded for his effort, Bill experiments beyond the group.

In this example, Bill benefited from a willingness to relate adaptively within the group. He did not need to learn why, at a deeper level of insight, he had related domineeringly in the past. Some therapists would unravel sources, usually located in early family relationships. Thus, unresolved sibling rivalry might emerge which he could then explore in the *here and now* (Yalom and Leszcz 2005)

Insight (self-understanding)

In their early attempt to classify therapeutic factors, Corsini and Rosenberg (1955) used the term 'intellectualization' to identify a process of learning that leads to insight. This distinction between intellectualization and insight is problematic since the former has been used to identify a defence mechanism. Yalom (1995) argues that interpersonal insight is the form of learning most relevant to group therapy, psychogenetic insight (understanding the origin of symptoms) subsidiary.

Insight follows feedback from, and interpretation by, other members, both patients and therapists. It operates when patients: (1) learn something important about themselves (understanding overt behaviour, assumptions, underlying motivations, uncovered fantasies); (2) learn how they come across; (3) learn more clearly about the nature of their problems; and (4) learn how such behaviour evolved (psychogenetic insight).

Universality

Before entering the group, the patient commonly perceives himself as uniquely burdened. Universality operates within the first few sessions: 'We're all in the same boat' soon replaces 'I am unique'. In one early group, Peter's disclosure of shame about masturbation was followed by the men sharing problems about sexuality. He was relieved not to be deviant. The therapist reinforces this with comments like: 'It seems as if everyone shares this problem in one way or another'.

Instillation of hope

The patient begins treatment with the expectation of gaining relief from problems (Frank and Frank 1991). The factor operates when a patient sees peers improve and that the group is beneficial; he becomes optimistic about change.

Altruism

A unique benefit is the group's potential to facilitate mutual help. The occasion frequently arises for a patient to support a co-member, to enjoy the sense of giving of himself: 'I can be useful to others and I am therefore of value'. This is particularly useful in patients who suffer from poor self-esteem. Altruism reduces morbid self-preoccupation.

Guidance

We saw earlier that pioneering group therapy was didactic. Advice still plays a role but much less so. In early meetings, the therapist shapes the culture by promoting interaction and self-reflection. As the group matures, these functions are increasingly held by members themselves. Less helpfully, they slip into advice on how to solve problems: 'Why don't you simply discuss it with your wife?' or 'You should change jobs'. Although this reflects caring and should not be undermined, it usually has negligible benefit. The group comes to see that no short-cut remedies exist.

Vicarious learning

A member has, in his peers, models from whom to learn. Herein lies a distinct advantage of the group. Not every patient has to tackle a shared problem but benefits in seeing how a peer deals with it. Furthermore, each patient may have a quality which another wishes to emulate. For example, passive members may model themselves on assertive peers.

Identification can foster positive group norms. Noting how members take risks, reveal aspects of themselves and express feelings, encourages others to act similarly. The therapist also models, although this may work both ways. A passive, reticent therapist, for example, is unlikely to promote an interactive group.

Catharsis and self-disclosure

This pair of factors embraces ventilation of feelings like anger, anxiety, grief, guilt, and shame, and disclosure of previously concealed information, often embarrassing. Although they often occur together, they are distinctive. Emotional release has had a hallowed tradition in individual psychotherapy (see Chapter 1). The same is true for group therapy. But catharsis itself is of limited value unless the patient makes sense of the experience. What happened when I cried so bitterly? What was the significance of the tears? What should I do now that I have a greater understanding?

Through self-disclosure the patient divulges hidden aspects of himself about the past, current life, fantasies, or held-back feelings about members. Its value lies in sharing, which reduces isolation, demonstrates trust, and is often the first step in exploring the ramifications of 'secrets'.

Group therapy in practice

What happens in a group depends on the leaders, members, their goals, time available, and negotiation of inherent developmental phases. It is history written by many hands, an evolution of nature shaped by nurture.

The role of the leaders

Leaders assist members to realize the group's potential. The effective group has the capacity to move from a position of apprehension and relative ignorance to a maturity typified by solidarity and trust. The leader acts as an 'expert guide' in this progression (Aveline 1993). See also the classic account of the 'work group' by Bion (1961).

Two therapists are generally better than one since they place multiple perspectives at the service of the group. Their first task is to create and maintain the group, the second to promote a facilitative culture. They determine the givens of the group—size, frequency and time of meeting, duration, and whether open or closed. They arrange for a comfortable room free from interruption. They select and prepare members. They hold the boundaries of the group.

Once the group is launched, leaders have many means to help members to realize its potential. They encourage members to address each other directly; create a space for reticent members; are respectful and even-handed; attend to neglected issues; adjust the pace to minimize harm; foster a sense of responsibility; release therapeutic forces in members and in the group as a whole; encourage members to act determinedly at opportune moments; model openness, spontaneity, and honesty; and cultivate a reflective attitude. Exercising these effectively requires an appreciation of the continuing experience of each member and the group generally, its history, and developmental phase. Leaders work with process as well as individual narrative.

Developmental phases

A group in which therapeutic factors operate optimally does not arise automatically. Clinical observation and systematic research suggest that it passes through a series of stages before achieving maturity. There may be movement back and forth between stages, and not every patient is in the same stage at the same time. How a group copes with adversity, for example, intense conflict or discouragement after a setback may be crucial in determining its course (MacKenzie 1994).

Schutz's (1958) illuminating account is useful. *In-out* is the stage of dependency. The leaders have created the group and members await their guidance. Dependency is heightened by the group's apparent uncertainty. Sessions have no explicit agenda; each patient is more aware of his personal goals than of the group's to evolve into a mature system.

Top-bottom is the stage in which counter-dependence replaces dependence. The leaders inevitably disappoint the group since they are not ideal and cannot be totally relied on. Novice therapists may collude with the patients' infantile wishes by attempting to be all-caring and wise. An experienced therapist, however, provides cues that he expects the group to assume responsibility.

Counter-dependence manifests itself as competitiveness. The patient has to secure his place other than through dependency and he has rivals. This is a time of, frustration and anger, the latter directed at both therapists and co-patients. Commonly, the former will be criticized for 'not telling us what to do'. Unpunctuality and absenteeism can reflect patient frustration. Peer criticism manifests as sniping, scapegoating, and impatience. Carl Rogers (1973) in discussing the comparable stage of an encounter group suggests that expression of negative feelings is the patient's way to test the group's trustworthiness: 'Can I really express myself, even negatively?'

Top-bottom is stressful but patients learn they can express anger without disastrous repercussions, and take risks.

Near-far is the stage of intimacy. With a more realistic view of the leaders, conflict wanes. Passage through the top-bottom phase brings relief. Patients 'pulling one another apart' is replaced by 'pulling together'. Now the quest is for intimacy. 'Can I get closer (nearer) to others?' Negative feelings may still be expressed but occur in a more secure framework.

The alliterative sequence 'forming, storming, norming, performing, and adjourning' is another well known, similar formulation of stages in group development (Tuckman 1965).

Problems arising during group development

The passage between creation and transformation into a mature group has taken many weeks, even months, and called for skilful leadership. Threats to its welfare are encountered, even by experienced therapists. Loss of membership is inevitable no matter how rigorous the selection. Morale is undermined when a patient departs, with others ambivalent about continuing. Eight patients can stand the loss of one or two peers but greater attrition calls for replacement. Two caveats are pertinent. Addition of a pair of members is less anxiety provoking for the newcomers. A new patient should not be introduced if the group is in crisis as there is a danger that he will be scapegoated. All newcomers require the same preparation as foundation members, plus help to examine their expectations of entering an established group. Similarly, the group needs to prepare for the change.

Absenteeism and lateness also undermine the group's welfare. Regular, punctual attendance is crucial and the leaders need to reinforce its importance, by comment and commitment. A member unable to attend or knowing he will arrive late should inform the group. Absenteeism or unpunctuality invariably represent salient communications: resistance, anger, defiance, testing (does the group care about me?), and the like. For example, Jenny repeatedly arrived late and demanded a résumé of events she had missed. The group soon resented her but she seemed to thrive on this. It became clear that only by acting provocatively could she feel part of the group.

Dropouts, missed meetings, and tardiness always need to be dealt with head-on. Similarly, leader-determined absences and holiday-breaks will be significant and their meaning needs to be explored.

The mature working group

Following this developmental sequence, the group becomes a mature working system (Bion 1961). With cohesiveness achieved, patients are well placed to tackle their problems. Now the therapeutic factors are fully operative.

At all stages, therapy is facilitated by a *here and now* focus. Change is a consequence of patients evaluating ways they relate and then taking action to change. The pre-therapy goals compiled by the patient emphasize a future orientation, reinforced by periodic review. As the patient learns more about himself, he is encouraged to be future-minded: 'What options do I have? How will I choose between them? How will I translate choice into action?' A *there and then* focus is discouraged. 'There' refers to events outside the group, most commonly crises. The danger is that the group becomes crisis-bound. Crises in members' lives are inevitable and may be significant but a focus on them jeopardizes the core purpose, that of change catalyzed by interaction. When such external events occur, the leaders bring them into a *here and now* context.

'Then' implies a search for causes of behaviour. The danger here lies in preoccupation with the sources. A patient's disclosure of his family and personal history is helpful in allowing members to know him better and aiding self-understanding but the group can get bogged down in archaeological exploration.

There are infinite ways to maintain a *here and now* approach, the choice depending on clinical circumstance. Some illustrations follow:

'Who do you feel closest to/most intimidated by/most dominated by/etc. in the group?' (The patient has referred to intimacy, fear of others, or submissiveness.)

'Who in the group is most like you with respect to indecisiveness/passivity/aggressiveness etc.?' (Patient has indicated that he has one of these traits.)

'What has been the most difficult thing to share with the group today?'

(The patient has mentioned his difficulty in acting spontaneously.) *Here and now* comments may also focus on the group as a whole:

> 'Each of you seems buried in private thoughts.' (Following an extended silence.)
>
> 'How does each person see the meeting today?' (Halfway through a tense session.)
>
> 'How do you feel about Peter's absence?' (Peter has not arrived after 15 minutes and has not left any message.)

Another feature of the mature group is its ability to examine and understand its own dynamics, that is, the how and why of events, communications, interactions, and moods. Beyond what occurs overtly, the group operates at several levels. Dealing with content is obviously necessary, as is following through on how events in members' lives are tackled, but these are not sufficient. The group needs to examine the process of group events.

Commenting on process tends to be the leaders' task. Patients are too mired in the happenings in the group to view what lies behind them; they may also resist emotionally charged interaction. This task is undoubtedly demanding for leaders who need to keep the group process moving forward. Even Whitaker's (1985) excellent account does not suffice to cover the myriad complexities involved. Group analysis has produced many useful concepts including matrix, mirroring, resonance, polarization, and scapegoating (Aveline 1990; Roberts and Pines 1992).

Commonly made comments on dynamics follow; these may be addressed to the group, a subgroup, or a particular patient.

Group-directed

'There is a tension in the room today as if we were all on tenterhooks awaiting Jim's arrival'. (An absent member has not informed the group that he would not attend.)

'The group is split, those supporting Claire and those critical of her'.

'The group is being protective of Ann. Perhaps there is part of them in Ann they would like to protect too'. (Projection and mirroring.)

'It feels like we are unable to identify with Jack and his problem'. (Silence following his disclosure about his homosexuality.)

'The group is finding fault with Jim for not being entirely open. Surely this is something that everyone in the group is struggling with'. (Scapegoating.)

'There feels to be a lot of sadness in the group. I wonder if we're feeling the pain that Bill does not appear to be in touch with when he tells his story. (Projective identification.)

'The group has moved completely away from Jane as if her distress is too painful to bear'. (The group is in flight, as described by Bion (1961).)

'What is going on now?' The *reflective loop* is an important concept. The group reaches an impasse or gets stuck in a repeated pattern and is invited to analyse what went on. 'How did the pattern start? What did you feel about what was happening and what were the consequences? What did you do or not do?' John, a newcomer, had yet to say much about himself. The group bombarded him with questions and elicited partial disclosure but at the cost of incapacitating discomfort. Collectively, this was a restrictive solution as it spared other members from presenting their own issues. Individual dynamics played a part and were opportunities for learning. Bill was punitive in his scorn for John's failure and thus highlighted a propensity to react sadistically to vulnerability. Joan identified with John's predicament but felt helpless and could not speak up to defend him, a typical reaction. Marcia was glad not to be in the 'hot seat', a position she avoided to her disadvantage. Once the impasse is understood, the group can try out other solutions.

Patient-directed

'You come across as extremely angry in talking about Paul's lateness'.

'You tell us things are O.K. but your body tells another story; you look shaky and tense'.

'I have the feeling that you're saying to the group "I want the group's attention on my terms or not at all"'.

Since the group roams boundlessly, an infinite number of comments are possible. Some general points apply. The main objective is to facilitate learning, not to display the therapist's observational skills, his wit (although there is a distinct place for humour; see Bloch et al. 1983), or his cleverness. A patient only benefits from the therapist's comments if he understands, integrates, and can make use of them. The clearer the link between *here and now* content and the comment the better. Putting it another way, the more inferential, the less effective its impact. Statements are preferable to questions. In the face of uncertainty, it is reasonable to preface a comment with: 'I have the feeling that...' or 'I could be off the mark but...' 'Why' questions are unhelpful and again should be replaced by a statement (e.g. 'James seems critical of you today' rather than 'Why do you think James is critical of you today?').

Comments on non-verbal behaviour like seating arrangements, lateness, change in appearance, or silences are as pertinent as those on verbal content.

Timing of interventions is best related to *here and now* material. Sometimes, it is better to defer a point to when the patient is less distressed, the level of inference less ambiguous, or the therapist better able to highlight a consistent pattern. For instance, it may be more effective to wait before commenting: 'Chris has been relatively quiet for the last few meetings and participates only when invited. His mind seems to be elsewhere'. There is also a risk of flooding the patient with comments to the extent that he becomes perplexed.

The written summary

This technique has been described elsewhere (Yalom et al. 1975). The therapist prepares an account of each meeting (about two pages) and mails it to members. The summary contains a narrative of events interleaved with commentary. Although not objectively tested, therapists who have prepared such summaries are impressed by their utility. They serve several functions: help to bridge sessions; offer a second chance to the therapist to press home a point; enable her to reinforce group norms; and facilitate new observations not conceived of during the meeting. The summary allows an absent member to keep up. The therapist also profits from its preparation; since it is a 'public' document, she must ensure accuracy and clarity, and be tactful. Ethical issues arise over confidentiality and the right to receive reports when a member's attendance is poor. Written reports also have a role in training (Aveline 1986).

Ending therapy

When a patient should end treatment is as much of an issue in group as in individual therapy. Should he stop treatment when he has achieved goals originally set? Should he 'graduate' with enhanced knowledge and experience on the premise that his 'education' will continue thereafter?

The process differs in group compared to individual treatment. The reason is obvious; the group can resort to a jury system to decide questions of when and how. Ideally, a patient raises the issue and asks members for their reactions. If there is consensus, it is likely that termination is reasonable. Disagreement suggests it is premature. The process of leaving should last weeks enabling the graduate to share what he has achieved, his hopes, and why he feels ready to depart. Both he and the group also need time to say farewell and to work through separation.

Termination based on consensus is a time to celebrate. The patient feels confident to manage independently. The remaining members are urged to note the change and to take encouragement; thus, they are reminded that they too are potential graduates.

In a closed group, termination is predetermined; all members ending together. An open group may also agree to terminate as a group on a set date because of factors, such as therapists moving to other jobs. As the group mourns the loss of a member who leaves, so must it work through its own termination.

Occasionally, the leaders in conjunction with the group have to take the drastic step of discharging a member; reasons include repeated breaches of rules, coming drunk to meetings, and forming an intimate relationship with a peer, which they refuse to discuss.

Ethical issues

Leading a group is a complex task. Leaders have to make many decisions whose consequences cannot be predicted. One moment, they are urging on the group, the next reining it back. The impact of members can be discouraging or uncomfortable for their peers; apathy may develop or collusion with unhelpful patterns like scapegoating and idealization. Crises emerge with members storming out or threatening self-harm, sometimes forcing the group into. The range of personality type, vulnerability, and the drive of external events in members' lives mean patients' needs for help and capacity to cope create a matrix of conflicting priorities.

The leaders have to strike a balance between upholding the rights of the individual to be themselves and the greatest good for the group as a whole. The balance is a fluctuating compensation for what they see as anti-therapeutic processes (Aveline 2003). Leaders have an ethical obligation to live up to the trust placed in them (*fidelity*) and, with their work of facilitating members being therapeutic, they have the task to respect member's *autonomy* while ensuring *justice*.

Other applications of groups

Space does not permit consideration of alternative models that have been applied to out-patient groups. These include, for example, the psychoanalytic, existential, cognitive behavioural, and one derived from Bion (see Recommended reading).

Although the focus has been on the long-term group, many groups have short durations of up to about 16 sessions. They are less ambitious in terms of promoting change. Often these are structured and frequently use a form of cognitive behavioural therapy to address Axis I disorders. Using a group setting to deliver a non-group therapy has been shown to be helpful in, for example, promoting social skills in patients with schizophrenia (Lieberman et al. 1998), reducing distress in cancer patients (Kissane et al. 1997; Sheard and Maguire 1999; Kissane et al. 2003), improving social relations in a dual diagnosis population (Weiss et al. 2000), and preventing anxiety in children (Dadds et al. 1999). Such groups may be deployed either to augment other therapies, such as pharmacotherapy, or deliver less formal models of change, such as the *12-step model* in drug abuse (Crits-Christoph et al. 1999). While treatments for severe personality disorder tend to be extended and intensive (Warren et al. 2003), shorter groups can be helpful (Budman et al. 1996). Integrated models are being developed (Fisher and Bentley 1996).

Process groups are deployed in in-patient and day-patient settings, their mode of application dependent mainly on whether the unit is run on therapeutic community (Kennard and Roberts 1998) or more conventional lines. In the latter, careful attention is paid to aims that can be achieved. Thus, in a ward where a patient's stay rarely exceeds 2 to 3 weeks it would be fanciful to expect that group membership could exert radical change. In this instance, a model is needed which enables realistically set goals to be accomplished.

One such model, devised by Maxmen (1978), involves inpatients in a small, open group where they are guided to 'think clinically and respond effectively to the consequences of their illnesses'; that is, they learn to identify maladaptive behaviours and to avoid circumstances likely to precipitate recurrence. Yalom (1983) advocates considering each session as a complete group in itself. Instillation of hope, acceptance, universality, and altruism are especially valued in ward groups, with a lesser role for self-understanding. Ward groups can counter the helplessness felt by many inpatients; they give voice to the muted. Inpatients may need help to encourage them to join groups and participate actively (Pam and Kemker 1993). Differentiating two levels of therapy, Yalom has devised two distinct approaches, one for high-functioning, the other for low-functioning patients. This advance gets away from the 'one-size fits all' tendency (Klein et al. 1994).

In the Vancouver/Edmonton project previously cited, supportive and interpretative streams are offered within a time-limited day-patient and evening program. Patients often need a variety of experience and one which is tailored to meet their capacity to engage in explorative therapy (Piper et al. 2001; Ogrodniczuk et al. 2002). Psychodynamically informed partial hospitalization is beneficial in the therapy of complex personality disorders, such as borderline personality (Bateman and Fonagy 1999; Bateman and Fonagy 2001).

There is a place for structured exercises in group therapy; these stem mainly from the traditions of psychodrama. Various forms of creative expression can be incorporated, many of which are suited for the format; dance, music, and art have been tried. Interested readers are referred to Aveline 1979; Remocker and Storch 1982; Davies 1988; Feasey 2001. In Germany, models of group support are being tried post-discharge. Via the internet, a weekly live chat room is provided for a 90 minute discussion of personal issues previously notified to the leader. Members build on their shared inpatient group experience (Golkamnay et al. 2003).

No chapter on group therapy would be complete without mention of the self-help group. Although the purist may demur from designating this as treatment, common ground is shared by self-help and therapeutic groups in terms of membership, underlying assumptions, and strategies. The self-help group, however, is distinctive in the sense that, classically, it is founded and run by its members (although they may consult). Alcoholics Anonymous is composed exclusively of people dependent on alcohol who meet in order to provide mutual help and support. Such a group is compatible with professionally led group therapy and can be synergistic (Yalom et al. 1978). New technology is affecting this area too. *Walkers in Darkness*, a US support group for people with depressive or bipolar disorder, has a live chat room for sufferers with occasional guest visits by mental health professionals (www.walkers.org).

Training

Ideally, training comprises supervised practice, observation of skilled therapists, participation in a training group and knowledge of the literature on theory and technique (Aveline 1988).

Supervised experience is paramount. Commonly, a pair of co-therapists meets with an experienced clinician weekly. Supervision should begin at the time of patient selection since the success of a group depends on this and trainees require guidance. Supervisory sessions ideally take place soon after each meeting while events are still fresh in mind.

Two difficulties are the time taken to report what occurred and the omission of material which may embarrass or threaten them. A method to reduce both is the written summary described earlier (Yalom et al. 1975). The summary sent to patients is shared with the supervisor. The leaders are less defensive since they have given a comprehensive overview of the session. Supervision is best continued throughout the group's life.

Leaders need to acquire knowledge of the salient aspects of theory, technique, and research. Without such knowledge, the therapist lacks a coherent framework in which to work. Familiarity with various theories is also necessary. Inevitably, a trainee selects the approach prevalent in the institution in which he is being trained. As we have limited information on the relative effectiveness of different schools, a newcomer would be advantaged in applying the model described above which tends to the non-doctrinaire. Attachment to a particular framework may arise which can be incorporated into her clinical work.

Novices often become participate in a training group, thereby acquiring valuable experience about personal and group. The aim is two-fold—the group conveys to the therapist what patients are likely to experience and she uses the opportunity for self-exploration. Whether individual therapy is also a requisite for training is debatable; a thorough training group experience probably suffices.

Viewing skilled therapists through a one-way screen or on video has a place; the former is preferable since discussion with the therapists follows immediately.

Summary

Group therapy has become an established mode of treatment in psychiatry. An interpersonal model has been offered in this chapter. Training in other schools may follow depending on preference and clinical need.

A group approach is applicable to diverse contexts, from the psychiatric ward to the self-help group. Space has permitted only brief mention of these. Again, the recommended reading contains a guide.

Appendix 1: Guidelines for potential group members

Outlined below are features of group therapy you need to know about before making a commitment. They form the basis of a successful group and we believe members should be guided by them.

1 The group works on the assumption that an important problem for all its members is difficulty in establishing and maintaining close and satisfying relationships. Members may experience their problems with other people in a variety of ways.

2 The group is a special place where you can explore in an honest way your relationships with other members and with the leaders. If you have difficulty in the way you relate, then a situation that encourages honest, open communication provides you with a good opportunity to learn valuable things about yourself.

3 It is important that you are honest with your feelings especially towards other members and the leaders. In many ways, this is an essential element of group therapy and involves taking risks. This becomes progressively more possible as you develop trust in the group and feel comfortable in participating.

4 Group therapy gives you the opportunity to try out new ways of behaving. It is important to recognize that this is probably the safest place in which you can experiment. The group encourages experimentation and provides feedback about its effectiveness.

5 Stumbling blocks occur along the way. As there is no agenda or formal structure to meetings, you may initially feel puzzled, even discouraged. We encourage you to weather the first few weeks. Working on personal problems and developing new ways of relating is not easy and can be stressful. Group therapy may involve emotional pain and distress but there are also many lighter moments.

6 We shall ask you to identify the main difficulties you experience in your relationships with others and that you will be working on. Every 4 months, we will review progress by asking you to assess any change with the rest of the group, including the therapists; they will be invited to offer feedback. New goals will then be set to cover the next 4 months. We hope this will prove helpful and enable us to maintain focus.

7 A basic aim is that each member accomplishes his set goals. Since problems requiring change have usually been many years in the making, members should commit themselves to at least 6-months' membership. Should there be unavoidable reasons for leaving, it is important to give notice as early as possible so that you and the others can come to terms with the departure.

8 In the event of contact between members outside the group, we ask you to share this so that the work is kept within the group context.

9 Regular attendance and punctuality are crucial. If you know you will be unable to attend a session or that you will be late, a message spares members' and therapists' anxiety.

10 What happens in the group is confidential. All members are duty-bound to respect that confidentiality. (The reader is directed to Appelbaum and Greer (1993), and Roback et al. (1993) for interesting commentaries on this important aspect of the group's culture.)

11 Smoking and drinking are not permitted in the group.

References

Appelbaum, P. and Greer A. (1993). Confidentiality in group therapy. *Hospital and Community Psychiatry*, **44**, 311–12.

Aveline, M. (1979). Action techniques in psychotherapy. *British Journal of Hospital Medicine*, **22**, 78–84.

Aveline, M. (1986). The use of written reports in a brief group psychotherapy training. *International Journal of Group Psychotherapy*, **36**, 477–482.

Aveline, M. (1988). Issues in the training of group therapists. In *Group Therapy in Britain*. (eds) (M. Aveline and W. Dryden). Open University Press, Milton Keynes, 317–336.

Aveline, M. (1990). The group therapies in perspective. *Free Associations*, **19**, 77–101.

Aveline, M. (1993). Principles of leadership in brief training groups for mental health professionals. *International Journal of Group Psychotherapy*, **43**, 107–129.

Aveline, M. (1997). Assessing for optimal therapeutic intervention. In *Client Assessment*. (eds) (S. Palmer and G. McMahon). Sage London, pp. 93–114.

Aveline, M. (1999). The advantages of formulation over categorical diagnosis in explorative psychotherapy and psychodynamic management. *European Journal of Psychotherapy, Counselling and Health*, **2**, 199–216.

Aveline, M. (2003). Ethical issues in group therapy. In *Forms of Ethical Thinking in Therapeutic Practice*. (eds) (C. Jones and D. Hill) Open University Press/McGraw Hill, New York.

Bateman, A. and Fonagy P. (1999). The effectiveness of partial hospitalisation in the treatment of borderline personality disorder—a randomised controlled trial. *American Journal of Psychiatry*, **156**, 1563–1569.

Bateman, A. and Fonagy) P. (2001). Treatment of borderline personality disorder with psychoanalytically oriented partial hospitalisation: an 18 month follow up. *American Journal of Psychiatry*, **158** (1), 36–42.

Bion, W. R. (1961). *Experiences in groups*. London, Tavistock.

Bloch, S., Browning, S. et al. (1983). Humour in group psychotherapy. *British Journal of Medical Psychology*, **56**, 89–97.

Bloch, S. and Crouch E. (1985). *Therapeutic factors in group psychotherapy*. Oxford University Press, Oxford.

Bond, G. R. and Lieberman M. A. (1978). Selection criteria for group therapy. In *Controversy in psychiatry*. (eds) (J. Brady and H. K. Brodie). Saunders, Philadelphia.

Budman, S. H., Demby, A. et al. (1996). Time-limited group psychotherapy for patients with personality disorders: outcomes and drop-outs. *International Journal of Group Psychotherapy*, **46**, 357–377.

Burlingame, G. M., Fuhriman, A. et al. (2002). Cohesion in group therapy. In *A guide to psychotherapy relationships that work*. (ed.) (J. C. Norcross). Oxford, Oxford University Press.

Burlingame, G. M., Strauss, B. et al. (2004). Small group treatment: evidence for effectiveness and mechanisms of change. In *Handbook of Psychotherapy and Behavior Change*. ed. (M. Lambert). Wiley: New York, 647–696.

Corsini, R. J. and Rosenberg B. (1955). Mechanisms of group psychotherapy: processes and dynamics. *Journal of Abnormal and Social Psychology*, **51**, 406–11.

Crits-Christoph, P., Siqueland, L. et al. (1999). Psychological treatments for cocaine dependence: National Institute on Drug Abuse Collaborative Cocaine Treatment Study. *Archives of General Psychiatry*, **56**, 493–502.

Crouch, E., Bloch, S. et al. (1994). Therapeutic factors: Interpersonal and intrapersonal mechanisms. In *Handbook of group psychotherapy*. (ed.) (A. Fuhriman and G. M. Burlingame). Wiley, New York.

Dadds, M. R., Holland, D. E. et al. (1999). Early intervention and prevention of anxiety disorders in children: results at 2-year follow up. *Journal of Consulting and Clinical Psychology*, **65**, 145–150.

Davies, M. (1988). *Psychodrama group therapy*. (eds) (M. Aveline and W. Dryden). Open University Press, Milton Keynes.

Feasey, D. (2001). *Good practice in psychodrama with an analytic perspective*. Whurr, London.

Fisher, M. S. S. and Bentley K. J. (1996). Two group therapy models for clients with a dual diagnosis of substance abuse and personality disorder. *Psychiatric Services*, **47**, 1244–50.

Foulkes, S. H. (1946). Group analysis in a military neurosis centre. *Lancet*(i), 303–10.

Frank, J. D. and Frank J. B. (1991). *Persuasion and Healing*. Johns Hopkins University Press, Baltimore.

Freud, S. (1955). Group psychology and the analysis of the ego. Hogarth, London.

Fuhriman, A. and Burlingame, G. M. eds. (1994). *Handbook of group psychotherapy*. Wiley, New York.

Gabbard, G. O., Coyne, L. et al. (2000). Evaluation of intensive inpatient treatment of patients with severe personality disorder. *Psychiatric Services*, **51**, 893–898.

Golkamnay, V., Dogs, J. et al. (2003). *Project Internet-Bridge: relapse prevention through internet chat groups: evaluation of acceptance and effectiveness*. 34th Annual Meeting of the Society for Psychotherapy Research, Weimar, Germany.

Jung, C. (1974). *Group psychotherapy and group function*. M. Rosenbaum and M. Berger. Basic Books, New York.

Kaul, T. and Bednar R. (1994). Pretraining and structure: Parallel lines yet to meet. In *Handbook of group psychotherapy*. (eds) (A. Fuhriman and G. M. Burlingame). Wiley, New York.

Kennard, D. and Roberts J. (1998). *An introduction to therapeutic communities*. Jessica Kingsley, London.

Klein, R., Brabender, V. et al. (1994). Inpatient group therapy. In *Handbook of group psychotherapy*. (eds) (A. Fuhriman and G. M. Burlingame). Wiley, New York.

Kissane, D., Bloch, S. et al. (1997). Cognitive-Existential Group Therapy for Patients with Primary Breast Cancer-Techniques and Themes. *Psycho-Oncology*, **6**, 25–33.

Kissane, D., Bloch, S. et al. (2003). Cognitive-Existential Group Therapy for Women with Primary Breast Cancer: a Randomised Controlled Trial. *Psycho-Oncology*, **12**, 532–546.

Lewin, K. (1951). *Field theory in social science*. Harper, New York.

Lieberman, R. P., Wallace, C. J. et al. (1998). Innovations in skills training for the seriously mentally ill: the UCLA social and independent living skills (SILS) modules. *Innovations and Research*, **2**, 43–59.

MacKenzie, K. R. (1994). Group development. In *Handbook of Group Psychotherapy*. (eds. A. Fuhriman and G. M. Burlingame). pp. 232–268 Wiley, New York.

Maxmen, J. (1978). An educative model for in-patient group therapy. *International Journal of Group Psychotherapy*, **29**, 321–38.

Ogrodniczuk, J. S., Piper, W. E. et al. (2002). Interpersonal predictors of group therapy outcome for complicated grief. *International Journal of Group Psychotherapy*, **52**, 511–535.

Pam, A. and Kemker S. (1993). The captive group: Guidelines for group therapists in the inpatient setting. *International Journal of Group Psychotherapy*, **43**, 419–438.

Piper, W. E. (1994). Client variables. In *Handbook of Group Psychotherapy*. (eds) (A. Fuhriman and G. M. Burlingame). pp. 83–113 Wiley, New York.

Piper, W. E., McCallam, M. et al. (2001). Patient personality and time-limited group psychotherapy for complicated grief. *International Journal of Group Psychotherapy*, **51**, 525–552.

Pratt, J. (1974). The tuberculosis group: An experiment in home treatment. In *Group psychotherapy and group function* (eds) (M. Rosenbaum and M. Berger). Basic Books, New York.

Ratigan, B. and Aveline M. (1988). Interpersonal group therapy. In *Group therapy in Britain*. (eds) (M. Aveline and W. Dryden). pp. 45–64 Open University Press, Buckingham.

Remocker, A. J. and Storch E. (1982). *Action speaks louder. A handbook pf non-verbal group techniques*. Churchill Livingstone, Edinburgh.

Roback, H., Purdon, S. et al. (1993). Effects of professional affiliation in group therapists confidentiality attitudes and behaviours. *Bulletin of the American Academy of Psychiatry and the Law*, **21**, 147–53.

Roberts, J. and Pines M. (1992). Group-analytic psychotherapy. *International Journal of Group Psychotherapy*, **42**, 469–94.

Rogers, C. (1973). *On encounter groups*. Penguin, Harmondsworth.

Roth, A. and Fonagy P. (2004). *What works for whom? A critical review of psychotherapy research*. Guilford, New York.

Scheidlinger, S. (1994). An overview of nine decades of group psychotherapy. *Hospital and Community Psychiatry*, **45**, 217–25.

Schutz, W. C. (1958). *Firo: A three-dimensional theory of interpersonal behavior*. Rinehart, New York.

Sheard, T. and Maguire P. (1999). The effect of psychological interventions of anxiety and depression in cancer patients. *British Journal of Cancer*, **80**, 1770–1780.

Strauss, B. M. (2000). Attachment and group psychotherapy. *Ricerche sui gruppi*, **5**, 41–53.

Sullivan, H. S. (1953). *The interpersonal theory of psychiatry*. Norton, New York.

Tuckman, B. W. (1965). Developmental sequence in small groups. *Psychological Bulletin*, **63**, 384–399.

Warren, F., Preedy-Fayers, K. et al. (2003). Review of treatments for severre personality disorder, Home Office Online Report 30.03 (http://ww.homeofice.gov.uk/rds/pdfs2/rdsolr3003.pdf.

Weiss, R. D., Griffin, M. L. et al. (2000). Group therapy for patient with bipolar disorder and substance dependence: results of a pilot study. *Journal of Clinical Psychiatry*, **61**, 361–7.

Whitaker, D. S. (1985). *Using groups to help people*. Routledge and Kegan Paul, London.

Yalom, I. D. (1983). *Inpatient group psychotherapy*. Basic Books, New York.

Yalom, I. D. and Leszcs (2005). *The theory and practice of group psychotherapy*, (5th edn) Basic Books, New York.

Yalom, I., Bloch, S. and Brown. S. (1975). The use of a written summary in group psychotherapy supervision. *American Journal of Psychiatry*, **132**, 1055–7.

Yalom, I. D., Bloch, S. et al. (1978). Alcoholics in interactional group therapy: an outcome study. *Archives of General Psychiatry*, **35**, 419–25.

Yalom, I. D., Brown, S. et al. (1975). The written summary as a group psychotherapy technique. *Archives of General Psychiatry*, **32**, 605–613.

Recommended reading

Aveline, M. and Dryden, W. (ed.) (1988). *Group therapy in Britain*. Open University Press, Milton Keynes. (Covers a range of theoretical models and applications as well as chapters on research and training.)

Bion, W. R. (1961). *Experiences in groups*. Tavistock, London. (The 'Tavistock' approach in which the theoretical ideas of Melanie Klein are central.)

Foulkes, S. H. and Anthony, E. J. (1973). *Group psychotherapy*. Penguin, Harmondsworth. (The approach of the London Institute of Group Analysis and influenced by psychoanalytic concepts and techniques.)

Fuhriman, A. and Burlingame, G. (eds.) (1994). *Handbook of group psychotherapy*. Wiley, New York. (A comprehensive volume, which presents a synthesis of empirical and clinical research on every conceivable aspect of group therapy.)

Kaplan, H. I. and Sadock, B. J. (eds.) (1993). *Comprehensive group psychotherapy*, 3rd edn. William and Wilkins, Baltimore. (Contains chapters dealing with therapy of special groups such as married couples, adolescents, and the elderly, as well as chapters on different schools.)

Whitaker, D. (1985). *Using groups to help people*. Routledge & Kegan Paul, London. (A clear, comprehensive account of group work by a leading figure in the field; useful practical orientation.)

Yalom, I. D. and Leszcz, M. (2005). *The theory and practice of group psychotherapy*, (5th edn). Basic Books, New York. (An excellent account of the theory and practice of interactive group therapy, with an important section on therapeutic factors.)

Part 3

Attempts at integration

Chapter 12

Cognitive analytic therapy

Ian B. Kerr and Anthony Ryle

Cognitive Analytic Therapy (CAT) is an integrative model of psychotherapy developed over recent decades by Ryle and subsequently further elaborated by others (Denman 2002; Ryle and Kerr 2002). Although devised as a brief therapy for 'neurotic' problems, it has become a mature model of development and psychopathology applicable to an expanding range of conditions. Committed to evidence-based practice, its origins lie partly in process research (Ryle 1980; Bennett and Parry 2003, 2004). Its evidence base is primarily naturalistic although formal outcome studies (notably for borderline personality disorder; BPD) are in progress. Generically, it conforms, as expected for a model with cognitive and psychodynamic roots, with criteria regarded as important for effectiveness (Ryle and Kerr 2002; Roth and Fonagy 2005; Parry et al. 2005). Characteristic features of CAT are its proactive, collaborative therapeutic stance and a relational approach stressing the interpersonal origins and context of most psychopathology. Significantly, a major part of Ryle's motivation was an attempt to devise a 'good enough' intervention for the vast numbers of patients encountered in public mental health services and this attitude of social responsibility still pervades the model.

CAT as a model of development and psychopathology

Background

The origins of CAT lie in part in Ryle's frustration with the limitations of psychoanalysis and behaviourism. He sought to create a 'common language' by restating certain psychoanalytic concepts in the framework of cognitive psychology. He was especially influenced by his repertory grid work, based on Kelly's personal construct theory, with its paradigm of 'man as scientist', actively, but often unconsciously, construing the world on the basis of previous interpersonal experience. Through Ryle's research (Ryle 1979, 1980; Brockman et al. 1987) it became apparent that repetitive patterns of thought and behaviour, evident early in therapy, accounted for considerable distress and dysfunction. Exploring these with patients helped to strengthen the therapeutic alliance and improved outcome. This led to an emphasis on early descriptive reformulation, still a key feature of CAT (see below).

This early research culminated in the 'procedural sequence model'. This was based on the key concept of the 'procedure' which remains fundamental to CAT. A procedure is a linked series of aims, actions concerned with relationships and self-management, and consequences which may be revised or be self-confirming. Failure to modify maladaptive procedures characterizes 'neurotic' presentations. Identifying these procedures, backed up at a research level by use of repertory grid techniques, became central to therapeutic work. A list of these maladaptive procedures ('traps', 'snags', and 'dilemmas'; Ryle 1980) was collected into the 'psychotherapy file'. Ryle's interest in the interpersonal origins of procedural sequences and recognition of the limitations of the 'information-processing' focus in cognitive psychology (see Bruner 1990; Aitken and Trevarthen 1997; Stiles 1997) led to the development of the 'Procedural Sequence-Object Relations Model' (PSORM).

This model has been further influenced by the work of Lev Vygotsky and the 'activity theory' tradition (Wertsch 1985; Ryle 1991) and by concepts of the social and dialogic self derived from Mikhail Bakhtin (Ryle and Kerr 2002). The Finnish psychologist, Mikael Leiman (1992, 1997, 2004) has been developing a more 'dialogical' version of CAT. The model has also drawn on recent developmental psychology stressing the intersubjective nature of the infant, who collaboratively and playfully participates in sign-mediated activity with its caregiver from a very early stage (Stern 1985; Aitken and Trevarthen 1997; Trevarthern and Aitken 2001). Key Vygotskian concepts are those of the *zone of proximal development*—the gap between what a child can do independently and what can be achieved with the help of an enabling other; *psychological tools*—sign-mediating cultural artefacts which influence mental activity; and *'internalization'*—a transformative process through which interpersonal processes shape intrapersonal ones.

CAT as a model of development

In the CAT model of the self, early, socially-derived patterns of interaction and dialogue are internalized to become the foundation of our relationship to others and of self-management procedures, including the 'conversations' within ourselves which contribute to consciousness. The latter, while relatively stable and self-reinforcing, can be influenced by further dialogue, including the dialogue of therapy. All mental activity, conscious and unconscious, is heavily influenced by the internalization of sign-mediated, interpersonal, and social experience, in the context of one's biological constitution.

This process results in the acquisition of a repertoire of reciprocal roles (RRs). These are complexes of implicit relational memory, including perception and affect. RRs have also been described as 'semiotic positions' (Leiman 2004). Enactment of a role, whether in behaviour or internal dialogue, always anticipates or attempts to elicit the reciprocal reaction of a current or an internalized other. Reciprocal role procedures (RRPs) therefore act as 'templates' for subsequent enactments in 'self–other' interactions and in internal 'self–self' management. RRs may be experienced consciously as internal conversations (dialogic voices), which may become a focus in treatment. Important reciprocal roles are concerned with nurturance-dependency, control-submission, and abuse-victimization. Examples include, at one end of a spectrum, '*well-enough cared for* in relation to *well-enough caring for*', through to, at the other end of this spectrum, '*abused* in relation to *abusing*' (see further examples in Figure 12.1).

Fundamental to a reciprocal role is the internalization of both parental/culturally derived and child-derived experience. A child who internalizes, for example, a 'bully-submissive' RR will tend to engage with others in terms of this pattern, playing either the originally child-derived 'submissive' role or the parent-derived 'bullying' one. Coping or 'responsive' (Leiman 2004) RRPs develop to deal with dysfunctional parental roles and may manifest as, for example, avoidant, submissive, or emotionally numb role enactments. These concepts have been confirmed empirically in developmental psychology (Cox and Lightfoot 1997; Trevarthen and Aitken 2001; Ryle and Kerr 2002) and have important implications for psychotherapy.

The social concept of self implicit in CAT is based on the idea that the individual is largely formed and sustained through a continuing dialogue with others. This represents a quite radical and counter-intuitive idea to many, challenging traditional Cartesian assumptions of the independent and free-willed individual. Such a concept is frequently a (therapeutic) challenge to many trainees and patients (Ryle and Kerr 2002).

CAT as a model of psychopathology

The internalization of unhealthy RRs, evident in self-perpetuating maladaptive procedural enactments, is seen in CAT to underlie most psychopathology. These may be evident in damaging relationships or poor self-care and may be reflected in internal dialogue. Equally important may be 'forbidden' or 'feared' enactments (such as 'assertion of own needs') which are 'prohibited' by cultural and parental 'voices' (Leiman 2004). These may also represent therapeutic targets. CAT differs therefore from CBT in not regarding psychopathology as malfunction of cognitive processes or as acquired behaviours but as enactments of underlying relational, psychological processes. Attending to symptoms (e.g. self-harm) may be necessary, but may collude with and reinforce underlying RRs (e.g. if experienced as 'controlling') if these are not also identified and worked on (Ryle and Kerr 2002). CAT also differs from psychodynamic models in integrating an account of behaviour, symptoms, and subjective distress, with insights into their interpersonal and developmental origins.

Borderline personality disorder (BPD) and other complex disorders

The CAT model also describes more extensive damage to the self as occurs in personality (Ryle 1997a,b; Ryle and Kerr 2002) and psychotic disorders (see below and Kerr et al. 2003). Here, disruptions of the normally well-integrated repertoire of RRs occur which impair self-reflective and executive function and cause major interpersonal problems. These occur notably in borderline personality disorder (BPD) which is seen as an essentially dissociative disorder due to chronic deprivation or trauma in possibly biologically vulnerable individuals (e.g. due to impaired impulse control). Poor integration of RRPs results in the tendency of such patients to 'switch' suddenly, especially under conditions of stress or adversity, into one or other of a range of self-states, each characterized by a separate RR. Such patients often experience anxiety and depression and 'coping' enactments may include, for example, substance abuse or self-harm. Confirmation of such self-states has been made through repertory grid analyses (Golynkina and Ryle 2000).

CAT as a model of therapy

General considerations

CAT is usually offered as a time-limited (normally 16 sessions) intervention. For many patients referred to outpatient psychotherapy departments this appears to be adequate. CAT is inclusive with regard to acceptance for therapy and regards lack of 'psychological-mindedness', poor 'motivation', or complex presentations as part of the problem rather than as exclusion criteria. However, therapy would not usually be offered to those with acute psychotic disorders, marked substance abuse, or if there is a major risk of violence.

Although a 16-session format is typical, for more severely disturbed patients (e.g. with personality or psychotic disorders) 24 sessions will usually be offered. With patients for whom the supportive aspects of therapy are paramount (e.g. with chronic psychotic disorders), CAT-informed work lasting years has been undertaken.

The *therapeutic focus* in CAT lies primarily in identifying and subsequently revising a patient's repertoire of RRs and their enactments and, in more disturbed patients, repairing disruptions to the integrity of the self. This is understood to occur through a therapeutic relationship in which a new RR is gradually internalized.

Collaborative construction of *reformulation documents* (a letter and diagram) is a key process. These act as 'route maps' for the therapy and are 'psychological tools', contributing to CAT's structured approach. Reformulation aims at making sense, in both 'paradigmatic' and 'narrative' ways, of the patient's story. The latter function ('bearing witness') is seen as important in itself. The letter aims to summarize the patient's story from the therapist's point of view while also identifying recurrent reciprocal role patterns, their origins, and how they have emerged as ways of coping. The ways in which reciprocal roles may be mobilized in the therapeutic relationship are also noted. Reading out a draft of this letter, which the patient is encouraged to modify, is usually a powerful and poignant moment and may be followed by silence or tears. It also reinforces the alliance, dropouts being uncommon after this stage. The letter is supplemented by summaries of key reciprocal roles and their enactments and consequences (target problem procedures—'TPPs', or 'key issues'). Many of these will have been identified by the patient from the 'psychotherapy file'. Finally, aims are articulated and both recognition and revision of TPPs are monitored using rating charts throughout therapy. These may range from the abstract, for example, 'recognizing and challenging an internalized criticising parental role and voice', to the more behavioural, for example, 'not always acting as a 'doormat' and placating people at work, and seeing what happens'). Keeping a diary is encouraged and its contents routinely discussed.

The diagram depicts key reciprocal roles, their habitual enactments, and their consequences (see Figure 12.1). These key psychological processes are described through joint exploration and discussion. This is ideally undertaken with a blank sheet and is led by the therapist using the patient's own words. Each diagram is therefore a 'one off'. The therapist sketches provisional RRPs and shows, non-judgementally, how they reinforce original roles in a vicious cycle and maintain symptoms (see Figure 12.1). Seeing such an overview can generate highly charged insights and understandings. Diagrams may also serve as 'transitional objects', enabling more disturbed patients to maintain a sense of the therapist and of the work done. They may also be used to communicate, where appropriate, to others, for example, relatives or other mental health professionals. Explicit acknowledgment of 'real world' factors which may influence outcome (e.g. lack of educational opportunities or of adequate housing) can also help using techniques such as 'power mapping' (Hagan and Smail 1997).

Transference and counter-transference

Maladaptive role enactments also occur between patient and therapist and are an important focus of therapy. These range from, for example, 'mutually admiring and idealizing', to, for example, the patient 'anticipating and acting as if the therapist will be uncaring and punitive and so provoking in the therapist an irritated reaction of being unappreciated'. These are discussed and incorporated in the diagram and letter. CAT thus works with transference and counter-transference, by identifying reciprocal role enactments which the therapist strives not to reciprocate. Inevitably, the therapist is drawn into collusions, but explicit reference to reformulation tools offers a means of addressing and resolving them. 'Forbidden' enactments may also be identified and efforts to try them out encouraged, sometimes as behavioural experiments.

CAT's style of '*doing with*' is fundamental to the model. Therapists are transparent and explicit about their concepts and convey the style of therapy from the start. They adopt, where appropriate, an unashamedly proactive and psycho-educational role. Therapists aim to operate within the patient's 'zone of proximal development' (ZPD), pacing therapy so that the concepts and experience it offers can be internalized. This approach demonstrably contributes to the alliance (Bennett and Parry 2004) and so to a low dropout rate.

An important aim in CAT is to reach an understanding that thoughts and feelings, previously assumed to be immutable and 'given', are rooted in a repertoire of reciprocal roles which can be identified, have a history, and which can be thought about, challenged, and modified. Such a 'dialogic challenge' may be the principal task in some therapies. It may be only gradually achieved but is frequently an emotionally highly charged experience. Therapy is also respected as an opportunity to process often-painful experiences and to grieve for lost opportunities or a life that was not possible to lead. It can also offer an opportunity, in relation to previous reformulation, to address more existential issues of meaning and purpose.

Duration of therapy and time limitation

Although CAT began as a brief therapy, it was never conceived of as a 'fast food' version of an ideally longer treatment. Focus on a time limit has both theoretical and empirical justification (Ryle and Kerr 2002; Parry et al. 2005). More complex patients may well require longer-term support and consolidation but a major pull to collusion inevitably lies in continuing to see a patient as needy and helpless and so offering 'just a bit longer'. Extension beyond an agreed limit may be justified, but this can perpetuate a dependent role and deprive the patient of the opportunity to experience a new role through 'ending well'. Adaptive mourning involves acknowledging loss and internalizing what was lost. Letting go may be conceived of as 'openly sharing vulnerabilities, losses, and anxiety with a trusted and secure other' rather than maintaining defensive or symptomatic enactments. Such indefinite enactments are a major therapeutic challenge with some patients, for example, a chronically depressed and 'needy' patient with whom it would be easy to reciprocate an indefinite 'caring and supportive' role, or in a narcissistically-disordered person where a special, 'admired–admiring' reciprocal enactment may easily be perpetuated. Most patients are doing well by follow-up despite possibly being anxious in the face of termination. Ending well, therefore, is seen as an aim in itself.

Phases of therapy

Initial phase

The initial phase, usually 3–4 sessions, is an assessment period during which presenting difficulties and their origins are explored and a coherent account of them is generated through the reformulation letter and diagram. Already the characteristic style of CAT of thinking about reciprocal roles and their enactments (including within therapy) will be evident. Some homework, for example, keeping a diary, will also be suggested during this stage.

Middle phase

Here, a more open exploration of current and past experiences may occur but always in the light of the reformulation. Maintaining focus in this way is crucial (Bennett and Parry 2003, 2004). The patient is encouraged to work in and beyond sessions on their aims, with recognition and revision of TPPs marked on rating sheets. Therapy may be the only safe place to experiment, for example, expressing anger or not being placatory. Most patients will be able to extend this experimentation to day-to-day life. RRPs refractory to insight, transference–counter-tranference challenges, or behavioural experiment, may require more emotionally-charged and intuitive approaches (e.g. role-play). For instance, a 'criticizing' parental voice may be experienced as unchangeable and as 'deserved' by a survivor of abuse and may only be shifted by such approaches. Creative methods like painting may help as may writing 'no-send' letters to important, sometimes deceased, others.

Ending

Ending therapy is always emphasized with sessions counted off from the outset. Ending is an issue even in longer-term supportive work since it frequently provokes anxiety in patient and therapist with recurrence of maladaptive role enactments. Brief 'goodbye' letters are written for the last session by therapist and patient reflecting on what has been experienced, what has or has not been achieved, and what may be anticipated for the future. These documents contribute to 'ending well' and have obvious symbolic value. Ending well constitutes a new role enactment although not all patients achieve this at this point.

Follow-up

At least one follow-up session is offered a few months after ending. Although most patients will have moved on, a minority require further help. The decision to offer extra sessions is undertaken with a supervisor or colleague since the pull to collusion is ever present. Some patients may be offered further therapy, for example, intermittent follow-up or several further sessions or an alternative, such as group therapy. Longer-term supportive therapy may also be indicated (see Chapter 10).

Considerations in treating borderline personality disorder (BPD) and other complex disorders

The tendency of patients with BPD to dissociate into different self-states and to enact extreme RRPs complicates engaging and working with them. These enactments often appear unpredictable, bewildering, and demoralizing to therapists and others. Rather longer treatment is usually offered (usually 24 or more sessions). This may be adequate, although some may need longer-term or supportive treatment. Identifying and revising underlying reciprocal roles and their enactments remains the principal task rather than trying to control symptoms (e.g. self-harm) although these may also require direct attention. Improving self-reflective function with the aid of a diagrammatic reformulation is of particular importance with such patients. Sketching out a rudimentary map early on helps to establish a therapeutic alliance. Extreme enactments (e.g. 'desperate help-seeking', 'seeking relief through self-harm', 'abused, vengeful rage') frequently create unhelpful systemic 'reactions' (as opposed to considered responses) around a patient in mental health teams and beyond (Kerr 1999). These range from 'sympathetic over-involvement' to 'angry or fearful rejection'. All too often, these reactions reinforce the original experiences (and consequent reciprocal roles) that a patient has suffered. From a CAT perspective, these reactions are an integral part of the problem as they are with other varieties of the so-called difficult patient. These systemic reactions may require the use of techniques such as 'contextual reformulation' where they can be additionally incorporated into a patient's diagram (Ryle and Kerr 2002).

Considerations in treating other complex disorders

CAT with other complex disorders may also require adaptation. For instance, in working with patients with psychotic disorders, probable neuro-cognitive vulnerability will need to be acknowledged, as will the need for multidisciplinary input and other treatments (e.g. medication). In eating disorders, life-threatening metabolic complications may need treatment and possible vulnerability due to, for example, 'perfectionist' personality traits may need acknowledgement. In such situations, the therapeutic aim may not be 'cure' but rather a fulfilling life in the context of enduring vulnerability (Ryle and Kerr 2002).

A clinical illustration (deidentified)

Jean, a middle-aged woman, was referred by her community mental health team (CMHT) which had been treating her severe depression with antidepressants, an antipsychotic, and general support. There was some concern that she might be developing a psychotic depression. She had dropped out of an assertiveness group claiming it made her feel worse.

Until the previous year, Jean had worked as a senior social worker combining casework and onerous administrative duties. She had been involved in a case concerning maltreated children that had gone badly and for which she had been criticized. Meanwhile her own son had been imprisoned for repeated stealing to support a long-standing drug habit. He had previously been excluded from the family home for stealing from them. Jean blamed herself for the way things had turned out. Her daughter, however, had 'done well' and was at University. Jean had experienced increasing exhaustion and hopelessness and feelings of guilt about her son, and a sense of inadequacy as a professional and as a mother. She felt she would be better off 'out of it' which would 'decontaminate' her family and the world.

Despite a risk of self-harm and her high doses of medication, she was offered 16 sessions of CAT. At the first meeting, she was clearly depressed. Her sleep was poor and she had recurrent dreams about being trapped in a cave and being pursued by a monster. She felt guilty about her inability to do her job and about being referred for therapy. This, she felt, confirmed that there was something 'really wrong' with her. She thought she ought to be able to 'pull herself together' and that many others 'out there' needed help more than she did. She did eventually concede, however, that a part of her was relieved, if apprehensive, to be offered therapy, stating also that she wanted to discover her 'real self'.

Jean read through the 'Psychotherapy File' (Ryle and Kerr 2002), which lists common 'dilemmas', 'traps', and 'snags' and also unstable states of mind. She recognized certain 'traps': the fear of hurting others, depressed thinking, trying to please, and social isolation. She identified these 'dilemmas': either keep feelings bottled up or risk rejection, either try to be perfect and feel depressed and angry, or, not try to be perfect and feel guilty, angry, and dissatisfied;

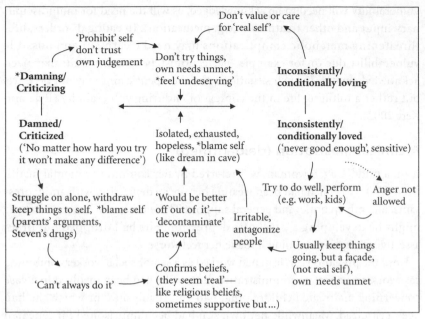

Figure 12.1 Sequential diagrammatic reformulation (SDR) of Jean. This highlights key reciprocal roles ('damning/criticizing in relation to damned/criticized' and 'inconsistently/conditionally loving in relation to inconsistently/conditionally loved') and their procedural enactments. The recurrent dialogic voice associated with the 'damning/criticizing' role is marked by an asterisk where it occurs at different points.

'dilemmas' in relating to others were: either get involved with someone and likely to get hurt, or, not getting involved and staying in charge but remaining lonely; and, as a woman either having to do what others want, or, standing up for rights and getting rejected.

From the descriptions of states she identified: zombie—cut off from feelings, cut off from others and disconnected; feeling bad but soldiering on; contemptuously dismissive of self; intensely critical of self; frightened of others. She identified only one of the 'difficult and unstable states of mind' (characteristic of BPD) namely that 'some states were accompanied by intense, extreme, and uncontrolled emotions'.

On the basis of Jean's history, the above responses, and the work of the first four sessions, a reformulation letter was drafted and discussed with her. The following are extracts:

Dear Jean,

This is the letter, which we discussed before, attempting to summarize the issues which brought you to therapy and to think about what might lie behind them and about how you might be able to move on. As I said, this is only my version and you may want to correct or modify any points which you feel are not quite right or are missing.

... When we first met you had been suffering from a severe depression for almost a year and had at times been feeling, I think, really very desperate, to the point that you seriously thought of ending your life. You had had various sorts of medication which, although they seem to have helped some of your symptoms, didn't seem, in your mind at least, to have got to the root of many of your problems. It seemed too that the idea that you had some sort of depressive illness had served to confirm your fears that there was something fundamentally wrong with you.

... From our discussions it has appeared that many of these current difficulties go way back to the early experiences you had, which we have discussed at some length, and to the ways in which, as a result, you have coped with life over the years.

... It sounds as if childhood was a very hard time for you particularly given, as you said, that you might have been naturally a bit more 'sensitive' compared, for example, to your brother who seemed to have had a 'thicker skin'. However, you wondered too if some of that might have been due to gender-related expectations of you as an elder sister. It seems as if the atmosphere in your family was really quite critical and only approving if you did well or behaved well. You noted that your family 'didn't really do feelings' and you were very much left to feel you ought to cope and manage on your own. In addition, you naturally tended to think that your parents' arguments might be your fault and it seems this too has contributed to your overall feeling that there was something wrong about you. Also, as you pointed out a lot of this stemmed from, and was reinforced by, the very religious flavour of your parents' own upbringing and their commitment to the church. You have noted that, although you too still have strong religious beliefs, it felt hard now to go to church because of your feeling that you had been a failure and were, as you put it, 'undeserving'. Disentangling some of these moral and religious views, which you quite reasonably hold, from some of the assumptions and beliefs you might have absorbed as you grew up has already seemed a very difficult issue in our sessions. This has also seemed connected with the struggle you have described, in the midst of everything, of not knowing who your 'real' self was, especially given what you described as that voice at the back of your head criticizing you. Among other things, you said, it seems recurrently to state: 'No matter how hard you struggle it won't make any difference' and you have said that you felt as if you were 'damned'. You can accept that falling ill and having your schooling disrupted was not your fault but you still felt it confirmed that you were not good enough. However, you did learn from your time in hospital that caring for others was a rewarding and commendable way of being, although, as we have discussed, this pattern of caring for others in the family and at work over the years has had its cost.

... As we noted when making the diagram, it seems that over the years you developed two main strategies for coping with these experiences and voices. These have been to struggle on alone and keep things to your self and also to try to do well and 'perform', both at home with your kids and at work. You have seemed very clear that this performing somehow obscured your real self. We have joked too about how even in therapy some of these roles have got enacted as, for example, when you have always turned up dutifully, in good time, and tried to be a 'good' patient. You were also amazed and upset for me to learn that some people didn't do this or might get quite angry in sessions which seemed, I think, almost inconceivable to you. I have sometimes felt quite strongly in our sessions this need in you to keep up a coping façade and behave well for fear I might otherwise reject you or that you might contaminate me too, as we discussed at one point. However, the cost of coping in these ways, as we noted, has been that you finish up exhausted, isolated and with your own emotional needs unmet. From what you have said it sounds as if this may have unwittingly contributed to the tension and difficulty you have described in your marriage which has also obviously reinforced your original fears and assumptions. Inevitably, over the years, particularly given the recent difficulties you have had with work and with Steven's drug problem (which, of course, you have blamed yourself for), it has been impossible to keep this up. Both at home and at work you described becoming irritable whereas normally, we noted, anger was simply 'not allowed'. This has of course provoked rejection and antagonism from your colleagues, thereby compounding the situation.

. . . It also seems that just when you haven't been able to cope then inevitably that critical voice from the past has 'kicked in', blaming you and reinforcing your original experiences and negative beliefs. As you noted, when things have been particularly difficult the self-critical voice seems even more real and somehow compelling. It seems too, as if this, often unconscious, self-critical tendency has sabotaged your own thoughts of being active or communicating and has somehow, as you put it, 'prohibited' you. All of this has seemed to reinforce both ends of the reciprocal roles which you had acquired (as we described on the diagram) and effectively become vicious circles. Ultimately, this seems to have become so intractable and hopeless that you felt so stuck (like in the dream of the cave) that you came to believe that if you weren't here it would be both a relief to you but also that the world would be better off and somehow 'decontaminated'.

. . . However, it has also seemed that there is a part of you that still hopes that things might change and, in particular, that there might still be hope of trying to rediscover who your real self might be. This seems to have brought you along to therapy and has helped you to try to stick with it even when it has stirred up painful memories. Given how hard things have been and how hopeless and exhausted at times you have obviously been, I have been impressed by your determination and courage in persisting with therapy. I think the work we have already been able to do in highlighting patterns and seeing their origins and costs has made an obvious difference. Being able to move on and do things differently will of course be easier said than done, particularly in terms of challenging that critical, damning voice, which obviously feels so real at times and so much part of who you are. Nonetheless, I do think that if we can work further on these issues it could make a big difference to your future, although of course there is no magic way in which we can undo painful events of the past. I shall also add to this letter a summary of what seem to be key issues for us to work on over the rest of your therapy and hope this will contribute to change for the better.

With best wishes,

Key issues (Target Problem Procedures)

1 Because you felt conditionally loved and somehow 'never good enough' you managed by performing and by caring for others or by putting up a

façade. This has led, in the end, to you not coping well, being exhausted, and leaving your own emotional needs unmet. Not coping and your resultant irritability can provoke rejection from others, leaving you isolated and blaming yourself, which confirms your original assumptions that you are no good and 'damned'.

Aim: Try to communicate your feelings and assert your own needs to a few others you can trust (as you have begun to do in therapy)—and see what happens.

2 Because you felt criticized and 'damned' by others and because this is perpetuated by your critical inner voice, you feel undermined, and sabotage your own plans and efforts, the result of which is to confirm your feeling that you really are no good.

Aim: Try to be aware when your critical and damning voice 'kicks in' and consider, as we have done together, where it comes from and how far you accept its validity.

The sequential diagrammatic reformulation (SDR)

The patterns described in the letter were also depicted diagrammatically. The final version is shown in Figure 12.1. Two main childhood-derived reciprocal roles are shown in bold. The consequences of procedural enactments deriving from the original reciprocal roles are shown with arrows. These also demonstrate the self-perpetuating nature of these patterns.

Further course of therapy

Reading the letter out to her was followed by silence and tears. She felt that both letter and diagram were accurate. However, the possibility that her response was partly an enactment of her need to please was also discussed later. She noted that, although she was familiar with most of the content, it was strange to have it all 'pulled together'. She struggled with her 'real' perception of not being good enough and being 'dammed'. However, she could gradually acknowledge that these ideas (voices), along with her strict religious morality, might stem in part from her childhood experience. Working on the first aim proved more feasible and with encouragement she eventually confided some of her worries (particularly about her blameworthy self) to a friend. She reported back with a big smile that the encounter had gone well. Her friend, in fact, had similar problems! This proved a turning point in her moving on from her 'ought to cope and struggle on alone' procedure. She then shared worries with her husband. Again she found to her amazement that he was sympathetic and not as she had expected. These sources of stress soon turned into sources of support as she continued to communicate her feelings.

Another turning point occurred midway through therapy when she was 'able' to say that she had felt anger towards the therapist for not taking her religious views seriously and 'reducing them' to role enactments. She also felt, perhaps correctly, that the therapist had not taken her experience of the oppression of women seriously enough (this had been identified as an issue in the psychotherapy file and in her experience of having to play an 'elder sister' role). She talked about these topics and noted that it was hard to disentangle genuinely held moral views from their formation through personal experience. She found this a pivotal discussion, relating it to her struggle to find her 'real' self. She was surprised that she could express (some) anger and have this conversation without disastrous consequences, such as the therapist rejecting her.

Challenging her self-critical voice proved more difficult although she became adept at recognizing it, sometimes humorously. Undertaking 'empty chair' work, when she revisited her child-self and parents and imagined whether she felt that the child warranted blame and considered the advice she might give to her parents, was productive. She was, tearfully, clear that she would not blame her younger self and that her parents might be a little kinder. Although she became more adept at recognizing this role enactment, it was clear from the rating sheets that revising it was hard, especially when things felt difficult and when she felt hopeless, at times, about anything changing in her life. She also wrote a 'no send' letter to her son in which she expressed her sorrow and sense of guilt but also anger for the trouble he had caused. This led her to reflect that his problems had not all been her fault and she was able to extricate herself to an extent from her sense of blame for his problems.

As therapy progressed, longer but more comfortable periods of silence occurred. However, as is often the case, her mood began to slip as the ending approached. She became anxious about the future and the prominent 'damning' voice reasserted itself. Nonetheless, she was able, almost automatically, to refer to the diagram to make sense of her enactments. She was clearly anxious in the final session when old enactments (such as 'ought to cope alone') were evident. However, she had written a moving, if brief, letter stating how much she felt she had made progress and sense of things. She noted how good it felt to share her worries. When feeling under pressure she could hear her therapists's voice challenging her usual assumptions. She expressed gratitude for the work they had done. In his own 'goodbye letter' the therapist acknowledged her effort and indicated how impressed he had been by this, but also anticipated how let down and angry she might feel after the ending.

At follow-up 3 months later, Jean reported further improvement (confirmed on routine psychometric measures) despite a fraught period following the last session. She had come off the antipsychotic and hoped to discontinue the antidepressant before long. There was no way she could go back to feeling 'trapped in the cave' although the old procedures and voices recurred intermittently. The 'damning' voice was 'more in perspective'. She was referred back to her CMHT for follow-up. She was eager to share her diagram with the community nurse at the handover meeting. This seemed a positive, practical, and powerfully symbolic outcome.

Evolving applications of CAT

Particular patient groups

CAT has been applied in an increasing range of clinical areas both as a therapy and in contributing to a re-conceptualization of aspects of various disorders (Ryle and Kerr 2002). Here we highlight innovative applications. CAT, in an extension of work with BPD, has been applied to the treatment of *survivors of sexual abuse* (Pollock 2003). In *forensic settings*, an understanding of patients' RRPs (and of reactions elicited from staff) can be valuable in understanding their offences and in management (Pollock 1997; Pollock and Belshaw 1998; Pollock et al. 2005; Wood 2004). CAT has also been used for people with *learning disabilities* with novel modifications, such as use of colour coding or of symbols on diagrams (Ryle and Kerr 2002). In *old age psychiatry*, CAT helps to challenge therapeutic nihilism (Hepple and Sutton 2004). Its concepts shed light on how the effects of dementia are magnified by society's negative attitudes. CAT also contributes to the reassessment and treatment of lifelong personality problems and the effects of unacknowledged, early trauma.

CAT has been employed in *consultation-liaison psychiatry*. Fosbury (1997, 2003), for instance, has shown that it is more effective than intensive education in maintaining diabetic control. Use of CAT for poorly-controlled asthma is reported by Walsh et al. (2000) and Cluley (personal communication). So-called 'non-compliance' in these situations proves to be, in most cases, unrecognized enactment of more general self-management and interpersonal reciprocal roles, such as '*neglectful to neglected*' (which may lead to a self-neglect enactment) or '*demanding to demanded of/guilty*' (which may lead to a 'resentful, passively resistant' enactment). It is easy to see how blaming, rejecting, or emotionally-neglectful attitudes can elicit these reciprocal enactments. Exploration of CAT for *psychotic disorders* has led to a re-conceptualization of aspects of psychosis and of therapeutic aims which may complement CBT-oriented work (Ryle and Kerr 2002; Kerr et al. 2003).

CAT and the therapeutic environment

Although CAT was devised as an individual therapy, it has evolved, as described earlier, into a model of development and psychopathology and, as such, has potential application in general patient management, staff supervision, and consultancy. Many 'difficult' patients are better understood when dysfunctional reciprocal patterns between them and treating teams (and their parent institutions) are recognized. The technique of 'contextual reformulation' where these systemic reactions are incorporated into a patient's diagram is described by Ryle and Kerr (2002). A CAT-based study of a dysfunctional hospital unit is reported by Walsh (1996). This work extends Tom Main's (1957) contribution, offering a way to help staff overcome 'systemic ignorance' (Kerr 1999) and guard against splitting and demoralization. A similar approach to supporting GPs in managing frequently attending, somatizing patients has been reported by Pickvance et al. (2005). A 'skills' level training for mental health professionals in applying CAT understandings in CMHTs has been evaluated with encouraging results. CAT's robust and accessible model of psychopathology and its collaborative emphasis proved welcome to CMHT members and improved function and morale (De Normanville and Kerr 2003; Donnison, personal communication). Such training should also be useful to other mental health professionals, including psychiatrists (Rees 2000). CAT applied to small group therapy has been productively explored (Simpson and Maple 1995), as has its application to the therapeutic community (Kerr 2000). A novel use of CAT has been explored in Australia in the field of early intervention for adolescents at risk of personality disorder. The aim, in addition to standard therapeutic goals, is to forestall deterioration and prevent adolescents from becoming established patients (Chanen 2000).

Training

Several forms of training have been developed. Most are based in the United Kingdom although training centres have been established in other, mostly European, countries. The basic training is that of 'practitioner level' (offered in some settings as a Master's degree). This is aimed at therapists with a recognized professional background (e.g. psychology, nursing) and aims to produce practitioners competent to offer CAT within their core profession. This level of training typically extends over 2 years part-time and involves the equivalent of 10 training days a year as well as weekly supervision and seminar groups.

Teaching covers theoretical and clinical topics. All candidates are required to undergo their own brief personal therapy, an experience considered vital in training in a relational therapy. Clinical work involves seeing 8 patients for 16 sessions each or equivalent. A longer 'advanced level' training extending over an additional 2 years at a similar intensity is offered in the United Kingdom. This enables trainees to obtain full 'psychotherapist' national registration. More recently a 'skills' level training has been developed offering a brief intensive training over 1 week, together with supervised case work and a brief, 'personal reformulation experience' in lieu of formal therapy. This level of training is aimed at generic staff and/or trainees from diverse backgrounds. It addresses the important challenge of improving the 'psychological literacy' of mental health, and other, professionals. Such training appears pertinent since mental health services are expected to offer treatment to more complex patients with, for example, personality disorders.

Further background information on training is available on www.acat.me.uk

Future developments

As an evolving, integrative model, CAT should have a useful role in comparative research which seeks to establish 'what works for whom' (Roth and Fonagy 2005) and to help advance the field beyond parochial, 'brand name' competition. CAT has a tradition of process and qualitative research, important in complementing the limitations of randomized controlled trials (Ryle and Kerr 2002). CAT is playing a larger role in informing generic mental health practice through 'skills' type training, supervision, and consultancy. This represents a trend to address more complex, interpersonal issues at the core of psychopathology and, correspondingly, to address the need for staff to be 'interpersonally literate'. This offers a counter position to the biomedical view of mental illness prevalent in many health care domains. CAT may prove valuable as an integrative force and a platform from which to base multi-modal programmes (McGorry 2000; Ryle and Kerr 2002). Growing understanding of mental health such as offered by CAT (and other relational therapies) should also make a sturdy contribution to the field of public mental health and beyond.

References

Aitken, K. J. and Trevarthen, C. (1997). Self/other organization in human psychological development. *Development and Psychopathology*, **9**, 653–677.

Bennett, D. and Parry, G. (2003). Maintaining the therapeutic alliance: (ed. D. Charman) Resolving alliance-threatening interactions related to the transference. In *Core processes in brief psychodynamic therapy: Advancing effective practice*. Erlbaum, Mahwah, N.J.

Bennett, D. and Parry, G. (2004). A measure of psychotherapeutic competence derived from cognitive analytic therapy (CCAT). *Psychotherapy Research*, **4**, 176–192.

Brockman, B., Poynton, A., Ryle, A., and Watson, J.P. (1987). Effectiveness of time-limited therapy carried out by trainees: A comparison of two methods. *British Journal of Psychiatry*, **151**, 602–609.

Bruner, J. (1990). *Acts of meaning*. Harvard University Press, Cambridge, Mass.

Chanen, A. (2000). Prevention and early intervention for borderline personality disorder in young people. *Reformulation* (ACAT newsletter), Autumn 2000, p.9. (Available through www.acat.me.uk).

Cox, B. D. and Lightfoot, C. (Eds) (1997). *Sociogenetic perspectives on internalisation.* Erlbaum, Mahwah, N.J.

De Normanville, J. and Kerr, I. B. (2003). Initial experiences of a CAT skills level training in a CMHT. *Reformulation* (ACAT Newsletter), **18**; 25–27. (Available through www.acat.me.uk).

Denman, C. (2002). Integrative developments in cognitive analytic therapy. In *Integration in psychotherapy: Models and methods.* (eds J. Holmes and A. Bateman) Oxford University Press, Oxford.

Fosbury, J.A. (2003). The case study: The therapy, the patient and the therapist. In *Core processes in brief dynamic psychotherapy: Advancing effective practice.* (ed. D. Charman) Erlbaum, Mahwah, N.J.

Fosbury, J. A., Bosley, C. M., Ryle, A., Sonksen, P. H., and Judd, S. L. (1997). A trial of cognitive analytic therapy in poorly controlled Type 1 patients. *Diabetes Care*, **20**, 959–964.

Hagan, T. and Smail, D. (1997). Power-mapping 1. Background and basic methodology. *Journal of Community and Applied Social Psychology*, **7**, 257–267.

Kerr, I. B. (1999). Cognitive-analytic therapy for borderline personality disorder in the context of a community mental health team: Individual and organisational psychodynamic implications. *British Journal of Psychotherapy*, **15**, 425–438.

Kerr, I. B. (2000). Vygotsky, activity theory and the therapeutic community: A further paradigm? *Therapeutic Communities*, **21**, 151–164.

Kerr, I. B., Burkitt, P., and Chanen, A. (2003). Clinical and service implications of a cognitve analytic therapy based model of psychotic disorders. *Australian and New Zealand Journal of Psychiatry*, **37**, 515–523.

Leimann, M. (1992). The concept of sign in the work of Vygotsky, Winnicott and Bakhtin: Further integration of object relations theory and activity theory. *British Journal of Medical Psychology,* **65**, 209–221.

Leiman, M. (1997). Procedures as dialogical sequences; A revised version of the fundamental concept in cognitive analytic therapy. *British Journal of Medical Psychology*, **70**, 193–207.

Leiman, M. (2004). Dialogical sequence analysis. In *The dialogical self in psychotherapy.* (eds H. Hermans and G. Dimaggio) Brunner/Routledge, Hove.

McGorry, P. (2000). Psychotherapy and recovery in early psychosis: A core clinical and research challenge. In *Psychosis: Psychological approaches and their effectiveness.* (eds A. Bateman, B. V. Martindale, M. Crowe, and F. Margison) Gaskell, London.

Main, T. (1957). The ailment. *British Journal of Medical Psychology*, **30**, 129–145.

Maple, N. and Simpson, I. (1995). CAT in groups. In *Cognitive analytic therapy: Developments in theory and practice.* (ed. A. Ryle) Wiley, Chichester.

Parry, G. D., Roth, T., and Kerr, I. B. (2005). Brief and time-limited psychotherapy. In *Oxford textbook of psychotherapy.* (eds G. O. Gabbard, J. Beck, and J. Holmes.) Oxford University Press, Oxford.

Pickvance, D., Parry, G., and Howe, A. (2005). A cognitive analytic framework for understanding and managing problematic frequent attendance in primary care. *Primary Care and Mental Health*, **2**, 165–174.

Pollock, P. H. (1997). CAT of an offender with borderline personality disorder. In *Cognitive analytic therapy for borderline personality disorder; the model and the method.* (ed. A. Ryle) Wiley, Chichester.

Pollock, P. H. (2003). (ed) *Cognitive analytic therapy for adult survivors of abuse*. Wiley, Chichester.

Pollock, P. H. and Belshaw, T. (1998). Cognitive analytic therapy for offenders. *Journal of Forensic Psychiatry*, **9**, 629–642.

Pollock, P. H., Stowell Smith, M., and Gopfert, M.J. (eds) (2005). *Cognitive analytic therapy for offenders*. Brunner/Routledge, Hove.

Rees, H. (2000). Cognitive analytic therapy—a most suitable training for psychiatrists. *Psychiatric Bulletin*, **24**, 124–126.

Roth, T. and Fonagy, P. (2005) (2nd edn) *What works for whom*. Guilford, New York.

Ryle, A. (1979). The focus in brief interpretative psychotherapy: Dilemmas, traps and snags as target problems. *British Journal of Psychiatry*, **134**, 46–54.

Ryle, A. (1980). Some measures of goal attainment in focused, integrated, active psychotherapy: A study of fifteen cases. *British Journal of Psychiatry*, **137**, 475–486.

Ryle, A. (1985). Cognitive theory, object relations and the self. *British Journal of Medical Psychology*, **58**, 1–7.

Ryle, A. (1991). Object relations theory and activity theory; a proposed link by way of the procedural sequence model. *British Journal of Medical Psychology*, **64**, 307–316.

Ryle, A. (1997a). *Cognitive analytic therapy and borderline personality disorder: The model and the method*. Wiley, Chichester.

Ryle, A. (1997 b). The structure and development of borderline personality disorder; a proposed model. *British Journal of Psychiatry*, **170**, 82–87.

Ryle, A. and Kerr, I. B. (2002). *Introducing cognitive analytic therapy: Principles and practice*. Wiley, Chichester.

Sheard, T., Evans, J., Cash, D., et al. (2000). A CAT-derived one to three session intervention for repeated deliberate self-harm: A description of the model and initial experience of trainee psychiatrists in using it. *British Journal of Medical Psychology*, **73**, 179–198.

Stern, D. N. (1985). *The interpersonal world of the infant: A view from psychoanalysis and developmental psychology*. Basic Books, New York.

Stiles, W. (1997). Signs and voices: Joining a conversation in progress. *British Journal of Medical Psychotherapy*, **70**, 169–176.

Sutton, L. and Hepple, J. (2004). *Cognitive analytic therapy in later life*. Brunner/Routledge, Hove.

Trevarthen, C. and Aitken, K. J. (2001). Infant intersubjectivity: Research, theory and clinical applications. *Journal of Child Psychology and Psychiatry*, **42**, 3–48.

Walsh, S. (1996). Adapting cognitive analytic therapy to make sense of psychologically harmful work environments. *British Journal of Medical Psychology*, **69**, 3–20.

Walsh, S., Hagan, T., and Gamsu, D. (2000). Rescuer and rescued: Applying a cognitive analytic perspective to explore the mis-management of asthma. *British Journal of Medical Psychology*, **73**, 151–168.

Wertsch, J. V. (1985). *Vygotsky and the social formation of mind*. Harvard University Press, Cambridge, Mass.

Wood, H. (2004). Psycho-analytic theories of perversion reformulated. *Sex, mind and emotion. The psychological treatment of sexual disorders and trauma*. (In (eds) J. Hiller, W. Bolton, & H. Wood) Guilford, New York.

Recommended reading

Burkitt, I. (1991). *Social selves: Theories of the social formation of personality*. Sage, London. (An overview of social and psychological theories of the formation of self.)

Cox, B.D. and Lightfoot, C. (eds) (1997). *Sociogenetic perspectives on internalisation*. Erlbaum, Mahwah, NJ. (A collection of articles on the process of internalisation, many based on observational and experimental work in infants.)

Holmes, J. and Bateman, A. (2002). (eds) *Integration in psychotherapy: Models and methods*. Oxford University Press, Oxford. (Contributions on the various conceptual, historical and clinical issues involved in psychotherapy integration.)

Parry, G.D., Roth, T. and Kerr, I. B. (2005). Brief and time-limited psychotherapy. In *Oxford textbook of psychotherapy*, G.O. Gabbard, J. Beck, and J. Holmes. (eds) Oxford University Press, Oxford. (An overview of developments in this field and their rationales.)

Ryle, A. (1997). *Cognitive analytic therapy and borderline personality disorder: The model and the method*. Wiley, Chichester. (An account of the use of CAT in treating borderline personality disorder.)

Ryle, A. and Kerr, I. B. (2002). *Introducing cognitive analytic therapy: Principles and practice*. Wiley, Chichester. (An introductory text to CAT theory and its application.)

Wertsch, J. V. (1985). *Vygotsky and the social formation of mind*. Harvard University Press, Cambridge, Mass. (A comprehensive account of the work of Vygotsky and 'the activity theory' tradition.)

Chapter 13

The conversational model

Russell Meares

Introduction

The Conversational Model is the name Robert Hobson (1920–1999) gave, in 1985, to an approach to psychotherapy that grew out of work with patients who had failed other treatments; many of these would now be called 'borderline'. Its main focus is on the sense of a life going on within us, its feelings, images, and various forms. William James (1890) called this experience the 'stream of consciousness'. It is what he understood as 'self'. It barely features in mainstream psychotherapies, yet a disturbance of this experience is fundamental, no matter the clinical presentation.

The enhancement of self involves the development of a particular form of relatedness, (Hobson called it aloneness–togetherness). The adverse effects of unconscious traumatic memory on a person's experience of self and relations with others are a second focus. These effects are evident in subtle changes in the 'therapeutic conversation'.

Most therapies tend to deal mainly with either self or trauma. Jung, Kohut and Winnicott are examples of the former kind of theory and those of Freud, Klein, and also cognitive behavioural, of the latter. Therapists in the second group attempt to alter 'distortions' of traumatic memory through transference interpretations or by addressing cognitions. The themes of both self and trauma are interwoven in the Conversational Model, in which the main aim is the integration of traumatic material (governed by laws different from ordinary consciousness), into the larger system of self.

Historical context

The Conversational Model evolved in the 1960s when Robert Hobson (a leading Jungian analyst) ran an in-patient psychotherapy unit for patients who could not be helped by conventional treatments. Working with these damaged people was like living in a country with no maps. No theoretical framework was available to guide therapeutic practice. Work towards a framework began with a focus on the 'minute particulars' through the use of audiotapes to study the therapeutic conversation. Here could be found, in microscopic form, not only systems destructive of the sense of personal being but also 'moments of aliveness'. These data provided (and continue to provide) the principal basis for the evolving model.

In 1971, Hobson launched the model, and a series of publications, when he sketched out ideas of what he hoped would be a 'testable model of psychotherapy'. Fostering 'aloneness–togetherness' was seen as central, an aim beyond that of correcting maladaptive forms of relating. Instead, the purpose is the generation of self, a process arising in conversation *between* people, as a third thing. Hobson also highlighted the 'healing power of imagination'.

In order to devise a model of therapy directed towards restoring what it means and feels like to be 'myself', a definition of this experience was needed. James provided it (Meares 1977; Meares and Hobson 1977).

Another key aspect was the notion that the experience of self has a particular feeling, which is highly charged and involves the tender emotions (Meares 1976). Out of this arises a sense of personal value. The latter can be damaged. The concept has been largely neglected in traditional theories with the consequence that inadvertent repetition of this form of traumatization is a risk, particularly in therapies relying heavily on interpretation (Meares and Hobson 1977). In fact, enhancement of self was seen to arise not through interpretation but through potentiation of a play-like and non-linear form of mental activity which is directed towards the co-creation of an imaginative, symbolically told 'narrative of self'. (Hobson 1971; Meares 1973).

The Conversational Model was subsequently adapted for short-term therapies and 'manualized' as Psychodynamic-Interpersonal Therapy. Leading figures in this initiative were David Goldberg, Else Gutherie, and Frank Margison in Manchester and David Shapiro in Sheffield. The main theoretical development has been in Sydney, Australia, where the principal focus has been borderline personality (see Meares 1993a, Meares 2000a; 2005). The model is a continuing project. Although core features remain constant, the theory has evolved on the basis of new data in such fields as neurophysiology, child development, linguistics, memory research, trauma studies, and, most importantly, accounts of personal experience, from the clinical setting and expressions found in art, literature, and philosophy.

Theory

The theoretical framework depends mainly on the development of self, and unconscious traumatic memory.

Development of self

This concerns the evolution of reflective consciousness, the mature state of mind William James called 'self'. He saw it as made up of one pole of inner events and another of awareness of those events. The 'double' consciousness self is not experienced by the child until about the age of 4 or 5. (Meares and Orlay 1988; Flavell et al. 1993) Consciousness is largely adualistic prior to this milestone. Particular responses are required of the social environment with the mother (or other caregiver) playing out the role of the double, at least initially. *Thus double consciousness of the mature adult first appears not as an intrapsychic experience but in the world*. The principal changes are shown in Table 13.1

The process begins when the mother typically plays a game with her new baby in which she sets up a pretend conversation. She speaks to the baby and then replies as if she were the baby. By about 2 months, the baby is able to join in the game, taking his own part. There develops an interplay which has rhythms and reciprocity resembling adult conversation ('proto-conversation'). It consists of a coordinated pattern of vocalizations, facial expressions, and body movements which gives pleasure to each partner but which neither could have generated alone.

Although the proto-conversation does not depend upon words, its mediation can nevertheless be conceived in terms of language, since language consists also of phonology, the sound of the voice, which conveys emotional states. Indeed phonology is the basic language since it is all the baby can use for the first 18 months or so. Syntax is the last element to emerge.

Table 13.1 A developmental schema of 'doubling' in play*

Birth	Conversational play Mother doubles as the child
2–3 months	Proto-conversation Mother (i.e. caregiver) as the other who is a double
10–12 months	Imitation Child now creates the double by means of the body
18 months–4/5 years	Symbolic play Child creates an illusory double to whom he talks (condensation of experience of the other as double and projection of the child himself)
5 years–maturity	Inner conversation The colloquy The double is now internalized

* Source: Meares (1999)

Behaviour of the mother during proto-conversation provides a model for the therapist's contributions to her conversation with the patient, particularly where development of the self has been impeded. The behaviour consists of coupling, amplification, and representation.

- Coupling involves responsiveness to, and linking up with, the baby's immediate emotional experience where this is of a positive kind, however muted and ill-developed. The mother creates a feeling for the baby of 'being with' another, the feeling at the core of self which James identified as 'warmth and intimacy'. Through tone, perhaps rising pitch, and facial expression, she connects with experiences of her infant.

- Through amplification the mother provides a responsiveness which is like the expression of her child, but emotionally larger. The interplay now escalates with mother's amplifications increasing in a stepwise way until one or other of the partners turns off a particular cycle.

- Through representation the mother's behaviour and expression 'match' the baby's state. She does not simply mimic but acts as a double. She shows, in her face, what the baby is experiencing. For instance, her beaming smile shows the baby what he is—happy. The mother's face has the effect of a mirror (Winnicott 1971).

Coupling, amplifying, and representation often happen together. The distinctions are heuristically useful, however, helping to define a certain kind of therapeutic responsiveness.

The consequence of the mother's activity, and the aim of the therapist's, is to bring into being an experience or kind of consciousness which arises as a third process, 'between' the partners, the beginning of self.

Coupling, amplification, and representation are the elements of a self-organizing system. At first, the game between mother and child has no self in it. This can be illustrated by considering Hobson's statement— 'I can only find myself in and between me and my fellows in a human conversation' (Hobson 1985, p. 135). This statement, which is highly condensed, has three words referring to personal existence; 'I', 'me', and 'myself'. The statement suggests that 'I', and 'me' are present before 'myself' can be found. This progression is supported by developmental studies. There is a limited 'I' at birth, a system of perception and response. The 'me', who-one-is-in-relation-to-others, appears at about 18 months, when children recognize their own image. Awareness of 'myself' is not present until considerably later. It is the development of this more evanescent aspect of personal existence with which we are concerned here.

The experience of self, which the adult senses as 'inner' and insubstantial, has its origins in the outer world and in physical things. Clothes, bits of bodies, bottles, and so forth—when manipulated and played with while in engagement with the mother—become the basis of self. The nature of this engagement is implied by Hobson's word 'fellow'.

A 'fellow' is 'One of a pair; the mate, marrow; a counterpart, match'. The 'marrow' is 'the innermost part; the vital part; the essence; the goodness'. These words convey the feeling of the necessary form of relatedness, implying both 'being with' and the notion of the double. The beginning of finding 'myself in and between me and my fellows', again talking heuristically, is at the point when the 'me' is formed. The child starts to play with toys and other things in a new way. Piaget called this 'symbolic play'.

Symbolic play

The child slowly takes on the doubling function for himself, first in pretend games involving imitation and then, between 1½ and 6 years, in symbolic play. The child is absorbed in apparently solitary play with toys or other objects, chattering as he plays. The talk is addressed not only to himself but also to someone else, for example, 'Look! He's climbing up. He's clever isn't he?'.

This talk is the precursor of the adult's experience of being lost in thought and engaged in 'inner conversation'. Symbolic play is the forerunner of the 'stream of consciousness'. The child's language now is of a peculiar kind. It is associative and apparently purposeless. It jumps, and is, at times, so condensed that it cannot be understood, leading Vygotsky (1962), who described it, to conclude that its function is not communicative. What, then, *is* its purpose?

During this kind of play, the focus is on the child's personal concerns, aspirations, imaginings, and so forth. His small stories are the atoms out of which his symbolically told 'narrative of self', is eventually made. Thus, the peculiar language of symbolic play is necessary for the bringing into being of self.

The child is only engaged in symbolic play for a small amount of time. For most of the day, he uses a second language, that of ordinary communication. It is logical, linear, and purposeful. In adult life, the two main forms of language are rarely found in pure form.

The colloquy, intimacy, empathy, and aloneness—togetherness

The child engaged in symbolic play exists in a strange reality which both Piaget (1959) and Winnicott (1971) identified. It is both inner and outer. When the child conceives of their difference, and the notion of 'innerness', some time between the ages of 3½ and 5½, a series of changes ensues in conversation, personal experience, and relating with others (Meares and Orlay 1988; Meares 1993a; 2005).

Further progression is by a form of conversation called the 'colloquy' (Hobson 1985). The child displays conversation similar to that in symbolic play but is now freed from the need for toys and other physical objects. The 'inner conversation' then emerges. There is now no other person in this experience. The other is 'assimilated' into self so that what remains is largely feeling. This feeling allows the person to experience 'aloneness' without a sense of isolation.

Awareness of an inner life arises together with an accompanying awareness that others have their own unique worlds which differ from one's own. The capacity for empathy is discovered. The possibility of a new way of relating emerges. The child now realizes he can choose to share something of that which is sensed as inner. Intimacy becomes possible.

The development of intimacy does not supersede attachment. Instead these two kinds of relatedness link and are joined by a third kind—affiliation. 'Aloneness–togetherness' is a way of talking about such intimacy which avoids unfortunate implications arising from popular usage of the term. Being together now involves the sense of interplay between two minds, my own and that of another different to my own, which is experienced empathically.

Traumatic memory

The experience of self as it emerges in the therapeutic conversation is, from time to time, overthrown by a form of consciousness that is adualistic and traumatic in origin. This irruption blocks development in the sphere of self. A second therapeutic aim is to identify these intrusions of traumatic memory in order to integrate them into ordinary consciousness.

Since this is only possible if the process of self is established, this is the primary aim of therapy. It depends a great deal on the therapist's sensitive capacity to make empathic representations of the patient's nebulous, inner states.

The traumatic impact on the self, may affect one or more of the various features of self, for example, the senses of agency, ownership, or boundedness (see Table 13.2).

The most critical effect is on the *feeling* of self (William James likened it to 'warmth and intimacy') which provides a sense of personal worth. Damage to this core is among the more debilitating of trauma which takes various forms, including shaming, ridiculing, and invalidation. Traumatic memories are anxiety-ridden and underpinned by alienation. Most importantly, they are frequently non-reflective.

An explanation of the characteristic non-reflective nature of traumatic memory depends upon the fact that memory is not a unitary phenomenon

Table 13.2 Main characteristics of Jamesian self

Duality (i.e. reflective awareness)
Movement
Positive feeling (including vitality)
Non-linearity (association, analogic)
Coherence and continuity
Temporality (a past and a future)
Spatiality
Content beyond immediate present (i.e. of the possible, the imagined, the remembered)
Ownership
Boundedness (privacy)
Agency
Intimacy and warmth

but made up of various kinds of memory which are usually coordinated. These different modules emerge at different points in human development. The last to emerge are, according to the theories of Hughlings Jackson, likely to be the most fragile. These late developing memory systems, the episodic or remote episodic (or autobiographical) involve the reflective function. An assault upon the brain-mind system causes a descent down a notional hierarchy of mental function established by evolutionary history and manifest in developmental data, causing the reflective system to fail, while other systems continue to operate. They include the system which involves our knowledge of the world, a catalogue of facts. The individual no longer has a reflective memory of the episodes in which these facts were learnt. What is remembered concerns the facts of the trauma, for example, one is helpless, incompetent, valueless, or uninteresting in the company of someone controlling, critical, or neglectful. These facts are not known to be memories. They are located in the present, so that the attributes of the original traumatizer and traumatized are given to those in the present. This is the zone of 'transference', and leads to a repetitive conversation that has the form of a 'script' (Meares 1998).

Intrusion of the unconscious traumatic memory into the conversation is often shown by such features as devitalization, negative emotional tone, outer orientation, loss of reflectiveness, and linear thinking.

A change in relating may be a prominent element. The 'facts' of the traumatic situation shape relatedness. Since the traumatic memory system is unassimilated into ordinary consciousness, it is as if 'loose', so that the subject may be 'inhabited' by the experience of the victim or traumatizer in a system of 'reversals' (Meares 1993b).

The patient in the grip of feelings relating to the trauma may begin to tell a story which has the features of the original trauma and *also* of what happened at the moment the memory was triggered. The trigger may be external (e.g. something the therapist did or did not say), or internal, paradoxically an emergent feeling of liveliness or creativity.

The unconscious traumatic memory system creates powerful subliminal signals that draw the therapist into its net (Meares 2000b; 2005). The sensitive therapist feels coerced to behave in a way that he is cast in the role of original traumatizer and is in danger of acting it out. Realization of this possibility affords a means to learn the circumstances of the original trauma. The experience is sometimes explained in terms of projective identification.

Process

The therapeutic process is dominated by the two main forces—a positive thrust towards selfhood, and a negative one towards its demolition. The therapist becomes part of this field and so able to change it. The process is considered below under three headings—the beginning, the self system, and the trauma system.

The beginning

Telling the story

The patient is allowed to tell his story. This is not as easy as it sounds. The therapist's agenda is hard to keep in abeyance. He has to 'stay with' what is given (Hobson 1985), particularly feelings, and to respond in a way which allows the patient to elaborate.

The patient's expression usually consists of complex verbal and non-verbal signalling. The therapist responds to that which is most personal, has feeling, and is spontaneous. For example, if the voice is flat, the therapist may sense anxiety or guardedness, and speak to this rather than to the actual words. He may remark on the 'difficulty' of the situation. A woman's words concerning the 'nice space' of the room may reflect the space she seeks after a life of being stifled. The room is a metaphor. The therapist might do nothing other than comment about the 'pleasure' of space for the conversation to develop. The use of metaphors of states of self is central to the process. Working in this way leads to the heart of a problem.

The practitioner becomes skilled in the use of 'familiar discourse', avoiding jargon and hackneyed 'therapy language' (e.g. 'How did that make you feel?').

The therapeutic attitude

The therapist's train of thought has three concurrent streams, which arise from—(1) close attention to the patient's expressions, including actual words spoken and non-verbal signals, such as vocal tone, facial, and postural; (2) attention to his own experience; and (3) holding in mind observations from (1) and (2) in order to develop a framework of understanding. The framework is fluid and evolves through constant monitoring of the interplay between the pair.

This account of the process shows that the conversation in which the patient tells his story is not unstructured, although it may appear to be so. Since it involves both partners, it is a 'co-structuring'.

Selection

Selection usually entails assessing whether a person is treatable by a particular method. The question is reversed in the case of the Conversational Model. Since the approach depends on principles and not rules, it can be modified to suit the needs of the patient. Rather than fitting patient to method, the method is made to fit the patient. Although applicable in various settings (e.g. for self-harm—see Guthrie et al. 2001), the focus here will be on conditions in which DSM Axis I diagnosis, such as depression, is complicated by underlying personality disorder and has failed other treatments, or personality disorder itself. Major substance abuse, the risk of violence to the therapist, organic deficits, poor motivation, and limited command of the therapist's language militate against application of the Conversational Model.

The frame

A description of the treatment is carefully given, in clear language, and avoiding terms like 'consciousness', using instead 'sense of yourself' or 'the feeling of who you are'. Explaining unconscious traumatic memory's role in disrupting ordinary living can be useful. Simple everyday examples are given. Reading matter may be recommended.

The responsibilities of both protagonists are identified and practical details, such as time and place of the session outlined. The patient is thus aware of the 'frame'. It is helpful to offer these details in writing and to have the patient agree to them. Duration or mechanisms for its review are discussed. The therapist makes clear that an agreement to work for a specified period is adhered to even if the patient shows rapid improvement.

The self system

The person who has suffered a disrupted development of self characteristically converses in the style of a 'chronicle' (Meares 1998) cataloguing events. He is as if 'stimulus entrapped' (Meares 1997). Events typically shared are recent, even current. A monotonous dysphoria, interspersed with episodes of anxiety and anger is common. There is no reflective awareness, no memories of a distant past.

This disturbed state of mind is part of an ecology whose other elements are a form of consciousness, a brain-state, a brain-mind interplay with the social environment, and a conversation mediating the interplay. No element can change in isolation (Meares 2005). To alter the debilitating, constricted, or in other ways unsatisfactory state of mind, the patient's typical interplay with others must develop anew. Since relatedness depends upon conversation, the aim of therapy is to transform a particular kind of conversation into another which will allow emergence of a more vital kind of consciousness.

Therapist responsiveness resembles those of the mother during periods of proto-conversation and symbolic play and can be characterized as coupling, amplification, and representation (see earlier on p. 289).

Coupling

Coupling is a linking to the most 'personal' element of what is offered. The therapist responds to potential moments of aliveness, not necessarily words, although these are the usual currency. Something is chosen which he senses has emotional or imaginative significance, is spontaneous, or is suggestive of metaphor. Hobson used William Blake's expression, 'the minute particulars', to refer to subtle shifts in conversation, the actual words used, the way they are said, their nuances, and associated feelings. A particular word or phrase for instance, may contain a 'micro-history' which can be fleshed out, and even illuminate a larger area of the patient's life.

People with severe disorders of self may offer very little with which the therapist can join, even when the process is well established. For example, a patient begins the session with a sigh and says in a dead voice: 'Not much change really'. A novice may be influenced by this implicit hopelessness and rush to consider medication or inquire about symptoms. The feeling of failure is likely to be compounded.

Another therapist, not wanting to 'reinforce' hopelessness, may inquire about an event which he thinks might have been pleasurable. 'How did the picnic go?' he asks. This could succeed. It could also come across as coercive. The therapist is only interested in happy occasions; the patient may think that is all she can mention.

What the therapist utters has the potential to devalue. To reduce this risk he may respond non-judgmentally, 'Uh Huh'. But to the patient this means that what she has just said is uninteresting. The therapist is simply waiting, so she imagines, for her to say something more interesting. So what does the therapist say? He has to *stay with* her. This often depends on him using her own words, perhaps taking them a little further. The therapist replies: 'Not much really'. His response is not an echo or an imitation. He gives the word 'really' a slight emphasis. 'Really' implies doubt, perhaps there *is* some change. The main communication here is phonological. The vocal tone, together with facial expression and gesture, is the principal means of conversing.

One experienced therapist, for example, aware of the patient's complex psychopathology conducted a productive conversation in which his responses were mostly limited to 'Yeah' and 'Uh, huh'. Into each utterance, he compressed a range of meanings—wonder, affirmation, disbelief, speculation.

The syntax of the therapist's response is also important. Like inner speech, it is abbreviated and not strictly grammatical. To contribute to the development of the desired 'fellow feeling', it must connect with what is offered. Syntax is a component of the connection. The syntax displays and structures the form of relatedness. A syntactical style which uses questioning, as in the medical mode, diminishes the sense of 'fellow feeling'. Questions are, in fact, best avoided as far as possible. Posing irritating questions like: 'How did that make you feel?' as used by the average intrusive television interviewer, are replaced, instead, by speculative attempts to understanding.

Amplification

Although certain principles can be seen to be followed, or not, we can only judge the effectiveness of a particular contribution to the therapeutic conversation by 'what happens next' (Meares 2001). For example: 'No. Just the same'. The therapist's contribution has failed, there is no movement. But her actual response is different. Her voice becomes more animated as she says: 'Well, except I—I'm getting angry with Sam and I think—I guess there's a bit of a change there'. This reply shows that he has joined with her opening remark. He has understood what is implied in the word 'really'.

The patient's anger with her husband, Sam, is good news since he constantly reminds her of her uselessness and incompetence. There *has* been change. She is standing up for herself. The therapist affirms this. 'Aha' he says in a tone of vitality. 'That—that seems a good thing'. The response is an amplification.

Amplification typically includes enhancing positive affect (which is very often muted). It might also entail recognition of other affects which are less salient. For example, pleasure may be in the forefront of the expression but a sense of regret is also present. A third kind of amplification extends the meaning of words spoken.

Representation

Representation concerns the attempt to express, as well as the therapist can understand it, what is essential in the patient's communication. This often has a speculative quality, as if the therapist is searching for the appropriate words. The sentence may be left unfinished, leaving the patient to complete the representation.

Empathic representation

Empathic representation extends beyond the attempt to grasp the crux of the patient's 'presentation'; it concerns that which is latent or implicit. The therapist attempts to put himself in the place of the other and to imagine what the experience is like. For example, soon after the therapist's 'amplification', the patient describes her husband's behaviour as 'like acid eating in to me'. The sympathetic response to hearing about the persistent erosion of her sense of worth by her husband might be 'How terrible!' Sympathy, however, is not empathy. The therapist's response is strange but empathic. He replies with a rising inflection on the last word. 'An acid eating in to you is—unreasonable'. This acknowledges the debilitating effect of this constant demolition but resonates with her doubt that perhaps the husband's conclusions are justified. What happens next? The emergence of dualistic consciousness shows that the therapist's response was effective.

Narrative of self

The representation of inner life largely depends upon metaphor, which has the function of representing that which cannot be seen and placing it before 'the mind's eye'. An openness to metaphor is a necessary feature of the 'symbolical attitude' required of the therapist. An elaboration of a central metaphor, together with introduction of new metaphors, becomes part of a thematic evolution of a personal story, symbolically told, the analogue of which is the child's story told during symbolic play. This will be discussed in the next section.

Trauma system

Ordinary consciousness is disrupted by unconscious traumatic memory. The form of conversation, in this case, is repetitive, resembling a 'script' (Meares 1998). The extent and form of the intrusion varies. In what follows, a patient with depression will be used to illustrate the approach to traumatic memory.

The main task is to transform this aspect of psychic life (linear and non-associative), into a different kind of material which resembles the consciousness of self. This allows the traumatic system, previously sequestered, to dissolve in the flow of ordinary day-to-day selfhood. Janet (1925) called this process 'liquidation of the trauma'.

The process of 'liquidation' is frequently impeded by systems of avoidance and accommodation. Avoidance is to protect the individual against re-experiencing the trauma. Accommodation allays repetition of the trauma of abandonment by emitting behaviours which are designed to maintain the bond or attachment to the other (Brandchaft 1993).

A case illustration

Jane's depression relates to the deterioration of her marriage.

1 *Identification of traumatic consciousness.* As she tells her story at their first meeting, the therapist hears about a recent row. Jane had yelled at her husband after he suggested she use the new tablecloth for dinner. It seemed as if he was implying she was incompetent. As he listens the therapist is processing Jane's conversation with at least three currents of thought operating. He listens to her speech which is poorly put together, interspersed with long pauses. She looks miserable, her eyes downcast. Soon she says that she will not be returning to therapy since she dislikes it and feels it will not help. In monitoring his own responses, the therapist realizes that the words at the periphery of his consciousness are 'Don't be stupid'. They are, of course, not uttered but he now uses them, together with his earlier observations to frame a speculative framework of understanding.

The words that came into his mind, he supposes, were an effect of the expectational field. He has become the original other. If he had spoken the words, he would have humiliated her, presumably repeating the developmental trauma. The incident regarding the tablecloth now makes sense. Her husband's inconsequential remark had evoked memories of past memories of shame, but since they were 'unconscious', she did not know she was in the grip of a traumatic memory system. She located the experience in the present, 'transferring' the attributes of the original figure who had shamed her on to her husband.

The therapist speculates that the form of the conversation in which he is now engaged is affected by the same system. In the jumbled opening of the session, Jane presumably felt herself in a situation of revelation in which the response of the other was potentially humiliating. He now realizes that his silence, uncharacteristically completely devoid of murmurs or other non-verbal vocalizations, provoked, in miniature form, the experience of shame, seeming to show her the worthlessness of her observations.

2 *Restoration of previous consciousness.* Having formed his hypothesis, the therapist does not pounce. He does not 'interpret' what has happened during the silences. Any remark made while Jane is in a state of traumatic consciousness will be understood by her in terms of the meanings which the traumatic complex will give to the relationship at this moment. His interpretation is likely to convey that, once again, someone is treating her as stupid.

The therapist, instead, aims to restore a state of consciousness more nearly resembling selfhood. He makes a connection with her by validating her immediate personal reality. He might acknowledge his part in contributing to her discomfiture and incoherence. In addition to this validation the therapist changes his behaviour by becoming responsive, and valuing her contributions.

3 *Setting the scene.* Having restored the relationship and corrected the disruptive effect of his silence, the therapist, with the patient, sets out the whole experience, describes the feelings, the sense of the situation, the attributions given to both partners during the beginning of the session. It is not necessary, however, to proceed with this immediately since it may not fit the conversational flow. In fact, the therapist, in a subsequent session acted as follows. Having made a remark which gave valuation, Jane replied: 'Well, Um', and changed the subject. She exhibited doubt. This small marker allowed him to set the scene. He remarked, 'Let's look at what happened just then'. It became apparent that his affirming of her conflicted with a traumatic reality which said she was worthless.

This process is carried out many times. The therapist focuses on shifts which are evoked by triggers that arise in the conversation. They may be due to the therapist's behaviour or arise internally. For example, as Jane began to develop confidence and energy, she set up a room in which she could make tapestries. Her voice brightened as she spoke of this initiative. However, her tone abruptly changed when she commented: 'But it's a stupid idea really. I've never been any good at those things'. This was a shift which could be worked with. As Jane and the therapist brought this experience to life, she realized it was the positive feeling about herself, the sense that she could be creative, that triggered, as if automatically, its negation.

Towards the end of the successful therapy Jane and her therapist would spontaneously laugh together when she used the word 'but'.

4 *Playing about.* Scene setting involves incidents in the session as well as from the patient's daily life. When they have been described in detail, Jane is invited to use them as objects of play, to wander around in the mind to see where they lead, to find links with other aspects of their experience. To 'just let it come to mind'. For example, Jane disclosed later that although she realized her parents had her best interests at heart, 'They always made me feel like an idiot'. The next step involves helping the patient to turn this generic memory into a specific one which is alive through bringing particular episodes to life.

5 *Changing the script.* The traumatic memory is encapsulated in a 'script' which, as it is repeated endlessly during the patient's life, has the same characters, feelings, and outcome. Many forms of psychotherapy make this complex,

which operates both overtly and covertly, the primary focus of therapy. For example, psychoanalysis uses interpretations designed to examine 'distortions' of the transference. Cognitive behaviour therapy seeks to change habitually maladaptive attributions. Although useful, they are insufficient to allow integration of the traumatic complex into the consciousness of self. The script must change in terms of the relationship which underpins it, the feeling attached to it, its form, and the attributions of self and other.

(a) The relationship begins to change from the outset when the therapist behaves in a way which is unlike the original other. For example, when Jane's therapist acknowledges his part in her discomfiture he is acting contrary to her expectation. Again, when episodes of disparagement from early life are recounted, the listener is supportive and empathic.

(b) The feeling in the original script is of such states as anxiety, coldness, isolation, and devastation. The new telling occurs after the therapist has established a feeling of safety and security; this new feeling dissipates the negative feelings at the core of the traumatic complex.

(c) The form of the complex changes when, through the effect of the therapeutic relationship, the patient enters an associative kind of consciousness. In this way, the complex can be dissolved and integrated with the self.

(d) Attributions change as the patient becomes aware and is able to reflect upon the debilitating traumatic system. She now considers other ways of responding to the triggers of the traumatic system.

6 *The narrative of self.* In many cases, the effect of trauma is reduced by the emergence of a more robust experience of self. The therapeutic movement is towards a 'narrative of self', in which positive and negative themes of self and trauma are integrated.

People can recount events of their lives ceaselessly, including the traumata, but nothing changes. The story must enter the zone of the symbolic and be retold, in a way reminiscent of the story told by the child at symbolic play. The patient who tells this symbolic story does not know that he has done so.

A boy of 16 was referred by a lawyer because he had been charged with a minor theft. He came from a semi-rural slum where he lived with his mother who had been abandoned by the husband. He was morose and monosyllabic. Therapy seemed a hopeless task. However, it emerged that he had a poster concerning the Australian bushranger, Ned Kelly, in his bedroom. The therapist felt it necessary to study Kelly's story about which he became fascinated. He and the boy talked about Kelly. It became clear that in the story of Kelly's hard, delinquent life, his tough mother, his rage, and sense of persecution, his omnipotence and, against all odds, his emergence as a hero, was a theme which resonated with the boy's deprivation and desire to overcome it. Kelly's story, in which self and trauma were interwoven, became a means of metaphorically retelling the boy's history. However, no direct connection was ever made between this symbolic narrative and the boy's own life. Nevertheless, a transformation occurred, the boy came alive and approached his future optimistically.

Termination

It is sometimes said that the aim of therapy is to end it. If therapy cannot end, neither can the necessary internalization of the experience of being-with-the-other. Termination is anticipated from the beginning when arrangements are made about ending.

The fears of abandonment cannot be left until termination. Facilitation of ending is made through careful use of therapy breaks. At first, in severely disturbed patients, a break risks deterioration, perhaps a suicide attempt. Medical cover for this period is required. Later breaks are used positively and planned by patient and therapist together. The successful negotiation of, say, the therapist's vacation is a cause of significant validation by the therapist.

Another means to anticipate termination is through the use of a journal, which is the patient's own. Maintaining it is not prescribed as a chore, but as a way of 'chattering', like the child does, in an associative way.

Perpetuation of dependence is, paradoxically, made more likely by distancing strategies of the therapist. Reducing dependence follows enhanced awareness of the patient's inner states, notably memory and imagination.

A chief aim of the termination period is to enhance the process of representation, with the patient assuming a larger responsibility. She reflects on the experiences she has undergone and how they will be used in the future.

Training

Training mainly revolves around viewing audio- or videotapes of the sessions. The trainee becomes sensitively aware of shifts in the therapeutic conversation and their significance. However, he should not feel scrutinized. The aim is to enhance a sense of creativity. The supervisor acts on the principle that his teaching style reflects a therapeutic style.

The neophyte is encouraged to potentiate his own reflective processing by discussing his feelings with his supervisor and by preparing process notes of each treatment session.

A course of seminars incorporating systematic reading of relevant literature and videotaped material on theory and its application, complements the supervised therapy.

Conclusion

The primary aim of the Conversational Model can be simply stated. It is to potentiate the emergence of that form of consciousness which William James called 'self', and which involves a reflective awareness of inner events. This is the necessary context in which the 'problems', for which the patient presents, are processed.

The experience of self depends upon a kind of relatedness in which the subject has a feeling of 'being with' another and, at the same time, an awareness of his own individuality. This state of 'aloneness-together' is mediated by a particular form of conversation, so that the therapeutic endeavour is to establish this kind of conversation.

Although the aim may be stated simply, the process is complex. The model evolves, based on evidence from developmental research, neurophysiology, and linguistics. The notion that the therapeutic conversation reflects a form of consciousness plus the structure of relatedness leads to the possibility that process can be studied via sophisticated linguistic analysis and lead to further advances. We are only embarking on the study of self, its disruptions by trauma, and the necessary therapeutic response.

References

Brandchaft, B. (1993). 'To free the spirit from its cell' In *Progress in Self Psychology*, (ed A. Goldberg) Vol. 9. pp. 209–230, Analytic Press, Hillsdale, NJ.

Flavell, J., Green F. and Flavell, E. (1993). Children's understanding of the stream of consciousness. *Child Development*, **64**, 387–96.

Guthrie, E., Kapur, N., Mackway-Jones, K., Chew-Graham, C., Moorey, J., Mendel, E.,Marino-Francis, F., Sanderson, S., Turpin, C., Boddy, G., and Tomenson, B. (2001). Randomised controlled trial of brief psychological intervention after deliberate self poisoning. *British Medical Journal*, **323**, 1–5.

Hobson, R. F. (1971). Imagination and amplification in psychotherapy *Journal of Analytical Psychology*, **16**, 79–105.

Hobson, R. F. (1985). *Forms of feeling: The heart of psychotherapy*. Tavistock, London.

Jackson, J. H. (1931–2) *Selected writings of John Hughlings Jackson*, Vol. 1 and 2 (ed. J. Taylor), Hodder, London.

James, W. (1890). *Principles of psychology*. Holt, New York.

Janet, P. (1925). Treatment by mental liquidation. In *Psychological healing*, (ed. P. Janet) Vol. 1 trans E. and C. Paul. pp. 589–698, Allen and Unwin, London.

Meares, R. (1973). Two kinds of groups. *British Journal of Medical Psychology*, **46**, 373–9.

Meares, R. (1976). The secret. *Psychiatry*, **39**, 258–65.

Meares, R. (1977). *The pursuit of intimacy: An approach to psychotherapy.* Nelson, Melbourne.

Meares, R. (1993a). *The metaphor of play: Disruption and restoration in the borderline experience.* Jason Aronson, Northvale, NJ. Revised edition, Routledge, London, 2004.

Meares, R. (1993b). Reversals: On certain pathologies of identification. In *Progress in self psychology.* (ed. A. Goldberg). Vol. 9, pp. 231–246, Analytic Press, Hillsdale, NJ.

Meares, R. (1997). Stimulus entrapment: On a common basis of somatization *Psychoanalytic Inquiry*, **17**, 223–34.

Meares, R. (1998). The self in conversation: On narratives, chronicles and scripts- *Psychoanalytic Dialogues*, **8**, 875–891.

Meares, R. (1999). The adualistic representation of trauma, on malignant internalization. *American Journal of Psychotherapy*, **53**, 392–402.

Meares, R. (2000a). *Intimacy and alienation: Memory, trauma and personal being.* Routledge, London.

Meares, R. (2000b). Priming and projective identification. *Bulletin of the Menninger Clinic*, **64**, 76–90.

Meares, R. (2001). What happens next? A developmental model of therapeutic spontaneity: Commentary on paper by Philip A Ringstrom. *Psychoanalytic Dialogues*, **11**, 755–769.

Meares, R. (2005*). The metaphor of play: Origin and breakdown of personal being* (3rd edn). Routledge, London.

Meares, R. and Hobson, R.F. (1977). The persecutory therapist. *British Journal of Medical Psychology*, **50**, 349–59.

Meares R. and Orlay, W. (1988). On self boundary: A study of the development of the concept of secrecy. *British Journal of Medical Psychology*, **1**, 305–16.

Piaget, J. (1959). *Language and thought of the child (3rd Edition).* Routledge and Kegan Paul, London.

Vygotsky L. S. (1962). *Thought and language.* ed. and trans. E. Hanfmann and G. Vakar, MIT Press, Cambridge, MA.

Winnicott, D. W. (1960) Ego distinction in terms of true and false self. In, *The maturational processes and the facilitating environment.* International Universities Press, New York, 1965.

Winnicottt, D. W. (1971). *Playing and reality.* Tavistock, London.

Recommended reading

Hobson R.F. (1985). *Forms of feeling the heart of psychotherapy.* Tavistock, London.

Meares R. (2000). *Intimacy and Alienation: Memory, trauma and personal being.* Routledge, London. Paperback, 2001.

Meares R. (2005). *The metaphor of play: Origin and breakdown of personal being,* (3rd edn). Routledge, London.

(The above three texts describe the essentials of the Conversational Model.)

Levenson E. (1972). *The fallacy of understanding*. Basic Books, New York. (A pioneering and lucid description of the intersubjective field.)

Winnicott D. (1974). *Playing and reality*. Penguin, Harmondsworth. (A classic study of the transitional experience and its relationship to therapy.)

Woolf E. (1988). *Treating the self*. Guilford, New York. (A clear account of the self-psychological approach which resembles the Conversational Model.)

Part 4
Specific clinical groups

Chapter 14

Child and adolescent psychotherapy

Ricky Emanuel

Winnicott famously said, 'There is no such thing as a baby'. Similarly, children (I shall use this term to cover adolescents as well) cannot be realistically considered outside their context. When they are therefore referred for help, the approach has to be systemic, that is, viewing them in their own right, with their own difficulties and as members of a family, school, and community, all of which may affect their difficulties or vice versa. The therapist has to consider parents or other caregivers although consent can be problematic, especially in older children and adolescents (who may be competent to give their own consent). If the school has identified difficulties, this has to be borne in mind. Nevertheless, it is essential to adopt a developmental perspective with children of all ages.

This may mean that change must be brought about in the family, home, or school environment to ensure a child's best possible development. The therapist commonly articulates the view of the child to the 'network' around the child while maintaining confidentiality. These aspects typify work with children although basic therapeutic concepts in working with adults pertain to treating children.

Child and adolescent psychotherapies have multiplied over the years. This chapter cannot do justice to all of them. I shall focus on individual psychodynamic therapy, including use of non-verbal communication, such as play, drawing, and enactment, since this approach is commonly applied and its underlying principles inform many other types of intervention.

Changing childhood adversity and treatment methods

Fundamental changes have occurred in the problems brought to attention and in professional services providing treatment. More children are identified as traumatized, the result of physical or sexual abuse, family breakdown, or disasters. The latter may be family-based as when a parent attacks another or public disasters resulting, for example, from war. Children are increasingly referred to social, medical, and educational services with emotional and behavioural disorders (especially with problems of attention and impulsivity) or resulting from neglect or inadequate parental care. Increased rates of deliberate self-harm, suicide (in adolescents), eating disorders, pervasive developmental disorders like Asperger's syndrome, autism, and psychosis, often associated with substance misuse, have occurred. There is increasing awareness of the political and social cost of leaving these problems untreated.

A striking change since the 1960s has been the evolution of new treatment methods in child and adolescent psychiatry (Shapiro and Esman 1992). Previously, efforts were limited to weekly individual therapy for the child, using psychoanalytic or client-centred methods in association with casework for parents. Group therapy for children was occasionally applied. Behavioural therapy played a part from the 1950s (Herbert 1994) while family therapy, flowered in the 1970s (Gorell Barnes 1994).

An effort has always been invested in treating parents with the expectation that children benefit indirectly. Parent training has evolved, for example, to help them to apply cognitive and behavioural principles to deal with their children's conduct disorders, with good results. (Bank et al. 1991; Callias 1994; Webster-Stratten and Hammond 1997). Similarly, brief interventions based on psychodynamic or solution focused principles have been developed to work with under 5's and their parents' to deal with infant mental health problems. (Daws 1999; Emanuel 2002b)

Cognitive behavioural and relaxation therapies, individual or group, have been applied for depression and anxiety (Kendall and Lochman 1994; Brent et al. 1998; Emslie 2003). A major increase in the use of medication, particularly for ADHD and depression, has taken place although this is controversial since many antidepressant drugs appear potentially harmful (Whittington et al. 2004).

Consultation with people like GPs, teachers, and social workers has become common, governed by the notion that they can enhance their understanding of children with mental health problems and improve their own therapeutic skills.

The scientific basis for these dramatic changes remains insecure. Although research on interventions in child mental health work is growing (Fonagy et al. 2002; Kennedy 2004), evidence for efficacy is still lacking.

Psychotherapies involving children are not incompatible with other approaches. On the contrary, treatments are often helpfully combined, sequentially or concurrently, since most disorders are co-morbid and, as mentioned above, the child's network has to be taken into account.

Historical developments

Anna Freud and Melanie Klein

Following Sigmund Freud's (1909) analysis of Little Hans, with the child's father as therapist and a single encounter with the phobic 6 year old in his father's presence, Anna Freud in Vienna, and later in London, and Melanie Klein in London, developed theories and techniques for the direct psychoanalysis of children. Despite areas of contention, they combined close observation of children with psychoanalytic theory (Liekerman and Urban 1999). Both Anna Freud and Klein were of the view that many disorders derived from unconscious conflict and improved as result of self-awareness and insight, assisted by therapeutic interventions which facilitated maturation of the ego. They held that insight required a process of 'working through'. In interaction with the therapist in play, drawing, and/or words the child repeatedly displayed basic conflicts; interpreting feelings, thoughts, and motives underlying the conflicts enabled the child to master them and so mature.

Klein (1961, 1963) was the first to equip a playroom with non-mechanical toys, (representing people, animals, cars, and trains) drawing and cutting-out material, water, and sand. Everything the child did was a meaningful transference communication (related to a repetition of past patterns of relating, anxiety, other emotions, and defences in the present situation). The analyst's prime tasks were to understand the anxieties manifest in the child's communication and to interpret the meaning of his play on the basis of a coherent theoretical framework (of child development and origin of symptoms). Klein also held that the analyst should be aware of the child's unique life situation and idiosyncratic experiences. The repeated re-enactment of anxiety-laden life experiences and the therapist's continuing commentary on their underlying meaning constituted the principal program of work.

Anna Freud (1946) took issue with Klein's view of the transference as dominant. She saw the therapist not only as a recipient of unconscious projections but also as a real person, even an educator. Non-transference aspects were especially pertinent for severely deprived children and for those with ego-deficits, that is, children whose functioning was impaired by constitutional factors (e.g. learning disabilities, developmental disorders). The therapist assumed the role of an 'auxiliary ego' for them.

There is less difference in current practice, all schools being influenced by the unique insights of the other. Moreover, the therapist becomes a model for identification, in containing and making sense of intense experiences. They may also serve as a mediator between child and parents, the school, and sometimes, the courts. Fatherless children, for example, may best be helped by a male therapist.

D. W. Winnicott

Donald Winnicott, a psychoanalyst and paediatrician, devised an original and imaginatively effective method to help children with neurotic states and their parents in the setting of an outpatient clinic. He requested parents to tell him about the problem—its development and background. He had a single, lengthy interview with the child, using his famous 'squiggle' game as the principal mode of communication. Taking turns, he and the child would draw a squiggle on a sheet of paper, get the other to complete the picture and comment on what it might represent. Because of his exceptional gifts (together with his original concepts): empathic understanding, serious concern, and the capacity to allow his own childhood self to participate playfully in the encounter, he often achieved more in one session than others could during prolonged treatment. Follow-up was often by telephone with the parents. While offering ample illustrations of his approach, Winnicott (1971a) himself influenced by Klein, did not establish a 'school' during his lifetime, but his ideas have endured: 'good enough' rather than perfect parenting that is essential for nurturing, a facilitating environment in which the child can thrive and a transitional object/space (half way between me and not-me and a space where play takes place) (Winnicott 1971b).

John Bowlby

Bowlby's work on attachment, separation, and loss (e.g. Bowlby 1979; Holmes 1993; and for a summary see Wolff 1989) constitutes a monumental contribution to knowledge about child development and has had an enormous impact on practice. His attachment theory has also influenced treatment for mothers of young children (Fonagy et al. 1994a; Murray and Cooper 1994). The effect on therapy has been to attend to the crucial importance of early relationships. Their quality provides a coherent basis to understand developmental difficulties, especially in deprived and traumatized children, and to know how to intervene helpfully. Tools to measure security of attachment in adults (Main and Goldwyn 1993), particularly the capacity to make sense of emotional experiences and form a coherent narrative about them, have influenced child therapy practice (Emanuel 1996) (see below). Several investigators have devised measures arising from attachment theory for diagnostic purposes with children (Hodges et al. 2003; Target et al. 2003).

Aims of child psychotherapy

Since many detailed descriptions are available of the range of children treated (Szur and Miller 1991; Daws and Boston 1997; Lanyardo and Horne 1999; Rustin and Quagliata 2000; Kennedy 2004), only a summary will be presented below.

An interest in unconscious processes and the child's inner experience of the world are common to all psychoanalytically based child approaches. Freud's aim of making the unconscious conscious is still relevant to enable patients to gain more control over their lives. However, there has been a move away from the original goal of unearthing repressed memories, especially traumatic ones, which were thought to be responsible for symptom formation or attempting to reconstruct an accurate narrative of the past (Barrows 2001). These aims are now considered to be erroneous since infant memories are inaccessible. Moreover, research shows that memory is freshly constructed from stored elements of the experience so that there is little 'real' truth in recovered memory (Solms and Tunbull 2002).

Transference distinguishes psychoanalytically governed work from other forms of therapy. 'Freud recognised that that which could not be recalled would inevitably be repeated, and it was the repetition of early situations and patterns of relating, within the transference relationship, that became the chief focus of analysis and interpretation.... Memory now re-emerged as enactment within the live and emotionally charged atmosphere of the therapeutic relationship' (Barrows 2001). Insights into these patterns are sought for in therapy. The aim of treatment thus shifts from relief of symptoms based on unearthing repressed memories to changing psychological functioning.

Klein's (1946) discovery of projective identification had an enormous impact on psychotherapy practice. She described how parts of the self and feelings are unconsciously split off and placed into other people; they are then felt to contain these parts and are related to by the patient as if they truly had these projected qualities. Barrows (2001) writes: 'In the case of aggression, for example, this would mean not only that aggressive feelings are projected—leading to a view of the world as a hostile, attacking place—but also that the part of the personality that experiences and owns such feelings is also projected'.

Both good and bad parts of the self can be split off. Excessive use of projective identification leads to weakening of the ego, depletion of the personality, and reduced capacity to relate to others. While the mechanism is ubiquitous and a feature of normal development, its excessive or rigid use leads to disturbed functioning (Bion 1962). The aim of therapy is to help patients gain contact with parts of personality they have split off, re-integrate them and take more responsibility for themselves and their actions. This may be challenging for children who are brought to treatment and may therefore not experience themselves as having problems that need to be tackled.

A knowledge of the role of projective identification allows clearer understanding of highly disturbed patients, such as those with borderline symptoms as well as severely deprived children (Boston and Szur 1983).

The process of therapy

Children communicate in many ways—through words, behaviour, games, play, and drawing. The idea that play is meaningful communication was first described by Freud (1920). An 18-month-old child repeatedly threw his toys under furniture and played with a cotton reel attached to a piece of string which he could throw out of his cot and retrieve again. Freud gave an account of these activities, including vocalizations which accompanied this play, as well as background from the child's life, especially the relationship with his mother and his reactions to her absences. Freud linked these and interpreted the meaning of the play as an attempt to come to terms with or master, separation from mother. Disappearance of the toys under the furniture and attempts to control their comings and goings with the string were thought to relate to feelings about mother's absences. Klein elaborated our understanding of play when suggesting that the child was exploring its inner world as well as external reality. Language of play and dreams were similar, both derived from unconscious sources in addition to reality. Closely observing play and its accompanying emotions as well as scrutiny of one's own feelings offered a rich understanding of what might be going on. Winnicott repeatedly equated the child's play as his work.

An example follows of a child who barely speaks in the session but conveys his central preoccupations through play. By understanding the language of play it is possible to learn what the matter might be. Let me illustrate with Sam's story.

Sam, a 3-year-old, lost his 6-year-old sister, Emma, through death a few weeks earlier from a virulent form of leukaemia. A younger sister, Lucy, is 18 months. Sam's parents were understandably devastated by what had befallen their young family in less than 5 months. Mum nursed Emma, usually at home, but also in hospital. Emma regressed and was incontinent at the end, needing 24-hour care like a baby. Mum was 'lost' to the other children and continued to be so in her grief. Sam was referred by the community nurse who was looking after the family at home. He had become aggressive and out of control, with a complete change of personality. He had been involved in the funeral and seen Emma 'in her box'. The parents had explained to him that Emma had gone to heaven. Sam often looked up to the sky.

When I met the parents soon after Emma's death to discuss assessing Sam, they were barely able to speak but told me how his aggressive behaviour was entirely out of character. He had begun to hit them both and was also becoming aggressive towards Lucy. He had never displayed jealousy of her before. His violence alternated with fear about being left alone. He insisted that one parent be with him, especially at night. He had been close to Emma but she had become hostile to him towards the end of her life, for example, she used to order him out of her room aggressively when he came in to see her.

The first assessment session

One usually can gather much information in the first contact with a child, so much so that later, therapy feels like working through issues brought up in the initial session. The following account focuses on play as communication and also on assessment. Sam's Mum asked to see me before the session, explaining that he had been especially angry and destructive at home. She was worried in that he had become anxious when his father dropped him off at his nursery (something he had readily managed before). Sam asked his Mum to remain with him in the consulting room; he seemed anxious at meeting me. Sam immediately launched into playing with the toys I had provided. He showed no distress when Mum left the room shortly afterwards for a session with her therapist and Dad. I assured Sam he could see her whenever he wished but he showed no inclination to do so during the first session. In fact, he was reluctant to leave at the end of our encounter.

He played at a whirlwind pace, focusing first on the 'knife' scalpel from the hospital set. He set up a hospital scene but became distracted by a crocodile. He made it attack the baby pig. The crocodile's violence was rampant, Sam clearly identifying with it, breathing heavily, panting loudly, and making mouthing and biting noises. The crocodile's targets were the baby and the mother pig, then the human family. He quickly identified a 'policeman' (the father) and the rest of the doll family were placed around the doll's house table to have a 'little talk'.

I attempted a trial interpretation to judge Sam's reaction to this way of working. I linked the people having a little talk to him and I having a little talk but he didn't seem to resonate to this. The crocodile savagely bit the mother doll, particularly her genitalia, as Sam growled. Sam asked if this was 'the hole' babies come from. (One must be prepared to discuss sexual issues with children or, for that matter, any topic they bring up, since there is no prohibition on any subject. It is important to clarify this with parents when seeking their informed consent. Not having the freedom to work in this way is a contraindication for therapy.) Yes, it was, I said, and asked what his name was for this hole (creating a shared vocabulary is useful). Sam did not reply but took glee in tossing the chewed mother into the upstairs section of the doll's house. He then became concerned as to how she could be got down since there were no stairs. He seemed to panic momentarily as the mother seemed lost or 'gone'. He set about building stairs in order to retrieve her. This idea of an attack on the mother, her loss, and then her retrieval preoccupied him.

I commented : ' The mummy (note—not *your* mummy) seemed to be all bitten up by the crocodile and then lost. How is she going to be found again?' (I was well aware how his mother must have been lost to him but it would have been premature to interpret this since he was expressing a deep unconscious phantasy about it through the play). It was the policeman's job to go up the ladder to get the mother back. When she was rescued, she was put into the hospital. However, the crocodile found her there and re-attacked. I commented that there did not seem to be a safe place anywhere.

Sam became preoccupied with guns and wanted to make one from plasticine. He told me he was a soldier who protected people. The gun seemed to have both a violent and a protective function. He told me his Mummy didn't like guns and he wasn't allowed them at home. He moved on to paint guns. The crocodile then began to rampage again, attacking anything it came across, with Sam growling and panting.

I talked about the crocodile's attacks and nobody to stop them. None of the guns, policeman, or soldiers could protect anybody. Sam looked at me very seriously, perhaps for the first time, then made the crocodile bite the baby doll. He then rushed over to the plasticine gun and shot the crocodile. (This was a response to another trial interpretation. It shows that if you get things wrong or your timing is poor with first interpretations, the child will ignore these.) He was preoccupied as to whether this violence could be contained, appearing to believe it could only be stopped violently. No one was strong enough to protect Mummy and her babies from the attacks.

It was difficult to get Sam to end. He wanted to take the guns home, perhaps to protect himself. He also wanted to make walkie-talkies since this was also equipment policemen needed. We made them with the plasticine. We communicated with each other although he couldn't maintain a conversation. Guns, walkie-talkies, policemen, and the army all seem connected, mostly in relation to quelling the unbridled violence.

What was this all about? It emerged with an urgency and seemed overwhelming. Sam expressed many themes in his play which he could not have done in another way. We knew he had become violent at home and was attacking his parents and sister. His attention focused first on the knife and the hospital; this suggests that he associated hospitals with violence. First, the baby is attacked, then the mother; she becomes 'lost' to him. Policemen then enter but are ambiguous in that they rescue the mother but also carry instruments of violence, as do the soldiers. They seem helpless to prevent the violence. His savage attacks on the genitalia of the mother, the place the babies come from, could not have been clearer. Sam's identification with the crocodile suggests that he feels his violence has been responsible for the attacks on mother and her babies, in other words, on Emma, and for her hospitalization. This violence has also lost him his mother.

His normal feelings of rivalry towards his mother and her new babies, which he apparently had not shown at the time of Lucy's birth, had become confused in his mind with making Emma die. Sibling rivalry customarily leads to aggressive feelings towards the abandoning or betraying mother and to the baby taking its place. Remember that Emma had regressed markedly before she died and that mother was preoccupied with her as if she were a new baby. Mum was lost to him as he poignantly showed in his play but he felt it to be his fault. He conceptualizes he will be savagely punished for these aggressive feelings since they appear to have come true.

The child is reassured that aggressive phantasies are not omnipotent by dint of the fact that people survive; mother's baby had not. Sam was convinced that his violent phantasies actually cause damage. The policeman father would thus be out to get him like with the gun shooting the crocodile. The policeman Daddy was not able to protect the family from death claiming one of its members. This was the anxiety that Sam manifested at night and whenever he was separated as he did not feel he could be protected as one of mother's babies. He also would be the target of retaliation for his own murderous attacks.

These themes re-emerged in subsequent sessions. I fed back my understanding to the parents along these lines. Sam couldn't wait to come to his sessions since they provided him with a means to express his intense anxieties. The parents could see how responsible he felt for Emma's death even though they had reassured him they would protect him. They knew that surviving children feel anxious about their parents' capacity to keep children well after the death of a sibling. It was essential for the well-being of the whole family to talk to them, especially Dad, about stopping Sam's violent attacks on them and Lucy, in a firm manner. Dad needed to show he could be a good policeman who would protect Mummy and her babies. They told me a few weeks later that Sam's violence had abated considerably. He was also able to separate more comfortably from them and remain in his own bed.

Bion's theory of container/contained (♀♂)

Any intimate relationship like a therapeutic one is bound to evoke intense feelings. We are all familiar with the phenomenon of 'taking your feelings out on those closest to you'. I will now examine more closely what this means and place it in the context of normal development in order to show how the feelings one has when working with children, the counter-transference, can be a powerful tool in understanding them. People often worry about feelings they have when in close contact with children, and see them as getting in the way of 'objective' understanding. On the contrary, they can be most helpful.

It is difficult to stay with painful feelings like hate, dislike, emptiness, meaninglessness, even positive feelings like love, when working with children. We try to put them somewhere using projective identification (as described above); blame the child, the parents, the government, the head teacher, society, or deny we are having feelings at all.

Babies and children respond similarly to anxiety by seeking to rid themselves of it through behaviour if they do not have language. While this form of communication persists in all of us, it is most prominent in infancy. There is a link between experiences in early life and the capacity to think. Thinking in this sense is intimately related to emotional development. Neuroscientific investigators, particularly Damasio (1999, 2003), are increasingly confirming the psychoanalytic view that emotional experience is primary and underpins cognition. A baby needs someone to receive and contain his communications of distress which he experiences as unpleasant bodily emotions. As the word designates, emotion, is about motion, and is a hard-wired part of our mind—body apparatus. Emotions of an infant can feel terrifying in the sense of imminent disintegration or states of unpleasure which need evacuation. Hunger can be experienced as persecutory gnawing at the baby from the inside. He needs someone who can hold the *unbearable* feelings he cannot manage and make them bearable; he needs an attachment figure to process his emotional experiences.

Bion's theory of container/contained is a coherent framework to understand these processes.

If a baby is distressed, it may evoke distress in the mother using projective identification (No. 1 in Figure 14.1). The emotion, the contained, the raw stuff of sensory experience (an α element as Bion's terms it) has to be deposited in the container. The mother/container/attachment figure then has to sort out what this distress is, to reflect on it (called reverie or α function—No. 2 in the figure), before being able to respond. She makes sense of it by the unconscious process of 'affective attunement' (Stern 1985), relating it to her own internalized experience as a baby, how she was mothered, by using her experience of the baby hitherto. This is represented in Figure 14.1 as her making use of an internalized container/contained system. If she can make sense of the feelings aroused in her, she can respond accordingly (No. 3 in the figure). The baby is not only comforted but also able to take inside himself the experience of being understood. This enables him to develop his own capacity to think and have a space in his own mind. It is akin to a baby bird being unable to tolerate raw food until it has been predigested by the mother.

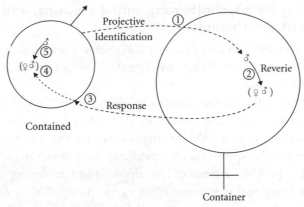

Fig. 14.1 The development of (♀♂) mental apparatus (Bion).

   Through such repeated experiences and by being able to make sense of them, that is, think about them, the baby becomes stronger and less overwhelmed. The baby gradually identifies with his mother's containing functions and develops its own container/contained system (No. 4 in the figure). He uses this apparatus to identify feelings after having learned differential responses to various emotional states contained by the mother (No. 5 in the figure). This is the crucial apparatus to make sense of emotional experiences and learn from them—the basis for a resilient personality (Fonagy et al. 1994). Neuroscientists are now able to show the neurobiology of these processes. 'Mirror neurons' have been identified which represent in an individual's brain the movements that are seen in another and simulated, so we actually feel another's experience (Damasio 2003). These processes link a person's bodily/emotional responses to another and form the neurobiological basis of projective identification. A right-brain to right-brain communication link is established when feelings are transferred from one person to another in the way described above, as noted by Schore (2000).

   Awareness of feelings evoked when with another person can help a person understand what is communicated and thus modify his response. Attunement to the child in order to be receptive to the minutiae of what is emotionally exchanged is a primary task of psychotherapy (Hunter 2001). We have to sort out what is coming from the child and what belongs to us (personal analysis helps in this respect). If the therapist can accept projections, let them enter and survive in his psyche, without falling prey to them, then the child can develop a belief that a container exists for his primitive feelings. A skill (or art) in working in this way is to decide when or if to try to hand the feelings back through an interpretation.

The setting for psychotherapy, initial sessions, and qualities of the therapist

The psychodynamic therapist's primary task then in working with children is to help them make sense of their emotional experience and thus develop a self-reflective function.

The first step is to establish a setting in which the child can communicate his innermost feelings. The same room laid out in the same way without intrusion of other children's drawings or equipment, a consistent time and attention to therapy breaks offer predictability and security to the child. The therapist provides a range of toys, drawing and modelling equipment to facilitate emotional expression. Water can be used for many purposes in symbolic play. Toys are placed in a box solely for the child's use. There may be shared toys like a doll's house but a distinction is made between how the child can treat their own and shared toys. The child is allowed to do what he pleases with his own toys, up to a point, which does not compromise safety; shared toys have to be protected. Toys and drawings are kept in the box at the end of a session to ensure confidentiality. Children often object to this as being unfair but come to understand how the room, equipment, and relationship are part of the security of the setting necessary for 'our work'. The sessions are denoted as *work*, toys as *equipment* to 'help show what is on your mind as many children find it easier to draw or to play than to talk'. The child is made aware about the limits of confidentiality, the therapist stressing that what is said or shown remains between child and therapist. A distinction is made between privacy and secrecy. The sessions are private but the child is free to talk to whomever he wants. This is especially true for sexually abused children (Emanuel et al. 2002). The therapist clarifies that they will meet with the parents periodically to let them know how the child is progressing but details of the sessions will remain private. Exceptions are if the child is at risk when it is made clear that people will be alerted should there be a need for child protection.

Children are put at their ease in the first session with ground rules and limits explained. An ice breaker is to ask the child why he thinks he is there and to acknowledge that contact with parents has usually taken place (with older adolescents the setting is closer to that of an adult). The child often says he does not know, in which case enquiring how he felt about coming is apt. If the child is anxious, acknowledging this and indicating that 'it is hard to come into a room with a stranger' helps. With young children, sessions with the parents present may be necessary to help the child separate. If the child remains verbally frozen, inviting him to look into the toy box is a useful strategy. Once a child begins to play or draw and notes the therapist's interest one is in business! Commenting on the play usually promotes rapport.

A salient skill is to gather details about how the child responds to the treatment setting and to the therapist (Kennedy 2004). Training through infant observation aims to develop a capacity to record a range of observations which may have meaning upon reflection (Rustin 1999). No notes are taken during the session since this detracts from observing the necessary 'material' and transference/counter-transference phenomena. Notes can be written later. Infant observation training promotes the ability to recall details of the interactions and sequences.

Supervision provides the opportunity for 'second order' reflections and helps ensure that observations are not distorted by prejudice, professional interests, and the like (Rustin 1999; Kennedy 2004).

The therapist's receptive frame of mind, open to whatever the child communicates, is a key ingredient. The therapist pays close attention to what the child makes him feel, and thinks about what is being communicated. *Where appropriate*, he hands this back in a more understandable and bearable way to the child (interpretations). Interpretations should mainly focus on the immediate situation since this is where the possibility prevails of something being understood in a fresh way (Joseph 1985). They also should not be framed in theoretical terms, or focus on defences when an expression of hope for the future would be more 'growth enhancing' (Alvarez 1992). It can be a relief to the child when a negative transference is interpreted, especially at times of resistance. With children who have been abused, for example, the therapist may be perceived as an abuser (which can be a disturbing experience). But bearing the projection without retaliating is potentially a beneficial process for the child (Emanuel et al. 2002)

Developmental help and psychotherapy

For some children, life experience or genetic disposition has prevented them from developing the mental apparatus described earlier. It becomes the task of therapy to help them to use their minds to engage in the 'proper' process. In fact many children seen in treatment are so damaged that they lack a basic emotional vocabulary.

Many traumatized children's mental apparatus has been overwhelmed or shattered. The traumatic experience is often still raw even years later. These children and others for a variety of reasons who have not developed the mental apparatus have to learn to name the elements of their emotional experience (Hurry 1998). They first have to be able to talk about *what* has happened before they can begin to understand *how* it may have happened. This process can only occur in the context of a relationship with a receptive person. Over time, the child identifies with the functions of the therapist like a baby identifies with the functions of the container, who 'names' the baby's experience by her differential responses to varied emotional communications.

Relationship to the external world and parents

In psychotherapy, the *meaning* of the experience needs to be worked through. Seeing a therapist is not the same as talking with a friend, being the child's friend (although friendliness is necessary), or serving as a replacement parent. The therapist is often the last to know crucial 'facts' about the child's external life; this always surprises parents, 'Didn't he tell you his father is gravely ill?'. The therapist may have gathered that something was wrong and the child anxious but he would probably have communicated his anxiety that his rivalrous feelings had made the father ill. He may have feared punishment much in the way we saw with Sam in relation to his sister. It is not the external facts which are shared in therapy but the *meaning* of an experience for the child and his phantasy life. External factors are of course vital and need to be addressed when they come up. The therapist *always* follows the child's lead, something is seriously awry if this is not the case.

Most therapy is conducted concurrently with work with the parents who are usually seen by another therapist (but not always so). Involvement of parents and carers in assessment and treatment is pivotal (Rustin 1999). Parents have intense feelings about their child seeing a therapist, including envy, rivalry, suspicion, and idealization, and have difficulties with confidentiality. It may also be hard for parents to permit their child to continue in therapy if the problems they brought the child to treatment for have improved. Improvement, however, may be due to problems being 'contained' in the therapeutic relationship. Other parents may need their child to be the identified patient, having projected something from their own past into him. Treatment is often precarious when the child's relationship with the therapist is idealized and no problems manifest in the session.

The child may become hostile to, or fearful of, the therapist in the transference and resist therapy. If an aim of therapy is to help the child to manage unwanted split off parts, attempts at reintegration can be resisted. Holiday breaks can stir up feelings of rejection. Children may 'act out' and project a feeling of rejection into the therapist. Parents need help to understand all these possibilities. Talking about potential resistance when gaining their consent is advisable. It is helpful to discuss with parents how to handle resistance, for example, by their encouraging the child to attend the session even if it is to share negative feelings. Similarly, it is vital to stress the value of consistent attendance.

Regular reviews with parents, including the professional seeing the parents are essential; these allow them to learn how their child is getting on (while preserving confidentiality). This can be problematic in treating older adolescents. Here agreement must be negotiated about whether contact is made with parents.

Work with a confused, fragmented child

To illustrate the points made above, particularly acquisition of emotional language, let me describe therapy with Garry, aged 12. He was referred as a 'fragmented', confused child with controlling and obsessional traits. He had marked learning difficulties which seemed to relate to his control of how much he could let himself know things. Garry had 'cried and screamed every night from age 3 months to 3½ years'. His mother appeared cut off from her son raising questions in the therapist's mind about her ability to contain him. The following account is of a session 6 months into his twice-weekly therapy. The material was presented to me in supervision; my comments are in italics.

Garry walks into the room with an unusual gait, as if he is measuring something with his steps. He opens his personal toy box that contains his drawings. He exclaims 'Garry' after recognizing his name on the folder and laughs. The therapist mentions the forthcoming holiday and suggests making a calendar to show the remaining sessions, duration of the break, and the date of resuming. Garry laughs 'Holidays!' He picks out a drawing he has made of a pair of spectacles done early on in therapy. He pushes it away and sighs. The therapist asks him what is wrong with it. 'It is ugly ... I will leave it there'. (*Is this Garry's emotional response to the news of the break? After laughing disingenuously, he seems to identify with the ugly glasses being pushed away by the therapist for the holidays*).

Garry takes out another drawing he had labelled 'Red'. When he had done this drawing, he said red was angry and when you are angry you are sad. (*He has a rudimentary emotional alphabet*). As he looks at his red drawing, a cat meows outside. Garry laughs and explains that the noise is 'the scream of someone who has got scared ... or someone who is sad or someone who is happy' (*He has labels for emotional states but cannot identify them accurately*). He then exclaims, 'I have an idea! ... Let's make a calendar'. (*This suggests that the range of emotions—sad, angry, scared, or happy connect with his emotional reaction to the break, and need clarification*).

The therapist comments on the holidays making him feel all sorts of different things.

Garry does not work on the calendar but takes the red drawing and utters a few meows. 'So it was a meow, not the cry of a frightened person, or a sad or a happy one', he comments. He repeats 'sad, happy, frightened'. The therapist notes that he is interested in situations where people are sometimes happy, sometimes sad, and sometimes frightened (*The therapist is trying to differentiate various emotional states for Garry*).

'Why frightened?' Garry asks laughing. (*revealing mixed up emotions*)

The therapist replied: 'You may be frightened for many reasons, like when you are afraid of being not able to face something, or when you do not know how something will turn out' *(His therapist is aware that Garry's learning difficulties are linked to his fear of the unknown).*

Garry laughingly utters the words 'Fear!...holidays'.

'Maybe you are wondering if one has to be afraid of holidays and a break in our meetings?' asks the therapist.

Garry laughs and looks thoughtful.

(One can see Bion's process of reverie in slow motion as the meaning of the experience of the holidays is discovered and handed back to Garry in a form he is able to bear. The therapist's light touch enables Garry to contemplate his fear of the break).

Garry goes over to the sofa and repeats 'ticket' several times. Then he says, 'Holidays, holidays, just like the school holidays, holidays, holidays' again and again. *(He is making a link between the school holidays and the break in therapy).*

He moves to the air conditioning unit, 'Air conditioner—climate control' *(Another link to heat and summer).* 'Cool air ... going to the seaside'. He then retrieves the drawing of the spectacles 'I don't like it ... maybe I liked it earlier'. He places it under a chair where it cannot be seen. 'There, done' he states with satisfaction.

(Another painful emotional experience is being worked through, the rudimentary feeling that he is being pushed away by the therapist for the break, even though the 'happy' dimension of the break implies tickets and the seaside in hot weather. The break signals to him that the therapist may not like him which is so painful that he splits the feeling off and projects it under the chair. The over-determination may be the act of projective identification and a symbolic communication about feeling pushed out of sight for the holiday).

Garry darts around the room. The therapist tells him he is doing this because he has told him about the holidays and he is excited *(The therapist fails to take up his sense of rejection or feeling of ugliness).*

'Going on holiday,—we will not see each other for a while', remarks the therapist.

'We won't see each other? I am a bit sorry, a bit sorry', Garry whispers *(He minimizes sadness but is discovering what he feels).*

In this session we see Garry discovering feelings about the break,—sadness and happiness—but also splitting off painful feelings that he is ugly and disliked by the therapist. The therapist helps Garry make some sense of his emotional experience but the aim of reintegrating a split off part of himself is not yet dealt with. The work occurs at Garry's pace, the therapist sensitive not to overload him.

Duration and frequency

Child therapy ranges from a few assessment sessions (which can be inherently therapeutic) to much longer-term work. This is usually weekly; on occasion (as with Garry) twice-weekly sessions are held to maintain momentum. More intensive treatment is indicated when the severity and complexity of the problem warrants it and child and network can support it (Heinicke and Ramsay-Klee 1986; Fonagy and Target 1996; Kennedy 2004). Most children are seen for a planned number of sessions (e.g. 4–6), such as in parent–infant mental health work (Daws 1999; Emanuel 2002b) or with adolescents who do not want a longer-term commitment due to fear of dependency at the point they are, developmentally, moving away from the influence of the parental world. Up to four sessions is common to clarify the adolescent problem and to suggest further help if required (Salzberger-Wittenberg 1977).

The most common duration for psychoanalytically oriented therapy is about 6 months. In cases where the disturbance is marked or in pervasive developmental disorders, chronic, physical illness or disability, children may be seen for longer periods. Child therapists function in many settings— schools, social services, primary care, and general hospitals (Lanyardo and Horne 1999). Here they help staff to understand children's communications and phantasy life and how these influence behaviour (and the staff themselves) (Emanuel 2002a).

Termination

It helps to prepare a child for the end of therapy, including short-term. This is not always possible, especially if parents withdraw a child prematurely. The therapist then has to accept the decision although try to persuade them to bring the child to a farewell meeting. It is a painful aspect of child therapy when a child who is engaged is withdrawn prematurely.

Dependency is common but if termination is planned and worked through, it can lead to further growth. Awareness of the meaning to the child of termination in the light of past losses facilitates a positive ending. Negative feelings about ending have to be faced, including disappointment that not everything is better. The notion that true independence arises from dependence on internal figures, 'in-dependence' as Bion put it, is pertinent. How the child internalizes the work done becomes a focus as well as whether the therapist will keep him in his mind. Review sessions, letters, or emails following termination can help but are best decided on in co-operation with the child.

Evidence-based practice and research

The first systematic review of the evidence base for psychoanalytic child psychotherapy was reported by Kennedy (2004). The following is a summary of the 32 studies she analysed. Five were randomized controlled trials (RCTs), one in process (Trowell et al. 2003). There were several non-randomized trials. Beneficial effects were found on a range of measures—educational adjustment, behaviour, symptoms, relationships, family functioning, and psychiatric and psychological disorders. Deterioration in family functioning was seen in one trial where children were treated without parallel work with the parents.

Most studies were undertaken with routine clinical samples which add to their validity. Many children were severely disturbed. Brief, less intensive interventions were effective in less impaired children whereas more intensive work was required for those with more severe problems. Benefits were sustained over a considerable follow-up. Younger children were more apt to improve. Work with the parents or family was pivotal with younger children. In summary, psychoanalytic psychotherapy was effective for children and young people with a variety of disorders.

Which children benefit from child therapy has not been clarified fully. For instance, it was thought that autistic children would be harmed by therapy but Reid et al. (2001) have reported encouraging results. Research is still needed to ascertain potential beneficiaries. Motivation in the child, parents, and network (e.g. social services) is essential to assess, as for all psychotherapies. Severely deprived, abused, or traumatized children (Trowell et al. 2002), those who are depressed (Trowell et al. 2003), and anxious, and those with 'internalizing/emotional' conditions (Fonagy and Target 1996) are all able to benefit. Children with 'externalizing' problems like conduct disorders (unless there is associated anxiety), are more resistant to therapy, especially if they are unwilling to take any responsibility for their behaviour (Baruch et al. 1998).

Training

Personal psychotherapy is highly desirable to enable the therapists to know themselves better and sort out what belongs to them and what to the patient. Moreover, prospective therapists should explore their motivation in wanting to work with children, including inappropriate rescue phantasies.

Other facets of training are infant observation, seminars on child development and psychodynamic theory and technique, and regular supervision. Working with parents, under 5's and adolescents, and family and group therapy, are useful additional training components. Consultative work with related professions is necessary given that this 'applied work' is commonplace in child services.

Trainees from other pertinent disciplines, such as child psychiatry, are commonly supervised on psychoanalytic lines. This should be provided by a qualified practitioner to prevent prejudice against the role of psychoanalytically oriented therapy. With the right patient and quality supervision, a supervisee from another discipline can obtain an accurate impression of how children communicate through play, and the impact of the inner world on behaviour.

A psychotherapeutic perspective in a multidisciplinary team exposes members to the value of a way of thinking, particularly the child's point of view.

Presentations of child psychotherapy cases also assist other disciplines to appreciate this way of working.

Conclusion

The purpose of psychoanalytically based child psychotherapy is well summarized by Urwin (2000): 'Child psychotherapists have long appreciated that psycho-analytic work with children cannot simply be about analysing conflicts, removing repressions, or reconstructing the past. More often it involves enabling processes and structures to develop to allow for the possibility of thought, reflection, and sustained emotional experience in the first place'. The approach is not directed merely at symptomatic relief but capitalizes on the enormous growth and developmental potential in children and adolescents before problems became entrenched. Early intervention hopefully prevents later personality or psychiatric problems though this is notoriously difficult to prove. Nevertheless, opportunities to reduce the severity and duration of distress are considerable as is the chance to exert a positive influence on the lives of children and those of their families.

References

Alvarez, A. (1992). *Live company—Psychoanalytic psychotherapy with autistic, borderline, deprived and abused children.* Routledge, London.

Bank, L., Marlowe, J. H., Reid, J. B., Patterson, G. R., and Weinrott, M. R. (1991). A comparative evaluation of parent-training interventions for families of chronic delinquents. *Journal of Abnormal Child Psychology*, **19**, 15–33.

Barrows, P. (2001). The aims of child psychotherapy: A Kleinian perspective. *Clinical child psychology and psychiatry*, **6**, 371–385.

Baruch, G., Fearon, P., and Gerber, A. (1998). Evaluating the outcome of a community-based psychoanalytic psychotherapy service for young people: One year repeated follow up. In *Rethinking clinical audit*, (ed. R. Davenhill, and M. Patrick,) pp. 157–182. Routledge, London.

Bion, W. R. (1962). *Learning from experience.* Heinemann, London.

Boston, M. and Szur, R. (1983). *Psychotherapy with severely deprived children.* Routledge and Kegan Paul, London.

Bowlby, J. (1979). *The making and breaking of affectional bonds.* Tavistock, London.

Brent, D., Kolko, D., Birmaher, B., Baugher, M., Bridge, J., Roth, C., and Holder, D. (1998). Predictors of treatment efficacy in a clinical trial of three psychosocial treatments for adolescent depression. *Journal of American Academy of Child and Adolescent Psychiatry*, **39**, 906–914.

Callias, M. (1994). Parent training. In *Child and adolescent psychiatry: Modern approaches (3rd edn).* (ed. M. Rutter, E. Taylor, and L. Hersov,), pp. 918–35. Blackwell, Oxford.

Damasio, A. (1999). *The feeling of what happens. Body, emotion and the making of consciousness.* Heinemann, London.

Damasio, A. (2003). *Looking for Spinoza. Joy, sorrow and the feeling brain.* Heinemann, London.

Daws, D. and Boston, M. (1977). *The child psychotherapist and problems of young people.* Wildwood House, London.

Daws, D. (1999). Brief psychotherapy with infants and their parents. In *Handbook of child and adolescent psychotherapy—Psychoanalytic approaches* (ed. M., Lanyardo, A., Horne) Routledge, London.

Emanuel, L. (2002a). Deprivation x 3. The contribution of organizational dynamics to the 'triple deprivation' of looked-after children. *Journal of Child Psychotherapy*, **28**, 163–179.

Emanuel, L. (2002b). Parents united: Addressing parental issues in work with infants and young children. *International Journal of Infant Observation and its Applications*, **5**, 103–117.

Emanuel, R. (1996). Psychotherapy with children traumatized in infancy. *Journal of Child Psychotherapy*, **2**, 214–239.

Emanuel, R., Miller, L., and Rustin, M. (2002). Supervision of therapy of sexually abused girls. *Clinical Child Psychology and Psychiatry*, **7**, 581–594.

Emslie, G., Mayes, T., Laptook, R., and Batt, M. (2003). Predictors of response to treatment in children and adolescents with mood disorders. *Psychiatric Clinics of North America*, **26**, 435–456.

Fonagy, P., Steele, M., Steele, H., Higgit, A., and Target, M. (1994). The theory and practice of resilience. *Journal of Child Psychology and Psychiatry*, **35**, 231.

Fonagy, P. and Target, M. (1994a). The efficacy of psychoanalysis for children with disruptive disorders. *Journal of the American Academy of Child and Adolescent Psychiatry*, **33**, 45–55.

Fonagy, P. and Target, M. (1996). Predcitors of outcome in child psychoanalysis: A retrospective study of 793 cases at the Anna Freud Centre. *Journal of the American Psychoanalytic Association*, **44**, 27–73.

Fonagy, P., Target, M., Cottrell, D., Phillips, J., and Kurtz, Z. (2002). *What works for whom? A critical review of treatments for children and adolescents.* Guilford Press, London.

Freud, A. (1946). *The ego and the mechanisms of defence.* Hogarth. London.

Freud, S. (1909). Analysis of a phobia in a five year old boy (Little Hans). *Standard edition of the complete psychological works of Sigmund Freud*, **10**, 3–150.

Freud, S. (1920). Beyond the pleasure principle. *Standard edition of the complete psychological works of Sigmund Freud*, **18**, 14–15.

Gorell Bames, G. (1994). Family therapy. In *Child and adolescent psychiatry: Modern approaches (3rd edn).* (ed. M. Rutter, E. Taylor. and L. Hersov), 946–67. Blackwell, Oxford.

Heinicke, C. and Ramsay-Klee, D. (1986). Outcome of child psychotherapy as a function of frequency of session. *Journal of the American Academy of Child and Adolescent Psychiatry*, **25**, 247–253.

Herbert, M. (1994). Behavioural methods. In *Child and adolescent psychiatry: Modern approaches (3rd edn).* (ed. **M. Rutter, E. Taylor.** and L. Hersov), pp. 858–879, Blackwell, Oxford.

Hodges, J., Steele, M., Hillman, S., Henderson, K., and Kanuik, J. (2003). Changes in the attachment representations over the first year of adoptive placements story stems. *Clinical Child Psychology and Psychiatry*, **8**, 351–363.

Holmes, J. (1993). *John Bowlby and attachment theory*. Routledge, London.

Hunter, M. (2001). *Psychotherapy with young people in care: Lost and found*. Brunner-Routledge, Hove, UK.

Hurry, A. (1998). *Psychoanalysis and developmental therapy*. Karnac, London.

Joseph, B. (1985). Transference: The total situation. In *Psychic equilibrium and psychic change—Selected papers of Betty Joseph*. (ed E. Bott-Spillius, M. Feldman). Tavistock/Routledge, London.

Kendall, P. and Lochman (1994). Cognitive-behavioural therapies. In *Child and adolescent psychiatry: modern approaches (3rd edn)*. (ed. M. Rutter, E. Taylor, and L. Hersov) pp. 844–57. Blackwell, Oxford.

Kennedy, E. (2004). *Child and adolescent psychotherapy: A systematic review of psychoanalytic approaches*. North Central London Strategic Health Authority. Downloadable from www.nclondon.nhs.uk/publications/workforce/child_and_adolescent_systematic.review.pdf

Klein, M. (1946). Notes on some schizoid mechanisms. In *Envy and gratitude and other works*. Hogarth Press, London.

Klein, M. (1961). *Narrative of a child analysis*. Hogarth Press, London.

Klein, M. (1963). *The psychoanalysis of children*. Hogarth Press, London.

Lanyardo, M. and Horne, A. eds. (1999). *Handbook of child and adolescent psychotherapy—Psychoanalytic approaches*. Routledge, London.

Leikerman, M. and Urban, E. (1999). The roots of child and adolescent psychotherapy in psychoanalysis. In *Handbook of child and adolescent psychotherapy—psychoanalytic approaches* (ed. M. Lanyardo and A. Horne). Routledge, London.

Main, M., Goldwyn, R. (1993). Adult attachment rating and classification systems. In *A typology of human attachment organisation assessed in discourse, drawings and interviews*(ed. M.Main) Cambridge University Press, New York.

Murray, L. and Cooper, P. (1994). Clinical applications of attachment theory and research: Change in infant attachment with brief psychotherapy. *In the clinical application of ethology and attachment theory*, (ed. J. Richer) pp. 15–24. Association for child Psychology and Psychiatry, Occasional Report, No. 9.

Reid, S., Alvarez, A., and Lee, A. (2001). The Tavistock autism workshop approach. In: *Autism—The search for coherence*, (eds. J. Richer, S. Coates) Jessica Kingsley, London.

Rustin, M. (1999). The training of child psychotherapists at the Tavistock Clinic: Philosophy and practice. *Psychoanalytic Inquiry*, **19**, 125–141.

Rustin, M. and Quagliata, E. (2000). *Assessment in child psychotherapy*. Duckworth, London.

Salzberger-Wittenberg, I. (1977). Counselling young people. *In The child psychotherapist and problems of young people*. (ed. D. Daws and M. Boston,) Wildwood House, London.

Schore, A. (2000). Attachment and the regulation of the right brain. *Attachment and Human Development*, **2**, 23–47.

Shapiro, T. and Esman, A. (1992). Psychoanalysis and child and adolescent psychiatry. *Journal of the American Academy of Child and Adolescent Psychiatry*, **31**, 6–13.

Solms, M. and Turnbull, O. (2002). *The brain and the inner world. An introduction to the neuroscience of subjective experience*. Karnac, London.

Stern, D. (1985). *The interpersonal world of the infant: A view from psychoanalysis and developmental psychology*. Basic Books, New York.

Szur, R. and Miller, S. (1991). *Extending horizons. Psychoanalytic psychotherapy with children, adolescents and families.* Karnac, London.

Target, M., Fonagy, P., and Shmueli-Goetz, Y. (2003). Attachment representations in school-age children: The development of the child attachment interview (CAI). *Journal of Child Psychotherapy*, **29**, 171–186.

Trowell, J., Kolvin, I., Weeramanthri, T., Sadowski, H., Berelowitz, M., Glasser, D., and Leitch, I. (2002). Psychotherapy for sexually abused girls: Psychopathological outcome findings and patterns of change. *British Journal of Psychiatry*, **180**, 234–247.

Trowell, J., Rhode, M., Miles, G., and Sherwood, I. (2003). Childhood depression: Work in progress. *Journal of Child Psychotherapy*, **29**, 147–169.

Urwin, C. (2000). Reviews of psychoanalysis and developmental therapy by Hurry, A. *Journal of Child Psychotherapy*, **26**, 124–128.

Webster-Stratten, C. and Hammond, M. (1997). Treating children with early onset conduct problems. A comparison of child and parent training interventions. *Journal of Consulting and Clinical Psychology*, **65**, 93–109.

Whittington, C. J., Kendall, T., Fonagy, P., Cotrell,D., Cotgrove, A., and Boddington, E. (2004). Selective serotonin reuptake inhibitors in depression: systematic review of published versus unpublished data. *The Lancet*, **363**, 1341.

Winnicott, D. W. (1971a). *Therapeutic consultations in child psychiatry.* Basic Books, New York.

Winnicott, D. W. (1971b). *Playing and reality.* Penguin, London.

Wolff, S. (1989). *Childhood and human nature: Development of personality.* Routledge, London.

Recommended reading

General

Boston, M. and Szur, R. (1983). *Psychotherapy with severely deprived children.* Routledge and Kegan Paul, London. (An application of child psychotherapy techniques with a series of case studies illustrating work with severely disturbed and deprived children arising from advances in clinical theories especially Bion.)

Daws, D. and Boston, M. (1977). *The child psychotherapist and problems of young people.* Wildwood House, London. (The first book published showing the range of work child psychotherapists do and describing the training of child psychotherapists.)

Hunter, M. (2001). *Psychotherapy with young people in care: Lost and found.* Brunner-Routledge, Hove. (An excellent collection of case studies on work with children in the care system.)

Lanyardo, M. and Horne, A. eds. (1999). *Handbook of child and adolescent psychotherapy—Psychoanalytic approaches* Routledge, London. (A more recent collection of papers focussing on the development and practice of child psychotherapy providing an up to date introduction to the profession. It illustrates the wide range of settings and direct and applied work done by child psychotherapists.)

Rustin, M. and Quagliata, E. (2000). *Assessment in child psychotherapy.* Duckworth, London. (A useful collection of papers illustrating different types of assessments for psychotherapy of a range of children and adolescents with different conditions.)

Szur, R. and Miller, S. (1991). *Extending horizons. Psychoanalytic psychotherapy with children, adolescents and families*. Karnac, London.(An update on the original Daws and Boston book of 1977 on the work of the child psychotherapist illustrating how the work of child psychotherapists has developed.)

Personality

Hindle, D. and Vaciago Smith, M. (1999). *Personality development—A psychoanalytic perspective*. Routledge, London.(A comprehensive overview from infant and to adult personality development showing the emotional tasks involved at each stage of development.)

Miller, L., Rustin, M., Rustin, M., and Shuttleworth, J. (1989). *Closely observed infants*. Duckworth, London. (A book describing the method and value of infant observation as part of a psychotherapy training as well as a research tool.)

Reid, S. (1997). *Development in infant observation: The Tavistock model*. Routledge, London. (The authors of this volume offer an overview of the current practice in infant observation and explore new concepts that have arisen from direct observation of infants.)

Waddell, M. (2002). *Inside Lives : Psychoanalysis and the growth of the personality*. Karnac, London. (A perspective of the relationship between psychoanalytic theory and the nature of human development tracing the interplay between external and internal influences on a person's character development.)

Child psychoanalysis and its application

Salzberger-Wittenberg, I. (1973). *Psycho-analytic insights and relationship—A Kleinian approach*. Routledge, London. (Using theoretical exposition and case material, the author demonstrates how Klein's concepts can be used in social work casework.)

Salzberger-Wittenberg, I., Henry, G., and Obborne, E. (1993). *The emotional experience of learning and teaching*. Karnac, London (A useful book showing how psychoanalytic ideas can be put to work in the classroom, especially ideas about phantasy, transference and counter-transference.)

Chapter 15

Psychotherapy with older adults

Jane Garner

Introduction

We can all think of well-known people, family, friends, and patients who age
well and enjoy the freedoms later-life may bring. However, the Western world in
the twenty-first century can be a difficult place to be if you are old, particularly
old and ill. The postmodern emphasis on individuality, achievement, celebrity,
fashion, and youth marginalizes older people who would be better recognized
if societies were more concerned with the sense of community. That many
more people are now able to reach old age is usually not regarded as an
achievement but as a 'problem' to be resolved. Old people are frequently
stereotyped in a denigrating or patronizing way: 'dirty old . . .', 'sweet old . . .'.
If they *are* praised, it is for looking younger than their years or for defying age.

Health professionals have tended to collude with these limited expectations
and gone along with the idea that later life is 'life in decline'. Even services set
up for older people have attended to the biological, to a lesser extent the social,
and rarely to the psychological, in a way that would not be acceptable to
younger people. Few psychotherapists have treated older patients, influenced
perhaps by Freud's comments in 1904 that '. . . people over the age of 50 are no
longer educable'—curiously uttered when he was 49 and possibly expressing
his own fears. This chapter will use a psychodynamic framework but will
allude to other approaches appropriate for older patients.

A psychodynamic framework

If assumptions underlying psychodynamic therapy are accepted, they will be
applicable to all people, with no arbitrary cut-off based on age. Evidence has
accumulated that older patients do as well in therapy as younger ones (Knight
1996; Woods and Roth 1996).

Aims

The aim of psychodynamic psychotherapy generally is to effect psychological change through increased self-understanding. For older patients, such

change may need to be qualified. Younger people can exercise emerging self-mastery through behaviour or lifestyle changes in the external world. Older people have less opportunity to take a new path, given financial constraint, mobility limitations, and physical illness. The desired outcome then is not a striving and impossible wish for life to be different, but accepting with equanimity what cannot change and taking up opportunities which may present in the future. For instance, a physical disability will not be altered by psychotherapy but any negative effect on patients and their relationships may be ameliorated. Moreover, adverse circumstances may be mitigated by enhanced psychological-mindedness in approaching them (McClean 1995). According to Erikson's model (1959), a positive outcome would be the patient seeing his life as the only one he could have led in the circumstances in which he found himself and avoiding regret that life is now too short to pursue a different course.

Selection

Selection criteria for older patients do not differ significantly from those for younger people. Diagnostic categories and disease-based explanations of distress are of limited utility in deciding on suitability. Instead, it is useful to think of people having difficulty in dealing with transition (e.g. retirement), bereavement, shifting family relationships, or regrets for the life they have led. Therapy is likely to be beneficial if people can think psychologically, be curious about the role they may have played in the relevant events and relationships in their lives, and tolerate frustration and emotional distress. A hospital-based and supported therapist can treat more psychologically disabled patients. Psychotropics are not a bar to therapy. Those who have had a depressive, psychotic, or other major psychiatric illness may need medication before therapy begins. Psychological intervention then has the advantage of promoting compliance.

Diagnosis is not a contraindication even in an organically based disorder, for example, a dementing illness. Memory in a direct sense, for example, recalling a sentence or reiterating an autobiography, is not essential for psychological therapy (Fonagy 1999). What the patient does not remember will be manifest in some form in the transference relationship. A psychodynamic approach to these patients, (O'Connor 1993; Garner 2004a) previously considered as quite unsuitable, can provide a sense of continuity and security. Family members, trying to cope with their relative's cognitive changes and all that brings in its wake, may benefit not only from advice and psychoeducation but also from a dynamic understanding of the situation, for example, unconscious conflict in fulfilling the role of carer.

Theory

Underlying assumptions in psychoanalytic work are that only a fraction of life is conscious. Some thoughts and memories are repressed. Dreams and fantasies reveal hidden motivations and urges. Symptoms and personality difficulties have hidden meaning. The relationship with a therapist respectful of these concepts may be diagnostic as well as therapeutic.

Psychoanalytic theory is one of development. Freud emphasized the early years but some analysts became interested in later phases of the lifecycle (e.g. Karl Abraham and Eliot Jaques). Following his split with Freud, Jung began to examine the psychology of the second half of life which he conceived to be governed by different principles from the first. In the 'morning of life', people focus on nature, the world at large, and the care of children whereas in the 'afternoon' more attention is directed towards the self. Jung (1931) was not referring to an obsession with oneself but rather to spirituality and the inner self (Bacelle 2004). The neo-Freudians reformulated Freud's theory in sociological terms, focusing on the external culture and how people interact. Out of this tradition, Erik Erikson (1959) postulated that development continued throughout the lifecycle, encompassing cultural and intrapsychic processes. His 'eight ages of man' (see Table 15.1) cover the particular developmental task for each phase of the cycle.

He conceptualized development as a series of alternative basic attitudes. If the negotiation between the alternatives succeeds, the balance is towards the positive (Garner 2004b). Stages remain active throughout life and may be stimulated by certain conditions. The value of Erikson's framework for older patients is the notion that development continues into the late stages of life and takes historical and social circumstances into account. The latter may be particularly pertinent since older patients will have lived much of their lives in different times from most of the staff who care for them.

Table 15.1 Erikson's eight stages

Basic trust vs mistrust
Autonomy vs shame and doubt
Initiative vs guilt
Industry vs inferiority
Identity vs role confusion
Intimacy vs isolation
Generativity vs stagnation
Ego integrity vs despair

According to Erikson, the psychosocial task in the eighth age is to negotiate between the polarities of ego-integrity and ego-despair. Those who have developed an attitude of integrity see their lives to be the only lives they could have had and their positions in the world to be the only possible ones. Those who lack integrity will be despairing. Despair may be clothed in disgust, contempt, and displeasure, that life is too short and there is not now sufficient time to take an alternative route, and the person fears for the future because of 'not being' rather than taking pleasure and value from 'having been'. The patient may feel in a state of physical and psychological disintegration. The therapist provides a sense of containment in which these anxieties can be altered. Losses, anger, and grief need to be acknowledged for mistakes made, opportunities missed. At the same time worthwhile aspects of life, for example, having loved and been loved, need to be appreciated. Struggling with the specific developmental task may reactivate the mark left by earlier struggles. Increasing dependency or fear of anticipated dependency may bring the first task for the baby, basic trust, to the fore (Martindale 1989). A disability in old age may require the most personal care to be undertaken by another. The fear may arise that the carer will feel disgust and hate. If the experience of dependency in early life was good enough, this can be revived in old age so that the patient trusts the carer to treat him benignly.

Other analysts have taken up the theme of psychological development in adult life (Colarusso and Nemiroff 1981). Nemiroff and Colarusso (1985) discuss 'developmental resonance'—the therapist respecting the patient's experience from all periods of life even if he has not 'been there'. The body–mind relationship emphasized in child development tends to be ignored in work with adults even though they may well be preoccupied by bodily changes. Old age does not happen suddenly, we age gradually and are aware of changes in appearance and in function. Therapists may avoid this aspect since it echoes their own anxieties and the narcissistic injury involved as they are no longer so strong, smooth limbed, or attractive. They do need to be aware of biological realities and help their patients to accept and adapt to them.

Hildebrand (1982), who ran a workshop at the Tavistock Clinic for staff with older patients in therapy, adopted and elaborated a psychodynamically informed developmental psychology. He delineated particular developmental tasks and difficulties which need to be negotiated for successful later life (see Table 15.2).

Hildebrand posited that old people come to therapy when developmental adaptation breaks down—the person has failed in negotiating one or more of the above tasks.

Table 15.2 Hildebrand's developmental tasks and difficulties in later life

Fear of diminution/loss of sexual potency
Threat of redundancy in work roles, the fear of being replaced by younger people
The need to reconsider and possibly remake the marital relationship after children have left the family home
Awareness of one's own ageing, illness and possible dependence
Awareness that what one can now achieve is limited
The feeling of having failed as a parent (paradoxically exacerbated in the childless)
Loss of a partner and of intimacy
The fact of one's own death in terms of narcissistic loss and pain.

People not only take into old age past and new difficulties but also attributes and skills developed over the years. Cicero (1923) wrote in 45 BC: 'It is not by muscle speed or physical dexterity that great things are achieved, but by reflection, force of character, and judgement; in these qualities old age is usually not only not poorer but is even richer'. The older population of course are a varied and heterogeneous group. Those with sufficient internal resources can use even the negative experiences of later life creatively to stimulate positive development.

A common theme in therapy with older people is loss of the real and tangible—jobs, homes, relationships—and also of status, esteem, and future potential. Although any loss can stimulate depression or anger, moving into a new situation always entails a degree of loss. We need to give up things in order to move on in life. Similarly in psychotherapy, the patient has to forego maladaptive behaviour, erroneous beliefs, unrealistic wishes, and illusions (Wolff 1977). Salzberger-Wittenberg (1970) sees the potential for loss to strengthen character, develop courage, and create a deeper concern for others.

Sexuality in old age is a taboo subject (Garner and Bacelle 2004). Clinicians often share a negative stereotype of a sexual life in later years with their older patients so that this area of experience remains unexplored (Gussaroff 1998). However, the need for intimate connectedness continues throughout life. Research tends to concentrate on quantitative rather than qualitative aspects of sexuality, whereas emotional tone and communication in the sexual relationship become more cogent.

Sexual anxieties may continue throughout life; there is a timelessness to many themes in the unconscious (alongside physiological problems) which may contribute to dysfunction. Despite possible resistance in both patient and therapist, the sexual dimension is always present in psychodynamic work, whatever the age.

When seeing a patient with a dementing illness the emotional quality of the relationship between therapist and patient needs particular attention. Freud (1914) emphasized that what the patient does not remember will be repeated in the transference relationship. He was referring to patients with repressed memories but the same seems true for those with cognitive impairment. The relationship is still used for communication. An emotional life continues without language. It is easy to attribute everything about a patient with a dementing illness to organically based impairment but in doing so, one misses the complexity and subtlety of human experience and interaction as well as the opportunity for psychotherapeutic intervention.

Damasio (1994) argues that the distinction between diseases of the brain and of the mind into biological and psychological reflects a basic ignorance of the link between the two. For instance, the patient who believes his parents are still alive is usually considered to be exhibiting further evidence of a seriously impaired memory. Miesen (1993) terms this phenomenon 'parent fixation' and regards it as an equivalent of attachment behaviour, a response to the fear of abandonment and feeling of loss evoked by the dementia. Therapists therefore need to be dependable attachment figures.

The main focus of therapy with the partner of the patient with dementia will be dealing with the grief of losing the person they knew, who may have seemed lost from the early stages of the disease (Garner 1997) and anticipating future losses including through death.

Process

The foundation of all psychological therapies is mutual respect and collaboration. At the beginning the therapist spends time using straightforward language to explain the process to someone who may be quite naïve about this form of treatment. As with any dynamic therapy the patient is seen regularly, at a consistent time. How regularly depends to some extent on available resources but more particularly on the individual. Weekly sessions are common although every other week may be preferable to 'process' the previous session. Some older patients can feel disheartened if treatment feels too fast or pressurized. Once a frequency has been determined, it persists until there is a compelling reason to change and this is discussed and understood before arrangements alter.

In the initial sessions, virtually as an extended assessment, the focus may need to be on the value of the patient since he may have internalized the prevailing view of the worthlessness of older people and that the time should be given to the young. 'I've had my innings' is often heard. The recognition of loss implicit in this type of comment is part of the therapy from the outset.

However, loss is specific; appreciating that many losses are occurring does not do justice to the nature of the losses specific to the patient and his circumstances (Knight and Satre 1999). George Pollock (1982) invokes the concept of mourning-liberation in later life. Ageing well depends on the ability to mourn for oneself in such a way that it opens up possibilities and freedoms in subsequent years. Old age is then seen as a different phase rather than the end phase. The final anticipated loss, one's own death, may not be as feared in later life as it is for some who are younger. Coming to terms with one's mortality is a task for middle life (Knight 1986), although some older patients view death as a persecutory anxiety (Segal 1958). There is a shape to life which has a beginning, a middle, and an end. This may provide comfort. Conceptually, it is a strain to think of immortality. In stories and legends in which the protagonist cannot die, he longs for release, for death, for 'not being'.

Techniques used are the same as with younger patients—free association by the patient and active listening by the therapist. The latter also observes his own reactions to what happens in therapy distinguishing what it is the patient is stimulating in him and what is a reaction to events and people in his own life. The therapist also is aware how his attitudes and beliefs (even misinformation) about older people may affect treatment.

The therapist needs to be more flexible in a range of ways. The consulting room on an upper floor in a building with an unreliable lift is not a reason to exclude a patient of limited mobility from therapy but rather a reason to borrow a room on the ground floor. Older people often are dealing with chronic illness and social stigma, the therapist should not compound these difficulties by adhering rigidly to theory or responding prejudicially.

Therapeutic factors parallel those in treating younger patients. The therapist is open to hearing what is said (and *not* being said). Thus, the therapist does not impose either society's or his own values but demonstrates empathy, warmth, and respect. There is a skill involved in being emotionally engaged and also, at the same time, having sufficient detachment to observe the interaction and the therapist's personal reactions. The core feature is the relationship. Therapy is not given as a tablet may be given and taken by a passive patient; both protagonists collaborate and reach joint understanding. Instilling hope is essential, not the vain hope that 'everything will be fine' but the appreciation that a way may be found through the present difficulties.

Clinical illustration

Mr T was referred by his GP to an Old Age Psychiatry department at the age of 78 with no previous psychiatric history. The usual practice was to see a new patient initially in their home and to interview a relative. Mr T insisted adamantly on being seen as an outpatient and was clear that he did not wish his wife to know of the referral. His main complaint was of 'things not being right'. Although he was an intelligent, articulate man, he had difficulty characterizing this further. An exploratory approach was adopted with the idea of referring him on for therapy. The dissatisfaction of 'things not being right' was clarified during subsequent meetings—his wife was not right and he was becoming extremely irritable with her; his health was not right, particularly pain in his left hip which slowed him down and some shortness of breath which alarmed him; his sleep was not right disturbed as it was by nocturia which his GP attributed to an enlarged prostate (Mr T considered it an humiliating 'old man's' problem); his days were not right—although retired for the past 13 years he had still not managed to use his time in a way that suited him; it was not right that he and his wife were childless; and it was not right that his father had left his mother for another woman.

The decision was made that medication was not appropriate but psychotherapy was an option. Although not sophisticated in his knowledge about therapy he was attracted by the idea that there was an area of his life of which he might be unaware. This echoed much of his life which was full of secrets (including the referral being kept from his wife).

Mr T was born in 1920. His father was unable to settle to domestic life after returning from gruesome experiences in the First World War with medals for bravery. He had difficulty holding down a job and in 1925 left his wife and moved to a different part of the country with another woman. He tried unsuccessfully to contact his son. Mr T did not regard father as leaving mother but as leaving him. A lifelong hatred of his father followed. Mother and son moved in with the widowed maternal grandmother. He was always 'a good boy' for mother and grandmother and charming to their friends but at school, although bright and doing well academically, he behaved badly, but never enough for the school to notify his mother. This was an early example of a double life with secrets. He left school at 16 taking any job that came along and studying at night school.

He was called up for service in the Second World War. He felt fortunate that it was the Royal Air Force. He had dreaded the idea that he might have had to be a soldier like his father since to be anything like him felt intolerable. Determined to be unlike father he sort out a 'good job' after being demobilized. He worked his way up to a responsible position in management. The values of the business were at odds with his personal political views. However, his colleagues at work and his socialist friends never met and through evasions and direct lies did not know of one another.

He always knew how to charm women and had many girlfriends. At age 30 he married Betty, wanting to be a better husband than his father had been. In many ways he was. His steady job brought a good income. They enjoyed each other's company, shared political ideas, and had a satisfying sexual life. Notwithstanding, he had many secret affairs. Their marriage deteriorated after he retired. Together most of the time, petty grievances grew out of proportion. He initiated rows such that at times Betty retreated to her sister's home for a few days peace. Not having children was a serious loss to both of them. Mr T had difficulty coming to terms with not having a son whom he would treat so much better than his own father had treated him. He envied his father for his ability to have children despite the defects he saw in his character. He and Betty avoided blaming each other and the joint feeling of loss kept them united for some years.

He had never really taken women seriously; he had taken it for granted that he would get what he wanted from them—he had found it easy to delight his mother; secretaries at work were always ready to assist him; he had usually pleased his wife (while also cheating on her); he had seduced, pleased, and then left his mistresses at will.

Unusually he seemed unnerved that he was not able to charm the female therapist 30 years his junior, into giving him extra sessions, seeing him at a different time, or speaking to him on the phone. The therapist was a little charmed by him, seeing him as good looking and romantic with a slightly scary edge; perhaps like her own father had been. He made her think of Greek myths. A turning point came when she referred to the myths. He liked this. He had been fond of classics at school and liked the idea of examining his 'odyssey'. He teased the therapist, was she the faithful Penelope or the sorceress, Circe?

Betty died one year into Mr T's therapy. This was a difficult time for him. He had been reaching the point when he thought he could tell her about the therapy and offer regrets and apologies for his irritability. There had been a few occasions when he had not obtained an erection and he blamed her. In retrospect he wondered if his irritable behaviour was due to his feeling that his life was not better than it was and he did not want to give anyone anything, including sex to his wife. He felt pleased with this new idea; it also took away a feeling that he was a failure. Unfortunately, Betty died before he could share these thoughts with her.

A few months after the death he visited her sister and disclosed that he was in therapy and spoke of his regrets about aspects of the marriage. He was pleasantly surprised at the sympathetic reaction of his sister-in-law. He had imagined Betty would have told dreadful tales about him. On the contrary,

Betty had discussed him fairly and lovingly. He was pleased to hear this but sad that he could not make up for his previous behaviour.

In reconsidering his father, he said in a self-deprecating, grimly jocular way that at the age of 80 the time had come to forgive him. He regretted he had never taken up his father's suggestion to meet. He wished he had known more about him as a person, not only as a hated object. In particular, he wondered what had happened to him as an infantryman in World War I.

How he should write his will was a real problem; the question emphasized his childlessness. He wanted his money to achieve something worthwhile. Eventually he decided to contribute to his favoured political causes and to the charity Age Concern since he thought that in his earlier life he had not given much thought to old people except to be disgusted by his grandmother when she developed dementia. He left the main part of his estate to his sister-in-law's children. He knew this would have been his wife's wish. He himself was pleased to have found in his sister-in-law someone to whom he could talk openly.

He succeeded in locating someone with whom he had been close for many years but they had fallen out, arguing over the niceties of political ideology. They had not met since. Mr T remembering the friendship which had been eclipsed by this row felt he should swallow his pride and make the first move to a reconciliation. Fortunately, his friend reciprocated. They spent hours reminiscing. Together they joined an organization which campaigned to increase pensions and welfare benefits for older people.

In the relationship with the therapist Mr T had initially seen her as a woman he might control. Later, he saw her as the daughter he had never had. There were times when he felt 'persecuted' by her ending the sessions on time, by her going on holiday, and by her not taking everything he said literally. By termination, he felt sorry that he would not see her regularly but pleased that he was sorting out his life and feeling better about his father. He had found the therapeutic relationship comforting at the time of his wife's death. For the therapist she had always liked Mr T, at times charmed but also irritated by his self-assurance with women. At the beginning when he tried to subvert the rules of treatment, she had felt like a strict mother of an exasperating little boy. Following the death of his wife, she very much wanted to hug him but subsequently felt satisfied that she had maintained the boundary and used understanding and words instead.

The anticipated ending was discussed from early on in the work. Would it end with the immense sadness he had felt at not becoming a parent, or with his wife dying before he could divulge his secrets? Would it end with the intense feeling of abandonment he had experienced when his father had left?

A date was set 6 months ahead (after 2 years in treatment) to give time to work through these concerns. Mr T had enjoyed going to the theatre. He was well aware of Jaques disquisition on the Seven Ages of Man in '*As you like it*' and thought Shakespeare had been wrong in typifying old age, '. . . *sans* everything'. He felt he still had the possibility to enjoy positive experiences. He recalled the playwright Strindberg's comment 'Old age isn't nice but it is interesting'. He was inclined to agree.

Termination

The 20-year-old patient may feel little pressure to change quickly; he has all the time in the world. For the 70-year-old, the recognition that the time left to him may be brief can accelerate psychological change. He may leave feeling he has renewed energy and anticipation, and a belief he can execute desired courses of action. Other patients linking termination with death may need to feel that the therapist will always be available. This does not mean that the therapist has to see the patient forever but not discharging him absolutely indicates that the patient may return in the future if the need arises. Martindale (1998) highlights the difficulty for the unconscious in knowing about the 'cessation of experiencing', in knowing about not being. There is a notion that a psychic life persists so it may also be useful to explore the patient's ideas about life after death.

Termination may be forced upon the therapy by external circumstances. A move into residential care or serious physical ill health may be dealt with by the therapist meeting the patient in a different location. However flexible the therapist, a move may make it logistically impossible, for example, to another part of the country. Communicating by letter about any unfinished business has a place. The loss involved in the ending of therapy will have been anticipated from the beginning. It will also have been linked with other losses discussed in the sessions: loss of people, familiar environments, work, status, youth, potential, time and, eventually, life.

Problems encountered in therapy

Patients will inevitably be older, even much older than their therapists. In the transference, the latter will be experienced as a range of other people; for example, child, sibling, parent, grandparent, figures from childhood, and also from the adult past. The patient may envy the younger therapist: his youth, health, holidays, sexuality although knowing nothing in reality about the therapist's life.

Working with older patients evokes particular feelings in therapists. The patient may be the idealized parent or grandparent the therapist never had or conversely denigrated in these roles. The patient may represent for the therapist his own feared later life. His concerns about his own old age may be in collusive identification with the patient's difficulties and negative thoughts and feelings.

An overtly fit young therapist and a disabled old patient may seem in an ostensibly unequal relationship which may stimulate unhelpful feelings of pity in the therapist or occasionally sadism (Garner 2002) accompanied by guilt and reparative wishes to make things better.

There is no cure for old age and if accompanied by chronic disability therapists feel it a blow to their therapeutic narcissism. This may stimulate hostility, frustration, and helplessness. Identifications may be painful—'this may be me in two, three, four, or more decades'. Sharing these sentiments with an understanding supervisor certainly helps. If the patient dies, supervision becomes invaluable. Death from suicide or causes unrelated to the reason for therapy can make the therapist feel guilt, anger, and sadness, all of which are part of normal grief.

Dependency or fear of it may be an issue for both partners. Increasing dependency is a reality for many older people. How the patient deals with this is influenced by how dependency was negotiated in early life. Some may adopt a pseudo-independent style proclaiming they can still do what is now obviously impossible. Others assume a more dependent role than is realistically necessary. Yet, others fear a future subjugated by unsympathetic carers. Therapists may also harbour anxiety about patient dependency, fearing that this will trap them and make unrealistic demands at a time in their lives when they should be attending to their own needs (Martindale 1989).

Within the intimacy of the therapeutic relationship attention is paid to boundaries so that patients are touched emotionally but not physically. However, if they need a hand to stand up it would seem churlish not to give it. Whatever the outcome of the therapists' internal debate about this, their behaviour needs to be spoken about with the patient in the session (Ardern 1997).

In work with a patient requiring help in daily living, Hausman (1992) has pointed out that an obstacle may be the family's resistance to the patient entering therapy. They may sabotage treatment by not reminding the patient of an appointment. Splitting can be painful for relatives particularly if the therapist is idealized and the family denigrated.

Training

This type of work is demanding. Supervision is essential. Even the experienced therapist needs space to think about the patient and about feelings within him which may be provoked by the relationship. Supervision provides a safe setting in which to explore these complex dynamics.

Principles of dynamic psychotherapy for adults of any age are similar and training required no different—studying relevant theory, treating cases under regular supervision, and, ideally, having an experience of personal therapy. Outcome is enhanced if the therapist is not only generally well qualified but also has specialized training in working with older adults (Pinquart and Sorensen 2001).

Therapists need to be familiar with the realities of their patients' lives, for example, how much is a state pension and what will it purchase?; what is the impact of giving up driving?; what is it like to be unable to walk to the end of the street?; what if the only visitor is the person who delivers 'meals on wheels'? The substance of a patient's life may not be changed by therapy but understanding its impact on their inner world, fantasies, and relationships may be achieved. Understanding is the cornerstone of this type of work and is why supervision is vital. Understanding is not only about what the patients communicate in words but also about how they make the therapist feel. He needs to examine his own feelings about the patient, old age, and the range of material brought to the sessions.

Other therapeutic approaches for older patients

Group therapy

There are many accounts of the value of group therapy with older people (Evans 2004). It is not helpful to have only one older person in a group since she may easily be scapegoated or made to carry a stereotyped 'wisdom' for the group. Group composition should either reflect a range of ages or be limited to older people. If the latter, the phenomenon of ageing can be readily explored. Evans (1998) extends Zinkin's (1983) idea of 'malignant mirroring' to include older people. Why do they not want to go to clubs or day centres or even join a therapy group—'it is full of old people'. These projections can be examined and understood in a group setting. Both positive and negative aspects of ageing can be explored so the members gain a more balanced view.

Therapeutic factors as outlined by Yalom (1995) apply to groups with older members. Evans (2004) suggests that two of these factors have particular relevance. The first is *universality*, the sense that problems are shared, and the second *altruism*, the sense that one is of value reduces self-preoccupation. Evans et al. (2001) point out that psychological-mindedness can be learnt, and autonomy and self-esteem enhanced through participating in a group.

The group can also encourage members to see themselves from the perspective of their fellows which in turn prompts adaptive coping to deal with the challenges and demands of ageing.

Reminiscence therapy

Spontaneous reminiscing is adaptive and increases socialization. Reviewing one's life is involved in many models of psychotherapy as a precursor to change (Butler 1963). It is a prerequisite for successful 'individuation' (Jung 1929) and 'integration' (Erikson 1959). Helping people make sense of their lives—in terms of values, accomplishments, and disappointments paves the way to resolve unfinished business (Knight 1986).

'Reminiscence therapy' is valuable for those who resist the idea of formal 'psychological' treatment. This may begin with the apparently simple act of taking a psychiatric history. The patient is helped to shape a narrative of their life, to consider successes and regrets and the role they played in their story. In a comparison of life review and cognitive therapy groups, Weiss (1994) found the treatments equally effective, including for people over 75. In a meta-analysis of 20 controlled outcome studies, Bohlmeijer et al. (2003) found a significant effect of a life review approach on depressive symptoms in the elderly.

Reminiscence techniques are applicable for those who are depressed and those who have a dementia and may be added to a programme in a residential unit. Talking about one's life increases interaction, socialization, self-esteem, and mood. Moreover, the more staff know about the patient's past life, the better they can understand current behaviour and personal preferences.

Life review is added to other therapy modalities with older patients, for example, cognitive therapy (Koder et al. 1996) and systemic family therapy (Hughston and Cooledge 1989). In the latter, the older family member is then viewed as a person with resources and knowledge, and with something to offer to the family. By reflecting on past experience, the family may avoid repeating previous mistakes and be more creative in thinking of the future.

Family therapy

A systems approach has been combined usefully with dynamic ideas as well as with a developmental perspective of the family with tasks, with tasks to be negotiated at points in its lifecycle (see chapter 18). Key family therapy concepts are still relevant when including older family members. Moreover, the opportunity becomes available for the therapeutic use of the family narrative. Systems work focuses on the here and now and it is about distress *associated with*, not *caused by*, relationships. This needs to be explained carefully since it is not uncommon for an older person as the identified patient to say: 'It's me, it's my fault, don't bother the family'. Finding fault is not the therapist's task—understanding is.

Systems thinking is well suited to family work with older people. Families need guidance to cope in situations which cannot actually improve. For instance, therapy reframes the way chronic illness and increasing dependency is considered. Roper-Hall (1992) writes of 'co-creating alternative ways of understanding the situation'.

Circular questioning (see page X) improves communication between identified patient and family members over transitions, for example, 'What do you think your mother feels about going into a nursing home?' Another element of the work is challenging cultural beliefs, for example, negative stereotypes of old age.

Conclusion

The value of the psychotherapies for older people has been established and is a crucial compliment to the biological and social management usually offered. Reviewing one's life and relationships is a normal human activity, undertaking this task with a facilitating therapist in later life may be a liberating experience for those facing a wide range of difficulties. Older patients should be offered the same opportunities as those at other points in the lifecycle to benefit from a therapeutic relationship, and the application of psychological principles relevant to their needs.

References

Ardern, M. (1997). Psychotherapy and the elderly. In *Advances in old age psychiatry: Chromosomes to community care*. (eds. C. Holmes and R. Howard) pp. 265–276. Wrightson Biomedical, Petersfield.

Bacelle, L. (2004). On becoming an old man: Jung and others. In *Talking over the years: A handbook of dynamic psychotherapy with older adults*. (eds. S. Evans and J. Garner) pp. 29–41.Brunner-Routledge, London.

Bolmeijer, E., Smit, F., and Cuijpers, P. (2003). Effects of reminiscence and life review on late-life depression: A meta-analysis. *International Journal of Geriatric Psychiatry*, **18**, 1088–1094.

Butler, R. N. (1963). The life review: An interpretation of reminiscence in the aged. *Psychiatry*, **26**, 65–76.

Cicero, M. T. (1923). *De Senectute*. Trans. Falconer, W. A. On old age. Harvard University Press, Cambridge, Mass.

Colarusso, G. A. and Nemiroff, R. A. (1981). *Adult development: A new dimension in psychodynamic theory and practice*. Plenum, New York.

Damasio, A. R. (1994). *Descartes' error*. Putnam, New York.

Erikson, E. H. (1959). *Identity and the life cycle. Psychological issues monograph, No. 1.* International Universities Press, New York.

Evans, S. (1998). Beyond the mirror: A group analytic exploration of late life depression. *Ageing and Mental Health*, 2, 94–99.

Evans, S. (2004). Group psychotherapy: Foulkes, Yalom and Bion. In *Talking over the years: A handbook of dynamic psychotherapy with older adults.* (eds. S. Evans and J. Garner) pp. 87–100.Brunner/Routledge, London.

Evans, S., Chisholm, P., and Walshe, J. (2001). A dynamic psychotherapy group for the elderly. *Group Analysis*, 34, 287–298.

Fonagy, P. (1999). Memory and therapeutic action. *International Journal of Psychoanalysis*, 80, 215–223.

Freud, S. (1904). On psychotherapy. *Standard Edition* Vol 7, 257–268, Hogarth Press, London.

Freud, S. (1914). Remembering, repeating and working-through. (Further recommendations on the technique of psycho-analysis II). *Standard Edition* Vol 12, 145–156. Hogarth Press, London.

Garner, J. (1997). Dementia: An intimate death. *British Journal of Medical Psychology*, 70, 177–184.

Garner, J. (2002). Psychodynamic work and older adults. *Advances in Psychiatric Treatment*, 8, 128–137.

Garner, J. (2004a). Dementia. In *Talking over the years: A handbook of dynamic psychotherapy with older adults.* (eds. S. Evans and J. Garner). Brunner-Routledge, London, 215–230.

Garner, J. (2004b). Growing into old age: Erikson and others. In *Talking over the years: A handbook of dynamic psychotherapy with older adults.* (eds. S. Evans and J. Garner) pp. 71–85.Brunner-Routledge, London.

Garner, J. and Bacelle, L. (2004). Sexuality. In *Talking over the years: A handbook of dynamic psychotherapy with older adults.* (eds. S. Evans and J. Garner) pp. 247–263. Brunner-Routledge, London.

Gussaroff, E. (1998). Denial of death and sexuality in the treatment of elderly patients. *Psychoanalysis and Psychotherapy*, 15, 77–91.

Hausman, C. (1992). Dynamic psychotherapy with elderly demented patients. In *Caregiving in dementia.* (eds. M. M. Jones and B. M. L. Miesen) Routledge, London.

Hildebrand, H. P. (1982). Psychotherapy with older patients. *British Journal of Medical Psychology*, 55, 19–28.

Hughston, G. A. and Cooledge, N. J. (1989). The life review: An underutilised strategy for systemic family intervention. *Journal of Psychotherapy and the Family*, 5, 47–55.

Jung, C. G. (1929). Aims of psychotherapy. In *Collected Works Vol 16*, Routledge, London, 36–52.

Jung, C. G. (1931). The stages of life: In *Collected Works Vol 18*, Routledge, London, 387–403.

Knight, B. G. (1986). *Psychotherapy with older adults*. Sage, London.

Knight, B. G. (1996). Psychodynamic therapy with older adults: Lessons from scientific gerontology. In *Handbook of the clinical psychology of ageing.* (ed. R. T. Woods). Wiley, Chichester.

Knight, B. G. and Satre, D. D. (1999). Cognitive behavioural psychotherapy with older adults. *Clinical Psychology: Science and Practice*, 6, 188–203.

Koder, D. A., Brodaty, H., and Anstey, K. J. (1996). Cognitive therapy for depression in the elderly. *International Journal of Geriatric Psychiatry*, **11**, 97–107.

Martindale, B. (1989). Becoming dependent again: The fears of some elderly patients and their younger therapists. *Psychoanalytic Psychotherapy*, **4**, 67–75.

Martindale, B. (1998). On ageing, dying, death and eternal life. *Psychoanalytic Psychotherapy*, **12**, 259–270.

Miesen, B. M. L. (1993). Alzheimer's disease, the phenomenon of parent fixation and Bowlby's attachment theory. *International Journal of Geriatric Psychiatry*, **8**, 147–153.

McClean, D. (1995). Two models, one mind: Integrating the biological and psychological. *Psychoanalytic Psychotherapy*, **9**, 133–144.

Nemiroff, R. A. and Colarusso, C. A. (1985). *The race against time: Psychotherapy and psychoanalysis in the second half of life*. Plenum, New York.

O'Connor, D. (1993). The impact of dementia: A self psychological perspective. *Journal of Gerontological Social Work*, **20**, 113–128.

Pinquart, M. and Sorensen, S. (2001). How effective are psychotherapeutic and other psychosocial interventions with older adults: A meta-analysis. *Journal of Mental Health and Aging*, **7**, 207–243.

Pollock, R. G. (1982). On ageing and psychotherapy. *International Journal of Psychoanalysis*, **63**, 275–281.

Roper-Hall, A. (1992). Better late than never? Family therapy with older adults. *Clinical Psychology Forum*, **48**, 14–17.

Salzberger-Wittenberg, I. (1970). *Psychoanalytic insight and relationships: A Kleinian approach*. Routledge and Kegan Paul, London.

Segal, H. (1958). Fear of death: Notes on the analysis of an old man. *International Journal of Psychoanalysis*, **39**, 173–181.

Weiss, J. C. (1994). Group therapy with older adults in long-term care Settings: Research and clinical cautions and recommendations. *Journal for Specialists in Group Work*, **19**, 22–29.

Wolff, H. H. (1977). Loss: A central theme in psychotherapy. *British Journal of Psychology*, **50**, 11–19.

Woods, R. T. and Roth, A. D. (1996). Effectiveness of psychological interventions with older people. In *Psychotherapy: What works for whom?* (eds. A. D. Roth, and P. Fonagy,) Guilford, New York.

Yalom, I. D. (1995). *The theory and practice of group psychotherapy*. 4th edition. Basic, New York.

Zinkin, L. (1983). Malignant mirroring. *Group Analysis*, **16**, 113–129.

Recommended reading

Ardern, M. (1999). Psychodynamic aspects of old age psychiatry. In *Everything you need to know about old age psychiatry*. (ed. R. Howard) pp. 253–266. Wrightson Biomedical, Petersfield. (Incorporates dynamic thinking into the work of a multidisciplinary old age psychiatry team to the benefit of patients and staff.)

Ardern, M., Garner, J. and Porter, R. (1998). Curious bedfellows: Psychoanalytic understanding and old age psychiatry. *Psychoanalytic Psychotherapy*, **12**, 47–56. (The authors discuss the place that psychoanalytic theory and practice can have in an old age psychiatry service and serve as an adjunct to biological, social and other psychological approaches.)

Culverwell, A. and Martin, C. (1999). Psychotherapy with older adults. In *Older people and their needs*. (ed. G. Croley) Whurr, London. (Points to seeing older people as individuals, that they develop wisdom is as much an illusion as the view that people necessarily decline; 'like wine some mature better than others'.)

Evans, S. and Garner, J. eds. (2004). *Talking over the years: A handbook of dynamic psychotherapy with older adults*. Brunner/Routledge, London. (Examines how old age has been represented in different psychodynamic frameworks and clinical applications.)

Garner, J. (2004). Identity and Alzheimer's disease. In *Identity and health*. (eds. D. Kelleher and G. Leavey) pp. 59–77, Routledge, London. (The self is a multi-layered entity of many components. This chapter looks at the changing self in dementia. From philosophical, sociocultural and psychological considerations it takes the view of the patient, the family and the professional.)

Hess, N. (1987). King Lear and some anxieties of old age. *British Journal of Medical Psychology*, **60**, 209–215. (Draws on Shakespeare's King Lear and the author's clinical work to highlight the dread of being abandoned to a state of utter helplessness: A defence is often narcissistic tyranny.)

Hepple, J. and Sutton, L. eds. (2004). *Cognitive analytic therapy and later life*. Brunner/Routledge, London. (Counteracts the pessimism and stereotypes associated with later life. Of particular interest is Hepple on 'Ageism in therapy' and Dunn on 'Why so few become elders'.)

Mouratoglou, V. M. (1999). Family therapy with older adults. In *Everything you need to know about old age psychiatry*. (ed. R. Howard) pp. 267–284.Wrightson Biomedical, Petersfield, (An introduction including indications, family therapy ideas and principal theoretical frameworks.)

Sinason, V. (1992). The man who was losing his brain. In *Mental handicap and the human condition: New approaches from the Tavistock*. Free Association, London. (The author, who is also a poet, has written a moving account of therapy with an academic who had to retire early due to Alzheimer's disease. She has no illusions about a 'cure' but presents an understanding that organic loss shares an existence alongside emotionally caused impairment.)

Wilde, O. (1998). *The picture of Dorian Gray*. Oxford University Press, Oxford. ('Youth! Youth! There is nothing in the world but youth!' To Dorian Gray the idea of getting old is such an anathema that he gives his soul for eternal youth. His ageing self is split off and projected into the feared and hated portrait, kept out of sight.)

Chapter 16

Couple psychotherapy

Michael Crowe

The institution of marriage, especially in Western societies, is in a state of flux. Pressures exist which both idealize and undermine couple relationships. There is increased public interest in exploring the nature of couple interaction and a parallel process which questions the basis of couple relationships and seeks more individual freedom and fulfilment. It is not surprising therefore that there is a high demand for couple therapy (Crowe and Ridley 2000).

Marriage itself is becoming less popular, having reached a peak in the 1960s. Added to this, many forms of unofficial pairing exist, which often include cohabitation, and sometimes also involve the rearing of children. The divorce rate is now above 40% in many Western countries (National Statistics Office 1998), and it is probable, although the figures are not available, that the rate of break-up of common-law relationships is even greater.

Many factors are coming together to weaken the status of marriage. Women often seek to combine the satisfaction of a career with the rearing of children, and may then feel that their independence is more attractive to them than remaining in an unhappy marriage. Although men have to some extent responded to the challenge of sharing household and family responsibilities (Rabin 1996), tension still typifies many relationships as to the equitable division of duties (Oakley 1974). More women are opting to become single parents, either *ab initio* or following a divorce or separation. On the other hand, divorce and single parenthood tend to disadvantage children. They do less well at school and in work, and suffer depression, low self-esteem, and neurotic symptoms more commonly than those who have two biological parents living together (Rodgers and Pryor 1998). Problems for children increase further when the principal custodial parent remarries and a 'blended' family is created (Robinson 1991). Divorce also has a negative effect on the partners themselves, with increased alcoholism, heart disease, cancer, accidents, depression, and suicide in the first year.

It is appropriate to see couple therapy as a possible way to overcome these problems by reducing the divorce rate. Helping couples to stay together is not, however, its sole purpose. It can also be an effective way to deal with a wide range of problems that affect partners in a relationship. There is a correlation between couple relationship problems and psychiatric illness (Crowe 2004). For example, a wife's depression can be exacerbated by her husband's lack of empathy; if the husband can be helped to understand her better the depression may be relieved. It was found by Parker and Ritch (2001) that, in patients with 'non-melancholic' depression, the attitude of the partner had a significant influence on the outcome, with a worse couple relationship being associated with a worse prognosis. Again, a jealous man may, through his behaviour, make his wife even more distressed than himself; couple therapy can help to reduce the impact of the jealousy on the partner as well as to alleviate the jealousy itself.

Definition

Couple therapy is a method of treating a couple with relationship difficulties, usually by seeing both partners together. It is usually short term, although psychodynamic practitioners use a longer treatment period. It is similar to, but not identical with, couple counselling. Couple counselling was established earlier than couple therapy, having been first practised in the United Kingdom in the 1930s. It combines giving advice on practical issues, such as finance, children, and living arrangements, with a largely psychodynamic approach to understanding problems such as resentment and anger. Couple therapy, on the other hand, which dates from the late 1940s is a more radical approach, and may be based on one or more of several theories. These include psychodynamic, systemic, and cognitive-behavioural, as well as various combinations of these. 'Behavioural-systems couple therapy', the approach that I shall be highlighting here, is one example of these combined forms of therapy.

In therapy, the couple are generally seen together by a single therapist, but in some (e.g. psychodynamic couple therapy) the partners may be treated separately in parallel by two therapists who receive joint supervision. The aim of all forms of couple therapy is to make a real and lasting difference to the satisfaction and stability of the relationship.

Theory and practice of the different approaches

Let us briefly review some of the large variety of models that have been applied to couple relationships.

A central concept of the *psychoanalytic* position, (see Daniell 1985 and Clulow 2001), is that the internal (mostly unconscious) world of the two partners determines the nature of their interaction and their response to changing circumstances. This is historically based on an understanding of object relations theory (Greenberg and Mitchell 1983) but in recent years the concept of adult attachment (Bowlby 1969) has also been widely adopted. The combination of the two leads to a formulation of the couple's problems in terms of two individuals, each with their own defence mechanisms and patterns of insecure attachment, in a relationship which becomes problematic. Their difficulties can be interpreted in terms of their primitive needs and the defences, including mutual projections, which have been developed to deal with them.

Therapy aims to help the partners to become aware of these internal worlds and their origins, enabling them to reduce misunderstandings through insight and to get in touch with their own feelings and those of the partner. Transference is often interpreted. A central focus is on infantile feelings and 'repetition-compulsion' which leads to the person treating his/her partner similarly to the way he/she felt about the opposite-sexed parent (Scharff and Scharff 1997). A principal outcome is that of liberating the relationship from past adverse influences. Therapy is relatively extended and the pace of change gradual, but the improvement was found in one study to be enduring (Crowe 1978).

The *behavioural* approach (behavioural marital therapy or BMT) examines current observed and reported behaviour on the premise that the troubled couple have reached a low level of mutual positive reinforcement and are using coercive methods to try to control each other's behaviour. Stuart (1980) and Jacobson and Margolin (1979) emphasize the need for sensible negotiation of rights and duties, and work on everyday tasks to achieve this end. Two main forms of therapeutic activity take place: reciprocity negotiation (RN) and communication training (CT). In RN, the partners request changes in behaviour and negotiate how this can be achieved through mutually agreed tasks. In CT, the couple are encouraged to speak directly to each other about feelings, plans, or perceptions, and to feed back what they have heard and understood. Origins of behaviour or deeper meanings behind the partners' attitudes are not dealt with explicitly. The emphasis is entirely on change in the 'here and now' and the immediate future.

Although the behavioural and psychoanalytic models appear incompatible, they can be partly reconciled by regarding them as concentrating on different levels (conscious and unconscious) of the mind. Thus, psychoanalytic concepts, such as the internal worlds of the partners, their shared fantasies, and the need for personal insight and mutual understanding, do not necessarily contradict the behaviourist's formulation of failed mutual reinforcement and the need to negotiate everyday exchanges. As an example of their compatibility, Segraves (1982) has devised a combined psychodynamic-behavioural approach in which the underlying cause of the couple's problems is understood as relating to conflicting internal fantasies about themselves and each other. Intervention, however, is directed to helping them to understand these and increasing reality-based communication and ability to negotiate.

Aaron Beck (1988) has applied his *cognitive-behavioural* model to the problems of couples, identifying in their communication misunderstandings, generalizations, and a concentration on negative aspects of a problem—all typical of depressive thinking. His approach uses a similar therapeutic process to those which have been successful in treating depression: challenging assumptions, reducing expectations, relaxing absolute rules, and focusing on the positive rather than the negative (see chapters. . . . .).

The *systems* approach derives partly from concepts developed by family therapists, such as Salvador Minuchin (1974) and Jay Haley (1980), and partly from a more focused approach to couples, such as that of Carlos Sluzki (1978) (see chapter 18). A central concept is 'enmeshment'; an excessive involvement by one person in what is essentially the 'private business' of another. It is most acutely seen in the teenagers' struggles to separate and individuate from their parents, and the difficulty some parents have in 'letting go'. Enmeshment is closely related to the concept of intimacy. This is quite a complex issue, and often misunderstood, especially in popular parlance. Intimacy refers to four kinds of interaction: sexual, physical, emotional, and 'operational' (Crowe and Ridley 2000), of which the last refers to sharing plans and information with one's partner. Conflicts may arise over how close each partner wishes their relationship to be. Systemic therapy attempts, among other goals, to achieve an optimum 'distance' between the partners.

Another key concept is homeostasis—the tendency for partners to maintain the *status quo*, no matter what external factors may impinge on them. Negative feedback systems operate to restore the relationship following a change that could potentially alter its nature. Symptoms in one partner may form part of a negative feedback process which stabilizes an otherwise unstable relationship.

Underlying systems thinking is circular causality. In a relationship, events do not occur merely because one partner 'causes' them, but rather result from a complex cycle of interaction in which both partners participate actively. Moreover, a person's actions in a relationship stem not just from a single cause, whether in the immediate or remote past, but result from a continuing chain of causation to which both partners contribute and which affects them both. A systemic therapist would therefore not direct his therapy at one partner (e.g. using medication or individual therapy) but would expect both partners to be active participants, and both to be prepared to change.

The behavioural-systems approach

The approach selected for detailed consideration, behavioural-systems couple therapy (BSCT, Crowe and Ridley 2000), combines concepts and techniques from two theoretical models. The behavioural aspect, similar to that of Stuart (1980) and Jacobson and Margolin (1979), comprises reciprocity negotiation and communication training. The more complex systems component includes systems thinking, structural moves during the session, tasks and timetables, and paradoxical injunctions (see below).

BSCT is a practical easy-to-learn approach, widely applicable to a variety of presenting problems. It serves well as a foundation upon which the therapist can add other approaches, such as psychosexual therapy. The various components can be incorporated at different points in the therapy session. Tasks, timetables, and paradox are usually reserved for the 'message' at the end of the session, when homework tasks are being given. Negotiation, communication training, and structural moves, by contrast, are used during the session in order to alter the couple interaction at the time.

Indications and contraindications

If a relationship problem is identified by one or both partners, and they are willing to work on it, then in most cases they are suitable for BSCT. The breadth of the approach, the proven efficacy of the behavioural components, and the fact that the systemic components are suitable for those with psychiatric symptoms, allow for a wide range of positive indications. In addition, there is no limitation to the use of this kind of approach with those couples or individuals who are poorly educated, since the concepts are easily understood.

Those couples where both partners agree that they have relationship problems are highly suitable for BSCT. Where one partner is less motivated than the other, therapy is still possible providing they can both be persuaded to attend. The therapist should not, however, challenge the 'unwilling' partner too hard in the early stages, in order to avoid premature dropout.

Another indication is the situation where, perhaps in individual therapy, a patient complains repeatedly about the partner. Similarly it sometimes happens that the partner of a patient in individual therapy begins to suffer from depression or other symptoms which are attributed to the patient's therapy; again, couple therapy, accompanied perhaps by suspending the individual therapy, may help with the relationship problems.

Many problems with sexual function are suitable for couple therapy, especially where there is a disparity of sexual desire (see below), or where there is a specific phobia of sex. In some such cases, where there is an associated history of childhood sexual abuse, combined individual and couple therapy is usually the best option.

Couples in which one partner experiences depression or anxiety, especially if the symptoms are connected with relationship problems, may be suitable for couple therapy. Indeed, couple therapy was found to be more acceptable in such couples than antidepressants, and just as effective in treating the depression, in a study by Leff et al. (2000). Jealousy, as long as it is not of delusional intensity, is again suitable for couple therapy; a specific programme for this problem within BSCT has proven clinically effective (Crowe 1995). Couple therapy is one of several approaches advocated for treatment of jealousy by de Silva (1997).

There are, however, limitations to the utility of couple therapy. An acute psychotic condition in one partner is generally a contraindication, although including the partner in a psychoeducational approach is beneficial once the acute phase is over (McFarlane 2000). Severe alcohol or drug dependency problems often preclude couple therapy, because the dependent patient is unavailable psychologically and their behaviour is too inconsistent. This is unfortunate, given that in earlier and milder cases couple interventions can be useful. When psychiatric symptoms have been present long before the relationship began, individual therapy rather than couple therapy is indicated.

The most common limitation on the usefulness of couple therapy is a relationship which has gone beyond the point of no return, in that the partners are in a constant state of hostility and divorce is imminent. Here it often happens that the partner who is reluctant to end the relationship pushes for couple therapy, but it becomes clear when they first attend that the other partner wants nothing but a clean break. In these circumstances, an alternative option is mediation, a process which ideally involves both legal and counselling input for the couple (and any children involved), and which shares many features with couple therapy (Robinson 1991).

Assessment and selection

Little preselection is necessary for BSCT, except the exclusion of acute psychosis, severe substance abuse, and imminent divorce as mentioned above. Couples are referred, usually by general practitioners or counsellors, and when seen for the first time they often bring a letter of referral, giving basic details of the problem. Assessment is incorporated into the first therapy session. Several issues are considered: the ability of the partners to empathize with each other, their pattern of communication, the degree of their commitment to the relationship, their situation in the 'family life cycle' with its associated stresses, and their flexibility in responding to therapeutic interventions. This first session is therefore akin to a formal assessment, but would rarely result in the couple not being given another appointment. The main task for the therapist is to assess their motivation and their potential for responding to behavioural tasks which are given quite soon after the session begins. Even if they are not successful in this, they will often be given a more systemic intervention (see below) designed to improve their motivation and co-operation, rather than being excluded from therapy.

The process of BSCT

The components of BCST are used by therapists throughout the therapy in various combinations. However, it is more fruitful to use the behavioural interventions where the couple is trying actively to work on improving the relationship. Systems interventions are used when the situation is complex, either because of psychiatric symptoms, such as one partner becoming depressed, or because the couple are finding it hard to work together, and are sticking to their previous maladaptive behaviour.

In order to facilitate therapists' understanding and use of BSCT, we have developed the 'hierarchy of alternative levels of intervention' (ALI hierarchy). This links each type of intervention to a specific clinical situation and makes it easier for the therapist to select an appropriate level at which to work.

Figure 16.1 shows the ALI hierarchy diagrammatically. The vertical axis represents the couple's presenting problems, the horizontal axis the therapist's potential interventions. As symptoms or specific complaints about the partner's behaviour become more prominent, or as the system seems to be more rigid, so the therapist moves from a behavioural, problem-solving approach towards a more systems-orientated one (see the section on specific techniques below).

BSCT is generally short term—5 to 10 sessions over a period of 3 to 6 months. Preparation includes studying the referral letter and any other information available, and devising a formulation that could shed light on the nature of the presenting problems. The formulation will often, for example, take into account the couple's stage in the family life cycle (e.g. recent birth of a child or the 'empty nest') or a life event such as retirement or a serious illness.

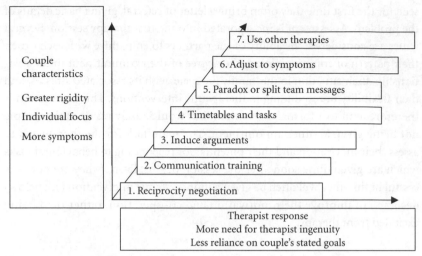

Fig. 16.1 The hierarchy of alternative levels of intervention (ALI) (after Crowe and Ridley 2000).

The formulation may include a 'hypothesis' about contributing factors, but this is not thought of as being a true explanation of the causes, but rather a means of constructing hunches and framing strategies for use in later stages of therapy. A decision is also made in relation to the level of the ALI hierarchy at which to start working.

When BSCT was first developed, it was common for therapists to be assisted by a team of observers behind a one-way screen. The main advantage of the screen is in training (see below). However, for trained therapists it has proved satisfactory to practise BSCT in the conventional consulting room; this is how most therapists work today.

Several therapeutic tasks are required in the first session:

- developing rapport with both partners, without favouring either;
- keeping reasonable control of the session (not letting one partner dominate or allowing the session to be characterized by mutual complaints);
- maintaining momentum, and
- maximizing opportunities for the couple to experience a change in their interaction

A useful initial step is to request the partners to face and talk to each other rather then addressing the therapist—the so-called process of 'decentring' (Minuchin 1974). Maintaining this configuration during the session enables the therapist to observe the couple's interactional pattern, and allows them to negotiate directly about aspects of their joint lives on which they need to achieve a compromise. Decentring also makes it possible to encourage arguments on everyday issues (stage 3 on the ALI hierarchy), which in turn helps them to reduce inhibitions about talking openly, and enables the 'weaker' partner to be more assertive. However, it is not necessary to maintain this position throughout. Other techniques, such as circular questioning (see below), in which the therapist takes a central position, may bear more fruit at other stages.

It may be difficult to preserve the decentred position, since the partners often try to address the therapist instead of each other. The therapist too may be tempted to intervene directly. One way to participate and yet remain decentred is to request the partners to ask each other questions on topics that the therapist considers relevant. For example, he/she might say: 'You seem to differ on this; I wonder if you could seek your wife's views so that we can discover what the differences are'. Again, if one partner turns to the therapist for an opinion, the therapist might reply: 'It's more important to know what your partner thinks about that. Could you ask her first?' In this way, the session continues in the decentred mode, the couple talking with each other rather than with the therapist. When partners ask the therapist for a judgement as to which of them is right, it is useful to explain that he/she is not a judge but a referee, ensuring fair play.

The therapist should try to achieve a balance between lightness and seriousness. Some partners tend to dismiss each other's concerns as 'neurotic' or 'overreacting'. The therapist should draw them away from these attitudes, without taking sides, by urging them to treat each other with more respect, or asking them both to comment on a particular issue. However, the therapist should also introduce lightness at different stages of the session, to get the couple away from pessimistic perceptions of their relationship. In the messages at the end of sessions, for example, the therapist can bring in a lighter note, perhaps by referring back to a humorous episode during the session.

Focusing on interaction rather then on individual symptoms or behavioural problems of one partner is crucial. Therapists with other backgrounds who are trained to show empathy to individual patients may find this an unappealing way to practise. However, effective couple therapy is promoted if the therapist can interrupt long-winded complaints about the behaviour of one partner, and refocus on the relationship. This is not always easy, and it is important not to be seen to be one-sided in doing it. In a similar vein, although information about the partners' histories is useful, it is better not to spend much time eliciting these, since it may distract from the therapy itself.

A couple may be concerned with serious ongoing issues, such as an extramarital affair or the imminence of divorce. These issues have to be handled with respect, but when they occupy too much time in therapy they may need to be challenged, for example, by indicating that the primary task is to improve the couple's interaction and help them to communicate more effectively on all issues, including the one they are spending time on in the session.

Another impediment to progress occurs when one partner persists in talking in long monologues as a spokesperson for both of them, while the other allows or even encourages this to occur. The more reticent partner is often the one who has psychiatric symptoms, or at least has a psychiatric label, whereas the other feels a need to take responsibility in order to help them and the therapist. One way to overcome this is to ask the 'ill' partner to speak on their own behalf, or alternatively the therapist might emphasize ways in which the 'ill' partner can help the more competent one with other issues (thus restoring the balance of power to some extent).

The therapist's own style of working may slow down momentum. It is of course essential to show accurate empathy to both partners, but when this becomes an end in itself rather than a means to improve their interaction, progress may be inhibited. Decentring (described above) or asking circular questions (see below) may be tried in order to overcome this block. Trainee therapists can be given feedback to help them to overcome this tendency to revert to traditional counselling techniques.

The partners are encouraged to communicate openly with each other, at both practical and emotional levels. Some couples are very good at the practical side, but communicate poorly on emotional matters, and their conversations may resemble a committee meeting. Issues which are not part of the 'agreed agenda', such as feelings of sadness or anger, are suppressed or ignored. In other couples there is a discrepancy between, say, a husband who is logical and self-controlled and his wife who readily expresses feelings. In both this and the 'committee meeting' situation, it is important to increase the flexibility of emotional expression. This can be done by highlighting the problem, and then encouraging the unemotional partner to speak more freely. In some couples, a planned argument on a trivial issue (see below) will provoke healthy emotional expression without the danger of raising topics which might be too sensitive.

Circular questioning derives from systems theory, and is particularly useful where the 'system' is rigid, and the therapist is struggling to produce change, or even in some cases persuading the couple that their problems are susceptible to relationship therapy. They may be demanding medical treatment for the 'ill' partner, or simply having difficulty in carrying out homework tasks. In circular questioning, the therapist assumes an active role, deliberately asking questions of one partner about the other, following the answer by a second question asking the other partner about the first one, and so on. A sequence of interaction ensues in which both partners may begin to challenge what the other has said, or they may end with a lively discussion about their relationship. Since people are less defensive when talking about others than about themselves, circular questioning can bring out information which is otherwise concealed. The usual outcome of a sequence of circular questioning is the framing of a paradoxical message (see below), which is similarly designed to unlock a rigid system.

The end of a session is something which needs to be planned, and usually involves the assignment of homework exercises (see below). These may be in the form of a negotiated set of mutual tasks (ALI level 1), a timetabled activity (level 4), or a paradox or 'split-team' message (level 5). After the next appointment is arranged, it is best for the therapist to ensure that the couple leaves the room, to prevent the dilution of the impact of the message by discussing it at length with him/her after the session is over.

Specific techniques

Reciprocity negotiation (RN)

At the first level of the ALI hierarchy (Figure 16.1), and at an early stage in a typical first session, the most commonly used interventions involve reciprocity negotiation. This form of therapy is simple to apply and to understand, and it forms a central component of behavioural couple therapy, the therapeutic approach which consistently shows the highest degree of effectiveness in controlled studies of outcome (Baucom et al. 1998).

In RN, the partners state their complaints in everyday terms. The therapist then helps them to consider how to change their interaction in order to reduce complaints and to ensure that both partners get what they want from each other without disputes. The theory behind RN is partly operant conditioning, with mutual positive reinforcement, and partly the *quid pro quo* principles of social exchange theory (Thibault and Kelley 1959). The assumption is that satisfaction in a relationship depends on each partner receiving positive reactions to their interactional behaviour ('maximum reward from minimum cost'). A corollary of this is that each partner is prepared to do things which the other finds rewarding as long as the favour is returned. Couples in difficulty reward each other at low levels or the rewards are unevenly distributed. In either case, the relationship is seen by one or both partners as unrewarding, and both may use coercive tactics to try (usually ineffectively) to motivate the other. This negative approach is particularly prone to occur in distressed couples (Weiss 1978). Moreover, it has been found that distressed couples show little positive reinforcement, much aversive interaction, and inadequate problem solving (Schindler and Vollmer 1984).

RN is a staged process. The initial step is for one partner to state a complaint. This is translated into a wish for changed behaviour, and this wish is converted into a positive task. The second partner is asked to do the same thing. The tasks become part of the couple's homework between sessions. At the end of a session, the partners should have about two tasks each to fulfil before the next meeting with the therapist. Tasks are most fruitfully based on daily life, and usually refer to activities around the house. It should also be agreed by both partners that the tasks set are both practicable and acceptable. The following case illustrates the typical process (Caroline and Douglas are a composite of three couples seen by the author).

> Caroline claims that her husband Douglas always keeps her in the dark about his life, friends, and plans. Douglas does not appreciate that she needs to know about these aspects. She says: 'You never talk, you have your head under the bonnet of the car, or you are out with your friends, or watching football . . . She is brought back to the point by the therapist because she has stated too many complaints to be used in one session. The therapist then clarifies whether Douglas is willing to share more of his plans with her, and he agrees to do so. They are asked to specify how long the 'information sessions' at home should be, and how often they should take place. Because the couple are not in the habit of talking together without complaining, the therapist asks them to practise their talk session there and then, and they do so without much difficulty, keeping to the topic and avoiding negative comments. The question then arises what Douglas would like from Caroline, because the tasks should be bilateral. He wants her to stop complaining. Since this is a negative task, the therapist decides not to use it at this stage. In any case, she may be expected to be less negative to him if the information sessions go well. He then asks them to socialize more as a couple; the therapist seizes on this as a suitable task suggesting that they organize an evening out or entertain at home at roughly fortnightly intervals.

This is a simple example of RN, and the key steps are:

- complaints become wishes;
- wishes become tasks;
- tasks are positive (if a negative task is set it is turned round so that it becomes an opposite or incompatible positive one);
- tasks are specific and preferably repeatable on a daily basis;
- tasks are reciprocal, and
- tasks are practicable and agreed upon by both partners.

Communication training

The next strategy in the ALI hierarchy is communication training. The couple are asked to converse with each other in a decentred way (see above) and their mode of communication observed by the therapist. It may, for example, be clear that the couple do not make eye contact, or converse on a purely intellectual level, or they may use monologues or rehearse old arguments.

Since Virginia Satir's (1964) pioneering contribution on family communication patterns, other workers (e.g. O'Leary and Turkewitz 1978; Olson et al. 1983) have developed communication-training programmes. Olson has emphasized positive communication skills, such as empathy, reflective listening, and supportive comments, in enabling couples (and families) to share their perceptions and changing needs.

Problems in communication encountered include lack of empathy; inability to express emotion; failing to listen; monologues with no break for feedback; one partner is the spokesman and the other is silent; mind-reading (where partner A claims to know better than partner B what is in partner B's mind); wandering off the topic; continual criticism; and the sting in the tail (where a positive comment is followed by criticism).

Communication training is a more demanding type of therapy than reciprocity negotiation. Like RN, it depends on good motivation, but it also requires a degree of verbal sophistication, flexibility, and willingness to try out new ideas.

The therapist first decentres, and asks the couple to converse about an everyday topic. A communication problem will soon emerge. The therapist then asks them to try to rephrase what they have said in a way that is more respectful to the partner, leaves more opportunity for response, and avoids misunderstandings. The therapist may encourage more mutual feedback, ask one partner not to 'mind-read' or point out that the emotion behind the message has been misread. Through these interventions the partners are helped to: speak for themselves, use 'I' at the start of the sentence; to communicate feelings to each other; using a tone of voice congruent with what they are saying; speak briefly and wait for an answer; stick to the topic; and attend to non-verbal as well as verbal aspects of communication. A case example will illustrate this approach.

> Joe, a professional experienced in public speaking was attempting to keep his wife Sandy from panicking when they hosted dinners. He gave impressive advice (without actually looking at her), saying that there was no need to worry as long as she had the food prepared exactly at the time when the wine would have been opened for the requisite 2 hours. He did not notice her quiet crying until the therapist pointed it out. Although Joe then became concerned and comforted her, he needed help to understand that, for her, his demands were stringent, and she had good reason to panic if he became impatient over the issue of 'the wine'. The therapist pointed out that Joe had not been listening very well to what Sandy had been saying, asked Sandy to speak up when she felt she needed to be heard, and encouraged Joe to listen more carefully. However, it was crucial that the therapist did not actually side with her, even though

Joe seemed unreasonable. By remaining neutral the therapist kept both partners motivated to continue successfully with the therapy. Indeed, Joe was later able to express his own insecurity and to seek Sandy's understanding.

Structural moves in session

These include raising arguments in session, reversed role-play, and 'sculpting'. The argument is the technique most frequently used, and is especially useful in couples who are inhibited or avoid expressing their differences because of one partner's sensitivity to conflict. This may be associated with a degree of depression in the sensitive partner, and is also often found in those who are inhibited sexually. The dominant partner, usually confident verbally and more socially at ease, may effortlessly take the spokesperson's role. The other partner is either reticent most of the time or spends considerable energy trying to placate the other and so reduce conflict.

The strategy is to ask them to argue over something trivial. A classic example is the issue of whether the toothpaste tube is squeezed from the bottom or the side! The topic chosen should reflect a genuine difference of opinion, but not be too serious. Issues such as religion or the education of the children might lead to dangerous rifts, with later complications if they cannot resolve them.

Having identified an issue on which they can disagree, the therapist encourages them to discuss it without inhibition, and urges the more submissive partner to participate with conviction (which may be foreign to him/her). The discussion may end with one partner giving in, but it is more satisfactory if at the end they can 'agree to differ', still respecting each other's point of view. If the exercise has been successful, a homework task may be set—to argue about another trivial matter for a prearranged time, using a timer, and to end by agreeing to differ. A further case, again taken from the author's experience, will illustrate the approach.

> Derek, an engineer married to Sarah for 32 years, had become reluctant to approach her sexually. She was outspoken and irritable, and complained bitterly about the lack of sex. He, in contrast, was quiet and diplomatic. They had had Masters and Johnson orientated sexual therapy without effect. In the third session, the therapist asked whether there was any issue on which Derek might have a different opinion from Sarah. After some hesitation, he offered the question of whether the toilet seat should be left up or down after he had used it. He thought it did not matter, while her opinion was firmly that it should be left down. They had a lively argument about it, the liveliest, according to them, in their entire marriage. The therapist encouraged Derek not to give in too quickly. Sarah expressed her admiration for the way he had argued, and later that week they had intercourse for the first time for months. The outcome was good in the longer term, their sex life became more regular, and they never lost their taste for lively discussion.

Another intervention providing a novel experience is reversed role-play. Here the partners address an issue on which they have contrary opinions, but they each assume the other's position, by changing places physically and arguing the opposite case. The exercise promotes mutual understanding. They feed back afterwards how it felt to express the opposite viewpoint and to see themselves in a new light.

A third form of intervention is 'sculpting', in which the partners position themselves and each other so as to express their perceptions of their relationship. For example, a husband who feels downtrodden might put his wife standing on a chair, with himself kneeling on the floor and her hand on his head. When her turn comes, however, she might place them both standing, embracing, and looking into each other's eyes. This contrast in perception then provides a lively topic to explore in the session and for later homework.

All these interventions in the session are designed to alter the couple's experience of their relationship. They gain experiential insight into each other and themselves, as well as trying out new modes of interaction in session, hopefully laying the foundation for subsequent change.

Timetables and tasks

Much homework is expected to be done between sessions. At the end of the session, the therapist offers the couple a message in the form of a brief review of what has been discussed, plus a homework task. This may be behavioural (arising from reciprocity negotiation, as above) or may arise from the therapist's systemic understanding of the couple. In the latter case, the task is likely to be based on an aspect of their behaviour which is perceived to be out of control. For example, in the case of a jealous husband, the couple might be asked to discuss his accusations, and for him to indulge in cross-examination, for half an hour a day, at a set time (Crowe 1995). If the subject is raised at any other time the partner is instructed to reply that she is happy to discuss it, but only at the appointed time.

A timetabled task can be applied in other situations. For instance, if the man is much more enthusiastic for sexual intercourse than the woman (Crowe and Ridley 1986), the couple is asked to compromise on a frequency for sex which is acceptable to the woman and tolerable to the man. They then agree on which night each week it will take place. This may seem artificial, but it does not have to continue for long before they can revert to a more spontaneous pattern. The advantage is that it takes the heat out of the disputes about sex, and both partners feel more satisfied. The enthusiastic one is assured that he will have sex at a predictable frequency, while the reluctant partner can relax when sex is prohibited and prepare for it when it is planned.

Timetables can be arranged for many types of behaviour. For example, if a couple regularly argue over dinner, they are asked to plan an argument to take place instead over breakfast. Timetables can also help to reduce psychiatric 'labelling' as applied to one partner's behaviour. A partner whose jealous outbursts are timetabled will be reassured that they are serious and worthy of his partner's attention, although they are clearly unwelcome to her, thus helping to 'normalize' the behaviour while controlling its frequency for the sake of the partner.

Other tasks may be more straightforward and encompass the idea of 'having fun'. In couples, especially those in midlife, who lead dull lives, a good idea might be a regular evening out.

A frequently set task is a 'talk' timetable, whereby the couple arrange a time, perhaps two or three times a week, in which they sit together without distraction for some 20 minutes to discuss a topic. This may simply be to talk about their news of the day, to debate a planned activity or to exchange feelings about something important like their son's schooling.

Although sex therapy is dealt with separately in Chapter 17, it should be mentioned here that many relationship problems have both a sexual and a non-sexual dimension. Where the sexual difficulty is predominantly to do with motivation rather than technique, couple therapy is a fruitful approach, with or without specific sexual exercises. If such exercises are needed, non-genital sensate focusing (Masters and Johnson 1970) to get the couple back into the habit of loving physical contact without the pressure of intercourse, is a suitable homework task.

Paradoxical interventions

In the event of the above interventions proving ineffective, which may occur in a couple who have a rigid way of interacting or experience many individual symptoms, paradoxical injunctions derived from systems theory (see Selvini Palazzoli et al. 1978) may be useful.

Paradox is always applied cautiously and sympathetically. It usually helps to carry out circular questioning first (see above). Having done this, a common form of paradox is 'prescribing the symptom', that is, advising the couple that it is best 'for the time being' for them to persist with the problematic behaviour (together with the partner's response) which brought them to therapy. They are offered a plausible and challenging rationale for this (a 'systemic explanation') consistent with the therapist or the therapeutic team's appraisal of the relational dynamics. An example may help to clarify the use of paradox.

Miles and Betty, a professional couple in their forties, had had a tense relationship for many years, characterized by conflicts and power struggles. These had increased since she had returned to teaching after the children had left home. He had ostensibly approved of the move, but they had begun to fight about the domestic chores. Miles would advise Betty on washing clothes, clearing the kitchen and the like. Betty, believing that her performance was satisfactory, resented his interference. Reciprocity negotiation was ineffective, and by the fifth session, the therapist was beginning to despair of helping them, especially since they were so reasonable towards each other in session. The observing team suggested a paradox in which the therapist would also 'put himself down' in order to motivate them further. This was the message:

'My colleagues have criticized me for naively leading you on to believe that an easy solution to your problem exists. In fact, they now think that, following the departure of your children, you need arguments to enliven your relationship. Therefore you should go on, Miles, picking Betty up on all that she does, and you, Betty, should resist his advice and go your own way. You will then avoid the boredom of an 'empty nest' and play out a parent–child scenario which, despite its painful aspects, is better than the realization that you are middle aged'.

This intervention exerted an immediate effect. They commended the therapist for his diligence, and asserted that the earlier therapy had not been wasted. Second, they accepted the team's view and realized that they had been trying too hard for the ideal relationship, resolving to be less demanding and critical of each other in future.

When a paradox is offered it matters little whether it is 'obeyed' or not. Rather, it is the understanding it provides which liberates the couple from the vicious circle they are in. They understand that they can have a degree of control over the seemingly hopeless situation they are in; they are partly responsible for having created the circumstances they profess to dislike; and the therapist does not seek to control them by imposing solutions.

A paradox has four elements: 1) positive connotation of the couple and their problem; 2) a description of the 'symptom' or unwanted behaviour in one partner and the reciprocal behaviour in the other; 3) a prescription of both symptom and reciprocal behaviour; and 4) a systemic reason for continuing both.

It has become less common to present a paradox boldly. It is often presented as a 'split team message' in which the therapist expresses a hope that the couple will be able to solve their problems by the previous straightforward therapeutic tasks, but that colleagues in the team have doubts, and these then form the paradoxical part of the message.

There are limits to the use of paradox. It would not be ethical or sensible to prescribe behaviour which is illegal, involves violence to self or others, or is irresponsible. Paradox is best kept in reserve until other techniques have proved ineffective, or the partners are so entrenched in their pathological interaction that no intervention makes any difference (see the ALI hierarchy, fig. 16.1)

Beyond the hierarchy

Some couples are unable to be helped in their relationship problems by any of the above techniques. No solution may be available other than to adjust to the presenting problem. This intervention has something in common with paradox, since it honestly accepts the *status quo* and reduces unrealistic expectations. It may lead logically to ceasing therapy, and also to the possible referral of one or both partners to individual therapy.

Termination

It is customary to prepare the couple for termination two sessions before the end. It is usually obvious to both the therapist and the couple when to end therapy. The problems are less pressing. The partners show a greater ability to manage their relationship without help, perhaps through longer intervals between sessions. It then becomes easy to say that 'the next session will be the last', and then at the last session to offer a follow-up meeting at the couple's discretion (sometimes referred to as 'one in the bank').

It is not always easy to finish therapy. Some couples value longer- term involvement, and this can be offered if the therapist feels that continued therapy can yield more benefits. It may extend for up to 3 years, at monthly or bi-monthly intervals. The interaction between therapist and couple changes in such cases, resembling perhaps a form of supportive therapy.

Sometimes a conflict may occur between a therapist who judges that treatment should end and a couple who wish to continue. A compromise is typically reached in which the session become more spaced out, leading eventually to termination. More common is the situation in which a couple drops out before the therapist thinks they are ready. The best that the therapist can do in these circumstances is to write or telephone offering a further appointment.

Training and supervision

In BSCT, as in all other forms of psychotherapy, supervision is crucial. It acts as a form of 'quality control' on the work of the therapist, both ethically and professionally. Supervision also guards against the risk of the therapist imposing inappropriate goals or solutions. In couple therapy, this risk is probably less than in individual therapy, since the partners can compare their relative perceptions of treatment. The possibility still exists, however, in suggestible couples; supervision is a sensible precaution.

Live supervision has always been available in BSCT, using a one-way screen and observers. Other forms of supervision are audio- or videotaping of sessions, or the traditional method in which the therapist provides an account of the session to a supervisor or supervisory group. The supervisor will examine periodically problems in treatment that derive from the therapist rather than the couple, but personal therapy is not mandatory to practise BSCT.

Other approaches to couple therapy incorporate their own recommendations for supervision. In psychodynamic couple therapy, for example, there is an interesting combination of therapy and supervision in which two therapists each see one partner in therapy, and then come together for joint supervision; this is as if the therapists themselves have a surrogate marriage which can facilitate the lessons of supervision being conveyed to the couple. In behavioural and cognitive-behavioural couple therapy training, a greater emphasis is placed on technique and knowledge than on examining therapist feelings, but personal style may also be a focus, especially in live supervision.

Factual knowledge needs to be acquired, with an emphasis on the sociology of marriage and similar relationships, as well as cultural differences, including religious and marital issues.

In training for BSCT specifically trainees need to grasp both behavioural and systems theories, and understand the strengths and limitations of alternative approaches. They should also understand the principles of both outcome and process research.

The greater part of the training is practical. Much use is made of role-play, where trainees play the part of the couple and therapist. Role-play, apart from being a good introduction to technique, also helps them to empathize with their patients. For example, they may become familiar with feelings of helplessness and frustration. It is also useful for them to 'cross sexes' when role-playing, so as to gain insight into what it feels like to be a member of the opposite sex. Therapeutic techniques practised include decentring, managing reciprocity negotiation and communication training, initiating arguments and giving timetables and paradoxical messages. Exercises may be videotaped and discussed at future training sessions.

Trainees benefit from observing experienced therapists from the beginning of their training, and can join them as observer and later as co-therapist. They will proceed to treat several couples as the lead therapist (with the team in support), and they will have observed many more during the training period.

Conclusions

There is still a dearth of outcome studies on the efficacy of couple therapy, although Baucom et al. (1998) have carried out a comprehensive review, and found that certain forms are consistently effective. Untreated couples usually experienced no improvement, whereas behavioural approaches mostly showed significant improvement, which was maintained during follow-up.

Where different forms of therapy have been compared (see Crowe 1978; Emmelkamp et al. 1984; Johnson and Greenberg 1986 and Snyder and Wills 1989) systemic, insight orientated, and behavioural treatments had similar effects except that the latter produced results more rapidly.

Couples therapy, whatever the model, is proving to be an effective way to tackle not only relationship problems but also those of a psychiatric nature, such as depression and jealousy, where there is a relationship component. It has the added advantages of being readily acceptable to the couples (Leff et al. 2000), and of reducing the labelling of many forms of behaviour as 'psychiatric' (thus avoiding stigma).

There are few contraindications for couple therapy, which may be used as a treatment in its own right, or as an adjunct in treating conditions, such as depression, schizophrenia, and sexual dysfunctions. If it can also contribute to reducing the high current divorce rate, it will have played a part in lessening the sum of human suffering.

References

Baucom, D. H., Shoham, V., Mueser, K. T., Daiuto, A. D. and Stickle, T. R. (1998). Empirically supported couple and family interventions for marital distress and adult mental health problems. *Journal of Consulting and Clinical Psychology*, 57, 39–46.

Beck, A. T. (1988). *Love is never enough*. Harper and Row, New York.

Clulow, C. (ed.) (2001). *Adult attachment and couple psychotherapy*. Brunner Routledge, London.

Crowe, M. J. (1978). Conjoint marital therapy: A controlled outcome study. *Psychological Medicine*, 8, 623–36.

Crowe, M. (1995). Management of jealousy in couples. *Advances in Psychiatric Treatment*, 1, 82–8.

Crowe, M. (2004). Couples and mental illness. *Sexual and Relationship Therapy*, 19, 309–10.

Crowe, M. J. and Ridley, J. (1986). The negotiated timetable: A new approach to marital conflict involving male demands and female reluctance for sex. *Sexual and Marital Therapy*, 1, 157–73.

Crowe, M. and Ridley, J. (2000). *Therapy with couples: A behavioural-systems approach to couple relationship and sexual problems*. (2nd edn). Blackwells, Oxford.

Daniell, D. (1985). Marital therapy, the psychodynamic approach. In *Marital therapy in Britain*, Vol 1 (ed. W. Dryden). Harper and Row, London.

De Silva, P. (1997). Jealousy in couple relationships: nature, assessment and therapy. *Behaviour Research and Therapy*, 35, 937–85.

Emmelkamp, P. M. G., van der Helm, M., MacGillavry, D. and van Zanten, B. (1984). Marital therapy with clinically distressed couples: A comparative evaluation of system-theoretic, contingency contracting and communication skills approaches. In *Marital interaction: Analysis and modification* (ed. K. Hahlweg and N. Jacobson). Guilford, New York.

Greenberg, J and Mitchell, S. (1983). *Object relations in psychoanalytic theory*. Guilford, New York.

Haley, J. (1980). *Leaving home*. McGraw Hill, New York.

Jacobson, N. S. and Margolin, G. (1979). *Marital therapy: Strategies based on social learning and behavioral exchange principles*. Brunner/Mazel, New York.

Johnson, S. M. and Greenberg, L. S. (1985). Differential effects of experiential and problem-solving approaches in resolving marital conflict. *Journal of Consulting and Clinical Psychology*, **53**, 175–84.

Leff, J., Vearnalls, S., Brewin, C. R., Wolff, G., Alexander, B., Asen, E., Dayson, D., Jones, E., Chisholm, D. and Everett, B. (2000). The London depression intervention trial. Randomised controlled trial of antidepressants v. couple therapy in the treatment and maintenance of people with depression living with a partner: Clinical outcome and costs. *British Journal of Psychiatry*, **177**, 95–100.

Mc Farlane, W. (2000). Psychoeducational multi-family groups: Adaptations and outcomes. In *Psychosis: psychological approaches and their effectiveness* (ed. B. Martindale, A. Bateman, M. Crowe and F. Margison). Gaskell, London.

Masters, W. H. and Johnson, V. E. (1970). *Human sexual inadequacy*. Little, Brown, Boston.

Minuchin, S. (1974). *Families and family therapy*. Tavistock, London.

National Statistics Office (1998). *Population trends*. HMSO, London.

Oakley, A. (1974). *The sociology of housework*. Blackwell, Oxford.

O'Leary, K. D. and Turkewitz, H. (1978). The treatment of marital disorders from a behavioural perspective. In *Marriage and marital therapy* (ed. T. J. Paolino and B. S. McCrady). Brunner/Mazel, New York.

Olson, D. H., McCubbin, H. I., Barnes, H., Larsen, A., Muxen, M. and Wilson, M. (1983). *Families: What makes them work?* Sage, Los Angeles.

Parker, G. and Ritch, J. (2001). The influence of an uncaring partner on the type and outcome of depression. *Journal of Affective Disorders*, 66, 207–214.

Rabin, C. (1996). *Equal partners: Good friends*. Routledge, London.

Robinson, M. (1991). *Family transformation through divorce and remarriage*. Tavistock, London.

Rodgers, B. and Pryor, J. (1998). *Divorce and separation; the outcome for children*. Joseph Rowntree Foundation, York.

Satir, V. (1964). *Conjoint family therapy*. Science and Behavior Books, Palo Alto, CA.

Scharff, J. S. and Scharff, D. E. (1997). Object relations couple therapy. *American Journal of Psychotherapy*, **51**, 141–73.

Schindler, L. and Vollmer, M. (1984). Cognitive prospectus in behavioural marital therapy: Some proposals for bridging theory, research and practice. In *Marital interaction*, (ed. K.Hahlweg and N. Jacobson). Guilford, New York.

Segraves, R. T. (1982). *Marital therapy: A combined psychodynamic-behavioural approach*. Plenum Press, New York.

Selvini Palazzoli, M., Boscolo, L., Cecchin, G. and Prata, G. (1978). *Paradox and counter-paradox*. Jason Aronson, New York.

Sluzki, C. E. (1978). Marital therapy from a systems perspective. In *Marriage and marital therapy*, (ed. T. J.Paolino and B. S. McCrady). Brunner/Mazel, New York.

Snyder, D. K. and Wills, R. M. (1989). Behavioural vs. insight—oriented marital therapy: Effects on individual and interpersonal functioning. *Journal of Consulting and Clinical Psychology*, **57**, 39–64.

Stuart, R. B. (1980) *Helping couples change*. Guilford, New York.

Thibault, J. W. and Kelley, H. H. (1959). *The social psychology of groups*. Wiley, New York.

Weiss, R. L. (1978). The conception of marriage from a behavioural perspective. In *Marriage and marital therapy*, (ed. T. J. Paolino and B. S. McCrady). Brunner/Mazel, New York.

Recommended reading

Bancroft, J. (1989). *Human sexuality and its problems* (2nd edn). Churchill Livingstone, Edinburgh. (An excellent all-round textbook for sexual problems and their treatment.)

Clulow, C. (ed.) (2001). *Adult attachment and couple psychotherapy*. Brunner Routledge, London. (An up-to date reappraisal of the psychodynamic approach to couple therapy.)

Crowe, M. (2005). *Overcoming relationship problems: A self-help guide using cognitive-behavioural and systemic techniques*. Constable and Robinson, London.

Crowe, M. and Ridley, J. (2000). *Therapy with couples: A behavioural-systems approach to couple relationship and sexual problems* (2nd edn). Blackwell, Oxford. (A clear and practical account of the behavioural-systems approach to couple therapy, with many case examples.)

Dryden, W. (1985). *Marital therapy in Britain*, Vols. 1 & 2. Harper and Row, London. (A good guide, despite its age, to the various marital therapy approaches, with case examples of each.)

Robinson, M. (1991). *Family transformation through divorce and remarriage*. Tavistock Routledge, London. (A well researched discussion of divorce, remarriage and step-families.)

Chapter 17

Sex therapy

John Bancroft

Since the third edition significant changes have occurred in treating sexual dysfunction in men. This has mainly resulted from the introduction of drugs, such as sildenafil (Viagra), which have had a major impact on the treatment of erectile dysfunction, and other pharmacological agents aimed at improving low sexual desire (e.g. apomorphine) or treating premature ejaculation (e.g. serotonin re-uptake inhibitors) (Leiblum and Rosen 2000). Female sexual dysfunction has not benefited in the same way, but not for want of trying. Vigorous attempts to find the 'Viagra for women' have brought new attention to the sexuality of women, and not a little controversy (e.g. Tiefer 2001; Bancroft 2002a). This has reinforced the idea that women's sexuality differs from men's in being less genitally focused and more readily inhibited, either by a greater vulnerability to the latter or a wider range of inhibiting factors in women. Testosterone has been reported as effective for low sexual desire in women, but only, it would seem, in those who may be more sensitive to its effects (Bancroft 2002b).

To some extent these pharmacological developments have led to a retreat from sex therapy, but it remains relevant, either because it can produce more long-lasting changes without the need for continued medication or because it complements drug treatment. More attention is now required to identify criteria for using sex therapy on its own or in combination with pharmaco-therapy.

While Masters and Johnson (1970) continue to be a major influence in the field of sex therapy, modifications incorporating the principles of cognitive behaviour therapy and other theoretical approaches have emerged in the last few years (e.g. Heiman 2000; Pridal and LoPiccolo 2000). In my experience as a sex therapist, however, I have found little need to change the basic principles, in particular, the specific behavioural steps used. However, as shown in this chapter, I am now taking a more theoretical approach to defining the rationale of sex therapy. Masters and Johnson (1970) introduced this form of sex therapy without any theoretical basis; and it became widely used because it proved effective. The interface between psychological mechanisms and physiological sexual response, fundamental to any psychologically based therapy, has, however, received little attention. The exception has been the work of Barlow and his colleagues (see Cranston-Cuebas and Barlow 1990 for a review). On the basis of experimental studies they concluded that distraction from attention to sexual stimuli was a key factor in failure of sexual response. In recent years, we have adopted a theoretical approach, the Dual Control (DC) model, which postulates that sexual arousal and response depend on interaction between excitatory and inhibitory systems in the brain, which are relatively independent of each other (Bancroft and Janssen 2000). The model also emphasizes individual variability in the propensity for both sexual excitation and sexual inhibition. A psychometrically validated method of measuring such variability has been established for men (Janssen et al. 2002) and a comparable method for women (Graham et al. in press). The DC model has shown itself relevant to sexual dysfunction and high-risk sexual behaviour in men, and promises to be equally pertinent in women. In this chapter, we will explore how this DC model may influence the approach to sex therapy. However, as with Barlow's earlier model, research demonstrating its clinical value has yet to be done.

The DC model highlights the role of inhibition of sexual response as an adaptive mechanism for most people. Some individuals, however, have high or low propensities for inhibition which are maladaptive. The model also postulates that individuals vary in their propensity for sexual excitation. Again, the normal part of the range is adaptive, where as lower and higher parts can be problematic. Most physical factors which adversely affect sexual response probably do so by lowering the capacity for sexual excitation. Psychologically mediated processes which have an adverse effect, on the other hand, are likely to involve inhibition or distraction. We need to distinguish between 'inhibitory tone' (e.g. as responsible for maintaining a flaccid penis), and increased inhibition in response to the immediate situation ('reactive inhibition'). Sexual arousal and response results, it is assumed, from a reduction in 'inhibitory tone', combined with an increase in excitation. Problematic inhibition may result from high baseline levels of inhibitory tone which are consequently more difficult to reduce sufficiently, or 'reactive inhibition', which counteracts the required reduction, or a combination of the two. Individuals with high 'inhibitory tone' are likely to be vulnerable to sexual dysfunction, compounded by an accompanying increase in 'reactive inhibition' in sexual situations due to concern about performance failure.

The instrument developed to measure excitation and inhibition proneness in men (Janssen et al. 2002) is comprised of three scales—SES, a measure of sexual excitation proneness, and two inhibition scales—SIS1, described as 'inhibition due to the threat of performance failure' and SIS2, 'inhibition due to threat of performance consequences'. High SIS1 may reflect high inhibitory tone as well as a tendency to react to sexual situations with 'reactive inhibition' due to the threat of failure, whereas SIS2 reflects the likelihood of reactive inhibition in a variety of contextual situations, such as a problematic relationship. SIS1 also reflects the impact of distraction on sexual response (see Bancroft and Janssen 2001 for more comprehensive consideration of these postulates). The instrument for assessing excitation and inhibition in women (SESII-W; Graham et al. in press) produces two scales—sexual excitation and sexual inhibition, and a range of sub-scales. Examination of these scales in relation to female sexual dysfunction is at an early stage.

The above theoretical framework is relevant to sex therapy in a number of ways. Sex therapy, as we define it here, may reduce 'reactive inhibition' by identifying factors relevant to the individual or the couple, which invoke inhibition, and finding ways to make them less threatening. Problems stemming from relationship difficulties are in this category; similarly, problems resulting from poor communication between the couple, and misinformation about normal sexual response. In people with long-standing negative attitudes about sex, involvement in sexual activity may also provoke inhibition. Therapy aims at modifying negative attitudes. High 'inhibitory tone' may be more difficult to resolve. However, by adopting a structured approach, the compounding effects of 'reactive inhibition' due to 'fear of failure' can be reduced, and ways of adapting to the high inhibitory tone established, by changing expectations and seeking modified behavioural and sexual response goals. Inhibition-reducing drugs, such as phentolamine, may be usefully combined with sex therapy in these cases (Bancroft and Janssen 2001).

Problems resulting from low excitation proneness may be more difficult to modify with sex therapy. Drugs such as sildenafil (which acts peripherally to enhance genital response) and apomorphine (which acts centrally to enhance sexual desire) may be combined with sex therapy in such cases (Bancroft and Janssen 2001).

Sex therapy is primarily intended for helping couples, but the principles can be used in individual therapy, as we will consider later. This account applies to heterosexual couples, but is also relevant to same-sex couples.

Goals of sex therapy

Goals can be defined as

- helping each person to accept and feel comfortable with his or her sexuality

- helping the couple to establish trust and emotional security during sexual interaction
- helping the couple to enhance the enjoyment and intimacy of their lovemaking

These goals are achieved by identifying factors, either in the current relationship, or in the person's past experience, which are related to inhibition of sexual response and need resolution before change is likely, and helping both partners to understand the relevance of these factors.

It is noteworthy that these goals do not encompass reversal of specific sexual dysfunctions. Certain interventions may be used, for example, for premature ejaculation or vaginismus, but otherwise the expectation is that normal sexual function (in terms of sexual desire, arousal, or genital response) will return once the above goals are achieved. The exception is impairment of sexual function not dependent on psychological processes (e.g. neurological or vascular disease). In such cases, the above goals of sex therapy may still be appropriate, even though expectation of change in sexual response is lessened as a result of the physical impairment. Alternatively, sex therapy in these cases may be combined with medication. The decision to prescribe, however, is not necessarily made at the outset, but may become more obviously appropriate in the early stages of sex therapy.

Assessment

There are three stages to assessment; first, to facilitate the decision whether sex therapy is appropriate; second, to identify issues that are relevant to the sexual problem; and third, to determine whether medication or other treatments are required. Assessment begins at the initial consultation, and continues at the start and during the course of therapy.

Although, when couples present for sex therapy, one of them is usually regarded as having the problem, both partners need careful assessment.

Is sex therapy appropriate?

The therapist considers whether, on the basis of the initial assessment, the couple presents with a difficulty that may benefit from sex therapy, (keeping in mind that this may not become clear until treatment is underway). One key factor is the likelihood of the couple being able to work together in improving their sexual relationship. In several respects, the best way to answer the question is to seek the decision of each partner, once they have been fully informed and the implications of treatment are clear to them.

The motivation of the partners is crucial. In order to assess it adequately, the therapist conveys in detail what the treatment involves, and what its goals are.

The need for an 'adult–adult' relationship in which the couple are willing to carry out the recommended tasks, is stressed. (This issue has been discussed in Chapter X). The therapist makes this point explicitly at the outset and returns to it repeatedly, either because expectations of medical care in the past have regarded the clinician as the 'parental expert' or the tendency to slip into a passive-dependent role needs to be thwarted. Failure to work collaboratively with the therapist is associated with poor outcome.

Consistent with this alliance is the need to agree on frequency and timing of treatment sessions, and the opportunity for the couple to carry out assignments, free from distractions, such as moving house, changing jobs, or having mother-in-law to stay! It may be useful to postpone treatment until circumstances are more or less stable.

The therapist should evaluate carefully, at the initial assessment, the mood of each partner. Moderate or severe depression in either may be a barrier to effective participation. Consideration should be given to treating the depression itself first. A related issue is the use of antidepressant medication, which may be contributing to the sexual problem; the most predictable side effect is impairment of orgasm or ejaculation. When this is central to the couple's presenting problem, consideration should be given to withdrawing the antidepressant, reducing the dose, or changing to a medication less likely to have sexual side effects.

Assessment during therapy

Once the decision to proceed with therapy is made, another assessment session is arranged, focusing on each person separately. While one partner is being interviewed, the other reads a copy of our counselling notes (see Bancroft 1989, pp. 535–544), which describe the sequence of steps to be followed, plus basic principles and information about normal sexual response. Each interview aims to establish rapport and to explore earlier significant sexual experiences, not necessarily within the current relationship, but of possible relevance to the current problem. Each partner also shares their reactions to the counselling notes, since this can shed light on their attitudes and expectations. With both interviews completed, the first behavioural assignment is described and the next appointment scheduled.

It is unrealistic to expect the couple to feel secure enough, either with therapist or with each other, to reveal all relevant sensitive material at the start. Fortunately, an advantage of this treatment approach is its effectiveness in revealing and illuminating key underlying issues as treatment proceeds. The key elements of the therapeutic process are:

1 Clearly defined tasks are given and the couple asked to attempt them before the next session.

2 Those attempts, and any difficulties encountered, are examined in detail.

3 Attitudes, feelings, and conflicts that make the tasks difficult to carry out are identified.

4 These are modified or resolved so that subsequent achievement of the tasks becomes possible.

5 The next tasks are set, and so on.

The key is the nature of the tasks set. These are well suited to identifying relevant issues. The tasks are behavioural in nature, and sufficient in some cases to produce change.

Should other methods, such as medication, be used?

This decision may need to wait until a more thorough assessment has been done, often during the course of therapy.

The process of assessment, in its totality, can be defined as looking at each partner through three conceptual windows.

We look through the first window at the current relationship and the couple's life generally. Are there circumstances that might increase inhibition of sexual interest and response, such as stress, fatigue, or unresolved conflict in the relationship?

We examine each partner's sexual history through the second window. To what extent has either reacted to difficulties at various stages in his or her sexual life with inhibition, or, using our DC model, shown a propensity for sexual inhibition? Such individual differences may result from genetic or early learning factors, or sexual trauma.

We look through our third window at whether physical, pharmacological, or hormonal processes might be interfering with sexual response.

Therapy is usually effective if there are identifiable issues through the first window contributing to reactive inhibition. The effect of treatment when problems are detected through the second window is more difficult to predict. We may be dealing with long-established patterns. If the history reveals that these have recurred but not persisted, remission is clearly possible. Long-standing problems may be more difficult to shift, but may benefit from adjusting the couple's expectations to take these into account. Problems identified through the third window are unlikely to improve from sex therapy alone, but may do so if combined with medication or other treatment modalities. The impact of a physical process, such as a drug side effect, or a hormonal or neuro-physiological condition is commonly magnified by the individual's psychological reaction to it. This presents a challenge in assessment.

Questionnaire methods to measure proneness to inhibition or impaired arousability, as described earlier, can be a helpful adjunct to the assessment process.

Process

The treatment process under consideration here is a combination of behavioural assignments, to demonstrate problem areas, and psychotherapeutic techniques. We will now consider the requisite steps, the issues likely to emerge, and psychotherapeutic interventions to deal with them.

Part one: non-genital

Self-assert and self-protect

Each partner is instructed to practise 'self-asserting'; and 'self-protecting'; that is, making clear what 'I' like, prefer, or find unpleasant or threatening. Stating 'I would like . . .' or 'I feel hurt because . . .' instead of the more usual 'shall we . . . ?' or 'why don't you . . . ?' is often difficult. A typical pattern of communication, regarded as unselfish, is to think or guess what the partner would like rather than putting one's own wishes first. Given a reluctance to hurt the partner, misunderstandings remain concealed and persist. However, providing both partners state their own wishes, there is no cause for resentment, and differences are resolvable through open negotiation. The therapist advises the couple to try this style of communication in relatively trivial, non-sexual situations before applying it to sexual tasks (e.g. 'I would like a cup of tea, would you?'). The emphasis on 'I' is maintained throughout the course of treatment.

An explicit agreement is made to ban attempts at genital or breast contact or intercourse, to reduce performance anxiety and to allow both partners to feel safe. Moreover, the non-genital stages of interaction are valuable in their own right. The couple is advised to have no more than three sessions of lovemaking before their next appointment to avoid too much happening; only a limited agenda can be properly covered at each meeting. The couple decides when those sessions occur, and the more spontaneous they are the better. However, they are specifically asked to alternate in who suggests and initiates a session.

Stage 1. The sexual goal is *touching your partner without genital contact and for your own pleasure*. The person who has 'invited' touches the partner's body, other than out-of-bounds areas, in whatever way is pleasurable; the objective is for the toucher to enjoy the experience. The partner being touched has only to 'self-protect' (i.e. to say 'stop' if anything unpleasant is felt). Roles are then reversed. They should not expect to get strongly aroused, but may do so. The goal is to relax and enjoy the process.

The therapist ensures that these steps have been carried out with both partners feeling secure before proceeding to Stage 2.

Stage 2. '*Touching your partner without genital contact, for your own AND your partner's pleasure*' is now the goal. Sessions continue as before, the couple alternating as initiator, with active touching carried out by one person at a time. Now, however, the person being touched gives feedback as to what is enjoyable as well as what is unpleasant. The toucher can use this information to give as well as to receive pleasure. The ban on genital contact persists.

A partner may express concern that the ban on intercourse will lead to unresolved sexual arousal and frustration. Reassurance is given that such frustration only arises if one is not clear what to expect. Explicit acceptance of limits obviates this. However, if after a session either partner is left aroused and in need of orgasm, it is acceptable to masturbate on one's own.

Issues often identified during stages 1 and 2

1 *Misunderstandings about the treatment and motivation for change.* Precise 'homework' assignments quickly demonstrate whether the couple are motivated. Difficulty in understanding and accepting the assignments may stem from a failure to clarify the process adequately or from a negative therapeutic relationship. In some cases, treatment style conflicts with personal values about sex. Commonly, a couple complains that they dislike the lack of spontaneity— the feeling that the therapist not only instructs them but looks over their shoulder at what should be an intimate affair. Although these feelings are perfectly understandable, it is gently pointed out that treatment is a temporary bridge between the problematic situation and a rewarding sexual relationship. The therapist also explains that these two stages are of sufficient relevance to a normal sexual relationship that it would be worthwhile for any couple to go through them periodically. Finally, it is pointed out that the therapist's initially very directive role will change as treatment proceeds and control is progressively handed back to the couple.

Difficulty in accepting the approach may reflect a reluctance in one or both partners for treatment to succeed. At an unconscious level, they seek failure to justify ending the relationship, accepting a non-sexual one, or engaging in an extramarital affair.

Accepting limits, especially on genital touching and intercourse, is commonly problematic and discussion of such problems is often fruitful. Although failure to understand the rationale behind the limits may be responsible for this difficulty, other factors are more often involved. The limits may be rejected on the grounds, for example, that it is unreasonable to expect a 'normal' man to become sexually aroused and not be able to follow through to orgasm.

2 *Issues of trust and interpersonal security*. The above steps are an effective way to test trust. Breaking the ban or reluctance to maintain it, when examined closely, provides valuable information to the therapist. It may emerge that one partner believes the other is unlikely to keep to the ban once sexually aroused. This is an opportunity to inform the couple that feeling secure is key to the realization of sexual pleasure in any relationship. An essential feature of sexual pleasure is being able to let one self go and become 'sexually abandoned'. At the same time, this involves letting down one's defences, making one vulnerable to hurt or rejection in the process. By the same token, exposing oneself in this way, in the presence of another person, and surviving the experience emotionally unscathed, has a binding effect. Thus, insecurity is likely to impair sexual enjoyment. This insecurity may reflect a fear of rejection or sexual betrayal.

3 *Other problems in the relationship*. Common unresolved problems stem from the couple's difficulty in adapting to each other. The most crucial form is veiled resentment, often related to the bartering aspect of a sexual relationship, when one partner is participating in sex at least partly to gain non-sexual benefits from the other in return. When a sexual problem occurs in such a relationship, 'sabotaging' therapy may occur when one partner feels that the sexual difficulty is being 'resolved' before the other conflicts have been addressed.

4 *Relevant sexual attitudes*. Stage 1 is often difficult for couples (especially the male partners) to grasp as they are conditioned to think of sexual touching as a way of giving rather than receiving pleasure. This may lead to recognition of deeply held attitudes such as 'you should only enjoy sex if you are giving pleasure to your partner', which may be central to the overall problem. This 'touching for one's own pleasure' is often a fruitful first step in treatment.

The requirement for clear alternation of who invites and initiates sessions is an effective way to elicit problematic attitudes, such as the widely held belief that 'nice' women do not initiate sex, they wait for their partners to do so. Providing structured, therapist-sanctioned alternation helps the reluctant initiator to overcome this difficulty.

The emphasis on 'self-assertion' and 'self-protection' often elicits relevant problems in the non-genital phase. The idea that it is alright to assert one's wish to do something specific sexually, confident that one's partner will indicate clearly if it is unacceptable, is revolutionary for many couples. Implementing this principle, which is relevant to close relationships in general, avoids 'second guessing' what one's partner wants. The common assumption that 'you should know what your partner enjoys' is challenged, and the importance of ongoing effective communication is highlighted. One should not assume that because your partner enjoyed some specific activity on one occasion, it would be equally enjoyable on another.

Part two: adding the genital component

As an introduction to this second part, the therapist provides basic information about the anatomy and physiology of sexual response in both sexes, emphasizing those aspects, which are often misunderstood and underlie dysfunction. This account is given no matter how sophisticated the couple since it is rare for them to be entirely knowledgeable. This is also an opportunity to introduce the vocabulary to be used for discussion and reporting back once genital contact begins.

Before giving the next set of assignments, the therapist stresses how important it is for the couple to maintain changes achieved in the non-genital phase. It is all too easy, when genital contact becomes involved, for either or both partners to lose sight of open communication, the principles of 'self-assert and self-protect' and the value of 'touching for one's own pleasure'.

Stage 3. Touching with genital contact included. Alternating who initiates and who touches still applies, with genital areas and breasts now included. Continuing with enjoyable types of non-genital touching identified in stages 1 and 2 is still emphasized. The couple is encouraged to explore positions to engage in genital touching. Questions about their reactions to different positions may reveal important feelings and attitudes.

Communicating what one finds pleasurable about being touched often presents difficulties at this stage. The therapist emphasizes that pleasure will vary, making open communication important. Their goal is to relax and enjoy the experience. The partner being caressed may or may not become sexually aroused; if ejaculation or orgasm happens it does not matter and need not signify an end to the session.

The couple have been warned from the outset about the 'spectator role'— that is, being a detached observer of oneself or one's partner rather than an active participant. This detachment generates performance anxiety and interferes with normal sexual response. A useful method is to concentrate on the local sensations experienced while touching or being touched (i.e. 'lend oneself to the sensations'). If this fails a simple relaxation procedure can be used. If that does not work, the partner is informed that a problem has arisen and a temporary halt requested. The session is resumed after a short period of conversation or other activity.

If premature ejaculation is a problem, the couple are introduced at this stage to the 'stop–start' (Kaplan 1975) or 'squeeze' (Masters and Johnson 1970) techniques and asked to incorporate either of them into the touching sessions (see references for details of these techniques). In the case of vaginismus, gradual vaginal dilatation with finger or graded dilators are used. The timing of these techniques and whether they should be carried out individually or conjointly, will be discussed further in relation to individual therapy.

Stage 4. Simultaneous touching with genital contact. Touching is now done by both partners simultaneously. They need to be comfortable with preceding stages before trying this. Difficulty in taking the initiative and asserting oneself is often identified at this point.

Stages 5 and 6. Vaginal containment. Once genital and body touching is progressing well and the man is achieving a reasonably firm erection (or has started to gain control over ejaculation during manual stimulation), the couple includes some vaginal containment. The use of these structured assignments has helped discourage the couple from regarding lovemaking as divided into foreplay and intercourse. During a touching session, the woman adopts the female superior position and, at some stage, introduces the penis into her vagina. This not only makes it easier for her to guide the penis but also allows her partner to remain in a 'non-demand position', with the woman in control and able to stop or withdraw whenever she wants. The couple are instructed to try vaginal containment for short periods at first, without other movement or pelvic thrusting, concentrating on the sensations of the 'penis being contained', or the 'vagina being filled'. Duration is gradually extended. Stage 5 merges into Stage 6 when movement and pelvic thrusting are allowed, although initially for brief periods only. Again, one is breaking down the 'big divide' between foreplay and intercourse which, if present, provokes anxiety whenever the step from one to the other is anticipated. Instead, behavioural steps merge into intercourse.

The couple are encouraged to practise stopping at any point at the request of either partner to counter the common notion that love play once begun must continue until its physiological conclusion, with no escape *en route*. The confidence that either partner can say 'stop' at any stage, without incurring anger or hurt in the other, is a basic feature of a secure sexual relationship. The couple are also advised to experiment with different positions and methods of touching to discover what satisfies them.

Issues often identified during Part 2

5 *Performance anxiety*. Concern that one will not respond sexually or will lose one's response is a common feature of sexual problems. As indicated

earlier, this is one way in which inhibition of sexual response can be invoked. The use of graded behavioural steps helps to identify when 'performance anxiety' arises. It may become clear that the partner's expectations aggravate this problem. The therapist counsels that there is no need for any particular response to occur at any particular time; that for many couples responses occur on some occasions but not others; that pleasure and intimacy can occur without genital response, as experienced during the first part of the program; that each partner should feel free to call a halt at any stage without worry that the other will become upset or critical.

6 *Ignorance or incorrect notions about sex.* Misunderstandings are numerous. A widely held notion is that an erection indicates advanced sexual arousal and the need for intercourse, at a time when the woman may only be starting to respond. Erection is obvious to both partners whereas internal vaginal lubrication, the equivalent female physiological response, may pass unnoticed. Both occur, however, with similar speed and often as the initial response to sexual stimulation. The belief that if an erection subsides it cannot return needs correction. Another common belief is that 'normal sex' means simultaneous orgasm. The notion that a woman should experience orgasm from vaginal intercourse alone and that failure to do so or that reliance on clitoral stimulation indicates an abnormality needs to be dispelled. The therapist stresses that only a small proportion of women on a minority of occasions achieve orgasm without clitoral stimulation, either by themselves or their partners.

7 *Negative sexual attitudes.* These are usually acquired during childhood or adolescence and precede the current relationship. They often involve a sense that sex is a 'necessary evil' for the purpose of reproduction, and that sexual pleasure is somehow wrong, at best justified if it gives pleasure to one's partner. There may be distaste about the exchange of 'bodily fluids' during sex, which highlights the close proximity of the sexual and excretory organs (often felt by fastidious people). A concern about 'loss of control', because it is wrong or frightening, may occur. This may be a particular problem with the experience of orgasm, which may disrupt the sense of intimacy which makes sexual activity 'respectable'. Many other examples could be provided.

Negative attitudes following childhood sexual abuse or other unpleasant early sexual experiences, are particularly difficult to deal with. The trauma and fear caused by the abuse may result in an understandable aversion or fear of subsequent sexual contact. The sense of betrayal by someone in a position of trust may make it difficult for the abused person to feel emotionally secure in a sexual relationship. Another form of damage results from the notion that a normal child is asexual. The assumption by the adult world that the child was sexually unresponsive may confuse the child who, at some stage of the abusive experience, was aware of pleasurable feelings. This may lead to a sense of being not only 'sexually abnormal' but also responsible for the incident. Such a belief makes sexual response difficult to accept later in life. The abused person is often anxious that her partner in adult life will blame or reject her if she discloses the abuse.

The psychotherapeutic component

So far we have considered the behavioural steps and factors making them difficult to carry out that are commonly identified. What else can the therapist do to help resolve these issues, reducing inhibitory responses in the process and allowing the couple's basic sexual responsiveness to be mutually enjoyed?

Facilitating understanding

Understanding why one has difficulty in carrying out a particular task is crucial since this leads to reappraisal of the problem and related beliefs and values. For example, a woman is reluctant to initiate lovemaking, since she feels this reflects improper enthusiasm. She then feels vulnerable to her partner's refusal should she try to initiate, and this is yet further evidence of the behaviour's unacceptability. Men are conditioned differently. Rejection of their advances is much less threatening to self-esteem. By re-examining such assumptions, acknowledging, for example, that it is appropriate for the woman in an established relationship to take initiatives, and that both partners may decline at any time, 'cognitive restructuring' follows. This allows previously unsettling behaviour to be dealt with. Cognitive restructuring may continue implicitly, and between therapy sessions. What can the therapist do to facilitate it?

- Setting further tasks may help to focus on the specific problem. Identifying differences in the reaction to two subtly different tasks may be particularly useful. Why, for example, is it easier to show a partner what is unpleasant than to convey what is pleasurable?

- Encourage examination and labelling of feelings experienced at the time of difficulty (e.g. fear, guilt, disgust, or anger).

- Encourage the couple to work out an explanation for their difficulty in carrying out a task. Therapists may offer likely hypotheses and evidence for and against, but the couple should be encouraged to provide their best explanation. This underlines the educational aspect of the therapy process, and the importance of the couple understanding why they overcome a problem; they can then take a similar approach should problems recur. However, this is not likely to happen unless the couple experience a need to understand their difficulty. The therapist can facilitate this by asking the couple to repeat the homework assignments. 'Socratic questioning' may help; the therapist, with an explanation in mind, poses questions encouraging the couple to view the situation in a particular way. He may offer more than one explanation, inviting the couple to consider the options.

The cognitive restructuring inherent in the above may suffice to remove obstacles to behavioural change. If not effective, other strategies are available.

Making explicit the couple's commitment to specific changes

As obstacles are encountered, the therapist establishes explicitly whether the couple want to surmount them (e.g. does the woman want to be able to initiate? Does the man who finds his partner's genitalia repellant want to overcome that feeling?) In other words, is the obstacle a 'resistance' regarded by the patient as unwelcome (i.e. ego-alien), or is it consistent with his or her value system and therefore not in need of change?

Setting further behavioural steps designed to tackle the difficulty

Problems stemming from fears of a 'phobic' kind require a graded approach. A woman who fears vaginal entry is asked briefly to insert her own finger a short distance. Such a small step does not overwhelm the patient with anxiety, and she can then be encouraged to 'stay with' the anxious feelings until they start to subside.

Reality confrontation

The causes of anxiety can be challenged on a rational basis. When anxiety is ego-syntonic and the patient does not wish to overcome a resistance, the therapist considers how incompatible this is with the aims of treatment. Thus, a suggestion that masturbation may help to achieve orgasm or overcome inhibition may be rejected on the grounds that it is an unacceptable behaviour. An alternative approach should be offered, possible if she is in a sexual relationship. If, on the other hand, a patient objects to touching his or her partner's genitals, the incompatibility of this position with the goals of treatment is emphasized.

Patients may need to be confronted with other inconsistencies between belief and action or between their understanding and the facts. For instance, the view that 'normal' women experience orgasm from vaginal intercourse has to be challenged. Giving permission, often a crucial role, may involve the therapist pointing out inconsistencies between the values of patient and therapist.

Facilitating the expression of emotion

Negative emotions play a part in establishing or maintaining sexual dysfunction. The first step in coping with these is to label them correctly. Resentment within the relationship is common. More often than not, its appropriate expression is required before it resolves. The therapist assists in three ways: (1) educates the couple about ways that unexpressed emotions adversely affect them and about benefits of appropriate expression; (2) helps the couple to identify instances when unexpressed emotions are likely to cause problems; and (3) encourages the couple to work out adaptive ways to communicate feelings.

A final general series of points on the psychotherapeutic component follows. As mentioned earlier, a common reason for a couple's reluctance to carry out an assignment is inadequate understanding of its purpose or lack of confidence in the therapist and his approach. These aspects are particularly pertinent in the initial stages before a sound therapeutic alliance has been forged. The rationale of therapy may need to be clarified more than once. It is often better understood after the first attempts at the behavioural assignments. The couple are told that treatment recommendations are based on common sense, not magic. The therapist carefully explains why an assignment is necessary and the patient is encouraged to seek clarification of any matter that is ambiguous or uncertain. This not only allows the patient to voice doubts about therapy, but also highlights its educational function.

Other relevant non-specific features include reassurance, promoting hope, showing warmth and empathy, reinforcing specific behaviour by responding to it with pleasure or praise, and 'inoculating against failure' by preparing the couple for possible setbacks so that when they do arise, they will not feel discouraged but rather make constructive use of them.

These strategies have no special mystique. Obviously, there is considerable scope for expertise, and therapists will vary not only in their initial aptitude but also in their capacity to learn from experience. Therapists from different backgrounds may find training and experience with other types of therapy helpful in dealing with the psychotherapeutic component, provided, that the 'adult–adult' quality of the patient–therapist relationship is maintained.

Individual therapy

Whatever the advantages of couple therapy, circumstances may only allow for working with the individual alone; it may even be the most suitable option. This obviously applies to people without partners, and to those with partners who are unwilling to participate. Such refusal is relevant since it implies a negative relationship, or at least lack of commitment to the relationship, which may be central to the sexual problem. Individual treatment in such cases is only indicated if there is a clear-cut goal which does not depend on the co-operation or even involvement of a partner. For example, the person with inhibited sexual attitudes or who feels uncomfortable with his or her body and sexual responses comes into this category. Other examples include vaginismus (the woman is unable to allow anything to enter her vagina, such as tampons, her own, or the doctor's examining finger) and the inability to experience orgasm during masturbation in men or women. Sometimes, when erectile difficulties or premature ejaculation are marked, occurring even during masturbation, individual therapy may be worthwhile.

Should we work with such a person individually when the partner is prepared to co-operate in couple therapy? We should keep an open mind about this. In women with vaginismus, especially those with marked phobic features or personality problems, individual therapy may usefully precede or even obviate the need for couple therapy.

Having decided to work with a person rather than a couple, the behavioural programme is usually more varied. However, goals of treatment in many cases are related to 'increasing comfort with one's body' and self-touching and exploration, comparable to stages 1, 2, and 3 of couple therapy are appropriate. Sexual aids like vibrators may assist, particularly in helping women to experience orgasm for the first time. Their place in couple therapy remains less certain.

Anxiety about the other sex or the likelihood that the opposite-sex parent played a role in reinforcing negative attitudes points to the advantages of an opposite-sex therapist.

Whereas the behavioural programme in individual therapy requires more planning, psychotherapeutic tactics are similar to those used in couple therapy. Obvious differences in the one-to-one relationship do exist; extra care, for instance, should be taken to avoid dependency.

Clinical illustrations

Jeff and Amanda

Jeff, 62, and Amanda, 32, had recently married after a 9-year relationship. Jeff presented with erectile problems and difficulty ejaculating intra-vaginally.

His history included a childhood marred by emotional and physical abuse. He described himself as having a 'tainted view of sex'. He first married when aged 20, attracted by his wife's 'normal' family. He regretted the marriage from an early stage. Having children was a major issue; she wanted several, he did not. He would pretend to ejaculate inside her. After they had two children, sexual activity declined markedly.

Jeff suffered from long-standing depression and had received a variety of antidepressants continuously for 15 years.

Amanda described the relationship as good but felt that sex presented 'a wall' between them. She wanted to feel closer sexually and was keen to have a child. She had stopped taking oral contraceptives 6 months previously, and had found herself more easily sexually aroused since. Jeff felt he was too old and not healthy enough to have another child.

Jeff's history revealed significant factors through all three 'windows'. Through the first window was continuing difficulty in their current relationship, which was, in part, related to the child issue. A clear history of Jeff's negative attitude to sex going back to his childhood was obvious through the second window. He did not feel comfortable about enjoying sex. There was also the potentially relevant point about 'pretending to ejaculate' with his first wife. Was this a manifestation of a long-standing ejaculatory difficulty or did it reflect a long-standing conflict over having children? The use of antidepressants was seen through the third window. To what extent was his ejaculatory difficulty due to drugs like sertraline and fluoxetine that Jeff had been taking?

Before starting sex therapy agreement was obtained from Jeff's psychiatrist for a trial withdrawal of sertraline; bupropion, an antidepressant which he had also been taking, which is not associated with sexual side effects, would be continued. With no consequent worsening of his depression, a 'limited contract' (five session) course of sex therapy was started. An agreement was also negotiated to avoid pregnancy for 6 months.

During stages 1 and 2, Jeff experienced a distinct reduction in 'performance anxiety'. He had difficulty initially touching for his own pleasure; giving Amanda pleasure was in the forefront of his mind. After a while, he enjoyed and valued the touching ('it was a lot of fun') since he was able to dissociate this non-genital touching from the negative aspects of sex he associated with sexual intercourse. Amanda felt at first that the assignment was artificial and 'forced', but then found that touching 'made me feel close'. She had difficulty keeping to the limits, and was quite aroused by the end of these early sessions. Jeff, interestingly, found himself wondering 'what's coming next' when Amanda touched him, an indication of his concern about her 'breaking the ban' and putting pressure on him to respond.

As they continued with stage 2, both of them felt aroused. They 'broke the ban' on one occasion, with Jeff touching Amanda's vulva. This resulted in her having a series of orgasms, whereas Jeff lost his erection. Following this, Jeff was reluctant to initiate further sessions. At the next meeting with the therapist, they were asked to move on to stage 3 and genital touching, with Jeff paying particular attention to when and why he started to feel any performance anxiety, given that there was still a clear ban on vaginal entry. He was also instructed not to attempt to ejaculate. They progressed well over the next few sessions. Jeff revealed, however, that he had difficulty communicating verbally during the sessions, and was instructed to practice talking. This was clearly related to his negative attitudes about sex. He was also prescribed sildenafil to enhance his erections, while still maintaining the ban on vaginal intercourse. He had tried the drug in the past but without benefit. This time, taking the sildenafil initially made him feel greater performance anxiety, but this settled down. Amanda then started to express distress about her wish to have a child.

The couple continued to make good progress, with Jeff's sexuality much improved. The combination of medication (i.e. sildenafil) with sex therapy worked well. Longer-term improvement, however, will probably depend on resolving the issue about having a child.

How can this treatment be viewed from our theoretical perspective? Jeff completed our questionnaire during the early assessment. He had a high SIS1 score (a measure of propensity for inhibition due to the threat of performance failure) suggesting a high inhibitory tone and susceptibility to performance anxiety. His SIS 2 score (inhibition due to the threat of performance consequences) was moderately raised, consistent with his 'reactive inhibition' associated with Amanda's wish to get pregnant. His SES, (propensity for sexual excitation) was somewhat low, reflecting his age and possible effects of medication or other health issues. Sex therapy was effective in enabling them as a couple to deal with Jeff's performance anxiety, and this had the added benefit of enabling the sildenafil to be more effective at improving his low arousability. Therapy also achieved cognitive restructuring of negative sexual attitudes and beliefs which had been a barrier to sexual pleasure, with consequent reduction of reactive inhibition during sexual activity.

Mary and Peter

Mary and Peter had lived together for 4 years. Mary complained that she only experienced orgasm during masturbation, not during intercourse. A crucial issue arose when the stage 1 assignment was presented. Peter doubted he could accept the ban on genital touching and intercourse. The rationale was carefully explained a second time. Notwithstanding, he feared that he would become sexually aroused during a session and felt he could not be held responsible for what might ensue. Once aroused, he expected to continue with intercourse. He attributed this to his 'normal maleness'. Would he be in danger of raping his partner if he became aroused? Peter admitted this was unlikely.

He conceded he had been able to accept limits during courting days, before they started to have intercourse.

Asked if she would lose control were she to become aroused, Mary replied negatively. Both were confronted with the stereotypes of the controlled woman and the uncontrolled man. Offered a reasoned argument that such stereotypes were imposed by societal not biological forces, Peter was asked if he preferred to see himself as a 'sexual animal' and did he feel more masculine as a result. What did control mean to Mary? She described how, given her insecurity during lovemaking, she was unable to let go. Could this be relevant to her orgasmic difficulty? Peter felt that it probably was. With the importance of feeling safe in a sexual relationship highlighted, Peter agreed to accept the limits of Stage 1.

This couple revealed highly relevant attitudes in their reaction to the initial behavioural assignment, which helped to explain why Mary was probably, though unwittingly, inhibiting her arousal and orgasm.

Jane and Bob

Jane and Bob, both 25 and married for 3 years, had stopped all sexual activity when Jane found herself unable to touch Bob's genitals. After participating without difficulty in stages 1 and 2, a key issue arose during stage 3, once genital touching was on the agenda. Jane felt a strong feeling of disgust but could not explain it. The therapist suggested that her disgust might be a mixture of attraction and repulsion (an interesting idea, with therapeutic value, as it allows for a positive component of an otherwise negative emotion). Jane was then requested to define the difference between touching Bob's penis, and other parts of his body she was prepared to touch. After an unconvincing attempt to do so in terms of texture and shape, she was asked what it meant to be disgusted by something Bob found pleasurable. She then expressed the fear he would lose control if she made him aroused. Bob was surprised at Jane's lack of trust.

Following this session, Jane began to touch Bob's penis, although initially she felt mildly nauseous while doing so. Over the following 2 weeks she began to enjoy her own genitals being touched, a new experience, and described feeling aroused. She was, however, still reluctant to touch Bob's penis more than briefly. Why was she able to enjoy being touched but hesitant to give Bob his pleasure. She felt confident she herself would not lose control but expected Bob to do so when he approached orgasm. What did this loss of control mean to her and, what consequences did she fear? She described the break in communication that occurs when partners are approaching and experiencing orgasm. The break constituted a threat to her; she needed to remain in contact. She was invited to describe other situations where a similar break in communication might occur—such as, Bob falling asleep. This was not a concern because she knew she could wake him if necessary. Asked how the timescale of Bob going to sleep compared with his reaching orgasm, she acknowledged with surprise that the latter 'time out' was, by comparison, brief.

This couple illustrates how a behavioural assignment can, with appropriate inquiry, expose relevant attitudes and beliefs which are difficult to sustain when they are clearly identified and challenged (a clear example of cognitive restructuring). Mary's 'reactive inhibition', invoked by the threat of 'losing contact' with Bob when he was experiencing orgasm, may be similar to Jane's need to feel that the situation was under control. It may also, however, reflect a long-established tendency for Mary to feel that sex was justified if it involved expressions of love and intimacy, which were threatened by the departure from 'intimacy' that Bob's orgasm entailed.

Some practical considerations

Although sex therapy varies in duration, 12 sessions over 4–5 months is typical. The therapist adjusts to the particular needs. Treatment begins weekly with the interval between sessions extended once major issues like unexpressed resentment, communication problems, or undue passivity have been dealt with. The last two or three sessions are spaced out over a few months so that the couple have an opportunity to consolidate their progress and cope with any setback before termination.

Open-ended arrangements about length of treatment are best avoided. A specified number of sessions are agreed on at the outset with the proviso that progress will be assessed and a decision made on that basis whether to continue for longer. In cases with reasonable prospects, a contract of 10 sessions with scope for a further 2–4 is sensible. A couple's ability to benefit is usually evident by the fourth session. Hawton and Catalan (1986) found that early response to treatment predicted a good outcome, whereas couples that drop out usually do so around the third or fourth session. Where the therapist is uncertain about prospects at the outset (e.g. a partner is ambivalent about the relationship or overt hostility makes collaboration unlikely), a limited contract of three or four sessions is advisable, and the couple told that further treatment would depend on progress made.

Masters and Johnson (1970) advocated a dual-therapist (male and female) team, but this requires justification on economic grounds. Although superior results using two therapists rather than one were not shown in early controlled studies (Bancroft 1989), advantages are obvious: both male and female points of view are represented and collusion between therapist and one partner more easily avoided. Moreover, one therapist can remain more objective while the other is interacting with the couple. Against this, the co-therapist relationship is not necessarily easy, making the choice of co-therapist crucial. Co-therapy requires time outside treatment sessions for adequate discussion between therapists. Co-therapy is definitely a valuable model for training provided that the experienced therapist does not monopolize.

In the case of therapy with an individual, guidelines are elusive since objectives and the nature of the therapist's involvement vary more. However, similar principles apply.

Training

Because of its psychosomatic nature, sexual dysfunction has causal factors of a medical type in a substantial proportion of cases. For this reason, sex therapy is best provided in a setting with access to medical expertise. Once these medical aspects have been clarified, however, features of a suitable therapist are determined more by personality, experience, and training than by a particular professional background. In my experience as a trainer, doctors, psychologists, social workers, nurses, and marriage guidance counsellors have all proved effective therapists.

Training often starts with the co-therapist format described above. In addition, regular supervision groups in which continuing case management is discussed are essential. Role-playing, in which the trainee takes the role either of the patient or the therapist, can be particularly illuminating in such sessions.

Conclusion

Sex therapy is indicated for problems of wide-ranging complexity. At one extreme, a behavioural programme with little therapist intervention will suffice; at the other, considerable psychotherapeutic skills are required. Most cases fall between these extremes. The basic framework is, however, similar across the range. This is of undoubted advantage to the novice.

References

Bancroft, J. (1989). *Human sexuality and its problems*. 2nd edn. Churchill Livingstone, Edinburgh.

Bancroft, J. (2002a). The medicalization of female sexual dysfunction. *Archives of Sexual Behavior*, 31, 451–455.

Bancroft, J. (2002b). Sexual effects of androgens in women: Some theoretical considerations. *Fertility and Sterility*, **77**(Suppl. 4), S55–S59.

Bancroft, J. and Janssen, E. (2000). The dual control model of male sexual response: A theoretical approach to centrally mediated erectile dysfunction. *Neuroscience and Biobehavioral Reviews*, **24**, 571–579.

Bancroft, J. and Janssen, E. (2001). Psychogenic erectile dysfunction in the era of pharmacotherapy: A theoretical approach. In *Male sexual function: A guide to clinical management*, (ed. J. Mulcahy) pp. 79–89. Humana Press, Totowa, NJ

Cranston-Cuebas, M. A. and Barlow, D. H. (1990) Cognitive and affective contributions to sexual functioning. *Annual Review of Sex Research*, **1**,119–161.

Graham, C. A., Sanders, S. A. and Milhausen, R. R. Assessing propensity for sexual inhibition and sexual excitation in women: Development of the SESII-W. *Archives of Sexual Behavior*, in press.

Hawton, K., and Catalan J., (1986) Prognostic factors in sex therapy. *Behaviour Research and Therapy*, **24**, 377–385.

Heiman, J. R. (2000) Orgasmic disorders in women. In *Principles and practice of sex therapy*. 3rd edn (eds. S. R. Leiblum and R. C. Rosen) pp. 118–153. Guilford, New York.

Janssen, E., Vorst, H., Finn, P. and Bancroft, J. (2002). The Sexual Inhibition (SIS) and Sexual Excitation (SES) Scales: I. Measuring sexual inhibition and excitation proneness in men. *Journal of Sex Research*, **39**, 114–126.

Kaplan, H. S. (1975). *The new sex therapy*. Bailliere Tindall, London.

Leiblum, S. R. and Rosen, R. C. (2000). Sex therapy in the age of Viagra. In *Principles and practice of sex therapy*. 3rd edn (eds. S. R. Leiblum and R. C. Rosen) pp. 1–16. Guilford, New York.

Masters, W. H. and Johnson, V. E. (1970). *Human sexual inadequacy*. Churchill, London.

Pridal, C. G. and LoPiccolo, J. (2000) Multielement treatment of desire disorders: Integration of cognitive, behavioral and systemic therapy. In *Principles and practice of sex therapy*. 3rd edn (eds. S. R. Leiblum and R. C. Rosen) pp. 57–84. Guilford, New York.

Tiefer, L. (2001) Arriving at a 'New View' of women's sexual problems: Background, theory and activism. In *A New View of women's sexual problems* (eds. E. Kaschak and L. Tiefer) pp. 63–98. Haworth, Binghampton.

Recommended reading

Bancroft, J. (1989). *Human sexuality and its problems*. 2nd edn. Churchill Livingstone, Edinburgh. (A comprehensive text covering all aspects of sexual behaviour, problems and treatment.)

Hawton, K. (1985). *Sex therapy: A practical guide*. Oxford University Press, Oxford. (A useful, concise and practical text.)

Heiman J. R. and Meston C. M. (1997) Empirically validated treatment for sexual dysfunction. *Annual Review of Sex Research*, **7**, 148–194. (A comprehensive review of the literature on controlled outcome studies of psychological treatments.)

Kaplan, H. S. (1975). *The new sex therapy*. Bailliere Tindall, London. (A balanced and eclectic account; particularly recommended are chapters on psychological causes and basic principles of treatment.)

Leiblum, S. R. and Rosen, R. C. (ed.) (2000). *Principles and practice of sex therapy.* 3rd edn. Guilford, New York. (A multi-author text covering most aspects of treatment.)

Masters, W. H. and Johnson, V. E. (1970). *Human sexual inadequacy.* Churchill, London. (A classic text, albeit a little dated, on the various forms of sexual dysfunction.)

Chapter 18

Family therapy in the adult psychiatric setting

Edwin Harari and Sidney Bloch

The term 'family therapy' covers a variety of approaches. At one extreme it is a method drawn from one or more of a range of theoretically based schools that seek to help an individual patient who presents with a clinical syndrome. At the other extreme family therapy is a way of thinking about psychotherapy in general; the intervention may involve the individual alone, the nuclear family, or an extended network, but the focus is the relationships between people. According to this view, psychopathology reflects recurring, problematic interactional patterns among family members and between the family, and possibly, other social institutions, and may include doctors and helping agencies. Midway between these two positions is one that views the family as acting potentially as a resource or as a liability for an identified patient; different interventions are thus needed to enhance the positive effects of family relationships as compared with those that seek to minimize or negate their noxious effects. As we will elaborate in this chapter such a range of interventions makes it tricky to define and research family therapy.

Historical and theoretical developments

The family has long been recognized as a fundamental unit of social organization in the lives of human beings. Regardless of the specific pattern of family life, the foundational narratives, myths, legends, and folklore of all cultures emphasize the power of family relations to mould the character of the individual and serve as an exemplar of the moral and political order of society.

In the past 150 years, new academic disciplines, among them anthropology, sociology, and social history, have devoted much attention to the diverse forms of family structure and function found in different cultures at various historical periods. Constrained perhaps by Western medicine's focus on the individual patient, psychiatry has been tardy in formulating

Based on our chapter on family therapy in *Oxford textbook of psychotherapy*, edited by G. Gabbard, J. Beck, and J. Holmes. Oxford University Press, Oxford, 2005.

a view of the family other than as a source of genetically transmitted diseases, hence the emphasis on inquiring about the prevalence of mental illness among relatives.

Scattered through Freud's writings are interesting comments about marital and family relationships and their possible roles in both individual normal development and psychopathology (Sander 1978). Freud's description of unconscious processes, such as introjection, projection, and identification, explained how an individual's experiences could be transmitted across the generations in a family. Freud's successors elaborated on his formulations, for example, in 1921, J. C. Flugel published the first detailed psychoanalytic account of family relationships (Flugel 1921).

Strongly influenced by the work in the United Kingdom of Anna Freud, Melanie Klein, and Donald Winnicott, the child guidance movement devised a model of one therapist working with the disturbed child and another with the parents, most often the mother on her own. The two clinicians collaborated in order to recognize how the mother's anxieties distorted her perception and handling of her child, which compounded the child's own developmental anxieties. This work, however, was conducted by psychiatric social workers and only a minority of psychiatrists.

Proliferation of 'schools'

Transgenerational

Things took a different turn in the United States. There, Ackerman (1958), who coined the term 'family therapy' in the 1950s, had introduced the idea of working with the nuclear family of a disturbed child using psychodynamic methods. An interest in working with the family, including two or more generations, arose concurrently in several psychiatric centres. Most of the pioneers of so-called 'transgenerational family therapy' were analysts who used many of the concepts of object relations theory that they recast into their own conceptual language.

Thus, Murray Bowen (1978) in his work with psychotic children found that their capacity to differentiate themselves emotionally from their families (especially from mother) while retaining a sense of age-appropriate emotional belonging was impaired by the legacy of unresolved losses, trauma, and other upheavals in the lives of parental and grandparental generations. Bowen also devised the genogram, a schematic depiction of family structure, with a particular notation for significant family events; this forms a standard part of contemporary family assessment in clinical practice (see figure 18.1).

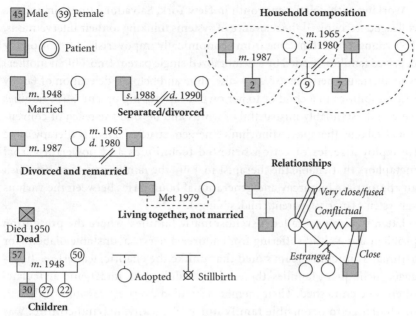

Fig. 18.1 Genogram conventions.

Boszormenyi-Nagy and Spark (1984) in their contextual therapy also addressed this transgenerational theme by describing how family relationships between generations and between adults in a marriage were organized around a ledger of entitlements and obligations; this conferred on each person a sense of justice about their position. This, in turn, reflected the experience in childhood of neglect or sacrifices made on a person's behalf for which redress was sought in adult life.

Systems oriented

Bowen had also introduced the principles of systems theory into his work with families. A system may be defined as a set of interrelated elements that function as a unity in a particular environment. General systems theory (GST) was propounded in the 1940s by the German biologist, Ludwig von Bertalanffy (1968); he outlined the principles by which any system (inanimate, animate, or ideational) can be described. Key concepts of GST are hierarchy, the emergence of new properties in the transition from one level of organization to another, and formulations derived from thermodynamics, which describe the exchange of energy between the system and its environment. A family may be considered a partially open system that interacts with its biological and sociocultural environments.

Working with delinquent youth in New York, Salvador Minuchin and his colleagues recognized the relevance of systems thinking to their interventions. The youngsters often came from economically impoverished, emotionally deprived families, headed by a demoralized single parent (most often mother) who alternated between excessive discipline and helpless delegation of family responsibilities to a child or to her own disapproving parent. Such families were understandably mistrustful of words and beyond the reach of conventional 'talking' therapies. Minuchin's emergent structural family therapy came to deploy a series of action-oriented techniques and powerful verbal metaphors that enable the therapist to 'join' the family, and to re-establish an appropriate hierarchy and generational boundaries between the various subsystems (marital, parent/child, siblings).

Later, treating so-called 'psychosomatic families' where the presenting problem was a child suffering from anorexia nervosa, unstable diabetes, or asthma, Minuchin's team noted that unlike the chaotic, leaderless disengaged 'delinquent families' these, while middle class, intact, and articulate, often were enmeshed. Their members avoided overt expressions of dissent or challenge to ostensible family unity. Typically, marital conflict was detoured through the symptomatic child, resulting in maladaptive coalitions between parent and child, or between grandparent and child, the inclusion of third parties (e.g. a helping agency) into family life. All this led to a loss of appropriate boundaries. Because words were used to avoid change in these well-educated families, Minuchin and Fishman (1981) again looked to actional strategies to challenge their unspoken fears of conflict and change.

Jay Haley's (1976) Strategic Therapy combined aspects of Minuchin's model with ideas of the psychotherapist, Milton Erickson; his hypnotherapy techniques had skilfully exploited the notion that a covert message lurks behind overt communication that defines the power relationship between people. This applies to a patient's ties with his family and their professional helpers.

Another important series of theoretical developments took place in Palo Alto, California, where a group of clinicians gathered around the anthropologist Gregory Bateson (1972) in the 1950s. In his fieldwork, Bateson had noted two relational patterns:

1 symmetrical, in which each participant's behaviour induces the other to do more of what they were already doing as equals. Power struggles in a marriage or between parents and an adolescent, arguments over compliance with medication or family conflict preceding psychotic relapse or an alcoholic binge exemplify such symmetrical escalation;

2 complementary, in which participants arrange themselves such that, for example, one is dominant and the other subordinate. The doctor–patient relationship or the parent–child relationship often is of this type, while a pattern of rigid complementarity characterizes the marriages of many patients suffering from chronic anxiety states, agoraphobia, and chronic dysthymia.

The ability to switch from complementary to symmetrical patterns and vice versa, and to alternate between dominant/subordinate and co-equal positions at different times and on various matters are skills that the Bateson approach teaches. It views psychopathology as the product of people getting stuck in once relevant but now dysfunctional modes of relating and problem solving. Bateson's group also noted that implicit in communication were tacit, nonverbal 'metacommunications' that defined the relationship between the participants. Contradiction or incongruence between these two levels when each message carried great persuasive, moral, or coercive force to the recipient formed part of what they labelled a 'double-bind'. When combined with a tertiary-level injunction that forbade escape from the field of communication, this double-bind was proposed as a possible basis for schizophrenic thinking (Bateson et al. 1956, 1962).

Systems oriented: further developments

All these aforementioned system-oriented approaches assume that the family is a system observed by the therapist. However, therapists are not value neutral. As described, in some models they take an active role in advocating and orchestrating specific changes in accordance with a preconceived model of family functioning. Yet these models ignore therapists' biases as well as the relevance of their relationships with families. This probably reflected the determination of certain American family therapists to distance themselves from psychoanalytic theory, and also led them to neglect the family's history, how it altered during the life cycle, and the relevance of past notable events.

In response to these criticisms there was a move away from the here-and-now, problem-focused approach that had characterized most behavioural and communicational views of psychopathology. The Milan school (Selvini-Palazzoli et al. 1980; see pp. 62–64 in the section on course of therapy), whose founders were all psychoanalysts, developed circular questioning, a radically new method of interviewing families. Furthermore, observers behind a one-way screen formulated hypotheses about the family-plus-therapist system and its relevance to the clinical process. A Norwegian group (Andersen 1991) developed the 'reflecting team dialogue' in which, following a therapy session, the family could observe the therapists discussing their problem, possible causes, and unresolved factors, which might have led them to seek certain solutions they had persevered with despite obvious lack of success, while neglecting alternative solutions.

Postmodern developments

Family therapists also began to consider that families might be constrained from experimenting with new solutions to difficulties because of the way they had interpreted their past experiences or internalized the explanatory narratives of their family, the expert's, or society at large.

This led to a shift from regarding the family as a social system defined by its organization (i.e. roles and structures) to a linguistic system. According to this view, the narrative a family relates about their lives is a linguistic construction that organizes past experience and relationships, and their significance, in particular ways. Other narratives are excluded from consideration. When a family with an ill member talks to health professionals, conversations are inevitably about pathology (a problem-saturated description). The participants ignore times when the problem was absent or minimal, or when they successfully confined it to manageable proportions. A different story might be told if they were to examine the context and relationships that might have led, or could still lead, to better outcomes.

A number of narrative, social constructionist, or solution-focused approaches (these overlap to a degree) make use of these concepts (De Shazer 1985; Anderson and Goolishian 1988; White and Epston 1990). Philosophically, they align themselves with postmodernism, a movement that challenges the idea that there is a basic truth or grand explanatory theory known only to experts.

Criticism of systems approaches

Many criticisms of the above systems approaches to family therapy have been levelled. These include: disregard of the subjective and intersubjective experiences of family members; neglect of the family's history; denial of unconscious motives that influence individuals in a relationship; although people are reciprocally connected in a family system the power they exert on one another is not equal (this is highlighted particularly in the problem of violence against women and in various types of child abuse); inequality and other forms of injustice based on societal attitudes towards differences in gender, ethnicity, class, and the like, are uncritically accepted as 'givens'; minimizing the role of therapeutic relationship, including attitudes family members develop towards the therapist and her feelings towards each of them and to the family as a whole.

This critique has led to an interest in integrating systems-oriented and psychoanalytic concepts, particularly those derived from object relations theory. Attempts at a general level are those of Flaskas and Perlesz (1996), Braverman (1995), and Cooklin (1979), and the feminist perspective (Luepnitz 2002); specific disorders such as schizophrenia (Ciompi 1988), "psychosomatic" illness (Stierlin, 1989) and anorexia nervosa (Dare 1997) have also been targeted. One variant of integration is John Byng-Hall's (1995) masterful synthesis of attachment theory, systems thinking, and a narrative approach.

A further criticism of systems-oriented therapies is their minimizing the impact of material reality, such as physical handicap or biological forces, in the cause of mental illness, and socio-political phenomena, such as unemployment, racism, and poverty. These are obviously not merely the result of social constructions or linguistic games. The distress they inflict are real in the extreme.

The 'psychoeducational' approach, 'family crisis intervention', and 'family-sensitive practice' have evolved in the context of the burden that schizophrenia places on the family, and the potential for responses of members to influence the course of the illness. This has paved the way for a series of interventions: educating the family about what is known regarding the nature, causes, course, and treatment of schizophrenia; providing the family with opportunities to discuss their difficulties in caring for the patient and to devise appropriate strategies; clarifying conflict in the family not only about the illness but also about other issues; regularly evaluating the impact of the illness on the family as individual members and collectively; helping to resolve other conflicts not specifically related to the illness, but which may be aggravated by the demands of caring for a chronically ill person (Magliano et al. 2005).

This type of work may be carried out with several families meeting together. Whatever the case, promising results have been achieved in reducing relapses and frequency of hospital admission (McFarlane et al. 1995). The limitations of psychoeducational programs for psychiatric disorders and vulnerability to relapse after a psychotic episode have been shown to reflect the emotional climate of the family. It is noteworthy that these potentially disruptive patterns of interaction often are not detectable by the clinician who interviews the patient alone rather than observing him in the context of a family interview (Thompson et al. 2000). Furthermore, the difficulties therapists encounter working with such families vary at different phases of treatment.

While the conventional view claims critical comments are significantly correlated with relapse, it also appears that, at least in some patients with bipolar disorder, a comparative excess of genuinely positive and supportive comments by family members may also be associated with relapse (Rosenfarb et al. 2001).

Family crisis intervention, initially devised for families with a schizophrenic relative but since applied to other clinical states, operates on the premise that deterioration in mental state or a request by the family to hospitalize a member may well reflect a change in a previously stable pattern of family interaction. Convening an urgent meeting with patient, spouse, and other key family members, even in a hospital emergency centre, is associated with a reduced rate of admission (Langsley et al. 1969).

Cognitive-behaviour approaches

While integrating some concepts from systems, postmodern, and psycho-educational approaches, cognitive behaviour therapy emphasizes the importance of identifying and directly modifying dysfunctional ideas and behavioural patterns of family members. When families are in distress they frequently perceive each other's reactions (behavioural and emotional) in a distorted way, which may in turn elicit counterproductive reactions. Persistent deleterious cycles are set up in which family members continually misperceive and/or misinterpret one another and react accordingly.

Therapy aims to help family members correct their selective negative biases, negative attributions of one another, negative predictions, dysfunctional assumptions, and unrealistic standards. Cognitive behaviour therapists work to help family members increase positive behavioural changes, engage in pleasurable activities, and improve communication and problem-solving skills (Epstein and Schlesinger 2003).

Indications for family therapy

Notwithstanding the application of these various approaches in adult psychiatry for at least three decades, indications remain ill defined compared with other forms of psychotherapy. Moreover, controversy has dogged the subject. This is not altogether surprising. Pioneering family therapists acted perhaps with a touch of hubris when claiming that their innovative approaches were suited to most clinical conditions. Ambitiousness rode high. With the passage of time, a more balanced view evolved that encompasses the notion that a systemic context is advantageous in assessing and treating any psychiatric problem, although it is not axiomatic that family therapy will be the treatment of choice (or even indicated).

We should bear in mind that family therapy is a *mode* of psychological treatment, not a unitary approach with one central purpose. One only has to note the diversity of theoretical models we discussed earlier, with their corresponding variegated techniques. Attempts to link indications to specific models have proved ill advised and contributed little to the field overall.

It has also become clear that conventional diagnoses as listed in DSM-IV or ICD-10 do not serve well as a source to map out indications for family work. DSM-IV has a minimal section, the so-called V diagnoses, covering 'relational problems', which are not elaborated upon at all (American Psychiatric Association 1994). All we are told is that the problem in relating can involve a couple, a parent–child dyad, siblings, or 'not otherwise specified'. ICD-10 ignores the relational area entirely.

In mapping out indications, we need to avoid the complicating factor of blurring assessment and therapy. A patient's family may be recruited in order to gain more knowledge about his diagnosis and subsequent treatment. This does not necessarily lead to family therapy. Indeed, it may point to marital or to long-term supportive therapy. Thus, we need to distinguish between an assessment family interview and family therapy *per se*.

Finally, a typology of family psychopathology that might allow the diagnostician to differentiate one pattern of dysfunction from another and identify appropriate interventions accordingly is elusive. Here, empirical evidence is inconclusive and clinical consensus lacking. An inherent hurdle is determining which dimensions of family functioning are central to creating a family typology (Bloch et al. 1994). Communication, adaptability, boundaries between members and subgroups, and conflict are a few of the contenders proffered (we offer our own classification below).

It does not help that there are no clear associations between conventional psychiatric diagnoses and family type (Friedmann et al. 1997). Efforts to establish links, such as an anorexia nervosa family (Minuchin et al. 1978) or a psychosomatic family (Clarkin et al. 1979) have not been fruitful. Similarly, work in the area of the family and schizophrenia (e.g. Bateson et al. 1956 and Bowen 1978) has not yielded durable results. Instead, research supports the view that no particular type of family dysfunction differentiates between specific types of mental illness (as designated on Axis 1 of DSM-IV). Rather, having a mentally ill family member acts as a general stressor on the family that may lead to impaired functioning across a range of family-related activities (Epstein and Schlesinger 2003). Consistent with the systemic view, such illness-induced family dysfunction may aggravate the course of the illness or complicate its management.

What follows is our attempt to distil past clinical and theoretical contributions, particularly the work of Walrond-Skinner (1978) and Clarkin et al. (1979). There are many ways to cut the pie; resultant categories are not mutually exclusive entirely given the considerable overlap in clinical practice; and a particular family may require family therapy based on more than one indication. We also must stress that family dysfunction is obvious in certain clinical situations but more covert in others, and often concealed by a specific member's clinical presentation. Six categories emerge:

1 The clinical problem manifests in explicitly family terms; the therapist readily notes family dysfunction. For example, a marital conflict dominates, with repercussions for the rest of the family or tension between parents and an adolescent child dislocates family life with everyone ensnared in the conflict. In these sorts of situations, the family is the target of intervention by dint of its obvious dysfunctional pattern and family therapy the treatment of choice.

2 The family, nuclear or extended, has experienced a life event, stressful or disruptive in type, which has led to dysfunction or is on the verge of doing so. These events are either predictable or accidental and include, for instance, accidental or suicidal death, financial embarrassment, serious physical illness, the unexpected departure of a child from the home, and so forth. In all these circumstances, any family equilibrium that previously prevailed has been disturbed, the ensuing state becomes associated with family dysfunction and/or the development of symptoms in one or more members. In some instances, family efforts to rectify the situation inadvertently aggravate it.

3 Continuing, demanding circumstances in a family are of such magnitude as to lead to maladaptive adjustment. The family's resources may be stretched to the hilt, external sources of support may be scanty. Enduring physical illness, persistent or recurrent psychiatric illness, and the presence in the family of a frail elderly member are typical examples.

4 An identified patient may become symptomatic in the context of a poorly functioning family. Symptoms are an expression of that dysfunction. Depression in a mother or an eating problem in a daughter or alcohol misuse in a father, in family assessment, is adjudged to reflect underlying family difficulties.

5 A family member is diagnosed with a specific condition, such as schizophrenia, agoraphobia, obsessive-compulsive disorder, or depression; the complicating factors are the adverse reverberations in the family stemming from that diagnosis. For example, the schizophrenic son taxes his parental caregivers in ways that exceed their 'problem-solving' capacity; an agoraphobic woman insists on the constant company of her husband in activities of daily living; a recurrently depressed mother comes to rely on the support of her eldest daughter. In these circumstances, family members begin to respond maladaptively in relation to the diagnosed relative and this paves the way for a deterioration of his condition, manifest as chronicity or a relapsing course.

6 Thoroughly disorganized families, buffeted by a myriad of problems, are viewed as the principal target of help, even though one member, for instance, abuses drugs, another is prone to violence, and a third exhibits antisocial behaviour. Regarding the family as the core dysfunctional unit is the relevant rationale rather than foci on each member's problems individually.

We reiterate that family therapy may be a treatment of choice in all these categories, but not necessarily the only one. Thus, in helping a disturbed family struggling to deal with a schizophrenic son, supportive therapy and medication for the patient is likely to be as important as any family treatment. Similarly, an indication for family therapy does not negate the possibility of another psychological approach being used for one or more members. For instance, an 18-year-old adolescent striving to separate and individuate may benefit from individual therapy following family treatment (or in parallel with it) while the parents may require a separate program to focus on their marital relationship.

Contraindications for family therapy

These are more straightforward than indications; they are self-evident and therefore mentioned briefly.

1 The family is unavailable because of geographical dispersion or death.

2 There is no shared motivation for change. One or more members wish to participate but their chance of benefiting from a family approach are likely to be less than if committing themselves to individual therapy. (We need to distinguish here between poor motivation and ambivalence; in the latter, the assessor teases out factors that underlie it and may encourage the family's engagement.)

3 The level of family disturbance is so severe or long-standing or both that a family approach seems futile. For example, a family that has fought bitterly for years is unlikely to engage in the constructive purpose of exploring their patterns of functioning.

4 Family equilibrium is so precarious that the inevitable turbulence (Goldenberg and Goldenberg 1996) arising from family therapy is likely to lead to decompensation of one or more members, for example, a sexually abused adult may do better in individual therapy than by confronting the abusing relative.

5 A member with a psychiatric condition is too incapacitated to withstand the demands of family therapy. The person in the midst of a psychotic episode or someone overwhelmed by severe melancholia is too affected by the illness to engage in family work.

6 An identified patient acknowledges family factors in the evolution of his problem but seeks the privacy of individual therapy to explore it, at least initially. For example, a university student struggling to achieve a coherent sense of identity may benefit more from her own pursuit of self-understanding. Such an approach does not negate an attempt to understand the contribution of family factors to the problem.

Assessment

Family assessment, an extension of conventional individual psychiatric assessment, adds a broader context to the final formulation. Built up over a series of interviews, the range and pace of the inquiry depends on the features of the case. Its four phases are: history from the patient, a provisional formulation concerning the relevance of family issues, an interview with one or more members, and a revised formulation.

In some cases, it is clear from the outset that the problem resides in the family as a group (see indications); in this context, the phases below are obviously superfluous.

History from the patient

The most effective way to obtain a family history is by constructing a family tree. This provides not only representation of structure but additional information is obtained about important events and a range of family features. Scrutiny of the tree also becomes a source of noteworthy issues warranting exploration and, eventually, of clinical hypotheses. Personal details are recorded for each member, such as age, dates of birth and death, occupation, education, and illness, as are critical events (e.g. migration, crucial relational changes, major losses, and achievements), and the quality of relationships.

An erudite discussion of the family tree—its construction, interpretation, and clinical uses—is presented by McGoldrick and Gerson (1985). Useful guidelines are to work from the presenting problem to the broader context, from the current situation to its historical origins and evolution, from 'facts' to inferences, and from non-threatening to more sensitive themes.

Commonly, questions are preceded by a statement such as: 'In order to better understand your problems I need to know something of your background and your current situation'. This is enriched by questions that refer to interactional patterns: 'Who knows about the problem? How does each of them see it? Has anyone else in the family had similar problems? Who have you found most helpful, and least helpful thus far? What do they think needs to be done'. Attitudes of members can thus be explored and light shed on the clinical picture.

The presenting problem and changes in the family

Questions aimed at understanding the current context include: 'What has been happening recently in the family? Have there been any changes (e.g. births, deaths, illness, losses). Has your relationship with other members changed? Have relationships within the family altered?'

The wider family context

At this point a broader inquiry flows logically—in terms of members to be considered, and in the time span of the family's history. Information about parents' siblings and their families, grandparents, and a spouse's family may be pertinent. Other significant figures, which may include caregivers and professionals, should not be forgotten.

Apart from information about the extended family's structure, questions about the family's response to major events can be posed: for example, 'How did the family react when grandmother died? Who took it the hardest? How did migration affect your parents?' Relationships should be explored at all levels covering those between patient and other members and between those members themselves. Conflicted ties are illuminating. Understanding the 'roles' adopted by members is also useful, for example, 'Who tends to take care of others? Who needs most care? Who tends to be the most sensitive to what is going on in the family?'

Asking direct questions about members is informative but a superior strategy is to seek the patient's views about their beliefs and feelings and to look for differences between members; for example: 'What worries your mother most about your problem? What worries your father most?' Several lines of inquiry may reveal differences:

- Pursuing sequential interactions: 'What does your father do when you say your depressions are dreadful? How does your mother respond when your father advises you to pull up your socks? How do you react when she contradicts your father?'
- 'Ranking' responses: 'Everyone is worried that you may harm yourself. Who worries most? Who is most likely to do something when you talk about suicide?'
- Looking for changes in relating since the problem: 'Does your husband spend more or less time with you since your difficulties began? Has he become closer or more distant from your daughter?'
- Hypothetical questions dealing with imagined situations: 'How do you think your relationship with your wife will change if you do not improve? Who would be most likely to notice that you were getting better?'

Triadic questions help to gain information about relationships that go beyond pairs; for example: 'How do you see your relationship with your mother? How does your father see that relationship? How would your mother react to what you have told me if she were here today?'

Making a provisional formulation

Two questions about the family arise following the above interview: (1) How does the family typically function, and (2) Do any family features pertain to the patient's problems?

How does the family function?

A schema to organize ideas about family functioning builds from simple to complex observations: structure, changes, relationships, interaction, and the way in which the family works as a whole.

◆ The family tree will reveal the many family *structures* possible—single parented, divorced, blended, remarried, sibships with large age discrepancies, adoptees; unusual configurations invite conjecture about inherent difficulties.

◆ Data will be obtained about significant family *changes* and events. Timing of predictable transitions such as births, departures from home, marriages, and deaths is pertinent. Have external events coincided with these transitions? (times at which the family may be more vulnerable). How have demands placed on the family by such changes been met?

◆ *Relationships* refer to how members interact with one another. This is typically in terms of degree of closeness and emotional quality (e.g. warm, tense, rivalrous, hostile). Major conflicts may be noted as may overly intense relationships.

◆ Particular *interactional patterns* may become apparent. These go beyond pairs. Triadic relationships are more revealing about how a family functions. A third person is often integral to defining the relationship between another pair. A conflict for instance may be rerouted through the third person, preventing any direct resolution. A child may act in coalition with one parent against the other or with a grandparent against a parent.

◆ At a higher level of abstraction, the clinician notes *how the family works as a whole*. Particular patterns, possibly a series of triads, may emerge, which may have recurred across generations. For example, mothers and eldest sons have fused relationships, with fathers excluded, while daughters and mothers-in-law are in conflict. Idiosyncratic shared beliefs may be discerned that explain much of the way the family does things. 'Rules' governing members' behaviour towards one another or to the outside world may flow from these beliefs. For example, a family may hold that 'you can only trust your own family; the outside world is always hostile', they may therefore avoid conflict at any cost, and prohibit seeking external support.

Evidence of family difficulties may be found at each of these five levels. If they are, the question arises whether these relate or not to the identified patient's problems.

Are family factors involved in the patient's problems?

Links between family functioning and the patient's problems take various forms, but the following categories cover most clinical situations. More than one will often apply: the family as reactive, the family as a resource, and the family in problem maintenance.

The family as reactive

The patient's illness, or its exacerbation, may have occurred at a time of family upheaval. The precipitant for the upheaval may have been the illness itself. An escalating combination of the two may pertain. The illness may have occurred in the face of family stress; it pressurizes the family all the more, and this in turn exacerbates the illness.

The family as a resource

The family may be well placed to assist in treatment. This may be as straightforward as supervising medication, ensuring clinic attendance, and detecting early signs of relapse or providing a home environment that promotes recovery and its maintenance. The family may also call on friends and agencies, professional or voluntary, to offer support.

The family in problem maintenance

Interactions revolving around the patient's illness may act to maintain it in one of three chief ways. First, the illness itself becomes a way of 'solving' a family problem, the best that can be achieved. For example, anorexia nervosa in a teenager due to attend a distant university may lead to her abandoning this plan as she feels unable to care for herself. Were she to leave, parental conflict would become more exposed and her mother, with whom the patient is in coalition against her father, would find herself unsupported. The illness therefore keeps the patient at home and enmeshed in the parental relationship, and provides a focus for shared concerns and an ostensible sense of unity.

Second, maintenance of the illness does not solve a family problem but may have done so in the past. An interactional pattern persists even though it lacks utility. In the previous example, the father's mother died 9 months later. His wife subsequently expressed feelings of closeness, feelings not experienced by him for years; their relationship gradually improved. Both parents, however, continued to treat their daughter as incapable of achieving autonomy, reinforcing her own uncertainty about coping independently if she were to recover.

Third, persistence of illness reflects a perception by the family of themselves and their problems, to which they are bound by the persuasive power of the narrative that they have shaped for themselves; the narrative may have stemmed from the helping professionals' explanatory schemas.

Interview with key informants

The clinician will by now have made an initial assessment of the patient's problems and of the family context. An interview with one or more informants, usually family members, is the next step. Several purposes are served: to corroborate the story, to fill in gaps, to determine influences impinging on the patient, and to recruit others to help. A family meeting is most effective in order to accomplish these goals.

Problems may arise in trying to implement the session. The patient may resist family members being interviewed for all sorts of reasons, for example, symptoms have been kept secret, the patient regards it as unfair to burden others, he is ashamed of seeing a psychiatrist, he is fearful the family will be blamed, or he is suspicious of them. These concerns need ventilating, particularly if the family is pivotal and treatment will be enhanced by their involvement. The patient will agree in most cases. Where the health or safety of a patient or others is threatened, refusal may be overridden on ethical grounds. Otherwise, refusal must be respected. The question of a family session can be raised later after a more trusting relationship has been cemented.

Who should be seen depends on the purpose of the interview; generally, all those living in the household and likely to be affected by the identified patient's illness should participate. Of course, some family members may be living elsewhere but are very much involved. The more family factors pertain, the more desirable the attendance by all members. The patient's views should be sought as he will provide insight into who he considers are key people.

The family interview

The clinician will have garnered substantial information by the time the family is seen. He should reflect on any biases that may have crept into his thinking about the family, and how the situation might influence them to draw him into alliances. This may well happen when conflict prevails. The clinician strives to act neutrally; his sole interest that of 'helping in the situation'. A non-judgemental stance is paramount. Introductions are made, names and preferred modes of address clarified. The clinician then explains the meeting's purpose. The details may well influence future participation. Everyone is then invited to share their views about the nature and effects of problems they have encountered.

The clinician may have an idea about how the identified patient's problems relate to family function and can test it out by probing questions and observing interactions. This idea is typically kept to himself as it is unhelpful to present a hypothesis prematurely. Instead, he seeks details about everyday events and infers patterns thereafter. For example, rather than focusing on 'closeness', he enquires about time spent together by the family, whether intimate experiences are shared, who helps with family tasks, and so on. Triadic relationships can be scrutinized both through questioning (What does A do when B says this to C?) and observation (What does A do when B and C reveal tensions?). The scope for circular questioning is enhanced if several members participate. A third person may be asked to comment on what two others convey to each other when a particular event occurs. This approach of not asking predictable questions to which the family may by now have stereotypical responses often challenges them to think about their relationships in a fresh way.

Information is elicited that elaborates the family tree. Observations are made concerning family structure and functioning, for example, who makes decisions, who controls others and in what areas, the quality of specific relationships, conflict, alliances, how clearly people communicate and how they approach problems. The discussion then extends to all spheres of family life: beliefs, traditions, rules, and values. Religious and spiritual beliefs and beliefs and practices may be relevant, either as a resource or as a contributory factor to the family's difficulties (Moncher and Josephson 2004).

Throughout the interview the clinician affirms the experiences of all members by not only attending to concerns, but also acknowledging strengths and their efforts to tackle their difficulties. The interview ends with a summary of what has emerged. The clinician may ask to continue the assessment on a second occasion or may recommend family therapy at this point. If the latter, he then explains its aim and rationale. Arrangements are set for a follow-up session, purportedly the launch of the family therapy *per se*, but in essence a continuation of the 'work' in progress.

Revised formulation

As more information becomes available at each of the aforementioned levels, the initial formulation can be revised as necessary. The five observational levels of structure, transitions, relationships, patterns of interaction, and global family functioning are re-examined in terms of the family as reactive, resourceful, or problem maintaining. Appropriate interventions can be planned, at least for a follow-up session. We are now ready to turn to the course of typical family therapy.

The course of therapy

With the phase of assessment concluded and a family approach agreed upon, therapy begins. We should recall, however, that a family may be referred as a group from the outset on the premise that the problem is inherently a family-based one. In this case, the initial stage incorporates assessment and this is made explicit. Given the plethora of 'schools' of family therapy, as described earlier, it would be laborious to map out the course of treatment associated with each of them. Instead, we will focus on the approach pioneered by the Milan group (Selvini-Palazzoli et al. 1980) but we should stress that it has undergone much elaboration and refinement over 25 years. Our account tends to highlight the original features. First, we need to comment briefly on the roles the therapist may assume.

Role of the family therapist

Beels and Ferber (1969), who were among the first observers to consider various roles for family therapists, divided them into 'conductors' and 'reactors'; the differentiation remains useful as it transcends schools. The therapist as *conductor* is represented in the work of practitioners, such as Satir, Bowen, and Minuchin. Virginia Satir (1967) is a good illustration. With her emphasis on communication, she espoused the notion that the family therapist is a teacher who shares her expertise in optimal communication by setting goals and the direction of treatment. In her case, she guided the family to adopt a new form of language in order to resolve problems in communication that she saw as the root of their troubles.

Additionally, the therapist instils confidence, promotes hope for change, and makes them feel comfortable in the process. In Satir and fellow conductors, the therapist is an explicit authority, who intervenes actively in implementing change. The therapist as *reactor* plays a different role by resonating with, and responding to, what the family manifests. Therapists in the psychoanalytic tradition belong to this group as do what Beels and Ferber label system purists. Typically, the therapist shares observations about patterns of relating that emerge during the sessions. We will illustrate this aspect when describing the Milan approach (Selvini-Palazzoli et al. 1980). We have selected it arbitrarily as we cannot possibly give accounts of every school.

Whatever role the therapist occupies, forming a positive therapeutic relationship with the family is a core task (Rait 2000).

The Milan approach—as illustrative of a course of family therapy applying systems theory

With assessment complete, the therapist (sometimes a pair) meets with the family. With her preparatory knowledge, she shapes a hypothesis about the nature of the family's dysfunction. As a reactor, he has the opportunity, on observing patterns *in vivo*, to confirm her ideas. Such patterns usually emerge from the start making the therapist's job correspondingly easier. Apart from hypothesis testing, another task in this session is to engage the family fully so that they will be motivated to reattend. We could interpolate a dictum here: a primary aim of the first session is to facilitate a second session. A key element in encouraging engagement is for the therapist to promote a sense of curiosity in members so that they raise questions about themselves and the family as a group (Cecchin 1987).

The chief strategy used is circular questioning, which we touched on in the assessment section (Tomm 1987). Although it is easy to imagine doing, it is tricky to do well. The main purpose is to address the family's issues indirectly; this avoids pressurizing particular members and perhaps provoking their resistance. For example, the therapist asks questions of an adolescent about how his parents get on with each other; or a mother about how her husband relates to the eldest son; or a grandmother about which grandchild is closest to the parents; and so forth. This mode of inquiry generates illuminating data about individual members and about the family as a group. In this phase, it helps to clarify the hypothesis, to engage participants, and affords the therapist greater facility to remain neutral and thus avoid forging alliances with an individual or subgroup. Because the system and not the identified patient is the target of change, the therapist is wary of showing bias. (This does not preclude transient alliances adopted for strategic purposes; these, however, need to be limited in time and distributed throughout the system.)

The therapist and family 'work' together for an hour or so on the basis of promoting curiosity, circular questioning, and neutrality. A number of options then follow. If the therapist is part of a team, her colleagues will have been observing the proceedings through a one-way screen. The family's consent, of course, will have been obtained previously. During a break the team—observers and therapist(s)—systematically pool impressions (Selvini-Palazzoli 1991). This is invariably a rich exchange as team members often note something others may have missed. As a result of these deliberations, a consensus about family functioning evolves. Conclusions are drawn and converted into 'messages'. The therapist returns to the family briefly to convey them. This is akin to the Delphic Oracle. The actual messages and their oracular quality comprise a potent intervention but not necessarily more cogent than interventions in the form of circular questions made earlier. Indeed, the advent of the narrative school has brought with it a de-emphasis on the 'therapist's message' on the premise that 'truth' is a shared construction.

The messages, usually between one and three, are given crisply and with maximal clarity. 'Homework' may be assigned and another session planned unless termination was set for this point. Messages have several purposes including the promotion of intersessional 'work'. Three or 4 weeks is commonly set aside between meetings, and for good reason. During this time, the family, armed with new ideas, will tackle them in their day-to-day lives. It is not critical *how* they do so but important *that* they do so. To get back to the point about curiosity, and as Cecchin (1987) has argued, the family's interest in their own functioning should have been so aroused that they will be motivated to continue looking at themselves between sessions.

One of the authors (see Allman et al. 1992) has conducted research on the nature of the message that led to devising a classification. Messages are divisible into three broad groups: supportive, hypothesis related, and prescriptive. In the first, the message has a reassuring, encouraging, or otherwise supportive quality but it is not related to the hypothesis. A complimentary message might be that, 'the team were impressed by how open you all were in the session' and a reassuring one that, 'this is like a new start for the family; there are bound to be uncertainties'.

Hypothesis-related messages refer to the hypothesis worked out by the therapeutic team, and may assume diverse forms. It may be stated directly, for example, 'Susan has assumed the role of therapist for her parents and sister in order to prevent the family's disintegration'. There may be reference to change, such as 'The team can see John taking responsibility to look after himself; John and his father's improved relationship has allowed this to occur'. The family may be offered options, an outline of possible choices related to the hypothesis, for example, 'The family could risk being more open or you could continue to keep things to yourselves'. Paradoxical messages are a means to communicate a hypothesis that invites the family to revisit a feature of their functioning so that the family's difficulties are positively promoted and explicitly encouraged, for example, 'The team sense that your problem is working for the good of your marriage; sticking with your illness can save the marriage'. The paradox may also be split in that the family is told about a divergence of opinion in the team (Papp 1980). For instance, the family may be informed that some team members believe it too risky for them to communicate openly, whereas others suggest this can be done safely.

Through a prescriptive message the family is given a task directly. This may or may not be related to the hypothesis. For example, the family is urged to meet on their own before the next session in order to explore what inhibits a member from relating closely to the others.

Whatever the form of message, the therapist attempts to de-emphasize the pathological status of the identified patient and to apply what the Milan group refers to as positive connotation. The latter, a brilliant innovation, rests on the premise that all behaviour is purposeful, and that the purpose can be construed positively. An adolescent's 'symptom of open grieving' is reframed as serving the family by sparing *them* the anguish of grief. This quality of message calls for creative thinking and flies in the face of the customary view of symptoms as evidence of psychopathology. Again, curiosity enters the picture as the family hears this positive communication concerning an issue that they have hitherto regarded as negative and abnormal.

The above process continues during succeeding meetings and attention is paid to what occurs in the family between sessions. Duration of therapy depends on how entrenched the family dysfunction is rather than on the status of an identified patient's problems. Thus, systemic change is aimed for and the family encouraged to consider a substitute mode of functioning that is feasible and safe. In practice, sessions range in numbers from one to a dozen. If progress has not been achieved by about session 8, it is likely that alternate ways of helping the family and/or the identified patient are called for.

Termination is less problematic than in individual or group therapy. The reason is obvious. The family has come as a living group and will continue to be one after the therapist bows out. In most approaches, even when the therapist is a prominent conductor, the family's own intrinsic resources are highlighted so that these can be drawn on and exploited further upon the therapist's exit. Determining the endpoint is usually straightforward in that there is a shared sense that the work has been accomplished. A hypothesis (or set of) has been introduced, tested, and confirmed. The family system has been carefully examined in order that impediments are recognized and understood and better modes of functioning devised and implemented. The family does not have to leave functioning optimally. Instead, termination occurs when there is agreement that the family is equipped with new options and feels confident to try them out over the long term.

As alluded to earlier, this may be determined alongside a judgement that an identified patient (or other member occasionally) requires another therapy in his or her own right. A clear example is an adolescent who has felt unable to separate and individuate. While family work has explored the system that blocked 'graduation' to adult psychological status, the sense prevails that he could benefit from individual or group therapy by building on changes already achieved. In another example, the parents may conclude, with the therapist's support, that they have an agenda that is not pertinent to their children and therefore best handled in couple therapy.

Problems encountered in therapy

Where assessment has been carried out diligently and motivation for change sustained, treatment proceeds smoothly. This is not to negate a possible crisis buffeting the group. But rather than being derailed, the family is encouraged to regard the crisis as a challenge with which to grapple.

Family treatment does not always succeed. Indeed, deterioration may take place, albeit in a small proportion of cases (Gurman and Kniskern 1978). What are the common difficulties encountered? The non-engaging family is problematic in that while evidence points to the need for family intervention, members cannot participate, usually because they resist letting go 'the devil they know'. In another variation, engagement of particular members may fail. This is particularly so in the case of fathers who tend to see the target of therapy as the identified patient rather than the family as a whole.

Missed appointments may punctuate therapy, often linked to turbulent experiences between sessions or apprehension about what a forthcoming session may reveal. Like any psychotherapy, dropout is possible. On occasion, this is reasonable inasmuch as the indication for family therapy was miscon-strued. In other circumstances, dropout is tantamount to failure and may derive from such factors as therapist ineptitude, unearthing of family conflict that they cannot tolerate, and inappropriate selection of a family approach based on faulty assessment.

We have referred to the possible occurrence of a family crisis. Given that the family continues as a living group during treatment, they are exposed to all manner of vicissitudes, and these may disrupt the therapeutic work. For example, an overdose by the identified patient, abrupt marital separa-tion, or a psychiatric admission may take its toll and serve to jeopardize treatment.

In discussing the ending of the treatment, we commented on outcome. Obviously, not all families benefit. The family's dysfunction may be so intractable as to be impervious to change, hypotheses may be 'off the mark', the family may lack adequate psychological sophistication, members may retreat in the face of change because of insecurity, and so forth.

Occasionally, dependency becomes a problem as the family senses a greater security when relying on the therapist. The latter may inadvertently foster dependency by assuming a role of authoritativeness that impedes a growing partnership. The family's own resources are then not given expression.

Finally, a family subgroup may harbour a secret that threatens the principle of open communication between members. The therapist may be inveigled into this group, although he stressed at the onset that keeping secrets is not conducive to the therapeutic process. For example, a call to the therapist from a spouse that she is having an affair that she will not disclose to her husband or children imposes a burden on both therapist and the family work.

Astute judgement is required in these situations. No ready-made prescriptions are available but instead a keen awareness in the therapist that difficulties are possible even in a highly motivated and well-selected family. The general principle, however, is to prevent their evolution if at all possible or to recognize them early and 'nip them in the bud'.

Research in family therapy

In appraising the contemporary state of adult family therapy research, the choice is to see the glass as either half full or half empty. We opt for the more optimistic scenario. We need to remind ourselves that adult psychiatry family therapy is a toddler, dating only from the 1970s. During this time, immense strides have been made, particularly in the development of theoretical concepts. Pioneers in the field were chiefly therapists, working with families and tantalized by the nature of the process rather than its effectiveness. In hindsight, this makes sense. Models were completely lacking, the *how* to conduct treatment crying out for creative ideas. As can be seen in the theoretical part of the chapter, these have emerged bounteously, and continue to do so. The result is a rich array of therapeutic approaches, including several comprehensive theoretical contributions (Gurman and Kniskern 1991). The growth has occurred at a dizzy pace with the inevitable consequence of overload. How can we make sense of the competing offerings? Is integration needed in order to forestall fragmentation of the field? Have we reached the point to reflect on what the terrain looks like? Are we now better placed to carry out outcome studies and to evaluate relative effectiveness? Tough questions, and the research pathway is obstructed by many hurdles. Observers of family therapy research, among them Gurman et al. (1986) and Bednar et al. (1988) have sought to clarify evolutionary themes and options for further work. Notwithstanding this collective endeavour, we have still not reached the enviable position say of an integrated model, such as cognitive behavioural therapy that, by dint of its relatively integrated status, has been systemically investigated, both its process and outcome, so that we are building up knowledge about how cognitive behaviour therapy works and for what types of patients.

A complicating aspect of family therapy research is to define components of the approach, namely the therapist assembling a natural group of varying composition, in which a dominant goal is to alter its functioning. This is altogether a more daunting matter compared with the relatively straight-forward task of examining the effectiveness of say a well-described treatment given to a single patient presenting with a well-defined depressive syndrome.

Even if we were able to design solid outcome studies, we would be left with the conundrum of what constitutes the desired outcome and how to measure it. We can illustrate this by citing the conclusions of Asen and his colleagues (1991) in their investigation of 18 London families. Fundamental differences among the researchers emerged when handling the data. The team had decided to apply a multidimensional set of measures to assess change and at individual, dyadic, and family levels. At follow-up they noticed changes at the first two levels but not in the family as a group. The latter involved ratings of, *inter alia*, communication, boundaries, alliances, adaptability, and competence. The researchers were refreshingly candid in sharing their doubts about how to deal with the findings. Several contradictory interpretations were offered, for example: an absence of change in family functioning; the measure of that functioning nonreactive to treatment as it was a trait measure; and an inappropriate model of family therapy applied in the first place. Asen et al. concluded that the 'assumptive worlds' of therapists and researchers were being approved rather than the families themselves, a conclusion that makes good sense and an issue continuing to ensnare researchers. (These ethically related dimensions are discussed by Bloch et al. 1994, in *The family in clinical psychiatry*.)

A research team in Oxford (Bloch et al. 1991) encountered similar difficulties in their evaluation of 50 consecutive families treated in an adult family therapy clinic. Whereas two-thirds of the patients were judged to be improved at termination, only half the families were rated as functioning better or much better. Again, like the Asen team, the investigators were left with questions as how to determine what had actually been achieved. A methodologically simpler way to wrestle with the issue is to focus solely on the identified patient's progress. Hafner et al.'s (1990) work exemplifies this choice—a case-controlled evaluation of family therapy in an inpatient setting with subsequent hospital admission data applied as the chief change criterion. Satisfactory as this study is in terms of design, the omission of a family-system outcome measure leaves us hankering for more information about the group's functioning following the intervention.

With these tricky matters in mind, let us consider what research in the adult family therapy field needs to sort out. The diffuse question of whether family therapy works or not in this setting is of limited utility, and is reminiscent of the sterile debate that typified psychotherapy outcome research in the wake of Eysenck's throwing down the gauntlet in 1952 (Alexander et al. 1994). While subsequent meta-analyses demonstrated that psychological interventions overall exerted useful effects across a range of conditions, the field was still open to the criticism that efficacy of a specific therapeutic approach for a particular clinical state remained unanswered. The NIMH collaborative study on the treatment of depression was an advance. Family therapy should not repeat the same error and so squander opportunities and time. Instead of posing the futile question of whether family therapy works in adult psychiatry, we should instead ascertain whether a specific approach, whose character is well identified and adherence by therapists to it confirmed, is useful for both the identified patient, with a specific presentation, and the family's functioning, again well defined.

Research has begun to fulfil these desiderata. Many studies exploring interventions in families containing a schizophrenic member have described principles of treatment, the rationale upon which it is based, aspects of the process, and outcome measures in the patient and (in some cases) the family (see, for example, Falloon et al. 1986; Bellack et al. 2000; Mueser and Fox 2002 and Barrowchough et al. 2001). Helpful reviews can be found in Dixon and Lehman (1995) and Mueser and Bellack (1995). Although not as advanced as developments in schizophrenia, research conducted in the area of affective disorders has been innovative, and should pave the way for formal outcome studies (see Weber et al. 1988; Keitner 1990 and Miklowitz et al. 2000). The Maudsley study on anorexia and bulimia nervosa aptly illustrates how outcome research can contribute to the clinician (Russell et al. 1987). In a well-controlled study, 80 patients were randomized to either family therapy or 'routine individual supportive therapy', following their discharge from an inpatient weight/restoration program. Treatment of the family involved an average 10 sessions, and individual treatment 15 sessions, spaced out over a 1-year period.

Family therapy focused on engaging the family and providing them with information about the eating disorder and the effects of starvation. Parental anxiety was acknowledged and efforts made to help parents take control of their daughter's diet. In parallel with improved physical status, therapy turned progressively to typical adolescent issues of separation and individuation and how these might be accomplished. A structural approach was applied, with systemic and strategic measures incorporated when progress slowed down.

Family therapy of a specific type can be applied to the family as a group in the light of system dysfunction. Thus, while the above research concerning particular psychiatric states, and involving an identified patient, is necessary for progress, this does not preclude outcome studies where the family is the principal target of change. We illustrate this with a particular form of family grief therapy derived from empirical research on the outcome of family grieving in an oncology setting (Kissane et al. 1998). A 13-month follow-up yielded 5 family clusters of which 2 were distinctly dysfunctional, 2 functional, and an intermediate group at risk of maladaptive grieving. Three dimensions of family functioning were critical: cohesion, managing conflict, and expressiveness. The investigators then devised a model highlighting the goals of promoting cohesiveness, expressiveness, and optimal management of conflict. A corresponding screening instrument was applied to identify dysfunctional families.

Fifteen therapists were trained to use the emergent treatment guidelines and to work under close supervision in order to ensure that they adhered to the model. The randomized controlled trial (RCT) showed clearly the model's suitability and feasibility. Treatment began prior to the death of a terminally ill parent and extended into the bereavement period. Outcome measures included individual psychosocial morbidity and adaptation and the family's functioning. The model and its practical application are described in detail in *Family focused grief therapy* (Kissane and Bloch 2002). The findings of the RCT can be found in Kissane et al. 2006, in press.

In 2002 a landmark publication (Sprenkle 2002) provided a comprehensive review of the research evidence for the efficacy of marital and family therapy in a wide range of clinical disorders, accompanied by discussion of the conceptual and methodological difficulties of such research encounters, the difficulties in translating research findings to the complex, emotionally variegated clinical context and the political dimension of the increasing demand for evidence-based practice in the field. An overview of these matters has been provided by Sprenkle (2003) and Carr (2004).

Unlike the early attitudes in the field which we alluded to above, contemporary researchers are mindful of the biological and specifically genetic bases of many diseases, including some of the most severe forms of mental illness. The reciprocal interactions between genes and environment, and how such interactions influence the clinical picture of a chronic illness over time, including the specific phases of the family life cycle, has many implications for prevention, early detection, and treatment (Rolland and Williams 2005).

This necessarily schematic account of research developments on family therapy in adult psychiatry suggests likely future trends. We can best summarize what research should strive for as: 'Specificity is of the essence'. While postmodernist foundations of narrative therapies might suggest that they are less amenable to traditional research of the sort we have described, this has not proven to be entirely so. (See, for example, the special section in *Family Process*, edited by Steinglass 1998). A group of researchers in London studied the accounts by family members of their experiences caring for an acutely psychotic relative, and discerned two patterns of narrative. In one that was described as having meaning, members' stories depicted themes of reparation and restitution and integrated the illness into ongoing family life. In the other, described as frozen or chaotic narratives, members viewed the illness as a series of random events (affinity with Byng-Hall's model—Byng-Hall 1995; Stern et al. 1999). The clinical implications of these two patterns and their relation to empirical studies of relapse prevention await elucidation.

Psychoeducational interventions for children whose parents suffer from a major affective disorder have been modified to pay attention to the children's narratives of their experiences. Initial findings indicate the possibility of improving the children's resilience and coping with their parents' illness (Focht and Beardslee 1996). This research approach is promising in terms of its preventative potential and could be extrapolated to the adult sphere.

Training

From a few charismatic figures practicing idiosyncratic, innovative methods of family therapy, the field has developed into a skilfully marketed enterprise in many countries, particularly the United States, with hundreds of books, scores of training courses, several dozen journals, and a year-round program of local, national, and international conferences and workshops (Liddle 1991). Formal training may occur in one of three contexts (Goldenberg and Goldenberg 1996).

1 University-based, degree-granting programs view family therapy as a distinct profession, with its own corpus of knowledge, and offer diploma, masters, Ph.D., and postdoctoral training.

2 Free-standing institutes also tend to see family therapy as a distinct discipline and provide part-time training, usually of shorter duration than most university-based programs. A prerequisite for entry in most of these is that the candidate has completed basic training in one of the health professions.

3 Within university-affiliated hospitals and clinics that provide professional training in psychiatry, psychology, social work, and occupational therapy,

many provide a brief course in the theory and practice of family therapy as part of general professional training.

Although there is a vast spectrum of training experiences to which students are exposed, most programs include:

1 Live supervision of clinical work with the supervisor (and often other students) observing the trainee and family from behind a one-way screen. Some clinicians consider the one-way screen to be dehumanizing and too objectifying of the family as well as adding to the trainee's performance anxiety. They advocate instead a model of co-therapy (trainee and supervisor), often with other students sitting in the interview room in full view of the family.

2 Video recording of the trainee's work, which is then reviewed by her in the presence of supervisor and fellow students is widely used. Tapes of particular models conducted by eminent therapists are also popular.

Whether training requires familiarity with concepts and techniques of a variety of schools or whether it is preferable to develop expertise in only one school remains debatable. Free-standing institutes tend to be run by therapists of a particular school, so that after a generally cursory overview of the field training is restricted to a specific model. This is more likely when the program is part of general education in psychiatry, psychiatric nursing, psychology, and social work.

Diversity of schools and training reflects an uncertainty as to whether family therapy is a distinct profession, a method of conceptualizing psychopathology, or a set of therapeutic methods to add to the armamentarium of the mental health professional. This issue is further compounded by the aforementioned trend towards integrating psychodynamic, attachment, systems, feminist, and narrative approaches.

Conclusion

Family therapy has the potential to contribute much to the mentally ill and their families. As we have tried to illustrate in this chapter, research points to many promising areas of therapeutic activity. We hope newcomers to the psychotherapies will seriously consider the role of family therapy, and as informed practitioners. They will be amply rewarded in doing so.

References

Ackerman, N. W. (1958). *The psychodynamics of family life*. Basic Books, New York.

Alexander, J., Holtzworth-Munroe, A., and Jameson, P. (1994). The process and outcome of marital and family therapy: Research review and evaluation. In *Handbook of psychotherapy and behaviour change* (eds A. Bergin and S. Garfield). 4th edn, pp. 595–630. Wiley, New York.

Allman, P., Bloch, S., and Sharpe, M. (1992). The end-of-session message in systemic family therapy: A descriptive study. *Journal of Family Therapy*, **14**, 69–85.

American Psychiatric Association (1994). *Diagnostic and statistical manual of mental disorders*, 4th edn (DSM-IV). American Psychiatric Association, Washington DC.

Andersen, T. (1991). *The reflecting team: Dialogues and dialogues about dialogues*. Norton, New York.

Anderson, H. and Goolishian, H. A. (1988). Human systems as linguistic systems: Preliminary and evolving ideas about the implications for clinical theory. *Family Process*, **27**, 371–393.

Asen, K., Berkowitz, R., Cooklin, A., Leff, J., Loader, P., Piper, R. and Rein, L. (1991). Family therapy outcome research: A trial for families, therapists, and researchers. *Family Process*, **30**, 3–20.

Barrowclough, C., Haddock, G., Tarrier, N., Lewis, S., Moring, J., O'Brien, R., Schofield, N. and McGovern, J. (2001). Randomized controlled trial of motivational interviewing, cognitive behaviour therapy, and family intervention for patients with comorbid schizophrenia and substance abuse disorders. *American Journal of Psychiatry*, **158**, 1706–1713.

Bateson, G. (1972). *Steps to an ecology of mind*. Ballantine, New York.

Bateson, G., Jackson, D. D., Haley, J., and Weakland, J. H. (1956). Toward a theory of schizophrenia. *Behavioural Science*, **1**, 251–64.

Bateson, G., Jackson, D. D., Haley, J., and Weakland, J. H. (1962). A note on the double-bind. *Family Process*, **2**, 154–61.

Bednar, R., Burlingame, G., and Masters, K. (1988). Systems of family treatment: Substance or semantics? *Annual Review of Psychology*, **39**, 401–34.

Beels, C. and Ferber, A. (1969). Family therapy: A view. *Family Process*, **8**, 280–332.

Bellack, A., Haas, G. and Schooler, N. et al. (2000). Effects of behavioural family management on family communication and patient outcomes in schizophrenia. *British Journal of Psychiatry*, **177**, 434–439.

Bertalanffy, L. (1968). *General systems theory: Foundation, development, applications*. Braziller, New York.

Bloch, S., Sharpe, M., and Allman, P. (1991). Systemic family therapy in adult psychiatry: A review of 50 families. *British Journal of Psychiatry*, **159**, 357–64.

Bloch, S., Hafner, J., Harari, E., and Szmukler, G. (1994). *The family in clinical psychiatry*. Oxford University Press, Oxford.

Boszormenyi-Nagy, I. and Spark, G. M. (1984). *Invisible loyalties: Reciprocity in intergenerational family therapy*. Brunner-Mazel, New York.

Bowen, M. (1978). *Family therapy in clinical practice*. Jason Aronson, New York.

Braverman, S. (1995). The integration of individual and family therapy. *Contemporary Family Therapy*, **17**, 291–305.

Byng-Hall, J. (1995). *Rewriting family scripts. Improvisation and systems change*. Guilford, London.

Carr, A. (2004). Thematic review of family therapy journals in 2003. *Journal of Family Therapy*, **26**, 430–445.

Cecchin, G. (1987). Hypothesizing, circularity, and neutrality revisited: An invitation to curiosity. *Family Process*, **26**, 405–13.

Ciompi, L. (1988). *The psyche and schizophrenia. The bond between affect and logic.* Harvard University Press, Cambridge, MA.

Clarkin, J., Frances, A., and Moodie, J. (1979). Selection criteria for family therapy. *Family Process*, **18**, 391–403.

Cooklin, A. (1979). A psychoanalytic framework for a systemic approach to family therapy. *Journal of Family Therapy*, **1**, 153–65.

Dare, C. (1997). Chronic eating disorders in therapy: Clinical stories using family systems and psychoanalytic approaches. *Journal of Family Therapy*, **19**, 319–51.

De Shazer, S. (1985). *Keys to solution in brief therapy.* Norton, New York.

Dixon, L. and Lehman, A. (1995). Family interventions for schizophrenia. *Schizophrenia Bulletin*, **21**, 631–43.

Epstein, N. B. and Schlesinger, S. E. (2003). In *Treatment of family problems in cognitive therapy for children and adolescents* (eds M. Reineeke, F. Datrilio, and A. Freeman). 2nd edn, pp. 304–37. Guilford, New York.

Falloon, I., Boyd, J. L., and McGill, C. (1986). *Family care of schizophrenia: A problem-solving approach to the treatment of mental illness.* Guilford, New York.

Flaskas, C. and Perlesz, A. (ed.) (1996). *The therapeutic relationship in systemic therapy.* Karnac, London.

Flugel, J. C. (1921). *The psychoanalytic study of the family.* Hogarth Press, London.

Focht, L. and Beardslee, W. R. (1996). 'Speech after long silence': The use of narrative therapy in a preventive intervention for children of parents with affective disorders. *Family Process*, **35**, 407–22.

Friedmann, M. S., McDermutt, W. H., Solomon, D. A., Ryan, C. E., Keitner, G. I., and Miller, I. W. (1997). Family functioning and mental illness: A comparison of psychiatric and nonclinical families. *Family Process*, **36**, 357–67.

Goldenberg, I. and Goldenberg, H. (1996). *Family therapy. An overview.* Brooks-Cole, Pacific Grove, CA.

Gurman, A. and Kniskern, D. (1978). Deterioration in marital and family therapy: Empirical, clinical, and conceptual issues. *Family Process*, **17**, 3–20.

Gurman, A. and Kniskern, D. (ed.) (1991). *Handbook of family therapy*, Vol. II. Brunner-Mazel, New York.

Gurman, A., Kiniskern, D., and Pinsof, W. (1986). Research on marital and family therapy. In *Handbook of psychotherapy and behaviour change* (ed. S. Garfield and A. Bergin). 3rd edn, pp. 565–624. Wiley, New York.

Hafner, J., MacKenzie, L., and Costain, W. (1990). Family therapy in a psychiatric hospital: A case-controlled evaluation. *Australian and New Zealand Journal of Family Therapy*, **11**, 21–5.

Haley, J. (1976). *Problem-solving therapy.* Jossey-Bass, San Francisco, CA.

Keitner, G. (ed.) (1990). *Depression and families: Impact and treatment.* American Psychiatric Press, Washington DC.

Kissane, D. and Bloch, S. (2002). *Family focused grief therapy.* Open University Press, Milton Keynes, UK.

Kissane, D., Bloch, S., McKenzie, M., McDowall, A., and Nitzan, R. (1998). Family grief therapy: A preliminary account of a new model to promote healthy family functioning during palliative care and bereavement. *Psycho-Oncology*, 7, 14–25.

Kissane, D., McKenzie, M., Bloch, S., Moskowitz, C., McKenzie, D., and O'Neil, I. (2006). Family focused grief therapy: A randomized controlled trial in palliative care and bereavement. *American Journal of Psychiatry*, in press.

Langsley, D. G., Pitman, F. S., Machotka, P., and Flomenhaft, K. (1969). Family crisis therapy: Results and implications. *Family Process*, 7, 145–58.

Liddle, H. (1991). Training and supervision in family therapy: A comprehensive and critical analysis. In *Handbook of family therapy* (ed. A Gurman and D. Kniskern) Vol. II, 2nd edn, pp. 638–97. Brunner-Mazel, New York.

Luepnitz, D. A. (2002). *The family interpreted: Psychoanalysis, feminism and family therapy*. Basic Books, New York.

Magliano, L., Fiorillo, A., Fadden, G., Gair, F., Economou, M., Kallert, T., Schellong, J., Xavier, M., Goncalves, P., Gonzales, F., Palma-Crespo, A., and Maj, M. (2005). Effectiveness of a psychoeducational intervention for families of patients with schizophrenia: Preliminary results of a study funded by the European Commission. *World Psychiatry*, 4, 45–52.

McFarlane, W. R., Link, B., Dushay, R., Marchal, J., and Crilly, J. (1995). Psychoeducational multiple family groups: Four-year relapse outcome in schizophrenia. *Family Process*, 34, 127–44.

McGoldrick, M. and Gerson, R. (1985). *Genograms in family assessment*. Norton, New York.

Miklowitz, D., Simoneau, T., George, E. et al. (2000). Family focused treatment of bipolar disorder: 1-year effects of a psychoeducational program in conjunction with pharmacotherapy. *Biological Psychiatry*, 48, 582–592.

Minuchin, S. and Fishman, H. C. (1981). *Family therapy techniques*. Harvard University Press, Cambridge, MA.

Minuchin, S., Rosman, A., and Baker, L. (1978). *Psychosomatic families: Anorexia nervosa in context*. Harvard University Press, Cambridge, MA.

Moncher, F. and Josephson, A. (2004). Religious and spiritual aspects of family assessment. *Child and Adolescent Psychiatric Clinics of North America*, 13, 49–70.

Mueser, K. and Bellack, A. (1995). Psychotherapy and schizophrenia. In *Schizophrenia* (ed. S. Hirsch and D. Weinberger). pp. 626–48. Blackwell Science, Oxford.

Mueser, K. and Fox, L. (2002). A family intervention program for dual disorders. *Community Mental Health Journal*, 38, 253–270.

Papp, P. (1980). The Greek chorus and other techniques of paradoxical therapy. *Family Process*, 19, 45–58.

Rait, D. (2000). The therapeutic alliance in couples and family therapy. *Journal of Clinical Psychology*, 56, 211–224.

Rolland, J. and Williams, J. (2005). Toward a biopsychosocial model for 21st century genetics. *Family Process*, 44, 3–24.

Rosenfarb, I. S., Miklowitz, D. J., Goldstein, M. J., and Harmon, L. et al. (2001). Family transactions and relapse in bipolar disorder. *Family Process*, 40, 5–14.

Russell, G. F., Szmukler, G., Dare, C., and Eisler, I. (1987). An evaluation of family therapy in anorexia nervosa and bulimia nervosa. *Archives of General Psychiatry*, **44**, 1047–56.

Sander, F. (1978). Marriage and family in Freud's writings. *Journal of the American Academy of Psychoanalysis*, **6**, 157–74.

Satir, V. (1967). *Conjoint family therapy*. Science and Behaviour Books, Palo Alto, CA.

Selvini, M. and Selvini Palazzoli, M. (1991). Team consultation: An indispensable tool for the progress of knowledge. Ways of fostering and promoting its creative potential. *Journal of Family Therapy*, **13**, 31–52.

Selvini-Palazzoli, M., Boscolo, L., Cecchin, G., and Prata, G. (1980). Hypothesising-circularity-neutrality: Three guidelines for the conductor of the session. *Family Process*, **19**, 3–12.

Sprenkle, D. (2002). (ed.). *Effectiveness research in marital and family therapy*. American Association of Marriage and Family Therapy Press, Alexandria, VA.

Sprenkle, D. (2003). Effectiveness research in marriage and family therapy: Introduction. *Journal of Marital and Family* Therapy, **29**, 85–96.

Steinglass, P. (1998). Researching narrative therapy. *Family Process*, **37**, 1–2.

Stern, S., Doolan, M., Staples, E., Szmukler, G. L., and Eisler, I. (1999). Disruption and reconstruction: Narrative insights into the experience of family members caring for a relative diagnosed with serious mental illness. *Family Process*, **38**, 353–69.

Stierlin, H. (1989). The psychosomatic dimension: Relational aspects. *Family Systems Medicine*, **7**, 254–63.

Tomm, K. (1987). Interventive questioning: Part II. Reflexive questioning as a means to enable self-healing. *Family Process*, **26**, 167–83.

Tompson, M. C., Rea, M. M., Goldstein, M. J., Miklowitz, D. J., and Weisman, A. G. (2000). Difficulty in implementing a family intervention for bipolar disorder: The predictive role of patient and family attributes. *Family Process*, **39**, 105–20.

Walrond-Skinner, S. (1978). Indications and contra-indications for the use of family therapy. *Journal of Child Psychology and Psychiatry*, **19**, 57–62.

Weber, G., Simon, F., Stierlin, H., and Schmidt, G. (1988). Therapy for families manifesting manic-depressive behaviour. *Family Process*, **27**, 33–49.

White, M. and Epston, D. (1990). *Narrative means to therapeutic ends*. Norton, New York.

Recommended reading

Ackerman, N. (1958). *The psychodynamics of family life*. Basic Books, New York.
(A classic text by a pioneer family therapist, illustrating the relevance of family dynamics and the family context to the treatment of disturbed children.)

Goldenberg, I. and Goldenberg, H. (1996). *Family Therapy: An overview*. 4th edn. Brookes-Cole, Pacific Grove, CA.
(A comprehensive overview of the main schools of family therapy, their key concepts and research aspects.)

Luepnitz, D. A. (2002). *The family interpreted: Psychoanalysis, feminism and family therapy*. Revised edition. Basic Books, New York.
(A thoughtful critique of family therapy from a feminist perspective, which argues that the patriarchal but father-absent modern family generates many difficulties that

are best understood by integrating object-relations psychoanalytic thinking and feminist concerns about the organization of family life with systemic family therapy.)

Simon, F., Stierlin, H., and Wynne, L. (1985). *The language of family therapy: A systemic vocabulary and sourcebook*. Family Process. Press, New York.

(A useful dictionary of common terms and concepts in family therapy although a little dated in that it does not include post-modern and narrative therapy concepts; but is still valuable in clarifying systems thinking and its clinical application.)

Index